Aviation and the Role of Government

Harry Lawrence

KENDALL/HUNT PUBLISHING COMPANY
4050 Westmark Drive   Dubuque, Iowa 52002

Book Team

Chairman and Chief Executive Officer *Mark C. Falb*
President and Chief Operating Officer *Chad M. Chandlee*
Director of National Book Program *Paul B. Carty*
Editorial Development Manager *Georgia Botsford*
Developmental Editor *Angela Willenbring*
Vice President, Operations *Timothy J. Beitzel*
Assistant Vice President, Production Services *Christine E. O'Brien*
Senior Production Editor *Mary Melloy*
Senior Permissions Editor *Colleen Zelinsky*
Cover Designer *Janell Edwards*

All Shutterstock images used under license from Shutterstock, Inc.

Cover Images:
Flag, © Christopher Penler, 2008, Shutterstock
Eagle, © FloridaStock, 2008, Shutterstock
Planes, © Robert Ford, 2008, Shutterstock

ISBN 978-0-7575-4803-1

Printed in the United States of America
10 9 8 7 6 5 4 3 2

TO SUSAN

And to Garrett, Lee, Colburn, Lachlan, Greyson, Sarah, Sadie, Conner (born on the 100th anniversary of the Wrights' epic flight), Reid, Alex, Ruby Jo, & Grace—memories of my first solo flight in a small, yellow airplane on July 16, 1956, cause me to paraphrase these thoughts to you:

" As I run my hand over the wing and take in the poised majesty of this small machine, you should know that this plane can teach you more things and give you more gifts than I ever could. It won't get you a better job, a faster car, or a bigger house. But if you treat it with respect and keep your eyes open, it may remind you some things you used to know— that life is in the moment, joy matters more than money, the world can be a beautiful place, and that dreams really, truly are possible. And, because airplanes speak in a language beyond words, I will take you up in the evening summer sky and let the airplane show you what I mean. "

From the "Eyes of a Child," *Flying Magazine,* February 2000

CONTENTS

Table of Statutes   xi
Table of Cases   xiii
List of Figures   xv
Preface   xxi
About the Author   xxv

PART I   **Foundation   1**

CHAPTER 1   **Beginnings   3**

CHAPTER 2   **The Industrial
                    Revolution   7**

CHAPTER 3   **The Railroads   11**
The Railroads, Laissez-Faire Economics,
   and the Basis of Regulation   15
The Interstate Commerce Act of 1887   16
Endnote   17

CHAPTER 4   **The Industrial Age and
                    the Rise of Unionism   19**
Endnote   23

PART II   **Dreamers   25**

CHAPTER 5   **The Beginnings
                    of Flight   27**
Balloons   28
Dirigibles   29
Gliders   31

CHAPTER 6   **Prelude to Powered
                    Flight   37**
Endnote   39

CHAPTER 7   **The Wright Brothers   41**
Endnotes   52

PART III   **Pioneers   53**

CHAPTER 8   **Glenn Curtiss   55**
Endnotes   62

CHAPTER 9   **World War I   63**
The National Advisory Committee
   for Aeronautics (NACA)   65

CHAPTER 10   **Airmail Story   67**
A Rough Beginning   67
Scheduled Airmail Service   69
Transcontinental Airmail   72
The Lighted Airway   73
Endnotes   73

CHAPTER 11   **Horsepower   75**

PART IV   **Regulation   79**

CHAPTER 12   **The Privatization
                    of Airmail   81**
The Airmail Act of 1925 (The Kelly Act)   84

CHAPTER 13   **The Founding
                    of the Airlines   87**
The Morrow Board   87
The Air Commerce Act of 1926   88
Lindbergh   88
The Daniel Guggenheim Fund for the Promotion
   of Aeronautics   91
Airways—from Lighted Beacons to Radio
   Navigation   92
Amelia Earhart   93
From Mail Carriers to Airlines   97
United Air Transport   97
North American Aviation   97
Aviation Corporation   97
Transcontinental Air Transport—
   A Novel Idea   98
Progenitors of the Big Four   98
The Airmail Act of 1930
   (McNary Watres Act)   99
Endnotes   103

CHAPTER 14   **New Deal—
                    The Roosevelt
                    Administration   105**
A New Broom Sweeps Clean   105
The Airmail Act of 1934
   (The Black-McKellar Act)   106
The Railway Labor Act   108
Endnotes   110

CHAPTER 15   **State of the Airlines before the Civil Aeronautics Act   113**
The National Advisory Committee on Aeronautics (NACA)   113
The Big Four   114
  American Airlines   114
  Eastern Air Lines   114
  TWA   115
  United Airlines   119
The Lesser Lines   120
Pan American Airways   120
Summary of Airlines' Condition   129
Endnotes   131

CHAPTER 16   **The Civil Aeronautics Act of 1938 (McCarran-Lea Act)   133**
Endnote   136

CHAPTER 17   **World War II   137**
The Lend Lease Act   138
The Chosen Instrument   139
The Airlines at War   139

CHAPTER 18   **A New Beginning   143**

CHAPTER 19   **On the Way to the Jet Age   149**
Jets   150
The British Comet   153
America Catches Up   154

CHAPTER 20   **The Federal Aviation Act   159**

CHAPTER 21   **The Next Jets   163**
The Really Big Jets   165

CHAPTER 22   **The Department of Transportation   169**
The Federal Aviation Administration   170
Regulation   171
Certification   172
  Airmen   172
  Aircraft   172
  Air Carriers   173
  Air Navigation Facilities   173
  Air Agencies   173
  Airports   173
  Designees   173
Investigation   174
Enforcement   174
Operations   175
  Air Traffic Control   175
  Radio Aids to Navigation   175
  National Airports   175
  Monroney Aeronautical Center   175
  William J. Hughes Technical Center   176
Education   176
Funding   176
Registration and Recordation   176
Commercial Space Transportation   176
Dual Mandate   177
The National Transportation Safety Board   177
Endnote   180

CHAPTER 23   **Airports   181**
Federal Airport Act of 1946   183
Airport Security   184
Evolution of a New National Airport Policy   185
Endnotes   186

PART V   **Deregulation   189**

CHAPTER 24   **Prelude to Deregulation   191**
The Economic Nature of Transportation   191
The Nature of Regulated Transportation   192
Endnote   195

CHAPTER 25   **The Airline Deregulation Act of 1978   197**
Braniff—A Case History Under Deregulation   198
The United States Bankruptcy Act   198

CHAPTER 26   **The Age of Lorenzo   201**
Texas International   201
People Express   203
Takeover at Continental Airlines   204
Computer Reservation Systems   205
Takeover at Eastern Air Lines   209
Takeover at People Express   209
DOT Approves the Eastern Takeover   210
Lorenzo Departs   211
Endnotes   212

CHAPTER 27 **Carl Icahn and TWA** **213**

CHAPTER 28 **Pan American and Deregulation** **217**

Endnote 223

CHAPTER 29 **Airline Labor Relations** **225**

Major Airline Unions 226
Strife and Presidential Interventions 227
The Mutual Aid Pact 228
Airline Labor Relations after Deregulation 229
ALPA and the Crew Size Issue 230
The PATCO Strike 231
Concession Bargaining 232
Two-Tiered Wage Agreements 232
Airline Union Characteristics 233
The Progression of Labor Impacts due to Deregulation 233
Summary 235
Endnotes 235

CHAPTER 30 **The Progression of Deregulation** **237**

Airline Fares 237
Passenger Travel 238
Number of Carriers 238
Market Share 239
Safety 239
Employment 239
The Evolution of Operating Practices 240
Hub and Spoke 240
Low Fare, Point-to-Point Service 242
The Regional Jet 242
The Fourth Wave—Demise of the Legacy Airlines Business Model 245
Endnotes 245

CHAPTER 31 **Deregulation and the Significance of Competition** **247**

A Look Back at the Arguments for Deregulation 247
Barriers to Entry—Limiting Competition 249
Slots 249
Gates 251
Perimeter Rules—LGA and DCA 251

Marketing Strategies—Frequent Flyer Programs 253
Marketing Strategies—Code Sharing and CRS 253
The Internet and Airport Competition Plans 254
Summary 254
Endnotes 254

CHAPTER 32 **Antitrust Enforcement after Deregulation** **255**

The Sherman Antitrust Act—Price Fixing and Trusts 256
The Clayton Antitrust Act—Mergers, Acquisitions, and Predation 256
The Civil Aeronautics Act and the Department of Justice 256
The Department of Justice and CAB— 1978 to 1985 257
The Department of Transportation— 1985 to 1988 257
The Department of Justice—1988 258
How Proposed Mergers and Acquisitions Are Reviewed 258
The Department of Transportation after 1988 259
Predation and Competitive Responses of Airlines 259
Anticompetitive Practices at Airports 261
Endnotes 261

CHAPTER 33 **Airports and Deregulation** **263**

Airport Ownership 264
Airport Funding for Operations and Capital Improvements 264
Airport Revenue Bonds 264
Airport Improvement Program Funds (AIP) 264
Airport User Charges 266
Passenger Facility Charges (PFCs) 266
State and Local Government Programs 266
Airport Facilities Use Arrangements 266
Residual Use and Lease Agreements 266
Compensatory Use and Lease Agreements 267
Hybrid Use and Lease Agreements 267

Gate Leasing Arrangements   267
   Exclusive-Use Arrangements   267
   Preferential-Use Arrangements   268
   Airport-Controlled or Common-Use
     Arrangements   268
DOT Interest in Airport Practices—
   Unfair Competition   269
Airport Privatization   269
Wendell H. Ford Aviation Investment and Reform
   Act for the 21st Century (AIR-21)   270
Endnotes   272

CHAPTER 34   Airports and the
                Environment   273
The Air Pollution Act and The Clean Air Act   273
   Aviation Impacts   274
   Aviation-Generated Air Pollution   274
Aircraft Noise   277
   Aircraft Noise Abatement Act of 1968   277
   Noise Control Act of 1972 and Aviation
     Safety and Noise Abatement Act
     of 1979   277
   Airport Noise and Capacity Act
     of 1990   278
Endnotes   279

CHAPTER 35   Deregulation in the
                Nineties   281
The Economy   281
Liquidations and Chapter 11   282
Southwest Airlines   283
American Airlines   283
Foreign Code Sharing   283
United Airlines   284
A New Wave of Startups   284
Good Times Are Here Again   284

CHAPTER 36   Airlines at the Beginning
                of the 21st Century   287
September 11, 2001   287
The Air Transportation Safety and System
   Stabilization Act   289
Aviation and Transportation Security Act   290
Homeland Security Act of 2002   290
Aftermath of September 11   291
   Security Mandates   291
   Liability Insurance   293
   Load Factors   295

   Labor   295
   Fleet   296
   Bankruptcies   296
Beyond 9-11—Another New Beginning   299
   A Glance over the Shoulder   299
   Taking Stock   300
Legacy Airlines vs. Low-Cost Carriers   304
Looking Forward   305
Vision 100—Century of Aviation Reauthorization
   Act of 2003   308
   Next Generation Air Transportation System
     (NextGen)   308
Why NextGen Is Necessary   310
Endnotes   310

PART VI   **International Civil**
                  Aviation   311

CHAPTER 37   **Treaties and International**
                Civil Aviation
                Organizations   313
International Aviation Relations   313
The Warsaw Convention—1929   314
   The Hague Protocol and the Montreal
     Agreement   314
   IATA Inter-Carrier Agreement and IATA
     Measures of Implementation
     Agreement   315
   The Montreal Convention—1999   315
   The Chicago Conference   316
   The Chicago Convention—1944   316
   The International Air Transport
     Agreement   316
   The Transit Agreement   317
   The Bermuda Agreement   317
Additional Conventions   317
   International Recognition of Rights in Aircraft
     (Geneva Convention—1948)   317
   Damage to Third Parties on the Surface
     Caused by Foreign Aircraft (Rome
     Convention—1952)   318
   Air Offenses Convention (Tokyo Convention
     of 1963)   318
   Hijacking Convention (Hague Convention
     for the Suppression of Unlawful Seizure
     of Aircraft—1970)   318

*Convention for the Suppression of Unlawful
Acts against the Safety of Civil Aviation
(Montreal Convention—1971)   318*
*Plastic Explosives Convention (Convention
on the Marking of Plastic Explosives for
the Purpose of Detection—1991)   318*
The International Civil Aviation Organization
(ICAO)   319
The International Air Transport Association
(IATA)   320

**CHAPTER 38   Europe after World
War II—The Rise of the
European Economic
Community   323**
The European-American Relationship   323
The Marshall Plan   324
The Evolution of the European Community   326
Institutions of the EEC   327
*The Treaty of Rome and Air
Transportation   328*
Endnotes   329

**CHAPTER 39   American Deregulation
and the European
Union   331**
Liberalization of Air Transport in the European
Community   332
Advent of the European Union   333
Competition Rules in Air Transport   333
Predation and Merger   333
Government Subsidies   334
Aviation Agencies of the European Union   336
*The European Civil Aviation Conference
(ECAC)   336*
*The European Joint Aviation Authorities
(JAA)   336*
*European Aviation Safety Agency
(EASA)   338*
European Air Traffic Control   339
SESAR (Single European Sky ATM Research
Program)   339
The Case for Convergence   340
Summary   341
Endnotes   341

**CHAPTER 40   Global Deregulation
Takes Off   343**
The First Multilateral Open Skies Agreement   345
Deregulation and the United Kingdom   345
*Breakthrough—Open Skies Agreement
between the United States and the
European Union   345*
Summary   346
Endnotes   346

**CHAPTER 41   Global Aircraft
Manufacturing   347**
European Aircraft Manufacturing   347
The Concorde   348
Airbus Industrie   351
The Competition Begins   353
The American Giants   355
The U.K. Rejoins Airbus   356
Funding the "Family"   356
International Aircraft Production into the
21st Century   359
Large Commercial Jet Engines   361
The Global Supply Chain—Major Suppliers   363
United States   363
Europe   364
Russia   364
Japan   365
China   366
South Korea   367
Taiwan and Indonesia   367
Airbus vs. Boeing: International
Trade Background   367
The World Trade Organization   371
Airbus vs. Boeing: The Road to War   371
*Airbus vs. Boeing: A Review of the
Grievances   372*
The U.S. Position   374
The EU Position   374
Overview of the Dispute   375
Airbus Restructured   376
Regulatory Nationalism   377
Challenge to America   378
Why It Matters   380
An Uncertain Future   387

Airbus Beginning the 21st Century   388
    The A380   388
    The A350   390
Boeing Beginning the 21st Century   391
    The 787   392
    The 747-8   396
Beginning the 21st Century—The Global
   Duopoly   396
Endnotes   398

CHAPTER 42   Beyond Earth   401
The Founding Fathers of Rocketry   401
Space: The New Frontier   404
    Sputnik   404
Scientific Cooperation—Precedent for Space   405
The Antarctic Treaty   406
The Space Race Begins   406
Who Owns Outer Space?   407
Terrestrial Precedents   407
Treaties Affecting Outer Space   409
    The Limited Test Ban Treaty of 1963   409
    The Outer Space Treaty of 1967   409
    The Rescue Treaty of 1968   410
    The Liability Treaty of 1972   410
    The Registration Convention of 1976   412
    The Moon Treaty of 1979   412
    *The International Space Station
      Agreement*   413
Commercial Space Transportation—
   End of a Government Monopoly   414
    *The Commercial Space Launch Act
      of 1984*   414
    Commercial Space Launch Activity   415
    Commercial Launch Sites   417
SpaceShipOne (SS1)   418
    Reusable Launch Vehicles   422
The NASA Centennial Challenges   423
    *The Bigelow Aerospace Competition—
      America's Space Prize*   424
Vision for Space Exploration—A Statement
   of National Purpose   424
    A Brief History   424
    The Vision   425
The Role of Government   426
Endnotes   427

APPENDIX 1   **Excerpts from the
Address of Dr. Alexander
Graham Bell in Presenting
the Langley Medal to
Mr. Gustave Eiffel and
to Mr. Glenn Curtiss
in 1913   429**

APPENDIX 2   **Excerpts from Remarks
of Dr. Alexander Graham
Bell before the Board
of Regents of the
Smithsonian Institution
on February 13, 1913
on the Award of the
Langley Medal   433**

APPENDIX 3   **Blazing the Trail to
Chicago   435**

APPENDIX 4   **Excerpts from
Lindbergh's Log of His
Solo Flight from New
York to Paris   437**
New York to Paris   437
The Flight   438
Endnote   440

APPENDIX 5   **Women in Early
Aviation   441**
Endnote   444

APPENDIX 6   **Calbraith Perry
Rodgers   445**

APPENDIX 7   **Accidents Involving
Passenger Fatalities   449**
U.S. Airlines (Part 121) 1982–Present   449
U.S. Commuters (Part 135) 1982–Present   452

GLOSSARY   455

BIBLIOGRAPHY   463

INDEX   471

STATUTES

1862 Pacific Railroad Act

1887 Interstate Commerce Act

1890 Sherman Antitrust Act of 1890

1903 Elkins Act

1906 Hepburn Act

1910 Mann-Elkins Act

1914 Clayton Antitrust Act

1925 Airmail Act of 1925 (Kelly)

1926 Air Commerce Act of 1926

1926 Railway Labor Act

1928 Foreign Airmail Act

1930 Airmail Act of 1930 (McNary-Watres)

1932 Norris-Laguardia Act

1934 Airmail Act of 1934 (Black-McKellar)

1935 National Labor Relations Act (Wagner Act)

1935 Motor Carrier Act

1936 RLA Made Applicable to Airline Industry

1938 Civil Aeronautics Act

1941 Lend Lease Act

1944 Surplus Property Act

1946 Federal Airport Act of 1946

1955 Air Pollution Act

1958 Federal Aviation Act of 1958

1963 The Clean Air Act

1966 Department of Transportation Act

1968 Aircraft Noise Abatement Act

1968 Civil Service Reform Act

1969 National Environmental Policy Act

1970 Airport and Airway Development Act of 1970

1970 The Clean Air Act, Amended

1972 Noise Control Act of 1972

1973 Airport Development Acceleration Act

1974 Independent Safety Board Act of 1974

1976 Airport and Airway Development Act Amendments

1977 Air Cargo Deregulation Act

1978 Airline Deregulation Act

1979 Aviation Safety and Noise Abatement Act

1980 Motor Carrier Act of 1980

1982 Airport and Airway Development Act of 1982–FAA

1984 The Commercial Space Launch Act

1990 Airport Noise and Capacity Act (ANCA)

1994 FAA Authorization Act of 1994

1994 Independent Safety Board Act of 1994

1996 Airport Privatization Program

1999 Wendell H. Ford Aviation Investment and Reform Act for the 21st Century (Air-21)

2001 Air Transportation Safety and System Stabilization Act

2001 Aviation and Transportation Security Act

2002 Homeland Security Act

2003 Vision 100-Century of Aviation Reauthorization Act

2004 The Commercial Space Launch Amendments Act

Antitrust Legislation

1890 Sherman Antitrust Act

1914 Clayton Antitrust Act

The United States Bankruptcy Act

The bankruptcy laws of the United States have been consistently amended since 1801.

CASES

Massachusetts Commonwealth v. Hunt

National Labor Relations v. Bildisco

Nouvellas Frontieres

Pan American World Airways Inc v. United States

Panama Refining Co. v. Ryan

Parker v. Brown

United States v. CAB

FIGURES

1-1   The rate of technological advance.

2-1   Important events in industrial and technological development.

3-1   An early steam engine.

3-2   The Louisiana Purchase provided much of the land needed for the proposed transcontinental railroad.

3-3   The transcontinental railroad.

3-4   The emergence of cities, 1880.

5-1   An observation balloon during the Civil War.

5-2   Types of airships.

5-3   Otto Lilienthal and his glider.

5-4   Otto Lilienthal in flight—"to fly is everything."

5-5   Octave Chanute.

5-6   Lilienthal-type glider tested by Octave Chanute.

5-7   Box-type glider (double decker) design later used by the Wright Brothers.

5-8   Box-type glider showing dunes near Lake Michigan where Chanute held experiments.

6-1   Samuel Langley.

6-2   Samuel Langley and Charles Manly.

6-3   The Aerodrome atop Langley's barge.

6-4   The crash of the Aerodrome.

7-1   The Wright Brothers' kite—1900.

7-2   The Wright Brothers' kite, also flown as a glider.

7-3   Glider—1901.

7-4   Glider turning—1902.

7-5   The first powered flight—December 17, 1903.

7-6   The third powered flight—December 17, 1903.

7-7   Flyer II at Huffman Prairie—1904.

7-8   Flyer III at Huffman Prairie—1905.

7-9   Flyer III—the world's first practical Airplane—1905.

7-10   Wilbur Wright flying in France—1909.

7-11   Orville Wright at Fort Myer, Virginia—1908.

7-12   Lt. Thomas Selfridge and Orville Wright prior to a take off at Ft. Myer, Virginia—1908.

8-1   The Baldwin dirigible equipped with Curtiss motors, was delivered to the Aeronautical Division of the U.S. Army Signal Corps in Washington in the summer of 1908. Baldwin operated the controls of the craft from the rear, while Glenn Curtiss took care of the engine forward. The airship succeeded in meeting government specifications during its two-hour trials.

8-2   Members of the Aeronautical Experiment Association (From Left to Right) Glenn Curtiss, J. A. D. McCurdy, Alexander Graham Bell, Frederick W. Baldwin, Thomas E. Selfridge.

8-3   White Wing.

8-4   June Bug with Glenn Curtiss at the controls—1908.

8-5   Glenn Curtiss seated in the June Bug.

8-6   Glenn Curtiss winning the Scientific American Trophy with the June Bug—July 4, 1908.

8-7   Lt. Thomas E. Selfridge and Dr. Alexander Graham Bell at Baldwin Trials, August 18, 1908.

8-8   Eugene Ely performing the first take off from a Naval vessel—November 1910.

8-9   Eugene Ely making the first landing aboard a Naval vessel, January 1911.

8-10   Curtiss flying boat—Model E.

8-11   The NC-4, the first plane to cross the Atlantic.

10-1   President Woodrow Wilson at the inauguration of airmail—May 15, 1918.

10-2   Major Reuben Fleet (on the left) briefs airmail pilot Lt. George Boyle before he begins his flight on May 15, 1918.

10-3   Lt. George Boyle takes off for Philadelphia.

10-4   The first civilian airmail pilots (from left to right): Edward Gardner, Captain Benjamin Lipsner, Maurice Newton, Max Miller, and Robert Shank.

10-5   De Havilland—DH-4 with a Liberty engine.

10-6   DH-4.

10-7   Wild Bill Hopson, airmail pilot.

10-8   Original Transcontinental Airmail Route.

10-9   The lighted airway system as of December 31, 1927.

11-1   Frederich B. Rentschler.

12-1   Benoist flying boat—1914.

12-2   Benoist flying boat—1914. Inauguration of the St. Petersburg—Tampa airboat line.

12-3   Aeromarine 50-U8D.

12-4   Charles Lindbergh on CAM 2, flown between Chicago and St. Louis.

12-5   Ford Trimotor.

12-6   Ford Trimotor loading mail.

13-1   Charles Lindbergh pays a visit to Orville Wright at Wright Field, Dayton, OH, June 22, 1927.

13-2   Juan Trippe and Charles Lindbergh.

13-3   Schematic of the four-course radio range.

13-4   Amelia Earhart.

13-5   Route of Transcontinental Air Transport—depicting night and day portions of the route.

13-6   Airmail Airways.

14-1   1934 airmail routes.

15-1   Eddie Rickenbacker.

15-2   The Boeing 247 was to be a great leap forward with its low mono-wing, and two engines instead of three that were mounted into wings in nacelles that greatly reduced drag.

15-3   DC-1, designation for the Douglas Commercial Number 1. This was the only one ever built.

15-4   DC-3—The plane that changed the world.

15-5   Boeing 307.

15-6   Howard Hughes, the eccentric multimillionaire and aviation pioneer.

15-7   Progress in airmail transport service, 1926–1936.

15-8   Source of revenues of the airline companies.

15-9   Fokker F-7 to Havana, Pan American 1928.

15-10   S-38.

15-11   Igor Sikorsky and Eddie Musick.

15-12   Charles Lindbergh and S-38 in Miami.

15-13   Charles Lindbergh and S-38.

15-14   The Consolidated Commodore was originally designed as a patrol boat for the United States Navy, but was converted to commercial use by September 1929.

15-15   Pan American Airways Route Map 1933.

15-16   The S-40 was the first aircraft to address the problem of range of miles over the vast Pacific Ocean.

15-17   S-40. Approaching Pan Am's Dinner Key Terminal, FL.

15-18   S-40. taking off from Biscayne Bay, FL.

15-19   The S-42 had a range of 2,520 miles.

15-20   S-42.

15-21   S-43—on glassy water.

15-22   In October 1935 the first M-130 Martin flying boat was delivered.

15-23   M-130 and Commodore at Dinner Key Terminal.

15-24   M-130 at Dinner Key.

15-25   The B-314 was the largest aircraft to be used in scheduled service until the arrival of jumbo jets in the late 1960s.

15-26   Inside Pan Am's Dinner Key Terminal.

15-27   Passengers boarding a Pan Am flight for an adventure.

16-1   The beginnings of air traffic control—Earl Ward (left) organized the Newark, New Jersey air traffic facility in the mid-1930's. Here he tracks a flight with the aid of a calipar as R.A. Eccles watches. The pointed markers are representing aircraft were moved across the map as flights progressed.

17-1   Military airmen in Training with Pan Am.

18-1   The DC-4 became available to the domestic fleet in 1946.

18-2   The Constellation was much more expensive to maintain than other comparable aircraft.

18-3   General aircraft utilization domestic airlines.

18-4   Less time to cross the continent.

19-1   The DC-6 was launched in coast-to-coast service on April 27, 1947 with one stop enroute for fuel.

19-2   Boeing 377, Constellation 049, and DC-4.

19-3   Germany's Jumo-004 engine.

19-4   The Comet entered into service on British Overseas Airways Corporation in May 1952.

19-5   A KC-97 refueling a B-47.

20-1   Pete Quesada being sworn in at the FAA in the fall of 1958.

21-1   The Caravelle was a prototype with the aircraft's engines on the side of the fuselage near the tail of the aircraft.

21-2   Boeing 727.

21-3   Douglas DC-9.

21-4   Boeing 737.

21-5   The Boeing 747 flew faster than previous models.

21-6   Comparison of the interiors of the L-1011 (top) and the F-7 (bottom).

21-7   Lockheed L-1011.

21-8   DC-10.

22-1   Estimated controller losses and planned hires, fiscal years 2006–2015.

22-2   NTSB's Organization.

22-3   Number of accident investigations completed by NTSB by mode, fiscal years 2002–2005.

22-4   Key laws, regulations, and NTSB policies for investigations by mode.

22-5   Fatalities by transportation mode, 2005.

26-1   Frank Lorenzo at a press conference, June, 1984.

27-1   Carl Icahn began buying up shares of TWA in 1985, and by April he had acquired enough stock in the company to trigger the mandatory public filings with the Securities and Exchange Commission.

28-1   Boeing 747 (top), Boeing 314 (middle), Fokker F-7 (bottom).

28-2   Pan American Field at Miami before the sale by Pan American to the city of Miami.

28-3   Pan American Dinner Key Terminal.

29-1   Airline employee compensation as a share of total operating expenses, 1968–2005.

29-2   Employees.

30-1   Median fares have declined almost 40 percent since 1980 as measured in 2005 dollars.

30-2   Safety record of U.S. airlines—fatal accidents per million aircraft miles.

30-3   Accident rates.

30-4   A wide array of "regional jets."

30-5   Uses of regional jets.

30-6   U.S. regional airline growth, 1978–1996.

31-1   Summary of slot exemptions granted by DOT under AIR21 and Vision 100 as of September 2006.

32-1   Major air carrier mergers, acquisitions, purchases, and consolidations through 2001.

33-1   Airport activity statistics of certificated air carriers.

34-1   U.S. aircraft emission trends, 1970–1995.

34-2   Significant progress in reduction of aircraft noise.

34-3   Population expected to benefit from noise funding.

33-2   98% of airport revenue comes from airport users: U.S. Airport Sources of Revenue, 2001.

35-1   Jet fuel price 1989–1991. In July 1990, fuel price was at 57 cents. By October 1990, fuel price had soared to $1.14 a gallon.

35-2   Passenger traffic 1990–1991 showing dramatic decline in international travel.

36-1   Boeing 757.

36-2   The Manhattan skyline prior to the terrorists' attacks of September 11, 2001.

36-3   Organization of the Transportation Security Administration (TSA).

36-4   Financial impact of post 9-11 Policies. Post 9-11 taxes, fees, and unfunded mandates have added more than $4 billion to the industry's annual burden.

36-5   Taxes and fees on a $200 roundtrip ticket.

36-6   Federal aviation taxes and fees.

36-7   Aviation taxes have outpaced inflation, airline labor costs, and airfares.

36-8   Airline Insurance Costs: 2001–02.

36-9   Comparison of fuel spikes and economic recessions.

36-10   Market price of jet fuel.

36-11   Breakeven passenger load factor at record highs.

36-12   Net change in mainline operating fleet—ATA U.S. members. ATA members are Airborne Express, Alaska Airlines, Aloha Airlines, America West Airlines, American Airlines, American Trans Air, Atlas Air, Continental Airlines, Delta Air Lines, DHL Airways, Emery Worldwide, Evergreen International, FedEx, Hawaiian Airlines, JetBlue Airways, Midwest Airlines, Northwest Airlines, Polar Air Cargo, Southwest Airlines, United Airlines, UPS Airlines, and US Airways.

36-13   Aircraft orders and options backlog—ATA U.S. members.

36-14   U.S. airline employment.

36-15   Fuel prices U.S.

36-16   Passenger load factor.

36-17   Employees.

36-18   Legacy airlines have recorded nearly $25 billion in operating losses since 2001.

36-19   Stage length cost curves, 2000 and 2003.

36-20   Unit cost differential, 1998 to 2003.

36-21   Percentage change in airline fares and demand since 2000.

36-22   Airline profits and losses, 1998–2003.

38-1   Western Europe after World War II, showing countries that received aid under the Marshall Plan.

39-1   Examples of airline privatizations since the 1980s.

41-1   Concorde.

41-2   The Airbus family.

41-3   Evolution of Airbus.

41-4   Airbus family.

41-5   Large civil aircraft orders.

41-6   Large civil aircraft engines in service.

41-7   Large civil aircraft engines delivered.

41-8   U.S. major suppliers.

41-9   European major suppliers.

41-10   Trade facts.

41-11   Stock ownership of Airbus Industrie.

41-12 R&D scientists & engineers in aerospace and as % of all industries.

41-13 Aerospace manufacturing employment.

41-14 Federal aerospace procurement and R&D expenditures FY 1993–2001.

41-15 Trade balance by industry, 2005 (best five vs. worst five).

41-16 Aerospace employment.

41-17 Aerospace industry sales.

41-18 Aerospace industry sales.

41-19 Aerospace foreign trade.

41-20 FY 1987—FY 2007 DoD budget authority.

41-21 Aerospace share of national R&D funding.

41-22 A380 orders.

41-23 Specifications.

41-24 Joint effort: Parts for the Boeing 787 are manufactured around the globe.

41-25 Boeing 787 orders and options.

41-26 Last schedule flight of the British Concorde, October 24, 2004.

41-27 Orders and deliveries.

42-1 Konstantin Tsiolkovsky.

42-2 Robert Goddard on March 16, 1926.

42-3 Hermann Oberth (foreground) Wernher von Braun (near right).

42-4 GSO satellite and launch demand.

42-5 NGSO satellite and launch demand.

42-6 Combined GSO and NGSO launch forecasts.

42-7 U.S. Space Transportation Industry.

42-8 U.S. spaceports.

42-9 White Knight lifting SpaceShipOne.

42-10 SpaceShipOne.

42-11 Hybrid rocket engine used by SS1.

42-12 Saturn V, space shuttle, and shuttle-derived launch vehicles (Areas 1, Ares IV, & Ares V) shown by relative size.

App 5-1 Harriet Quimby was the first American woman to earn her license from F.A.I. on August 2, 1911.

App 6-1 Cal Rodgers just before beginning his cross-country odyssey on September 17, 1911.

App 6-2 Flight of the "Vin Fiz," 1911.

For the last 100 years, the evolution of commercial aviation has been a worldwide phenomenon. It has been the result of a combination of individual and corporate effort, and it has proceeded because of, and sometimes in spite of, the involvement of governments. In the United States, commercial aviation developed under principles of private enterprise in tension with government in its role of protecting the public interest. In contrast, throughout most of the rest of the world, governments have assumed the lead in innovation, development, and promotion of civil aviation, consistent with their more socialized economic systems and philosophies.

The cornerstone of the American experiment is government-protected individual freedom, in the words of the Declaration of Independence, the right to "life, liberty, and the pursuit of happiness." This freedom extends to business: the freedom to risk capital and ingenuity in return for financial gain. Failures resulting from these risks are borne individually or corporately, while the fruits of success often accrue to the benefit of the many.

The government of the United States traditionally has not been an intrusive government; rather, it was created in reaction to intrusive, oppressive foreign government. The powers of the federal government are derived from the people and are granted specifically in the Constitution of the United States. The government has no other source of power. Involvement of the federal government in the affairs of its citizens is authorized only as a result of duly enacted legislation (statutory law) by the Congress, and then only as to those matters over which it is given jurisdiction by the provisions of the Constitution.

When the American government was created, land transportation was primarily a private affair. The federal government took cognizance of its admiralty (maritime and shipping) responsibilities, but otherwise gave little heed to matters of travel. The obligation of government to attend to the "public welfare" extended to matters of interstate commerce, banking, defense, and the delivery of mail through the Post Office Department. The government experimented with trail improvement on its western margins (Ohio Territory, for instance) and road building (Post roads) incident to the delivery of the mails, but did little else. As the technological advances of the Industrial Revolution proceeded, so did the manufacturing and commercial enterprises that utilized them. Corporate forms of existence came into general use. Westward migration followed the steam locomotive and the telegraph across the country. The government was increasingly drawn into subsidy and regulation. These developments were followed by the reciprocating gasoline engine, the automobile, and the telephone. The transmission of electricity, wireless communication, commercial radio, and the airplane came after. The role of government continued to expand as the technological advances of the Industrial Revolution increasingly impacted the nation's commerce and its people.

The concepts of the federal maritime law were applied to the railroads when they appeared, and the law was modified as necessary to account for differences between these two modes of transport. Government experience with the railroads was applied to the new air transport industry when, in turn, it appeared. The result has been the development of a similar government methodology for the treatment of all forms of commercial transportation. Government in the United States remained mostly in the background even into the early part of the 20th century, but it remained ready to apply a steadying hand to prevent excesses of private or corporate self-interest.

The other primary interest of government in modern transportation involved issues of safety, which was legally appropriate under the Constitution in the interest of the public welfare. Government involvement in transportation safety issues first appeared in connection with railroad employees, who were suffering egregious personal injury due to the nature of railroading in the late 19th and early 20th century. Government's first involvement with aviation safety issues, in 1925, related to certification of pilots and aircraft, and airworthiness concerns. Safety would become the overriding governmental interest in commercial aviation as the twentieth century progressed and as economic regulation by the government was phased out, beginning in 1978.

The early involvement of the government of the United States in transportation issues was mainly reactive, but also partly proactive. The railroad industry-government relationship was fairly well-established by the time the first practical airplane was developed. The railroads were privately owned, but the government actively regulated them. The United States experimented with government ownership of the railroads during World War I, but ended up returning them to corporate ownership after the war.

When the airplane appeared, there was no practical reason, nor any legal justification, for any government involvement. The audacious and romantic notion of flight was not put to practical use for over a decade after the Wright's first flight, then in war in Europe in 1914. By war's end in 1918, in the United States the airplane was quickly returned to curiosity status, being used in barnstorming exhibitions, banner towing, and the occasional sightseeing flight. In the first part of the 20th century, America ran on wheels, steel ones and ever increasingly on rubber tired wheels, and it did not have any immediate need for the airplane.[1]

In Europe, a limited commercial success had already been seen in Germany with the rise and deployment of dirigibles by 1909. European governments soon appreciated the potential commercial use of the airplane, particularly given the ruinous state of Europe's railroads after the devastation of World War I. The

English Channel lay between London and Paris, separating two of the premier commercial and cultural metropolitan centers of the world, and it provided an obvious reason for commercial aviation to succeed. European governments owned the railroads. It was natural that the first commercial airlines created after World War I would also be owned by European governments.

But the United States was staunchly capitalistic. If aviation for any purpose was to succeed in this country, it was going to be up to a new breed of adventurer and entrepreneur to make it happen. Who they were and how they made it happen is the larger part of the account of the first century of flight. The story of airmail, the politics of the Great Depression, the creation of private airlines, the impact of World War II, the dawning of the jet age, the deregulation of the airlines, and the advent of world competition are all part of that adventure. The achievements of the first century of flight required the best from many worlds. The realms of business and finance, of engineering and science, and of government struggled together to overcome the uncertainties at the leading edge of a new technology. These struggles continue even today as the air transport industry, the flying public, and the government attempt to define the role that air transportation should play in the 21st century.

At the beginning of the new millennium, government has now been called upon to play perhaps its most decisive role ever in air transportation: the protection of the traveling public from international terrorism, and the pursuit of its ultimate defeat.

Endnote

1. In 1900, there were 8,000 automobiles registered in the United States. By 1920, there were 8 million automobiles registered. *Wall Street Journal* 5/17/03.

Harry W. Lawrence is a member of the adjunct faculty of Embry-Riddle Aeronautical University, College of Career Education, and holds the rank of Adjunct Assistant Professor. He is shareholder emeritus at the law firm of Lowndes, Drosdick, Doster, Kantor, and Reed in Orlando, Florida.

He received his Juris Doctor degree from the University of North Carolina at Chapel Hill, 1965, and was admitted to practice in Florida, Tennessee, and the District of Columbia. He was admitted to practice before the Supreme Court of the United States and Courts of the Fifth, Sixth, and Eleventh Circuits of the United States. He served as counsel for Seaboard Coast Line Railroad and Clinchfield Railroad Company (now CSX). He is Board Certified in Civil Trial Law by the Florida Bar. His practice of law had an emphasis on maritime, aviation, and railroad transportation issues.

He holds a Commercial Pilot Certificate with instrument, multiengine, glider, seaplane, and jet type ratings. He has been corporate owner and operator of fixed-base operations for general aviation, including turbojet commercial aircraft.

PART I

Foundation

© Stephen Strathdee, 2008, Shutterstock.

Chapter 1 Beginnings

Chapter 2 The Industrial Revolution

Chapter 3 The Railroads

Chapter 4 The Industrial Age and
the Rise of Unionism

Beginnings

This is a story that begins with man's earliest reported technological accomplishment, the invention of the wheel, and continues with an ever-increasing intensity. A curve plotted on one axis as time and on the other as the rate of technological advance will depict a flat to gradually rising line, becoming at a point a rapidly rising line, disclosing a recent very high rate of technological accomplishment. (See Figure 1-1.) Between 1790 and 1870, for example, there were just over 40,000 patents granted in the United States for that entire 80-year period. During the 30 years between 1870 and 1900, the Patent Office granted over 400,000 patents, a ten-fold increase in slightly more than one third of the time. In 1870, there was nothing in America that could be called a steel industry; but by 1900, over 10 million tons of steel were being produced annually, more than the rest of the world combined. As men struggled to fly, the rate of technological innovation was beginning to move up, but it had been a long time coming.

All modern day accomplishments are based, to one degree or another, on the efforts and accomplishments of those who went before. The ancient Phoenicians sailed the confines of the Mediterranean Sea by reference to land, and also by reference to the sun and stars. The length of the Mediterranean, its east and west limits, were known to them as Asu (east) and Ereb (west), the word roots that form the names of Asia and Europe in use today. Ocean travel was coastwise. Improvements were made to the shapes of sails and hulls used in early maritime commerce. Insurance and accounting came into vogue in the maritime trading centers around the Mediterranean, in the city-states such as Venice. Gunpowder arrived by the ninth century and, by the late twelfth century, the magnetic compass was coming into common use on land and sea.

But the rising curve of progress really only begins with the rise of Western Civilization and the Rule of Law. Circumstances conducive to invention and innovation depend on many factors, including incentive to innovate—like the profit motive—and protection for the results of invention, like patent law. These and other relevant factors depend on a stable, progressive and lawful society, and a strong government. Magna Carta (The Great Charter), in 1215, establishing for the first time limitations on the arbitrary powers of the King of England, is widely regarded as the cornerstone of personal liberty. Its principles have evolved into broad constitutional concepts embraced today. In 1420 began a period of progress and enlightenment known as the Renaissance (rebirth), a time of advances in astronomy, anatomy, engineering, physics, and

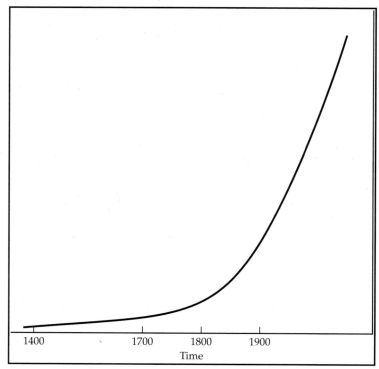

FIGURE 1-1 The rate of technological advance.

art. Great leaps of mind made by the luminaries of that day included the idea that man might actually fly—or so believed Leonardo da Vinci (1452–1519). His sketches depicting wings to support manned flight disclose that he understood the same basic airfoil concept used today. His ideas on the subject were lost for a period of 300 years before rediscovery.

❝ When once you have tasted flight, you will forever walk the earth with your eyes turned skyward, for there you have been, and there you will always long to return. ❞

Leonardo da Vinci

That enlightened period was followed by the era of European exploration and discovery, of long distance open water navigation, and the opening of extended trade routes still in use today, along with a commercial appreciation of the meaning of time and distance. Latitudinal position, or north-south location, had for some time been capable of being established by reference to the celestial bodies, using instruments from early times like the gnomon or the Arabian kamal, and later the astrolabe, the cross-staff, and in 1731, the sextant. While a laborious methodology using the sextant could approximate longitude after 1731, the lack of a definitive longitudinal reference had prevented from time immemorial the accurate determining of positions of longitude, which resulted in costly navigation errors, loss of life and property, and commercial uncertainty.

In 1714, British Parliament offered a prize of twenty thousand pounds sterling for a reliable method of determining longitude on a ship at sea. The best minds in Europe, including noted astronomers and physicists, worked on the project for 50 years without success. John Harrison, who was an uneducated carpenter and clockmaker, reasoned that if a ship's local time at sea could be compared to the time at the port of origin, the calculation could readily be made to find the ship's longitudinal location. But no clock existed that would keep accurate time at sea, due to the water's motion. After years of painstaking effort, he finally produced such a timepiece, a chronometer, in 1764. The missing universal frame of reference, the Prime Meridian, was officially established in 1884 at Greenwich, England, at which Universal or Zulu time is now found.

In transportation, while marginal improvements were seen in matters nautical, no significant advance had been otherwise made since the dawn of time. Motive power for land transport was provided either by animals or by men themselves. George Washington, for instance, in 1776, was unable to travel from Philadelphia to New York any faster than Julius Caesar could cover the equivalent distance from Rome to Pompeii. In the middle of the eighteenth century, the problem was the lack of motive power.

We will begin the study of aviation, and the role of government, with the advent of the Industrial Revolution. The fruits of this period in world history would, for the first time, drastically alter essentially every aspect of human existence, and would, within the space of 54 years in the twentieth century, accomplish a journey from the bicycle age to the space age.

CHAPTER 2

The Industrial Revolution

© Dan Barnes, 2008,
Shutterstock, Inc.

The City of London, although of ancient Roman origin (Londonium), had little to distinguish it from the other potential candidates of Europe and the Middle East (Paris, Venice, Athens, Alexandria) for the honor of becoming the jumping off place for the economic and military conquest of the world. One might have thought, for example, that such a place might more logically be somewhere in the Cradle of Civilization—the Middle East—or at least the Mediterranean, where for centuries commerce had steadily proceeded as invaders and traders crisscrossed the area bartering food, raw materials, and spices. Those people developed new and better sailing ships and means of propulsion (such as the triangular sail as an improvement on the square rigger), and they had a leg up when it came to understanding and practicing the art of politics, the use of centralized power, the formulation of ideas, and the development of institutions through centuries of inheritance. The earliest cities, governments, law codes, and alphabets were of Middle Eastern origin, as were the earliest forms of religion—Judaism, Christianity, and Islam.

The roots of the Industrial Revolution, however, can be found in English inventiveness. In 1750, most people in the world lived in relative self-sufficiency, filling their needs from the sea and through the husbandry of their own or others' land. People produced not only their food, but also their clothes, fuel, candles, and even furniture. Items that could not be produced locally, such as spices, tea, and precious stones, could be purchased in limited quantity from entrepreneurial efforts. The issue of labor was rather simple: one essentially did for oneself.

But there was a difference between England and the rest of Europe. England had developed a type of middle class, a mercantile base that dealt in the leather and wool trades, shipping, and banking. Most of Europe was still stuck in the vestiges of the feudal system of the Middle Ages where one's future was defined by his status at birth. In England, trade had become a leveler of class distinction to some degree, where the opportunity to engage in free market exchange brought the opportunity for financial gain. Financial success meant escape from dependency on the upper classes and service to those with wealth and property. A lack of dependency brought with it not only self-sufficiency, but also freedom from the servile bondage of a class-bound society. It brought hope to the common man, and it invigorated him.

Production of woolen goods was revolutionized by invention, like the flying shuttle in 1733 by John Kay, and the spinning jenny in 1764 by James Hargreaves. These and other inventions led to machinery that provided a mechanized means of production whose places of operation came to be known as factories. Factories required people to operate the machines, men and women who could offer their labor in return for wages. In a society that was primarily agrarian, employment opportunities were not widespread. But among the descendents of feudal peasantry, the opportunity to work for a wage, and thus gain a measure of independence, was a step up.

The implementation of the factory system brought with it a significant change in the organization of work. While the production of goods had always been an individual endeavor, requiring the application of some skill in the craft, the factory system introduced a repetitive, routine, and boring set of hand–eye coordination that required, at the most, minimal skill. Over time, workers became more restive, dissatisfied, and unconnected.

Perhaps the most seminal of all developments during this time was the 1769 appearance of the reliable steam engine by Scottish inventor, James Watt. This invention would institutionalize the factory system, both in terms of the development of the labor movement and in terms of the efficient production of goods. It would change the course of the maritime trade, beginning with the installation of a steam engine on a barge to provide motive power, the forerunner of the steamship. Not long after, the steam engine would inaugurate an entirely new mode of transportation on land when installed on a carriage, the precursor of the locomotive.

The Industrial Revolution set the stage for the modern age to come. Figure 2-1 lists important events in the Industrial and Technological Revolution. It provided the impetus for the creation of the modern corporation, as a legal entity, which developed as the vehicle by which to raise the large sums of money that were required to engage in the business opportunities that were generated by the Industrial Revolution. It provided the means necessary to commence the first land mass transportation system, the railroads. As the relationship was being established between the

railroads and labor, and between both of them and with government, the paradigm for the airlines in these same areas was being set. Procedures among the various maritime countries of the world, defining the relative rights and obligations of nations engaged in international shipping, would similarly be made applicable to the airlines.

The Industrial Revolution caused a new involvement by government in the affairs of business, and spawned an era of regulation and legislation. It gave rise to the labor movement and cast the die for early labor-management strife. It created a new demand for manufactured goods, ranging from steel for use in the construction of railroad tracks, locomotives and cars, to denims for their workers, a consumerism that continues unabated today. It fueled an explosion of new industries, and new companies within each industry to compete under primitive free enterprise, or laissez-faire principles. And it produced a dependent worker class who, because of industrialization, urbanization, immigration, and specialization, were no longer self-sufficient.

An understanding of the history and experience of the railroads is important to our purpose for at least four reasons:

1. As the first modern form of national transportation, the railroads set the model in many ways for the succeeding modes of transport, particularly air transportation.

2. The experience of the railroads defined the relationship between carriers and the government, particularly in respect to the concept of the public interest.

3. The experience of the railroads defined the relationship between carriers and the public, the shippers and passengers.

4. The railroad experience saw the beginning of a cohesive labor movement that was inherited by the airlines and that has been central to the airlines' experience in the twentieth century.

We will review each of these developments in more detail in the next two chapters.

1452	(April 15) Leonardo born.
1492	Columbus discovers the New World.
1502	The first watch is made.
1512	Copernicus concludes that the Earth circles the sun.
1519	(May 2) Leonardo dies in Amboise; Magellan launches first round-the-world voyage.
1733	John Kay invents flying shuttle.
1765	James Hargreaves invents the spinning jenny, automating weaving the warp (in the weaving of cloth).
1775	Watt's first efficient steam engine.
1779	First steam-powered mills.
1793	Eli Whitney develops a device to clean raw cotton, called a cotton gin.
1801	Robert Trevithick demonstrates a steam locomotive.
1807	Robert Fulton's **Clermont** first successful steamboat.
1811–15	Luddite riots: laborers attack factories and break up the machines they fear will replace them.
1821	Faraday demonstrates electro-magnetic rotation, the principle of the electric motor.
1837	Morse develops the telegraph and Morse Code.
1844	First long-distance telegraph message (Washington to Baltimore).
1858	First trans-Atlantic cable completed. Cathode rays discovered.
1859	Edwin Drake strikes oil in Pennsylvania. Etienne Lenoir demonstrates the first successful gasoline engine.
1860	Science degrees awarded at University of London.
1863	Steel begins to replace iron in building: steel framing and reinforced concrete make possible "curtain-wall" architecture—i.e., the skyscraper.
1867	Alfred Nobel produces dynamite, the first high explosive which can be safely handled.
1873	Christopher Sholes invents the Remington typewriter.
1876	Bell invents the telephone.
1877	Edison invents the phonograph.
1878	Microphone invented.
1879	Edison invents the incandescent lamp.
1883	First skyscraper (ten stories) in Chicago. The Brooklyn Bridge opens. This large suspension bridge, built by the Roeblings (father and son), is a triumph of engineering.
1885	Benz develops first automobile to run on internal-combustion engine.
1888	Hertz produces radio waves.
1892	Rudolf Diesel invents diesel engine.
1895	Roentgen discovers X-rays.
1896	Marconi patents wireless telegraph.
1897	Joseph Thomson discovers particles smaller than atoms.
1900	First Zeppelin built.
1901	Marconi transmits first trans-Atlantic radio message (from Cape Cod).
1903	Wright brothers make first powered flight.
1908	Henry Ford mass-produces the Model T.

FIGURE 2-1 Important events in industrial and technological development.

The Railroads

The steam engine, first fitted to a wagon in 1804, evolved into a primitive railroad locomotive to pull the first railroad carriages in 1830. (See Figure 3-1.) The first chartered railroad, the Baltimore & Ohio Railroad, operated from Baltimore to Ellicott's Mills, a distance of just 13 miles. Short haul railroads like this began springing up all over the East Coast of the United States about this time. The noisy, dirty, and generally terrifying apparition of an early steam locomotive, spitting steam and hot coal cinders in its wake and upon the few discomfited passengers who may have been loaded in the open cars behind it, rudely intruded on the sedate horse and buggy countryside. Yet few questioned its future. It was, after all, the most significant transportation advance in the history of the world, even at its maximum speed of 16 miles per hour, and even though it had the worrisome tendency of setting fire to the countryside through which it passed.

Like most inventions, the locomotive was gradually improved through the contributions of many people until it worked smoothly and readily achieved its designed purpose. This was advanced technology. The various small lines began meeting up, forming interchange points and exchanging the relatively small amount of freight traffic available. Passenger service was tentative, and the destinations sparse. These early rail lines were constructed to meet local needs, and there was no overall plan for lines to serve the nation or any particular geographic region.

Railroads were considered, legally and practically, to be monopolistic enterprises. The large capital investment required to begin operations virtually guaranteed little competition. Land had to be purchased, then the land had to be made level—requiring fills or bridges to connect over low places, valleys, and rivers, and causing cuts or tunnels to be dug to eliminate hills and mountains. Once that was done, the roadbed, consisting of ballast, ties, and finally the rails themselves, had to be laid. This process was required in one form or another for every linear foot of road. Even as the road was laid, and large sums of money spent, the question was unanswered: How should and would the government consider this new industry?

This was a time of forging new relationships all around, relationships that, once defined, would extend into the as yet unimagined air age of the future.

➡ What was the responsibility of a railroad to passengers and shippers?

➡ Was there any responsibility to communities served?

➡ Where was the higher allegiance—to stockholders or to the public?

Source: U.S. National Atlas, 1970.

FIGURE 3-1 An early steam engine.

Prior to the construction of the great transcontinental road that linked the West Coast of the United States with the Midwest, government had generally refrained from intervening in the affairs of the infant railroad industry. There was no federal governmental interest in railroad regulation since, in the early nineteenth century, federal issues like the "public interest" or "interstate commerce" had yet to be framed. Local governments treated the small railroads as any other business. When it would later come, federal government intervention would be characterized as either "positive" or "negative." Positive intervention could be described as government action that is designed to support or benefit the railroad, such as favorable tax treatment, subsidies, land grants, and the like. Negative intervention takes the form of restrictive legislation, the curbing of pre-existing rights enjoyed by the railroads, and the forcing of certain behavior deemed to be in the public interest, such as prohibiting arbitrary or unequal treatment of shippers.

The sheer magnitude of the proposed transcontinental railroad construction dictated that the government's participation would be required. No corporation, group of corporations, no bank, or group of banks was big enough to make it happen. Only the government was big enough, and only the government had the money and other resources necessary (including the land), and the sovereignty necessary to assuage the conflicts, partisanship, separate interests, and legal questions guaranteed to arise in the vast undertaking. Much of the land over which the railroad would run had been purchased in 1803 from France. Known as the "Louisiana Purchase" (see Figure 3-2), this vast tract consisted of over 800,000 square miles and extended from the Gulf of Mexico to the Canadian border and from the Mississippi River to the Rocky Mountains. The land area of the United States was suddenly doubled by this acquisition, and from it would come, in **whole or part,** fifteen new states that would ultimately be admitted to the federal Union.

In 1860, there were 30,000 miles of railroad in the United States.

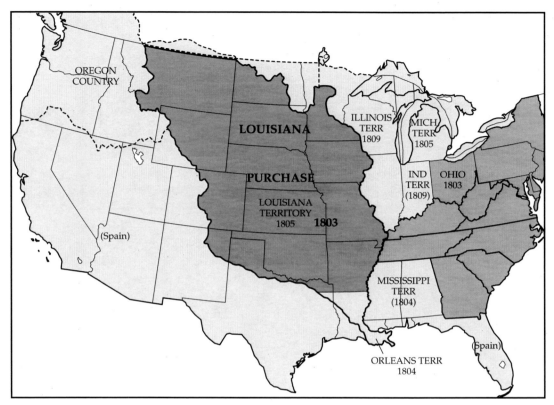

FIGURE 3-2   The Louisiana Purchase provided much of the land needed for the proposed transcontinental railroad.

The passage by the Congress in 1862 of the **Pacific Railroad Act** became the first of government's involvements in the world of modern transportation. The law provided for the creation of two private corporations, the Union Pacific (building from the East) and the Central Pacific (building from the West), whose charters were to build a railroad and a telegraph line[1] between the Missouri River and Sacramento, California. The government would issue its bonds, bearing interest at the rate of six percent, to the railroads for sale to the public. The improvements and the land on which they were placed would stand as security for the government's obligation to pay the interest on the bonds and to pay the face amount of the bonds when due. The government was not subsidizing the construction; rather, it was loaning its credit in order to raise the construction funds.

The government would, however, grant to the railroads the right of way (200 feet on each side) for the roadbed, and it would also deed land adjacent to the right of way in square miles amounting to 6,400 acres per mile. This was land expected to be used to entice settlers from the East who would create and work farms and ranches. The land would be used to build towns and to provide for industry, all of which in turn would provide passenger and freight traffic for the railroads and insure westward expansion and population of the Great Plains and points west. This was truly a win-win situation, even for the government, since the value of the remainder of the land that the government owned would be greatly enhanced by the efforts of the railroad companies and those who would follow them. The interests of the government would also be served by facilitating a viable railroad system to serve the nation and to advance the national economy and the public welfare.

The line began in the East on the Missouri River, at Omaha, Nebraska, and made its way west to Promontory Summit, Utah, where in 1869, the line of road that began in Sacramento, California, was joined. Along the way it laid down settlements which were to become the cities of the future, with names like Cheyenne, Laramie, North Platte, and Elko, names which fifty years later would also figure prominently in the annals of early flight as the first cross-country air mail service struggled to create yet another, but altogether different, fledgling transportation system. This transcontinental railroad is shown in Figure 3-3. With air transport, the government, once again, would take the lead and then step out of the way, leaving the captains of industry to their own devices in making the system run.

But turmoil lay ahead. It has been said that the years between 1860 and 1868 laid the foundation for the uprooting of the society of America. The Civil War, beginning in 1861, tore the country apart for four years, and the so-called Reconstruction era that followed effectively rendered the South a land occupied by a foreign power for many years. Centuries-old traditions in both the North and the South were eradicated or radically altered. Politics and social life changed.

> In 1870, there were 53,000 miles of railroad in the United States.

The impact of available and relatively fast railroad transportation on the stability of the population compounded the problem. People began to move and to follow the railroads as they connected sections of the country and both coasts, and as the heartland was settled. People could more readily live and work anywhere in the country, leaving behind their past, their established social networks, and sometimes their principles and mores. Political power was for sale in the legislatures of the states and in Congress as graft and corruption became prevalent.

The new opportunities afforded to corporations led to a time of unbridled capitalism at the hands of rapacious men of industry like the Vanderbilts, the Goulds, and the Carnegies. The power of corporations, like the Pullman Company, Standard Oil, and United States Steel,

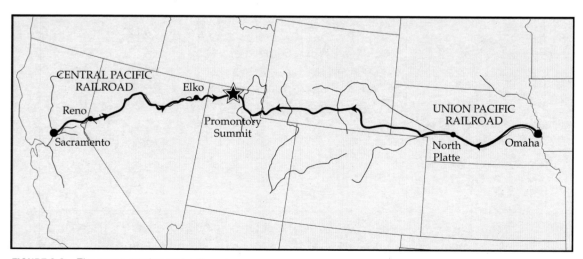

FIGURE 3-3 The transcontinental railroad.

joined with the new political structure to create a vast gulf between owners, known as the "robber barons," and workers. Labor was set against management in an epic struggle that would poison labor relations in the railroad industry for generations to come and that would be carried over to the airlines. The government's initial assistance, as positive legislation, would soon turn to regulation of the restrictive kind with the passage of the first comprehensive national legislation regulating transportation.

The Railroads, Laissez-Faire Economics, and the Basis of Regulation

As the railroads spread out from the East, they connected with other lines, North and South, and created interchange points between them. For the first time, goods began to be moved from origins far distant from their destinations. Markets that at one time had been local now became regional and even national. Manufacturing, meatpacking, farming, and the cattle business were becoming interdependent, and America was beginning to depend on transportation—the railroads—as the lifeblood of its commerce.

The railroads wielded vast economic power. Like government, they possessed the power of eminent domain. They set passenger fares as they wished. Freight rates varied according to the whim of the railroads, and were often discriminatory and unevenly applied.

Farmers, in particular, were at the mercy of the railroads in marketing their produce. Grain elevators were necessary as storage facilities for farmers, and these often were owned by the railroads.

Various states, in response to petitions from its citizens, enacted laws designed to curb the excesses of the railroads. But the railroads ran from state to state, and generally considered themselves immune from attempts at local regulation. These laws, therefore, were uniformly ineffective and were ignored or legally challenged by the railroads. It was not until shippers as a group began to assert influence on a national level that the Congress did eventually begin to address the problem.

In the United States, governmental authority to regulate lawful enterprises must be based on constitutional principles. In 1887, although these principles were not well defined, it was clear that the national government in Washington had express Constitutional authority to regulate commerce between the states. So it was that Congress that year debated the first regulation of transportation.

Historically, governmental regulation has been grounded on two primary concepts:

1. Economic necessity
2. Legal authority

The concept of economic necessity presumes (1) that there are certain businesses that are necessary in the public interest (e.g., transportation companies, gas companies, electric companies, etc.); (2) that these types of companies should be required to serve all of the public without discrimination; and (3) that these companies should be stable and be able to make a reasonable, but not too large, a profit. To assure that these conditions exist, the government has undertaken to regulate them. This regulation controls entry into the business (which controls competition, expertise, and financial stability), the rates that are charged the public, and to some extent the manner in which the business is operated.

In the United States, most businesses are run under the principles of private enterprise. While businesses that are considered necessary in the public interest are mostly privately owned, they are considered to be "quasi-public," that is, operated in the public interest. From 1887, when the regulation of transportation began, the federal government considered interstate transportation to be a quasi-public undertaking, thus a legitimate object of regulation.

The second basis of regulation is legal. The legal basis of regulation is founded in the U.S. Constitution and the laws that are enacted by Congress. With regard to transportation, the commerce clause of the Constitution is most often invoked to authorize regulation of companies conducting business among the states (interstate commerce). The commerce clause is based, in part, on the realization that the people of the various states must be guaranteed equal access to a necessary service. It is also recognized that, in matters between the states, the presumed impartiality of the federal government should make it, and not the states, the arbiter of the law.

Once enacted pursuant these constitutional principles, regulation is **implemented through** either the common law or statutory law.

➡ *Common law* is the law that has resulted from judicial decisions derived from litigated cases between individual parties. This law is contained in written opinions of judges and is referred to as "judge-made" law. The common law that existed in England before the American Revolution was applied in the American colonies, and after independence was won and the United States Constitution was adopted, English common law continued to serve as legal precedent in the new United States.

➡ *Statutory law* is the law that Congress or the state legislatures have enacted by vote of elected representatives in those bodies. On the federal level, this law is codified in the United States Code, a sequentially numbered series of volumes that contain all current federal statutory law. The United States Code is kept updated by means of supplements published on a regular basis. Some statutes provide for the creation of federal agencies, like the Federal Aviation Administration or the Interstate Commerce Commission, to administer the mandates set down in the statute. Such agencies are given rulemaking authority, which means they may conduct public hearings and make rules having the force of law to govern the manner in which the affected business or activity is conducted, like the Federal Aviation Regulations, for example.

The Interstate Commerce Act of 1887

The first legislation in the United States regulating transportation was the Interstate Commerce Act, in 1887. This statute heralded the era of "negative" legislation, or legislation that had the effect of curbing or restricting railroads in their conduct of business.

The thrust of the Act was to prohibit the railroads from paying rebates (kickbacks), from giving unreasonable preferences to shippers, and from discrimination against any shipper. Railroads were required to publish tariffs, which disclosed rates and schedules, and they were required to charge according to those tariffs. The Act brought uniformity to the relationship between the railroads and the public.

The Interstate Commerce Act and its amendments also created the Interstate Commerce Commission, the agency assigned the role of administering the terms and provisions of the statute. It was empowered to monitor railroads to ensure compliance with the terms of the statute, to hear complaints from the affected public, and to make rules and enter orders in furtherance of the statutory mandate.

Subsequent federal enactments continued the era of negative legislation toward the transportation industry, including:

➡ The **Elkins Act of 1903** (focused on person discrimination and established a system of fines and criminal penalties)

➡ The **Hepburn Act of 1906** (set maximum rates)

➡ The **Mann-Elkins Act of 1910** (focused on place discrimination)

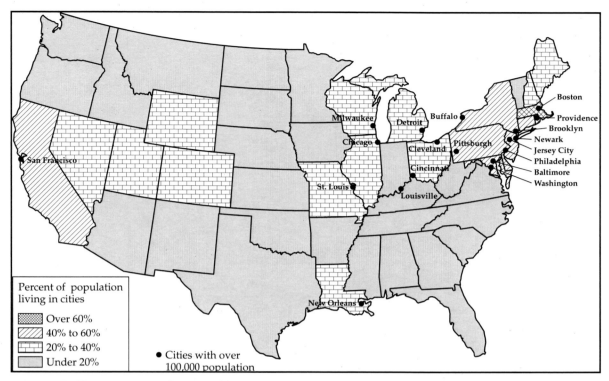

FIGURE 3-4 The emergence of cities, 1880.

The pendulum had swung too far in the early and energetic days of railroading, and the government was now catching up to balance things out in the public interest. The days of unbridled capitalism in the railroad business were over. In the early years of the twentieth century, the railroads were nearing what was to be their maximum trackage (miles of laid tracks), and they were just about to experience the effects of continuing industrial and technological development (Figure 3-4 displays the emergence of U.S. cities in 1880) that would lead to alternative forms of transportation that would overpower them. The days of the internal combustion engine, the open road, and the machines of the air lay just over the horizon.

In 1890, there were 164,000 miles of railroad in the United States. Railroad mileage would peak at 254,000 miles in 1916, and then begin a gradual decline.

Endnote

1. The government issued a patent for the telegraph in 1837 to Samuel Morse. The first intercity telegraph message was transmitted in 1844.

CHAPTER 4

The Industrial Age and the Rise of Unionism

© Alex Staroseltsev, 2008, Shutterstock.

Before proceeding further into the twentieth century, we need to visit the labor movement in the United States. This phenomenon became a force and an institution in American industry that, beginning in the middle to late nineteenth century, has had a significant impact on national modes of transportation.

The development of trade unionism is highly correlated to the progression of industrialization. Although trade guilds existed from medieval times in Europe, they were composed of artisans who banded together to promote their craft, and to improve their products and methods. As such, guilds had an exclusionary aspect not seen in modern trade unions, which are inclusionary of most kinds of wage-earners.

Trade unions were formed as associations of workers as a natural counter-balance to owners. Historically, the formation of such groups was illegal under the laws of most countries. These groups were seen as hostile to the order of the day, revolutionary even, and their objectives were often sought through disorderly and violent means.

Prior to the Civil War, most of what could be called "industry" was controlled by small individual owners, often families, or sometimes small partnerships. These industries included the cotton and woolen mills of New England, iron and steel factories of Pennsylvania and New York, the various short-line railroads that served their local areas all over the eastern U.S., oil drillers in Pennsylvania, and coal mining operations in the Appalachian Mountain chain. Most of the wealth of the country lay in land ownership. The United States was primarily a nation of farmers.

The Civil War spurred development in most areas of industry. The woolen mills were called upon to clothe a million men with uniforms. Boots and saddles were needed, the packing plants of Chicago were transformed, the manufacture of iron and steel products boomed, and Chicago became a transportation center. The railroads proved their efficiency during the war through the movement of troops and materiel. And the railroads demanded more coal, iron, and oil.

After the end of the Civil War, railroad construction exploded. Some 35,000 miles of track were laid from 1866 to 1873. Building railroads was an expensive undertaking, and the use of the corporation found favor as a means of raising money. Corporations also became the preferred form of business ownership and operation in most other industries. The shares of public corporations were traded on the stock exchanges of New York and Chicago, although large blocks of stock were owned by very wealthy individuals and families. In the days before any social regulation, corporations determined all the rules and working conditions of employment, including the hours to be worked and the rates of pay.

As industrialization grew, so did the organization of workers. Some of these organizations were more like fraternal organizations than unions, although they ultimately progressed into trade unionism and condoned work actions and strikes. Some of these groups were politically oriented, being populated by anarchists, socialists, and communists. The writings of Karl Marx, a German philosopher and bohemian, formed the basis of a philosophy of class strife, e.g., the haves against the have-nots, which was adopted by many groups. His Communist Manifesto, published in 1849, detailed the decline and fall of the capitalist economy and the ultimate triumph of the worker over the owner-class. Union leaders were usually the most aggressive of the workers.

The first railroad unions appeared in the 1860s. Their original purpose was to provide life insurance for their members, since life insurance companies refused to insure railroad workers due the high risk of injury and death. Railroads provided union organizers with the opportunity to organize workers on a national level instead of the local level usually associated with factories. Railroad unions were formed according to the class or craft of service that the employer rendered, whether engineer, fireman, conductor, or other.

After the Civil War, the railroads were the largest industrial employer in the United States. Money was flowing from the private sector into the railroads as they rapidly expanded, and as might be expected, the expansion rate proved to be too great. The overbuilding of the railroads, along with the great investment in money made by speculators, led to widespread economic failures. First profits dried up and then credit. The first industrially-induced recession, known as the Panic of 1873, resulted in bank closures and depositor losses. The crisis caused the failure of more than 18,000 businesses, and 89 of the nation's 364 railroads went bankrupt.

The relationship between the unions and the owners of the railroads was exceedingly antagonistic, with good cause on both sides. Although not illegal[1] unions were not recognized by business or by the government as quite legitimate. Union members often resorted to violence and civil disturbance; the railroads reciprocated with hired police forces and strike-breakers.

The economic conditions surrounding the Panic of 1873 resulted in the railroads cutting wages and terminating workers. In 1877, the first serious railroad strike of the new industrial age began on July 14 in Martinsburg, West Virginia, and spread along the lines of railroad into Pittsburgh and Philadelphia, then on to the Midwest, St. Louis and Chicago, becoming more violent as it went. Railroads across the country were brought to a standstill by rioting and bloodshed. In Chicago and St. Louis, a political group known as The Workingmen's Party, which was the first Marxist-influenced political party in the United States, organized mobs of up to 20,000 demonstrators who battled police and federal troops in the streets.

Gradually, the troops suppressed both strikers and rioters city-by-city and, 45 days after it began, the Strike of 1877 was over. But the unions came out of the fray empowered by the knowledge of what their combined action could produce. The unions became better organized, and their numbers and membership grew. Their leaders espoused the general belief that they were justified in resorting to any means to overcome the power of the corporations. The Strike of 1877 was to mark the beginning of a particularly violent period in labor relations in the United States.

During the next decade there would be thousands of strikes, lockouts, and work interruptions in American industry as management-labor relations deteriorated further. But railroad strikes gained the most notoriety of all because of the wide-spread effect they had on the transportation system of the country. The biggest of all, called the Pullman Strike, occurred in 1894.

The Pullman Palace Car Company manufactured luxurious railway sleeper cars that were used by most railroad companies in their passenger trains. Due to another cyclical economic downturn (known as the Panic of 1893), production at the Pullman plant located in south Chicago was severely curtailed. As a result, the work force was reduced from 5,500 to 3,300, and the wages of the remaining workers were reduced by 25 percent. The workers at the Pullman plant were required to live in Pullman City, where the plant was located, in houses built by the company and leased to the workers. Everything in the town was owned by the company, and the company provided everything for the people, except saloons. When wages were reduced, the workers petitioned for a reduction of lease payments, but the company refused. This led to a strike by the Pullman workers in May 1894.

The American Railway Union (ARU) had been established just the year before, in 1893, by Eugene V. Debs, a former railroad worker and union officer in the Brotherhood of Locomotive Firemen. The ARU was unlike railroad trade unions in that it included railroad workers of all classes and crafts. It shortly became the largest union in the United States with over 140,000 members by 1894. In August 1893, it had called a strike of the Great Northern Railroad in response to a series of wage cuts. The shut down of the railroad caused the company to reverse its wage decision. So when the Pullman Company cut wages, the ARU voted to join the Pullman strikers in order to bring all of the union's clout down on Pullman.

The largest strike in the history of the United States ensued, involving hundreds of thousands of participants and twenty-seven states and territories of the U.S. One hundred and twenty-five thousand railroad workers refused to handle Pullman sleeping cars or any trains in which they were placed. Thirteen railroads had been forced to abandon all service in Chicago and ten others were able to operate only passenger trains. The

New York Times announced that the strike had become the greatest battle between labor and capital that had ever been inaugurated in the United States. Public sentiment shifted against the strikers as the disruption dragged on and as national transportation remained interrupted. Still, there was no federal intervention.

In July, the railroads began attaching the Pullman cars to U.S. mail cars, which then caused a disruption of interstate mail. Debs and other union officials were arrested for interfering with the delivery of U.S. mail. On July 2, a federal court injunction was issued against the ARU and its leaders. On July 3, President Cleveland ordered in federal troops to end the strike and to operate the railroads. On July 4, mobs of rioters began roaming the streets and destroying railroad property. Fires set by the mobs on July 6 and 7 destroyed 700 rail cars and seven buildings. Twelve people were killed by gunfire.

Debs was arrested on July 7 for violating the court order, and the violence began to subside. Trains began to move again and the strike whimpered to an end. Debs spent six months in prison.

These violent conflicts between organized labor and business during the latter part of the 19th century would lead to a federal legislation in the years to come designed to address the legitimate concerns of both labor and management. Eugene Debs would later be a candidate for President of the U.S. for the Socialist Party of America, standing for election four times between 1904 and 1920. His best showing, 6 percent of the vote, occurred in the election of 1912, and is the highest voter result for a Socialist Party candidate.

The disruption and violence of strikes were unpopular, and the courts routinely issued injunctions against unions on the basis of the **Sherman Antitrust Act of 1890.** This statute, while enacted primarily to eliminate corporate monopolies, contained language that prohibited "every contract, combination in the form of trust or otherwise, or conspiracy, in restraint of trade or commerce." The courts interpreted this language as prohibiting strikes, which did, of course, restrain trade and commerce. In 1914, Congress passed the **Clayton Antitrust Act,** a further enactment against corporate trusts, but which contained provisions expressly exempting labor unions from the operation of the "restraint of trade" prohibitions found in the Sherman Antitrust Act.

The early part of the twentieth century saw many changes in the American way of life.

➡ Horses and buggies were giving way to the automobile.

➡ Factories were going full blast, turning out production goods as never before.

➡ The assembly line, perfected by Henry Ford in the production of automobiles, was further aggravating the relations between workers and owners.

➡ The entry of the United States into World War I caused many young servicemen to be exposed to foreign culture for the first time, and to the bohemian ways of European life.

Still, America was very conservative during this time. The Bolshevik Revolution in Russia in 1917 and its aftermath raised further concerns in this country as aggressive union activity seemed to bring the United States a step closer to socialist and communist ideology. Workers in heavy industry, such as mine workers, steel workers, and railroad workers, were highly organized and pursued a militant relationship with management.

The coming of the Great Depression during the 1930s and the Roosevelt New Deal, however, reflected a change in the way government looked at workers and their place in society. The New Deal brought a great wave of legislation directed toward fixing what was coming to be regarded as a broken economy and assisting those at the lower levels who functioned within it.

➡ Working conditions, hours, and rates of pay were the subjects of contention, and as the twentieth century progressed, these conditions gradually improved due to the American system of self-determination through legislation.

➡ Child labor laws and a minimum wage were enacted.

➡ Laws addressing the safety of workers were put on the books for the first time.

➡ Broad legislation protecting the right of workers to organize and to strike was passed.

➡ National work programs, like the Works Progress Administration (WPA), a relief program established by Presidential executive order, were instituted to alleviate the high unemployment numbers experienced due to the adverse economic conditions of the 1930s.

The postulations that Karl Marx had made with respect to the class warfare that, in his view, were inevitable were proved incorrect by the flexibility of the American governmental system. As substantial problems induced by the Industrial Revolution that affected the working population of the United States were perceived, Congress reacted with remedial legislation. These laws had the effect of acting like a relief valve in a pressure cooker, as workers perceived that their legitimate concerns were being addressed. Although union membership rose steadily from the latter part of the nineteenth century through the 1930s, it reached its peak in the 1950s. As economic conditions improved in the United States and worldwide, and as the workforce shifted from heavy industry to technology, union membership dropped off, and is still in the process of falling. Negative perceptions of thug-like union activity increased among the American population. Connections between some large unions, like the Teamsters, and the underworld or Mafia, were shown to exist. Unions have been accused of misappropriating members' pension funds, and union officials have frequently been indicted and successfully prosecuted. The good that some unions accomplished was often overshadowed by these events.

The most important observation that can be made concerning the course of labor and management relations over the last century and a half is undoubtedly the success of the American system of government in coping with the often diametrically opposed positions of these participants in business. That system, based on the structure of the Constitution of the United States, has proven stronger than the differences that divide its population, and it has enabled a cooperative endeavor between labor and management that has benefited the world.

We will later consider specific developments in the country's labor laws and their impact on the airline industry.

Endnote

1. Trade unions were adjudicated to be legal organizations in the 1842 case of Massachusetts Commonwealth v. Hunt.

PART II

Dreamers

© Stephen Strathdee, 2008, Shutterstock.

Chapter 5   The Beginnings of Flight

Chapter 6   Prelude to Powered Flight

Chapter 7   The Wright Brothers

The Beginnings of Flight

© Johnny Kuo, 2008, Shutterstock.

❝ Many wonderful inventions have surprised us during the course of the last century and the beginning of this one. But most were completely unexpected and were not part of the old baggage of dreams that humanity carries with it. Who had ever dreamed of steamships, railroads, or electric light? We welcomed all these improvements with astonished pleasure; but they did not correspond to an expectation of our spirit or a hope as old as we are: to overcome gravity, to tear ourselves away from the earth, to become lighter, to fly away, to take possession of the immense aerial kingdom; to enter the universe of the Gods, to become Gods ourselves. ❞

Jerome Tharaud, 'Dans le ciel des dieux,' in *Les Grandes Conferences de l'aviation: Recits et souvenirs*, 1934

It is generally acknowledged that the success of the Wright brothers' Kitty Hawk flight on December 17, 1903, was due to their success, for the first time, in combining into a machine the three essential elements needed for heavier than air powered flight:

1. a source of lift (the wings properly shaped),
2. propulsion (an engine of appropriate power versus weight, and efficient propellers), and
3. a means of control (a 'warping' or bending of the wings for banking, vertical rudders for turning, and an elevator for pitch.

To the date of their first successful flight, no one else had been able to assemble all three of these essential elements into one machine under conditions conducive to flight. It is generally acknowledged that the Wrights' machine was not so much an "invention" as it was a "development," one that relied upon the efforts, trials, failures and successes of many who went before. In spite of that fact, the U.S. Patent Office issued a patent to the Wrights in 1906.

The flight experience of mankind prior to the Wright brothers' success was limited to balloons, dirigibles, and gliders. Balloons and dirigibles are classified as "lighter than air" craft. The Federal Aviation Administration (FAA) classifies gliders as a category of aircraft separate from airplanes, but the essential and only significant difference is propulsion, or the lack thereof. The wing of the glider produces lift, just as with the airplane, and the control surfaces of the glider (the ailerons, elevator, and rudder) are the same as the airplane. Early work and experimentation with gliders

27

proved much more valuable to the long-term effort of sustained, controllable flight than did lighter than air experimentation. Since no history of flight would be complete without treatment of the history of all successful flight forms, we begin with the first flights of man.

Balloons

To fly has been a dream, although an elusive dream, of humankind from time immemorial. Through the ages, mockingly the birds of the air swirled and swooped with graceful ease over earthbound man. Man continued to look to the sky, and to dream on. The first flights of man were not to be patterned after the winged creatures; that had proven over the millennia to be too complex. Man's first exploration aloft was the result of the observations of two wealthy French brothers, Jacques Etienne and Joseph Michele Montgolfier, who happened to be paper-makers in Annonay, France. They observed that fire seemed to have the quality of supporting certain light solid objects, like paper, and that they were borne aloft on what they theorized was a lighter than air gas. Experimentation led to the first hot air balloon ascent in 1783. This was followed that same year by a successful two-hour flight of a balloon filled with hydrogen gas, the brainchild of a French chemist, Jacques Alexandre Cesar Charles. Hydrogen gas had been first isolated in 1766 by the British chemist Henry Cavendish. The first ascent by humans in a balloon was also recorded in 1783 near Paris, piloted by Jean Francois de Rozier.

Within two years, there were people who called themselves "aeronauts," and who devoted significant effort to getting off the ground and going somewhere. In 1785, aeronaut Jean Pierre Blanchard, accompanied by an American, John Jeffries, made the first successful crossing of the English Channel from Dover to Calais.

Balloons immediately found a use as observation platforms during the French Revolution, and later, during the American Civil War. (See Figure 5-1.) War again provided function to the balloons in the Franco-Prussian War (1870–1871) as observation vehicles, and even as an escape vehicle when French minister Leon Gambetta floated out of the besieged city of Paris to the very great consternation of the opposing forces. Progressing from war to war, it seems, once again balloons were used for observation in World War I, but now they were joined by, and opposed by, fighter aircraft.

Until the modern age, the record for distance traveled in piloted balloons stood from 1914, when the balloon, Berliner, covered a distance of 1,896 miles from Bitterfeld, Germany to Perm, Russia. Toward the middle and latter twentieth century, extraordinary feats have accompanied balloon flight. In 1960, Capt. Joe Kittinger of the U.S. Air Force ascended in a

FIGURE 5-1 An observation balloon during the Civil War.

Source: National Archives and Records Administration.

polyethylene balloon to an altitude of 102,800 feet, setting an altitude record. He then bailed out of the gondola to set a free-fall parachute descent record. The balloon altitude record was broken the next year during an ascent to 113,700 feet. In 1984, Kittinger piloted a 3,000 cubic meter balloon from Caribou, Maine to Montenotte, Italy, covering 3,543 miles. He thus became the first, and only, person to solo a balloon across the Atlantic Ocean.

Dirigibles

The second entry into the lighter than air category was the craft known as the dirigible. The marked distinction between a balloon and a dirigible is the elongated shape of the dirigible, the control planes to allow pilots of the dirigible to turn, descend and climb, and the presence of engines to provide thrust.

Both balloons and dirigibles used hydrogen gas to provide a lifting substance until the gas helium was extracted from natural gas in 1917. Since the United States had a monopoly on helium, no other country was privileged to use it in their airships. Instead, they were required to continue to rely on the very flammable hydrogen gas.

The first dirigibles (the term used here interchangeably with the term "airship") flew in France between 1851 and 1884. The word dirigible is derived from the French "diriger," meaning to steer. Airship, on the other hand, is a literal translation of the German, Luftschiff (airship).

Airships are of two main types, rigid and non-rigid. (See Figure 5-2.) The rigid airship was highly developed after the turn of the twentieth century by Ferdinand Adolf von Zeppelin, a former German cavalry officer, who became acquainted with balloons during a visit to the United States. His LZ-1 became the first rigid airship to fly in a 17-minute sojourn over Lake Constance in 1900. This craft was 420 feet in length, supported by hydrogen gas, and cruised

at 20 miles per hour with two 16 horsepower engines. Count von Zeppelin became a national hero because of his development of the very imposing and exciting "Zeppelins," which could be seen overhead proceeding majestically through the German countryside. In 1909, Count Zeppelin formed the first passenger line for the carriage of passengers by air, Deutsche Luftshiffahrts A.G. (DELAG). DELAG, the airship company, carried passengers all over the country of Germany after its inauguration, and by 1913 had conducted over 1,600 flights, carrying 35,000 passengers without mishap.

With the advent of World War I, Germany and England geared up to produce airships by the hundreds. The British navy produced 200 airships between 1915 and 1918, more than Germany, and almost all of them were used for anti-submarine patrol. Germany produced 125 Zeppelins between 1914 and 1918, and employed them in offensive engagements over the English countryside, dropping bombs and otherwise wreaking havoc among the terrified population. The Zeppelins proved quite vulnerable to anti-aircraft battery fire and to fighter aircraft. Of the 125 Zeppelins manufactured and placed in service during the war, only 6 survived.

Several countries produced airships after the war. Both England and France built dirigibles, but accidents and mysterious disappearances caused the French to cancel their program in 1923. England continued operating dirigibles until 1930. Aerodynamic improvements were made as the technology advanced. The English R-34, completed in December 1918, had a total air resistance of only seven percent of a hypothetical flat disc of the same diameter. The United States built its own dirigibles and even received a Zeppelin as a war prize from Germany after the cessation of hostilities in 1918. The 660-foot ZR-III was the 126th Zeppelin constructed by Germany and was later renamed 'Los Angeles' and placed in service by the U.S. Navy.

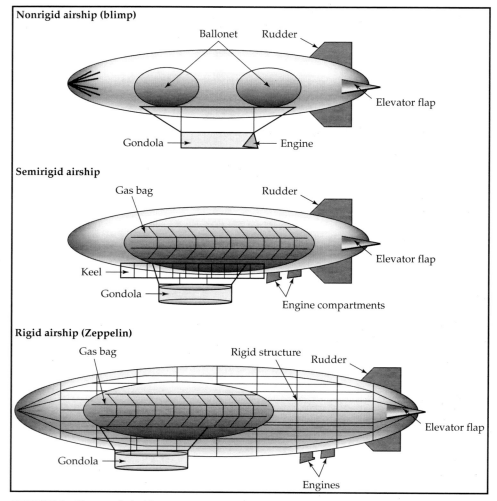

FIGURE 5-2 Types of airships.

After the war, the Zeppelin continued to be used in passenger service between America and Germany, as well as between Germany and South America. Zeppelin flights continued until the occurrence of the Hindenburg disaster in Lakehurst, New Jersey, in 1937. The Hindenburg was undoubtedly the greatest airship ever constructed, boasting restaurants, staterooms, lounges, and other amenities for the enjoyment of its trans-atlantic passengers.

The Goodyear Company built airships for the United States, including the Akron in 1931, commissioned for service in the U.S. Navy, and the Macon in 1933, also a Navy craft. Both the Akron and the Macon were lost to weather, the last of a long line of airships that had come to similar grief. It was believed that the rigid airframe employed in the dirigibles was not sufficiently flexible, given its rather large dimensions, to withstand the vicissitudes of rough air and storms.

The days of the rigid airship thus came to an ignominious close with their last production in the 1930s. The non-rigid airship, or blimp, was placed in service by the United States Navy in World War II in convoy operations, and proved effective as an anti-submarine weapon. The only service to employ blimps in World War II, the United States Navy, worked 170 of the non-rigid airships over the Atlantic during the war, escorting 89,000 ships and logging some 500,000 hours flying time.

Today, blimps are used almost exclusively as promotional devices, employing television cameras for golf event coverage or other sporting events, or displaying brand names of commercial products on their ample sides. The advent of international terrorism after September 11, 2001, however, has caused renewed interest in the subject of blimps as a potential countermeasure against terrorist attacks in the United States.

Gliders

From the early to mid nineteenth century, to the Wright brothers' success in 1903, controllable flight of "heavier than air" craft was a preoccupation throughout the civilized world among dreamers, engineers, and assorted tinkers. The sketches and writings of **Leonardo da Vinci** in 1505 were the only known serious, theoretical treatment of the subject of flight until the publication in 1810 of a series of articles by the Englishman, **Sir George Cayley.**

Today, Cayley is considered to be the founder of the science of aerodynamics because of his pioneering experiments with wing design and the effects of lift and drag, and his formulations concerning control surfaces and propellers. He concluded, by observing birds, that a curved surface (a wing) would support weight and, under the proper configuration of fuselage and other accoutrements, would permit flight. As a scientist, he kept meticulous records of his observations and the results of his experiments. In years to come, this documentation would greatly assist those who followed him in the quest for flight.

In 1804, Cayley built and flew a model of a glider that incorporated the principles of the cambered wing, and in 1808 he flew a full-scale version of this glider as a kite, thereby proving his basic wing theory. Cayley worked on his the-

ories all his life. Between 1849 and 1853, he designed and built the first human carrying gliders in history. His research probed the engineering essentials of aircraft design today, including the ratio of lift to wing area, the determination of the center of wing pressure, the importance of streamlining, the concept of structural strength and the concepts of stability and control. Cayley's work became the foundation of most of the future experimentation of flight.

Throughout the course of the nineteenth century, many pioneers contributed to the persistent quest of manned flight. Some got the cart before the horse, like the Englishmen, **John Stringfellow,** and his cohort, **William S. Henson.** In their zeal they attempted to form a company called the "Aerial Steam Transit Company" in 1843, for the purpose of operating an international airline. The first problem the company had was the absence of any form of aerial conveyance, such as an airplane. There also was no form of propulsion to make the aerial conveyance go anywhere, although Stringfellow apparently worked at high pitch to develop a lightweight steam engine to be placed on the yet undesigned airplane. The attempt came to naught when the English House of Commons rejected the motion to form the company, with great laughter.

In apparent recognition of the unlikely commercial success of their venture, Henson got married and moved to the United States, where no record has been located to support evidence of any further aeronautical involvements. But Stringfellow persisted and, in 1848, he was successful in developing a three-winged model aircraft on which he placed a lightweight steam engine that actually flew a distance of 120 feet. He is thus credited with producing the first engine driven aircraft capable of free flight and, under the auspices of the Aeronautical Society, exhibited his machine at the world's first exhibition of flying machines held in the Crystal Palace in London in 1868.

Others, such as the French sea captain **Jean-Marie Le Bris,** are noted more for their efforts than their successes. His legacy was a series of crashed gliders occurring after short, unmanned flight. **Francis Wenham** was an Englishman who pursued the elusive reality of flight without success, but who did design and build the first wind tunnel. Wenham was a marine engineer, as was the Frenchman **Alphonse Penaud,** who brought to their interest in flight an engineering discipline that would enhance the ultimate success of achieving manned flight.

Penaud's work was important to the Wright brothers' success, by their own admission. Penaud is known for his experimentation with model aircraft, with results long studied by aeronautical engineers and historians. Penaud had shown that models are effective for purposes of experimentation. He demonstrated the usefulness of the twisted rubber band as a means of propulsion for model airplanes. These models were among the first powered, heavier than air objects ever to fly and went far to encourage experimenters that manned, powered flight was possible. Penaud's "planaphore," a model monoplane with tapered dihedral wings, an adjustable tail assembly, and a pusher-type propeller mounted on the tail of the airplane, flew as a demonstration in 1871 in Paris. The planaphore covered a distance of 131 feet and is acknowledged to be the first recorded flight of an inherently stable aircraft.

Efforts to find a workable means of propulsion, or thrust, for aircraft were the primary interests of two other engineers. **Clement Ader,** a French electrical engineer, and **Hiram Maxim,** chief engineer for an early electric utility, experimented with steam engines, at the time the only known reliable form of moveable power.

During the 1880s Ader built flying machines to which he attached 40 horsepower and 20 horsepower steam engines. The engines were effective in producing sufficient power to propel his clumsy and unwieldy machines, all of which were completely without any effective means of control, and by turns they all suffered the ignominy of the crash and burn.

In 1893, Hiram Maxim built an enormous biplane. It was 200 feet in length with a wingspan of 107 feet, and he mounted on it not one but two 180 horsepower steam engines. The platform for the engines, the boiler, and the three-man crew was 40 feet long and 8 feet wide. The machine was effectively affixed to the ground by attachments to a track over which it ran. It was made to move along the track at speeds of up to 42 miles per hour in a fashion described at the time by a journalist at the scene:

> When full steam was up and the propellers spinning so fast that they seemed to become whirling disks, Maxim shouted, "Let go." A rope was pulled and the machine shot forward like a railway train with the big propellers whirling, the steam hissing and the waste pipes puffing and gurgling, it flew over the 1800 feet of track in much less time that it takes to tell it.

Otto Lilienthal (see Figures 5-3 and 5-4), a German engineer who believed that glider flight was a necessary prerequisite to powered flight, constructed and tested a series of monoplanes in the nature of what we today would call hang gliders. He made the most accurate and detailed observations about the properties of curved surfaces, presenting for the first time observations concerning aspect ratio, wing shape, and profile, and conducted various experiments in his workshop that were built on the already proven idea of the cambered wing. In 1889 he published "Birdflight as the Basis of Aviation," which contained the findings and conclusions from his experiments and which were presented in tabulated format. Beginning in 1894, he proved, through repeated successful glides of distances of over 1,000 feet, that manned flight was possible. Between 1891 and 1896, Lilienthal made over 2,000 gliding flights, many over distances in excess of 1,000 feet, and for this period there are 137 known photographs of him in flight. He wrestled with the concept of

Source: Library of Congress.

FIGURE 5-3   Otto Lilienthal and his glider.

Source: Library of Congress.

FIGURE 5-4   Otto Lilienthal in flight—
"to fly is everything."

control, using dexterous movements of his body to keep the glider in proper attitude, but was unable to develop an otherwise effective means of control. On August 9, 1896, the lack of control took its toll when his glider stalled at an altitude of 50 feet and plummeted to the ground, fatally injuring him. As he lay dying in the open field where he crashed, he was heard to have said, "Opfer mussen gemacht werden." Thus was started the tradition that has transcended the epoch of aviation, in the translation of his last words, "Sacrifices must be made."

Lilienthal's exploits were publicly acknowledged, and photographs, interviews, and publication of his experiments and calculations were widely circulated. **Percy Pilcher,** a Scotsman and marine engineer and lecturer in naval architecture at Glasgow University, was intrigued by Lilienthal. He fashioned his own form of glider, but did not fly it until after he was permitted a visit to Lilienthal with the opportunity to practice in his proven machines. Pilcher died in his own gliding crash in 1899. He was later cited by Wilbur Wright as having influenced the brothers' experiments, who credited both Pilcher and Lilienthal in the success of the Wrights' experiments.

Octave Chanute was arguably the most important single influence on Orville and Wilbur Wright as they relentlessly pursued their goal of manned, powered flight. Chanute was an accomplished and successful civil engineer, president of the American Society of Civil Engineers, and designer of the first railroad bridge over the Missouri River. (See Figure 5-5.) His interest in flight can be best understood as a hobby until he was in his sixties, when he published a book called "Progress in Flying Machines," which compiled

FIGURE 5-5 Octave Chanute.

his extensive investigation of flight experimentation and research up to that time. (See Figures 5-6 and 5-7.) In 1896, Chanute began a series of glider experiments using gliders of his own design and construction. A short train ride from Chicago to the south lies the Indiana state line, along the shore of Lake Michigan. In June of that year, Chanute, his associate Augustus Herring, and two others established a campsite outside of Miller Junction, Indiana, among the famous dunes along Lake Michigan. Winds from the Lake and the elevation of the dunes provided a very suitable venue for glider experimentation, and the isolation of the region provided some degree of privacy. (See Figure 5-8.) These physical characteristics of the topography were later noted by the Wrights in the selection of the Outer Banks of North Carolina for similar, although even more favorable, characteristics.

During this encampment, the Chanute party experimented with Lilienthal glider designs, making modifications that to them seemed appropriate. Progress was made, particularly in the six-winged version known as the "Katydid." The party returned to the area in August 1896, and continued experiments with gliders, this time concentrating on the double-deck kite version that would become the model for the Wright's successful efforts a few years later. Chanute was encouraged by the results of the double decker tests, and upon his return to Chicago he published the results in an article entitled "Recent Experiments in Gliding Flight." The next year he followed this up with an article in the "Journal of the Western Society of Engineers,"

FIGURE 5-6 Lilienthal-type glider tested by Octave Chanute.

FIGURE 5-7 Box-type glider (double decker) design later used by the Wright Brothers.

sonian Institution, who was also in the process of experimenting with the idea of manned flight, and in that way became aware of the efforts of Chanute. Wilbur Wright corresponded with Octave Chanute first in 1900, and expressed particular interest in the structural engineering concept of strut and wire bracing that Chanute first introduced to aircraft design with the double decker. From this developed a lengthy and prolific correspondence and association between Chanute and the Wright brothers that extended for a decade, until his death in 1910.

Chanute became a friend and confidant to the Wrights, and even accompanied them to the Outer Banks on several occasions. As a man of some stature as compared to the unknown Wright brothers, he defended them and vouched for their accomplishments during the secretive five-year period following their first successful controlled and powered flight in 1903, when, as we shall see, no one else would.

wherein he recounted not only the 1896 experiments but also additional flights conducted by Augustus Herring in 1897. This free distribution of information was typical of the generous Chanute, who was genuinely committed to the advancement of manned flight regardless of any issue of credit for it.

The Wright brothers became seriously interested in the subject of manned flight in 1899. They wrote to Secretary Langley at The Smith-

❝ All agreed that the sensation of coasting on the air was delightful. ❞

Octave Chanute, regarding first glider flights, 1894

FIGURE 5-8 Box-type glider showing dunes near Lake Michigan where Chanute held experiments.

CHAPTER 6

Prelude to Powered Flight

© egd, 2008, Shutterstock, Inc.

As the Wrights continued their experiments at the Outer Banks of North Carolina in the fall of 1903, there was serious competition for the honor of completing the first manned, powered flight. Efforts were underway around the world, using the combined knowledge and experience of all of the preceding pioneers of flight. Of all such competition, the most formidable was that of Samuel P. Langley (see Figure 6-1), an astronomer, professor of mathematics at the U.S. Naval Academy, and the third Secretary of the Smithsonian Institution in Washington, D.C.

Langley began experimentation in heavier than air flight in 1886, using both gasoline and steam-powered engines. In 1893, Langley built a steam-powered model weighing a little over 14 pounds, which he called Aerodrome Model No. 4. He concluded that a launch of the craft could most easily and reliably be accomplished over water. He purchased a fishing scow and erected on it a platform on which he mounted, in turn, a series of launching devices. The launch of Aerodrome No. 4 was unsuccessful when the wing structure failed.

After the completion of modifications, Langley launched Aerodrome No. 5 on May 6, 1896, which flew successfully for over one half mile.[1] Two years later, with the United States at war with Spain, President McKinley asked Langley

Source: U.S. Air Force.

FIGURE 6-1 Samuel Langley.

to pursue the development of a manned aerodrome as a potential weapon of war, and Congress funded the project with $50,000. Langley pursued his experiments diligently for the next five years, exploring workable power sources for his full scale, man-carrying aerodrome. He concluded that steam engines were too heavy to be practical and became convinced that the internal combustion engine was the answer. By 1900, Langley's assistant, Charles Manly (see Figure 6-2), had successfully designed a 5-cylinder radial engine that weighed only 125 pounds but produced an impressive 53 horsepower.

A full-sized version of the Aerodrome was completed by 1902. (See Figure 6-3.) Delays in completing the project caused earlier plans to use ballast or dummy passengers to be amended, primarily on the insistence of Charles Manly that he be allowed to pilot the craft. On September 7, 1903, all was in readiness for the launch.

Contrary to the practice employed by the Wright brothers, the press was in full attendance as Manly assumed his place in the airplane and signaled for the catapult launch. What happened next is described by Dr. A. G. Bell in a speech in 1913:

> . . . but when the catapult was released the aerodrome sped along the track on the top of the house-boat attaining sufficient headway for normal flight; but at the end of the rails it was jerked violently down at the front, and plunged headlong into the river.

Langley was lampooned in the press, his aircraft maligned as a "buzzard," and his launch platform and houseboat ridiculed as the "Ark." Despite the very public failure, the commitment to flight remained steadfast. Manly was unhurt, the engine was undamaged, and the Aerodrome was repairable. On December 8, 1903, with the Wright brothers in residence at Kitty Hawk, all was again in readiness for history to be made. According to Dr. Bell:

> This time the rear guy post was injured, crippling the rear wings, so that the aerodrome pitched up in front and plunged over backwards into the water . . .

FIGURE 6-2 Samuel Langley and Charles Manly.

The Washington Star headlined on December 9, 1903, "AIRSHIP FAILS TO FLY," accompanied by a distressing photograph of the Aerodrome just after launch, captioned "Collapse of the Airship." (See Figure 6-4.) Within 3 years Langley was dead, the object of ridicule. Controversy concerning the cause of the failure, i.e., whether in fact but for a faulty catapult Langley's airplane would have been the first to fly, would continue for years. In 1913 Dr. Bell believed that the catapult was the only problem:

> It will thus be seen that Langley's aerodrome was never successfully launched, so that it had no opportunity of showing what it could do in the air. The defect lay in the launching mechanism employed and not in the machine itself, which is recognized by all experts as a perfectly good flying machine, excellently constructed and made long before the appearance of other machines.

Source: National Air and Space Museum, Smithsonian Institution (SI 2003-35050).

FIGURE 6-3 The Aerodrome atop Langley's barge.

In 1914 the refurbished Aerodrome was fitted with floats and was successfully flown by Glenn Curtiss from Lake Keuka in New York. Funds for this effort were contributed by Dr. Bell and others. It is asserted that significant modifications, based on developments in aircraft design during the intervening 11 years, had been performed to the Aerodrome by Curtiss before its flight. As will be seen in chapter 8, Dr. Bell and Glenn Curtiss were closely associated in developing aircraft prototypes beginning in 1907 in a group called the Aerial Experiment Association (AEA). There would be competition and rivalry between the Wright Brothers and the AEA, and AEA member Glenn Curtiss in particular, as these two groups strived to produce the world's first practical aircraft in the early years of the twentieth century. Trade secrecy, patents, and litigation were to be the spin off from these efforts. But someone had yet to be the first to fly.

Source: National Air and Space Museum, Smithsonian Institution (SI 2002-16637).

FIGURE 6-4 The crash of the Aerodrome.

Endnote

1. Dr. Alexander Graham Bell was in attendance. See Appendix 1 for his comments.

CHAPTER 7

The Wright Brothers

© Dan Barnes, 2008, Shutterstock, Inc.

❝ More than anything else the sensation is one of perfect peace mingled with an excitement that strains every nerve to the utmost, if you can conceive of such a combination. ❞

Wilbur Wright

In 1908, Wilbur Wright responded to an inquiry concerning the circumstances of his and Orville's interest in flight. He said:

> Late in the autumn of 1878, our father came into the house one evening with some object partly concealed in his hands, and before we could see what it was, he tossed it into the air. Instead of falling to the floor as we expected, it flew across the room till it struck the ceiling, where it fluttered awhile, and finally sank to the floor. It was a little toy, known to scientists as a "helicoptere," but which we, with sublime disregard for science, at once dubbed a 'bat.' It was a light frame of cork and bamboo, covered with paper, which formed two screws, driven in opposite directions by rubber bands under torsion. A toy so delicate lasted only a short time in the hands of small boys, but its memory was abiding.

Later, the boys became experts in kite building and in flying them until their age made this activity unseemingly childish. They also built model "helicopteres," making them larger and larger. The larger they become, they discovered, the less they flew. In this way they began to learn the rudimentary physics of aerodynamics, that a machine having only twice the linear dimensions of another would require eight times the power to achieve lift. Thus, were they introduced to coefficients of aerodynamic lift.

In the late nineteenth century, the bicycle was advanced technology, and its popularity made its commercial appeal very great. The Wrights opened a bicycle shop in Dayton, Ohio, and became adept at machinery and mechanics. In the middle of the decade of the 1890s, the brothers had some limited knowledge of the small group of engineers and scientists who had conducted experiments with gliders and flying machines. But it was not until the death of Otto Lilienthal, in 1896, that they seriously took up the study of aeronautics. They began reading works by Chanute, Lilienthal, Langley, and articles published by the Smithsonian Institution. They saw at once that the field of aviation was neatly divided between the advocates advancing theories and experimentation related to propulsion, or

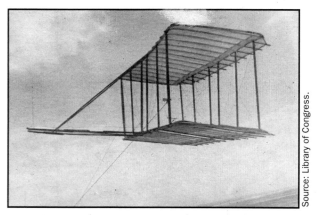

Source: Library of Congress.

FIGURE 7-1 The Wright brothers' kite—1900.

Source: Library of Congress.

FIGURE 7-2 The Wright brothers' kite, also flown as a glider.

powered flight, like Langley and Maxim, and those advocates of soaring flight, like Lilienthal, Mouillard, and Chanute. The sympathies of the Wright brothers lay with the latter group, based on the sound logic that until the problem of control of an aerial vehicle could be solved, the question of power would not be relevant. They, therefore, zeroed in on the problem of control.

As they educated themselves with the available literature, they also noted that the years between 1895 and 1900 represented a brief time of heightened activity in aeronautics, and a time of great public expectation that a solution to the problem of flight would be found. But successful flight did not materialize. Maxim, after spending $100,000 in the effort, abandoned his work. The Ader machine, built at the expense of the French government, was a failure. Lilienthal and Pilcher were killed in experiments, and Chanute and most others seemed to be having little success. The Wrights concluded that the public, distressed and disappointed by the failures and tragedies, had given up on the idea of manned, powered flight. As they said, the whole process seemed to have been shuffled off to that purgatory of science and engineering that was concerned with such things as the perpetual motion machine.

So it was that they harked back to their days of kite flying. They began their active experimentation in October, 1900 at Kitty Hawk. (See Figure 7-1.) They chose that venue for its constant, substantial breezes, and because of the elevation of the sand dunes and unobstructed terrain that joined the sea. Their machine was designed in large part from the work of Chanute with its struts and wire bracing, and from the Lilienthal tables from which the coefficient of lift could be calculated. It was to be flown tethered to the ground, as a kite with a man aboard, and also as a glider. The 1900 experiments failed to confirm published data on wind pressures and lift, although they did confirm the basic effectiveness of lateral and vertical control, innovations that were original to the Wrights. The main problems of lift and drag were daunting, but as the brothers left Kitty Hawk as winter approached, they were encouraged enough to plan improvements to be tested the next summer.

On their return to North Carolina on July 11, 1901, the design of the glider was essentially the same (see Figure 7-2), except that it was made larger and the camber of the wings was increased in order to attempt to provide for greater lift. Still, the amount of lift achieved was disappointing. The brothers reluctantly concluded that the published data of flight, particularly as concerned lift, could not be trusted. The center of pressure calculated from the tables was too far forward, resulting in a nose heavy trim. Even attempts to manipulate the "warping mechanism" of the wings while attempting on-board gliding did not result in the satisfactory trials experienced the year before. Wilbur and Orville were so dispirited that they broke camp a month earlier than they had planned, and returned to Dayton. As recollected by Orville:

> . . . we doubted that we would ever resume our experiments. Although we had broken the record for distance in gliding, and although Mr. Chanute, who was present at that time, assured us that our results were better than had ever before been attained, yet when we looked at the time and money which we had expended, and considered the progress made and the distance yet to go, we considered our experiments a failure. At that time I made the prediction that men would sometime fly, but that it would not be within our lifetime.[1]

On their return to Dayton, Wilbur and Orville began to believe that the information that had previously been developed, particularly the Smeaton coefficient and data compiled by Otto Lilienthal regarding pressures, were in error. They determined to verify all of the necessary data, such as coefficient of lift and wind pressures from their own experimentation. Rather than secure this information from building and crashing more gliders, they set about to make these determinations more scientifically. They constructed a state of the art wind tunnel and developed instruments to quantify lift and drag. They tested over 80 different wing configurations in their wind tunnel and, in the process, confirmed that prevailing data on coefficient of lift was wrong. They also were able to identify an optimum shape of wing, one much longer and narrower, for their new machine. Tests also provided insight into the need of a vertical "vane" as they called it; what today is known as a rudder. (See Figure 7-3.)

The design of the 1902 glider (see Figure 7-4), incorporating the results of their testing in the wind tunnel, was the first aircraft that solved the fundamental problems of soaring flight, lift and control, and it constituted a major departure from their first two gliders. They returned to Kill Devil Hills in the late summer of 1902 and by the middle of September, they had begun kiting experiments. In a letter to Milton Wright on October 2, 1902, Wilbur wrote:

> Our new machine is a very great improvement over anything we had built before and over anything any one has built. We have far beaten all record for flatness of glides as we in some cases have descended only 5 1/3 degrees from the horizontal while other machines descended from 7.5 to 11 degrees. . . . This means that in soaring we can descend much slower, and in a power machine can fly with much less power. The new machine is also much more controllable than any heretofore

FIGURE 7-3 Glider—1901.

Source: Library of Congress.

Source: Library of Congress.

FIGURE 7-4 Glider turning—1902.

built so the danger is correspondingly reduced. We are being careful and will avoid accident of serious nature if possible. Yesterday I tried three glides from the top of the hill and made 506 ft, 504.4 ft, and 550 ft, respectively in distance passed over. Everything is so much more satisfactory that we now believe that the flying problem is really nearing its solution.

Upon completion of the 1902 tests, the Wrights returned to Dayton, and they were now ready to confront the only remaining problem: propulsion.

Motive power, thrust, or propulsion, all words of similar meaning, was shown to have been effective using the steam engine. Weight and complexity of the steam engine, with its water, boiler, and piping, argued forcefully for a gasoline engine. But a lightweight gasoline engine did not exist. A mechanic in their own shop, Charles Taylor, decided that he could build

one and shortly produced a four-cylinder engine with a power to weight ratio superior to any known at the time. Although extremely primitive (it had no carburetor), the engine barely had the horsepower (it produced 12 horsepower) to provide the thrust needed for the 1903 experiments.

The second part of the propulsion problem was the propeller. There was no available data on aircraft propellers, and their research into marine propellers turned out to be a dead end. They approached the problem in the same way as they had approached the wing lift. They just rotated the wing 90 degrees, put a twist in it and they had created a propeller. The efficiency of the propeller designs was tested in the wind tunnel until the best was found.

There was no guesswork in the 1903 experiments. The Wright brothers had brought the scientific method to their task, and the total design had been proven on paper. They also possessed the skills of mechanics and craftsmen to put it all together in the final product and in workmanlike manner. Free, controlled, and sustained powered flight was at last achieved on December 17, 1903 in their design known as the Flyer I. (See Figures 7-5 and 7-6.) This craft was damaged after its fourth flight (852 feet in 59 seconds), although it was salvaged and returned to Dayton, Ohio. In 1928, Orville sent it for display to the London Science Museum. Since 1949, it has been on display at the Smithsonian Institution.

The Wrights continued their research and development at Huffman Prairie, Ohio, beginning in 1904. They built a second powered model, the Flyer II (see Figure 7-7), that was virtually identical to the Flyer I, but 320 pounds lighter. They attempted short hops in the Flyer II, but they were having difficulty with the underpowered engine and the lack of the favorable winds enjoyed at Kitty Hawk. In September 1904, they developed a catapult launching system to get the airplane quickly up to flying speed. This system allowed them to again concentrate on flying and on extending the range of their flights. Control problems continued, several public-flying displays ended badly, and their press became negative. Yet they persevered, and by the end of 1904 they had made 105 successful flights and logged a total of 45 minutes flying time.

In 1905 the Flyer III was launched (see Figure 7-9). After a series of serious mishaps, the Wrights made several significant changes to the Flyer based on their conclusion that longitudinal stability was the problem. They increased the area of the elevator to almost two times its former dimension. Believing that the elevator was too close to the wings, they extended it to a point almost twice as far from the leading edge of the wing as previously. When testing resumed, it was immediately apparent that these changes had made the Flyer truly airworthy. This was regarded by the Wrights as their final design,

Source: Library of Congress.

FIGURE 7-5 The first powered flight—December 17, 1903.

Source: Library of Congress.

FIGURE 7-6 The third powered flight—December 17, 1903.

Source: Library of Congress.

FIGURE 7-7 Flyer II at Huffman Prairie—1904.

having with it solved all major control problems, and it became generally acknowledged to be the world's first practical airplane. On October 5, 1905, the Wrights completed a flight of 24 miles in 38 minutes, landing only when the gas tank on the airplane ran dry. Being highly satisfied with their design, but wondering of what practical use the airplane could be put, they lob-

Source: Library of Congress.

FIGURE 7-8   Flyer III at Huffman Prairie—1905.

bied the U.S. government, suggesting that the airplane might be used for military scouting and reconnaissance. The War Department was not interested, advising the Wrights that the United States had 'no requirements' for their invention.

The Wrights had applied for, but still had not secured, a patent in 1905 and they were not willing to make the details of their product public. After the negative press received in 1904, reporters were not invited to view the machine or its performance and the few articles published about it during this time were generally inaccurate. Their sole support came from Octave Chanute, who had seen the aircraft, had seen it fly, and who knew the details of its construction. His correspondence with his contacts throughout the world was about the only sustaining force that kept the Wright's accomplishments above rank rumor. When visitors began to come to Dayton to view their machine and to interview them, the Wrights shunned all publicity and even disassembled the Flyer and stowed away the parts from view for almost three years. The Flyer did not fly again until 1908 when it was adapted to carry two people.

Rejected at home, the Wrights turned to Europe, where aviation was taking hold. The asking price for the aircraft was $200,000, a very large sum in those days. Although they guaranteed its performance, they refused to demonstrate it to a prospective purchaser until a price had been negotiated and paid. Not surprisingly, no sales were recorded. At the same time, experimenters were proceeding with their own individual designs and making progress, although none had come close to accomplishing what the Wrights had. This fact, in addition to the secrecy that surrounded the Wrights' 1905 experiments, produced widespread skepticism in the aviation community. Skepticism even took the form of sarcasm and taunting. Consider the tone of the following article from the very prominent *Scientific American* magazine, entitled "The Wright Aeroplane and Its Fabled Performance."[2]

Source: Library of Congress.

FIGURE 7-9   Flyer III—the world's first practical airplane—1905.

A Parisian automobile paper recently published a letter from the Wright brothers to Capt. Ferber of the French army, in which statements are made that certainly need some public substantiation from the Wright brothers. In the letter in question it is alleged that on September 26, the Wright motor-driven aeroplane covered a distance of 17.961 kilometers in 18 minutes and 9 seconds, and that its further progress was stopped by lack of gasoline. On September 29 a distance of 19.57 kilometers was covered in 19 minutes and 55 seconds, the gasoline supply again having been exhausted. On September 30 the machine traveled 16 kilometers in 17 minutes and 15 seconds; this time a hot bearing prevented further remarkable progress. Then came some eye-opening records. Here they are:

➡ October 3: 25.535 kilometers in 25 minutes and 5 seconds. (Cause of Stoppage, hot bearing.)

➡ October 4: 33.456 kilometers in 33 minutes and 17 seconds. (Cause of Stoppage, hot bearing.)

➡ October 5: 38.956 kilometers in 33 minutes and 3 seconds. (Cause of Stoppage, exhaustion of gasoline supply.)

It seems that these alleged experiments were made at Dayton, Ohio, a fairly large town, and that the newspapers of the United States, alert as they are, allowed these sensational performances to escape their notice. When it is considered that Langley never even successfully launched his man-carrying machine, that Langley's experimental model never flew more than a mile, and that Wright's mysterious aeroplane covered a reputed distance of 38 kilometers at the rate of one kilometer a minute, we have the right to exact further information before we place reliance on these French reports. Unfortunately, the Wright brothers are hardly disposed to publish any substantiation or to make public experiment, for reasons best known to themselves. If such sensational and tremendously important experiments are being conducted in a not very remote part of the country, on a subject in which almost everybody feels the most profound interest, is it possible to believe that the enterprising American reporter, who, it is well known, comes down the chimney when the door is locked in his face—even if he has to scale a fifteen-story sky-scraper to do so—would not have ascertained all about them and published them for broadcast long ago? Why, particularly, as it is further alleged, should the Wrights desire to sell their invention to the French government for a "million" francs. Surely their own is the first to which they would be likely to apply.

We certainly want more light on the subject.[3]

On May 22, 1906, the U.S. Patent Office granted Patent No. 821,393 to the Wrights for their design. The patent was broad enough to cover the entire craft, although the main claim in the application was to the means of control. Diagrams, accompanied by step-by-step explanations of the workings of their three dimensional means of control, clearly show the originality of their design.

Ultimately, the infant aviation community did not accept that the work of the Wright brothers was worthy enough as to command royalties. In Europe, the patent was to be ignored and the Wrights' lateral control innovations were to be shamefully duplicated, as in the Bleriot monoplanes, for example. In the United States, Glenn Curtiss would begin developing designs of airplanes with a form of aileron control without payment of royalties. But he maintained, probably correctly, that the incorporation of the "aileron" into the wing was outside of the Wrights' patent.

In 1907, though, things began to improve for the secretive Wrights. The War Department that year announced a competition for an air-

plane for government use. The specifications tracked those that the Wrights had earlier advertised to the government. The Wrights returned to Kitty Hawk, a more isolated venue than Huffman Prairie, re-established their camp, and began testing their modified Flyer, which now had two side-by-side seats mounted in the upright position. This version was known as the Model A.

By 1908, the Wrights were satisfied with their modified design and were ready, not only for the Army competition, but to begin the European marketing of the Flyer. The Wrights decided to divide their efforts. Orville returned to Dayton and prepared a machine for demonstration. Wilbur journeyed to France to fulfill the terms of a contract that had finally been successfully negotiated for the sale of the Flyer. The terms of the French contract varied significantly from the bid submitted by Orville to the U.S. War Department.

The bid to the United States government was for one aircraft, for $25,000, deliverable in 200 days with an additional 30 days allowed for flight demonstration. The French contract agreed to deliver four aircraft, for $4,000 each, and to receive a lump sum payment of $100,000 and a 50% interest in the French purchasing company. The French contract also required that the aircraft successfully complete flights of 31 miles each, while carrying a passenger, and that the Wrights teach three students to fly and solo.

Wilbur was to be the subject of extensive ridicule on his arrival in France, where the terms of the contract had been widely publicized, and where it was generally believed that no aircraft was capable of accomplishing the requirements of the contract. As far as the French knew, the successful short flight of M. Santos-Dumont in 1906 outside of Paris not only established him as the first to fly, but also created the "operations envelope" for the "aeroplane" in general (that original flight covered a distance of 200 feet). Wilbur set up operations outside of Paris and resolutely went about preparing to meet his part of the bargain. After flawless demonstrations in August 1908, not only of the capabilities of the Model A but also of his piloting skills, the combination of which greatly surpassed anything the French had ever seen, he almost overnight became a national hero. Wilbur then began a series of record setting accomplishments:

1. September 21, 1908—A record for distance and duration that brought a $1,000 prize from the Aero Club de France.
2. October 7, 1908—The first flight with a female passenger, Mrs. Hart O. Berg.
3. October 10, 1908—A record for distance and duration with a passenger.
4. November 18, 1908—An altitude record of 90 meters, earning a prize of 1,000 French francs from the Aero Club de Saitte.
5. November 23, 1908—A new altitude record bring with it a prize of 2,500 French francs.
6. December 31, 1908—A new duration and distance record (2 hours, 18 minutes) for the Coupe de Michelin Trophy and a prize of 20,000 French francs.

Wilbur became the toast of France, the recipient of medals, commendations, and the honoree of testimonial dinners. He was even given a standing ovation by the French Senate. Flights were conducted throughout Europe for the remainder of 1908 and into 1909 with increasing acclaim from the Europeans. (See Figure 7-10.) Audiences were had with King Alfonso of Spain, King Victor Emmanuel of Italy, and King Edward VII of England. During the demonstrations in Italy, the American industrialist J. P. Morgan chanced to see one of the flights and was later instrumental in helping the Wrights secure financial backing from wealthy investors in New York. In England, the Wrights met Charles Rolls of Rolls-Royce renown, who purchased a Wright flyer for his personal use, the first private airplane purchase in history.

Meanwhile, in September 1908, Orville began the demonstrations for the U.S. government in Ft. Myer, Virginia. (See Figure 7-11.) The demonstrations were attended by Lt. Thomas Selfridge, as a government representative, and he was authorized to accompany Orville as a passen-

Courtesy of Special Collections & Archives, Wright State University.

FIGURE 7-10 Wilbur Wright flying in France—1909.

FIGURE 7-11 Orville Wright at Fort Myer, Virginia—1908.

FIGURE 7-12 Lt. Thomas Selfridge and Orville Wright prior to a take off at Ft. Myer, Virginia—1908.

ger on one of the flights being evaluated by the government. (See Figure 7-12.) As we will see in the next chapter, Selfridge was a member of the Aeronautical Experiment Association (AEA), which had designed and, for the first time in America, publicly flown an airplane. The Wrights, in fact, regarded the activities of the AEA as an infringement on their patent.

Orville was not pleased that Lt. Selfridge was to be given an up close look at the Flyer, but the flight proceeded aloft with the two antagonists aboard. As the aircraft flew at 80 feet, one of the propellers somehow struck a bracing wire, causing it to snap in two. Orville was unable to control the Flyer, and it dove almost vertically into the ground in front of the horrified spectators. Lt. Selfridge was killed, becoming the first fatality due to an airplane accident, and Orville was very seriously injured. The demonstrations were cancelled.

❝ If you are looking for perfect safety, you will do well to sit on a fence and watch the birds; but if you really wish to learn, you must mount a machine and become acquainted with its tricks by actual trial. ❞

Wilbur Wright, from an address to the Western Society of Engineers in Chicago, 18 September 1901

After his release from the hospital, Orville traveled to France as a part of his recuperation and participated along with Wilbur and their sister Katherine in the victorious tour of Europe. When the Wrights returned to the United States in May 1909, they were welcomed as national heroes. President Taft feted them at the White House and awarded them a Congressional medal.

The War Department had extended the time for completion of flight tests that had begun in 1908 until Orville could recover from his injuries. The tests were resumed on June 29, 1909 with a new model of the former Model A flyer. This version was called the Military Flyer, weighing 740 pounds and with a Wright 4-cylinder 34 horsepower engine, which offered more speed. On July 12, Orville completed the duration portion of the Army requirements by staying aloft for one hour and 12 minutes with Army Lt. Frank Lahm aboard the aircraft, exceeding the test parameters. Orville next began the flight to meet the Army speed requirement of 40 miles per hour. He climbed the Flyer to 400 feet and, assuming a slight nose down attitude, streaked past his launching derrick at 42.583 miles per hour. He flew a victory lap around Arlington National Cemetery and landed. The first military aircraft had just been purchased at a cost of $30,000 ($25,000 contract price plus bonus of $5,000 for the extra two miles per hour attained in the test). Wheels were installed on this version in 1910.

The Wright Company was formed in November 1909 as an aircraft production company with the backing of New York financiers, and the brothers continued to improve on the Model A design. The Model B was the first production airplane with a 75 horsepower Rausenberger engine, and was the first Wright aircraft to fly without a canard in front. It was also the first to have a single elevator located aft, although it continued to use wing warping for banking control. The military version of the model B adopted ailerons for the first time for lateral control.

The Wright Company produced a number of different models through 1916, the last year of production, with various design modifications, although Orville Wright sold his interest in the company to a group of financiers in 1915. The Model F was the first Wright airplane to adopt a fuselage, on which the elevator was placed atop the rudder located on the tail of the aircraft. The Model K was the first tractor (forward facing propellers) airplane produced by the Wright Company, and on the K model wing warping was finally abandoned completely in favor of aileron control.

Wilbur Wright died of typhoid fever in 1912, and although Orville remained in the aviation arena for years, he was never to take another principle role.

> **❝** It may be that the invention of the aeroplane flying-machine will be deemed to have been of less material value to the world than the discovery of Bessemer and open-hearth steel, or the perfection of the telegraph, or the introduction of new and more scientific methods in the management of our great industrial works. To us, however, the conquest of the air, to use a hackneyed phrase, is a technical triumph so dramatic and so amazing that it overshadows in importance every feat that the inventor has accomplished. If we are apt to lose our sense of proportion, it is not only because it was but yesterday that we learned the secret of the bird, but also because we have dreamed of flying long before we succeeded in ploughing the water in a dugout canoe. From Icarus to the Wright Brothers is a far cry. **❞**
>
> **Waldemar Kaempffert, *The New Art of Flying*, 1910**

Endnotes

1. Kelly, Fred. *The Wright Brothers: A Biography authorized by Orville Wright* (New York, Ballentine Books, 1956).
2. January 13, 1905, Vol. XCIV, No. 2, page 40.
3. See Appendix 2, an address by A. G. Bell on the presentation of the Langley Medal to Gustave Eiffel in 1913. In this speech Dr. Bell provides a then contemporary explanation of the confusion and general lack of awareness that the public and the scientific community labored under regarding innovations of flight.

PART III

Pioneers

© Stephen Strathdee, 2008, Shutterstock.

Chapter 8   Glenn Curtiss

Chapter 9   World War I

Chapter 10   Airmail Story

Chapter 11   Horsepower

Glenn Curtiss

Glenn Curtiss' efforts were to overlap the Wrights and, as has been said, he was to really take off where they left off. He began as a young man excelling in bicycle racing in 1896, becoming champion for western New York State. In 1900 he started his own bicycle shop where he built a version he called the Hercules. Almost immediately he took to installing on these bikes a one-cylinder gasoline engine kit, which he modified due to its poor construction. Before long he had designed and produced a motorbike that was handily defeating all competing models, and by 1907 he had become internationally known for his lightweight, powerful engines. That year, atop his V-8, 268 cubic inch, 40 horsepower model, at Ormond Beach, Florida, he set the record for the fastest speed in the world at 136 miles per hour.

Not only was Curtiss becoming interested in the reports of powered flying machines, but aviation enthusiasts were also becoming interested in the powerful, lightweight engines he produced. One such was Thomas Scott Baldwin, who was building a "dirigible balloon" in California when he happened to see a new motorcycle with a Curtiss motor. Baldwin began collaboration with Curtiss that resulted in both improvements to the airship and in the motors supplied by Curtiss, which were now being oriented to aviation pur-

poses. At the St. Louis World's Fair in 1904, the Curtiss-Baldwin "dirigible balloon" proved the only success of all those brought from all over America and Europe. (See Figure 8-1.) Soon all such airships were driven by Curtiss motors.

The U.S. government then commissioned Baldwin and Curtis to build a dirigible balloon for use by the Army Signal Corps, with the requirement that it achieve a two-hour endurance flight, at a speed of twenty miles per hour, and that it be steerable in any direction. Flight tests in the summer of 1905 met those specifications handily and the government accepted the airship.

Curtiss came to the attention of Dr. Alexander Graham Bell, the inventor of the telephone, and the two met in New York in 1905. Dr. Bell was interested in Curtiss' motors for use on his "tetrahedral kites," a form of aerial contrivance he called "aerodromes." Invited to Bell's Nova Scotia quarters in 1907, Curtiss was introduced to two of Bell's assistants, J. A. D. McCurdy and F. W. Baldwin, recent graduates of Toronto University in mechanical engineering. Also present was Lt. Thomas Selfridge who, as we have seen, was to become the first fatality as a result of a powered airplane flight in the Wright Flyer A. Lt. Selfridge was a military expert in gliders and aeronautics and had previously corresponded

Source: Library of Congress.

FIGURE 8-1 The Baldwin dirigible equipped with Curtiss motors, was delivered to the Aeronautical Division of the U.S. Army Signal Corps in Washington in the summer of 1908. Baldwin operated the controls of the craft from the rear, while Glenn Curtiss took care of the engine forward. The airship succeeded in meeting government specifications during its two-hour trials.

with the Wright brothers about some aspects of their experiments. The Wright brothers, in spite of their penchant for secrecy, had provided Selfridge with some details of the Flyer from their patent documents. Nevertheless, there was much skepticism concerning the Wrights' claims. Few people had seen the Wrights fly. The only thing known for certain was that on August 22 and 23, 1906, M. Santos-Dumont was able to publicly launch his strange looking craft aloft, and to cover a distance of 200 feet at a speed of 25 miles per hour. This was the first public flight in the world.

This group of five individuals committed itself to form a scientific association to study aeronautics, and to design and build a practical airplane. They called the group the "Aerial Experiment Association." (See Figure 8-2.) A charter was drawn up and signed on September 30, 1907, wherein it was agreed to share expenses and to jointly own any successful inventions that might be conceived. They set to work immediately, and on March 12, 1908, they succeeded in accomplishing the first public flight

in America of a motor-driven, heavier than air mechanical machine. This flight was made on frozen Lake Keuka at Hammondsport, N.Y.

The machine was Number One, ostensibly designed by Lt. Selfridge, although all members contributed to the final product, and they dubbed it "Red Wing." The Red Wing was propelled by the Curtiss V-8, 40 horsepower air-cooled engine and it sat on ice runners. Although it resembled the Wright's Flyer in some respects, it was significantly different, and it did not incorporate "wing warping" for lateral control. The group at AEA was aware of the wing-warping design in the Wright patent and avoided using it, since by law a royalty would have to be paid. Because all of the group's experiments were public, and given the reputation of Dr. Bell, the decision was made to take pains not to infringe the Wright patent. The one and only flight of the Red Wing covered a distance of 318 feet, 11 inches, and it was demolished on landing due to lateral control problems.

After the crash of Red Wing, a second craft was built. "White Wing" was nominally

Source: Library of Congress.

FIGURE 8-2 Members of the Aeronautical Experiment Association (From Left to Right) Glenn Curtiss, J. A. D. McCurdy, Alexander Graham Bell, Frederick W. Baldwin, Thomas E. Selfridge.

designed by Casey Baldwin (see Figure 8-3), as the group apparently took turns in crediting their designs to specific individuals in the group in turn. It incorporated the salvaged engine from Red Wing and sported motorcycle wheels and tires. An innovative steerable nose wheel was fashioned allowing a more controllable take off. White Wing, however, had a more innovative feature designed by Dr. Bell, a feature that would become the subject of a bitter and infamous patent infringement lawsuit brought by the Wright brothers. The innovation, dubbed "aileron" or little wing, provided moveable wing tips, the forerunner of the modern aileron used throughout the world of aviation today. White Wing flew on May 21, 1908, but crashed on its fourth flight when piloted by John McCurdy. Glenn Curtiss, however, had first managed to keep it aloft for a distance of over 1,000 feet on its third test.

At about the same time, the weekly magazine, *Scientific American,* along with the Aero Club of America, offered a beautiful silver trophy to any aviator who could achieve prescribed flying goals in each of three successive years. The goal for the first year was that the airplane must

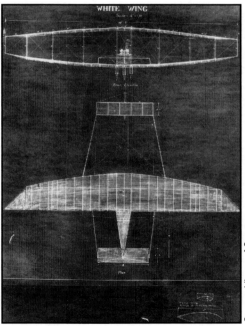

Source: Library of Congress.

FIGURE 8-3 White Wing.

fly in a straight course for a distance of one kilometer (3,281 feet). This was a feat already easily accomplished by the Wright Flyer, but the additional requirements set by the contest were that

Source: National Air and Space Museum, Smithsonian Institution (SI 2003-35048).

FIGURE 8-4 June Bug with Glenn Curtiss at the controls—1908.

Source: Library of Congress.

FIGURE 8-5 Glenn Curtiss seated in the June Bug.

the feat be accomplished in public and that the aircraft take off and land on wheels. The Wrights at this time were deep into their secretive mode and were not in the least interested in any public demonstrations of the Flyer. Moreover, the Flyer still employed the catapult rail for launch, without wheels. Glenn Curtiss, however, was interested, and he set about modifying the White Wing design in order to produce an entrant for the Cup competition. This design was to be known as the June Bug (see Figures 8-4 and 8-5), and with the latest modifications, including enlarged ailerons, it made its first flight on June 21, 1908. Curtiss flew the June Bug for a distance of over 3,000 feet, and the AEA was ready to try for the Scientific American Cup.

The June Bug was able to complete the distance requirement for the Cup at the hands of Curtiss on July 4, 1908 before a large and incredulous crowd, practically none of whom had ever before even seen an airplane. The June Bug flew 5,360 feet in one minute and 40 seconds and won the Scientific American trophy. (See Figure 8-6.) The aviation community and, indeed, the world at large were taken by storm, much to the consternation of the secretive Wright brothers. Orville Wright wrote to Curtiss after the competition reminding him and the

AEA that they had not consented to the use of their control system in exhibitions or in any commercial way. The AEA, however, did not concede that their "aileron" design in any way infringed the Wright's patent, and they continued to experiment and improve.

The most successful of the three airplanes that the AEA built after the June Bug was named "Silver Dart," and it flew on February 23, 1909, as the first airplane to fly in Canada. The AEA disbanded in 1909 and Curtiss combined in business with Augustus Herring, a former associate of Octave Chanute. The ensuing years brought success after success to Curtiss, even as the sun began to set on the Wrights as leaders in the aviation community. Curtiss was awarded the Scientific American trophy for the second time on July 17, 1909, flying a distance of 25 miles. On August 29, 1909, flying the "Gold Bug" (also known as the Golden Flyer), Curtiss won the speed competition (Gordon Bennett Cup) over a closed course at Rheims, France against stiff competition, like Louis Bleriot, who made the first international flight on July 25, 1909 by flying the English Channel between Calais and Dover.

In 1910, Curtiss won $6,600 in prize money in the categories of fastest speed, endurance, and quick starting at the San Diego International Air

Source: Library of Congress.

FIGURE 8-6 Glenn Curtiss winning the Scientific American Trophy with the June Bug—July 4, 1908.

Meet. Following a mild setback due to his partner's mismanagement of the Herring-Curtiss Company, and a poor showing at a Governors Island demonstration in 1910, Curtiss redeemed his reputation and achieved, arguably, his most notable accomplishment to that time by winning the New York City-Albany endurance flight on May 21, 1910. The challenge carried with its successful conclusion a $10,000 prize for completion of the 152-mile distance, allowing two landings enroute and completion within a period of 24 hours. It was the first official cross-country airplane flight in the United States.

The Wright brothers, exasperated with the publicity and success of Curtiss around the world, filed a patent infringement lawsuit against Curtiss and the Herring-Curtiss Company in August 1909, alleging that their lateral control system had been and was being used without permission and without the payment of royalties. The Gold Bug, in the meantime, had been purchased by a group known as the Aeronautic Society of New York, becoming the first commercial sale of an aircraft in the United States. The Aeronautic Society, which was flying the craft at commercial exhibitions, agreed to pay the Wrights a royalty, but Curtiss refused. The ensuing litigation was slow, tedious, and very expensive. The strain of it was said to have contributed to the death of Wilbur Wright of typhoid fever in 1912, and bad blood rose amongst those

Source: Library of Congress.

FIGURE 8-7 Lt. Thomas E. Selfridge and Dr. Alexander Graham Bell at Baldwin Trials, August 18, 1908.

in the formerly close, collegial aviation community. Octave Chanute reportedly was disgusted at the Wrights for their greedy and litigious attitude, while others seemed dismayed at the stubbornness of Glenn Curtiss. But perhaps the best illustration of the feeling of the public at the time was expressed in the Evansville (Illinois) Courtier of December 2, 1909:

> For the purpose of controlling absolutely in this country and Canada all aviation by means of heavier-than-air machines, the Wright Company, backed by financiers controlling probably nearly a billion dollars, was formed several days ago. The men behind the latest, The Flying Machine Trust, are nearly all prominent in financial and trust affairs. The capital of the company is modestly placed at $1,000,000, and it is

Source: Florida State Archives.

FIGURE 8-8 Eugene Ely performing the first take off from a Naval vessel—November 1910.

announced that there is no stock for sale. The company, which has been formed to take over all of the Wright's patents and to prosecute infringements, claims as an asset even the principle of the plane and the control of the equilibrium of the machine.[1]

With the advent of World War I in 1914, a patent "pool" was organized with the assistance of the United States government that halted all patent litigation in the United States and provided, instead, for nominal payments to be made to patent holders. The purpose of the arrangement was to promote the free exchange of ideas and inventions for the collective good of the country in wartime. The unintended consequence of the arrangement, however, was the ultimate termination of the litigation between the Wrights and Curtiss, with no clear winner. By war's end in 1918, Orville Wright had sold out his former interests in the patents, and the litigation was never resumed. It is noteworthy that prior to the war, Dr. Bell had applied for patents as trustee for the AEA for innovations in flying machines, listing some 28 such improvements, including Bell's ailerons. The U.S. Patent (1,010,842) was granted to the AEA in December 1911.

Source: Florida State Archives.

FIGURE 8-9 Eugene Ely making the first landing aboard a Naval vessel, January 1911.

In the meantime, Curtiss began to actively consider the airplane market potential of the U.S. Navy. In November 1910, a pilot employed by Curtiss, Eugene Ely, was the first to take off an airplane from a Navy vessel, the U.S.S. Birmingham. (See Figure 8-8.) Two months later in January, Ely became the first to land an airplane back aboard a vessel, the U.S.S. Pennsylvania, utilizing in both cases specially constructed wooden platforms on the ships. (See Figure 8-9.) These demonstrations were followed by a successful landing of a float plane beside the Pennsylvania, followed by the hoisting of the plane aboard the ship, and then the redeployment of the airplane to the water for take off and return to shore.

Curtiss' exploits and accomplishments were by no means limited to flying prowess, speed, or endurance. His pioneering efforts in the design and construction of aircraft and engines continued with the development of the flying boat and amphibious aircraft. Although he had experimented with floats on the June Bug in 1908, it was not until 1910 that a craft was fitted with one centrally fitted float apparatus, actually a canoe, which was the forerunner of the future design of fuselage to be known as the "flying boat." Experiments showed that significantly greater engine power was required to permit a take off on water as compared to land; so various hull designs were tested.

Experimentation with hulls disclosed that a "stepped" configuration essentially solved the problem of the water takeoff. The "stepped" hull design incorporated a recessed aft section, so that the bottom of the aft section of the hull was higher than the forward portion of the hull. As speed increased, the aft section of the hull came out of the water first, which greatly reduced drag

and produced a planing effect of the hull on water that later came to be know as "being on the step." These original designs were modified and improved, spray patterns were controlled, and the improved hulls ultimately allowed take off from the water with close to the same horsepower as that required from land. By 1912, the Curtiss-designed aircraft hull had become state-of-the-art for the world. Further improvements were made as engines were mounted on the upper frame of the airplane, and as airframes were redesigned to account for pitch changes caused by these changes in the center of thrust. The Curtiss flying boats proved highly popular and sales were made to many foreign countries over the world.[2] (See Figure 8-10.)

In 1914, Curtiss Aeroplane and Motor Company designed the airplane that was to be known as the "Jenny," a combination of two separate versions of biplane (the "J" and the "N" models). The Jenny was too slow, and too underpowered, and it lacked the general performance capabilities required of fighter aircraft in World War I. It was, therefore, relegated to trainer duties. After the war, modifications made to the Jenny's wing would lead to the introduction by Curtiss of the first postwar airplane designed for the private sector, a plane named the "Oriole" placed on the

Source: U.S. Navy.

FIGURE 8-10 Curtiss flying boat—Model E.

market in 1920. These airplanes flew in the competitive market for almost twenty years.

Also in 1914, Curtiss produced the first twin-engine flying boat, and in 1919, the largest flying boats, the NC-1 through the NC-4 (see Figure 8-11) were launched. Three of these very large (for the time) aircraft began what was to be the first successful transatlantic crossing along a route beginning in Canada and terminating in Portugal. Only one of the airplanes, the NC-4, successfully completed the trip. Although Curtiss did not produce more of the flying boats, the design advances made by Curtiss were replicated or became the starting point for all future improvements on aircraft hull design. Boeing became the leading flying boat exponent in the United States, along with Martin and Sikorsky, and produced the beautiful Clipper Ships of Pan American fame.

The operations and experiments of Curtiss and the Aerial Experimentation Association at Hammondsport led to burgeoning regional public interest in aviation that resulted in large attendance at public demonstrations, and the establishment of a flight school through which passed many early contributors to aviation. Curtiss also later established a flight school in San Diego, California, where the first Navy pilots were trained, and where his testing of flying boats continued.

Endnotes

1. The Wright's commercial venture, like many to come, could only be deemed a failure. Orville Wright sold his interest in the company on August 26, 1915 for $250,000, one-fourth of its initial capitalization.

2. See remarks in Appendix 2 by Dr. A. G. Bell on February 13, 1913, to the Board of Regents of the Smithsonian Institution regarding Curtiss' contributions to flight safety using floatplanes.

Courtesy of the National Museum of Naval Aviation.

FIGURE 8-11 The NC-4, the first plane to cross the Atlantic.

World War I

In 1913, the state of aeronautical advance in the United States was primarily represented by the accomplishments of Glenn Curtiss. Conversely, leaders in Europe had invested heavily in aircraft technology. Competitions were regularly sponsored to encourage advances in aircraft speed, range, and altitude. Europeans had also incorporated aircraft units in their armed forces prior to the war. In 1913, the United States had only six pilots in the entire U.S. Army.

As in most wars, technological advances in weapons and support were greatly accelerated between 1914 and 1918. The United States was late entering the conflict (1917) and did not participate in the major aircraft innovations that occurred during the war. European manufacturers and designers had jumped ahead in aircraft and engine design, partly out of necessity. On the Allied side, the French Nieuport, followed by the SPAD, manufactured by the French company Societie des Productions Armand Deperdussin (hence the acronym), and the English S. E. 5, Sopwith Pup and Sopwith Camel, provided the fighter aircraft. In 1918, close to the end of World War I, Glenn Martin was responsible for contributing the only American design for combatant aircraft in the war with his MB-1 bomber. On the Axis side, the German manufacturers Junkers and Albatros Werke Gmbh produced formidable

Country	Aircraft	Trained Pilots
France	260	171
Russia	100	28
Germany	46	52
Great Britain	29	88
Italy	26	89
Japan	14	8
United States	8	14

TABLE 9-1 Aircraft and Trained Pilots in 1914
Source: Holley, *Ideas and Weapons*, p. 29.

fighter aircraft, but the Fokker designs proved to be the best, particularly the D.VII, which is widely regarded as the best fighter of the war. This aircraft was flown by Hermann Goering, who was to become the confidante of Adolf Hitler in the 1930s and the leader of the German Luftwaffe during World War II.

Although the Curtiss Aeroplane and Motor Company was the largest aircraft manufacturer in the world during the war, producing 10,000 planes by 1918, the JN-4 did not come close to matching European models in speed, power, and reliability. First produced in 1916, the Jenny mounted the OX-5 engine, 90 horsepower and water-cooled. When Curtiss improved his O model engine in 1913, he wanted to publicize its advances by designating it the "O Plus." But neither the "O Plus" nor the "O+" designation looked particularly good when printed, and the "+" could even be confused with the letter "T." Someone suggested rotating the Plus sign by 45 degrees, depicted as "OX," and the new series of engines became known as the OX-2.

The Curtiss models, although behind the Europeans, were higher performance machines than those built by the Wrights. The Wright Company had fallen by the wayside in aircraft design by World War I, its designs being almost entirely based on the outmoded Flyer models.

Manufacturing in the United States upon its entry into the war was made subject to the oversight and control of the Aircraft Production Board, which decreed that the United States should gear up to produce 22,000 aircraft for delivery to France within a year. Isolated between two great oceans, America was far removed from the vast destruction war had brought to Europe just since 1914, and the world was about to appreciate how valuable the heavy manufacturing reserve of the United States could be. But America was too far behind the design performance standards of aircraft already in use in Europe, so much of the American production effort was limited to manufacturing aircraft under license from European designers.

The DeHavilland DH-4, a single engine bomber/observation plane, was the primary military airplane built in the United States during the war. The Dayton-Wright Company built the most, 3,106 planes, followed by Fisher Body at 1,600, and Boeing, which produced 150.

The Wright Company concentrated on the production of engines under license, notably the 150 horsepower Hispano-Suiza aircraft engine, much in demand by the French. The French government in 1915 placed orders in the United States for 800 engines, which were required to be built in the United States due to the lack of

capacity in Europe during the war. The Wright Company contracted to supply 450 of these. To facilitate filling the order, the Wright Company arranged a merger with Glenn L. Martin in 1916 to form the Wright-Martin Aircraft Company. By the end of the war, the company had produced over 10,000 of the engines, known as the Wright-Hispano. In 1919, the Martin combination was dissolved and the company became the Wright Aeronautical Corporation. Much was to be heard from this company for its contributions to aircraft engine development during the 1920s.

With the entry of the United States into the war, the Aircraft Production Board ordered the production of 44,000 American-built aircraft engines to be used in conjunction with the ambitious goal of manufacturing over 22,000 aircraft. The immediate problem was, however, that the United States did not possess an aircraft engine capable of providing sufficient horsepower or speed for military airplanes. Packard Motors happened to have in its design inventory an experimental, but tested, eight-cylinder automobile engine that was to prove to the basis for America's greatest contribution to the war effort. On May 29, 1917, automobile engineers at Packard began a redesign of the engine with the purpose of supplying the ordered military aircraft engine, and five days later, a revised design was presented for aircraft use. But it was still an automobile engine, having battery ignition instead of magnetos, for example. It was redesigned again, this time expanding its power to twelve cylinders like the British Rolls engine, and with magneto ignition. The new design, the water-cooled Liberty, weighed only 710 pounds and, producing 410 horsepower, it surpassed the performance of all other aircraft engines in the world. By war's end, some 17,935 Libertys had been produced, of which 5,827 had been delivered to Europe for use in aircraft there. The Liberty was installed in the DH-4, and by November 1918 deliveries to the Army numbered 3,431 airplanes. Of these, 1,213 arrived in Europe, but only 248 ever flew at the front.

When the Armistice was signed, so many airplanes and engines had been produced for war use that engine and airplane manufacturing literally stopped cold. Surplus equipment was everywhere, and it was cheap. Curtiss Jennys were so numerous that, for $500, a student pilot could receive his instruction and upon solo be awarded a Jenny in the bargain.

As peace settled once again over the world, as the railroads were returned to their owners by the government, as the automobile began hitting the open roads being built by the government, and as all of the planes appeared to be sitting on the ground, many wondered what would become of aviation in America.

The National Advisory Committee for Aeronautics (NACA)

Although the United States had lost the initiative in aviation even before the start of World War I, in 1915 the government acknowledged the importance of aviation to the country when it established the National Advisory Committee for Aeronautics (NACA). From the beginning, NACA has been on the cutting edge of aeronautical research, its mission being to "direct and conduct research and experimentation in aeronautics with a view to their practical solution."

It was apparent to those in the Wilson administration that the United States lagged far behind European countries in its aviation capabilities, and those in government and in aviation found the situation untenable, to say nothing of the loss of national pride. As we will see, this competition between Europe and America has continued into the twenty-first century. Europe was clearly ahead of the United States in individual and governmental accomplishments, organized research, and government funding for military aviation. In 1917, NACA established the Langley Memorial Aeronautical Laboratory in Virginia for the pursuit of advanced test and experimentation in aeronautics.

Among its initial activities, NACA advised the national government on such matters as the desirability of beginning the airmail service, including the feasibility of night flight for mail delivery purposes. NACA was instrumental in securing the Manufacturers Aircraft Association agreement that curbed patent litigation and resulted in the sharing of ideas and inventions during World War I.

As we progress through the history of aviation and the role of government in this book, we will continually come back to the role of NACA as appropriate to illustrate its specific role in the evolution of aviation and the law related to aviation in the United States.

CHAPTER 10

Airmail Story

© Johnny Kuo, 2008, Shutterstock.

It was not long after the Wright brothers were first successful in marketing their airplane to the French and to the U.S. Army, in 1908 and 1909, that the idea occurred to someone in the Post Office Department that the airplane could be useful in delivering the mail—and faster than the railroads. Federal funding for airmail delivery was not forthcoming in spite of a bill introduced in Congress in 1910 by Congressman Morris Sheppard for that purpose. Beginning in 1911 without specific government funding, limited experimentation with airplanes hauling mail (15 pounds a load) was initiated. Congress was not convinced that the entire process of flying mail to a point over a United States Post Office, and dropping it from various heights to the ground, was not too hare-brained to be dignified by appropriations. Only in 1916 did Congress finally approve limited funding ($50,000 from the "Steamship Fund") for the establishment of a trial airmail route, in large part because of the rapid improvement and reliability of aircraft. In 1918 specific funding was finally approved (the Sheppard bill had been hung up in Congressional debate for 8 years) with a $100,000 appropriation for the purchase, operation, and maintenance of airplanes for use by the Post Office Department.

A Rough Beginning

Operations began by using airplanes and pilots furnished by the Army Signal Corps. It soon was clear that the airmail experiment was, in reality, a training device and exercise for the Army, and that delivery of the mail often amounted to an afterthought. It also became clear that the lack of training and experience of Army pilots, particularly in cross-country flying and navigation, was going to be a problem. Otto Praeger was Second Assistant Postmaster General of the United States from 1915 to 1921. He believed that the carriage of mail by air would be a logical next step in mail service to the country, and he also believed that the carrying of mail would have the secondary benefit of proving the use of the airplane for commercial purposes. After World War I, it seemed that business interests in the United States could not figure out how to put the airplane to any beneficial or productive purpose. This was the age of barnstormers, daredevils, adventurers, and a sideshow mentality that overshadowed most other thinking on the subject of airplanes. Banner towing, the selling of rides, and the occasional charter hop from one municipality to another was about the extent of commercial benefit associated with aviation. Besides, flying was fraught with danger.

The aircraft available after World War I were numerous, but they were mostly JN-4s, the latest version of which was the H model. This airplane had an average speed of 50 miles per hour, 60 tops, and could carry some 150 pounds of mail. The route fixed as the first experimental airmail route was between New York and Washington, D.C., a distance of 218 miles, with an intermediate stop at Philadelphia, and the date set for its inauguration was May 15, 1918. An airplane would depart both New York and Washington at the same time. In Washington, President Woodrow Wilson was in attendance, attesting to the magnitude and portent of the event, as was Otto Praeger and other Post Office dignitaries. (See Figure 10-1.)

The pilot selected for the Washington departure, Lt. George Boyle, was chosen more for his family contacts than for either his experience or skill. (See Figure 10-2.) As the President watched, Lt. Boyle called "contact" and the propeller was pulled through for start, but nothing happened. After several attempts, amid an embarrassing silence from the august assembly, someone thought to check the airplane's gas tank. It was empty. Upon being filled, the engine coughed to life and presently brand-new airmail pilot Boyle was finally airborne, and the airmail service had been launched, much to the relief of the Post Office and Army officials gathered there. (See Figure 10-3.) But there was yet another problem.

A pilot wishing to fly from Washington to Philadelphia is required to follow a generally northerly course, owing to the fact that Philadelphia is north of Washington. Lt. Boyle, however, turned to the south shortly after take off and landed in a pasture farther away from Philadelphia than when he started. The day was saved by the southbound mail, which arrived in Washington three hours and twenty minutes after it left New York. The second leg of the northbound route, from Philadelphia to New York, was salvaged when Boyle's difficulties became known, whereupon the second leg pilot loaded his airplane with Philadelphia mail and took off for New York.

FIGURE 10-1 President Woodrow Wilson at the inauguration of airmail—May 15, 1918.

FIGURE 10-2 Major Reuben Fleet (on the left) briefs airmail pilot Lt. George Boyle before he begins his flight on May 15, 1918.

Courtesy of the National Postal Museum, Smithsonian Institution.

Courtesy of the National Postal Museum, Smithsonian Institution.

Courtesy of the National Postal Museum, Smithsonian Institution.

FIGURE 10-3 Lt. George Boyle takes off for Philadelphia.

Scheduled Airmail Service

The experimental airmail service continued for about three months, until August 10, 1918, with an impressive record of 88% completion of flights attempted. The experiment using Army personnel had come to an end, and since it was the intention of the Post Office to use civilian pilots to operate the new, permanent airmail system, six new pilots were hired and new planes were put in service. (See Figure 10-4.) On August 12, 1918, the world's first regularly scheduled airmail service was begun between New York and Washington. On May 15, 1919, service was commenced between Cleveland and Chicago, the first segment of what was to ultimately become the transcontinental airmail route of the United States Post Office. Service on the segment from New York to Cleveland was deferred due to the adverse terrain, the Allegheny Mountains, which lay between those two cities.[1] Attempts to inaugurate that service in December 1918 had failed due to the fact that every airplane sent aloft had been forced down by weather. But by July 1, 1919, that service had been begun as well. The New York-Chicago

FIGURE 10-4   The first civilian airmail pilots (from left to right): Edward Gardner, Captain Benjamin Lipsner, Maurice Newton, Max Miller, and Robert Shank.

route segment would come to be known as the "graveyard run," and it would claim the lives of eighteen airmail pilots.

The mail was mostly flown in Curtiss Jennys from the beginning of experimental service, but it was clear that more powerful and larger airplanes were needed. The Army had developed an appreciation for Glenn Martin's airplanes during World War I, and was about to order the improved MB-2 bomber when the Post Office took over airmail delivery from the Army. In 1919, the Post Office applied some of the Congressional airmail appropriation to order six Martin MPs (mail planes), specially designed with nose cargo compartments capable of holding up to 1,500 pounds of mail, which were put into service in 1919 and 1920. Pilots crashed four of the new Post Office MPs on the New York to Chicago route, and the Post Office finally transferred the other two to the Army Signal Corps.

The Jennys gave way to the De Havilland DH-4 with Liberty engines, also leftovers from the war, that had earned the name "flying coffins" because of their propensity to catch fire on crashing, a not uncommon occurrence. (See

Figures 10-5 and 10-6.) These planes generally had as instrumentation an airspeed indicator, an altimeter of sorts, and an oil compass. The planes had to be flown visually, by reference to horizon, sky, and land outside of the cockpit. Navigation was also by outside reference, referred to as "pilotage," "contact flying," or "ded reckoning."[2] Landmarks on the ground were the prime navigational reference for these early cross-country pilots, and when clouds or fog obscured these, finding one's way became problematical, indeed. The airmail service did not operate at night; the mailbags were delivered to the trains for continuation of the journey until the next day, when once again the mail flew.

These two incapacities severely hampered the fledgling airmail service from fulfilling its promise.

→ First, the lack of instrumentation to fly "blind" or by instruments alone, was a problem that had to be addressed by the aircraft manufacturers, their vendors, and by the pilots themselves.

→ Second, the lack of any navigational infrastructure by which airplanes might find their way at night or in adverse weather conditions was a problem too big for individuals or the fledgling aircraft community.

A navigational infrastructure was an undertaking for government.

The first airmail pilots (see Figures 10-4 and 10-7), like Max Miller and Wesley Smith, began pushing the limits of "blind" flying, usually in order to extricate themselves from situations inadvertently encountered, like flying into clouds or fog. Smith is said to have taken a half empty bottle of whiskey aloft, which he placed on top of his instrument panel, to practice flying wings level with the whiskey level. Soon, he found that a curved tube filled with liquid and containing a ball, like a carpenter's level, was available, and this he fastened to his instrument panel. And so it went. It was found that turns

FIGURE 10-5 De Havilland—DH-4 with a Liberty engine.

Courtesy of the United States Air Force Museum.

FIGURE 10-6 DH-4.

Courtesy of the National Postal Museum, Smithsonian Institution.

FIGURE 10-7 Wild Bill Hopson, airmail pilot.

Courtesy of the National Postal Museum, Smithsonian Institution.

made at a constant, steady rate could be timed and the airplane could be rather accurately rolled out on predetermined headings. Sperry introduced a two axis gyroscopic instrument that allowed a pilot to determine whether his airplane had inadvertently entered a turn. This was followed up with a three-axis instrument that disclosed changes in pitch attitude.

At the same time, experimentation was proceeding on various fronts, including with radio, not only as a means of voice communication from air to ground, but also as a means of navi-

gation. By May 15, 1920, airmail service had been extended westward from Chicago to Omaha, Nebraska, establishing a through route all the way from New York. On August 16, 1920, a route was added southward from Chicago to St. Louis. On September 8, 1920, the transcontinental route was completed to San Francisco. Although the airmail service operated only during daylight hours, the railroad coast-to-coast mail time was bettered by 22 hours.

The promise was yet unfulfilled. Moreover, Otto Praeger was concerned that the entire airmail program might be cancelled if better results were not soon achieved. Night flying was the only way to free the airmail service from its earthbound dependence on the railroads. Flying at night had been experimented with, and successfully under certain conditions, like clear, moonlit nights, for short distances. But what about transcontinental distances on a regular schedule? Could it be done?

Transcontinental Airmail

On February 22, 1921, the first attempt at a through, continuous transcontinental airmail service was made. The plan called for a westbound plane to leave New York to fly the initial segment of the route to San Francisco, and an eastbound plane to leave San Francisco initiating the first segment to New York. (See Figure 10-8.) The trip each way would be sequentially flown by fresh airplanes and pilots, like the Pony Express, handing off the mail at predetermined points along the route. Two aircraft were assigned to begin at each end of the route.

The first airplane to leave New York discontinued shortly after take off. The second plane flew to Chicago but was grounded due to weather. The first plane out of San Francisco crashed in Nevada, but the second plane made it to Reno, and 12 hours after leaving San Francisco, the mail arrived in Cheyenne. Another plane took the mail on to North Platte, Nebraska, and there it was turned over to the next segment airmail pilot, Jack Knight.

A combination of ground personnel and volunteers built bonfires along Jack's route, which was to be traversed at night, and he made it to Omaha, his segment complete, by 1:00 A.M. There he learned that the plane scheduled to meet him in Omaha had not left Chicago due to weather. He volunteered to continue, armed only with an automobile road map to guide him over unknown terrain, a landscape he had never flown. This part of the country is chilly in February, and this night was accompanied by cold, ice, and snow, along with the low clouds that produce snow. He was unable to land at Des Moines, Iowa, as planned. He continued to Iowa City, and arriving, searched for the airport that was unlighted because the ground crew had left for the evening, believing that no sane person would fly in the prevailing conditions. A lone employee at the airfield heard his engine, lit a flare and watched as Jack Knight glided in with an empty gas tank. After refueling and accepting a quick cup of coffee, Knight gamely flew on to Chicago, finally landing at Checkerboard Field at 8:40 A.M. From there, the mail relay was continued to New York, and when the results were announced, the mail had been successfully carried coast to coast in slightly more than 24 hours.

The best that the Post Office had been able to do up to that time using the railroads was a transcontinental transit of 3 days. The experimental policy of flying the mail during daylight hours and handing the mail off to the railroads at night had only marginally improved savings in time, and was generally considered to be not cost effective. But with the grand experiment of February 21, 1921, it was now clear that flying the mails for the entire route could be done.

The success of the this first attempt caused Congress to favorably consider appropriations sought by the Post Office, granting a splendid

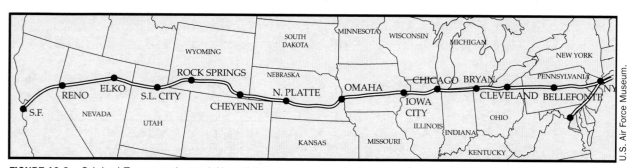

FIGURE 10-8 Original Transcontinental Airmail Route—compare to the Transcontinental Railroad, Figure 3-3.

sum for that time, $1,250,000, for airmail extensions. Paul Henderson, who became Second Assistant Postmaster General in 1922, was committed to the Otto Praeger principle that the mail could be flown. But it was clear that the mail had to be flown both night and day, and that bonfires as a means of nighttime navigation probably had only the most limited of possibilities.

The Lighted Airway

In 1923, Congress granted an appropriation to fund the construction of a system of sequential lighting on the transcontinental airmail route. The first segment completed was between Chicago and Cheyenne, a stretch of flat country most conducive to this original effort, and centrally located along the route. Airplanes launched at first light on either coast could reach the lighted segment by nightfall under most circumstances.

Beacons were placed on 50 foot steel towers constructed every ten miles along what had come to be known as the "airway." The beacons rotated so as to allow pilots to see their flash from 40 miles away in good weather. If the beacon were located at a landing field, the beacons showed a green course light, if not, then red. Morse code, which is still used as part of the FAA navigation scheme today, was introduced into the airway system at the time of this first construction. Each beacon flashed an identifier in Morse code that corresponded to the number of the beacon within the airway segment.

Regular scheduled airmail service was begun on July 1, 1924, just over six years from the inauspicious kick-off in Washington, D.C. with Lt. Boyle. Due to prevailing winds, eastbound mail crossed the nation in 29 hours, while that mail bound for the West took 34 hours. This provided a savings in time of at least two full business days in mail going from coast to coast compared with mail carried by rail. Within the first full year of operation, the lighted airway system had been completed coast to coast. (See Figure 10-9.) American aviation, with the leadership of an enlightened government, had made a quantum leap into a technologically-advanced civilian navigation system. Nothing like it existed in the world.

The American scene was almost set for the beginnings of a viable commercial aviation transportation system, but not quite. Still to come were more reliable engines, sturdier airplane designs, flight by reference only to aircraft instruments, involvement of the banking and financial community, acceptance by the public of aviation as legitimate transportation and, lastly, those visionaries and adventurers, both physically and financially, who would make it all happen.

Endnotes

1. See Appendix 3 for Max Miller's narration of his survey flight to Chicago across the Allegheny Mountains.

2. Or "dead reckoning." There does not appear to be agreement concerning the use of the term "ded reckoning" or "dead reckoning." "Ded reckoning" is based on contraction of "deductive reckoning."

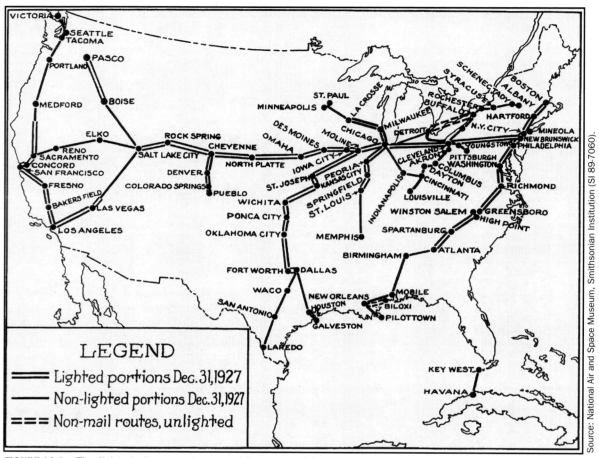

FIGURE 10-9   The lighted airway system as of December 31, 1927.

CHAPTER 11

Horsepower

© egd, 2008, Shutterstock, Inc.

F ate had set apart a place for Fred Rentschler in the Age of Aviation just beginning. Today, his is not a name that springs to mind as central to the development of commercial aviation in the United States, but it should be.

Fred Rentschler (see Figure 11-1) came from solid German stock. His father, Adam Rentschler, an immigrant from Württemberg, established a foundry in Hamilton, Ohio, where pig iron and machine castings were the mother's milk of his upbringing. Hamilton is but a stone's throw from Dayton, not only the home of the Wright Brothers, but in early years of the twentieth century the locale of the National Cash Register Company, its biggest business. The Rentschler foundry supplied the company with castings for its cash registers, and Adam Rentschler became a friend of Edward Deeds, NCR's vice president. Deeds, along with Charles Kettering, started a little company by the name of Dayton Engineering Laboratories to manufacture an innovation thought up by Kettering, an electric self-starter that could be applied to automobiles. DELCO, as the company was to be known, was to be credited with taming the horseless carriage, eliminating the need for the manly and strenuous art of hand cranking required at the time. The first starter was installed in the 1912 Cadillac and rapidly spread throughout the

FIGURE 11-1 Frederich B. Rentschler.

Source: Vought Aircraft Industries, Inc.

automobile industry. DELCO forged close ties with the automobile industry. In 1916, Kettering and Deeds sold DELCO to United Motors Corporation for the whopping sum of nine million dollars.

With the profits from the DELCO sale, Deeds and Kettering formed the Dayton Airplane Company and then brought in Orville Wright as consultant. The name was changed to the Dayton-Wright Company with the idea of producing airplanes for private use. When the United States entered the war in 1917, Deeds volunteered for work on the Aircraft Production Board in Washington. He was placed in charge of all aircraft procurement and given the rank of Colonel in the Army. The Dayton-Wright Company thereby received contracts from the government to produce 5,000 deHavilland warplanes under license. With no American aircraft engine design available, it was Deeds who engaged his automobile industry contacts in the redesign of the Liberty engine (discussed in chapter 10), which became America's greatest contribution to the war, and which was installed in the DH-4s. For his part, Kettering designed a successful pilotless "flying bomb" for targets up to 50 miles away, which the Dayton-Wright Company produced in 1918, but too late to be used in World War I. Although this device was patented, the government kept it a military secret until World War II when the same technology was employed by the Nazi German government, the "buzz bomb," with terrifying effect against the English countryside.

When Fred Rentschler came to Deeds looking for a job in the war effort in 1917, Deeds wangled a place for him as an inspector at the Wright-Martin plant in New Jersey where the Hispano-Suiza engine was being produced under license. Fred Rentschler's machinery background soon evolved into a love for aircraft engines.

As we have seen, Glenn Martin left the Wright-Martin enterprise after the war, and the company became Wright Aeronautical Corporation. The glut of airplanes and engines that existed at that time foretold a difficult future for aircraft engine production, and even as Rentschler's cohorts departed the company for greener pastures in the automobile business, Fred

Rentschler stayed on and continued making Hispano engines in limited quantity for the Army and Navy. The Navy, concerned about the unreliability of the available water-cooled airplane engines due to its mission of over water flight, believed that air-cooled engines, without radiators and the associated plumbing required in water-cooled engines, could be superior. The Navy encouraged Wright Aeronautical to develop such a dependable powerplant.

Air-cooled engines were in production in only one place in 1923, a small New York plant by the name of the Lawrance Company, located in Manhattan. Charles Lawrance was making the promising J-1 radial engine at the time, but the company lacked the funds and expertise required to work out all the problems necessary to bring the engine up to military standards. Wright Aeronautical purchased the company, and Rentschler and his engineers proceeded to solve its cooling problems and enhance its fuel economy. The 200 horsepower J-5 was completed in December 1925, and became known as the Wright "Whirlwind." This engine was to prove satisfactory to the Army and Navy, and it went into widespread production in 1926. It was to play a large and important role in the advancement of aviation in the United States, and was to be the engine that carried Lindbergh across the North Atlantic a little over a year later.

Rentschler knew that the basic radial design could support much more horsepower than the Whirlwind could produce, but he could not convince the Wright board of directors to invest in the research necessary to develop larger engines. Rentschler and his top engineers decided to leave Wright Aeronautical before completion of the J-5 project and to form their own company. Rentschler learned that his old benefactor, Colonel Deeds, was now chairman of a Hartford, Connecticut, based concern called Pratt & Whitney Tool Company, and that the company was sitting on piles of cash from World War I operations. A financial arrangement was agreed, including up front funding and plant space at the Hartford location. Colonel Deeds also agreed to allow Rentschler to adopt a variant of the tool company name; the new company was to be known as Pratt & Whitney Aircraft Company. Rentschler's group, wishing to remain independent, retained most of the common stock of the company and later paid off the advances made by Pratt & Whitney Tool.

Chance Vought, the aircraft manufacturer, was a friend of Rentschler. Vought disclosed that the Navy wanted a 350 horsepower air-cooled radial engine for use in an airplane to be flown from a new class of ship known as an aircraft carrier, then in the planning stages. Vought agreed to build the airplane if Rentschler could come up with the engine. Rentschler and his engineers set about designing an even bigger engine, one with 400 horsepower, and by March 1926, it was ready. Tests proved that it exceeded even the 400 horsepower design specification, and the Navy liked it. The new engine, dubbed the Wasp after the sound that some of the engineers said it made, went immediately to the Navy, and they kept coming. By 1929, over 2,500 Wasps had been delivered, and the engine was to remain in production until 1960. When the last Wasp was turned out, the production run numbered 34,966. While the Wasp was still in development, engineers at P & W were already designing an even bigger engine, the 525 horsepower Hornet. It, too, would be enormously successful, and with the Wasp would be the mainstay of the fleet for years to come. In 1927, when the first large carriers, the Lexington and the Saratoga, were launched, all 160 airplanes on deck had either Wasp or Hornet engines.

But P & W was in for some competition. After the departure of Rentschler and his engineers from Wright Aeronautical, the company gradually regrouped. By 1929, the company had developed the Cyclone, a 575 horsepower air-cooled radial that saw extensive service for many years in both civilian and military aircraft, including in the DC-3 and B-17. Wright Aeronautical merged with Curtiss Aircraft on July 5, 1929.

P & W became United Aircraft and Transport Corporation in 1928 and, as we shall see, was instrumental in forging the first transcontinental airline company with William Boeing. In 1934, the company name was changed to United Aircraft Company with four operating divisions, Chance Vought Aircraft, Pratt and Whitney Aircraft, Hamilton Standard, and Sikorsky Aircraft. Chance Vought would become a separate corporation in 1954.

The development of these powerful aircraft engines for the military, beginning in the 1920s, enabled commercial aviation, with the aid of other developments that we will see, to finally take off. Fred Rentschler would continue to figure prominently in the development of the United States air transportation system when the airlines made their debut later in that decade. The time was also approaching when the government would become a principle player as the era of aviation regulation was about to begin.

PART IV

Regulation

© Stephen Strathdee, 2008, Shutterstock.

Chapter 12   The Privatization of Airmail

Chapter 13   The Founding of the Airlines

Chapter 14   New Deal— The Roosevelt Administration

Chapter 15   State of the Airlines before the Civil Aeronautics Act

Chapter 16   The Civil Aeronautics Act of 1938 (McCarran-Lea Act)

Chapter 17   World War II

Chapter 18   A New Beginning

Chapter 19   On the Way to the Jet Age

Chapter 20   The Federal Aviation Act

Chapter 21   The Next Jets

Chapter 22   The Department of Transportation

Chapter 23   Airports

The Privatization of Airmail

The railroads had been taken over by the government during World War I. At the end of the war it was argued by some that the government should remain in control and operation of the railroads, as was the practice in Europe. But that was not to be in this country, and the railroads were again delivered to the owning railroad companies. The railroads had for decades delivered the intercity U.S. mail, and with the return of the railroads to their owners, they once again were the mainstay of the mail system. The airmail service operated by the Post Office was actually a relatively small part of the total intercity carriage of mail, but for several reasons the railroads were vigorously opposed to the government being in the long distance mail carriage business, as were all sectors of private enterprise.

It was never the plan for the government to remain in the airmail transport business, anymore than it was its plan to be in the railroad business. The time had come in 1925 to turn over the operation of the transportation of the airmail delivery system to private enterprise. The government had already laid the foundation for an airline industry. The building of infrastructure had begun with the funding of the lighted airway system, and the government had clearly undertaken the responsibility for creating and maintaining that infrastructure. A viable government program for the delivery of airmail had been created and was now in place as the basis for subsidy paid to private carriers. A small but growing aircraft and engine manufacturing sector had emerged and had demonstrated its engineering, production, and fiscal competence, and the banking and financial sector had been drawn into the picture and was becoming comfortable with financing the fledgling industry. The confidence of the public in the legitimacy and safety of aviation and the desirability of air travel, while still skittish, was beginning to grow.

From the Wright's first flight in 1903 to the middle of the 1920s, there had been only two known attempts to start a scheduled passenger flying service, or airline, in the United States. The first was the St. Petersburg-Tampa Airboat Line inaugurated on January 1, 1914 to serve the 18-mile over water route between the two Florida cities with a 26-foot Benoist XIV flying boat. (See Figures 12-1 and 12-2.) Although the little air service carried 1,200 passengers over the twenty-three minute route during the next several months, at a fare of $5.00 each, business sagged with the departure of the northern tourists and their money in the spring, and the company folded.

FIGURE 12-1 Benoist flying boat—1914.

FIGURE 12-2 Benoist flying boat—1914. Inauguration of the St. Petersburg—Tampa airboat line.

Manhattan Cadillac dealer Inglis M. Uppercu was the force behind the other airline attempt. Uppercu ran an aerial sightseeing service in New York that he had started as an offshoot of having manufactured seaplanes (see Figure 12-3) (Aeromarine Corp) for the Navy during Word War I. In 1920, he bought out a small Key West-to-Havana mail line and began to supplement the cargo with passengers. Prohibition (which outlawed the sale of alcoholic beverages) was in effect in the United States beginning in 1920, and Uppercu correctly figured that Cuba and the Bahamas, with their plentiful rum and sunshine, would make a fetching destination for thirsty and cold Americans. He formed Aeromarine West Indies Airways and during his first year carried 6,814 passengers in seven flying boats, flying 95,000 miles. He noted that people who seemed to be terrified of flying at altitude over land appeared to have no fear of flying a few feet above water in a flying boat. The airline published schedules and met them. During its second year, the fleet was expanded to 15 aircraft, which carried 9,107 passengers on two thousand flights. After two widely publicized accidents, resulting in the deaths of several passengers, and receiving exceedingly bad press that emphasized the complete absence of any kind of government mandated safeguards for the flying public, the bloom was off the rose. Uppercu shut down his airline in 1923.

Henry Ford, who by the middle of the 1920s was quite successful as the manufacturer of automobiles, saw that he had a legitimate business use for airplanes in the middle 1920s. Ford Motor Company had automobile plants in various locales, including Detroit, Cleveland, Chicago, and Dearborn, and it was necessary to carry parts and machinery between them on a regular basis. Ford became acquainted with William E. Stout, an idea-man and former airplane designer, who had a passion to build an all-metal airplane. The craft would be built of duralumin, not quite as light as aluminum but twice as strong. Ford decided to back Stout who did, in fact, produce a single engine high wing monoplane constructed almost completely of metal, all as advertised. Its corrugated metal sides and thick wings looked remarkably like those produced in Germany by the Junkers Company, but no one said anything. It was powered by the Liberty water-cooled engine, carried 8 passengers and was dubbed "Maiden Detroit."

Ford not only bought the plane, he bought the plant as well. He started Ford Air Transport and began a regular service between his plants.

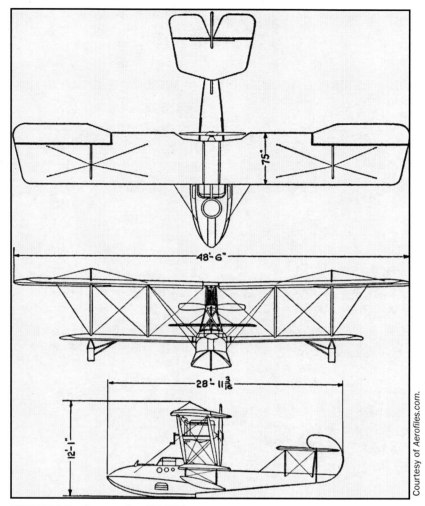

FIGURE 12-3   Aeromarine 50-U8D.

Courtesy of Aerofiles.com.

He then set Stout on a course to develop a bigger all metal airplane, one that would go down in history as the Ford Trimotor.

In 1924, Stout's efforts resulted in the trimotor Ford 3-AT, a bulbous-nosed monstrosity configured with the pilot seated in an open cockpit above the high-winged fuselage. The design was so horrendous that Ford retired Stout and turned the design function over to his team of engineers, which included William McDonnell. McDonnell's name was destined to later lead the merged McDonnell Douglas Corporation in 1967.

The story goes that progress on converting the mongrel 3-AT to a more aesthetically pleasing and efficient design was slow, until one day in 1926 when a Fokker F-7 trimotor monoplane showed up in Dearborn, under the command of Admiral Richard E. Byrd. The airplane was gratuitously hangared for the night at Ford's field, and it is said that Ford's design team did not get much sleep that night. In due course, the Ford 4-AT trimotor emerged from the Ford team's plans and sketches, bearing a striking likeness to the Fokker F-7. The Ford Trimotor, affectionately dubbed the

"Tin Goose," sported the same heavy cantilevered wing without wire bracing as did the F-7, and its dimensions and engine mountings were similar. The airplane conveyed a sense of sturdiness and stability to the fourteen passengers it could carry at 100 miles per hour over a distance of 250 miles. Refinements in this basic design were continued into the 1930s, with 199 Trimotors ultimately produced.

The Airmail Act of 1925 (The Kelly Act)

" Recently a man asked whether the business of flying ever could be regulated by rules and statutes. I doubt it. Not that flying men are lawless. No one realizes better than they the need for discipline. But they have learned discipline through constant contact with two of the oldest statutes in the universe—the law of gravity and the law of self-preservation. Ten feet off the ground these two laws supersede all others and there is little hope of their repeal. "

Walter Hinson, 24 July 1926, *Liberty Magazine*

Congress passed the Kelly Act (so-called after the name of the bill's sponsor) on February 2, 1925. The act was appropriately titled "An Act to Encourage Commercial Aviation and to Authorize the Postmaster General to Contract for the Mail Service." The statute called for the Postmaster General to seek competitive bids to operate the airmail feeder routes to the transcontinental main airmail trunk line between New York and San Francisco.

Advertisement for bids was published in the middle of 1925, and bids were received from 10 companies. Although eight routes were to be awarded, financial responsibility concerns caused the Post Office to delay assigning some of them until later.

Six contract airmail (CAM) routes were awarded at the beginning of 1926:

1. CAM 1-*Boston-New York,* awarded to a group including Juan Tripp, later to found and operate Pan American Airways. Colonial Air Transport operated the airmail service.

2. CAM 2-*Chicago-St. Louis,* awarded Robertson Aircraft Corp., a forerunner to American Airlines. Robertson hired Charles Lindbergh as Chief Pilot. (See Figure 12-4.)

3. CAM 3-*Chicago-Dallas,* awarded to National Air Transport, a forerunner of United Airlines.

4. CAM 4-*Salt Lake City-Los Angeles,* awarded to Western Air Express, a forerunner of TWA.

5. CAM 5-*Elko, Nevada-Pasco, Washington,* awarded to Varney Air Lines, a forerunner of United Airlines.

6. CAM 6-*Detroit-Cleveland,* awarded to Ford Air Transport.

7. CAM 7-*Detroit-Chicago,* awarded to Ford Air Transport.

Courtesy of the Minnesota Historical Society.

FIGURE 12-4 Charles Lindbergh on CAM 2, flown between Chicago and St. Louis.

Ford was the first to begin service, on February 15, 1926, with the others following within four months. The last to begin service was Colonial Airways on CAM 1. Subsequent awards that year were:

8. CAM 8-*Los Angeles-Seattle,* awarded to Pacific Air Transport, a forerunner of United Airlines.

9. CAM 9-*Chicago-Minneapolis,* awarded to Charles Dickenson. Northwest Airlines began operating the route in 1926.

10. CAM 10-*Atlanta-Jacksonville,* awarded to Florida Airways Corp, a forerunner of Eastern Air Lines.

11. CAM 11-*Cleveland-Pittsburgh,* awarded to Clifford Ball, later absorbed by United Airlines.

12. CAM 12-*Pueblo, Colorado-Cheyenne, Wyoming,* awarded to Western Air Express.

The next year saw more awards of airmail routes. National Air Transport (NAT) added the lucrative Chicago to New York mail route to its Chicago-Dallas service. In addition to this, Western Air Express began flying passengers on a non-airmail route between Los Angeles and San Francisco. By 1928, over five thousand souls had flown the route with Western Air.

The aircraft available to serve the new airmail companies were limited. The Post Office had largely relied on the World War I DH-4, but its Liberty engines were pretty much used up. Varney had to begin airmail service with the underpowered Swallow biplane, and Western Air Express bought the Douglas M-2, all six of them. Ford had the first of the Ford Trimotors (see Figures 12-5 and 12-6), producing fourteen in 1926. Juan Trippe of Colonial Air Transport, impressed by Fokker's monoplane design and its absence of wires and struts, ordered the first three Fokker trimotors produced, but they would not be available until 1927. In 1928, Western Air added Fokkers for its Los Angeles-San Francisco passenger service.

FIGURE 12-5   Ford Trimotor.

Courtesy of the Minnesota Historical Society.

FIGURE 12-6   Ford Trimotor loading mail.

Courtesy of the National Postal Museum, Smithsonian Institution.

The Post Office Department continued to make awards across the country for its feeder routes, as it phased itself completely out of the airmail carrying business. During the nine years that the Post Office Department carried airmail, 32 pilots—about one out of every six—were killed in the service.

One fall day in 1926, William E. Boeing, who had flown the first international mail route between Vancouver and Seattle in 1919 under contract with both Canada and the United States, learned that the main trunk transcontinental airmail route was soon to be offered for bid. The Chicago-San Francisco segment would be first.

The most advanced airplane so far built by Boeing was the Model 40, but it had the old water-cooled Liberty engine of World War I fame. The route between Chicago and San Francisco was challenging viewed from any angle: the weather, the Rockies, the distance, and the fact that flying at night was a requirement. The B-40, with the Liberty engine, was a marginal airplane for this route, and both the businessman and the pilot in William Boeing knew it.

❝ I've tried to make the men around me feel, as I do, that we embarked as pioneers upon a new science and industry in which our problems are so new and unusual that it behooves no one to dismiss any novel idea with the statement that "it can't be done!". Our job is to keep everlasting at research and experimentation, to adapt our laboratories to production as soon as possible, and to let no new improvement in flying and flying equipment pass us by. ❞

William E. Boeing, founder, The Boeing Company, 1929

As we have seen, Fred Rentschler, under the auspices of Pratt & Whitney Aircraft, had designed and produced the first air-cooled engine of any significant horsepower under contract for the Navy. The Wasp was in production primarily for the Navy at this time, but the Navy was not at war, and there were no rumors of war. An arrangement was made for Boeing to step ahead of the Navy for delivery of these engines, at the rate of five per month, and the Boeing 40A, with a single Wasp engine mounted up front, was born. Boeing low-balled the transcontinental airmail bid and won, knowing that carrying the mail in the B-40A was as much about selling airplanes as it was about carrying airmail. Varney Airlines, on the route between Elko and Pasco, was the first to order the Boeing with the Wasp.

Although the Kelly Act had been twice amended to increase the rate of compensation paid to airmail contractors, these airline pioneers needed and wanted to carry passengers along with the mail. It was generally acknowledged that the passengers who flew with the mail were, more than anything, adventurers of similar stripe to the pilots themselves. Most of the airplanes available in the middle 1920s were more suited to carrying cargo or other inanimate objects than human beings. The 40B-4, a revised version of the 40A, had design changes that allowed 4 passengers to be seated inside the fuselage forward of the open pilot cockpit, with 2 windows on each side. The B-4 layout provided relative comfort for the passenger, but flying was still a frightening thing for many.

CHAPTER 13

The Founding of the Airlines

© Terry Alexander, 2008, Shutterstock.

It is a curious historical fact the two men who arguably did the most for the advancement of commercial aviation in the 1920s were completely unacquainted while they each made their early contributions, but would wind up being related to each other by marriage. Dwight Morrow did not know of Charles A. Lindbergh when, in 1925, President Coolidge selected Morrow to head a board appointed by the President to investigate circumstances relevant to the fledgling aviation community and to establish a national aviation policy. Morrow was a Wall Street banker, intelligent, and well connected. He took his appointment seriously and conducted very effective hearings on the subject.

The Morrow Board

His board heard the testimony of Herbert Hoover, then Secretary of Commerce in the Coolidge administration, which said that the government was obliged to lend its support to commercial aviation, as it had always done in the maritime industry. Hoover pointed out that the government had for a century maintained aids to navigation in the coastal waters of the country, provided education and competency standards for ships' officers, required federal inspections of ships, and funded improvements in and about the navigable waters, including ports. He noted that the twenty-five years since the flight of the Wright brothers in 1903 had brought little advance in commercial aviation, and that America was lagging the Europeans in engaging the subject of transport by air.

The Morrow Board heard from another strong voice in support of governmental action. By the early 1920s, the National Advisory Committee for Aeronautics (NACA)[1] had become a loosely organized group of scientists and engineers who were developing into leaders in aeronautical research and experimentation. NACA conducted pure research in its Langley Laboratory unconstrained by bureaucratic influences. Independence from political pressures contributed greatly to NACA becoming the premier aeronautical research facility in the world beginning in the 1920s. By the time the Morrow Board was convened, NACA had even then gained a level of respect that caused the Board to heed its recommendations. NACA laid the foundation for initiating the examination and licensing of pilots and the imposition of airworthiness standards for aircraft, as well as for the creation of an Aeronautics Branch within the Department of Commerce to administer these activities.

Based on all of the testimony produced before his board, Morrow prepared a report that was to become the blueprint for the development of commercial aviation for years to come. The report concluded:

1. Aviation is vital to the national defense. The means of aircraft design and production must be supported in the national interest, and a military procurement program should be initiated.

2. Non-military aviation, comprising the largest potential for commercial development, serves a national purpose, and deserves the support of the government.

3. The government should enhance the safety and reliability of flying by establishing standards for pilots and aircraft. It should establish and maintain airways for navigation and enlarge its support for airmail contract carriers under contract with the Post Office. All this would have the collateral effect of bolstering both public and banking confidence in aviation.

The Morrow board was central to the second major federal statute affecting commercial aviation, the Air Commerce Act of 1926.

The Air Commerce Act of 1926

Prior to this enactment, there had been no official government statement identifying what role, if any, the federal government would play in the field of aviation. There had been no structure, no plan, no strictures, and no standards. In one fell swoop all of this uncertainty vanished, and in its place was laid a solid foundation for the building of a national commercial aviation industry.

The purpose of the act was to promote air commerce. It specifically charged the federal government with the obligation of creating and maintaining a national system of navigational aids and of adopting rules and regulations to promote safety of flight.

The Department of Commerce, in turn, was charged with the responsibility of promulgating

and enforcing safety regulations, including the registration and licensing of aircraft, producing aeronautical charts, providing meteorological advice and reports, investigating accidents, and certification and medical examination of pilots. The Aeronautics Branch of the Department of Commerce was created to administer and carry out the requirements placed on the Department. This agency was renamed the Bureau of Air Commerce in 1934 and assumed all safety responsibilities. The Interstate Commerce Commission assumed all rate and fare authority.

The black letter law was on the books, the Commerce Department had its marching orders, the banking community had taken note, the manufacturing sector was enthused, and the entrepreneurs were emerging. Still, the hearts and minds of the public were with the railroads. Those in government and in aviation wondered how the public imagination could be captured.

Lindbergh

Charles Lindbergh had been hired by Robertson Aircraft, one of the original airmail contractors, following a short career in which he fully qualified as an all-around daredevil. He parachuted from a plane in 1922, even before he had soloed an airplane for the first time. He adopted an itinerate life first as a wing-walker and stunt man and then as a barnstormer pilot. With Robertson, he flew the mail between St. Louis and Chicago, a route known for its range of temperatures and volatile weather.

An offer of $25,000 prize money had been made in 1919 by a New York businessman, Raymond Orteig, to anyone who successfully completed a non-stop flight between New York and Paris. Although the Atlantic had been successfully crossed in 1919 in three separate efforts, including one non-stop flight from St. Johns, Newfoundland to Clifden, Ireland, no one had succeeded in claiming the prize by 1927. Several attempts had been made during the intervening years, including French World War I ace, Rene Fonck, in 1926. In early 1927, Fonck was rumored to be readying another attempt, and Admiral Richard E. Byrd was said to also be preparing to make the crossing in his Fokker tri-motor. Advances in technology by 1927 made the chances of success increasingly likely, and the race was heating up with great publicity.

Lindbergh was backed by a group of St. Louis businessmen, but his budget was limited to $15,000. No airplane existed for that sum of money that had any chance of making the 3,600-mile flight successfully. He decided to fly solo, a controversial decision in an otherwise foolhardy endeavor, but a decision that lent itself to a smaller airplane, one that could possibly be built for a cost within his budget. The Ryan Airplane Company, a small aircraft manufacturer located in San Diego, California, agreed to build the airplane to his specifications for $6,000, plus the cost of the engine. He decided on the Wright Whirlwind engine, whose endurance had been proven earlier in 1927 when two pilots kept their Bellanca aloft with it for a period of 57 hours.

Lindbergh decamped to San Diego where he supervised the construction. Although the airplane type had never before been built (it was a custom job), it was completed in 77 days, and with the Wright Whirlwind installed, the total price was $10,580. To save weight, the Spirit of St. Louis, named in honor of his backers, had no brakes and no radio. Gasoline tanks occupied the forward portion of the cockpit where a windshield would normally be placed. To see forward he was required to use a small periscope. The airplane's range was 4,200 miles, just 600 miles over the flight-planned distance necessary to reach Paris.

Lindbergh had accumulated just over two thousand hours of flying time, but his airmail experience had given him exposure to practically all types of weather conditions. He felt that he was ready. He flew the Spirit of St. Louis from San Diego to New York on what was really a "shake down" flight, stopping in St. Louis to refuel, and in the process he set a coast-to-coast record of slightly less than 22 hours. The press coverage of the transcontinental flight only served to heighten the public attention that had been building.

The Spirit of St. Louis left Roosevelt Field on Long Island at 7:52 A.M. on May 20, 1927, with 450 gallons of gasoline, half the total weight of the airplane. Thirty-three hours and thirty minutes later, Parisians flooded the field at Le Bourget to welcome Lindbergh, and the entire world was entranced.[2]

" Science, freedom, beauty, adventure: what more could you ask of life? Aviation combined all the elements I loved. There was science in each curve of an airfoil, in each angle between strut and wire, in the gap of a spark plug or the color of the exhaust flame. There was freedom in the unlimited horizon, on the open fields where one landed. A pilot was surrounded by beauty of earth and sky. He brushed treetops with the birds, leapt valleys and rivers, explored the cloud canyons he had gazed at as a child. Adventure lay in each puff of wind.

I began to feel that I lived on a higher plane than the skeptics of the ground; one that was richer because of its very association with the element of danger they dreaded, because it was freer of the earth to which they were bound. In flying, I tasted a wine of the gods of which they could know nothing. Who valued life more highly, the aviators who spent it on the art they loved, or these misers who doled it out like pennies through their antlike days? I decided that if I could fly for ten years before I was killed in a crash, it would be a worthwhile trade for an ordinary life time. **"**

Charles A. Lindbergh, *The Spirit of St. Louis*

FIGURE 13-1 Charles Lindbergh pays a visit to Orville Wright at Wright Field, Dayton, OH, June 22, 1927.

Source: Library of Congress.

If the flying feat itself were not enough to sufficiently impress the mind, then the proceedings that followed, conducted on the world scene, would certainly do the trick. He went on a triumphant tour of European capitals, and was given audiences with the kings of Belgium and England. President Coolidge sent a United States warship to fetch the young Lindbergh home, where he was met by the dirigible U.S.S. Los Angeles and a ticker tape parade. He was awarded the Congressional Medal of Honor and commissioned a colonel in the Army Reserve. He was also introduced to Dwight Morrow.

He went on a three-month tour, sponsored by the Guggenheim Fund, of all 48 states, parading in 82 cities, and flying over 22,000 miles in the process. He was a fine hero, conducting himself at all times in his trademark modest and dignified manner. (See Figure 13-1.) He was invited to Mexico by Dwight Morrow, who was then ambassador there, for a Mexican tour and then for a sojourn through Latin America. Ambassador Morrow's daughter, Anne Spencer, met Lindy on one of his visits to the ambassador's residence in Mexico and, mutually taken with each other, in due course they were married.

It would be difficult to overstate the effect that Lindbergh had on the nascent airline industry in the late 1920s. Dormant aviation stocks across the board ignited as money poured in from all quarters. In 1926, total passenger enplanements in the United States had numbered less than six thousand. By 1930, the flourishing

airline industry carried over 400,000 adventurous souls. Production of aircraft soared.

Back in New York, what might have been the first of all celebrity endorsements occurred when Lindbergh joined the new airline, Transcontinental Air Transport (TAT), lending his name to a commercial product in return for cash and stock. Juan Trippe, (see Figure 13-2) having been deposed from Colonial Air Transport, also signed him up as a technical adviser to his new airline venture, Pan American Airways. This was

FIGURE 13-2 Juan Trippe and Charles Lindbergh.

Courtesy of www.panamair.org.

the beginning of a long-standing relationship between Lindbergh and Trippe[3] that would play a key role in the expansion of air commerce around the world, and with it, American influence.

The Daniel Guggenheim Fund for the Promotion of Aeronautics

In the middle of the 1920s, aviation in America was emerging from its long period of confusion and stagnation. But aviation in Europe had captured the imagination of the people and of industry almost immediately after the Wright brothers' tour of Europe in 1908–9, and it still led the way. The United States government had been significantly involved in promoting aviation at least since 1918 with subsidy and direct investment in infrastructure, and in 1926 it would begin to legally promote safety and standards in aviation in order to boost the public confidence. But the job was big. The list of individual citizens with ardent interests in aviation in the 1920s was long, and the record of their contributions was even then impressive. Corporate America, as well, had shared in the promotion and advancement of aviation. But the going was still slow.

One of the more beneficial byproducts of the American system of private enterprise is the philanthropic activity of its successful practitioners. The giving of one's time, interest, and assets to causes of one's choosing is a time-honored tradition in America. The Guggenheim family of New York made its money in the mining industry. In 1924, Daniel Guggenheim and his wife, Florence, established a foundation to promote a variety of charitable causes. One of their sons, Harry Guggenheim, was a pilot during World War I and became committed to the advancement of aviation. Father and son established, in 1926, a separate fund called the Daniel Guggenheim Fund for the Promotion of Aeronautics, and by 1930 the family had given almost $3 million to aviation-related projects.

The Guggenheims believed, like the government, that the public would embrace air travel if confidence could be established in its safety. A significant part of the safety of air travel depended on reliably designed and constructed aircraft, yet there was no such thing as an aeronautical engineer in 1925. The Guggenheims began to fund the establishment of schools at universities across the country, and by 1929 aeronautical engineering programs or research centers had been set up at the California Institute of Technology, Stanford, the Massachusetts Institute of Technology, Harvard, Syracuse, Northwestern, the University of Michigan, and others.

In 1927, the Guggenheims offered a prize of $100,000 for the construction of safe aircraft in a contest called the "Safe Aircraft Competition." The prize went to the Curtiss Tanager, which had incorporated into its design the first short takeoff and landing (STOL) characteristics ever demonstrated.

The Fund subsidized an operation in California by Western Air Express (WAE) in 1928 known as the "Model Airway," between Los Angeles and San Francisco. Airmail was not carried on this route since no award had been made by the Post Office to WAE. Instead, the airline carried only passengers along the corridor in an effort to show that commercial passenger service was feasible without airmail subsidies, as well as safe and reliable. The Fund provided a Fokker F-10 Super Trimotor to WAE for this scheduled service and had implemented a weather-reporting regimen along the route that utilized two-way radio. This was the first PIREPS (pilot weather reporting system) in history. The passenger operations ended in 1929, and although the experiment was not profitable, it did demonstrate that passenger only (non-airmail) service was feasible and popular with the public. At a time when one of the most frequent causes of airplane crashes was allocated to adverse weather conditions, not one weather-related incident was recorded. Upon the termination of the experiment in June 1929, the weather bureau assumed the reporting of aviation weather locally, and the practice ultimately spread all across the country.

When Charles Lindbergh in 1928 suggested that it would be helpful to navigation if the names of cities and towns could be painted on the roofs of large buildings, the Guggenheims funded the cost. The Postmasters of some 8,000 communities arranged for the painting on rooftops of their towns' names in large letters, with arrows pointing to the north and, if available, to the nearest landing field.

The Guggenheims made a very significant contribution to advances in instrument flying by funding research involving gyroscopic instrumentation invented by Elmer Sperry (directional gyrocompass and artificial horizon) and Paul Kollsman (precision altimeter). Guggenheim-funded engineers worked with the Aeronautics Branch of the Commerce Department and the Bureau of Standards to advance radio navigation, and with Jimmy Doolittle to test and implement instrument procedures in 1929 that made safe instrument flight routine within a decade.

Airways—from Lighted Beacons to Radio Navigation

By the end of 1927, the government had extended the lighted portion of the airway system from New York to Salt Lake City on the transcontinental route, and on portions of feeder and parallel segments, such as Los Angeles to Las Vegas, New York to Atlanta, Chicago to Dallas, and between Los Angeles and San Francisco. That year there were 4,121 miles of lighted airways operated by the Aeronautics Branch of the Department of Commerce. By 1933, there were 1,500 beacons in place, extending the lighted airway systems for a length of 18,000 miles. While the lighted airway was of significant aid in navigation, it had serious limitations in the context of an all-weather air carrier system. It was still a

visual navigation system, dependent on reasonably good weather in order to operate.

The Bureau of Standards in the Department of Commerce began, in 1926, to work with radio as a means of communication and navigation. As government involvement in aviation began to kick in as a result of the Air Commerce Act, money and effort were applied to solve problems and to attempt to eliminate limitations on the commercial development of air commerce. In 1926, for instance, there was no two-way voice communication possible with aircraft in flight. This constituted serious limitations in safety, including a lack of pilot awareness of developing weather. By 1927, the first transmitter was established at Bellefonte, Pennsylvania, allowing communication with aircraft in a 150-mile radius.

In 1928, the Bureau of Standards developed a new radio beacon system of navigation, the first non-visual navigation system in the world. The Aeronautics Branch, which had authority over the lighted airway system, took over the installation and control of the new radio navigation system in 1929. The system was known as the "four course radio range," and it would provide the first step in allowing a true all-weather air carrier system to begin to develop, and it would remain the standard navigation system in use until World War II.

The four course radio range utilized low frequency radio waves (190 to 535 kHz radio band) transmitted from powerful 1,500-watt beacons spaced 200 miles apart on the airway. The beacons transmitted two Morse code signals, the letter "A" and the letter "N." In Morse code, these signals are opposite, "dot-dash" for A, and "dash-dot" for N. When the aircraft was centered "on the beam," these signals merged into a steady, monotonous tone. If the aircraft ventured to one side of the airway, the signal heard was either the Morse A or N, depending on the aircraft's position from the beacon. (See Figure 13-3.)

Each beacon defined four airways, thus the name "four course radio range," and the beacon's

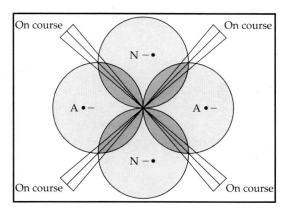

FIGURE 13-3 Schematic of the four-course radio range.

identification was broadcast in Morse code twice each minute. The so-called beam width was 3 degrees, so that at the half-way point of 100 miles between beacons, the on-course deviation was about +/–2.6 miles. Station passage was marked by a "cone of silence," at which point the aural tone would disappear as the aircraft passed overhead. Distance from the station was later provided by marker beacons placed along the airway at intervals of 20 miles or so.

By today's standards, the four course radio range was primitive. Low frequency radio was subject to electrical static and other weather aberrations and distortions, but it constituted a quantum leap forward over the visual, lighted beacon system in use at the time. Pilots became very adept at flying the four course system, and as the airlines began establishing schedules on their new routes, all-weather navigation allowed adherence to schedules that theretofore would have been impossible due to cancellations for weather and low visibility conditions.

Amelia Earhart

Lindbergh was not to be the only aviation celebrity of the late 1920s. Building on the women pioneers before her,[4] Amelia Earhart was to emerge shortly after the Lindbergh flight as the foremost female aviator up to that time, and arguably, even to the present day. (See Figure 13-4.) She certainly captured the public imagination in much the same way that Lindbergh had, and thereby contributed to the enthusiasm that helped to create the airlines.

When Earhart soloed in 1922 at a small field in south Los Angeles, California, there were fewer than 100 female pilots in the United States. Her flight instructor, Neta Snook, was one of those women. The right to vote had been achieved by women only three years before, in 1919. Earhart purchased a yellow Kinner "Airster" prototype for $2,000 and began making a visible impression in the area, being featured in the *Los Angeles Examiner* declaring that she intended to fly across the continent. She immediately set a new women's altitude record (of 14,000 feet) and was advertised as one of only two female pilots in an air meet at the Glendale airport. She was awarded a flying certification in

Source: Library of Congress.

FIGURE 13-4 Amelia Earhart.

May 1923 from the Federation Aeronautique Internacionale, although flying licenses were not required, nor even issued by the U.S. government. The certification was necessary in order to have official recognition for any record breaking or record setting achievements.

In 1924, Earhart moved with her mother to Boston, Massachusetts, arriving there by a "motorcar" which she drove all the way from California by way of Banff, Canada. This was a daring adventure at the time, as the U.S. Army had only performed the first sustained cross-country convoy in 1919. In Boston, her flying activities once again prompted curiosity from local interests, including *The Boston Globe,* in which she was featured in an interview in June 1927, shortly after the Lindbergh flight. She was billed as "one of the best women pilots in the United States" and began to be mentioned increasingly in the local press. Earhart bore a remarkable resemblance to Charles Lindbergh, and some say that was the main reason for the

❝ You haven't seen a tree until you've seen its shadow from the sky. ❞

Amelia Earhart

event that set her career skyward. She was to be the first woman to fly the Atlantic Ocean.

We have already seen what excitement Lindbergh's spectacular solo transatlantic flight had caused in 1927. By 1928, women in both Europe and America were making plans to be the first woman to make the crossing, but with a difference—they planned to have the flying actually performed by male pilots. (See Box 13-1.)

Amelia Earhart had no such plans. The flight that was to make her famous was entirely planned and paid for by others. She had nothing to do with the selection of pilots, the selection of aircraft, or with flight planning. She was, in effect, chosen. At the time, she was making a living as a social worker with immigrants in Boston.

The adventure began in early 1928 when another female patron, the wife of a wealth Londoner, Frederick E. Guest (she was formerly Amy Phipps of Pittsburgh), purchased a Fokker Trimotor from Commander Richard E. Byrd with plans to hire a pilot to fly her to England. Mrs. Guest was soon dissuaded from this venture by her family, but she stuck with the plan for the trip to be made by "an American girl with the right image,"[5] and a committee was formed to find her replacement.

On the committee was George Palmer Putnam, a New York publisher and writer. He had, in fact, published Lindbergh's **We,** the firsthand account of the first solo transatlantic crossing, and was in the process of publishing Richard E. Byrd's chronicle of his flying and exploring adventures in the book, *Skyward.* He heard of Amelia Earhart, then residing in Boston, and invited her to New York for an interview. It went well, and the agreement was sealed in April 1928.

Earhart would be a passenger on the "Friendship," a Fokker F-7 Trimotor fitted with floats that was already scheduled for a transatlantic attempt in June. The crew consisted of a mechanic, Bill Gordon, and the pilot, Lou Stultz, the latter of whom was proficient in multi-engine aircraft, float plane flying, and instrument flying. Amelia Earhart had none of these qualifications, nor for that matter, did many male aviators. Nevertheless, she was billed as the "Commander" of the flight, which left Newfoundland on June 17, 1928 and arrived in New South Wales the next day after a flight of 20 hours and 49 minutes.

Gordon and Stultz were soon forgotten, but the public embraced Amelia much as they had Lindbergh. This was a matter of some embarrassment to Earhart, who felt that she had done nothing to deserve such adulation and that the credit should go to the crew, and she had the courage to say so. But the public clamor continued. She received congratulations from many government

Box 13-1   Who Would Be the First Woman Across the Atlantic?

The first attempt was by Princess Anne Lowenstein-Wertheim, a German aristocrat who for some years had exhibited an affinity for aviation and who held several aviation records in her own right. She departed England on August 31, 1927, bound for Ottawa, Canada with two experienced Royal Air Force pilots, Leslie Hamilton and Fred Minchin, at the controls. Although the aircraft was spotted once enroute, it disappeared.

Another, Ruth Elder, was only a student pilot when she announced in August 1927 plans to fly the Atlantic. Her flight instructor was George Haldeman, and she acknowledged that he would do the flight planning and most of the flying. The route he chose was the longer southern route via the Azores. The aircraft chosen for the flight was a Stinson Detroiter, a single engine monoplane that Elder had named "American Girl." The project was a promotion for the manufacturer, Stinson, and was likened to a publicity stunt. The pair left Roosevelt Field, Long Island, New York, on October 11, 1927, for Paris and completed most of the planned flight route (over 2,600 miles) but the craft was forced down just 300 miles short of their destination by an overheating engine caused by a leaking oil line. A passing ship off the Azores rescued them. Their return to New York was celebrated almost as if the flight had succeeded, which, admittedly, it nearly did. Ruth Elder continued to fly and, in 1929, placed fifth in the first Women's Air Derby.

Frances Grayson was another female patron with money. She hired an all male crew for her attempt in a Sikorsky amphibian, which was readied for the flight at Curtiss Field on Long Island. Ruth Elder and George Haldeman were preparing for their departure at the same time from the same airfield. Francis Grayson flight planned the shorter northern route to Europe. This aircraft took off from Newfoundland on December 23, 1927, and was never seen again.

quarters, including President Coolidge, and under the tutelage of George Putnam, she embarked on a lecture circuit during 1928 and 1929 that gave her worldwide recognition. She thereby became acquainted with aviation luminaries of the time like Admiral Byrd and Colonel Lindbergh. Because of the physical resemblance to Lindbergh and the Atlantic transit similarity, she soon garnered the moniker "Lady Lindy."

After her return from Europe in 1928, Earhart began to earn the celebrity that had been handed to her by fate. She crossed the continent solo from New York to Los Angeles in September 1928. She was swamped with offers to endorse products in advertising media, she began writing articles for national magazines, including *Cosmopolitan* and *McCall's,* and she was hired by Transcontinental Air Transport (the Lindbergh Line) as Assistant to the General Traffic

Manager. She acquired a Lockheed Vega and began entering air races around the country and set several speed records.

In 1929, she was largely responsible for inaugurating the Women's Air Derby, a grueling nine-day race from Santa Monica, California to Cleveland, Ohio, dubbed by Will Rogers as "the Powder Puff Derby," a name that has remained with the event. The race was limited to women who had been licensed and who had logged at least 100 hours of solo time. It was estimated at the time that only 30 women could qualify for the event. Twenty fliers started the race, fifteen finished, and there was one fatality. Earhart finished third.

Earhart improved her flying proficiency, particularly in instrument qualification. With her publicist (and now husband) George Putnam, she planned and advertised her intention of becoming the first woman to solo the Atlantic. On May 19, 1932, AE (as she had begun to sign her name) left Harbor Grace, Newfoundland for Paris. Mechanical difficulties enroute, including a leaking reserve fuel line, an inoperative altimeter, and a broken weld on an engine manifold, caused her to alter course for Ireland. Fifteen hours and eighteen minutes after leaving Harbor Grace, AE landed the Vega in a sloping field outside of Londonderry. Her acclaim rose higher and higher, and she had earned it.

Amelia Earhart was destined for even bigger accomplishments, and for tragedy, as the decade of the 1930s unfolded. We will jump ahead in our chronology of the development of aviation to briefly consider the rest of her story. So far, Earhart had only tried to duplicate what men had done. She had set no significant records for the first time in aviation on a genderless basis. But on January 11, 1935, she left Wheeler Field in Hawaii and successfully soloed her new Vega across 2,400 miles of Pacific Ocean to Oakland, California. No person, man or woman, had ever done that before. The Vega performed flawlessly and required only eighteen hours and fifteen minutes enroute. She followed this up with other aviation firsts, a nonstop flight from Burbank, California to Mexico City on April 20, 1935, and from there she flew nonstop across the Gulf of Mexico and on to Newark, N.J., in fourteen hours and nineteen minutes on May 8 that year.

In June 1935, AE took on a new role as visiting aeronautics advisor at Purdue University, which had begun an ambitious plan to develop one of the nation's first academic aviation curricula. As it turned out, this assignment would provide Earhart with the airplane with which she would make her final mark—her unsuccessful attempts to circumnavigate the globe. The Lockheed Electra 10E was purchased by Purdue to be used for research purposes in connection with AE's duties, but soon after taking possession of the Electra in July 1936, she flew it in the 1936 Bendix air race from New York to Los Angeles.

Shortly thereafter, the airplane was fitted for long distance flight and the latest radio navigation equipment.

Earhart made two attempts to fly around the world in the Electra, both on a flight-planned route close to the equator of over 29,000 miles.[6] In both attempts she carried navigator Fred Noonan, who had flown the Pacific extensively with Pan American. The first attempt was planned from east to west, beginning in Oakland with the initial stop in Hawaii, and then on to tiny Howland Island. This effort was abandoned when Earhart ground looped the Electra on take off from Hawaii on March 19, 1937, with serious damage to the airplane. The plane was shipped back to the Lockheed plant where it was repaired.

For her next attempt, AE decided to reverse course and fly the route from Oakland to Miami, thence to South America, and on to Africa and points east. The Pacific itinerary was to be the last part of the flight, but it still included Howland Island, which is truly a relative speck of land in the vast Pacific Ocean. By late June 1937, the route had been successfully flown all the way to Lae, New Guinea, a distance of 22,000 miles. On July 2, Earhart and Noonan departed New Guinea for the long over water flight to Howland Island. In spite of all precautions, including the Coast Guard vessel *Itasca* standing off Howland to broadcast homing signals, and to plot her position, the Electra never made landfall at Howland. Although she was heard on several occasions attempting to make contact with Itasca, her location was never established, and no trace of her, Noonan, or the Electra has ever been found.

While Amelia Earhart had little direct effect on the establishment of commercial aviation in the United States, her efforts to overcome and transcend the boundaries encountered by the aviation pioneers of the 1920s and 1930s engendered public admiration and a greater acceptance of the new industry of flight. She became a model for both male and female aviators, and like many of them, her time was too short.

From Mail Carriers to Airlines

As the airmail contract carriers began to proliferate, and aviation groups not so lucky as to have garnered an airmail route simply started up, the field was beginning to get crowded. Before 1930, at least 44 different companies had jumped into the airline business. Some were better financed; others more experienced, and possessed of more natural talent and engineering expertise. All were eager.

During the late 1920s, the new aircraft industry came under the control of a few large companies that combined several different disciplines, including airmail carriers, airplane manufacturers, and engine manufacturers. Three groups, in particular, formed the core of these vertical holding companies that were to figure prominently in the future of the airline industry. These groups were

1. United Air Transport
2. North American Aviation (NAA)
3. Aviation Corporation of America (AVCO)

United Air Transport

Bill Boeing and William Rentschler had been personal friends ever since Boeing's airplanes had begun flying with Rentschler's engines. In 1929, amidst the great public enthusiasm generated by Lindbergh's flight, the two friends set up a holding company they named United Air Transport, combining the Boeing Aircraft and Transport Company and the Pratt & Whitney Aircraft works. Included in the new company were Chance Vought and the propeller manufacturer, Hamilton Aero Manufacturing Company. They added Sikorsky, Northrop, Stearman, Standard Steel Propeller, and Stout Airlines.

North American Aviation

North American Aviation was the brainchild of Clement Keys, a vice president of the Curtiss Aeroplane and Motor Company during World War I. He gained control of the company during the early 1920s and began acquiring an assortment of companies, including National Air Transport, which had the lucrative New York to Chicago airmail route. Next, he lined up and bought out several airmail routes operating between the Northeast and Florida (which would ultimately form the basis for Eastern Air Lines), while continuing to fly the mails on the midwestern routes. Before the great Wall Street crash of 1929, he merged the Curtiss holdings with Wright Aeronautical Corporation, creating Curtiss-Wright, completing the triad acquisition of companies capable of airplane building, engine manufacture and air carriage. General Motors would gain controlling interest in NAA for a time in the early 1930s. At this time, NAA's holdings included Eastern Air Transport, Transcontinental, and Western Air, and a substantial interest in Douglas Aircraft.

Aviation Corporation

Aviation Corporation was the work of Averell Harriman and Robert Lehman, New York financiers. Robert Lehman was of the Wall Street banking house of Lehman Brothers. Harriman was to later serve in key government posts, including lend-lease administrator, ambassador to the Soviet Union, Secretary of Commerce, and was to be a confidant of Presidents. Together they salvaged the Fairchild Aircraft Company in 1929 through a stock sale before the financial crash in October of that year. The new company proceeded to acquire five airmail carriers, themselves holders of eleven airmail routes; they bought all sorts of aviation properties, including aircraft and engine plants, and even some airports. The air carriers were combined to form American Airways.

Harriman and Lehman did not remain in the aviation business very long, losing out in a proxy fight to E. L. Cord in the early 1930s. Harriman then began his government service, while Lehman returned to Wall Street. But Lehman would be heard from again, this time with Yellow Cab magnate John Hertz at TWA.

Transcontinental Air Transport— A Novel Idea

Flying was not yet very appealing to travelers in the late 1920s. Forced landings, cancellations due to weather, airsickness from the heat, noise, and sometimes-violent motion of the primitive aircraft combined to make the experience more of an adventure than a reliable mode of transport. The passenger service that was available was short-haul, and there were parts of the country where there was no service at all, like between New York and Chicago, which was the heavily traveled train route through the Allegheny Mountains. The experience of the early airmail pilots over that route, as well as the subsequent trials of the contract airmail carriers, had convinced National Air Transport (Clement Keys), which flew the mails over the route, not to attempt passenger service. Still, Keys believed that airline service was destined to be a marketable and time-saving device for transcontinental passengers.

In 1928, Keys seized upon the idea of providing air transportation by day, then turning the passengers over to the trains for the standard luxurious Pullman service by night. He established a joint venture with the Pennsylvania Railroad in the East and the Santa Fe in the West to round out the full passage. The air carriage portion of the deal was carried out by the newly formed Transcontinental Air Transport (TAT), which had no mail routes, and it had to rely solely on passenger fares for its income. The westbound trip

began in New York at Penn Station, where passengers boarded the Pennsylvania Railroad for the overnight run to Columbus, Ohio. Once beyond the Alleghenies, TAT took over at Columbus, flying passengers all day on the next leg to Waynoka, Oklahoma, where they again boarded a Santa Fe overnight train to Clovis, New Mexico. From there, they continued in Ford Trimotor discomfort to Los Angeles. The complete itinerary could be completed, at least on paper, in forty-eight hours, saving a full day over the fastest through train schedule then being operated. (See Figure 13-5.)

The operation, although highly touted by the railroads and accompanied with big-name fanfare (Charles Lindbergh himself was at the controls of the inaugural flight), was really only a novelty. The Ford Trimotors held ten to fourteen seats, but the passenger load was usually only six or seven passengers, and sometimes just three. With no airmail subsidy, the airline lost money, $2.7 million in eighteen months. The Wall Street crash of 1929 impoverished many of the potential passengers, and by 1930, TAT was barely hanging on.

Progenitors of the Big Four

The premier airlines that actually did the flying were to become known as the "Big Four":

1. Boeing-Pratt & Whitney (United Airways) group,
2. the Robertson, Colonial, Texas Air Transport (American Airways) group,
3. the Western Air Express, Transcontinental Air Transport (TAT), Maddux Air Lines (TWA) group, and
4. Eastern Air Transport (Eastern Air Lines). There was also Panagra, the New York, Rio, and Buenos Aires Line (NYRBA), and Pan American Airways, which flew the routes outside of the continental United States. But

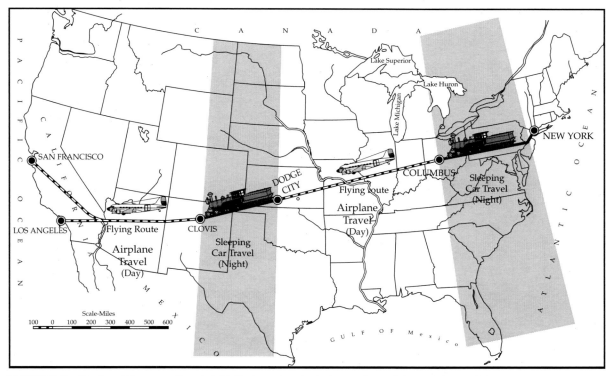

FIGURE 13-5 Route of Transcontinental Air Transport—depicting night and day portions of the route.

Juan Trippe had decided that rather than compete within the boundaries of the United States for the available mail routes, Pan Am would simply carry the mail to and from the United States borders—all of it.

Other airlines, like Curtiss Flying Service and Gorst Air Transport, were substantial and proud, but fell outside of the area of main strength.

The Airmail Act of 1930 (McNary Watres Act)

Former Secretary of Commerce Herbert Hoover was elected President of the United States in November 1928, and took office in 1929. He appointed Walter Folger Brown as his new Postmaster General. Brown knew very little about

aviation, and less still about the infant airline industry. But he was intrigued, and his appointment carried with it the mandate to "encourage commercial aviation." The Postmaster General was the only government office charged with awarding lucrative contracts to commercial air carriers, oftentimes the only thing that separated such carriers from extinction.

Brown set about to learn as much as possible about the fledgling airline business. He was well aware that, by law, government contracts had to be awarded competitively. He noticed that sometimes desperate, smaller companies foolishly submitted unrealistically low bids in order to get the business, and then played games with the weights of mail carried in order to increase their income. The Post Office set its postal rates, in part, to encourage the public to use the airmail system. The airmail contractors, however, were paid on the basis of weight. The difference between rate and weight amounted, in truth, to a subsidy paid to the carriers. It was not unknown for some operators to mail telephone books or steel machine parts to themselves, paying the Post Office postal rate on the front end, then subtracting that as an operating cost from the much larger air carrier rate charged to the Post Office.

Brown did not like this. It was about this time that a notorious proxy fight was being waged for control of National Air Transport (NAT), which held the New York-Chicago airmail route, between the Boeing-Rentschler group (United Air Transport), which had the San Francisco to Chicago mail route, and North American Aviation (NAA), the holding company to which NAT belonged. Rentschler's proposal to merge NAT with United in order to establish the nations first transcontinental carrier was rebuffed by Clement Keys of NAA, and what appeared to be a contest of personalities and wills had soon exploded. After a series of corporate maneuvers reminiscent of the Gould and Vanderbilt railroad era of the late nineteenth century, accompanied by contentious and unpleasant litigation between the route holders, the United group finally prevailed. United took over National Air Transport from NAA, and consolidated its route system coast to coast. Brown felt that this kind of personal and corporate self-serving activity was wasteful of both assets and energy, and not particularly in the national interest. After all, United now had a monopoly on transcontinental airmail service, which to Brown was not a good thing.

Within a relatively short time after taking office, Brown had formed well-researched and thought-out conclusions about what was wrong with the airmail service. Brown believed that the Post Office was paying too much for the carriage of mail, partly because the airline passenger business had not been developed. He believed that by developing passenger traffic, a new, untapped source of income would become available to the airlines. This new income would then

be available to help offset the cost of airline operations. Brown thought that tying the mail contracts to the size of aircraft (bigger) and requiring on-board state of the art communication equipment (radios) and instrumentation would have the effect of making airline flying safer and more acceptable to the potential flying public.

He noted that a system of illogical short routes had been created through the process of competitive bidding, and that competitive bidding had resulted in a nonsensical pay schedule to the airmail contractors with rates of pay varying from 62 1/2 cents to the maximum of $3.00 per pound. He believed that competitive bidding on airmail contracts was counterproductive and that a system of appointing qualified, well-financed, and experienced operators rendered a more stable and efficient system. He felt that those operators who had 'pioneered' airmail routes in certain parts of the country, and who had expended effort and money in promoting the airmail system, developing good will, and encouraging aviation should be given preferred consideration in the award of airmail contracts. (See Figure 13-6.)

On December 9, 1929, Brown appeared before the Appropriations Committee of Congress and related his concerns and suggestions about the airmail system in place, and the lack of an efficient passenger service. Members of the Committee were receptive to Brown's ideas and requested that he draft a bill and send it to them as soon as possible.

On February 4, 1930, Brown sent to Congress a proposed bill that contained the majority of his ideas about how to fix the system. The bill expressly allowed the Postmaster General to award contracts based on negotiated rates rather than competitive bidding. Although the bill was reported favorably out of committee, a minority report was filed containing objections by two members of the committee to the proviso allowing awarding contracts on other that a competi-

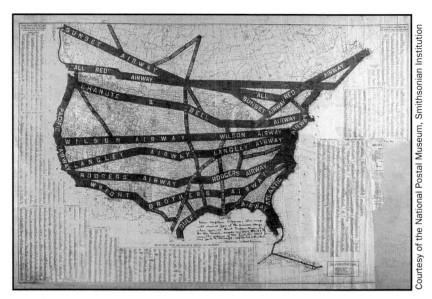

FIGURE 13-6 Airmail airways.

tive bid. One of those was Representative Kelly, the sponsor of the Airmail Act of 1925 (Kelly Act) and the 1928 Kelly amendments to the Act (reducing airmail postage and providing for ten-year airmail contracts).

The form of bill that was passed by Congress was substantially the same as the draft submitted by Brown, with the exception of the removal of the proviso allowing award of contracts based on negotiation and the removal of references to allowing consideration of 'equities' or 'pioneering rights' to carriers based on prior contributions. The bill became law when signed by President Hoover on April 29, 1930.

Accordingly, the main provisions of the act required that the carriers would no longer be paid on the basis of weight, but by the volume of the available space in the aircraft for the carriage of mail. This encouraged the carriers to invest in larger aircraft to earn more money. It further provided that bonuses would be paid if the aircraft were multi-engined and had certain navigational devices installed.

The act also contained certain provisions relating to the manner in which contracts were awarded. These provisions departed significantly from the traditional, straight competitive bid. The Postmaster was authorized, for instance, to circumvent the actual low bidder in favor of the "lowest responsible bidder." A "responsible bidder" was defined in the act as one that had flown daily scheduled service over a 250-mile route for a period of at least six months. Further, Brown went outside of the actual requirements of the act, and invoking what he considered his "discretionary" authority, subjectively required the applicant to have flown that route regularly not only during daylight hours but at night. In effect, the deck was being stacked in favor of the larger, more experienced airmail carriers.

Immediately after passage of the legislation, Brown summoned to Washington representatives from the major lines around the country, who assembled in the Postmaster General's office on May 19, 1930. It was his belief, he said, that the mail should be carried by substantial, established air carriers, the vast majority of which fell within the ownership of the three largest holding companies, United Air Transport, NAA, and AVCO. He explained his master plan to them, in conjunction with the expressed and unexpressed terms of the new law. He decreed that there could be no monopoly of transcontinental service, but that competition along that route would be required, to the dismay of United. Brown explained, in effect, that the country would be carved up among a few lines, with United flying the transcontinental route to San Francisco, another line flying the New York-Los Angeles route by way of Pittsburgh and St. Louis, and still another line proceeding from New York via Washington, Atlanta, and Dallas, thence on to Los Angeles.

Not surprisingly, the strong-willed leaders of the industrial and financial interests that controlled these carriers were unable to agree among themselves, as directed by the Postmaster General, as to how the country should be split up. Representatives of the carriers remained in Washington, attending meetings with each other until June 4, 1930. On that date, the carriers reported to the Postmaster General that they were unable to agree on allocating the five major routes in the country, including the two transcontinental routes, and submitted the issues back to Brown. The carriers advised the Postmaster General that they would agree to be bound by his decision as to the route awards.

During June and July 1930, negotiations and correspondence continued between the parties with a view toward an agreement that would be fair to all concerned and that would take care of smaller lines having some "equity" due to their "pioneering" efforts. Brown suggested that the central transcontinental route should go to the beleaguered TAT, the plane and train airline, which had been flying without airmail subsidy. TAT had no night flying experience, however, and was ineligible for consideration for the transcontinental route because Brown had added

this experience requirement under his "discretionary" authority. Western Air Express, however, did have the requisite night flying experience. Brown, in effect, ordered the merger of TAT with Western Air Express. This merged airline was to be TWA, or Transcontinental and Western Air. As consolation for sacrificing its independence, Western Air Express was allowed to survive as an independent entity and retain its passenger service between San Diego and Los Angeles, and between Los Angeles and Salt Lake City.

United kept its New York-San Francisco route through Chicago, and was allowed to expand northwest. Eastern was assigned New York-Miami, along with Atlanta, New Orleans and Houston. TWA got New York-Los Angeles through St. Louis and Kansas City. American would fly New York-Los Angeles via Nashville, Dallas, and points in the southwest.

Although the smaller lines were not invited to the meetings in May, representatives of several operators showed up, including Southwest Air Fast Express (SAFE), owned by oilman Erie Halliburton, Pittsburgh Aviation Industries, U.S. Air Transport, Curtiss Flying Service, Delta Air Service, and Thompson Aeronautical Corporation. During the summer of 1930, prior to the request for bids being sent out by the Post Office, discussions and negotiations continued. The financial interests of some of the smaller lines were taken into consideration, like SAFE and Delta, and mergers and buyouts were agreed to between them and the larger carriers who would be serving the routes on which the smaller lines had "pioneered." The parties even agreed that Walter Folger Brown would be the arbiter of the value of the stock transactions made to complete the arrangements. Some of the smaller operators received "extensions" of the major routes as additional consideration for the overall agreement.

The airlines paid lip service to the requirements of the Watres Act by going through the motions of competitive bidding with all of the carriers duly submitting bids. The only thing was, none of the Big Four submitted competing bids on the routes that had been assigned by Brown to others. Lower bids on the assigned routes submitted by small carriers were rejected as "not responsible." In this way, modern commercial aviation was born.

Hindsight will not compel a uniform judgment of Brown's actions. It cannot be doubted that the struggling world of commercial aviation was given a mighty boost by the arrangements put in place, and that it evolved at a much accelerated pace over what would otherwise have been the case. At the end of Brown's tenure in 1933, passenger traffic was rising, and the airlines were competing on their transcontinental routes. The cost to the government was less than it had been 4 years before, down from an average of $1.10 per mile in 1929 to half that in 1933, $.54 per mile. The airlines were in good shape financially. It is clear, therefore, that the public interest was served. As we shall see in the next chapter, the 1932 election of Franklin D. Roosevelt as President of the United States (he assumed office in 1933) would have a profound effect on the new commercial aviation community. The allocation of airmail routes and the award of airmail contracts would be the subject of a Congressional investigation, and Walter Folger Brown, himself, would be the subject of intense scrutiny and criticism.

No evidence would be adduced that would even suggest any financial or material gain by Brown. His actions appear to have been the result of a sincere desire to promote aviation, and he did so with success. It is, however, beyond dispute that the procedures employed by Brown were outside of the requirements of the Watres Act. The Congress did not remove the requirement of competitive bidding in 1930, yet that requirement was not observed. The bill that was passed by Congress had removed consideration being given to "pioneering" efforts of some of the operators, yet such consideration was given. In structuring the airmail routes in 1930, Walter Folger Brown proceeded as if his views were superior to the mandate of Congress. With the aid of hindsight, it can be seriously argued that his vision for the future of aviation was far superior to any of his peers.

It should also be noted that Congress had established a benchmark in 1928 with the Foreign Airmail Act, which gave wide discretion to the Postmaster General in awarding overseas mail contracts.[7]

Although the results of Brown's actions would be undone at the beginning of the next administration, the reality is that the Big Four put in place by the Brown policy were still the Big Four for the ensuing 48 years, until deregulation in 1978, in fact. It was then, in 1978, that the country would finally have the chance to glimpse what might have happened during the 1930s had it not been for Walter Brown.

Endnotes

1. For a more detailed discussion of NACA, see chapter 15.
2. See Appendix 4 for details of Lindbergh's flight, including hourly log entries.
3. Lindbergh served as technical advisor to Pan American for 45 years.
4. See Appendix 5.
5. Moolman, Valerie, *Women Aloft,* Time-Life Books, 1981.
6. By contrast, the around the world flight in 1938 by Howard Hughes was 14,456 miles in length, incorporating the itinerary New York-Paris-Moscow-Omsk-Yakutsk-Fairbanks-Minneapolis-New York. Except for New York, Paris, and Minneapolis, all stops were above 55 degrees north latitude. Hughes' flight set a new around the world speed record of 3 days, 19 hours, and 8 minutes, beating both of Wiley Post's world records of 8 days and 16 hours in 1931 and 7 days 19 hours in 1933 along a route similar to that flown by Howard Hughes in 1938.
7. See discussion of Pan American in chapter 15.

CHAPTER 14

New Deal— The Roosevelt Administration

© Alex Staroseltsev, 2008, Shutterstock.

A New Broom Sweeps Clean

The Great Depression was getting seriously underway in 1933, at the time that the Republican Hoover Administration was vacating office and the Democratic Franklin Roosevelt Administration was sweeping in with reform on its mind. Big business had ruled during the roaring twenties. The stock market increasingly through that decade had reflected in price the explosion in commerce and development, much money had been made and people were happy. But in 1933, the bread lines were long and were filled with disillusioned and angry men. The majority of voters had voted, in effect, to "throw the bums out." And so it was that the Democrats arrived in town with an agenda, a mandate even, to begin to set things straight. In the process, a rare opportunity was seen to make a little political hay and find out who and what was to blame for the mess the country found itself in.

Hugo Black came to the U.S. Senate in 1926 as a Democrat from Alabama, where he had enhanced his political career by winning local judicial elections and with membership in the Ku Klux Klan. While a lawyer there, he mostly sued corporations representing personal injury claimants. He considered himself a populist, and was re-elected to the Senate in 1932.

He was a supporter of Franklin Roosevelt's bid for the presidency, and after Roosevelt's election, he was an ardent supporter of New Deal (anti-corporate) initiatives.

Black was given the job of investigating government mail contracts. Soon, the original Brown meetings attended by the heads of the airlines in 1930 became known as the "Spoils Conferences." Small airline operators told of being excluded, and how on the subsequent submission of bids, their lower bids were rejected in favor of higher bids submitted by the larger lines.

To a populist in the 30s, this was rank favoritism, to say nothing of being blatantly against the law. Black used the subpoena power of his senate committee to seize correspondence and documents, using Interstate Commerce Commission agents with synchronized watches to swoop down on the aviation companies without warning. What he discovered led Black to conclude that the airlines had exploited the public through inflated contract rates charged to the government, that the airlines' manufacturing arms had made huge profits from military procurement contracts and that speculation in airline stocks had profited them all. And now the soup lines stood long.

Black was unsympathetic to evidence produced at the hearings that supported the Brown position and that what he had done was in the public interest. Nor was the undisputed fact that the airlines were stable and rendering to the nation the anticipated, though still formative, air transportation system of much consequence to him. Of what interest were airlines to a populace that did not have enough to eat? This was a pertinent, if shortsighted, question.

James Farley was appointed Postmaster General in the new Roosevelt administration. To him fell the duty to carry out the verdict of Black, sanctioned by the President by way of presidential order, that all of the existing airmail contracts held by the airlines then operating were to be cancelled forthwith. The airmail, decreed Farley, would be carried by the Army Air Corps.

Army pilots were basically untrained in cross-country flying and had neither knowledge of nor experience in flying the routes that the mails took across the country. Their airplanes were all open cockpits and contained few of the instruments that had become standard in just a few short years due to Brown's enticements to the airlines. By the end of the first week of flying, five pilots had been killed in accidents and six were critically injured. The Army pilots began flying only in daylight hours. Within five weeks, twelve Army pilots had died. It became clear that a major mistake had been made. New bids to reinstate private carriage of the airmail were called for, but under a revised set of rules.

A temporary arrangement had to be put in place immediately, pending adoption of legislation. Postmaster General Farley called a meeting of airline representatives, like Walter Folger Brown before him. But this time, none of the airlines involved in the "spoils conferences," nor any of the executives who attended them, could participate in the new round of bidding. No bidding airline could also be involved in the manufacture of aircraft designed to be used in the airline business, like the Boeing-Rentschler combination at United. Vertical holding companies that exercised control over the actual airlines were disallowed. Rectitude reigned supreme in

public, but in private, practicality ruled the day. Cosmetic name changes by the Big Four were accepted as serious compliance with the new rules, changes like American Airways becoming American Airlines and Eastern Air Transport becoming Eastern Air Lines. In fact, after the bids were opened on April 20, 1934, the commercial airline industry looked very much the same as it did before Black started his quest for delayed justice the year before.

Two significant changes did occur. An upstart airline named Braniff Airways beat out United on the Dallas-Chicago route, and the crop dusting C. E. Woolman, operating as Delta Airlines, had secured the Dallas to Charleston, S.C. route. Each of these new airlines would ultimately make the most of their opportunity.

Walter Brown would continue unrepentant and dignified amidst the righteous alarums of Black and other politicians who sought to capitalize at the expense of his reputation. The airlines whose contracts had been terminated, although back in the airmail business within a short time, had lost a significant amount of money by continuing operations in the interim, but only the United group of airline companies resorted to litigation against the government because of the contract cancellations. That litigation would drag out for another ten years. And, when finally concluded, it would uphold the government's right to terminate the airmail contracts. *Pacific Air Transport v. U.S., et. al.*[1] The court did, however, award money damages to the United group for contract payments earned prior to the cancellations. The opinion, which is 104 pages in length, is a detailed chronology of the events that transpired after passage of the Watres Act.

The Airmail Act of 1934 (The Black-McKellar Act)

The Black-McKellar Act, passed by Congress in June 1934, codified the arrangements for the award of airmail contracts made in April 1934, (see Figure 14-1) and repealed the powers and prerogative of the Postmaster General as established in the Watres Act. Competitive bidding was reinstated. The newly named airlines bid on the routes. Airline executives involved in the Brown meetings were prohibited from occupying positions of authority in the new airlines. The vertical structure of the airlines and manufacturing companies was prohibited. United Aircraft and Transport, for example, was dismantled and its operations split three ways:

➡ Boeing took over all operating properties in the West,

➡ All eastern U.S. functions were assumed by United Aircraft Corporation (today known as United Technologies), run by Rentschler,

➡ Finally the airline itself, United Airlines, became a separate and independent entity.

The air carrier industry was reorganized under the Act by separating oversight and regulatory authority among

1. The Post Office, which would continue to award contracts, designate routes, and establish schedules;

2. The Interstate Commerce Commission, which would establish reasonable rates through competitive bidding oversight;

3. The Department of Commerce, which through the Bureau of Air Commerce would attend to safety.

Ultimately, the effect of the Act would be to divest the other large airline operations from their holding companies. Aviation Corporation (AVCO) divested itself of American Airlines, now to be run by C. R. Smith as an independent

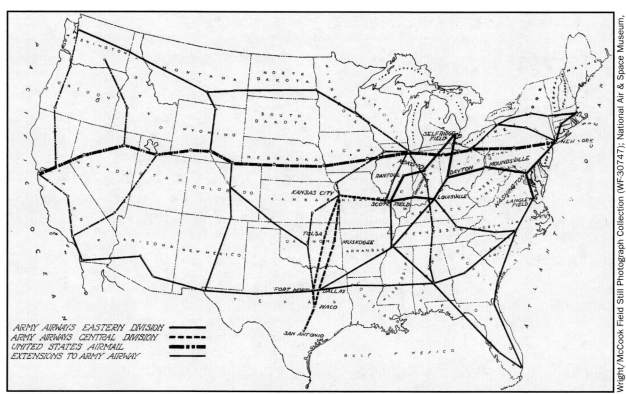

FIGURE 14-1 1934 airmail routes.

corporation. North American Aviation (NAA), a complex and diverse entity, was the parent of both TWA and Eastern Air Transport, and had substantial manufacturing interests. NAA first sold off TWA, now run by Jack Frye, a pilot's pilot. In due course, Eddie Rickenbacker cobbled together Wall Street financing to the tune of some 3.5 million dollars and bought out the Eastern Air Lines interest. Thus, all of the Big Four were positioned independently for the advent of commercial air transportation and the first comprehensive federal regulation of it.

Pan American, meanwhile, had been unaffected by the so-called Brown scandal and still had its airmail contracts. The Brown philosophy that the international airmail business should not compete with the domestic airmail business, and vice versa, was intact. The international trade routes that had emerged from the Brown era were not in the least affected by the new law, nor by anything that Black had done, and Pan American was set to become the premier airline of all.

The Railway Labor Act

Transportation during the 1920s was the domain of the railroads, which carried nearly all of the intercity passengers in the nation. The railroads delivered essentially all of the freight of the nation, and employed by far the most workers of any industry in the country.

The hazards of being a railroad employee, particularly those working as members of train crews, like brakemen, conductors and engineers, or those working on the bridges, tunnels, and rights of way of the railroad, had resulted in a level of deaths and maiming previously unknown. Congress, taking note of the plight of railroad workers, passed a spate of remedial legislation aimed at improving their working conditions and safety. Examples are the Boiler Inspection Act to lessen the risk of locomotive boiler explosions, the Safety Appliance Act to establish safety standards regarding ladders, handholds, and coupling devices on freight cars, and Air

Brake law requiring the installation of air brakes on railroad cars.

Congress also addressed the concerns of workers who had little or no control over their wages or working conditions, and the concerns of railroad management and the public regarding disruptions of the nation's primary transportation system through labor strife, work stoppages, and violence carried out by railroad workers. The result was the Railway Labor Act of 1926.

The Railway Labor Act, for the first time, provided a legislative scheme to insure workers the right to organize themselves into legally recognized bargaining units, or unions. This required railroad management to accord the workers a voice in their conditions of safety, wages, and working conditions. At the same time, the law restricted the unions' right to disrupt the nation's transportation system through work stoppages and strikes except under the most controlled conditions, and only after federally mandated mediation between workers and management proved fruitless. Even then, the law provided that the President of the United States could require, under certain conditions, that employees continue to work under their existing labor agreements so as not to paralyze the nation's commerce.

Except for the enactment of the Railway Labor Act in 1926, there had been no meaningful federal legislation affecting the larger world of workers and management since the Clayton Antitrust Act of 1914. That statute had exempted labor unions from the constraints of the Sherman Antitrust Act, legislation that had been used by the courts to great effect in enjoining union strike activity. In 1932, Congress passed the Norris-LaGuardia Anti-Injunction Act,[2] which further severely limited the power of courts to issue injunctions in labor disputes.

When the Roosevelt administration took office in 1933 amidst the distress of working people during the Great Depression, it turned its attention to the general condition of workers outside of the railroad industry. In 1935, Congress passed the Social Security Act to provide protection to workers to cover the risks of old age, death, and the dependency of children, and to provide for the payment of unemployment benefits. Congress also, in 1935, passed the National Labor Relations Act (the Wagner Act),[3] which extended to workers in the nation generally the right to organize, bargain collectively, and to "engage in concerted activities for the purpose of collective bargaining or other mutual aid and protection."

At this point, recognizing that the fledgling air carrier industry, similar to the railroad industry before it, appeared to be on the threshold of assuming some of the transportation needs of the country, Congress exempted airlines and their workers from the broader labor relations law of the Wagner Act and placed the air carrier industry under the Railway Labor Act (RLA), where it has remained. The pilots' union, the Air Line Pilots Association (ALPA), maintains that this result came about, at least in part, because of lobbying efforts by their organization in the early 1930s.

The first airline employee's union, ALPA, was formed in 1931, but it had no legal standing. The airlines required pilots to fly 120 hours a month, but during the depression in 1933, they announced that flight hours would be increased to 140 per month, and at a lower pay scale. A strike was called by the pilots and, in the absence of any law governing the situation, the parties agreed to refer the issue to mediation. Judge Bernard Shintag of the New York Supreme Court took evidence and ruled, among other things, that pilot monthly flight time should be limited to 85 hours per month. Although without the legal standing of enforcement, the ruling, known as Decision 83, was ultimately incorporated into the Civil Aeronautics Act of 1938.

Under the provisions of RLA, airline workers were given the same rights of organizing and collective bargaining as were railroad workers, and airline employees were similarly constrained from conducting work stoppages except under the very specific provisions of the statute.

The main purposes of the Act are:

→ The statute intends to establish a system that resolves labor disputes without disrupting interstate and foreign commerce. The statute imposes on both labor and management the obligation to use every reasonable effort to settle disputes. This is the "heart of the Act", as stated by the Supreme Court.

→ The statute requires that no change in working conditions or wages be made during negotiations between labor and management. This is called "maintaining the status quo" and generally prohibits management from changing working conditions or wages and prohibits unions from striking or conducting any other type of "work action", like slow-downs or sick outs, during this time.

→ The statute prohibits management from interfering with any attempt by workers to organize themselves into collective bargaining units.

There are only two types of "issues" recognized under the Act. Every type of actual or potential disagreement or dispute between the parties is classified as:

→ A "major dispute" is one that concerns wages and benefits, working conditions, or rules. These types of disputes are also called "Section 6" disputes and may, after exhaustion of all remedies under the statute, and while the "status quo" is being maintained during negotiations between the parties, result in strike action.

→ A "minor dispute" describes all other disputes, and mainly concerns individual employee issues such a disciplinary action. Strikes are prohibited in minor disputes; instead binding arbitration is required in the event that the parties are unable to resolve the issue.

Procedures to be followed are:

1. The party desiring to change the provisions of the labor agreement must give a Section 6 notice of the desired change to the other side. This notice includes the initiation of negotiations after the "amendable date," or the date that the agreement becomes subject to change.

2. The parties must enter into negotiations within 30 days and bargain in good faith.

3. Either of the parties may request mediation by the National Mediation Board (NMB), which appoints a mediator to assist in the negotiations. The NMB may not require either party to agree or to take any other action with respect to the issue.

4. If the NMB concludes that an impasse has been reached, so that no settlement of the issue is likely, it may offer to arbitrate the issue and issue a decision that will be binding on the parties. Both parties must agree to be bound.

5. If either party refuses binding arbitration, a 30-day "cooling off" period begins, during which mediation usually continues.

6. If no agreement is reached by the end of the 30-day period, either side may resort to "self help," that is, a strike by labor or the imposition of new wages or working conditions by management.

7. If certified to the President by the NMB, a Presidential Emergency Board (PEB) may be convened to prevent "self help." The PEB has 30 days to investigate and report to the President, after which time an additional 30 days (a total of 60 days) is imposed on the parties to maintain the "status quo." During this time, considerable pressure is exerted both by government officials and by the media (public opinion) to cause a resolution of the issue.

8. Congress is empowered upon a failure of all preceding efforts to legislate a resolution that is binding on the parties.

No Presidential Emergency Boards were convened during the 1930s, nor until after World War II. In fact, the first labor agreement in the airlines was not negotiated until 1939.[4]

It should be noted that the RLA was extended only to airlines, or "carriers" as defined in the Act, and not to other forms of transportation. The trucking industry, buses, and shipping under the Merchant Marine fall under the NLRB.

Significant developments in airline labor relations, both before and after the deregulation of the airlines in 1978, will be discussed beginning in chapter 30.

Endnotes

1. 98 Ct. Cl. 649 (1942).
2. 27 USC § 101–115.
3. 29 USC §151–166.
4. Presidential Emergency Boards under the Railway Labor Act <http://www.ilr.cornell.edu/library/e_archive/miscellaneous/airlines/emergency.pdf>

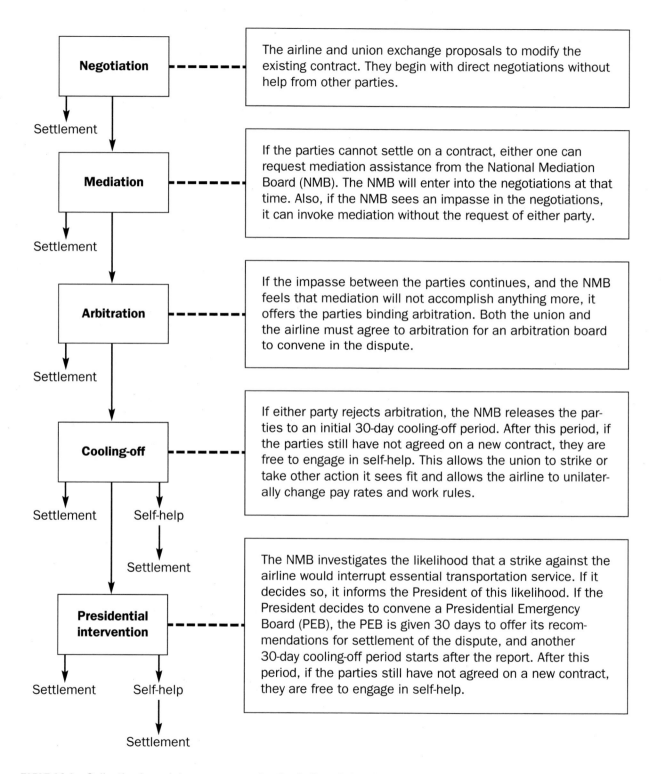

Negotiation

The airline and union exchange proposals to modify the existing contract. They begin with direct negotiations without help from other parties.

Settlement

Mediation

If the parties cannot settle on a contract, either one can request mediation assistance from the National Mediation Board (NMB). The NMB will enter into the negotiations at that time. Also, if the NMB sees an impasse in the negotiations, it can invoke mediation without the request of either party.

Settlement

Arbitration

If the impasse between the parties continues, and the NMB feels that mediation will not accomplish anything more, it offers the parties binding arbitration. Both the union and the airline must agree to arbitration for an arbitration board to convene in the dispute.

Settlement

Cooling-off

If either party rejects arbitration, the NMB releases the parties to an initial 30-day cooling-off period. After this period, if the parties still have not agreed on a new contract, they are free to engage in self-help. This allows the union to strike or take other action it sees fit and allows the airline to unilaterally change pay rates and work rules.

Settlement   Self-help

Settlement

Presidential intervention

The NMB investigates the likelihood that a strike against the airline would interrupt essential transportation service. If it decides so, it informs the President of this likelihood. If the President decides to convene a Presidential Emergency Board (PEB), the PEB is given 30 days to offer its recommendations for settlement of the dispute, and another 30-day cooling-off period starts after the report. After this period, if the parties still have not agreed on a new contract, they are free to engage in self-help.

Settlement   Self-help

Settlement

TABLE 14-1 Collective bargaining process under the Railway Labor Act
Source: GAO analysis of NMB data.

CHAPTER 15

State of the Airlines before the Civil Aeronautics Act

© Johnny Kuo, 2008, Shutterstock.

The Big Four, having been established largely through the efforts of Walter Brown, and having survived the Black investigation and the resulting remedial legislation (Black-McKellar), were well positioned for the beginnings of the modern era of commercial air transportation. The airlines were hurting financially, however, due to the losses experienced during the stand down period when the Army had flown the mail after the cancellation of all CAM routes in February 1934, and because the new rates mandated by Black-McKellar were set to a maximum of 33.5 cents per mile, less than a third of the going rate in 1929.

But progress had been made. In 1929, the contract mail carriers (who were to become the country's major airlines) were still flying wood and wire airplanes, although a few had acquired the very latest technology in the Fokker or Ford trimotors. By the late 1930s, when the Civil Aeronautics Act was passed, great innovations in aircraft manufacture had occurred, largely due to a combination of commitments and risks undertaken by the airlines and by the aircraft manufacturers, and to government innovations achieved at the National Advisory Committee on Aeronautics.

The National Advisory Committee on Aeronautics (NACA)

NACA was created in 1915 during the administration of Woodrow Wilson as a governmental aeronautical research laboratory. It was recognized during World War I that the United States had fallen well behind the European countries in aviation, and the events in Europe during that conflict were pointing up that aviation was rapidly becoming an issue of national defense. The appropriation for the Committee ($5,000) was modest even for those times, but its mission was clear: "To direct and conduct research and experimentation in aeronautics with a view to their practical solution." It was also to establish a proud legacy during its existence from 1915 to 1958, when it was renamed the National Aeronautics and Space Administration (NASA).

In the early days, NACA advised the government in several pivotal issues, including the government's role in the early airmail service and the lighted airway system. It was largely on NACA's recommendations that the details of the Air Commerce Act of 1926 were fleshed out, including licensing and standardization of aircraft and pilots, inauguration of the aviation weather service, and the establishment of the Bureau of Aeronautics within the Department of Commerce. But one of its most notable early accomplishments was in the area of testing and experimentation in its large wind tunnel, which produced advanced technical information used by American aircraft manufacturers, particularly in connection with the design of engine cowlings, airfoils, and their drag characteristics.

The Big Four

American Airlines

American Airlines emerged as the surviving corporate entity after Black-McKellar. Aviation Corporation (AVCO) had been formed in early 1929 as a holding company by a group of New York financiers, and it rapidly proceeded to acquire aviation-related companies left and right. Its holdings included airports, instrument manufacturers, and engine makers, and finally totaled more than 80 separate companies, some having absolutely nothing in common with the others. In early 1930, AVCO consolidated its aviation holdings into American Airways, the name under which the airmail contracts would be serviced in the early 1930s.

American Airways had been formed from eleven smaller lines. Some had their beginnings as early as 1925, notably Embry-Riddle Company (first to be acquired), and 1926, such as Colonial Air Transport, Southern Air Transport, Robertson Aircraft Corp, and Southern Air Fast Express (SAFE).

E. L. Cord, who had bested Harriman and Lehman for control of Aviation Corporation, made C. R. Smith, who had come from Southern Air Transport, president of the new American Airlines in 1934. Smith had a penchant for detail worthy of his training and experience as a bookkeeper and part-time bank examiner, and he ran the company with a hands-on approach that, by 1939, would make American Airlines the nation's foremost air carrier in passenger miles flown.

Upon his election as president, and while American was flying a conglomeration of airplanes ranging from the trimotor monoplanes to the bi-wing Curtiss Condors, he immediately placed orders with Douglas Aircraft for the new DC-2. Then, in 1935, he ordered the DC-3, the airplane that was to revolutionize commercial air travel. The DC-3, in fact, was a direct result of collaboration between Smith and Douglas to make modifications that American wanted to the DC-2. The main change desired by Smith was a wider cabin, but in the process of this change, other significant changes in the DC-2 were made, including a new wing, a hydraulic system, insulation, and a much better landing gear and suspension system.

In 1937, American Airlines' route structure included New York to Los Angeles, the southern route, via Washington, D.C., Nashville, and Dallas. It also had New York to Boston and New York to Montreal, New York to Buffalo and thence to Chicago, St. Louis, and Oklahoma City.

Eastern Air Lines

Eastern Air Lines emerged in 1934 as the surviving entity following Black-McKellar. The predecessor company, Eastern Air Transport, was owned by the holding company, North American Aviation, which in turn was controlled by General Motors as of 1933. Eddie Rickenbacker (see Figure 15-1), World War I hero and fighter ace, was hired by General Motors as a consultant and then was made general manager of Eastern Air Transport in 1934. Eastern Air Transport was successor to the original line, Pitcairn Aviation, and it later absorbed the Luddington Line and New York Airways before becoming Eastern Air Lines. When General Motors tired of the airline business in 1938, Rickenbacker purchased the company and steadily increased its business and its mileage.

In 1937, Eastern Air Lines had routes from New York to Miami and to Atlanta and points south and west, New Orleans, Houston, and San Antonio, all through Washington, D.C. It also

FIGURE 15-1 Eddie Rickenbacker.

Source: Library of Congress.

flew the Chicago to Miami route through Indianapolis, Nashville, and Atlanta.

TWA

TWA was the designation taken by the airline combined at the behest of Walter Folger Brown. A combination of the former Transcontinental Air Transport (TAT) and Western Air Express, it flew the middle transcontinental route from New York to Los Angeles under the name Transcontinental and Western Air. After Black-McKellar, the airline simply added "Inc." after its name in order to comply with the prohibition of Postmaster General Farley that precluded those airlines which had participated in the Brown meetings from bidding on the new airmail contracts in 1934.

TWA had been a part of North American Aviation in the early 1930s, and General Motors controlled the holding company. After Brown-McKellar, General Motors sold its interests to John D. Hertz and Lehman Brothers, who then had effective control of TWA.

Jack Frye, at the age of twenty-six, was TWA's operational vice president in 1930. He had founded Standard Air Lines in the 1920s, after stints at flight instructing and stunt flying, and went with the company when it was purchased by Western Air Express. With the merger of Western and TAT, he suddenly found himself in charge of operations of a transcontinental airline. TWA, and most other airlines, relied heavily on the Trimotors in the early 30s. With the 1931 crash of the Fokker Trimotor in which Notre Dame football coach Knute Rockne was killed, government mandated inspections of that plane's wooden wing structure became cost-prohibitive, not to mention the fact that the flying public thereafter was not keen on stepping aboard that airplane. Frye needed new equipment.

In 1932, Frye had heard the buzz in the aviation community of a new prototype in the works at Boeing, the model 247. (See Figure 15-2.) This airplane was to be a giant leap forward with its low mono-wing, and two engines instead of three that were mounted into the wings in nacelles (taking advantage of NACA research) that greatly reduced drag. The 247 used stressed all-metal skin, retractable landing gear (a first), insulated cabin walls, and hot water heating and double ventilation systems. This airplane would fly from one coast to the other in only nineteen and one-half hours, twelve hours less than with the trimotors. Fueling stops were reduced from fourteen to six. Frye decided that TWA had to have these airplanes.

When he inquired, he was advised that United Airlines (the sister company to the Boeing manufacturing arm) had already placed an order for sixty of the new planes, an order that it would take all of two years to fill, thus precluding any deliveries to other airlines. The 247 became operational in June 1933.

In the fall of 1932, Frye wrote to a number of aircraft manufacturers setting out airplane performance specifications for new equipment that TWA would be interested in purchasing. Although

Source: National Air and Space Museum.

FIGURE 15-2 The Boeing 247 was to be a great leap forward with its low mono-wing, and two engines instead of three that were mounted into wings in nacelles that greatly reduced drag.

TM & © Boeing. Used under license.

FIGURE 15-3 DC-1, designation for the Douglas Commercial Number 1. This was the only one ever built.

the specifications included that the airplane have three engines, the engineers at a small company located in California, known as Douglas Aircraft, believed that the performance specifications could be met with a twin engine design, including the requirement for a 10,000 foot minimum service ceiling on one engine (necessary to clear the Rockies).

A prototype was fielded in July 1933, the DC-1 (see Figure 15-3), designation for the Dou-glas Commercial Number 1. If this had been poker, the DC-1 would have called the B-247 and raised it. The DC-1 engine mountings and cowl-ing were similar to the 247, incorporating the design developed by the National Advisory Com-mittee on Aeronautics, but the landing gear of the DC-1 folded up into the engine nacelles. The engines, Wright Cyclones, had been engineered to produce 710 horsepower due to 87-octane gasoline having become commercially available

Source: Florida State Archives.

FIGURE 15-4 DC-3—The plane that changed the world.

during the period of the plane's construction. Although the constant speed propeller was still a few years off, the DC-1 did have a 2-speed propeller that could be set either for takeoff or for cruise (a first). Additional firsts included an automatic pilot and efficient wing flaps. Flight tests showed that Frye's performance specifications had been met. Only one DC-1 was built and that one was purchased by TWA. It was placed in limited service in 1933.

When Postmaster General Farley sent his notice dated February 9, 1934, canceling all airmail contracts effective February 19, 1934, Frye decided to make his own statement. With Eddie Rickenbacker of Eastern Air Transport as co-pilot, on February 18, 1934, Frye took off from Los Angeles in the DC-1 loaded with airmail and flew it to Newark, with fueling stops in Kansas City and Columbus, in thirteen hours and four minutes, setting the transcontinental speed record at the time.

The DC-2, with 14 seats, was brought to production in 1934, and 193 were built. The next year, in 1935, Douglas came out with the DC-3 (see Figure 15-4) (21 seats) with 900 horsepower Wright Cyclones (DC-3A with 1200 horsepower P&W engines), and Douglas would, before it was

all over, build 455 of them for commercial use and 10,174 for the military. By 1936, the DC-3 had reduced the transcontinental flying time to about seventeen hours. The airplane was awarded the Collier Trophy in 1936 and became known as "The Plane That Changed the World." And, indeed, it was used all over the world—in World War II in Burma, this airplane which at normal configuration seated 21 passengers, set a load record of 72 refugees safely delivered, and 6 more stowaways were discovered on landing.

By late 1938, pressurized airplanes were on the drawing boards. Boeing designed a commercial transport, the 307 (see Figure 15-5), scheduled for delivery in 1939. It was based on the basic B-17 design with four 900 horsepower Wright R-1820 Cyclone engines. This airplane had a service ceiling of 26,200 feet and was the first commercial liner pressurized for high altitude flight. The airplane came to be known as the "Stratoliner." Jack Frye decided that TWA had to have them too, so he placed an order with Boeing for five of the new planes. But his board of directors, chaired by John D. Hertz of Lehman Brothers, did not agree. In December 1938, TWA's board voted to cancel Frye's order to Boeing for the B-307.

Jack Frye knew that this dispute represented an essential disagreement concerning his and the board's vision for the future of TWA. He also knew that this disagreement would likely mean his being removed if control of the company remained in the hands of the present directors. Jack Frye was acquainted with Howard Hughes (see Figure 15-6), the eccentric multimillionaire and aviation pioneer in his own right, who was then living in Los Angeles and involved in the movie making business. Hughes had an abiding interest in aviation and had even worked for American Airlines, under an assumed name, as a co-pilot in 1932, flying between Los Angeles and Chicago. He listened to Frye, sided with his logic in the B-307 dispute with the board of directors, and agreed to

Source: Florida State Archives.

FIGURE 15-5 Boeing 307.

Source: Library of Congress.

FIGURE 15-6 Howard Hughes, the eccentric multimillionaire and aviation pioneer.

buy the company. He began secretly buying up TWA stock. By April, it was public knowledge that Hughes was becoming a substantial stockholder in the airline, so much so that the significant interests represented by Lehman and Hertz decided to pull out of the company, the second time Lehman had departed the field. Control was effectively passed to Howard Hughes, the Boeing order for the 307 was reinstated, and the future of TWA remained firmly in the grip of Jack Frye, now with Howard Hughes. On July 8, 1940, the 307 was placed into service on the New York to Los Angeles route, reducing the transcontinental flying time to fourteen and one-half hours.

Hughes was a singular individual and unique in all known respects. He was born wealthy, son of the founder of the Hughes Tool Company of Houston, Texas. As soon as he could, he left Houston, began traveling the world, and wound up in Hollywood. He entered the film business and, in the process of directing his first film, *Hell's Angels,* a story of British pilots in World War I, he became fascinated with aviation and learned to fly.

Even as a young man, Hughes was obsessive, wanting to be the best, to know the most, and never to fail. With absolutely no concerns about money, he began the design and building of an airplane racer, the H-1, with which he would set a world's speed record of 352 miles per hour in 1935. He set a transcontinental speed record of seven hours and twenty-seven minutes with the H-1 in January 1936. He flew practically every commercial airplane in production over the next several years, gaining experience in long-distance navigation and planning, as well as execution at the controls, until he launched his most ambitious attempt yet: a round the world flight in the Lockheed Electra.

The record in 1938 stood from Wiley Post's solo circumnavigation in 1933 at seven days and eighteen hours. Hughes' route took him from New York to Paris in less than half the time it took Lindbergh, then across Europe into Russia and Siberia to Alaska. From Fairbanks he refueled in Minneapolis and returned to Floyd Bennett Field in New York triumphant in three and a half days, halving Post's record.

Hughes had some prior acquaintance with TWA; in fact, one of its vice presidents had been a stunt pilot for Hughes' movie, *Hell's Angels.* Hughes was also more pilot than businessman. As Jack Frye would later remark, "One thing about Hughes, he did have an understanding about the airplane." He fully understood the advantage of having an airplane that could top most of the weather, so he agreed with Frye's position on the Boeing 307.

United Airlines

United Airlines' name came through the Black and Brown affair unscathed. This was because each of the airmail carrying lines operated in their own names, for example, Boeing Air Transport, Pacific Air Transport, and United Air Lines Transport Corporation. The chief operating officers of the companies caught up in the Brown affair were banished. Thus, United's Phil Johnson left the stage and the presidency of United Airlines was assumed by Pat Patterson, a 34-year-old former banker who came up through the ranks from Pacific Air Transport.

Patterson is credited with initiating the in-flight passenger service staffed by young women, initially nurses, in 1930. The United group was the strongest of the airlines of the 1930s. It was United's lead that counted with the other airlines when Patterson decided to continue passenger and freight service in spite of the cancellation of the airmail contracts in 1934, as he said, "no matter what the losses." United maintained its schedules but at tremendous cost. Even with the return of airmail contracts, given the

reduced rate then paid and the losses suffered during the cancellation period, United lost more than two million dollars in 1934, and continued to struggle financially over the last years of the 1930s, falling behind American Airlines with revenues less than half of American by 1938.

The United group, in their individual operating names (Pacific Air Transport, Boeing Air Transport, etc.) had been the lone airline group to sue the government over the airmail cancellation decision in 1934. That litigation would drag on and not be finally resolved until 1942, when the decision of the U.S. Court of Claims was handed down.[1] The court upheld the right of the government to cancel the contracts, but awarded damages to United for those sums representing United's airmail carriage up to the date of cancellation. The language of the opinion is generally considered to be favorable to United and not in keeping with the tone of the Black investigation and the negative airline press it generated.

It can be argued that United's difficulties beginning in 1934 were due to an unfriendly relationship between the Roosevelt administration (which would remain in office until 1945) and United due to the litigation, and exacerbated by a general anti-corporate attitude in certain government quarters. For example, the Interstate Commerce Commission had assumed responsibility for rates and mergers as a result of Black-McKellar. In 1936, the ICC refused to approve a merger between United and a moneymaking line serving New York-Washington. When the Civil Aeronautics Authority took over the ICC function in 1938, it denied purchase authority for United's bid for Western Air Express (the split off branch that did not merge with TAT to form TWA). United, with its 10 passenger Boeing Model 247s, was struggling to compete against the larger and faster DC-2s and DC-3s of the other lines.

In 1937, United still had its transcontinental route, but that was in heavy competition with the other routes awarded by Brown. It did not have the strength of the eastern lines that resulted from their consolidation of the shorter route structure between cities of the more populous eastern United States. Not until the 1960s would United be once again the airline industry leader.

The Lesser Lines

In 1938 it was the Big Four and then everybody else. Some of the smaller lines would fade away; others would prosper under the new law. When the Civil Aeronautics Act passed Congress, notables among the small lines were Delta, Northwest, Western Air Express, Braniff, National, and Continental. Much would be heard from them in the future. And then there was Pan American.

Pan American Airways

Pan American Airways was to occupy a singular place in the annals of American aviation and in the relationship of an airline company with the U.S. government. What Pan Am came to be was mostly a product of the efforts of Juan Trippe, a true visionary, an indefatigable worker and thinker, a man of exceptional personal and professional contacts in both the world of business and government, and a man who stayed at the helm of his company longer than any of his contemporaries.

Trippe was instrumental in the formation and early operation of Colonial Airlines, one of the original airmail contract flyers in 1926, that ultimately became part of American Airways. His vision for that airline was much too aggressive for its conservative directors and stockholders, and Trippe was soon out. He had actually formed a small airline in 1924, before the financial benefits of airmail carriage became available, but it had been unable to survive. After Colonial Airlines, he was soon underway with his concept of an international airline, lining up financing from his wealthy friends and his father's Wall Street contacts.

By 1927, Pan American was in the firm control of Juan Trippe and his friends. That year, wheeling, dealing, merging, and negotiating their way, the young men of Pan American had an airmail contract for the Key West, Florida to Havana, Cuba route. The contract stipulated that service must commence at the latest by October 19, 1927, and since other companies were waiting in the wings hoping Pan American would default, it became a matter of some importance to meet the deadline.

The Fokker Trimotors that Trippe had ordered to service the route had not shown up by that date, so the inaugural flight of Pan American Airways was hastily arranged on the dock at Key West on the drop-dead date. A transient floatplane pilot, bound for a job in Haiti, made a fortuitous fuel stop that day and unwittingly became a part of the grand history of Pan American, for a cash fee of $175.00.

Trippe's vision was fueled not only by his expansive imagination and unbridled determination, but also by the circumstances in which America found itself in the late 1920s. The 20s had been a decade of progress, experimentation, expansion, and success. World War I had caused Americans to look outward, mainly toward Europe, but now toward the untapped vast South American continent and the Latin American connection. The region was ideally suited to air transportation because of its island-hopping availability. South America was also largely undeveloped, ruled with mountains, smothered by jungles, and had largely skipped the era of railroad transportation. Transportation was about to go from pack mule and water skiff directly to air travel.

Europeans, mainly Germans seeking respite from the turmoil, frustration, and inflation of their defeated nation, had opened up aerial trading routes to South America in 1919. They were expanding their influence along its eastern coast and up into the Caribbean. The expatriates formed a company called Sociedad Colombo-

Aleman de Transposes Aereos (SCADTA) under the laws of Colombia that had become, as one of the world's first airlines, an example of what aviation could do under extremely challenging conditions. In the process, SCADTA had become the pride of the people of Colombia.

The United States looked with some alarm at this development. The long-standing policy of the United States, as articulated in the "Monroe Doctrine,"[2] after all, essentially decreed the Americas for Americans, not Europeans, and certainly not the Germans. The governmental policy toward commercial aviation that was forming during the 20s held that, while competition among business interests within the United States was good for the public, competition between American businesses outside its borders could be harmful. To properly compete with foreign airlines that were strongly supported by their governments, American international aviation would have to have some form of American government support and should follow some kind of governmental policy.

Pan American was ideally positioned to take advantage of this political and economic situation, and Juan Trippe commanded the confidence of the right people to enhance Pan American's opportunities. The first Trippe ploy was to take advantage of a practice common in the domestic aviation market to 'extend' route authority by fiat of the Postmaster General. This he did by securing an extension authority to Miami from Key West. After Lindbergh's epic transatlantic flight and the ensuing public clamor and appeal that it engendered, Trippe signed Lindy up as a consultant, and Lindbergh became an integral part of the Pan Am strategy to extend its routes across the Caribbean and into Central America and then down into South America. In time, he would also figure prominently in Pan American's westward Pacific expansion.

The second significant development was the passage by Congress in 1928 of the "Foreign Airmail Act." This statute allowed the Postmaster General the discretion to grant routes to bidders that, in his opinion, were the "lowest reasonable bidders that can perform the service satisfactorily." The Act provided, in so many words, that only airlines capable of operating on a scale and in a manner that would project the dignity of the United States in Latin America would be granted the right to carry international mail.

The first three airplanes purchased by Pan American were land-based Fokker Trimotors. (See Figure 15-9.) With these, the first passenger service between Key West and Havana was begun in January 1928. Given the lack of airports over the region and the fact that most of the flying was over water, Pan American made two significant decisions about its near-term future:

1. The line would employ flying boats to the exclusion of other types of aircraft and

2. The line would fly only multiengine planes. These decisions weighed favorably with the public and with the government.

It was also required that a form of navigation be developed that would allow flight over the trackless ocean. There were obviously no railroads to follow, no landmarks to navigate by, and no open fields to land in. Celestial navigation, long used in maritime transportation, was available, but it had serious limitations as the sole method of navigation for relatively fast moving airplanes. Voice radio was being experimented with on domestic air routes, but the equipment necessary to be placed on board approximated the size and weight of a small piano. Pan American had decided that radio was a near necessity from a safety standpoint, and it was searching for alternatives. An employee of RCA well versed in radio, Hugo Leuteritz, began experimenting with radiotelegraphy with devices that were installed on some of the airplanes. The equipment on board was very light, and the signals were clear and not beset by the static that made voice communication at these latitudes almost impossible. The procedure

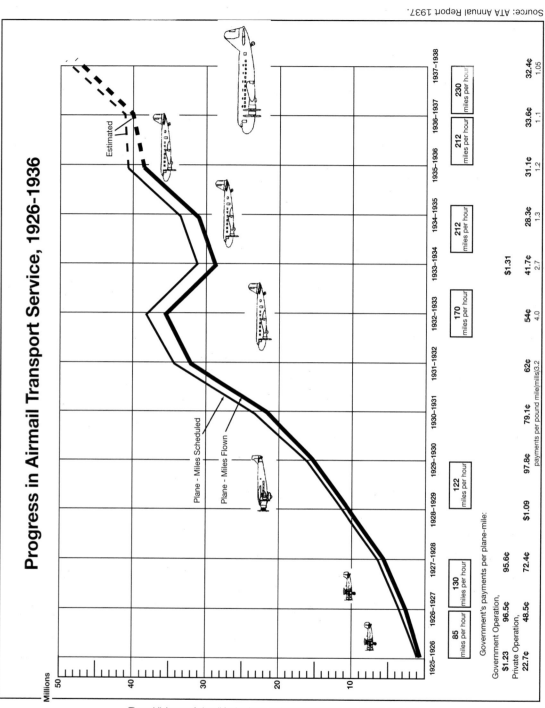

Source: ATA Annual Report 1937.

Progress in Airmail Transport Service, 1926-1936

The public's use of airmail for business and social purposes has mounted steadily.

(The decline during the fiscal year 1934, and in the subsequent interval required for repairing the decline, was caused by the cancellation of the airmail contracts.)

As volume has mounted, the unit cost to the government has steadily decreased. (Note figures at extreme bottom of chart.)

FIGURE 15-7 Progress in airmail transport service, 1926–1936.

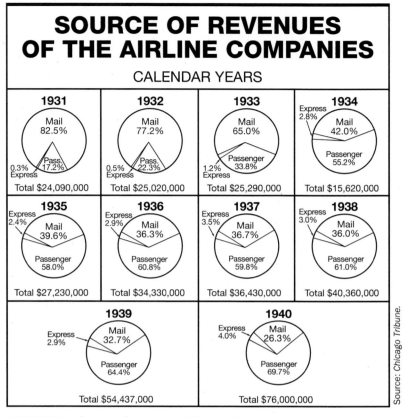

FIGURE 15-8 Source of revenues of the airline companies.

developed by Leuteritz utilized two land-based listening stations equipped with loop antennae that could pick up and then directionally locate the dots and dashes emitting from the enroute aircraft. When the two stations drew lines from their separate positions to that of the aircraft, and the two lines crossed, the latitude and longitude thus determined was transmitted by the shore station to the radio operator aboard the aircraft and its fix would be established. This method allowed pinpoint accuracy in making the desired landfall.

When the Sikorsky S-38 twin-engine flying boats arrived (see Figure 15-10), Pan American's chief pilot, Captain Eddie Musick (see Figure 15-11), began to make survey flights beyond Havana to anticipated destinations even before the Post Office advertised for bids. It

FIGURE 15-9 Fokker F-7 to Havana, Pan American 1928.

seemed that Pan American had an uncanny knack for already knowing where the routes were going to be offered, and for sewing up the local political and logistical support, including landing rights, necessary to make the routes immediately feasible and successful.

The next two routes awarded to Pan American were (1) from Havana to the Mexican island of Cozumel, then down Central America to Panama, and (2) from Havana to San Juan, Puerto Rico which suddenly increased Pan American's annual airmail revenues from $160,000 to $2 million. Passenger service was then initiated on February 4, 1929, with Lindbergh at the controls flying the 100-mile per hour S-38. With the first flying boats, service was commenced directly between Miami and Panama. (See Figures 15-12 and 15-13.) These two lucrative routes were soon followed by a third, from Miami to Mexico City, where linkups were made to the West Coast of the United States. Airmail revenues soon topped $3 million a year.

Airmail routes in the Caribbean, Central America and South America were consistently awarded only to Pan American in what was becoming the obvious policy of the United States government of allowing Pan American to be the 'Chosen Instrument' of U.S. foreign influence. This was despite the emergence of another American formed airline, the New York, Rio and Buenos Aires Airways (NYRBA), which began a head-on competition with Pan American in the region utilizing flying boats.

While Pan American went with the S-38, NYRBA ordered 14 of the Consolidated Commodore (see Figure 15-14), an amphibian designed as a patrol boat for the United States

FIGURE 15-11   Igor Sikorsky and Eddie Musick.

FIGURE 15-10   S-38.

FIGURE 15-12   Charles Lindbergh and S-38 in Miami.

Navy, but which was converted to commercial use by September 1929. The Commodore mounted two 575 horsepower Hornet engines beneath its high wing. It was put into service on the Miami to Santiago, Chile route down the west coast of South America, a 9000-mile route requiring seven days enroute. It was also used on the east coast route to Buenos Aires.

Big names associated with NYRBA, like James Rand (of Remington Rand), former Assistant Secretary of Commerce for Aeronautics William McCracken and William J. Donovan (credited with forming the Central Intelligence Agency), were unable by the middle of 1930 to secure even one foreign U.S. airmail contract. The airline was losing money on a then gargantuan scale ($50,000 a month) and, without help from the government, its backers saw no alternative to a sellout. On August 19, 1930, Pan American, with unofficial Post Office approval, bought out the NYRBA line. The next day, the post office department advertised the east coast of South America airmail route. Pan American, of course, was the only bidder and it bid the maximum allowable rate.

By 1930, Pan Am was flying 20,000 route miles to 20 different countries, and it was still within the Western Hemisphere. (See Figure 15-15.) Trippe was obviously the American government's "fair haired child," but his efforts at establishing transatlantic service were continuously thwarted by the British. Although the British agreed in principle with the proposition of bilateral rights between America and England, the standing position was that they were not physically or financially ready, and until they were, no American rights would be granted. Europe was not considered a feasible destination without landing rights in Bermuda, and since that island was strictly English, no European schedules of any sort were considered possible. Trippe turned his attention to the Pacific.

The range, in miles, of available aircraft was the most severely limiting factor in attempting a traverse of the vast Pacific Ocean. Sikorsky was the first to complete an aircraft design that attempted to address this problem, the S-40 flying boat. (See Figures 15-16 through 15-18.) This model boasted four engines, had a capacity of 44 passengers, and a range of 1,000 miles. The first S-40 was delivered to Pan American on October 10, 1931, and was christened by Mrs. Herbert Hoover at the Annapolis Naval Air Station. She broke a bottle of Caribbean seawater across the prow of the S-40,

FIGURE 15-13 Charles Lindbergh and S-38.

FIGURE 15-14 The Consolidated Commodore was originally designed as a patrol boat for the United States Navy, but was converted to commercial use by September 1929.

FIGURE 15-15   Pan American airways route map 1933.

FIGURE 15-16   The S-40 was the first aircraft to address the problem of range over the vast Pacific Ocean.

after which Juan Trippe dubbed the airplane a Pan American "Flagship." Thus was the appellation "Clipper" born.

Shortly thereafter, the S-42 (see Figures 15-19 and 15-20), with a range of 2,520 miles, came off

the line. This was still a bit short for the 2,410 mile San Francisco-to-Honolulu run, if any reserve of fuel for weather or other contingencies were to be made. Trippe turned to Glenn Martin for help, while at the same time flying the S-42 configured with extra fuel tanks to assure another 500 miles.

With Lindbergh's help, it was Trippe's plan that the Pacific would be conquered by way of Alaska, Japan, China, and points south, the kind of Great Circle route Lindbergh had used in 1927 to Paris. No airmail contract had been awarded to Pan Am, but Trippe was proceeding anyway. He bagged a majority interest in an airline with operating rights in China called the China National Aviation Corporation, but then, in 1934, Japan was becoming militarily aggressive, and the U.S. State Department advised against the proposed route. To go straight across the Pacific would require a route including Honolulu, Midway, Wake Island, and Guam before reaching Manila, Philippines. Aside from the fact that the Sikorsky aircraft was limited in range, there were absolutely no facilities on Midway, Wake, or Guam.

In typical fashion, Trippe had a freighter loaded with the necessary equipment, supplies, workmen, and supervisors and dispatched it to each of the proposed landing sites to construct the necessary passenger and aircraft support facilities, including terminals and hotels. With this service archipelago in place, and with landing rights in Hong Kong, Pan American was poised to be the first transpacific airline with service from the American to the Chinese coast.

In October 1935, the first M-130 Martin flying boat was delivered (the first of three). (See Figures 15-22 through 15-24.) This craft was larger than any other flying at the time. It had a range of 4,000 miles configured for mail and 3,200 miles with 12 passengers, a cruising speed of 163 miles per hour and redundant hydraulic and electrical systems. With the airmail contract secured, service was inaugurated for mail and cargo delivery on November 22, 1935, in a ceremony at the dock in San Francisco attended by

FIGURE 15-17 S-40. Approaching Pan Am's Dinner Key Terminal, FL.

FIGURE 15-18 S-40. Taking off from Biscayne Bay, FL.

Postmaster General Farley. In October 1936, with the support facilities now in place, passenger service across the Pacific Ocean began to Manila. A New Zealand route followed after Australia was blocked by the British, and then a second, southern transpacific route was initiated via Kingman Reef and Pago Pago. On April 21, 1937, the transpacific route was extended to Hong Kong, with connecting flights to destinations in China serviced by the Pan Am subsidiary, China National Aviation Corporation. Then, within a six-month period, December 1937 to the summer of 1938, Pan American suffered two highly publicized clipper accidents that brought unaccustomed criticism, both from the press and from government quarters. Chief Pilot Eddie Musick, who had surveyed the original Latin American routes ten years before, was at the controls of an S-40 off of Somoa when it exploded in midair. In July 1938, one of the three Martin 130 Clippers disappeared between the Philippines and Guam. The intense expansion of routes over the Pacific

FIGURE 15-19   The S-42 had a range of 2,520 miles.

Source: Florida State Archives.

FIGURE 15-20   S-42.

Source: Florida State Archives.

was taking a heavy toll and, while Pan Am banked over $1 million in profits from Latin American operations in 1938, it was losing large sums of money in the Pacific. Trippe turned his energies back to the Atlantic.

On February 22, 1937, the British Air Ministry issued Pan Am a permit to operate a regular air service between the United Kingdom and the United States via intermediate points in Canada, Bermuda, Ireland, and Portugal. The agreement by Pan Am to pool passengers and

cargo with the British airline, Imperial Airways, had a lot to do with this breakthrough. Technological advances, however, followed shortly on the heels of diplomacy. On order from Pan American since 1936, Boeing in 1938 produced its B-314 clipper (see Figure 15-25), the largest aircraft to be used in scheduled service then or thereafter until the arrival of the jumbo jets of the late 1960s. This airplane was configured in two decks, had a speed of 193 miles per hour and a range of 3,500 miles, enough range to

FIGURE 15-21 S-43—on glassy water.

FIGURE 15-22 In October 1935 the First M-130 Martin Flying Boat was delivered.

FIGURE 15-23 M-130 and Commodore at Dinner Key Terminal.

allow Pan American to fly right over Bermuda enroute to Europe. It carried 74 passengers seated or 40 passengers in the sleeping berth configuration. The Clipper went into the Pacific route service on February 22, 1939. (See Figures 15-26 and 15-27.)

In the Atlantic, Pan American launched its passenger service between New York and Marseille, France, on June 28, 1939 with the Dixie Clipper, a Boeing 314A, followed on

July 8, 1939, by Yankee Clipper service from New York to Southampton.

Summary of Airlines' Condition

The effects of the Great Depression were lessening by 1938. The economy was recovering, jobs were being restored, and manufacturing was picking up, including in the aircraft industry.

Source: Florida State Archives.

FIGURE 15-24 M-130 at Dinner Key.

Source: Florida State Archives.

FIGURE 15-25 The B-314 Was the largest aircraft to be used in scheduled service until the arrival of jumbo jets in the late 1960s.

Although the airlines' income from airmail carriage was down from what it had been before 1934, passenger revenues were up and exceeded airmail revenue for the first time. Airlines began to expand their passenger facilities and corporate infrastructure, and their traffic and sales departments. The airline industry was beginning to have an impact on the public and on the economy. As the government lost more control over the airlines because of the lessening effects of airmail revenue, and as the airlines began to develop passenger traffic and revenue, it was

FIGURE 15-26 Inside Pan Am's Dinner Key Terminal.

Source: Florida State Archives.

FIGURE 15-27 Passengers boarding a Pan Am flight for an adventure.

Source: Florida State Archives.

time for the government to put into effect some kind of comprehensive control of the industry. The situation was not unlike that of the railroad industry with the Interstate Commerce Act of 1887, or the trucking and bus industry in the Motor Carrier Act of 1935, except for one thing: The airlines wanted regulation.

Endnotes

1. Pacific Air Transport v. U.S.; Boeing Air Transport v. U.S.; United Airline Transport Corporation v. U.S., 98 Ct. Cl. 649 (1942).

2. The Monroe Doctrine was first expressed by President James Monroe in the State of the Union address to Congress on December 2, 1823. According to this policy, the American continents (North and South America, and including Central America) were to be henceforth free of any further colonization attempts by any European power. This statement of American national interest implied the use of American military and economic power in its enforcement. International adventures by Spain and Portugal triggered this policy.

CHAPTER 16

The Civil Aeronautics Act of 1938 (McCarran-Lea Act)

© egd, 2008, Shutterstock, Inc.

Since 1926, what little regulation the government had imposed on the aviation community had been administered by the Department of Commerce, specifically the Aeronautics Branch first and then the Bureau of Air Commerce beginning in 1934. In the meantime, flying had progressed from mail planes constructed of wood and wire with open cockpits to all metal stress skinned monoplanes flying in instrument conditions at speeds over three times that of early aircraft. In the middle 1930s, flying was still something of an adventure, for navigation facilities were primitive, instruments rudimentary, and weather prognostication an immature art form.

The TWA crash of the Fokker trimotor in 1931 that killed Knute Rockne was the most notorious domestic airline crash until the death of Senator Bronson Cutting on May 6, 1935, aboard another TWA airplane, a DC-2 on a transcontinental flight from Los Angeles to Newark. Cutting boarded the aircraft at Albuquerque, N.M., where it was reported that the plane's radio transmitter was faulty. The weather at Kansas City, which had been predicted to be good, had deteriorated to a ceiling of six hundred feet, one hundred feet below minimums, by the time of the flight's arrival in the area. Unable to communicate or to make the appropriate instrument approach, and with fuel low, the DC-2 crashed while attempting to fly visually at tree top level.

Senator Cutting was much beloved in the Senate. The congressional investigation of the crash centered on the Department of Commerce and its administration of aviation safety. It was determined that the Department had been lax in enforcing what few rules were in place. Then a controversy arose between the Department and TWA as to whether the 45-minute fuel reserve rule had even been properly published, or whether TWA was otherwise notified of the rule. There were questions of conflict of interest over the Department of Commerce investigating itself concerning the adequacy of existing rules and their enforcement. The Department was shown to have a propensity for laying blame on the pilot in command, a tendency, some may argue, that continues to this day. The press stirred the pot well, and the public reaction ranged from a loss of confidence in the system to outrage. The sense of the Congress was that the Department of Commerce had failed to keep pace with the ongoing progress of commercial aviation.

Then, on October 7, 1935, a United Airlines crash near Denver killed twelve people. On April 7, 1936, another TWA DC-2 crashed in Pennsylvania with twelve more fatalities. On August 6, 1936, a Chicago & Southern Lockheed went down in St. Louis with fatalities of all eight aboard, and on February 10, 1937, a DC-3 flown by United Airlines crashed in San Francisco and all eleven on board were lost. The winter of 1937, in fact, recorded five airline crashes with fatalities.

The airlines took it upon themselves to develop operating rules and regulations for the governance of their pilots, still a rather undisciplined lot, and who looked upon flying as another form of freedom, not restriction. The management of the airlines understood that, in order to win the confidence of the public and take their place as a legitimate form of public transportation that could compete with the railroads, order must be brought to the rather free-form society of aviation, up to that time primarily known for its airmail deliveries and stunt pilots.

In 1935, the airlines knew that someone had to control the growing number of airplanes plying the skies, particularly where they converged for landing, like in Newark, New Jersey. Newark Airport had a departure or an arrival every ten minutes. It was American Airlines that took the lead in designating a "boss," someone in charge who could direct planes to maintain separation by altitude, primarily, as they approached for landing. An agreement between six airlines created a company known as Air Traffic Control, Inc., and it was manned by employees of those companies.

The first facility was set up at Newark, (see Figure 16-1) followed by others in Chicago and Cleveland. At first, the controllers sought to track flights within fifty miles of the controlled airport, using blackboards, a large table map, a telephone, and a Teletype. Flight plans were filed by departing pilots who would then keep in contact with their company's radio operator, relaying their position at designated waypoints with their speed and altitude. This information would then be telephoned to the center guarding the destination airport, and the airplane's position would be marked using brass weights that were moved along the table map to represent the airplane's progress. When an aircraft approached one of the staffed centers, directions to the

FIGURE 16-1 The beginnings of air traffic control—Earl Ward (left) organized the Newark, New Jersey air traffic facility in the mid-1930's. Here he tracks a flight with the aid of a calipar as R. A. Eccles watches. The pointed markers representing aircraft were moved across the map as flights progressed.

Source: FAA.

incoming airplane would be issued by the controller to the airline's radio operator by telephone, who would then radio the pilot of the incoming airplane to descend to a certain altitude, to hold at the beacon, or that he was cleared for the approach.

The authority of the controllers was debatable, particularly among the more independent pilots who were used to doing things their own way and in their own time. It was at first considered by the pilots that the controllers' directions to them were advisory only, not mandatory, so that a direction to hold while another aircraft landed might or might not be honored. With air traffic control being taken over by the Commerce Department's Bureau of Lighthouses in 1936, procedures at last began to change. Discipline and self-control were becoming as much a requirement of good piloting technique as airspeed and altitude.

The regulations governing aircraft control adopted by the Commerce Department were actually not known to all airlines and pilots,

" Before take-off, a professional pilot is keen, anxious, but lest someone read his true feelings he is elaborately casual. The reason for this is that he is about to enter a new though familiar world. The process of entrance begins a short time before he leaves the ground and is completed the instant he is in the air. From that moment on, not only his body but his spirit and personality exist in a separate world known only to himself and his comrades. **"**

Ernest K. Gann, foreword to *Island in the Sky*

since they were not required to be published in the Federal Register, a publication whose purpose it was to advise of the adoption of agency regulations. The Supreme Court case of **Panama Refining Co. v. Ryan**[1] established the proposition that, in order to be binding, a regulation must be published in the Federal Register as notice to all concerned. The next year, 1937, saw the first codification of regulations promulgated by the federal government. They came to be known as the Civil Air Regulations. Not only did these first regulations establish rules governing the movement of airplanes within the designated airspace, they required, for the first time, that the airlines themselves draw up a detailed operations manual, approved by the government, containing procedures for that airline regarding weather, minimum altitudes, approach, departure, and enroute procedures. These Department of Commerce regulations did not apply to airport control towers, however, which remained under local city control until just before the United States entered World War II.

Standardization of aircraft procedures was only one aspect of the emerging airline industry that the airlines felt needed the steady hand of government control. Passenger traffic and airmail carriage had tripled since Black-McKellar, but the airlines were still suffering financially and had, in fact, all lost money each and every year since 1934. The airlines formed their own group, the Air Transport Association, and one of its first acts was to drum up support for and draft a bill creating federal rate and route regulation designed to stabilize the airline industry. The airline industry was demanding to be regulated.

The statute passed by Congress on June 23, 1938, provided a uniform basis of regulation for aviation in the United States and created three independent agencies to discharge the statute's mandate: the Civil Aeronautics Authority, the Administrator of Aviation, and the Air Safety Board. Although control of aviation matters had been removed from the Department of Commerce, with direct reporting to the President, there was a significant degree of overlapping authority among the three agencies. Almost immediately friction developed among the agencies, causing the President to order an investigation into the problems created under the new setup. Within a period of two years from its passage, the Civil Aeronautics Act was amended to resolve the situation inadvertently created by the legislation. Known as the 1940 Amendment to the Civil Aeronautics Act, it dissolved the three agencies originally created by the Act and redistributed their functions between two new agencies that would administer the Act for the next twenty years:

➡ the Civil Aeronautics Board (CAB) and

➡ the Civil Aeronautics Administration (CAA).

The CAB was established as an independent board of five individuals, who reported directly to the President, and whose function was primarily to exercise control over air carrier economic regulation, such as rates, routes, and mergers. The CAB was also given the responsibility to investigate aircraft accidents and for safety rulemaking.

The CAA was created as an agency, headed by an administrator, which was placed back within the Department of Commerce. Responsibility for all non-military aviation safety programs, air traffic control, and airway development now was assumed by the CAA. Enforcement became much more stringent, the rules now requiring pilots to obey the controller's instructions. Training centers were established to educate would-be controllers and to standardize their training. Coordination of all controllers followed, with towers and enroute centers falling under the CAA umbrella. The diminishing number of aircraft accidents reflected the wisdom of the new policy, and the public took note.

The Act also provided that anyone wishing to operate an airline business in interstate commerce would be required to apply for and receive a Certificate of Convenience and Necessity, the issuance of which would depend on the results of an appropriate review of the applicant's financial and experience qualifications and hearings conducted by the CAB to determine whether the granting of such an entry into the brotherhood of air carriers was in the public interest. The Act provided a Grandfather clause for all airlines that had provided adequate and continuous airmail service from May 14 to August 22, 1938. In 1938, there were sixteen such carriers in the United States and all of them were granted permanent Certificates of Public Convenience and Necessity to continue operations. But in all of the next forty years, the CAB would not grant entry to another major airline.

Endnote

1. 298 U.S. 388, 55 S.Ct. 241, 79 L.Ed 446 (1935).

CHAPTER 17

World War II

© Dan Barnes, 2008,
Shutterstock, Inc.

A year after the Civil Aeronautics Act was passed, Hitler invaded Poland to start World War II. Germany, Italy, and Japan comprised the Axis powers arrayed against the Allied forces which were to consist mainly of Great Britain, the United States, the U.S.S.R., Canada, Australia, and the various governments in exile of the conquered countries, notably France. Commercial aviation and aircraft manufacturing would be almost completely devoted to the war effort.

The United States did not immediately enter the war for reasons more fully discussed below. The inertia of pre-war planning for commercial aircraft carried on into 1939 and beyond. Howard Hughes by 1939 was well ensconced as the moving force behind TWA. He had countermanded the stop order on the pressurized Boeing 307 and five of the Stratoliners had been delivered to the airline. But he had bigger plans—plans that would create one of the most impressive airline shapes in the history of commercial aviation. They called it the Constellation.

Hughes knew that Douglas was working on the airplane that was to become the DC-4, and he knew that it was to be unpressurized and subject to the limitations of low altitude flight, particularly weather. On his first transcontinental flight in the H-1 racer in 1935, he had used oxygen to allow flight at higher altitudes, in more favorable winds, and out of most of the weather. Boeing had already produced its first version of a pressurized plane and was committed to the basic design reflected in the B-17 and the commercial, pressurized version in the B-307. Hughes approached Lockheed with the proposal that they design and build the world's fastest, high performance airplane, and that TWA would buy it. Hughes insisted on secrecy, believing that his specifications to Lockheed would produce an airplane that would give TWA a great advantage over the competition.

A young designer-engineer by the name of Kelly Johnson, who was to become a legend as the brains behind such super secret military projects as the U-2 and SR-71 spy planes developed in the famed Lockheed "Skunk Works" in later years, took on the assignment of the design, development and production of the Connie. He and the other designers at Lockheed agreed to Hughes's terms, including the requirement that TWA would get the first forty planes off the line, and that there be absolute secrecy. The deal was made with Hughes Tool Company, not TWA, both to ensure secrecy and because of the fact that Hughes Tool had the money. The project was begun, drawings were prepared, reviewed, revised, and by 1941 about one-half of the original prototype was done.

The war in Europe and Japan's military occupation of Korea, Manchuria, and parts of China caused the War Department to survey U.S. airplane manufacturers' plants with a view to ascertaining production levels in the event of the United States being brought into the hostilities. The Constellation design was thus disclosed. The war atmosphere had also caused the United States to create the War Production Board, whose job was to allocate the industrial and manufacturing resources of the country in a way to best ensure its defense and guarantee the production of essential goods. This higher cause was understood by all concerned, including the secretive Hughes, and by agreement it was determined that Pan American would participate in the Constellation project. Pan Am was the only international air carrier for the United States, and it was not a competitor of TWA. Further, Pan American had the international experience, the routes, the landing rights, and the foreign contacts that could make the best and highest use of the Connie's range and speed. Thus amended, the project went ahead under the auspices of the War Production Board.

The complexity and relatively difficult design shape of the Connie caused General Hap Arnold to stop production of the airplane numerous times during the next two years, in favor of the simpler and relatively inexpensive DC-4. The Connie would not actually fly until December 1943. After the first Connie was rolled out of the Burbank, California plant, as a part of its test flight regimen Howard Hughes and Jack Frye would fly it to Washington, D.C. in a new record time of under seven hours, nonstop.

The Connie would not contribute in any significant way to the war effort. The other four-engine aircraft, the DC-4, would. The DC-4 was a Douglas creation begun in the 1930s on orders from American Airlines and United for domestic service. It was the first production airliner with tricycle landing gear and, with the exception of the five Boeing 307 Stratoliners in service, was the first serious transoceanic aircraft to come available. It came available just as the United States had to have that very type of airplane, and it would fly in 1942. The airplanes came off the production line as the C-54 and some 1,162 of them were built for the military. The first ones did not go to the airlines that ordered them, but to their competitor, TWA, which was flying the southern transatlantic route to Africa for the military. During the war, these planes would log over a million miles a month over the Atlantic, some 20 sorties every day.

The Lend Lease Act

The United States did not immediately enter the war in Europe, partly because of the experience of World War I, and partly because of the geographical fact that two great oceans separated America from the hostilities being conducted in Europe and Asia. The country was politically and emotionally divided between those who favored involvement and those called "isolationists," one of whom was the most prominent man in the world of aviation, Charles A. Lindbergh. Sentiment ran high against becoming once again embroiled in "Europe's wars," which seemed to recur on a more or less regular basis and had done so since time immemorial. On the other hand, England, as the last hope of Western Civilization, stood alone against the totalitarian, fascist Nazi (NSDP) party of Germany. Germany, by 1940, had conquered virtually the entire European continent. A non-aggression pact between Russia and Germany had been concluded in 1939, protecting Germany's eastern flank, and the "Battle of England" raged in the skies over Great Britain between the Luftwaffe and the badly outnumbered Royal Air Force. German submarines prowled the Atlantic unchallenged, conducting unrestricted warfare, sinking prodigious amounts of tonnage of shipping and menacing the ships of the Royal Navy. Supplies, planes, and ships were running low for the forces of freedom, but the United States was diplomatically neutral.

England and the United States were historically bound together—by language, by culture, by common law—and England was calling on the United States, on President Roosevelt, for help. The Roosevelt administration was spiritually and emotionally with the British, and many believed that the defeat of Britain would be tantamount to a defeat of American interests worldwide. Slowly at first, but with increasing resolve, the United States began giving aid, comfort, and supplies to England. None of this was authorized by law. As debate swirled within the country, the country moved ahead with its aid plans without publicity.

The first planes supplied to England, seven Lockheed Hudson twin-engine bombers, were ferried via Gander, Newfoundland, to Aldergrove, Ireland on November 10, 1940, followed by some additional 30 aircraft that winter. On March 11, 1941, the supplying of material became legal with the passage of the Lend-Lease Act, which empowered the President "on behalf of any country whose defense the President deems vital to the defense of the United States, to sell, transfer title to, exchange, lease, lend, or otherwise dispose of, to any such government any defense article . . . not expressly prohibited." The United States, now legally empowered to do so, began wartime production of defense material and provided it to China, Russia, and to 35 other nations. TWA, the only airline with land-based four-engine aircraft, at government direction set up a training center in New Mexico for instructing American and British pilots how to fly the four engine bombers, the B-24 and the B-17. (TWA had purchased the new Boeing Stratoliner, the 307, in 1940. The 307 was the first pressurized airplane flown by any air carrier in domestic service.) Pan American also contributed to four engine training. (See Figure 17-1.)

The Army Air Corps formed a ferrying service to deliver aircraft to England and to shuttle ferry pilots back to North America. The industrial capacity of the United States was about to be tapped, and a mighty force it would prove to be.

And then on December 7, 1941, all of the fence sitters on the issue of involvement in the European and Asian war were unseated as the Empire of Japan bombed the Naval and Army Air Force facilities at Pearl Harbor. War was declared on Japan by the United States the next day, then Germany and the other Axis Powers declared war on the United States. Global war was on.

The Chosen Instrument

As the sole American airline with operations overseas, Pan American became an important asset of the United States during World War II. Pan American operated flying boats, in part, because of the lack of airfields. Nevertheless, Pan Am had experience in building airfields in remote areas. Roosevelt had secured rights to bases on many of the islands of the Caribbean from the British. He now called upon Pan American to build airfields on these islands as a part of a larger plan to supply the war effort against Germany. Airports would be built down through the Caribbean to South America, along its east coast, for ferrying equipment and supplies across the Atlantic narrows to Africa. The British were engaging the Germans in North Africa, and North Africa would be the location of America's first military engagements in World War II. Although the United States paid for all of the airport construction (some $90 million), Pan American held title to these facilities initially for appearance purposes since the United States was diplomatically neutral prior to its entry into the war. After the war, negotiations caused these improvements to revert to the United States, but with limitations on their use by airlines other than Pan Am.

The Airlines at War

At the beginning of the war, there were only some 365 transport aircraft in the United States. The airplane manufacturing community would

Source: Florida State Archives.

FIGURE 17-1 Military airmen in training with Pan Am.

shortly begin to produce 50,000 aircraft a year, the largest manufacturing activity in the United States for the duration of the war, and at war's end over 300,000 airplanes would have been produced. America's main contribution was in production, not development, for the existing weapons of war were considered sufficient, at least in the short run, to win the war if only there were enough of them. The P-51 Mustang was the only new development in airplane technology supplied by the United States after the onset of war. All the others produced were pre-war designs, and even the P-51 had a British engine.

The main production effort was, of course, directed toward fighter and bomber aircraft, although over 10,000 DC-3s, designated for the military as C-47s, were built, along with over 1,000 DC-4s (as C-54s). America needed every bit of transport potential it could muster during the years 1941–1945, including railroads and as well as air carriers, and while the railroads enjoyed a resurgence of their former glory during these years, the air carriers came into their own for the first time. Aircrews flew everywhere, either as military or civilian to military or civilian airports, on domestic and overseas routes. Flying northern transatlantic routes became routine, as did South American routes to Africa.

Domestically, the airlines discovered after the onset of hostilities that they had only 165 airplanes to service their routes. The armed forces had commandeered the rest for military purposes. Travel space on the relatively few air carrier aircraft was allocated according to a government imposed "priority system":

→ Priority One was for persons traveling under the authority of the President

→ Priority Two got military pilots a seat

→ Priority Three was other military personnel or civilians on essential wartime business

→ Priority Four was military cargo.

The remaining seats, of which there were precious few, went to everyone else. The lexicon of future airline travel was being established too. "Standbys" were those who hoped a priority above them would become a "no-show" so that a seat would become available. To be "bumped" was to have a higher priority passenger show up to take your seat.

American air carriers began to make money for the first time since 1934, and although the high load factor of domestic commercial operations contributed to profitability, the main effort of the airlines during the war was as contract carriers for the military.

The government allocated the airlines' responsibility during the war in logical fashion. Northeast Airlines was given the North Atlantic route as far as Greenland and then Reykjavik, Iceland. Northwest was assigned to the Alaska route, Eastern to the Caribbean and Brazil. American flew to South America and, in the process, caused a radio range to be built along its route from the United States. TWA had its five Boeing 307s, the only four-engine land-based transoceanic aircraft available at the time, commandeered by the military and was given the transatlantic route to Egypt, the most significant long distance route of any airline except Pan American. TWA set up its transcontinental division immediately at the beginning of the war, no doubt with an eye on the postwar period. At first, TWA flew to Africa via the South American route, and later, after Portugal granted landing rights, via the much shorter North Atlantic route by way of Prestwick, Scotland. TWA flew military supplies and equipment, like the other airlines, but it was the preferred carrier for VIPs and, in fact, TWA carried President Roosevelt to the three wartime conferences with Churchill in Casablanca, Tehran, and Yalta.

It is not surprising perhaps, that Pan American, as the only overseas carrier in existence before the war, was counted on as the major civilian arm of the military during the war. Yet, it is noteworthy that Pan American's five divisions, the Alaskan, Pacific, North Atlantic, Caribbean and Africa-Orient, flew half of all contract miles flown by all airlines for the U.S. military. In the process, Pan American began flying landplanes instead of the flying boats that had been its trademark during its early years, thus marking the end of the romantic and adventurous era of the Pan American Clipper. The range and speed of the DC-4 and the airplanes to follow, the availability of the airports that Pan American and others had built around the world, and the relative maintenance costs and requirements of amphibious planes over landplanes sounded the death knell of the flying boat airliner, and Pan American never ordered another one.

Most of the flying done during World War II was not by the commercial airlines but by the military forces created and trained by the government. The exigencies of war, shown once again to be a mighty motivating force, had caused a great technological leap forward in aircraft, engines, and systems. The feats of the noncombat pilots of the military lift branches, some 25,000 of them, during the four-year duration of the war testify to the great advance in air transportation over that short span of time. Feats only imagined a mere four years before were now commonplace. Distances had been covered and heights had been overcome for the first time in the airborne delivery of personnel and goods that would henceforth be considered routine. There was a confidence born not only of victory, but also of accomplishment.

Contrasted to the unspeakable devastation visited on the landscapes and structures of Europe that had been created by the most advanced civilization for the better part of two millennia, the homeland of United States emerged from the war unscathed, and with the mighty industrial plants that had supplied the weapons and material of war intact. America had:

➡ The pilots
➡ The planes
➡ The know-how
➡ The international presence on the ground
➡ The financial structure and stability to lead the world into the postwar realms of commercial aviation.

A New Beginning

Before the war, air travel had begun to catch on, and in 1941 domestic airlines carried four million passengers. With the war over in 1945, air travel quickly picked up again, and by the end of 1945 the airlines had enplaned some 7.5 million passengers. In 1946, the number almost doubled to 12.5 million passengers. The commercial airline fleet before the war provided about 6,200 seats. By 1946, the airlines had tripled capacity to 19,000 available seats. The cost of airline travel had fallen enough to be competitive with first class railroad fares, and the four-hour plane ride between Chicago and New York offered a real choice for any time-sensitive traveler over the sixteen-hour railroad Pullman. It was a new day in commercial aviation.

The development of transport aircraft had progressed rapidly during the war. The expectation was that the pre-war traffic would be promptly reclaimed and then exponentially developed using the new era of airliners. Some of the aircraft were suited to expanding the first class travel begun in the 1930s, particularly on the transcontinental and transoceanic runs. Modern airlines of the postwar era were on the verge of entering the first class travel market long held by the steamship lines and the transcontinental Pullman trains. While it was true that some airlines using DC-3s had offered berths for sleeping on overnight flights, now airliners could fly much higher and faster, and in pressurized and air-conditioned comfort.

TWA launched transatlantic service on December 5, 1945, with a VIP flight to Paris that was completed in the record time of twelve hours and fifty-seven minutes. Pressurized, and with a cruise speed of 280 miles per hour, the Connie was ready to contribute to the anticipated revolution in transatlantic and transcontinental air travel.

The number of airports used by the airlines more than doubled between 1941 and 1947, from 2,484 to 5,343. Outside the terminals, new sleek aircraft for the first time took on the look of flying in place with their new tricycle landing gear. Interspersed among the ubiquitous DC-3s that appeared to be sitting back on their haunches, these new planes stood tall over them and gave an impression of progress, comfort, and safety. The airplanes were getting larger than the terminals in some places. Mass transit, facilitated by the big airliners, was about to begin.

The DC-4, which had been commandeered by the military upon its appearance in 1942, became available to the domestic fleet in 1946. (See Figure 18-1.) Unpressurized, seating 44 passengers and barely able to muster 200 miles per hour at cruise, the DC-4 was outclassed by the Connie, yet it became in the late 1940s the four-engine airplane of choice. Its service during the war had proved it to be safe

Source: Florida State Archives.

FIGURE 18-1 The DC-4 became available to the domestic fleet in 1946.

and reliable, something yet to be proved in the Constellation and other advanced aircraft emerging from the war. The tapered lines of the Constellation, its more complex systems, its three vertical stabilizers, and the number of parts required to be stored and available also caused it to be significantly more expensive to maintain than the DC-4. (See Figure 18-2.) The straight lines of the DC-4 proved to be much cheaper to repair, maintain, and to fly.

The availability of these new aircraft increased the airlines' capacity and brought with them options for airline management that had never before been possible. This may be the point in history that the concept of the passenger seat as a "grapefruit," as in a perishable commodity, was articulated as a marketing truism. Every unfilled seat at takeoff was like spoiled grapefruit for that flight; it was forever lost to use. Competitive management thinking recognized that high density seating brought with it pure profit after boarding enough passengers to cover costs.

The scheduled airlines were, and had always been, of one class, and that was first class. When comparisons were made between the airlines and the railroads as to cost, an airline seat was compared to a Pullman berth (these

accommodations were seats during day travel and were converted to beds for night travel). The high cost of air travel could be favorably compared to first class rail fares because of the time-distance advantage between comparable points enjoyed by the airlines.

After the war, the CAB began loosening the regulations that bound the air-traveling public to the scheduled airlines (first class service). This allowed aircraft charter, or as some called it, the nonscheduled lines, or "nonskeds." Using DC-3s and then DC-4s, these charter operators flew at off hours, at night, and most importantly, with full airplanes. Not bound to a schedule, these operators were not required to leave the terminal at any particular time. Their schedule was simply dictated by the passenger count. And passengers flocked to them. Soon the nonskeds were going coast to coast and at prices that were thirty percent less than the scheduled airlines. They did the same thing on some international routes, notably to Puerto Rico.

Pan Am's official name had been changed in 1945 from Pan American Airways to Pan American World Airways. Juan Trippe was again ahead of the game and ready for the postwar contest. He saw that by seating five abreast in the DC-4, the passenger count could increase from 44 to 63. But the question remained in what market such a configuration could be put to use. And fares would certainly have to be reduced in order to induce anyone to put up with such crowding. Here, Juan Trippe was about thirty years ahead of his time, ahead of the day of deregulation that would come in 1978.

In 1948, Pan American began flying DC-4s from New York to San Juan, Puerto Rico. Puerto Rico was a relatively impoverished island, and most of its inhabitants could not afford expensive travel of either kind, ship or plane. The low standard of living in Puerto Rico and its mortality rate combined to provide motivation to some people to leave the country. Pan Am tapped this large market for mass air transit in the newly configured DC-4, which had no galley and only

Source: Library of Congress.

FIGURE 18-2 The Constellation was much more expensive to maintain than other comparable aircraft.

one flight attendant. Any Puerto Rican with $75 was given the opportunity to begin a new life in New York, which had a Puerto Rican population of seventy thousand at that time. By 1950, there would be two hundred and fifty thousand Puerto Rican residents in New York City. By 1975, five million of the island's former residents would have migrated to the United States.

Domestically, the airlines were losing money to the nonskeds, so they petitioned the CAB for authority to operate a second class of service. "Air coach," as it was called, was introduced by the scheduled airlines in 1948. Some of the crews began to refer to the new passengers as "cattle class." The airlines saw that they could compete with the railroads, not just for first class passengers, but also for coach passengers. Capital Airlines became the first established carrier to offer "coach-class" service, inaugurated on the New York–Chicago route. At a fare of two-thirds

the standard, there were few complaints of overcrowding, late night departures, or the lack of a meal service. TWA and American followed suit with their transcontinental service. By the end of 1951, nine domestic carriers offered coach or tourist class service to 34 cities. In 1952, fares were $99 coast-to-coast; $32 between Chicago and New York. Airline passenger traffic doubled in the five years between 1948 and 1952. By 1955, the airlines had passed the railroads for the first time in the number of passengers carried.

For a while the "coach" or "tourist" class flights operated as separate airplanes both domestically and internationally. The smaller international carriers complained to the International Air Transport Association (IATA) that they could not compete with larger airlines since they did not possess the necessary number of aircraft to operate both first class and tourist class airplanes. When IATA authorized them to operate their equipment carrying both first class and tourist in the same airplane, the modern form of aircraft configuration was born. TWA was the first to begin domestic operations with both fare classes on the same airplane after CAB approval.

A new group of air carrier, known collectively as local service lines or feeder lines, completed their first full year of service in 1946. While the CAB would not expand the total num-ber of trunk airlines beyond the sixteen that were grandfathered under the Civil Aeronautics Act of 1938, these smaller carriers received authority to operate on short routes to some 350 small cities. The average distance flown between stops was about 60 miles, and some of the communities served had populations of as few as 3000 people. By the end of 1951, there were 18 local service airlines operating 130 airplanes.

		(Selected Years)							
		1940		**1945**		**1948** 1/		***1949** 1/	
	No. of Engines	**No. Planes**	**Av. Mi. Per Day**	**No. Planes**	**Av. Mi. Per Day**	**No. Planes**	**Av. Mi. Per Day**	**No. Planes**	**Av. Mi. Per Day**
Beechcraft	2	—	—	0.8	66	6.5	219	—	—
Boeing									
247-D	2	34.9	468	—	—	0.8	800	—	—
SA-307B	4	3.1	1,354	3.6	2,094	5.0	1,326	5.0	1,306
377	4	—	—	—	—	—	—	7.0	306
Consolidated-Vultee									
Convair	2	—	—	—	—	9.3	907	92.0	834
Douglas									
DC-2	2	42.2	715	—	—	—	—	—	—
DC-3	2	145.2	1,198	314.4	1,756	429.2	1,194	404.0	898
DST	2	38.6	1,569	—	—	—	—	—	—
DC-4	4	—	—	—	—	155.0	1,317	158.0	947
DC-6	4	—	—	—	—	46.3	1,825	104.0	1,626
Lockheed									
Electra	2	33.8	58.3	1.3	727	—	—	—	—
Lodestar	2	4.4	661	17.7	1,545	12.0	258	11.0	909
Constelation	4	—	—	—	—	30.9	1,828	51.0	1,688
Sikorsky	2	6.0	203	2.0	184	—	—	—	—
Stinson									
Single Motor	1	—	—	10.9	404	7.0	439	—	—
Tri-motored	3	2.0	109	4.0	61	—	—	—	—
Martin 202	2	—	—	—	—	15.4	843	24.0	1,107
Curtiss 46	2	—	—	—	—	2.0	73	2.0	129

*1/includes local service and territorial lines. 1949 data for 10 months only.

FIGURE 18-3 General aircraft utilization domestic airlines.

LESS TIME TO CROSS THE CONTINENT

1858
Mail Coach
and Rail

1861
Pony Express
and Rail

1869
First
Transcontinental
Train

1921
First
All-Air Mail

1929
First Air-Rail
Passenger Service

1944
Regular
Air-Passenger
Service

☐ = 24 hrs.

The Continent Grows Smaller

Coast to Coast

1840	The ox-drawn Covered Wagon	6 to 8 months
1846	Sailing vessels around the Horn	6 1/2 months
1849	Steam vessels around the Horn	4 1/2 months
1858	Overland mail coaches and rail	24–30 days
1861	Pony Express and rail	11–13 days
1869	First transcontinental train	7 days
1903	First transcontinental automobile trip	61 days
1911	First transcontinental airplane trip Calbraith P. Rodgers: Sheepshead Bay, L. I. to Pasadena, California	49 days
1919	First transcontinental round trip by air: Lt. Belvin W. Maynard	9 days 4 hours 25 min.
1920	First air-rail mail: New York–San Francisco	72 hours
1921	First all-air mail: San Francisco–New York	33 hours 20 min.
1923	First non-stop coast-to-coast flight: Lts. John A. Macready and Oakley Kelly New York–San Diego, May 2–3	26 hours 50 min.
1924	Fastest transcontinental railroad trip	69 hours 7 min.
	Standard transcontinental railroad trip	87 hours
	Regular air mail, day and night schedule	32 hours
	First dawn-to-dusk coast-to-coast flight: Col. Russell L. Maughan,New York–San Francisco, June 23	21 hours 44 min.
1927	First coast-to-coast commercial air passengers: New York–San Francisco	31 hours 45 min.
1929	Round-trip record by Frank Hawks: New York–Los Angeles	19 hours 10 min.
	Los Angeles–New York	17 hours 38 min.
	First air-rail passenger service	48 hours
1930	New round-trip record by Frank Hawks: Los Angeles–New York, August 12	14 hours 50 min.
	New York–Los Angeles, August 15	12 hours 25 min.
1931	Record by Jimmy Doolittle: Burbank–Newark, September 4	11 hours 15 min.
1933	Regular coast-to-coast air passenger, mail, and express schedule	19 hours 35 min.
1934	Jack Frye and E. V. Rickenbacker in regular commercial transport plane: Los Angeles–Newark, February 18–19	13 hours 4 min.
	Jack Frye with mail: Los Angeles–New York, May 8	11 hours 30 min.
1935	Record by Leland S. Andrews and H. B. Snead: Los Angeles–Washington, February 20	10 hours 22 min.
1937	Record by Howard Hughes: Los Angeles–New York, January 19	7 hours 28 min. 25 sec.
1938	Westbound record by A. P. DeSeversky: Brooklyn–Burbank, August 29	10 hours 2 min. 55 sec.
1943	Regular schedule for passengers, mail, express	16 hours
1944	New record by Howard Hughes and 17 passengers in transport plane: Burbank–Washington, April 17	6 hours 57 min. 51 sec.
1945	Regular extra fare service: New York–Los Angeles	14 hours 35 min.
	Record in transport plane: Seattle–Washington, January 10	6 hours 3 min. 50 sec.

FIGURE 18-4. Less time to cross the continent.

CHAPTER 19

On the Way to the Jet Age

© Alex Staroseltsev, 2008, Shutterstock.

> **❝** To put your life in danger from time to time . . . breeds a saneness in dealing with day-to-day trivialities. **❞**
>
> **Nevil Shute, *Slide Rule: The Autobiography of an Engineer***

The last of the big airliners mounting reciprocating engines on their wings were stretched versions of the airliners that had gone before. The DC-6 and the DC-7 were from the DC-4 model with various refinements to go along with the increase in length, breadth, and power. The Super Constellation was 19 feet longer than the original. With increased length came additional seating and with more seating came more revenue. Range was extended so that non-stop service was possible—not only coast-to-coast but transatlantic.

The DC-6 was launched in coast-to-coast service on April 27, 1947, with one stop enroute for fuel. United advertised its service as ten hours total. (See Figure 19-1.) TWA's Constellations could do about the same, advertised as ten hours ten minutes.

Boeing, a late entry to the new postwar aircraft building party, in 1948 introduced the double-decked B-377 Stratocruiser, a four-engine landplane larger than either the DC-6 or Constellation and designed with an emphasis on

luxury reminiscent of the Pan Am Clippers. The airplane featured two decks with a cocktail lounge with leather seating located below, accessible by a curved stairway, and with a honeymoon suite in the aft section. Take off performance in the Stratocruiser was marginal, with the DC-6 routinely outperforming it, but it was bigger and faster at 340 miles per hour than any other airliner. It was also expensive, costing over $1.5 million, and its high operation costs did not help matters. It had engine problems (the P & W Wasp Major had 112 spark plugs in 28 cylinders and delivered 3,500 horsepower) and the propellers had a tendency to go flying off on their own. Still, these airplanes were the ultimate in passenger comfort. New York to London was a pleasant affair of 12 hours duration, including cocktails, a five-course dinner, a good night's sleep, and plenty of attention. But the Stratocruiser had the worst safety record of the postwar big planes; six were involved in fatal crashes with the loss of 108 passengers and 28 crew. United unloaded their Stratocruisers early; Northwest kept theirs for years. In the end, the airlines seemed glad to see them go. Figure 19-2 pictures the Boeing 377, the Constellation 049, and the DC-4.

The DC-7 proved to be the first true transatlantic airplane, flying either west or east with a

Source: Florida State Archives.

FIGURE 19-1 The DC-6 was launched in coast-to-coast service on April 27, 1947 with one stop enroute for fuel.

full load. With it, Pan American regained its leadership position over TWA, which was flying the Super Constellation. The DC-7 had engines that were reaching the limits of reciprocating engine power possibilities. With four Wright turbo-compound engines providing 3,250 horsepower, each weighing over 3,500 pounds, engine maintenance was a problem; American Airlines reported 10 engine failures a day on average. Westbound DC-7 service to the Pacific coast was advertised as non-stop, but with headwinds the advertised flying time of seven and one-half hours was often missed. Eastbound, American was able to adhere to its scheduled arrivals. The DC-7 made the first non-stop transatlantic crossing in 1957.

But the strain was showing; the limits of the reciprocating engine had been reached. It was time for the jet age.

Jets

It has been said that World War II advanced the airplane by fifty years. Yet it can also be accurately stated that there were really only two revolutionary technological advances to come out of the war—radar and the jet engine—and America had nothing to do with either. Not only were the Americans a bit slow at the beginning, they were even slower at appreciating how great a leap the jet engine represented in the potential for air commerce. This was demonstrated by the reluctance of American aircraft manufacturers and air carriers to pursue jet engine potential after the war.

The idea of turbine engines first manifested itself in England before the turn of the 20th century, when Charles Parsons developed a steam turbine that he applied to the generation of electric energy. He thereafter built a 100-foot vessel,

FIGURE 19-2 Boeing 377, Constellation 049, and DC-4.

Source: Florida State Archives.

the Turbinia, which he powered by means of a steam turbine to very impressive speeds. The British Navy subsequently built many of its warships utilizing steam turbines for propulsion.

In the early 20th century, attempts to apply the turbine technology to internal combustion engines, or gas turbines, met with disappointment. The design of the gas turbine called for the induction of air (as in a reciprocating engine) that would be compressed prior to ignition (as in a reciprocating engine). In the reciprocating engine, the compression is accomplished by means of the piston, but in the turbine engine, the compression is delivered by means of a series of rotating vanes (the compressor) located in front of the combustion chamber. Although the idea of the gas turbine proved workable, its fuel consumption was four times that of the internal combustion engine, and the economics of the invention simply prevented its adoption into commercial use.

The use of compressors in aircraft engines, however, did find continued use as the combined technology associated with aircraft engines and aircraft designs matured during the early years of aviation. As early as World War I, a turbocharger was fitted to a French aircraft to enable increased engine performance at higher altitudes. Turbochargers use the engine's exhaust gases to propel the turbocharger's compressor, thus making use of the free fuel source of the exhaust to compress air for induction into the engine's cylinders as the aircraft climbs into the thinner air at altitude. This technology was used to good effect in the design of the American fighters and bombers used in World War II. The B-17, for instance, could carry its bomb load to 34,000 feet.

The idea of utilizing the smooth, vibration-free rotation of a turbine, instead of the oscillating pistons of the much more cumbersome internal combustion engine, continued to occupy the minds of engineers and inventors. The first serious work on developing the jet engine, or turbojet, was commenced almost simultaneously in the 1930s in both England and Germany.

In England, Frank Whittle, an officer in the Royal Air Force (RAF), conceived that the application of the principles of the gas turbine might be applied, not to drive a shaft or propeller, but to produce a source of thrust for propulsion. In 1930, he was awarded a patent for his design, which was replete with compressor, combustion chamber, and turbine. Although his ideas and designs appeared to be workable, no assistance was forthcoming directly from the British government. The RAF did allow him to continue his work while on duty, and even assigned him the duty of securing engineering and advanced degrees at government expense, culminating in a master's degree from Cambridge. By 1935, Whittle had almost given up on his dream of producing a prototype jet engine when he was approached by two RAF officers willing to capitalize a company for this work. A company was formed, Power Jets, Ltd., and a workable prototype was achieved. At last, government interest was peaked, and direct funding of refinements of his engine was provided. Shortly, in 1939 and in conjunction with the Gloster Aircraft Company, Whittle was given a contract to produce England's first fighter jet airplane, the Meteor.

In Germany, Hans von Ohain, a physics student at the University of Göttingen, was similarly motivated to develop an efficient compressor for the gas turbine. His efforts led to early disappointments, but tests revealed enough success that his university mentors used their influence to introduce Ohain to Ernst Heinkel, the noted aircraft builder. Ohain found kindred spirits at Heinkel's company, and with that support a workable jet engine, of much simpler design than Whittle's, was incorporated into a newly designed airplane, the He 178, for its test flight in August 1939. The test was completely successful and ultimately produced the Jumo-004, (see Figure 19-3) later incorporated into the Messerschmidt 262 and Heinkel 280. These airplanes made limited but impressive appearances over the skies of Europe during World War II.

In October 1942, Hap Arnold, aviation pioneer and general officer in the Army Air Corps in World War II, on learning of Whittle's work, had one of his engines flown to Washington. General Electric Company, the most experienced turbine producer in the country, was given the assignment of producing an American model along the lines of Whittle's design. Bell Aircraft was appointed to build the airplane, and in 1943 the XP-59, known as the Airacomet, flew as the first U.S. jet aircraft. Arnold also knew of the German jet program and had kept his superiors fully informed. The result was a government decision in 1943 to begin initial studies by the four largest aircraft manufacturers in the United States to test the feasibility of jet bombers. From this initiative came the North American B-45 Tornado and the vastly superior Boeing B-47 Stratojet.

Boeing had engineered and put in service in 1944 a very large wind tunnel capable of design testing shapes at speeds close to the speed of sound. Engineers had been dealing with drag at lower speeds for decades, but compressibility was a phenomenon that had only manifested itself as aircraft gained speeds approaching the speed of sound. Drag also appeared to increase exponentially as the speed of sound was approached. The Boeing tests concentrated on these phenomena and, unlike the B-45, were to result in a sweepback wing design never before incorporated in production aircraft. This design had the effect of delaying the onset of compressibility and of raising the speed at which the exponential increase in drag occurred. In short, it facilitated faster flight. Interest in production jet aircraft in the United States was in military aircraft, as evidenced by the B-47 medium bomber

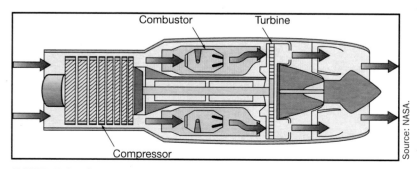

FIGURE 19-3 Germany's jumo-004 engine.

Source: NASA.

program, followed by the B-52 heavy bomber program. The first fully operational jet fighter, the Lockheed P-80, appeared in production in 1945 with its straight wings. The swept wing North American P-86 (designation changed to F-86) appeared in production in 1948 and set the world speed record that year at 671 miles per hour. These and the other jet aircraft of the time incorporated the conventional turbojet engine with all of its drawbacks and shortcomings. Chief among these drawbacks was fuel consumption, followed by high initial cost and frequent maintenance requirements. Airline chieftains were wary of the new, noisy technology. While there was little long-term operational data on jet engines available at the time, what was known was daunting. The consensus among American airline executives was that the jet was too risky, too unproven, and too expensive to be seriously considered as an addition to the fleet.

In the late 40s, a secret design concept for an improved jet engine, known as a "twin-spool turbojet" was in the works in military circles. The prototype of this engine would be known as the "J-57," and it was first tested aloft in 1951. After successful tests, it would be incorporated in a new generation of military airplanes, and it ultimately would make the difference the airline industry needed to consider turbojet propulsion in American commercial aviation. But in the early 1950s, the J-57 was still a military secret.

The British Comet

After World War II, commercial aviation interests in England conceded that the state of British aircraft technology and production was woefully behind that of the United States. The British, by necessity, had concentrated their efforts on fighter aircraft during the war, while the United States had been able to also pursue transport development. The British concluded that they could never catch up with the Americans in existing technology, but they saw a chance at leveling the competitive playing field with the United States by using the conventional turbojet in a new series of passenger transports.

In 1949, the de Havilland Comet began flight-testing with a design expectation of speeds of 480 miles per hour at flight levels of 35,000 feet. (See Figure 19-4.) While pressurized aircraft had been flying since the late 1930s, no airliner had faced the stresses that would be imposed at this projected altitude. The de Havilland Comet completed testing and entered into service on British Overseas Airways Corporation (BOAC) in May 1952, to the thrill and applause of the world. The first turbojet airliner halved flight times over BOAC's world routes. To the surprise of many, the Comet made money even though its operating costs were three times that of the DC-6, even charging regular fares. The difference was that the Comet flew virtually full on all flights, proving that high density seating was commercially feasible, at least on the vibration-free Comet. Next, Air France inaugurated jet service on some of its routes with the Comet. In the United States, it was still DC-7 and Superconstellation piston engine service.

Source: © Hulton-Deutsch Collection/CORBIS.

FIGURE 19-4 The Comet entered into service on British Overseas Airways Corporation in May 1952.

The Comet had three serious accidents in 1953. The third one involved the airplane coming apart in the air, possibly due to a design flaw, but it had occurred in connection with suspected thunderstorm penetration and was written off to the expected result of thunderstorm force. A fourth accident on January 10, 1954, grounded all seven of the Comets. This fourth Comet was lost over the Mediterranean Sea as it climbed above 26,000 feet. Its wreckage fell into the sea and was not immediately available for study. A commission formed in England to study the accidents came up with some fifty fixes to be incorporated into the Comet fleet. These adjustments were made and the Comets resumed service.

The wreckage of the Mediterranean crash was recovered and taken to the Civil Aviation Investigation Branch in England for analysis. As the investigation was proceeding, another Comet disappeared on April 8, 1954 on a flight from Rome to Cairo as it climbed to 35,000 feet. The fleet was again grounded and an all-out investigation was ordered to resolve the cause. It was fully appreciated that the future and reputation of the English aircraft production industry was now at risk, as was the entire future of commercial jet transportation.

The Royal Aircraft Establishment at Farnborough, headquarters for British aeronautical research, was given the task of solving the mystery of the Comets' crashes. A test procedure was contrived to expose the fuselage to a lifetime of pressurization and depressurization cycles, but at a rate 40 times faster than would normally occur. On June 24, 1954, the Comet's fuselage failed, developing a structural crack at the corner of one of the square windows, and expanding away down the fuselage. This indicated that the Comets likely had exploded, not unlike a bomb, due to the interior pressure of the aircraft. In August 1954, the last section of the doomed Rome to Cairo Comet was recovered. The investigators' conclusion of the cause of the crash was confirmed as the Comet's fuselage disclosed an almost exact duplication of the test results. The Comet 1 never flew again. Two later iterations of the Comet never flew commercially. The official findings of the British government's inquiry included that "more study both in design and by experiment" was needed to secure an economically safe life of the pressure cabin. These requirements were not met until 1958, at which time the Comet 4 made the first transatlantic jet commercial flight, on October 4, 1958. By then, the British advantage had been lost, and the United States aircraft production community was just getting started.

America Catches Up

The U.S. aircraft industry took its cue from its potential customers. The industry was obviously not interested in designing and building airplanes unless and until a market existed for them. The concept of the turboprop (the turbine jet engine used to drive a propeller) was considered the likely next commercially successful form of propulsion, and research and development efforts were stepped up both in military and commercial circles, particularly at Lockheed.

There was one other possibility. Boeing's reputation as a builder of military aircraft, mainly bombers and tankers, was unequalled. But Douglas and Lockheed were far ahead of Boeing in the commercial transport field. Boeing had taken a back seat to Douglas and Lockheed in every commercial airliner contest thus far—the B-247 ran second to the DC-3, the B-307 lost out to the Connie and to WWII, and the B-377 could not compete with the DC-7 and the Super Constellation. Boeing had built the C-97 piston engine tanker for the Air Force, but it was not adequate for fueling the new jet bombers, the B-47 and the B-52. The Air Force, Boeing reckoned, would be in the market for a new jet tanker.

Boeing decided to take the gamble. On April 22, 1952, Boeing's board of directors authorized the expenditure of one-fourth of the company's total net worth, $15 million, to develop a prototype. Neither the airlines nor the military had actually expressed an interest in purchasing such an airplane, nor had any appropriation been secured in Congress for replacing the C-97. Boeing officially designated the project the model 367-80, and it was known internally at Boeing as the "dash 80" thereafter. But the designation that the world would come to know was the "707."

Boeing had the largest and the only state-of-the-art wind tunnel for testing aircraft shapes. The development of this wind tunnel, in fact, had been responsible for the adoption of the swept wing design first incorporated in the B-47. (See Figure 19-5.) The 707 design was adapted through wind tunnel testing for over 4,000 hours. Redundant systems, overlapping structural components, multiple strength round windows, plug type doors for better pressurization seals, and spot welds set the standard for the jet aircraft production industry to come. The exterior shell of the 707 was engineered before the Comet disasters. Boeing decided that the skin of the aircraft would be aluminum, of a thickness that turned out to be 4 1/2 times as thick as the Comet's (the Comet's exterior shell was so designed in order to save weight). Boeing also incorporated a new alloy, known as titanium, that was as light as aluminum but stronger than steel to bolster the strength and fatigue resistance of the 707's skin. Then the engineers put the design through 50,000 pressurization cycles with no evidence of metal fatigue.

Tests revealed that the positioning of the aircraft's engines on pylons slung underneath the wings provided the best lift efficiency and had the added benefit of allowing easy access to the engines for maintenance. The wings were also designed to carry 17,000 gallons of fuel, thus allowing for non-stop transcontinental range.

In 1952, Douglas was investigating the feasibility of jet powered airliners but only went so

Source: Florida State Archives.

FIGURE 19-5 A KC-97 refueling a B-47.

far as to construct a full scale wooden mockup of what was to become the DC-8. The problem in the industry, with both manufacturers and carriers, was one of confidence. None of the industry leaders could seem to project a solution to the financial impact of the cost of construction of the high-flying jet airliner and its cost of operation, particularly from the fuel standpoint. The J-57 was still not available. Projections of cost per aircraft approximated $4 million, contrasted to the $1.5 million price tag of the DC-7. Aviation industry leaders were not convinced that jets were commercially viable. C. R. Smith of American Airlines was of the opinion that in order to justify going to jetliners, the cost of operating them should be no higher than the cost of operating the DC-6. Of course, no one knew what the costs of operation of a jet fleet would be. Fuel consumption could be projected, but some costs, such as parts, maintenance, and engine life (TBO) would have to await experience. Among the Americans, only Juan Trippe dissented.

Trippe had been interested in the de Havilland Comet when it first came out, and had placed orders for three of the airplanes subject to their specifications meeting the United States Civil Aeronautics Administration requirements.

There was, in fact, some concern that the CAA would not grant the Comet an airworthiness type certificate based on CAA reservations (prophetic, as it turned out) about the square corners of the windows in the aircraft. The CAA had recommended oval windows but de Havilland appeared to be satisfied with its design, citing design safety tolerances much in excess of expected stresses. Subsequent events would tragically vindicate the CAA's position, but without U.S. approval, Trippe was left in the age of piston aircraft. By the time that the problems with the Comet had been rectified in the redesign of the Comet 4, in 1958, the 707 was light years ahead of the old Comet design. The Comet, for instance, had seating for 67 while the 707's capacity was 130.

Boeing's gamble paid off when, in March 1955, it received its first order for the 707, not as the anticipated passenger airliner, but as the first jet tanker ordered by the Air Force. The first 707 was rolled out of its hangar at Renton, Washington, in May 1955, and completed its maiden flight on July 15, 1955. The 707 prototype would undergo flight testing for the next three years before being placed in commercial airline service. The largest aircraft then in commercial service was the Boeing Stratocruiser and the 707 was 15 times more powerful, twice as fast and almost twice as big. Douglas, now convinced of the feasibility of building civilian jet aircraft, announced that it would complete its design and begin production of the DC-8.

Pan American, alone among the American carriers, seemed interested in jets, despite their projected economic indicators. Trippe had seen how the public had abandoned piston-powered airplanes in droves for the Comet, and it was his purpose to be the first to supply the high-flying, vibration-free, 500-mile-per-hour airplane of the future to America. Just as he had been among the first to abandon the wood and wire airplane and put the Fokker trimotor all metal cantilevered monoplane in service in 1928 (Key West to Havana), the first to inaugurate extended over-water service in the great Clipper amphibians, the first to offer his airline passengers hotel accommodations in his own hotels at their destinations, and among the first to switch to pressurized aircraft, he was now the first to order the first U.S. produced commercial jet airliner. He did so against the prevailing industry tide in October 1955 with the announcement that he had ordered twenty Boeing 707s and, to the great delight of Douglas who did not actually have a real airplane in existence, twenty-five Douglas DC-8s. At a total capital outlay of $269 million, Pan American had committed to the largest airplane acquisition in the history of the industry.

The 707 and the DC-8 were so similar in appearance that it was hard to distinguish between them. But there were real differences to the potential customers, the airlines. First was cabin width, then length, then seating capacity, then the engines. The airlines seemed to prefer the DC-8 design. Before very long, Douglas had twice the orders for DC-8s than Boeing did for 707s. Boeing began making modifications, first to widen the fuselage to a dimension one inch wider than the DC-8, then to increase its length, wingspan, and range. Soon, it had another version of the original 707, and this time the airlines liked it. In 1955, Douglas outsold Boeing, only to be put in second place at the end of 1956. The airlines were now getting caught up in the idea of the jet age, and orders began to pour in. United States airlines bought, but so did foreign airlines. Eastern, Delta, KLM, SAS, Japan Air Lines, and Swissair all bought Douglas. American, Continental, Western, TWA, Air France, Sabena, and Lufthansa went with Boeing. Boeing had finally broken the old jinx of second best. All told, Boeing would win the numbers competition against Douglas by almost 2 to 1. The most satisfying event, though, might have been the selection by the President of the United States of the Boeing 707 as the first jet Air Force One, in 1959.

Lockheed declined to enter the competition, concentrating on the turboprop as its best guess of where the future of commercial aviation lay. Lockheed's contribution was to be the Electra, which in 1957 became the first propjet put in service by U.S. airlines. Only 169 planes were produced, some for the Navy, designated as the P-3. Convair submitted its 880 in 1959 but was unable to compete with the Boeing and Douglas jetliners, losing some $270 million for its efforts.

On October 26, 1958, Pan American became the first American air carrier to inaugurate scheduled jet service with the 707 on its New York to Paris flight. National Airlines was next on December 10, 1958, with a 707 leased from Pan Am that was put on the New York-Miami run to mark the first domestic jet service. Eastern was flying the same route with Lockheed Electras, and immediately began losing out to National. American followed domestically by putting the 707 to work on the transcontinental route, then TWA. United was out of action awaiting the delivery of the first DC-8s, still in the production phase. Eastern could not seem to accept that the jet age had really arrived, and was woefully late in acquiring its first jets, much to its economic disadvantage against its competitors.

On any competitive route in the late 1950s, jets trounced the piston airplanes. The flying public loved jets, and this translated into filled passenger seats. The load factor went up dramatically on jet routes, and their capacity was almost twice that of the DC-7. The airlines were surprised to find that the reliability of the new jet engines greatly reduced failure concerns which had become commonplace with the great turbo-compound piston engines, and that replacement parts and maintenance costs were much lower than expected. Time Between Overhaul (TBO) was a federally-mandated life expectancy of the piston engine used in commercial service in the late 1950s, and it was about 800 hours. The FAA found that jet engines could greatly exceed this limit, and gradually raised the TBO for jets to 4,000 hours. This artificial limit was ultimately discarded entirely in favor of a progressive maintenance schedule designed around the few critical components of the jet engine.

Passenger-mile costs proved to be about the same as on the DC-7. Although fuel consumption in the 707 was much higher than the DC-7, the actual passenger miles per gallon for the 707 was 42 compared to the 59 passenger miles per gallon for the DC-7. The lower cost for jet fuel (kerosene) compared to high-octane gasoline offset this slight difference. The economics of commercial jet travel were working out after all, and the flying public embraced the jet age.

CHAPTER 20

The Federal Aviation Act

© Johnny Kuo, 2008, Shutterstock.

Responsibility for aviation safety had been lodged in the Civil Aeronautics Authority (CAA) by virtue of the Civil Aeronautics Act of 1938, as amended in 1940. Over the course of the ensuing twenty years, aviation safety had dramatically improved, largely due to the reliability of aircraft and engines and the development of instruments and navigation aids. The skies were much more crowded in 1958 than they had been in 1938, no doubt; but progress had been made in refining the airway (navigation) structure since the days of the lighted (beacon) airways. Beginning in 1947, VHF Omnidirectional Radio transmitters (VOR) were installed across the country. An aircraft with a VOR receiver could track inbound from any point, directly to the station, by means of visual reference to the display shown in the onboard aircraft receiver. The direct routes between the VOR transmitters were established in 1950, designated as Victor airways, and were given numbers to distinguish one from another. Instead of flying from city to city as previously, or from one low-frequency radio transmitter to another (the radio range navigation system), aircraft that were equipped with these high-frequency radio receivers flew these routes as aerial highways.

The CAA was empowered to adopt rules and regulations pursuant to its mandate to administer safety concerns relating to aviation, and to establish through such rules and regulations standards for aircraft, engines, propellers, pilots, and mechanics, as well as for flight schools and the training of airmen. It was also charged with developing and administering the Air Traffic Control system (ATC), the system operated by the federal government that regulated the movement of aircraft throughout the United States. Control of aircraft by ATC could range all the way from taxi to takeoff, departure and enroute clearance, to arrival and landing clearance at destination. Most aircraft in the 1950s flew under Visual Flight Rules (VFR), which required little or no ATC control. Airline passenger operations, however, flew largely under Instrument Flight Rules (IFR), the procedure that was designed to ensure that an aircraft had airspace reserved specifically for it, so that no other airplane flying under IFR would occupy that same airspace.

These regulations were known as Civil Aeronautic Regulations (CARS) and were published in the Code of Federal Regulations. The CAA appears to have dutifully performed its administrative function regarding such matters. It can be argued with the aid of hindsight, however, that there was a lack of long-range vision within the CAA during its first twenty years of existence, between 1938 and 1958.

For one thing, the CAA was buried within the Department of Commerce along with the agencies that dealt with highways, maritime issues, textiles, the census, and myriad other matters. To make things worse, its appropriations had been slashed following World War II. Voice communication between pilots and ground controllers using high frequency radio had only been completely implemented in 1955. CAA air traffic control centers, which exercised control over all IFR traffic within large geographical areas throughout the country, now had direct voice contact with aircraft within their sectors. CAA controllers kept track of the location of each aircraft in the sector by means of position reports given by the pilots themselves. These position reports included time, altitude, last radio fix or location, next radio fix, and the estimated time of arrival at that fix. Position reporting was cumbersome and required extremely large blocks of airspace to be reserved for a single aircraft.

Radar, only recently invented (WW II), was slower to be adopted. Radar was first implemented by ATC only as an aid to making instrument approaches to airports during instrument or bad weather conditions. Gradually, as the number of large planes increased and began competing for the available airspace, it became more and more difficult for the air traffic control center personnel to keep track of aircraft. Distance Measuring Equipment (DME), the system that allowed an airplane to determine its distance from an equipped navigation facility, was incorporated into the VOR (Victor) airways system beginning in 1951. Now an aircraft could not only determine its azimuth location (bearing) from the station, it could determine its distance. DME was a big help in tracking aircraft in the "voice only" system, but even so, the control problem was becoming unmanageable.

In 1955 there were surveillance radars in place at thirty-two locations to service traffic arrival and departure at airports, but there were no long-range radars to control enroute traffic except in the mid-Atlantic region at Baltimore.

Concerns were raised that ATC traffic congestion increased the likelihood of mid-air collision. Extension of long-range radars to provide positive radar control for enroute traffic was discussed, but not implemented. Then, on June 30, 1956, a United Airlines DC-7 collided with a TWA Super Constellation over the Grand Canyon, in Arizona, killing 128 people.

The lack of enroute radar was not actually a contributing cause, nor would it likely have prevented the collision. Both aircraft were flying under VFR, clear of clouds in good weather, and under visual flight rules their flight crews assumed the obligation to each other to "see and avoid." Flying under VFR was much preferred at the time due to the zigzag routes that aircraft were required to fly in order to fly the Victor airways, or to go from one VOR to the next VOR. In addition, nothing prevented other airliners, or any other aircraft for that matter, from flying VFR in your reserved airspace. Without area radar by which the controller could actually see both the controlled aircraft as well as any other aircraft that may constitute a collision hazard, flying under IFR in good weather was considered more trouble than it was worth.

Nevertheless, the collision focused public attention on the increasingly crowded skies developing over America as commercial aviation grew. The addition of jets, flying at almost twice the speed of the fastest piston aircraft, would only increase the hazard, perhaps exponentially. Another problem was the mix of military aircraft with civilian aircraft in common airspace. Bomber and fighter jet aircraft operated under one set of rules run by the military, and civilian aircraft operated under a different set of rules administered by the CAA.

On January 31, 1957, a second mid-air collision occurred, this one between a Douglas Aircraft owned DC-7 and an Air Force F-89 near Sunland, California. Head-on closure at high speed was deemed the probable cause. After a collision of another jet fighter with a United Airlines DC-7 in April 1958, unified authority for rule making for control of all aircraft, military as well as civil, in United States airspace was placed in the CAB. With this change, the CAB had rule-making authority, and the CAA was authorized to uniformly administer the rules.

With unified administrative authority in the CAA, positive control was mandated for all aircraft flying above 24,000 feet, as well as on three designated transcontinental routes at altitudes between 17,000 and 22,000 feet, so that it was no longer legal to fly under VFR in that airspace. This was the first step in an overall larger plan to gradually increase the airspace over which positive control would be exercised. Senator Mike Monroney of Oklahoma was instrumental in encouraging and coordinating these significant changes in the interest of safety, and, in the summer of 1958, he authored the legislation that became the Federal Aviation Act of 1958. He was later honored when the FAA's new national aeronautical center in Oklahoma City was named after him.

The Federal Aviation Act of 1958 incorporated virtually all provisions of the Civil Aeronautics Act of 1938 that related to economic regulation, and retained authority for such regulation within the CAB. The Act greatly expanded agency authority over aviation safety, however, and attempted to address the complaints voiced about the shortcomings of the CAA during the preceding twenty years. The CAA was abolished, and in its place was created the Federal Aviation Agency, which was organized as an independent agency answerable to Congress.

The Federal Aviation Agency was given authority to make long-range plans and to implement such plans without interference from competing government interests. All air safety research and development was consolidated and placed within the new agency; thus, the work of the Airways Modernization Board, the Air Coordinating Committee, and the National Advisory Committee for Aeronautics was assumed by the Federal Aviation Agency. An example of the work of the National Advisory Committee for

Aeronautics includes the engine cowl research originally incorporated on the Boeing 247 and DC-1. Rule making was taken away from the CAB and placed in the new agency, as was the responsibility for recommendations regarding aviation legislation. Jurisdiction over suspension or revocation of airmen certificates was removed from the CAB and placed in the Federal Aviation Agency; the CAB was then designated as an appeals board to review the Administrator's certificate action with authority to reverse or modify the action taken by the agency against an airman. The CAB retained its responsibility for aircraft accident investigation as well as all aspects of economic regulation of the airlines.

In the fall of 1958, the first Federal Aviation Agency Administrator to be appointed was retired Air Force General Elwood R. "Pete" Quesada. (See Figure 20-1.) He stepped up enforcement procedures in the airlines, assessing fines and issuing suspensions for rules violations. He led the way for the adoption of military-style radar for control of civilian aircraft. His tenure with the Federal Aviation Agency was marked by stormy relations with the airlines and its pilots, as well as with general aviation, but it set the country on a course of placing safety first for the flying public, a priority constant to this day.

FIGURE 20-1 Pete Quesada being sworn in at the FAA in the fall of 1958.

CHAPTER 21

The Next Jets

FIGURE 21-1 The Caravelle was a prototype with the aircraft's engines on the side of the fuselage near the tail of the aircraft.

Source: National Air and Space Museum, Smithsonian Institution (SI 82-14081).

© egd, 2008, Shutterstock, Inc.

Boeing had upgraded the 707 in 1959 with the new J-75 engine. The DC-8 was flying. Big jets were flying long distances and setting records, and the public was enthralled. Governments the world over were buying these jets and setting up their own airlines. Flying in jets was a prestigious activity.

The government of France had been eclipsed in the jet design and production market. Its aviation representatives took note of something that was not in production and not even on the drawing boards—a medium-range jet that could carry 60 passengers up to 1,200 miles. This was the airplane for the European market, and presciently, was to become the airplane for the deregulated market of the future. This was the Regional Jet.

In response to a government-sponsored competition, Sud Aviation in Toulouse, France, came up with a novel idea in aircraft construction. They placed the aircraft's engines on the side of the fuselage near the tail of the aircraft instead of under the wings. They called this prototype the Caravelle (see Figure 21-1), a name given small sailing ships during the age of exploration. Production began, and in 1956 Air France contracted for the first twelve airliners to come off the line.

British European Airways, the government-owned airline, flew many of the same routes on the Continent using turboprops. Given the proven popularity of jets, already evident in the 1950s, Britain realized that it must build its own short-haul aircraft in order to compete. Its entry was the Hawker-Siddeley Trident, which incorporated the Caravelle aft-engine innovation but added a third engine housed within the vertical stabilizer and aft fuselage. The aircraft designers placed the horizontal stabilizer at the top of the vertical stabilizer, out of the way of the jet exhaust, an arrangement that provided more stability at low airspeeds.

Meanwhile, Boeing was testing the aft-engine concept with an aft-mounted engine attached to its 707 prototype, and it was pondering the viability of such an aircraft in the domestic market. Douglas had designed the DC-9, with its aft-mounted engines, in response to a request by United Airlines, but no other carrier expressed interest, and the design was put on hold. The airlines specified an aircraft with two or three engines, for cost effectiveness, that could operate from shorter runways like LaGuardia. Boeing's engineers were first to conclude that a three-engine airplane with a T-tail was the most likely airplane to succeed, borrowing from the Trident design, which had proven out in Boeing's tests. They designated the new airplane the Boeing 727 and incorporated the new Pratt & Whitney JT8D turbofan, with up to 17,500 pounds of thrust, as the power plant. Turbofans evolved from turbojets as early as 1960, mainly in response to complaints about the noise produced by straight jets, both while in taxi and airborne. The JT8D was not only quieter, it was more economical to operate than any other engine at the time.

The 727 was an aesthetically pleasing airplane. (See Figure 21-2.) It was said that building the 727 would have been warranted even if it couldn't fly. It utilized the same basic fuselage as the 707 and incorporated a new flap design that, at slow airspeeds, increased the wing area by twenty-five percent; thereby greatly reducing the aircraft stall speed. This reduction in speed enabled the 727 to operate from shorter runways, just as specified by the airlines.

The first production model of the 727 flew late in 1962 and immediately began to surpass its design criteria. It was faster, its fuel consumption was less, and its payload was greater. Short landing and takeoff was proven in operation, and its superb handling made it one of the most trusted and respected aircraft flying. Concerns arising from a series of four crashes occurring in 1965 were alleviated when it was determined that they were all caused by pilot error in allowing the airplane to descend at a rate from which recovery was difficult. These accidents established that the 727, in spite of its easy handling characteristics, had to be flown by the numbers, like most jets. The performance of the 727 would go on to earn

FIGURE 21-2 Boeing 727.

it a reputation as the most successful commercial transport aircraft in the history of aviation. By the early 1980s, Boeing had delivered or contracted to deliver almost 2,000 of the very unique airplanes.

After Douglas had placed its DC-9 plans on hold in the late 1950s, the emergence of the short-to-medium range aircraft market caused Douglas to dust off its DC-9 blueprints. In April 1961, Douglas announced that it would begin production of the DC-9. Although Douglas had no orders placed at the time of its announcement, within a month Delta disclosed its contract to purchase 15 of the new jets. Boeing did not respond to the DC-9 until 1965, the same year the first DC-9 went into service. (See Figure 21-3.) Then Boeing unveiled its plans for the 737. The 737 was not a sleek airplane, having a width equal to the 727 and 707 but not the length—it was shorter even than the DC-9. Lufthansa Airlines was instrumental in the design of the 737 because they were first to order the airplane, insisting that it carry 100 passengers, ten more than the DC-9. The 737 entered service in 1968. (See Figure 21-4.)

Sales of the 737 were initially depressed primarily because the Air Line Pilots Association (ALPA) took the position that ALPA crews would not fly the 737 with only two flight crew members; demanding that a flight engineer be

FIGURE 21-3   Douglas DC-9.

FIGURE 21-4   Boeing 737.

included in the cockpit. ALPA was playing catch-up from its earlier failure to require 3-man crews in the DC-9. This requirement made the 737's operating costs too high to be competitive, so the airlines largely rejected the airplane. ALPA abandoned its 3-crew position in 1974, partly because of worldwide recession based on the fuel crisis that year, and partly because of the untenable and obvious featherbedding aspects of its 3-crew position. Airlines then started buying the 737.

For the first time, feeder airlines began to buy the short-to-medium range jets and to bring jet service to the hinterlands of America. Piedmont, North Central Airlines, and Allegheny Airlines were able to expand their service, and in the later years of regulation, beginning in the early 1970s, these airlines were able to secure routes to destinations previously unavailable to them. These jets made routes between small airports—like Tri-Cities, Tennessee to Chicago, or to Washington, D.C., or to New York—convenient and profitable. The feeder lines preferred one class service and gave the world a glimpse of the age of deregulation to come. But first, the jumbo jets had to fly.

The Really Big Jets

In 1962, Lockheed won an Air Force contract to build the largest cargo plane ever conceived. The aircraft specified by the government included power plants of four 21,000-pound thrust turbofans, a range of 4,000 miles, and a useful load of 71,000 pounds plus fuel. When complete, the aircraft would be known as the C-141 Starlifter, and it would have shortcomings. Chief among these was the fact that the C-141 did not have the design volume required to house the cargo load specified. Already recognized by the Air Force was the need for a larger airplane. The Air Force had put out for competition the design of what was to be known as the C-5A, a truly mammoth creation. Lockheed won this competition too, even though Boeing's entry was a serious contender in the competition and, on reflection, perhaps the best of the three entries.

Second place Boeing decided to convert its design and engineering effort to commercial passenger use. Juan Trippe, ever on the cutting edge, had indicated an interest in such an aircraft. Boeing showed that its cargo plane could be modified to accommodate 450 passengers, at nineteen feet, five inches in width, and two hundred thirty-one feet in length. The JT9D turbofan, a high bypass ratio jet engine with 41,000 pounds of thrust, was chosen to power the aircraft. This airplane would also fly faster than previous models, at 625 miles per hour, and would be known as the 747. (See Figure 21-5.) Juan Trippe had long ago concluded that the key to making money in the airline

FIGURE 21-5 The Boeing 747 flew faster than previous models.

FIGURE 21-6 Comparison of the interiors of the L-1011 (top) and the F-7 (bottom).

business was to fill the airplanes with paying customers, like he did with the DC-4 in the late 1940s in the San Juan to New York migration. Now, this was a dream come true. He signed a letter of intent to purchase twenty-five of the "wide bodies," as they were to be known.

Boeing, just as it had during the design phase of the first American jet transport, the 707, took its safety responsibilities seriously. The "carnage factor" of a crash of such a large aircraft was daunting, and only increased Boeing's commitment to safety in the design stage. A "safety committee" was formed to review every aspect of the new aircraft. Concerns of the committee ran the gamut of engineering and construction, from hydraulics, to wing loads, and even to coffee pots. The airplane was so huge that Boeing did not even have a facility large enough to build it, so a new plant had to be constructed at Everett, Washington. It was the largest factory in the world.

The 747 first flew on February 9, 1969. Once again, Pan American was the first to place yet another new prototype airliner in service, this time the 747 Clipper Young America out of JFK for Europe. The 747 had initial problems, mostly because of its size. For instance, baggage facilities were overloaded at destination, causing delays; cabin attendants were overwhelmed by the number of drinks, meals, and related requirements caused by the passenger count; the lavatories seemed inadequate for the needs of passen-

gers; and so on. Each of the concerns was addressed, resolved, and the 747 gradually became a favorite of the flying public. The upper deck of the 747, complete with its cocktail lounge atmosphere for first-class passengers, which was sometimes converted to a restaurant, and its piano manned by a professional pianist, was reminiscent of the lower deck of the Stratocruiser of the 1940s.

In 1967, Lockheed completed its design for its wide-bodied entrant into the field, known as the L-1011 Tristar. (See Figures 21-6 and 21-7.) Lockheed utilized the fuselage tail-mounted engine of the original Trident, together with two wing-mounted engines, for its combined power plant, and it could accommodate 300 passengers.

Circumstances, primarily financial, had required Douglas to merge with McDonnell Air-

FIGURE 21-7 Lockheed L-1011.

FIGURE 21-8 DC-10.

craft of St. Louis. The new company was known as McDonnell-Douglas. Its submission to the wide-body contest was the DC-10, which bore a marked similarity to the L-1011. Both aircraft had three turbofans, one mounted under each wing and one tail mounted. The L-1011's rear engine's intake was built into the vertical stabilizer above the top of the fuselage, with the engine mounted at the rear of the cabin. In the DC-10, the third engine was mounted through the vertical stabilizer, with the intake and exhaust in a direct line fore to aft. (See Figure 21-8.)

In 1970, European aircraft builders, funded by their national governments and comprising a loose consortium of French and British interests that were later joined by the Germans, established their own aircraft production company, Airbus Industrie. The purpose, as they said, was "to reduce dependence on foreign equipment, facilitate survival of a struggling European aircraft industry and address a market opportunity not being met by the Americans." This consortium designed the Airbus 300, a 300-passenger entry actually built by Sud Aviation in Toulouse, France. The A300 had only two turbofan engines, either Rolls-Royce or General Electric, but for various reasons the A300 was slow to materialize. The A300 did not fly until 1972, over three years after the 747, and over one year after the DC-10.

Problems related to structural integrity were encountered by the DC-10 shortly after its inauguration. First, in June 1972, an American Airlines DC-10 out of Detroit suffered a decompression incident when a baggage door, located on the lower deck, blew off and collapsed the supporting deck of the passenger section above. Hydraulic lines had been designed and built to run the length of the aircraft through the floor or deck between the upper and lower compartments, and when the floor collapsed, some of these lines were severed, causing serious control problems for the flight crew. Only the ingenuity and skill of the crew allowed the stricken craft to be brought in for a safe landing.

The baggage doors were not the plug-type doors designed into many jet aircraft, but were dependent on latch mechanisms that, upon investigation, were found to be defective. An aircraft directive mandating corrective action was issued and the modifications were performed with the exception of two airplanes.

One of these was found and fixed; the other was not. On March 3, 1974, the airliner that had been overlooked, a Turkish Airline DC-10 from Paris to London, suffered a similar baggage door failure with a similar floor collapse. This time the crew was unable to fly the aircraft, which crashed, taking all 346 lives aboard.

In the DC-10, no further baggage door incidents occurred, nor were any other serious failures experienced for six years. Then on May 25, 1979, as an American Airlines DC-10 climbed out from Chicago O'Hare after takeoff, the left engine separated from the wing pylon, causing the aircraft to roll inverted and nose down, a condition that the crew was unable to correct at such a low altitude.

The wide-bodied experience of the American producers could be said to have been only marginally successful. Ultimately, McDonnell-Douglas sold 300 DC-10s while Lockheed sold only 244 L-1011s. By 1982 when production of the L-1011 was halted, Lockheed is said to have lost some $2.5 billion on the project.

Airbus, on the other hand, had managed to design a product that would crack the American airline market from Europe for the first time. The A300 had only two engines. This was of some concern initially for transoceanic flight, but it translated directly into reduced operating costs. Secondly, the A300 had incorporated composite, lightweight materials in its structure, adding to its cost effectiveness. As Air France began in 1974 to operate the A300 around the world, the airplane soon began to sell in the European and Asian airline market. Korean Air Lines, Lufthansa, Indian Air Lines and South African Airways bought the A300. Frank Borman of Eastern arranged a six-month trial of the A300 for its New York to Miami route, without any commitment to buy the airplane. This was an unprecedented deal, amounting to a manufacturer loss-leader arrangement whereby Airbus, in effect, loaned its airplane to Eastern on a trial basis. It turned out to be a brilliant stroke by Airbus that resulted in Eastern placing an order for 23 of the aircraft at the price of $25 million a copy, in April 1978.

With the Airbus 300, a trend began in airliner construction of wide-bodied, twin-engined, and lighter weight airplanes that still endures. Boeing contributed the 767 in 1983, using weight-saving composite materials and an advanced wing structure. Since the Boeing and Douglas face-off in the 1930s, beginning with the introduction of the 247 and the DC-1, the history of commercial airliner production competition had been an altogether American affair. Now, with the emergence of Airbus Industrie, combined with the shrinking number of American aircraft manufacturers, the contest is becoming not only international, but also specifically European versus American.

CHAPTER 22

The Department of Transportation

© Dan Barnes, 2008, Shutterstock, Inc.

Prior to the creation of the Department of Transportation, the broad function of the administration of transportation fell to the Undersecretary of Commerce for Transportation. The Department of Commerce, a cabinet level executive department under the direction of a secretary and also a member of the president's cabinet, had been the catch-all repository for the various forms of transportation. The nation's regulation of transportation was administered by agencies, like the Interstate Commerce Commission and the Civil Aeronautics Administration, within the department created to deal with specific modes of transportation. Aviation matters had been removed from the Commerce Department by the Federal Aviation Act of 1958 so that, in 1966, both the CAB and the Federal Aviation Agency (formerly the CAA) were independent agencies. Others remained within the Commerce Department. Administration of the nation's transportation system was fragmented. Some transportation modes were over-funded and over-regulated, while others were under-funded and operated under a system of benign neglect.

The needs of the country from the earliest times were seen as including an efficient and accessible transportation infrastructure. But no overall plan had ever emerged to develop or administer transportation.

In 1965, then administrator of the Federal Aviation Agency, Najeeb Halaby, recommended to planners in the Johnson administration that a cabinet-level Department of Transportation be created based, in part, on his experience as head of that agency. For one thing, Halaby believed that the Federal Aviation Agency had been frozen out of the deliberations surrounding the administration's consideration of a supersonic aircraft transport program. To Halaby, this aviation endeavor was something that the FAA should be consulted on. He wrote to President Johnson that there existed ". . . no point of responsibility below the President capable of taking an evenhanded, comprehensive, authoritarian approach to the development of transportation policies . . ." and that no means existed ". . . to ensure reasonable coordination and balance among the various transportation programs of the government."

Others in the Johnson administration also saw the need for unification of transportation activities, legislation, and oversight. At the urgings of Joseph A. Califano, Jr., special assistant to the president, and Charles Schultze, director of the Bureau of the Budget, a special Task Force was created to explore the wisdom and feasibility of creating such a cabinet-level department. In October 1965, Alan S. Boyd, then Undersecretary of commerce for transportation and who had been appointed to head the Task Force, forwarded to the President recommendations that included the creation of a Department of Transportation. The Task Force report further recommended that all separate sub-agencies that dealt with transportation matters be included in the proposed department. Representative of these were the Federal Aviation Agency, the Bureau of Public Roads, the Saint Lawrence Seaway Development Corporation, the Interstate Commerce Commission, the Civil Aeronautics Board, and the Panama Canal Administration.

Legislation was forwarded to Congress on March 6, 1966, with a letter from Johnson in which he stated: "America today lacks a coordinated transportation system that permits travelers and goods to move conveniently and efficiently from one means of transportation to another, using the best characteristics of each." The thrust of the proposed legislation sought to create one venue for the coordination and management of government-funded transportation programs, and to provide a center for the development of a national transportation policy and its administration.

Debate on the bill was lively, given that many bureaucrats, with their supporters in Congress, had long staked out their turf with respect to their own agencies and authority. The maritime industry opposed the bill, and some in the Federal Aviation Agency voiced fears that its newly won independent status (by the Federal Aviation Act of 1958) would be lost. Nevertheless, by October 1966, a compromise had been reached, and President Johnson signed the bill into law.

The Department of Transportation began operations on April 1, 1967, becoming the fourth largest cabinet-level department within the United States government. It combined over thirty transportation agencies and functions, and their employees, who numbered some ninety-five thousand. During the organizational phase of setting up the DOT were born the Federal Aviation Administration, the Federal Highway Administration, and the Federal Railroad Administration. DOT absorbed functions that previously belonged to departments other than Commerce. Urban mass transit, for example, was removed from the Department of Housing and Urban Development, which in turn caused the creation of additional agencies (the Urban Mass Transportation Administration, later renamed the Federal Transit Administration). The National Transportation Safety Board (NTSB) was created, which assumed the investigative responsibilities formerly carried out by the CAB's Bureau of Aviation Safety. The administration of aviation was placed in the new department and named the Federal Aviation Administration.

The Federal Aviation Administration

When the Department of Transportation Act created the Federal Aviation Administration (FAA), the function of the government in promoting, regulating, and enforcing aviation safety standards finally found a permanent home. A quick review of the history of the administration of aviation safety shows the torturous path that it had taken.

The Air Commerce Act of 1926 first authorized safety regulation, the administration of which was placed within the Department of Commerce. The Aeronautics Branch was created as an agency in the Department of Commerce and became the first government agency to concern itself with aviation safety. This agency was renamed the Bureau of Air Commerce in 1934. Under the Civil Aeronautics Act of 1938 (as amended in 1940), these functions were transferred to the Civil Aeronautics Administration (CAA) and remained within the Department of Commerce.

The Federal Aviation Act of 1958 significantly reallocated existing authority in aviation regulatory matters. The CAA was renamed the Federal Aviation Agency, removed from the Department of Commerce, and organized as an independent agency that reported only to Congress and to the President. The Federal Aviation Agency was given the responsibility previously exercised by the CAB for proposing air safety legislation (statutory) and for rule making, designated under the CAB as Civil Aeronautic Rules (CARs), and now known as the Federal Aviation

Regulations (FARs). All air safety research and development authority was consolidated within the Agency, including that previously carried out by the National Advisory Committee for Aeronautics, the Airways Modernization Board and the Air Coordinating Committee. The procedural responsibility in airman certificate actions was also transferred from the CAB to the Federal Aviation Agency. Under the Federal Aviation Act of 1958, the CAB retained its responsibility for the investigation of aircraft accidents as well as its economic regulation of the airlines, and it became an appeals review board for certificate action taken by the Federal Aviation Agency.

Under the provisions of the Department of Transportation Act, responsibility for aviation safety, and virtually all logical ramifications of safety issues, were placed within the authority of the FAA. Its basic mission is defined by its legislative mandate, particularly the Federal Aviation Act of 1958. In 1984, Congress authorized commercial space launches by the private (nongovernmental) sector for the first time under the Commercial Space Launch Act. Regulatory authority was initially placed within the Department of

Transportation in the Office of Commercial Space Transportation (AST), but in 1995 this function was moved over to the FAA under the same name (Office of Space Transportation (AST)). This office conducts the only space-related function within the FAA. FAA/AST regulates the commercial space transportation industry to ensure compliance with international obligations of the U.S. and to enhance safety and national security. It also licenses commercial space launches of both orbital and suborbital rockets and nonfederal launch sites, or spaceports.

The key functions of the FAA are outlined in the box below. A review of these functions will disclose how pervasive is the scope of FAA responsibility and authority. While safety has always been the mainstay of the FAA mandate, ongoing developments in aviation have caused new emphasis to be placed on related but separate concerns, such as security,[1] the environment, airport funding, international relations, and commercial space activities.

The functions of the FAA could logically be examined from several different perspectives, but for our purposes the following breakout of FAA responsibility should be the most instructive.

Key Functions of the FAA

1. Regulate and encourage aviation safety and security.

2. Develop, operate, and maintain a safe, secure, and efficient national air traffic management system.

3. Collaborate in developing a safe, secure, and efficient worldwide civil aviation system.

4. Regulate air commerce to fulfill the requirements of national defense.

5. Assist in the development of airports.

6. Help mitigate adverse environmental impacts of aviation.

7. Regulate the commercial space transportation industry.

Regulation

The FAA, as a government agency with rule-making authority, is required to follow certain procedures when originating or altering regulations that it issues. All federal agencies are required to issue Notices of Proposed Rule Making, published in the Federal Register, which are designed to allow those who may be affected by the proposed rule to be put on notice that a new regulation may be coming, and to allow input to the FAA on the impact of the proposed rule. Input from the aviation industry, or others who may be affected by the rule, often causes modification or abandonment of the proposed rule, and

---

See Chapter 42 for a full discussion of FAA responsibilities for commercial space launch activity.

is an important and practical aspect of the regulatory function of the FAA. Industry groups, such as the Airline Transport Association, Aircraft Owners and Pilots Association, National Business Aviation Association, and National Business Aircraft Association, closely monitor the FAA for these Notices of Proposed Rule Making.

Regulations adopted by the FAA are published in the Code of Federal Regulations, Title 14, and referred to in the aviation community as Federal Aviation Regulations (FARs). These regulations have the force of law and are primarily concerned with safety, although environmental (noise) and funding issues are also addressed. The FAA is required by the provisions of the Aircraft Noise Abatement Act of 1968 to consult with the Environmental Protection Agency (EPA) to establish noise standards and to enforce those standards by regulation. In addition to the FARs, the FAA issues mandatory orders that have the force of law in the form of Airworthiness Directives (ADs). These directives generally require inspections or modifications to aircraft that are already certified and in use in the aviation community, and may be prompted by accidents, operating experience, or observations of pilots and mechanics.

Certification

The FAA enhances the safe operation of aviation by controlling, through certification, who may legally function in civil aviation, and by certification of certain equipment used in domestic civil aviation. Certification by the FAA applies to seven major categories:

1. Airmen
2. Aircraft
3. Air Carriers
4. Air Navigation Facilities
5. Air Agencies
6. Airports
7. Designees (representatives of the Administrator)

Airmen

Certification is required of pilots, flight engineers, navigators, air traffic controllers, aircraft dispatchers, mechanics, repairmen, and parachute riggers. Certification of airmen includes procedures not only for the written and oral testing of applicants, but also the requirement of practical demonstrations of required levels of proficiency.

Minimum physical and mental health standards are applied through periodic medical examinations of airmen. The FAA issues separate medical certificates to airmen through its network of Aviation Medical Examiners. The amorphous standard that airmen possess "good moral character" has been consistently required of all certificate holders since passage of the Air Commerce Act of 1926.

Aircraft

The FAA issues three types of certificates applicable to aircraft and their components—Type, Production, and Airworthiness. The aircraft components that must be certified include aircraft engines, propellers, and appliances. Every civil aircraft manufactured in the United States is subject to this inspection and certification regimen beginning with the design of the aircraft. A Type Certificate is issued to the aircraft manufacturer after flight and static testing confirms that the design conforms to the standards adopted by the FAA and published in the FARs. The issuance of a Production Type Certificate follows on the manufacturer meeting all FAA standards designed to assure that all aircraft produced pursuant to the Type Certificate will faithfully conform to the approved design of the aircraft. This certificate is a sort of quality assurance requirement based on the manufacturer's production and inspection methods at its plant. The final requirement imposed by the FAA is the Airworthiness Certificate, which is awarded to each and every aircraft that comes off the assembly line and is required before the aircraft can be delivered to a purchaser. This certificate is valid only for a period of twelve months.

Air Carriers

There are two types of certificates issued by the federal government to air carriers in the United States. Air Carrier Operating Certificates are issued by the FAA under Part 121 of the FARs to carriers operating aircraft for hire with ten or more seats. The compliance requirements of Part 121 are numerous, but the two major areas addressed are the training of flight crews and aircraft maintenance programs. Air Carrier Fitness Certificates, also referred to as certificates of public convenience and necessity, are issued by DOT, not the FAA, and establish that the carrier has shown that it has the financial capacity and management expertise to carry on a scheduled airline operation. These are required only of carriers operating aircraft with 61 or more seats. While some Fitness Certificates authorize only cargo operations, the majority of such certificates apply to both passenger and cargo.

Air Navigation Facilities

Air Navigation Facilities include radio directional equipment and landing aids and are inspected and rated by the FAA to ensure compliance with safety operational standards. A certificate issued by the FAA as to such facility establishes such compliance.

Air Agencies

FAA regulations applying to aircraft repair stations and to maintenance technician facilities, pilot schools, and training centers include the requirement of meeting certifications standards relating to procedures, instructors, equipment, tools, and personnel.

Airports

Since 1982, the FAA has been charged with certificating operators of airports serving certificated air carriers (Airport and Airway Development Act). FAA regulations containing the requirements applicable to such airport operators are found in Part 139 and relate primarily to maintenance of minimum safety standards in airport operations.

Designees

The FAA designates individuals possessing certain skills, training, or education to assist it in carrying out its examination and inspection duties and through whom FAA certificates are issued. These individuals must first be certified, themselves, as representatives of the administrator and must hold that certificate issued by the FAA. These individuals include Aviation Medical Examiners who are issued a Certificate of Designation, and Pilot Examiners (Flight Standards Designated Examiner) who are issued a Certificate of Authority. In addition, Certificates of Authority are issued to Technical Personnel Examiners, Designated Aircraft Maintenance Inspectors, Designated Engineering Representatives, Designated Manufacturing Inspection Representatives, and Designated Airworthiness Representatives.

Investigation

The FAA conducts investigations of aircraft accidents subordinate to and in cooperation with the National Transportation Safety Board pursuant to an arrangement known as the Accident Investigation Selectivity Program. This program is formalized in an agreement between the NTSB and the FAA and is designed to delineate responsibility in accident investigations and to avoid conflicts. Previously, separate investigations conducted by the NTSB and the FAA sometimes resulted in contrary findings and conclusions, and were the occasion for embarrassment to one or both.

The types of accidents investigated by the FAA are normally limited to general aviation accidents or those that, by comparison to airline accidents, are relatively limited in scope or impact in the aviation community. It should be noted that the objectives of an FAA investigation are different from those of the NTSB. In particular, the FAA is looking for violations of the FARs, and it scrutinizes whether the accident was a result of deviations from standards adopted by the FAA. FAA investigations seek to determine whether FAA facilities were a factor and whether the FARs were adequate. The FAA also investigates aircraft incidents that do not result in accidents, such as "near misses" by passing aircraft or other instances when aviation safety may have been jeopardized. The FAA is also mandated by Congress to investigate all reports of violations of the FARs.

Enforcement

Since passage of the Federal Aviation Act of 1958, responsibility for carrying out enforcement

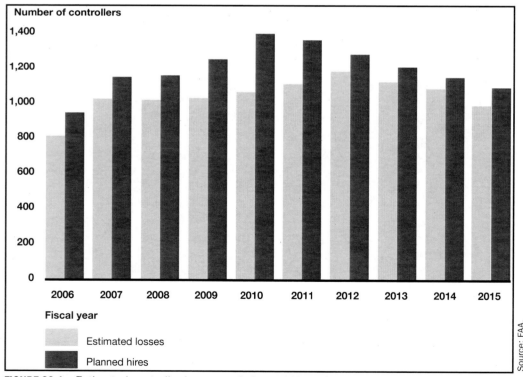

FIGURE 22-1 Estimated controller losses and planned hires, fiscal years 2006–2015

procedures for violations of the FARs has resided with the FAA. Enforcement options open to the FAA in any given case are normally dictated by considerations already well-established within the agency, and are generally handled either as administrative dispositions (warning notices and letters of correction) or by certificate action (suspension or revocation). Occasionally, civil penalties are assessed in lieu of certificate action (historically against corporations or against working pilots where certificate suspension is deemed too harsh).

Operations

The FAA is charged with the operation and maintenance of a vast array of facilities and equipment within the aviation system. We will briefly review the major categories of FAA responsibility.

Air Traffic Control

The ATC system includes airport control towers, air route traffic control centers (ARTCC), terminal radar approach control (TRACON), and flight service stations (FSS).

The FAA estimates that it will lose 10,291 controllers, or about 70 percent of the controller workforce, between 2006 and 2015 due to retirements. The large percentage loss is due to the unlawful PATCO strike in 1981, when President Reagan fired almost 11,000 controllers. From 1982 through 1991, the FAA hired an average of 2,655 controllers each year. These controllers will become eligible for retirement during the next decade.

In 1982, the FAA began a program of outsourcing operation at a limited number of VFR towers. As of 2006, 231 towers in 46 states participate in the FAA's Contract Tower Program.

In 2005, the FAA entered into a contract with Lockheed Martin to operate the 58 Flight Service Stations located in the contiguous United States.

Radio Aids to Navigation

These facilities include VORs, VORTACs, instrument landing systems (ILS), and microwave landing systems (MLS). The Global Positioning System (GPS) is operated by the Department of Defense, and Loran C is operated by the United States Coast Guard.

In 2003, the FAA inaugurated the Wide Area Augmentation System (WAAS) as a precursor for a new and extremely accurate navigation system. WAAS augments, or enhances, the Global Positioning System in order to provide the additional accuracy, integrity, and availability necessary for its use by the civilian aviation community. Previously, GPS data were unable to provide navigation capability for use in precision approaches. Through WAAS, precision approaches are conceivable for all 5,400 public use airports in the United States without local airport ground support facilities.

WAAS is an integral part of the FAA plan to replace ground-based Navaids entirely with satellite-based navigation capability, thus eliminating VORs, VORTACs, ILS, and MLS. (See Chapter 36 for the Next Generation Air Transportation System plan.)

National Airports

The FAA no longer is responsible for the two major airports located in and near Washington, D.C., Reagan National and Dulles, since their operation has been assigned to the Washington Metropolitan Airport Authority.

Monroney Aeronautical Center

The Center was named for Oklahoma Senator Mike Monroney, who was instrumental in securing passage of the Federal Aviation Act of 1958.

The Center is the repository for all aircraft registration, documents of title to aircraft, and lien recordations on United States aircraft (the Aircraft Registry). The Airman Records Branch contains the records pertaining to every person issued a certificate by FAA. It is the home of the FAA Academy, the training center for air traffic controllers, air safety inspectors, and other personnel. The Center also houses the Civil Aeromedical Institute (CAMI), which conducts research on various aspects of aviation safety, with an emphasis on human factors. CAMI specialists conduct tests on smoke toxicity, aircraft seats and restraint systems, air traffic controller selection and training methods, and the effects of fatigue, age, work, and rest schedules for ATC personnel. Teaching activities at CAMI include the training of pilots in water and arctic survival techniques and the sharing of the latest research in aviation medicine with designated Aviation Medical Examiners.

William J. Hughes Technical Center

Research and development programs are conducted at the technical center located just outside Atlantic City, N.J., on a former Navy airfield. Activities conducted at the Center include test and evaluation in air traffic control, communications, navigation, airports, and aircraft safety and security. The Center strives to develop innovative systems and concepts, new equipment and software, and modifications of existing systems.

Education

The FAA supports a large effort in the aviation community directed toward education of the flying public and the public at large. Periodic publications, such as the Advisory Circulars and Service Bulletins, and safety seminars for pilots, instructors, mechanics, and others reach out to all certificated airmen in an effort to facilitate improvements in all aspects of aviation safety.

Funding

Responsibility for distribution of federal grants under the Airport Improvement Program is assumed by the FAA under the Airport and Airway Development Act.

Registration and Recordation

A central registry for U.S. civil aircraft (N-numbered aircraft) is located at the Aeronautical Center in Oklahoma City. All aircraft operated within the United States are required to be registered, and it is the responsibility of the owner of every aircraft to secure the registration. The FAA issues its Certificate of Registration in the name of the owner upon satisfactory completion of the registration process. The Aircraft Registry also functions as the recordation site for establishing or determining legal title to aircraft, and is the one place that contains the entire chain of title of any aircraft. All legal encumbrances, or perfected security interests in aircraft, must be filed with the FAA at the Aircraft Registry.

Commercial Space Transportation

The responsibilities of the FAA discussed above grew and were assumed over time as civilian aviation sector activities developed. All of these responsibilities relate to civil aviation operations occurring on the surface of the earth and within the earth's atmosphere. When the United States began operations beyond the earth's atmosphere with the first space launch in 1958, and for many years thereafter, all U.S. space activities were the exclusive province of either NASA or the military.

With the passage by Congress of the Commercial Space Launch Act of 1985, the Office of Commercial Space Transportation (referred to as FAA/AST) was created within the FAA. Under this statute, AST has the responsibility to:

➡ Regulate the commercial space transportation industry, only to the extent necessary to ensure compliance with international obligations of the United States and to protect the public health and safety, safety of property, and national security and foreign policy interests of the United States;

➡ Encourage, facilitate, and promote commercial space launches by the private sector;

➡ Recommend appropriate changes in federal statutes, treaties, regulations, policies, plans, and procedures;

➡ Facilitate the strengthening and expansion of the United States space transportation infrastructure

FAA/AST is organized into three divisions:

➡ Space Systems Development Division (AST-100)

➡ Licensing and Safety Division (AST-200)

➡ Systems Engineering and Training Division (AST-300)

For a more thorough discussion of commercial space launch activities in the United States and the role of FAA/AST, please refer to Chapter 42.

Dual Mandate

The historic mission of the FAA has been to not only administer the requirements of safety in the aviation community, but to "promote" aviation in the overall national transportation scheme. The FAA has come under criticism from time to time that this dual role really amounts to a conflict of interest in promoting the airlines, on the one hand, and enforcing its regulations applicable to them, on the other hand. The issue resurfaced in the high visibility aftermath of the Valuejet crash in the Florida Everglades in 1996. The FAA had determined that the discount carrier was not in significant violation of the FARs, that FAA oversight and inspection of the airline had been standard, and reported its conclusion that the airline was

"safe." Within six weeks, the FAA had shut down the company based on additional findings of serious violations of regulations relating to the transportation of hazardous materials, which led to the conclusion that such violations were the direct cause of the catastrophic crash, with the loss of all lives on board.

In 1996, Congress revised the FAA's mission in the Federal Aviation Reauthorization Act, removing the "dual mandate" by repealing the duty of the administrator to "promote civil aeronautics." Instead, Congress directed the FAA to consider as its highest priority the "maintaining and enhancing of safety and security of air commerce."

The National Transportation Safety Board

The National Transportation Safety Board (NTSB) was created by the Department of Transportation Act of 1966 as an agency within DOT. The primary responsibilities given to NTSB were to investigate transportation accidents, to determine the "probable cause" of the accident, and to make recommendations based on its findings designed to assist in preventing similar accidents in the future. The range of transportation modes subject to the scrutiny of the NTSB was commensurate with the DOT itself, that is, railroad, highway, aviation, marine, and pipeline. It was assigned the additional role of acting as a review board for airman appeals from certificate actions or penalty assessments by the FAA.

In 1974, the NTSB was removed from the DOT and established as an independent agency answerable to Congress pursuant to the provisions of the Independent Safety Board Act. This action was taken by Congress because it was determined that, given its unique role in investigation and recommendation, the agency should be completely independent of other agencies and departments to ensure that it could be direct, impartial, and uninfluenced in making assessments of fault and recommendations for changes.

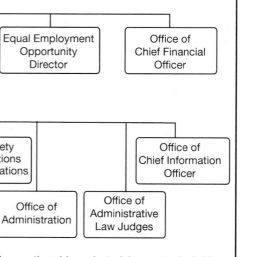

The agency is headquartered in Washington, D.C., and maintains 10 field offices nationwide and a training center in Ashburn, Virginia, in suburban Washington, D.C. In recent years, the agency has shrunk in size. In 2003, NTSB had 438 full-time employees compared with 386 in September 2006. During the same period, the number of full-time investigators and technical staff decreased from 234 to 203. (See fig. 3) NTSB's modal offices vary in size in relation to the number of investigators; as of September 2006, the aviation office had 102 investigators and technical staff; the rail, pipeline, and hazardous materials office had 31; the highway office had 22; and the marine office had 12 employees. An additional 36 technical staff worked in the Office of Research and Engineering, which provides technical, laboratory, analytical, and engineering support for the modal investigation offices. For example, it is responsible for interpreting data recorders, creating accident computer simulations, and publishing general safety studies.

Source: NTSB.

FIGURE 22-2   NTSB's Organization.

The investigative role of the NTSB dates back to the Air Commerce Act of 1926 when Congress gave the Department of Commerce responsibility for investigation of air crashes. An Aeronautics Branch of the Commerce Department was created to carry out this responsibility and it did so until renamed the Bureau of Air Commerce in 1934. In 1938, the CAB took over the investigative role and performed this duty until the creation of the NTSB in 1966.

To facilitate its investigative and reporting responsibility, Part 830 of the FARs requires aircraft operators to provide notification to the NTSB of certain accidents and incidents, and in certain cases to follow up such notice by required reports. This notification and reporting regimen is important to the role of the NTSB is staying current with problem areas in aviation safety.

The role of the NTSB was extended to the investigation of nonmilitary public aircraft acci-

Mode	2002	2003	2004	2005
Aviation[a]	1,949	1,997	1,870	1,937
Highway	52	45	45	33
Rail	11	9	12	8
Pipeline	1	2	2	1
Hazardous materials	2	1	2	1
Marine	6	6	7	4

[a]Aviation accidents include limited investigations in which NTSB delegates the gathering of on-scene information to FAA inspectors.

FIGURE 22-3   Number of accident investigations completed by NTSB by mode, fiscal years 2002–2005.
Source: GAO analysis of NTSB data.

dents under the provisions of the Independent Safety Board Act of 1994. Public aircraft, generally those aircraft owned or operated by various federal government agencies, were excluded

Mode	Key laws, regulations, and policies	Investigation policy
Aviation 	49 U.S.C. 1131 (a)(1)(A) 49 C.F.R. part 800 International Civil Aviation Organization annex 13	Investigates or causes to be investigated all civil and certain public aircraft accidents in the United States and participates in the investigation of international accidents where the United States is the state of registry, operator, designer, or manufacturer.
Highway 	49 U.S.C. 1131 (a)(1)(B)	Investigates selected accidents including railroad grade crossing accidents, which NTSB selects in cooperation with a state.
Marine 	49 U.S.C. 1131(a)(1)(E); 1131(b) 49 C.F.R. part 850 U.S. Coast Guard/NTSB memorandum of understanding from 9/12/2002	Investigates selected major accidents and incidents, collisions involving public vessels with any nonpublic vessel, accidents involving significant safety issues related to Coast Guard safety functions, and international accidents within the territorial seas and where the United States is the state of registry. Major marine accidents are defined as a casualty that results in (1) the loss of six or more lives; (2) the loss of a mechanically propelled vessel of 100 or more gross tons; (3) property damage initially estimated as $500,000 or more; or (4) serious threat, as determined by the Commandant of the Coast Guard and concurred with by the Chairman of NTSB, to life, property, or the environment by hazardous materials.
Railroad	49 U.S.C. 1131(a)(1)(C); 1116(b)(5) 49 C.F.R. part 840	Investigates railroad accidents involving a fatality, substantial property damage, or a passenger train.
Pipeline	49 U.S.C. 1131(a)(1)(D)	Investigates pipeline accidents in which there is a fatality, substantial property damage, or significant injury to the environment.
Hazardous materials	49 U.S.C. 1116(b)(5)	Investigates releases of hazardous materials in any mode that involves a fatality, substantial property damage, or significant injury to the environment. For all modes, NTSB also evaluates the adequacy of safeguards and procedures for the transportation of hazardous materials and the performance of other departments, agencies, and instrumentalities of the government responsible for the safe transportation of that material.
All modes 		Investigates selected accidents that are catastrophic or of a recurring nature.

FIGURE 22-4 Key laws, regulations, and NTSB policies for investigations by mode.

Source: GAO summary of law, regulations, and policies.

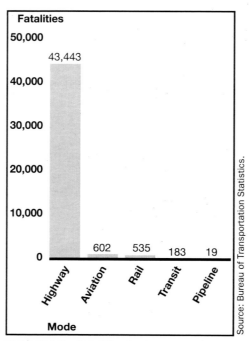

Source: Bureau of Transportation Statistics.

FIGURE 22-5 Fatalities by transportation mode, 2005.

The Primary Functions of the NTSB

1. Aircraft accident investigation
2. Probable cause determinations
3. Accident report preparation
4. Safety recommendations
5. Receipt of Part 830 notifications and reports
6. Appellate review of FAA certificate actions and penalty assessments
7. Disaster assistance

from compliance with the airworthiness and maintenance requirements of the FARs by the Federal Aviation Act of 1958. In 1993, the Governor of South Dakota, George S. Mickelson, was killed in the crash of a government aircraft in which he was a passenger. In the wake of the investigation into that accident, Congress rewrote the law to bring most nonmilitary government-owned or operated aircraft within the authority of the FAA and the NTSB.

In 1996, Congress further charged the NTSB, pursuant to the provisions of the Aviation Disaster Family Assistance Act, with the task of coordinating all federal assistance to survivors and families of victims of catastrophic transportation accidents. The NTSB strategic plan developed as a result of this mandate ensures that such people receive timely assistance from the carrier involved, and from all government agencies and community service organizations included in the program.

The primary functions of the NTSB are outlined in box shown on this page.

It should be noted that the NTSB has no authority over any other federal agency or any industry group. It has no regulatory or enforcement powers. Its effectiveness is enhanced by its resultant impartiality. The NTSB operates with a very small staff, historically fewer than 400 employees. Since 1967, the NTSB has investigated over 114,000 aviation accidents and issued more than 11,600 safety recommendations in all transportation modes. More than 80 percent of its safety recommendations have been adopted by those empowered to effect changes in the transportation system and in government agencies. At a cost of less than $.24 annually per citizen, it is said to be one of the best bargains in government.

Endnote

1. In 2001, responsibility for aviation security was transferred from the FAA to the Transportation Security Administration (TSA).

CHAPTER 23

Airports

© Terry Alexander, 2008, Shutterstock.

Before Herbert Hoover was President, he was Secretary of Commerce in the Coolidge administration. He was called on to testify before the Morrow Board in 1925. The Morrow Board had been created for the purpose of studying the state of aviation and recommending to the President an aviation policy for the nation. Aviation, as the newest form of commerce joining maritime and land-based transportation, naturally followed some of the paths previously established by the older forms. It was also recognized that the promotion of aviation was in the national interest, much the same as it had been acknowledged that the nation needed the Post Office, a merchant marine, and the railroads.

Secretary Hoover drew an almost complete parallel between the needs of the fledgling aviation industry and the government's policy toward maritime commerce in the United States. He pointed out that government had accepted the responsibility of providing aids to navigation in the nation's ports and waterways by establishing markers, buoys, and lighthouses, and by providing surveys and geodetic charting. The government had provided land grants to the railroads in order to open up the West, in the name of the national interest. Roadways, too, were within the realm of government responsibility in part to facilitate motor commerce. The analogy was complete. Aviation needed and deserved federal assistance and direction if it was to develop in an organized manner. Otherwise, a fragmented and chaotic system of air transportation could be expected.

Included within the analogy was the need for airports to serve the various cities of the country. In the 1920s airmail service was being provided to some cities but not to others, sometimes largely or completely based on the fact that no landing fields were available to receive the planes. Airports then were truly landing "fields," sometimes referred to as "all-way airfields" since landings and takeoff could be made in any direction. Runways were the exception. Notwithstanding the favorable national policy toward aviation, there was no authorization for the direct participation of the federal government in the construction of airports. Municipalities, counties, and state governments recognized that their participation in air commerce was going to be dependent, in large part, on their own financial contributions. The Air Commerce Act of 1926 authorized the Commerce Department to survey and rate airports, and by 1929 some 181 airports had been catalogued. Only half of the airports had some kind of "prepared" runway, ranging from an oil-treated surface to cinders and concrete. Major cities, including Cleveland, Detroit, Buffalo, Milwaukee, Denver, and Boston, had fields acquired and improved with local money. Indeed, prior to World War II, most of the airports of the country were financed, developed, and operated by local or regional government, since no federal airport program had ever existed.

New York's LaGuardia airport was a local project. It started out in 1929 as North Beach Airport and, when Mayor Fiorello La Guardia began his expansive program of municipal works during the 1930s, including the city's famous bridges, tunnels, and highways, the airport was included. New York had been a central maritime port for over a century and had developed into a major transatlantic passenger seaport by the 1930s. Its piers, visibly surrounding the island of Manhattan, provided a gateway to the world. They also provided an aviation analogy for the advanced planners of New York.

LaGuardia airport was only eight miles from the center of Manhattan, and Pan American had built its Marine Terminal there. There was a concrete apron for the parking of the new DC-2s and DC-3s, and its runways were a mile long. La Guardia took advantage of a Depression era program known as Works Progress Administration (WPA), which was begun to provide work for the millions of unemployed men during the 1930s. At a time when practically all construction of any kind was stopped by the rigors of the Great Depression, and with commercial aviation just beginning to emerge as a new and viable transportation medium, federal monies expended through the WPA program greatly enhanced the progress of commercial aviation in the 1930s.

The Civil Aeronautics Act of 1938 lifted the ban on direct federal contributions for airports. One of the first cities to be benefited was Washington, D.C., whose airport, Washington-Hoover Airport, was described at the time by historian John R. M. Wilson:

> Bordered on the east by Highway One, with its accompanying high-tension electrical wires, and obstructed by a smokestack on one approach and a smoky dump nearby,

the field was masterpiece of inept siting. Incredibly, the airport was intersected by a busy thoroughfare, Military Road, which had guards posted to flag down traffic during takeoffs and landings. In spite of such hazards, Washington-Hoover had a perfect safety record—for the simple reason that whenever even a slight breeze was blowing, planes refused to land there.[1]

By 1941, Washington National Airport had taken the place of Washington-Hoover, having been literally dredged up out of the swampy ground next to the Potomac. It immediately became the second busiest airport in the country.

Civil airport construction languished, largely because of World War II. During the war, the federal government had created many airfields for military use under a program known as Development of Landing Areas for National Defense, spending $3.25 billion. After the war, pursuant to the Surplus Property Act of 1944, about half of these bases were turned over to local and state governments. Still, airports of the size and quality for use by growing commercial aviation were few, and those few were abysmal. As reported in *Fortune* in 1946.[2]

> The half-dozen largest city airports handle millions of people a year. LaGuardia airport with 2,100,000 people, Washington with 757,000, Chicago with 1,300,000, and Los Angeles' Lockheed Air Terminal with 760,000 give clear indication of the size of the new air traffic. By standards of the huge railroad terminals, such as New York's Grand Central, which handles 65 million people a year, a million passengers is not so much. But a million passengers jamming through one small room, such as Chicago's filthy little air terminal, instantly creates a problem solvable only by a fresh start in new surroundings, by new design on functional lines.
>
> Chicago is the worst; its airport is a slum. Chewing gum, orange peel, papers, and cigar butts strew the floor around the stacks of baggage. Porters can't keep the

floor clean if people are standing on it day and night. At almost all hours every telephone booth is filled, with people lined up outside; the dingy airport cafe is filled with standees. To rest the thousands there are exactly twenty-eight broken-down seats. One must line up even for the rest rooms. The weary travelers sit or even lie on the floor. The drooping grandmothers, the crying babies, the continuous, raucous, unintelligible squawk of the loudspeaker, the constant push and jostle of new arrivals and new baggage tangling inextricably with their predecessors, make bus terminals look like luxury.

To say that the airports at San Francisco or Los Angeles are less squalid than Chicago is faint praise, for the difference is so slight that anyone passing hastily through would notice no real improvement. Almost all U.S. airports are utterly barren of things to do. The dirty little lunch counters are always choked with permanent sitters staring at their indigestible food; even a good cup of coffee is a thing unknown. The traveler consigned to hours of tedious waiting can only clear a spot on the floor and sit on his baggage and, while oversmoking, drearily contemplate his sins.

Federal Airport Act of 1946

In 1946, Congress authorized the expenditure of funds for use by the political subdivisions of state, county, and city governments in building or improving the airport infrastructure. Pursuant to the provisions of the Federal Airport Act of 1946, the government would contribute fifty percent of these improvements, and the local government would fund the rest. Small communities found it difficult to come up with even fifty percent of such large expenditures. The program worked better in large cities that could float bond issues to finance their portion of the cost. A series of amendments to the Act extended the duration and funding of the program and added provisions designed to guarantee proper standards of construction and operation, open and non-discriminatory access by the public, and appropriate zoning of lands adjacent to the airport.

New York utilized the program to construct a third major airport, named Idlewild (now JFK), and then expanded the original construction with $60 million of terminal buildings and parking areas. Los Angeles raised a bond issue in the amount of $60 million for its international airport. St. Louis expanded its airport and built a new terminal. The busiest airport in the country was Midway, in Chicago, with an arrival or departure every 80 seconds. The activity at Midway led to the building of O'Hare, which opened in 1955. Dulles airport, conceived to serve Washington, D.C., finally found a home in Chantilly, Virginia, in 1958. Still, it was generally realized and noted at the time that United States airports were not ready for jets, and that they were not keeping up with the growth of commercial air travel. The number of passengers enplaning on domestic flights would almost double between 1954 and 1959, from thirty-two million to fifty-five million. And it was reckoned that less than ten percent of the American population had ever set foot on a commercial airplane.

Airports faced new problems as a direct result of the larger piston airplanes, and these problems were compounded by the arrival of jets. Fuel storage facilities were inadequate, both in size and in type, since jets burned a form of kerosene, not the gasoline of piston engines. Taxiways had to be redesigned, relocated, and widened, due both to the size of the aircraft and to allow for the new, low positioning of jet engines on the pylons hanging below the wing. FOD, the new acronym for foreign object damage, was a major concern to the health and integrity of jet engines because they could not tolerate ingesting small rocks, gravel, and debris of any kind lying about the taxiway. Runways were too short for jet aircraft, particularly those needing a full load of fuel for transatlantic or transcontinental routes. These requirements were exceedingly costly to the airport owners, usually a governmental entity, whether city, country, or regional political subdivision.

Not only was it costly and time-consuming to enlarge and upgrade existing airports, new construction was becoming a contentious issue in the communities in which they were located. Noise associated with jet operations was becoming a serious environmental issue, an issue that had constitutional and legal ramifications that extended far beyond the boundaries of the airports. And if improvement of existing airport facilities was a problem, then the building of new airports was next to impossible to pull off. In 1952 when authorities began looking for a site near Washington, D.C., to relieve the already overcrowded National Airport, an exercised public in Fairfax County, VA, rose in protest. It would require six years of effort spent in negotiation, in cajoling, in conducting studies, and in spending lots of money before the eventual site for Dulles International Airport was selected and approved. It was worse in the metropolitan New York area. Attempts to locate an agreeable site anywhere in northern New Jersey were defeated; twenty-two other proposed sites in New York and New Jersey went down to defeat. A group comprised of the New York Port Authority, the FAA, and some airlines finally settled on a site forty-eight miles from the city, but opposition cancelled that one too. Plans to expand and upgrade the ancient White Plains Airport were defeated by local opposition. To this day, New York has the same three airports that it had in 1950.

The resistance was not limited to the Northeast. Attempts in Dade County, Florida, to build a new airport to serve Miami failed. Miami International Airport, like most metropolitan airports, has been situated in the same place since bi-wing, open cockpit airplanes first began using it. One exception was the Dallas-Fort Worth Airport, in Texas, which only came about because of the cooperation of the citizens and local govern-

ments of the two cities that it serves. Located midway between Dallas and Fort Worth, DFW was completed in 1974. It became a symbol of pride and progress for the area, and it was appreciated by its business and leisure travel communities. One motivating factor for success was the appallingly inadequate Love Field in Dallas, which it replaced, as well as the fact that Fort Worth had no commercial airport. After completion of DFW, no new airport would be built in the United States for another twenty years.[3]

The launch of the Airbus 380 in December 2000 created another challenge for U.S. airports, as well as airports all over the world. The size of the A380 will require that modifications he made at airports which will serve the new gigantic aircraft. Although the A380 can land on runways that will accept the Boeing 747, modifications to taxiways, terminal gates, and aprons will have to be made. Airports will also have to fund the purchase of new servicing vehicles for the A380. It is estimated that some 20 airports worldwide will be ready to receive the A380 by 2007, with that number increasing to 40 airports by 2010.

Airport Security

Exploding passenger traffic after World War II and the advance in aircraft technology were only part of the problem confronting airports. Aircraft hijacking began as a means for oppressed citizens from communist regimes to escape to freedom in the West. As long as the hijackings were of communist-controlled airlines and the destination was freedom, the public generally applauded this audacity. But when the hijacking traffic started moving in the other direction, from the United States to Cuba, people began to view hijacking a bit differently. The first such U.S. to Cuba effrontery occurred in 1961 when a National Airlines airliner was commandeered to Havana, and then more followed. It was unthinkable. No federal laws adequately covered the activity, so Congress hurriedly passed appropriate legislation making the hijacking of an aircraft a federal crime. Things then cooled off and it began to look as though the few hijackings from the United States had been an aberration. But in 1968, there were seventeen hijacking attempts; in 1969, there were thirty-three more.

Hijacking commercial airliners soon became a worldwide phenomenon when two Arabs grabbed a TWA flight bound for Tel Aviv. Hijacking was gradually evolving into terrorism; that is, hijacking for a political purpose. Palestinians seized a Pan American 747 in September 1970 and forced it to Cairo, where it was blown up. This kind of terrorism was repeated on several occasions, resulting in destruction of the aircraft amid full-blown television coverage. Hostages were taken; ransoms and the release of imprisoned terrorists were demanded.

The United States initiated a program of air marshals, G-men who rode anonymously aboard selected airliners for the purpose of foiling would-be hijackers. Eastern Air Lines began using metal detectors for boarding passengers. Then the infamous D. B. Cooper, a thief with no particular social or religious philosophy, took over a Northwest Airlines 727. He directed the aircraft to a designated landing site where he released the passengers but demanded and got $200,000 and four parachutes. After the aircraft departed, and while airborne over the vast forests of the northwestern United States, he lowered the 727's unique rear stairwell and disappeared, with his cash, into the night.

But hijackings worldwide were taking on a deadly and tragic caste. In October 1972, an Eastern 727 was hijacked to Havana by wanted murderers, and in November, an escaped convict and two accomplices seized a Southern Airways DC-9 and proceeded to take the airplane and crew on an extended twenty-nine hour odyssey, making eight landings. The airplane and crew finally wound up safely in Havana, even after agents in Miami shot out the tires during takeoff. The FAA responded by ordering the installation of metal detectors at all gates. In December 1972 the FAA changed the passenger airline business forever by ordering the airlines to carry out electronic screening of all boarding passengers, as well as the inspection of carry-on luggage.

In the years since the first electronic screening began, scrutiny of airline passengers has steadily intensified. The list of prohibited carry-on items has steadily lengthened. Surveillance methods and sources have increased. Many more security personnel have been employed. Since the terrorist attacks on September 11, 2001, security procedures have been greatly amplified, as well as modified to address the threat of international terrorism. Responsibility for airport security has been removed from the FAA and given to the new Transportation Security Administration (TSA).

Evolution of a New National Airport Policy

The operation of airports changed in many other ways. The physical size of new airports serving modern jet airline traffic, the noise considerations inherent in airport operations, the large facilities necessary to accommodate the millions of passengers passing through the airports, and the newfound safety concerns resulting from the criminal and social developments of the 1960s called for a new and aggressive national airport policy.

Under the Federal Airport Act of 1946, the Federal-Aid Airport Program (FAAP) had been the first peacetime program of financial aid aimed exclusively at promoting development of the nation's civil airports. It endured for 24 years, but the growing demands of modern commercial aviation rendered that program obsolete.

In 1970, Congress had passed the Airport and Airway Development Act in order to address the obvious shortcomings of the nation's airports and the airway system. The policy statement for this law recognized the inadequacy of the nation's airport and airway system, and committed the government to its substantial expansion and improvement in order to meet the demands of interstate commerce, the national defense, and the postal service. Congress created the Airport and Airway Trust Fund, from which grants would be made for the purposes of the Act. The statute provided for the collection of certain user fees to further fund the program.

In 1982, after deregulation, Congress amended the existing statute with the Airport and Airway Development Act of 1982, reestablishing the FAA's airport grants program (which had been inactive since 1981) and renaming the Trust Fund program the Airport Improvement Program (AIP). The Trust Fund was originally administered by the CAA in 1946, and sequentially thereafter by the Federal Aviation Agency and then the Federal Aviation Administration.

This Act also amended the Federal Aviation Act of 1958 by requiring, for the first time, that operators of airports serving certificated air carriers secure "Airport Operating Certificates" by application to the FAA, demonstrating the ability to conduct safe and properly equipped airport operations. These requirements are set forth in Part 139 of the Federal Aviation Regulations.

Endnotes

1. Wilson, John R. M., *Turbulence Aloft,* 34–35.

2. *Fortune* magazine, August 1946, 78.

3. Denver International Airport opened in 1995.

Aviation Taxes	Comment	Tax Rate
PASSENGERS		
Domestic Passenger Ticket Tax	Ad valorem tax	7.5% of ticket price (10/1/99 through 9/30/2007)
Domestic Flight Segment Tax	"Domestic Segment" = a flight leg consisting of one takeoff and one landing by a flight	Rate is indexed by the Consumer Price Index starting 1/1/02 during calendar year (CY) 2003 $3.00 per passenger per segment during CY2004. $3.10 per passenger per segment during CY2005. $3.20 per passenger per segment during CY2005. $3.30 per passenger per segment during CY2006. $3.40 per passenger per segment during CY2007.
Passenger Ticket Tax for Rural Airports	Assessed on tickets on flights that begin/end at a rural airport.	Rural airport: <100K enplanements during 2nd preceding CY, and either 1) not located within 75 miles of another airport with 100K+ enplanements, 2) is receiving essential air service subsidies, or 3) is not connected by paved roads to another airport 7.5% of ticket price (same as passenger ticket tax) Flight segment fee does not apply.
International Arrival & Departure Tax	Head tax assessed on pax arriving or departing for foreign destinations (& U.S. territories) that are not subject to pax ticket tax.	Rate is indexed by the Consumer Price Index starting 1/1/99 Rate during CY2003 = $13.40 Rate during CY2004 = $13.70 Rate during CY2005 = $14.10 Rate during CY2006 = $14.50 Rate during CY2007 = $15.10
Flights between continental U.S. and Alaska or Hawaii		Rate is indexed by the Consumer Price Index starting 1/1/99 $6.70 international facilities tax + applicable domestic tax rate (during CY03) $6.90 international facilities tax + applicable domestic tax rate (during CY04) $7.00 international facilities tax + applicable domestic tax rate (during CY05) $7.30 international facilities tax + applicable domestic tax rate (during CY06) $7.50 international facilities tax + applicable domestic tax rate (during CY07)
Frequent Flyer Tax	Ad valorem tax assessed on mileage awards (e.g., credit cards).	7.5% of value of miles
FREIGHT/MAIL		
Domestic Cargo/Mail		6.25% of amount paid for the transportation of property by air
Aviation Fuel		
General Aviation Fuel Tax		Aviation gasoline: $0.193/gallon Jet fuel: $0.218/gallon
Commercial Fuel Tax		$0.043/gallon

TABLE 23-1 Current aviation excise tax structure (Taxpayer Relief Act of 1997, Public Law 105-35).

PART V

Deregulation

© Stephen Strathdee, 2008, Shutterstock.

Chapter 24   Prelude to Deregulation

Chapter 25   The Airline Deregulation Act of 1978

Chapter 26   The Age of Lorenzo

Chapter 27   Carl Icahn and TWA

Chapter 28   Pan American and Deregulation

Chapter 29   Airline Labor Relations

Chapter 30   The Progression of Deregulation

Chapter 31   Deregulation and the Significance of Competition

Chapter 32   Antitrust Enforcement after Deregulation

Chapter 33   Airports and Deregulation

Chapter 34   Airports and the Environment

Chapter 35   Deregulation
in the Nineties

Chapter 36   Airlines at the
Beginning of the
21st Century

CHAPTER 24

Prelude to Deregulation

© Alex Staroseltsev, 2008, Shutterstock.

The Airline Deregulation Act of 1978 (ADA) was signed into law by President Jimmy Carter on October 24, 1978, bringing to a close 40 years of government oversight, control, and protection of the airlines of the United States. Only in the fields of aviation safety and international relations would the government henceforth concern itself with the "public interest" implications of the nation's airlines and their operations. The ADA was a departure from established government tradition dating back almost 100 years to the Interstate Commerce Act of 1887, the first regulation of the railroads, and the beginning of a governmental philosophy of broad regulation of the transportation industry.

The Economic Nature of Transportation

The nature of transportation is such that, unlike most consumer services, it is an intermediate product, only a means to an end. Hardly anyone flies in the airline system just to go for an airplane ride. The reason people fly is to accomplish another goal, whether it is for a business purpose or a personal one.

This characteristic of the transportation industry likens it to a commodity, for example, wheat or petroleum. Wheat is not purchased because anyone wants a bushel of wheat, but to create an end product, perhaps a cake or a loaf of bread. Oil has no use except to facilitate a secondary purpose, like the lubrication of machines or as a means of propulsion.

There are no unique characteristics within a class of commodity; one bushel of wheat is like any other. One quart of oil is indistinguishable, and worth no more, than any other quart of oil. Economic theory teaches that the price of a commodity will seek the lowest possible level based on supply and demand. If the supply of a commodity is adequate to the demand, unit profit on any given quantity of a commodity will be very small.

If an airline seat is like a bushel of wheat, its price will be valued like any other airline seat absent some distinguishing characteristic, assuming an adequate supply of airline seats. If the market in any commodity is cornered, so that the supply can be controlled, the price of that commodity can also be controlled, not unlike the OPEC states' control of a large segment of the world supply of oil.

Under regulation of the airline industry, the Civil Aeronautics Board controlled both the supply and the price of airline seats. With deregulation that control was to end, and the supply and price of airline seats was to be opened to the free market. Under economic theory, a deregulated or free market air carrier industry should make airline seats adhere to commodity supply and demand principles, and to reduced prices. In a free market economy within the air carrier industry, the risk still exists that control of supply (the availability of seats) may be manipulated by a cornering of the market through economic power or anticompetitive practices. We will review these concepts later in this Part in connection with factors that limit competition.

The Nature of Regulated Transportation

Since early in their history airlines had been considered by government to be, to some degree, instruments of national policy.

Airlines were used:

➡ To carry the mail

➡ To facilitate commerce between the cities and states

➡ To establish a fast and efficient passenger transportation system

➡ To function in the national defense system in times of emergency

➡ To carry the flag internationally

To carry out these functions, the airlines had to be financially stable, and they had to be dependable in the long run and reliable at all times.

For 40 years, entry into the airline business had been controlled by the Civil Aeronautics Board. No major new entrants had been permitted, although some smaller feeder lines were allowed to enter the market on a limited basis. The number of trunk lines had decreased from sixteen in 1938 to ten in 1978. That year the five largest airlines accounted for two-thirds of all domestic revenue. Competition was seen as good by the CAB, but not destructive competition, so routes were awarded among the existing carriers

based on the perceived needs of the communities and cities requiring service, and on the equitable allocation of routes to the airlines desiring and capable of delivering such service. Fares and rates were established mainly as a function of the airlines' cost of doing business, a system not particularly designed or administered to be cost efficient. But it was stable. Not one airline in 40 years had been allowed to go into bankruptcy.

Competition in the airline industry had been regulated, but it had not been eliminated. The more efficient the airline, the better its operating ratio and the more money there was at the bottom-line. The effect of airline economic regulation was to create both a financial ceiling and floor for the companies, guaranteeing that neither profits nor losses were excessive. While the support of the CAB limiting airline loss was comforting to management, the ceiling limiting innovation and profit was frustrating, particularly to the types of men who rose to run the airlines. The technological advance in aircraft and engine design kept airlines busy trying to stay ahead of one another in order to have the most appealing fleet available for the limited passenger market, most of which were business travelers. Aesthetics and service were high on the list of concerns, since these were two of the few discretionary operating decisions available to management. Marketing schemes were also highly competitive, the effort being limited to the best way to sell essentially the same product that every other airline sold. Each new innovation thought up by an airline, no matter how minor, was pushed as the reason to fly that airline. For instance, the introduction in 1965 of in-flight movies by TWA was highly advertised; it resulted in six to eight more passengers per flight. Airline management continually strived to bring some quality of uniqueness to their operations.

Until the 1960s and early 1970s, leadership of the major airlines had remained mostly in the hands of the young men who took over in 1934 after the Black investigation of the so-called "spoils conference" scandal. Newcomers like

Robert Crandall at American and Richard Ferris at United were natural competitors and often went head to head on issues like market share, computer reservation system development, and travel agent loyalty. Crandall preferred to compete within the established regulatory framework, while Ferris, who came from the hotel industry, was open-minded about deregulation.

The market for cheaper air travel had been recognized since shortly after World War II, when charter operators began flying, using war surplus DC-3s and later DC-4s. But CAB regulations governing charter operations were severely restrictive. Charterers could not sell individual tickets, nor could they fly published schedules. They were essentially relegated to selling the entire aircraft capacity to large, established groups by advance sales. The CAB monitored these operations carefully; ever watchful lest charter operations encroach on the CAB controlled scheduled airlines' established routes. The charter operators showed that a profit could be made with low fares, sometimes as much as fifty percent lower than CAB mandated fares, so long as the aircraft flew filled with passengers.

Charter operations failed to maintain market-share in a hostile environment controlled by the CAB, which often allowed the scheduled lines to meet the charter fares on a case-by-case basis. The trunk carriers in such cases would match the charter fares and, after the demise of the particular charter operation, the higher scheduled fares would be reinstated. Still, charter operators persisted and made money in specialty markets, particularly after the CAB began loosening the regulations applicable to charter operations in the 1970s.

Factors that contributed to deregulation of the airlines arose from several quarters, but came together at about the same time. By the 1970s, the railroad industry had been heavily regulated by the Interstate Commerce Commission for over eighty years, and the airline industry had been regulated by the Civil Aeronautics Board for almost forty years. The railroads were in serious financial trouble under regulation. Mergers entered into to stave off financial collapse, like the Pennsylvania Railroad and the New York Central, only succeeded in delaying the inevitable as the Penn Central entered bankruptcy in the 1970s. Railroad passenger service could no longer be sustained in the private sector, as Amtrak, subsidized by the government, was required to take over that service.

In the 1970s, the adversities realized by the railroad industry were perceived as a harbinger for the airline industry. It also seemed that the government was not trusted, nor was it respected as before, perhaps due to public disgust and unease created by the divisive issues of the 1960s and 1970s. It hardly mattered from which end of the political spectrum one viewed the situation. On the left, the Vietnam War and Watergate were examples of inept or corrupt leadership. On the right, the social experimentation of The Great Society programs of Lyndon Johnson, the rapid deterioration of inner cities, and civil disturbances seen nightly on the evening news were evidence of misguided governmental policy. Government seemed to be contributing to the problem, rather than offering rational solutions.

The anti-regulatory mood was also intellectual. Alfred Kahn, a professor of economics at Cornell University, produced a two-volume work, *The Economics of Regulation,* which basically postulated that the heavy hand of government regulation was inimical to the public interest, and that competition would naturally produce the best product for the best price for the public. Kahn had also become acquainted with a 1965 law review article in the *Yale Law Journal* written by Michael Levine, who as a law student had looked into the intrastate airline business in California. In comparing the intrastate airline fares with those mandated by the CAB, he concluded that CAB policies "fostered unnecessarily high fares, encouraged uneconomic practices, and limited the variety of services available to the public."

❝I really don't know one plane from the other. To me they are just marginal costs with wings.❞

Alfred Kahn, 1977

The anti-regulatory mood was not only emotional and intellectual, but also political. In 1974, Sen. Edward Kennedy had aspirations concerning the office of Presidency of the United States, and he was searching for an issue. Kennedy had on his staff a Harvard law professor, Stephen Breyer, in residence in Washington for a summer sabbatical. Breyer, who was to become an Associate Justice of the United States Supreme Court twenty years later on, was apparently genuinely concerned about what he saw within the CAB as an accepted pattern of price fixing of fares, to the detriment of the consumer. Politically, Kennedy could expose the price-fixing pattern of the CAB as a pro-consumer advocate, and he could propose the elimination of the agency on the basis of a fiscal conservative. Hearings on the matter began in February 1975.

Dissatisfaction with the regulatory scheme at the CAB came even from within the agency itself. Careerists at the agency seemed to have run out of tolerance for much of the silliness associated with the matters that were required to be decided by them, from the price of drinks on airplanes to special fares for skiers. In 1975 a staff study within the CAB observed that restrictions imposed on the airline industry were not justified, and, heretically, that the industry was not even monopolistic, but naturally competitive.[1]

In 1975, an individual by the name of John Robson took over as chairman of the CAB under President Gerald Ford. He had been an undersecretary at the Department of Transportation, a career Washington bureaucrat, and he knew little about the airline industry. But he soon came to understand the mood of the place. He began the relaxation of the myriad regulations that applied to charter operations, allowing the charter operators to fly more routes, longer distances, and with fewer restrictions, thus creating immediate competition for the scheduled airlines. This, in turn, caused the scheduled airlines to make application to the CAB for permission to make a legitimate, long-range competitive response to the charterers. The CAB then began granting those applications, thereby setting up an incipient competition theretofore unknown under regulation. This would come to be known as "de facto" deregulation.

The idea of deregulation, a concept truly iconoclastic in the annals of government, was beginning to catch on. When Jimmy Carter took office as President in 1976, he was a political newcomer. Sen. Kennedy still loomed on the horizon as likely competition to him for the hearts and minds of Democrats, if not a large segment of the entire voting population itself. Carter got behind the deregulation issue and supported it. He advised that Congress pass the legislation in order to "reduce Federal regulation of the domestic commercial airline industry" in the name of a less burdensome federal government. Carter had earlier appointed professor Alfred Kahn head of the CAB. Kahn not only continued the course begun by John Robson before him, he actively applied his deregulation philosophy to the matters coming before the Board.

The CAB had no jurisdiction over intrastate carriers like Southwest Airlines, and although Southwest could charge what it pleased subject only to the rules of the Texas Public Utilities Commission, its fares were substantially less than those mandated by the CAB regimen. Southwest was stiff competition for any airline flying within the very expansive borders of Texas, and that competition included interstate carriers Texas International and American Airlines. When Texas International sought CAB authority for its "peanut fares," (its regular, CAB mandated fare discounted fifty percent) in order to compete with Southwest, the CAB obliged.

Again, when American Airlines wanted to institute its "Supersaver" fare in March 1977, a flat out charter-like discount theretofore prohibited by CAB philosophy, the CAB approved. Significantly, the "Supersaver" fares applied to seats on regularly scheduled flights on which standard fare passengers had purchased tickets. Thus began the confusing and seemingly inequitable pattern of full-fare passengers seated beside someone who had paid a fraction of full fare. These fares also invited into the cabin leisure passengers, bringing with them their small children and babies, to occupy the center seat previously left unfilled. American Airline's coast-to-coast traffic soon increased by 61 percent. Nobody seemed to notice, but deregulation, for better or worse, had already begun.

De facto deregulation was limited to a revision of the "business as usual" regulation imposed by the CAB in only three major areas:

1. The loosening of the restrictions on charter operations
2. Approval of Texas International's "peanut fares" as a competitive response to Southwest and charter operations
3. Approval of American Airlines "Supersaver Fares" that allowed the first co-mingling of discounted fares with full fare passengers on the same flight

Still, in a regulated world the safety net was there. Carriers with financial problems could still rely on the CAB to make things right. The airlines were insulated from the Big Bad World of competition and all of the downside that unbridled competition can bring. But all of this was about to change.

Endnote

1. For a review of monopolies and the basis of regulation, refer to pages 15 and 16.

CHAPTER 25

The Airline Deregulation Act of 1978

© Johnny Kuo, 2008, Shutterstock.

The Airline Deregulation Act amends the Federal Aviation Act of 1958, stating as its purpose "to encourage, develop, and attain an air transportation system which relies on competitive market forces to determine the quality, variety, and price of air services." The Act completely changed the economic foundation for the domestic airline industry. It provided, among other things:

1. for the phase-out of the CAB and its authority over domestic routes and fares,

2. for the phase-out of existing economic regulations formerly constituting barriers to competition,

3. safeguards for the protection of air carrier service to small communities,

4. for the facilitation of entry of air carriers into new markets, and

5. for certain protection of airline employees who may be adversely affected by the results of the Act.

CAB route authority ended on December 31, 1981, and rate authority terminated on December 31, 1983. The CAB itself ceased to exist as of the close of business on December 31, 1984.

Prior law, as interpreted by the Supreme Court, had exempted the airlines from compliance with the antitrust laws governing commercial enterprise in the United States. After deregulation, upon the demise of the CAB, airlines became subject to these laws just the same as other corporations, with enforcement jurisdiction initially residing in the Department of Transportation.

With deregulation, there was no longer any requirement to secure from the CAB certificates of convenience and necessity before commencing service on a route. No longer were there artificial barriers to entry into the previously exclusive airline carrier club, nor was there any requirement to secure approval from the CAB for rate increases.

When deregulation became law, all of the pent-up competitive instincts of airline bosses were suddenly unleashed. Like adolescents let loose on a first unsupervised journey away from home, excesses might have been expected. The choices of how to proceed were practically unlimited. Unbridled optimism coupled with a fear of being left behind in the race to gain position on their competitors spurred frenzied activity of all sorts, and not a few miscalculations.

Braniff—A Case History Under Deregulation

Braniff's conclusion that deregulation would only be temporary, and that re-regulation was inevitable, was probably the biggest mistake of all. That conclusion prompted Braniff to believe that new routes should be established as quickly as possible, before the window of opportunity slammed shut, and that the equipment to serve these new routes should be immediately acquired before the aircraft manufacturers became backlogged with orders from all of the other airlines that were sure to come.

In 1978 Braniff International Airways was a successful, established carrier with a reliable business clientele responsible for about 70 percent of its traffic. When Postmaster General Farley ordered the re-bidding in 1934 for airmail routes after the so-called "Spoils Conference" affair of 1930, Braniff had acquired the coveted Dallas-Chicago route. Braniff was profitable and had been for much of its proud history as one of the 16 trunk carriers grandfathered under the Civil Aeronautics Act of 1938. After World War II, Braniff became the first international competitor to Pan American certificated by the United States government when it began service to South America along its East Coast. In December 1965, Braniff bought the 50 percent interest of W. R. Grace in Panagra, which served the West Coast of South America, and in March 1966 it completed this acquisition by buying out the remaining 50 percent interest from Pan American. Between 1975 and 1980, Braniff doubled in size.

Braniff's management decision after deregulation to rapidly expand its operations led to the purchase of many new aircraft, which in turn resulted in huge debt. The decision required expansion of its infrastructure at high cost to service the new, expanded route structure put in place after deregulation.

Beginning in 1980 and extending into the early years of the decade, fuel prices spiraled upward due to the OPEC oil crisis, interest rates shot up to 20 percent, and the attendant recession had a stifling effect on passenger traffic. When deregulation did not end, and upstart airlines continued to enter the field and pose significant competitive pressures on the Braniff's expanded routes, Braniff began suffering catastrophic losses. In order to maintain cash flow, Braniff began to sell off its newly acquired fleet of aircraft at distressed prices to its competitors, further weakening its position. It then turned to selling off its biggest prizes, its overseas routes, and the handwriting was on the wall.

By 1982, Braniff could no longer keep its doors open against the clamor of creditors, and it filed for Chapter 11 protection under the bankruptcy act. It was the first United States airline to do so since regulation was begun in 1938. Ultimately, the assets of the company were liquidated and it ceased to exist.

The United States Bankruptcy Act[1]

The Constitution of the United States (Article 1, Section 8) specifically provides that Congress be empowered to establish "uniform laws on the subject of bankruptcies throughout the United States." Congress has done so on repeated occasions since 1801. Bankruptcy in the United States, therefore, is mainly a federal exercise, administered in the federal bankruptcy courts, which are an adjunct of the United States District Courts located in each state across the land.

The concept of bankruptcy first implies that one's debts exceed his assets. This is called "insolvency." Under the laws of the U.S., a petition in bankruptcy can be initiated either by creditors of the insolvent debtor, called "involuntary bankruptcy," or by the debtor himself, called "voluntary bankruptcy." As we saw in Part I of this book, the industrial revolution, and particu-

---

[1] The bankruptcy law is codified at Title 11 of the United States Code. The U.S. Code is a series of books containing all of the laws of the United States arranged sequentially from Title 1 through Title 50A. Each Title is devoted to a particular subject matter. Title 49, for example, contains the federal statutes in the field of transportation.)

larly the advent of the railroads, caused the rise of the corporate form of business entity. Under U.S. law, corporations are entitled to the same basic privileges as individuals, including the protection of the bankruptcy laws.

The bankruptcy code is sub-divided into "Chapters," each one dealing with a separate kind of bankruptcy. The most common form of bankruptcy, known as "straight bankruptcy" is found in Chapter 7 of the Code and results in the shutting down of the business. This procedure provides for the appointment of a Trustee to liquidate all of the debtor's assets and to distribute the proceeds to the creditors. Chapter 11 is a more complex procedure that allows the debtor to remain in business under the supervision of the bankruptcy court while it goes through a "reorganization" of its debt structure and contractual obligations.

The intent of Chapter 11, in allowing a company to remain in business under reorganization, is to provide a way to pay most if not all of the creditors, to save jobs, to preserve the engine of profitability (which is the corporation's operations in place, good will, experience, and hope of the future), and to allow the business to earn a "fresh start." One trade-off to accomplish this result is the cancellation or renegotiation of pre-viously incurred debts and contracts, including labor contracts. This is accomplished either by compromise between the debtor and the creditors, or by rulings of the bankruptcy judge.

During the reorganization process, which may take months to years depending on the complexities of the reorganization, the debtor is considered "under the protection" of the bankruptcy court. This means that the debtor is shielded from lawsuits that could otherwise be brought by creditors, and from general harassment associated with its unpaid debts. At the same time, the operations of the debtor are subject to the scrutiny of the bankruptcy court and the creditors.

In the following chapters of this book, we will see how Chapter 11 bankruptcy has become an integral part of the air transportation business in the deregulated world. Other sophisticated free market techniques, previously unheard of in commercial aviation, would be brought to bear as airlines attempted to cope with the new world of competition. Hostile corporate takeovers, leveraged buyouts, downsizing, outsourcing, and employee pay givebacks and salary cuts were only some of the new developments that loomed over the horizon. Chief practitioner of these ideas was a Harvard MBA by the name of Frank Lorenzo.

CHAPTER 26

The Age of Lorenzo

> **❝** I think it is a pity to lose the romantic side of flying and simply to accept it as a common means of transport, although that end is what we have all ostensibly been striving to attain. **❞**

Amy Johnson, 'Sky Roads of the World,' 1939

Francisco A. Lorenzo had begun a career in New York City working in finance at TWA and Eastern Air Lines before branching out as an aviation financial consultant in the early 1960s. He and a partner formed Jet Capital Corporation and issued shares to themselves for pennies. They then took Jet Capital public, offering the shares at $10.00, and in that way raised $1.5 million. Lorenzo controlled most of the shares. (See Figure 26-1.)

Texas International

Lorenzo struck up an acquaintance with Donald Burr, a New York-based mutual fund financial analyst specializing in airline stocks, and they became good friends. One of Burr's stock picks by the name of Texas International Airlines, a small regional interstate airline, found itself beset with huge debt as a result of replacing prop planes with jets. Lorenzo was able to secure a

FIGURE 26-1 Frank Lorenzo at a press conference, June, 1984.

consultant position with the airline for the purpose of arranging refinancing to save the company. The deal finally agreed upon had Lorenzo's Jet Capital Corporation infusing most

201

of its $1.5 million into the airline, Lorenzo arranging for another $5 million in new equity for the company, and Lorenzo in control of voting shares. By 1972, Lorenzo had become the youngest airline president in the country.

In 1973 Don Burr joined Lorenzo at Texas International as a sort of second banana, although when he took the job, Burr believed he was to be co-chief executive with Lorenzo. Burr soldiered on anyway, and together Lorenzo and Burr began to lay plans to be able to compete with Southwest Airlines, an intrastate carrier over which the CAB had no control. Subject only to the rules of the Texas Utilities Commission, Southwest could charge any fare that it wanted, but its fares were considerably lower over the same routes than those mandated by the CAB for Texas International and the other interstate carriers. To compete, Texas International had to fill its airplanes' seats, and to do that it had to have lower fares. If the CAB approved a reduced fare structure, the company would have the additional leverage of lower fares against the other CAB regulated interstate carriers, as well. When the CAB unexpectedly approved the lower fares sought by Texas International, Lorenzo began a high profile marketing blitz touting his "peanut fares."

The consumer response was overwhelming:

➡ Passenger loads increased by as much as 600 percent

➡ People started flying instead of driving

➡ Texas International was the darling of both Wall Street and the consuming public

➡ Texas International's profits and loss statement showed what an airline could do if left alone by government.

This was all before the Airline Deregulation Act had passed, but Lorenzo was only warming up.

Texas International had grown to number sixteen in the size hierarchy of United States airlines by 1979, a year after deregulation became law, but for Lorenzo that was not big enough.

Growth is often accomplished by merger with another carrier, but that did not seem to be in the cards; none of the other airlines was interested. A hostile takeover, the process by which control of a corporation is achieved through stock acquisition, followed by election of a new board of directors and a new slate of officers giving control of the company to the takeover group, had never been attempted in the airline industry. But there was really nothing about the airlines after deregulation that differentiated them from most any other corporation. Times had changed since CAB Chairman James Landis, in 1947, had forced Howard Hughes out of the control of TWA with the words, "I don't believe one man should own a public utility."

Stock acquisition of an airline company, however, requires lots of money, and Lorenzo was not in the same league as Howard Hughes. Lorenzo did, however, have access to the assets of Jet Capitol, which had increased along with the value of Texas International stock. These assets could be used for acquiring the stock of another airline, at least in the short run. National Airlines was the ninth largest carrier in the United States in 1979, and Lorenzo discovered that it had practically no debt. The assets of the ninth largest airline unencumbered by debt are valuable collateral at the bank if one wished to borrow on those assets, something the management of National obviously did not wish to do. Lorenzo, however, saw these assets as a way to finance a possible takeover of National with a relatively small investment outlay. This process was the paradigm of what would come to be known in financial circles as the "leveraged buyout."

Jet Capitol began buying National stock in the open market until it had acquired almost 10 percent of stock outstanding. Lorenzo then conveyed his intentions to National's president, who immediately began to seek ways to fend off the hostile takeover. The simplest way to defeat a hostile takeover is to gain control of more shares of stock than the takeover group. That usually involves getting into a bidding war for the available stock which, in turn, causes the stock to increase in value. Pan American Airways, looking for domestic routes, of which it had absolutely none, joined in the bidding, and the stock of National went up and up. Lorenzo could not or would not compete with Pan American and decided to simply cash in his National stock—for $108 million, or about a $35 million profit. Pan American purchased 100 percent of National stock and it became a wholly owned subsidiary of Pan Am.

Lorenzo's war chest was now bigger than ever. He formed Texas Air Corporation in 1980 as a holding company. Texas Air owned Texas International and, as a holding company, began looking for opportunities. Using Texas Air, Lorenzo took the no frills concept to the East Coast, to New York City, and started a new subsidiary airline called New York Air to compete with the Eastern Shuttle between Washington, D.C., and Boston. To Lorenzo, a new airline company was much preferred for the main reason that it would be nonunion, unlike Texas International. Like most of the scheduled carriers, Texas International was burdened by union labor contracts that governed wage rates, seniority, and work rules. The pilots of Texas International were not happy to see their company's money being used to form a nonunion carrier instead of an extension of the Texas International network. An expansion of Texas International, as opposed to the creation of a new, nonunion airline, would bring with it new left seat opportunities for the Texas International pilots, openings for new co-pilots, and a larger union contingent. But this was contrary to Lorenzo's plan. Lorenzo was now beginning to build his reputation as the nemesis of organized airline labor, a union buster even, and there was nothing the unions could do about it. Somehow nobody had thought to mention this aspect of deregulation to the rank and file, or to the public.

New York Air began operations out of LaGuardia Airport. The limited landing and take-off slots at LaGuardia proved to be no problem through the political connections of Lorenzo and his new sidekick, Phil Bakes. Bakes, a Harvard law graduate, had worked on the staff of Archibald Cox in the prosecutions related to the Watergate break-in affair, as had Harvard associate Stephen Breyer. It was Breyer who recruited Bakes to work on the deregulation effort in 1975 on the Kennedy staff, and it was Bakes who was largely responsible for engineering the deregulation legislation successfully through Congress for Kennedy. He then worked on the unsuccessful 1980 presidential campaign of Ted Kennedy. Lorenzo had hired Bakes just as the dismal Kennedy campaign came to its sad end. Now, Bakes used his knowledge and contacts to deliver the slots to New York Air. New York Air was launched to great fanfare in New York, and the fare wars with the Eastern Shuttle commenced, to the delight of the traveling public. New York Air was the first in a long line of new airlines that would come to be known as the "Upstarts." And it was very successful.

People Express

In the meantime, Don Burr had decided that he wanted to be his own man and left Texas International in order to form his own airline, which he named People Express. People Express made its headquarters in an old abandoned terminal at Newark, and began operations with 737s purchased from Lufthansa. People Express was absolutely no frills, and did not provide the slightest amenities. There were no meals, beverages (coffee was $.50), or checked baggage. Passenger baggage that had been checked, for an additional charge of $3.00, was not even transferred to connecting carriers. This required the passengers to pick up their bags upon deplaning even if continuing on with another airline. People Express distinguished itself in other ways.

Fares were the lowest in the industry, perhaps ever. Greyhound Bus Lines lost business to People Express. Equality was the order of the day—there were no vice-presidents or secretaries, and employees were cross-trained and lent a hand where necessary. The airline's pilots were indistinguishable in their uniforms from cabin stewards and there were no nine to five days.

People Express began operations in May 1981 during one of the most turbulent economic times in memory. Interest rates, fuel prices, recession, and the air traffic controllers strike all combined to test the new theories of deregulation. In spite of the difficult economic situation, both New York Air and People Express began to thrive, and that was instructive. The no-frills concept took flying to the masses, where the main consideration was price. The effects of deregulation, good and bad, were beginning to be defined. We will return to People Express later.

❝ People Express is clearly the archetypical deregulation success story and the most spectacular of my babies. It is the case that makes me the proudest. ❞

Alfred Kahn, Professor of Political Economy,
Cornell University, 'Time,' 13 Jan 1986

Takeover at Continental Airlines

Frank Lorenzo next set his sights on Continental Airlines. He had earlier attempted to interest Robert Six, founder and chief executive of Continental, in a merger with Texas International, to no avail. Lorenzo began buying Continental stock in a hostile takeover bid, and ultimately acquired a majority through the open market. Al Feldman, who had turned around Frontier Airlines before joining Continental, had replaced Robert Six as CEO and became committed to saving Continental from Lorenzo, whom he did not admire. His efforts focused on joining with

Continental's labor unions to stave off Lorenzo, including attempting to secure financing for an employee stock ownership plan (ESOP). Lorenzo's reputation as a corporate raider, who cared little for the people or the companies taken over, was building, and the people at Continental frantically tried to find ways to retain control. In spite of all efforts, the ESOP failed.

When Lorenzo took over, a new board of directors was selected, including Alfred Kahn and John Robson, both former chairmen of the CAB and indirectly responsible for the emergence of Frank Lorenzo as mover and shaker in the airline industry. Lorenzo brought in Stephen Wolf from Pan Am as president. Texas International operations and aircraft were merged into Continental, the labor unions were called upon to give up pay hikes and other concessions, and the pilots were given an ultimatum to fly more hours for the same pay. As the consolidation proceeded, it soon became clear that Continental was in much worse shape than Lorenzo had been led to believe. If it was to be saved, and Lorenzo's investment salvaged, dire measures were going to be called for.

Phil Bakes, still Lorenzo's right hand man, determined that the airline's main expense challenge was the cost of labor. Pilots averaged around $90,000 per year, but flew only about a third of the month. Flight attendants drew $37,500 annually. Mechanics' wages were $40,000 a year. If Continental were to survive, labor would have to yield to the competitive market consequences of deregulation. Attempts at conciliation proved fruitless. The machinists union, International Association of Machinists (IAM), went out on strike at Continental in August 1983. On September 24, 1983, Continental became the second major airline to file for Chapter 11 protection under the bankruptcy act.

Lorenzo turned over operation of the airline in Chapter 11 to Phil Bakes. A recent decision of the U.S. Supreme Court, ***National Labor Relations Board v. Bildisco,***[1] established that labor contracts, to the extent that their provisions impaired the claims of other creditors, were not enforceable against the debtor corporation (the airline). This decision opened the way for Continental to unilaterally abrogate all wage scales and work rules, which it did immediately. In effect, Lorenzo was able to legally cancel all labor contracts that were in force at Continental. He then invited back its employees to work longer hours at half the rate of pay. Those who did not agree were simply out of a job. New hires were made in all areas of the company and, despite the fact that the company was in bankruptcy, the pilots' union called a strike. Through the efforts of Phil Bakes, schedules were largely maintained, additional pilots were brought into the company, fares were lowered to attract more passengers, and gradually the company took on a semblance of normalcy. Two years after Continental entered Chapter 11, it became the first airline to successfully emerge from bankruptcy and to pay its creditors close to 100 cents on the dollar. The restructured and reconfigured airline was now ready to cope with the deregulated world.

Computer Reservation Systems

Lorenzo was by no means through acquiring airlines. In 1985, just prior to Continental's coming out of reorganization, Lorenzo made a play for TWA. Some said this was because he needed its computer reservation system to manage the traffic in his growing conglomerate of airline companies. Computer reservation systems were proprietary with each of the Big Four, and it was realized that these systems gave huge advantages to those airlines by increasing their passenger market share, to the detriment of the smaller lines.

Travel reservations, the process of matching an available seat with a named passenger to occupy it, had always been a complex undertaking. Even with the railroads, where it was largely a matter of recognizing where passengers on the line of road were getting on and getting off, keeping up with the availability of seats was a daunting task. In the early airlines, as with the railroads, reservations were tracked manually, usually at a central location. Entries representing reservations were made in pencil so that they could be erased if the reservation was cancelled. When traffic picked up in the 1930s, ledgers became even more impractical, and the system was expanded to chalkboard displays in large rooms, also at a central location, on which entries and cancellations were noted. Clerks who took the reservation request from passengers handed off the information to runners who relayed the details to writers at the chalkboards. Chalkboards were replaced by electric light displays, also in large rooms, and despite the advanced technology of electricity, the process was still manual, cumbersome, and inaccurate. Increased service to multiple cities in random directions, even on one airline, exponentially increased the difficulties of keeping track of reservations manually. Booking seats on multiple airlines made the job even harder.

By the 1940s, efforts were being made to automate the process. Makers of computational equipment, like adding machines, were the logical choice to assist in solving these mathematical complexities, but in turn they advised that they could not handle the number of variables presented in the problem. C. R. Smith of American Airlines, himself an accountant and numbers man, was preoccupied with the reservations dilemma. Unable to secure assistance outside of the company, he authorized American's technical people to come up with a solution. The result was a massive mechanical monstrosity consisting of vertical cylinders, each one representing a different flight on a given day, which was filled with marbles representing available seats. When a seat was booked, an agent activated a switch that released one marble from the cylinder. A reciprocal arrangement at the top of the cylinder released a marble back into the cylinder for each reservation that was cancelled.

This arrangement was an improvement, but it was no match for the growing problem of reservations as traffic increased. With the beginning of the jet age in commercial air traffic, once again the problem was made exponentially more difficult. The process was not only marginally inaccurate, but also very costly for the company as personnel and terminals had to be added to the system.

IBM, through its primitive computer technology, during the 1950s was out front in developing solutions for the federal government related to the problems of monitoring the potential for incoming missiles. The acronym for the IBM program was SAGE, Semi-Automatic Ground Environment. SAGE was the first computer game in real time as strategic and tactical planners engaged each other in simulations of nuclear warfare.

Under contract with American, IBM began applying its SAGE technology to the reservations problem, and for almost ten years its best minds labored away. The project was originally known as SABER, Semi-Automatic Business Environment Research, and later as SABRE, and the first commercial activation of the system did not occur until 1962. At that time computer technology was truly rudimentary, and almost all commercial computers were engaged in solving mathematical equations, or in streamlining the problems of accounting in corporate America, like payrolls. And these applications were applied to dealing with numbers in a historical context, not real-time. With SABRE, real-time computing in business was born.

Now American Airlines had a real commercial advantage over its competitors. In the 1960s, the CAB was still in control of all meaningful decisions related to the running of an airline, so SABRE's function was expanded to not only solve American's reservations problems, and to assure consistent and accurate reservations for

the very first time, but also to track every passenger's name, address, personal information, and most details of that passenger's travel information, such as hotel usage. Not only could SABRE track customer information, but the technology was immediately expanded to begin to solve the company's day-to-day operational problems. But management at American was slow to realize the full potential of the advantage given them by the computer system they had developed.

The other airlines began their own experimentations with computers, particularly as applied to the reservations system. The technology was still relatively primitive, and the cost was enormous. In 1966, TWA committed $75 million to solving the problem, hiring Burroughs Corporation to come up with a proprietary computer reservations system. By 1970, no workable system had been achieved, although in time TWA would perfect a system known as PARS. United began its own program, called APOLLO, and made reasonable progress. At the same time at American, SABRE was losing its advantage as management failed to upgrade equipment, and as uninstalled computers sat in storage, allowing its competitors to catch up.

In 1970, in spite of their individual efforts up to that time, the major airlines realized that, from a cost effectiveness standpoint, it made a lot more sense to pool their resources to develop the ultimate computer reservations system than for each to go it alone, thereby duplicating effort and wasting untold sums of money. When presented with the airlines' plan, the Justice Department announced that it would consider such a combination between the major carriers to be a violation of the Sherman Antitrust Act, and would prosecute the airlines criminally if they proceeded. The airlines regarded the Justice Department position as a shocking miscalculation tantamount to a governmental abuse of power, but there was little that they could do. The opportunity was thus lost to have a single, unbiased reservations program developed for the benefit of all of the airlines and the public at large. The only course left for the airlines was for each of them to develop their own, proprietary system. Few in 1970 realized the commercial potential of the computer, or the great benefits that would inure to the owners of these proprietary systems. The joint plan proposed by the airlines would have allowed the unbiased computer reservations system to be used by all travel agents in servicing the flying public. Now the public would have to wait, as would the travel agents.

Around 1975, the travel agents got together to announce that they were planning to develop their own CRS. United had its APOLLO up and running, and by 1974 it was generally considered to be the best in the industry, having surpassed SABRE. It was, however, a work still in progress. No one at the major airlines believed that it was in their interest to lose control of CRS, and be faced with a giant travel agent computer network where all flights of all airlines would be available to all travel agents everywhere. It was deemed likely that such a system would require the airlines to pay a transaction fee for every reservation, in addition to the commission that they paid.

Another effort was made by the airlines to convince the government of the desirability of the joint approach. The CAB this time gave the airlines antitrust immunity, but only to permit the airlines to explore the possibilities of such a system—to talk, but not to proceed, with building such a program. It was at this stage, in July 1975, that United unilaterally declared that it would no longer participate in seeking government approval for the joint effort, and that it would go it alone. United, as the biggest bear in the woods, believed that it had a competitive advantage over the other airlines in its CRS, and it began to appreciate what favorable nuances could be incorporated into the program to heighten that advantage. United's plan was to gain control of the travel agent business by sup-

plying travel agents with its APOLLO program which would, of course, have built into it biases in favor of United.

The world of travel agents at the time was one of telephones and paper transactions. The Official Airline Guide (OAG) was a periodical publication containing all the world's airline departures and arrivals, displayed in a city pair format. The procedure was for the travel agent, upon receiving a request from a traveler for flight information preparatory to booking a reservation, to go to the OAG, discern the flight information and the airline that most closely matched the traveler's request, and then secure authority to book the flight. The travel agent would then telephone the airline, confirm the reservation, secure the airline's authority, and then telephone the traveler back with the confirmation. The agent would then write the ticket and ultimately transmit it to the traveler, usually by mail. The travel agent was paid a commission by the airline.

The United plan would simplify this procedure greatly. The plan was to install computer terminals in the travel agents' offices for a fee, and then provide the agents with all of the flight information available in the OAG on an interactive, real-time basis so that the travel agent would be able to confirm the reservation while the traveler was still on the phone, then the computer would issue the ticket. Unstated, but appreciated by some of United's competitors like Bob Crandall at American, was the fact that APOLLO would contain preferences for United through outright biased presentations that would likely cause the travel agent to favor a United flight over any other.

Typical of the types of bias that the computer could generate was positioning of the flight information on the computer screen. American had conducted research that showed that 50 percent of the time, travel agents selected the flight that appeared on the first line of the computer screen. Ninety percent of the time, the travel agent picked a flight that appeared on the first page of a multi-page computer display. If the proprietary CRS program were configured to offer its own flights on the first line, or at least in a favorable position on the first page, there was an advantage to that airline.

Dick Ferris of United and Bob Crandall of American, with their companies in a nip and tuck race to lead the industry in the middle 1970s, were head to head competitors. Crandall resolved to bring SABRE back up to a competitive level immediately, and to pitch SABRE to the travel agents as the best system for them. Crandall did his homework, made presentations at national travel agent conventions, conducted mail out campaigns, and before long, American was out in front again.

The agents who signed up with American were provided with terminals, computers, monitors, and the essentials for using the system in their business, and they were charged a fee. Only the largest "commercial" agencies could afford to participate, but the hardware was getting cheaper by the month. Then United struck back by providing some of the agencies with the equipment without a fee, and allegedly gave rebates (fees) to the agencies for using United's CRS.

The game was now on. It became a contest to program the airline's CRS to give the greatest advantage (bias) to that airline, preferably without disclosing its existence to the travel agent or anyone else. CRS owners were known for being slow to adjust changes made by their competitors in their schedules, particularly if those changes operated to the detriment of that CRS owner. Preferences were introduced, like providing advance boarding passes only to travel agents who were subscribers to SABRE. "Bonuses" were paid to travel agents. Dirty tricks were not out of the question. When Lorenzo's New York Air refused to pay the $3.00 transaction fee imposed first by American, and then by all other CRS owners, all New York Air flights were

dropped to the bottom of the last page. United dropped People Express completely from its APOLLO system. And the CRS owners began selectively charging booking fees to the smaller airlines, apparently on an arbitrary basis. This caused the CAB to order in 1984 that CRS owners desist from discriminating against the smaller airlines in booking fee charges.[2] So the CRS owners simply raised fees for everyone, and it was a huge burden. Midway Airlines is reported to have paid nearly $150 million in booking fees over a twelve-year period.

Travel agents in hub cities overwhelmingly used the CRS system owned and provided by the dominant hub carrier. The airlines candidly admitted that their computer screen displays favored their own airline, justifying the practice on the airlines' vast expenditure of funds in development of the CRS system. After a Justice Department investigation, the CAB in 1984, as one of its last official acts, ordered the airlines to cease all bias in their program's displays.

It was becoming increasingly clear as business and the public became more dependent on computers that the airlines were becoming increasingly dependent on computer reservations systems. By 1984, travel agencies were responsible for almost three fourths of all airline tickets sold. CRS was important before deregulation when all airlines charged the same fare as set for them by the CAB. With deregulation, CRS was indispensable, and Lorenzo did not have one.

Acquiring a computer reservations system is only one justification for waging a hostile takeover war. As Lorenzo was making his play, another wealthy financier, Carl Icahn, became enamored of owning an airline since in all his life he had never owned one. Deregulation, it appeared, allowed moneyed individuals the opportunity to buy and sell airlines not unlike a large Monopoly game. The vaunted concept of the "public interest," one of the main bases invoked for governmental regulation of public utilities, including the airlines, appeared to have been lost forever. When TWA got wind of Lorenzo's interest in them, they literally jumped into Icahn's arms, believing that anything would be better than a Lorenzo takeover. After engaging in a series of thrusts and parries, Lorenzo once again acquiesced and backed off, content with his multimillion dollar stock appreciation. Carl Icahn took control of TWA, discussed in Chapter 27.

Takeover at Eastern Air Lines

Eastern Air Lines, one of the venerable Big Four, had a proprietary computer reservations system. Eastern had largely grown and developed under the reign of Eddie Rickenbacker, World War I ace and champion racecar driver. Eastern's reputation in labor relations was not what one would call "progressive"; rather, it was contentious to the extreme, particularly with the machinists union under the leadership of Charlie Bryan. One might say that labor relations at Eastern were more like the railroads than the airlines. Eastern was losing money in 1983, so much so that insolvency appeared to Frank Borman, Eastern's CEO, to be a distinct possibility. The rigors of deregulation, along with the serious economic situation that existed in the early 1980s, were taking a toll. Borman, like others in the industry, went to the rank and file with pleas for help in the form of "givebacks," or voluntary wage cuts, in order to meet the emergency. Reluctantly, the pilots and the flight attendants cooperated, but the machinists did not. In fact, they demanded and got a 32 percent wage increase on threats of a strike, creating a rather incongruous situation among the respective crafts. The pilots were not happy, nor were the flight attendants, and morale plummeted. And still, Eastern lost more money.

In 1985, Eastern's debt approached $2.5 billion and income was dwindling. But it had a computer reservations system. Lorenzo loomed on the horizon as Borman desperately sought a way out of the financial morass. Last ditch

efforts to secure further givebacks from the unions fell short, primarily because the machinists under Charlie Bryan would not budge. It was soon realized that there was no alternative to the proposed sale to Lorenzo. After completing the finalization of the buyout with Borman, and while awaiting government approval of the Eastern purchase, Lorenzo turned his attention to People Express.

Takeover at People Express

❝ Be Luke Skywalker, not Darth Vader. Ultimately love is stronger than evil. ❞

Donald Burr, founder of People Express

People Express had done exceedingly well at the beginning, expanding its route structure and purchasing more and more aircraft. Revenues grew at an astonishing rate, from $38 million in 1981 to $1 billion in 1985. People Express even bought Frontier Airlines, headquartered at Denver, to give it a western hub and to rapidly increase its rate of growth. It also gave People Express an elementary CRS system, the lack of which Burr concluded was severely undermining his airline's ability to compete in 1985. But Frontier was a union airline, and its culture did not mesh well with People's, not that any conventional carrier could.

It was said that working at People Express was akin to being in a cult, with its emphasis from the top down on philosophical intangibles like love, equality, peace, and brotherhood. All this was the direct influence of Don Burr, who had been caught up in the message of a popular inspirational and self-help book called *The Greatest Salesman in the World.* The tenets of this book became the basis for his personal philosophy. Attempts to put these teachings into practice at Texas International inevitably brought him into conflict with Frank Lorenzo, who had a very different approach to running a corporation for profit. Now at People Express he was free to apply these teachings liberally, and he did, in upbeat posters, presidential messages, manuals, and meetings. Morale was high, and most employees joined in the upbeat new-age philosophy that infused the company, attending pep rallies in the company auditorium by chief cheerleader Burr. The employee stock purchase plan swelled, as workers paid out substantial portions of their salaries to the company in stock purchases, stock that seemingly never could go down.

Burr had pulled off the Frontier acquisition right out from under his mentor, Lorenzo, who was also vying for the property. But it had been costly. Lorenzo had offered twenty-two dollars per share in October 1985, but Burr had successfully lined up employee support at Frontier because of Lorenzo's anti-union reputation, and secured significant employee concessions. These, coupled with Burr's countering bid of twenty-four dollars per share, were enough to convince Frontier's board of directors to vote in favor of the People Express acquisition.

People Express's cash stores were immediately and firmly tapped in order to pay Frontier expenses. It was much worse than anyone had expected. Burr learned from his financial people right after the deal was closed that People Express could expect to lose $100 million in just the next few months covering Frontier's hemorrhaging. By June 1986, Burr realized he had to dump Frontier if People Express was to survive. Within the period of nine months after the Frontier acquisition, People Express was essentially out of cash.

There were not a lot of suitors interested in Frontier. United offered to take Frontier off Burr's hands for less than one-half of what Burr had paid just a few months earlier. But United's pilots soon put an end to the takeover discussions with People Express, and United pulled out of the discussions. With no more cash to infuse into Frontier, Frontier filed for Chapter 11 protection on August 28, 1986.

When all other possible deals had fallen through for People Express, Lorenzo became the only option. Burr had come full circle. On September 15, 1986, it was announced that Texas Air had purchased People Express.

DOT Approves the Eastern Takeover

The Department of Transportation gave its approval to the Eastern takeover by Texas Air later that year. That Eastern was a basket case was known, but, like Frontier, it had not been appreciated just how bad the situation was. Phil Bakes had performed well for Lorenzo after the Continental takeover. Under Bakes, Continental had been turned around and was profitable again. Like Continental, the most pressing problem facing Eastern was labor costs. But the labor problems at Eastern could not be handled like they were at Continental four years before by simply filing under Chapter 11, then unilaterally abrogating the labor contracts in place with the unions. Congress had passed legislation in 1984 that severely restricted the effect of the holding in *Bildisco,* so Chapter 11 would not be of any significant help in decreasing the labor burden faced by Eastern.[3]

Bakes relocated to Miami and took over the helm at Eastern. The magnitude of Eastern's problems dwarfed those encountered at Continental. The culture was different, the personnel were hostile, and the history of labor relations was dismal. Eastern's record of labor relations over the years was largely a chronicle of the intransigence of the International Association of Machinists, whose leader was the strange Charlie Bryan. Without a solution to the labor problem, for starters, there did not appear to be any way to salvage the airline.

Judging by subsequent developments, it appears that Lorenzo came to that conclusion early, that there likely was no way to salvage Eastern. Even as Bakes worked to solve the company's seemingly insurmountable problems, Lorenzo began the systematic dismantling of Eastern for the benefit of Texas Air and its viable holdings. Eastern's computer reservation system had been appraised for a sum between $250 million and $450 million, an astonishing fact when it is realized that the entire purchase price for the company was $615 million. Lorenzo had financed the purchase in such a way that less than half of the purchase money came from Texas Air, the rest of the money came from Eastern itself, validating once again the old leveraged buyout strategy that had worked so well. The computer reservation system was sold to Texas Air for the bargain price of $100 million, but the terms were even better: Texas Air put up no money, but gave Eastern a promissory note for the purchase price, payable at the end of a period of twenty five years at a severely discounted rate of interest. Texas Air then leased back the system to Eastern for a fee of $10 million a month.

❝ As a businessman, Frank Lorenzo gives capitalism a bad name. ❞

William F. Buckley

Lorenzo next transferred Eastern's newest airplanes to Continental, paying Eastern again by promissory note for part of the payment. Continental then sold the airplanes for cash, and at a profit. Continental bought eleven gates at Newark Airport for half price, again paid for by promissory note. The purchasing of fuel was outsourced to a subsidiary of Texas Air at a cost of $1 million per month. Eastern paid Continental another $2 million per month for the training of non-employee pilots who, ironically, would be used to replace Eastern's pilots in case of a labor disruption.

Eastern's service was also being curtailed for lack of cash flow, and was stopped completely at New Orleans, Seattle, and San Diego. Then came the sell-off of the routes, beginning with Eastern's shuttle, which was sold to Donald

Trump. The expected machinist strike came in March 1989, which marked the absolute beginning of the end. Although Eastern immediately went into Chapter 11, the reorganization amounted to little more than the gradual selling off of all remaining assets to raise operating cash. The bankruptcy court took control of the reorganization from Eastern in April 1990, appointing as Trustee Martin Shugrue, former Continental president. The court used the opportunity to judicially note that Lorenzo's stewardship of Eastern had been a catastrophe. The reorganization was turned into a liquidation of Eastern's assets and, in 1991, the charade finally ended. Eastern Air Lines was no more. Creditors were left holding the bag to the tune of almost $3 billion, and even the lawyers were shorted their fees, a most uncommon occurrence.

❝ Pilots are a rare kind of human. They leave the ordinary surface of the world, to purify their soul in the sky, and they come down to earth, only after receiving the communion of the infinite. ❞

José Maria Velasco Ibarra, President of Ecuador

Lorenzo Departs

Frank Lorenzo was obviously not cut from the same airline cloth as were the early aviation chieftains like Jack Frye, Eddie Rickenbacker and Juan Trippe, people who loved to build things and loved to fly. Lorenzo was first and foremost a financial guy, the quintessential MBA focused on finance, with little thought or care for tradition, history, or national concept. Whereas the airlines had been built by men who expected to make money from their efforts, not every decision they made was a financial one; not every action taken was with a view toward the bottom line. Empire building in the early days was done one step at a time, not in one fell swoop like the hostile takeovers, leveraged buyouts, and unrestrained mergers that became the *modus operandi* of the deregulated 1980s. Lorenzo had turned the venerable airline industry on its head: Continental had absorbed People Express (and Frontier) and New York Air. Texas Air, in turn, owned Continental, and had then acquired Eastern Air Lines. By 1987, Texas Air controlled 20 percent of the domestic airline market, and it had only 20 employees.

By the late 1980s, Lorenzo and his business methods were wearing thin in most quarters, including labor, the banks, other airlines, and the agencies of the federal government. His reputation was preceding him. It was said that the Berlin wall, before it began to come down in 1989, bore Lorenzo's name in red with a slash through it, signifying the negative. The ultimate industry rejection came from the bankruptcy order of Judge Burton Lifland, in his termination of Lorenzo's status as debtor in possession of Eastern. Judge Lifland noted that Lorenzo was "not competent to reorganize" the company. Lorenzo himself seems to have tired of the game. Pickets from Eastern regularly appeared outside of his home and there was some concern for his safety and that of his family.

Jan Carlzon had built SAS (Scandinavian Airlines System) into a niche airline operation within the continent of Europe, competing with the large state-owned airlines. His vision was to beat his European competition to the markets of America now opening due to deregulation. Thus, he began overtures in the middle 1980s to establish a relationship with a United States carrier. After negotiating unsuccessfully first with Eastern, then TWA, he approached Lorenzo with a proposition for a partnership arrangement with Continental, based out of Newark. This led to an agreement in October 1988 for SAS to purchase a minority interest in Texas Air for $50 million, to be followed the next year with another payment of $40 million. Texas Air, in the late 1980s,

was suffering hefty losses, and the experience with Eastern after its purchase by Texas Air was draining.

Lorenzo's reputation had made its way to Europe, where labor interests looked askance at the prospect of the Texas Air-SAS alliance. One European tabloid ran a cartoon depicting Carlzon and Lorenzo in bed together with the caption "It's fine if you go to bed just don't go to sleep." Even Lorenzo had to acknowledge that his reputation detracted from the ongoing success and potential of Texas Air holdings. In 1990, Texas Air was reorganized into Continental Air Holdings, and in the summer of that year Lorenzo struck a deal with SAS for the sale of his entire personal stake in the company for $50 million.

Seemingly always at the top of his game, and a master of timing, Lorenzo sold out just before Iraq invaded Kuwait in August 1990. The invasion and resulting worldwide reaction spurred fuel costs and depressed airline travel. Continental was unable to meet the financial strain imposed, and filed for Chapter 11 protection again in December 1990, prompting some wags to suggest that Continental was now in "Chapter 22."

Lorenzo made one last appearance on the airline scene in 1993. His idea was to inaugurate a new carrier called "Friendship Airlines." He made application to the DOT, as required by law, for a Certificate of Public Convenience and Necessity. Since deregulation, this procedure has been used to determine the "fitness" of an applicant to conduct an interstate air carrier operation. The DOT denied the application. Lorenzo was finally gone.

Endnotes

1. 459 U.S. 1145, 103 S.Ct. 784, 74 L.Ed. 992 (1983).
2. 14 C.F.R. 255; Regulation ER-1385, 49 Fed. Reg. 32540 (Aug. 14, 1984), aff'd *United Airlines v. CAB,* 766 F. 2d 1107 (7th Cir. 1985).
3. See Bankruptcy code, 11 U.S.C § 1113, et. seq.

CHAPTER 27

Carl Icahn and TWA

© Dan Barnes, 2008, Shutterstock, Inc.

> **❝**You learn in this business: If you want a friend, get a dog.**❞**
>
> **Carl Icahn**

T WA was one of the original "Big Four," created out of the so-called "Spoils Conference" in 1930 by the edict of Walter Folger Brown, which forced the combination of Western Airlines and Transcontinental Air Transport (TAT). TWA had participated in the major developments of American airline history under the leadership of Jack Frye, and later under the secretive and unpredictable Howard Hughes. It had pioneered both the early transcontinental routes and the early airliners used on those routes, like the DC-3 and the Constellation. TWA had contributed significantly to the war effort between 1941 and 1945, flying the only land-based four engine aircraft in existence at that time (the Boeing 307) on transatlantic routes to Africa from South America and to Europe. By war's end, TWA had gained transatlantic experience that only Pan American could rival. Howard Hughes, then firmly in control of TWA, changed the name of the company. Since 1930, the initials TWA had stood for Transcontinental and Western Airlines, but after the war the company name

became Trans World Airlines, still using the TWA brand.

Perhaps owing largely to its war effort, TWA was rewarded after World War II with the first transatlantic routes that went to any established American airline other than Pan American. On February 5, 1946, TWA made its first scheduled international flight, from New York to Paris. TWA was also granted access to London's Heathrow Airport, known as the "Gateway to the World," and it continued its international route expansion for years to come, including the polar route in 1957 from Los Angeles to London.

In 1961, TWA severed its relationship with Howard Hughes, who by that time had become a recluse, and by 1965 the company had redeemed all of his shares of stock. New management, led by Charles Tillinghast, made changes within the company that caused it to prosper. TWA's profits in 1965 were the largest of any airline.

TWA thrived under the regulatory scheme in place during the 1960s and 1970s, but with deregulation, things began to come undone. The very nature of TWA's routes, including many long distance ones, had mandated that its fleet be comprised of large airplanes. The use of large aircraft when smaller ones would have sufficed, with the resulting substantial expense differential, increased the financial burden. TWA was also slow to appreciate the hub concept, and its labor costs were way out of line. Its unions were not willing to grant the wage and working condition concessions that looked necessary. By the 1980s, TWA was losing money, some $100 million by the middle of the decade. TWA began to look appealing as a corporate takeover target. All of the symptoms were there, including low stock valuation, troubled management and relatively high asset value. This scenario drew the Wall Street raider types like sharks to blood in the water.

Carl Icahn (see Figure 27-1), as a young man, had some talent at chess and, it was rumored, at poker as well. He wound up on Wall Street in the stockbrokerage business and drifted into the super-specialty of arbitrage, the trading of both the long and the short side of stocks and options that allows the taking advantage of slight differentials in price. This led to trading in issues of companies rumored to be the object of takeover strategies, companies that usually experienced large and volatile price fluctuations. Icahn himself began initiating, or threatening to initiate, corporate takeovers against current management wishes. The tactic usually involved isolating a target, quietly starting to buy up its stock, running up its price, and then retiring from the field with a nice profit when the target's management successfully fought him off with counter offers for control.

Icahn began buying up shares of TWA in 1985, and by April he had acquired enough stock in the company to trigger the mandatory public filings with the Securities and Exchange Commission. Negotiations with TWA management came to nothing. Rather, the people at TWA who met with Icahn were appalled at his obvious disregard for the tradition, history, and contributions of the airline over the years. Icahn, they surmised, presumed to dismantle the company for its inherent value; they resolved to fight for their company. As the stock value rose, the company sought alternatives, looking for other investors more suitable to the company's traditions and purposes. They even entertained Frank Lorenzo as a partner more desirable than Icahn. Icahn continued to acquire stock. By the beginning of summer he had invested $100 million and owned at least one third of the outstanding shares.

Of the possible merger partners for TWA, only Eastern made any effort to investigate the possibilities. A combination of TWA and Eastern, two of the original "Big Four," would be a hard sell to the Justice Department, and even to DOT, on anti-competitive grounds, and it appeared to be equally problematical for the unions at Eastern. Eastern finally declined to participate.

Employee buyout plans at TWA as an alternative to a takeover did not develop. TWA's unions got wind of Lorenzo's interest, and they were decidedly on the other side of that issue from management; they wanted no part of Lorenzo. The unions at TWA started talking to Icahn, and soon their negotiations had yielded concessions from the pilots and the machinists in wages and working conditions designed to assist in rescuing the company. The unions were not willing to make the same concessions to Lorenzo. Apparently, they were not willing to make them to the current TWA management either.

FIGURE 27-1 Carl Icahn began buying up shares of TWA in 1985, and by April he had acquired enough stock in the company to trigger the mandatory public filings with the Securities and Exchange Commission.

© Bettmann/CORBIS.

In the end, it was labor that handed TWA to Icahn. Lorenzo, once again, pocketed a nice gain in the value of his stock acquired while pursuing control of the company—in this case $50 million. Icahn immediately set out to maximize his investment with further acquisitions by TWA.

TWA's main competition in St. Louis in 1986 was Ozark Airlines. In the middle 1980s the Department of Transportation under Elizabeth Dole was in charge of reviewing proposed mergers, and the stance at DOT at that time was to let unfettered private enterprise rule. This was, after all, the era of deregulation. Still, many people, like Alfred Kahn, the so-called father of deregulation, were concerned that the industry was rapidly becoming too centralized, too anti-competitive, and that the benefits of deregulation as they saw it would suffer from such lack of competition. Their views were largely dismissed as the DOT routinely signaled its approval of anticipated combinations in the industry.

Icahn closed the deal for the acquisition of Ozark for $239 million. The Justice Department decried the merger and came out against it. But it was the DOT's call (the DOJ would be given authority over mergers in 1988), and the merger was approved as expected. Icahn had engineered an almost complete abrogation of competition out of St. Louis. It came as no surprise that fares out of St. Louis were quickly raised, now that the CAB no longer existed, but it was clear that this was not what deregulation was supposed to be about. It also became obvious that the anti-competitive safeguards formerly monitored by the CAB, and now by the DOT, were being ignored.

Although the pilots and machinists had worked a deal with Icahn, the flight attendants had not. Their contract expired in 1986 and they walked out. Icahn hired replacements, at a significant savings to the company, and when the flight attendants called off the strike a few months later and wanted to return to work, Icahn refused to rehire them. The pilots and machinists were the next to learn what it was like to deal with Icahn, when he threatened to dismantle the airline if they did not extend their contracts at present wage rates. They did extend their contracts, even though the agreement had contemplated a "snap back" to rates paid prior to the concessions given when Icahn took over.

Next, Icahn sold all of the Ozark fleet of airplanes and then leased them back. This put cash into Icahn's pockets and placed the jets in the category of operating expense. The TWA computer reservation system, known as PARS, had been recognized to be a valuable asset of TWA, and this fact had not escaped Icahn's notice. Northwest Airlines did not have a CRS, so Icahn sold 50 percent of PARS to Northwest for $140 million. Some would term this sort of management style as "dismemberment," but Icahn insisted otherwise. But it did bear some resemblance to the treatment Lorenzo was giving to Eastern at about the same time.

In the late 1980s, things did not improve financially for the airlines, particularly the international airlines. In 1988, at a special meeting of shareholders, Icahn took the company private, finalizing the process of making TWA his personal, closely held company. The privatization took over $610 million cash out of TWA. Icahn realized $469 million personally and TWA overnight assumed over $539 million in debt. In 1991, Icahn sold TWA's routes to London from New York, Los Angeles, Boston, and Chicago for $445 million to American Airlines.

On January 31, 1992, TWA entered into Chapter 11 reorganization, and on May 1, 1992, Icahn, as debtor in possession, sold its London routes from Philadelphia and Baltimore to USAir for $50 million. TWA retained only the St. Louis to London route.

As a part of the reorganization and its restructuring in Chapter 11, Icahn agreed to resign as chairman of TWA and relinquish all control in the running of the company. The creditors' committee agreed to grant TWA's three primary unions a 45 percent equity stake in the company in return for concessions. In November 1993, TWA emerged from Chapter 11. Although TWA would briefly enter Chapter 11 again in 1995, it entered into a short period of stability during the late 1990s, modernizing its fleet with the largest aircraft order in its history for 125 Boeing and Airbus small jets like the B717 and A320, with options for 125 more. Still, TWA had not turned a profit since 1988.

By 2000, TWA was again on hard times, losing $353 million in 1999 and over $115 million in the first nine months of 2000. Agreement was reached with AMR Corporation, American's parent and also the parent of American Eagle, for the acquisition of TWA. It entered Chapter 11 for the third time in order to complete the acquisition process, and became TWA Airlines LLC. The Justice Department approved the merger based primarily on the financial condition of TWA, realizing that the merger would be, in this case, in the best interests of the employees and of the public. Without the merger, TWA would have been forced to liquidate. American would now control 22.6 percent of the entire airline market.

In September 2001, operations were consolidated with those of American with the release of 138,000 TWA employees and the closure of its JFK terminal. The name TWA ceased to exist.

CHAPTER 28

Pan American and Deregulation

© Terry Alexander, 2008, Shutterstock.

Among the trunk carriers of the United States, Pan American had enjoyed a monopoly on America's international traffic from 1927 until after World War II, with two exceptions. First, American Airlines was awarded a route between Dallas and Mexico City in 1942. Next, and the only other exception, was a small startup called American Export Airlines, originally a subsidiary of one of the largest shipping companies in the country, American Export Lines. Pan American successfully challenged the shipping line's ownership in court, and forced a divestiture of the airline operation. The airline became American Overseas Airlines and struggled along during the war flying mail and cargo mostly between New York and Ireland, using Vought-Sikorsky flying boats. After the war, Pan American's fortunes began a gradual decline in direct proportion to its loss of its monopoly. On July 5, 1945, the CAB approved the acquisition of American Export Lines by American Airlines, and granted routes across the North Atlantic to the United Kingdom and other European countries. Pan American had proposed to the government a continuation of the pre-war relationship that granted Pan Am "Chosen Instrument" status. But Congress rejected the idea of a continuing monopoly. Times had changed since pre-war days. The United States had nothing to fear from

foreign power competition, nor any need for a "Chosen Instrument" to represent the country in aviation internationally. In fact, the government decided that the more United States airlines spreading out over the world the better.

TWA was granted access across the Atlantic, Northwest Airlines began operations over the north Pacific, Braniff went into South America. But these airlines had domestic routes too. Pan Am had none. Everyone wanted to fly Pan Am's routes; almost twenty domestic airlines had applied for its Pacific routes alone. The applicants included passenger, cargo, scheduled, and charter airlines. Through the administrations of Truman, Eisenhower, and Kennedy (1944–1963), the previous monopoly enjoyed by Pan Am disappeared, but Pan Am was still in a competitive position. During the Johnson administration (1963–1968), however, everything went up for grabs. The chairmanship of the CAB, the body that would make the route awards, was a recent Johnson appointee friendly to Texas-based American Airlines and to Braniff. Juan Trippe retired in 1968, but earlier in the 1960s he had hired the second administrator of the Federal Aviation Agency (created by the Federal Aviation Act of 1958), Najeeb Halaby. Since Pan American was exclusively an international carrier with no domestic service, it had no boosters in the

Congress, unlike the major domestic carriers. Delta in Georgia, Eastern in Florida, and Northwest in Minnesota, for example, had their loyal delegations to lobby for them.

Pan American had pioneered all of the international routes and had represented the United States as the "Chosen Instrument" of American influence. Pan Am had served America's interests during the war and had even been largely responsible for the development and original use of the 707 and DC-8 jet fleet. But now it seemed like it was all politics. Routes to Hawaii went to Continental, Braniff, American, and Northwest. TWA got round-the-world rights and even Flying Tiger got the Pacific cargo routes. Although incoming President Nixon (1969) reviewed and amended some of the awards, the result was the same to Pan Am. And still, Pan Am could not get a domestic route from the CAB.

Merger talks were carried on between Pan Am and several carriers, including Braniff and American. But it was with TWA that the deal was struck to combine operations. Not only would the joining of the two international carriers render savings of $200 million a year, but merging the TWA-owned Hilton International hotel chain with Pan American's Intercontinental Hotel assets would mean that the new airline would own the most elite hotel system in the world.

The Antitrust Division of the Justice Department would have to approve the combination of TWA and Pan Am as posing no undue competitive threat to international commercial aviation. In spite of the plethora of carriers now plying the international routes since the end of the war, approval was not forthcoming. So Pan Am struggled on, knowing that it had to have domestic routes to survive. With losses mounting and market share dwindling, Pan Am's board of directors appointed a new president, a former Air Force general by the name of William T. Seawell. A West Point graduate, a B-17 Group commander during World War II, as well as a Harvard law graduate, Seawell had been a senior vice-president at American Airlines and president of Rolls-Royce Aero, Inc. Seawell came on board in 1971 as Pan Am was losing another $45 million, and by 1972, as Pan Am concluded a three-year losing period of $120 million, Seawell was made CEO and Halaby was out.

Seawell had not only been a general in the Air Force, he had been a general in the Strategic Air Command (SAC), with its iron-fisted rule by General Curtis E. Lemay. Many SAC pilots found the assignment to be sort of a purgatory. Pan Am's pilots wondered what the strict organizational procedures of SAC might mean to Pan American.

Seawell set about cutting and paring staff, offices, and expenses. The number of employees was cut to 27,000 from 42,000. Levels of management, like staff vice-president, were eliminated altogether. Service was curtailed and bases were closed. These measures were dictated not only by the bloat that Pan Am had acquired, but also by the first OPEC-generated fuel crisis that occurred in the early 1970s. Pan Am's fuel bill doubled. Although still *persona non grata* at the CAB and at the White House, the CAB did, in 1975, grant both TWA and Pan American some relief in approving some route swaps, thus lessening the competition between them. Still, Pan Am had no domestic routes.

Pan American lost $364 million in the early years of the 1970s. But by 1976, under the direction of Seawell, Pan Am started making a comeback. In 1976 it realized a net profit of $100 million. In 1977 it made $45 million, and in 1978 it was over $120 million. Still, all was not well. As shabbily as Pan Am felt it had been treated by the postwar administrations, particularly the Johnson and Nixon administrations, it was not prepared for the largesse bestowed on Pan Am's competitors by the Carter White House. There were more international routes for almost everyone: Delta to London, Braniff to London, and National to Paris and Amsterdam. Northwest was assigned Copenhagen and Stockholm. Pan American, incredibly, was losing even more market share.

With the passage of deregulation in 1978, Pan Am no longer needed the long-sought-after approval of the CAB. Under deregulation, Pan Am could fly wherever and whenever it wanted and charge any fare it pleased. The only problem was, so could everybody else. Pan Am did not have time to build a domestic route structure under these circumstances; it would have to find an airline to merge with or to buy.

The circumstances of the attempt by Frank Lorenzo to take over National Airlines in 1978 have already been considered above. We know that Lorenzo was not successful in that effort and that he lost out to Pan American after Pan Am trumped his best stock offer. Now we need to look at the results of the National takeover by Pan American.

National Airlines in 1978 was a tempting takeover target: undervalued stock price, low debt, and high assets. National was the first all-jet U.S. carrier. It had been flying the Atlantic since 1970 between Miami and London, and after that it went into Amsterdam, Paris, and Frankfurt. National, headquartered in Miami like Eastern, was also very similar to Eastern in its labor experience. Almost every contract renewal ended up in a strike. No trust existed between labor and management. The culture at National was much different from that at Pan American. National, in spite of its international routes, was really a southern airline dedicated to small destinations, while Pan American was the international sophisticate. The attitudes of its pilots said it all. From the early days of the Clippers, there had been a certain swagger to the Pan American pilots: their uniforms were patterned after the maritime officers of the deck, like the Queen Mary. They wore white hats. They were chosen, and superior, just like their airline. What's more, National's pilot roster was considerably younger than was Pan Am's.

It was an accepted fact that Pan American, in its zeal to get domestic routes, was caused to grossly overpay for National. All told, it cost Pan Am $374 million to acquire National, and the financial drain was just beginning. All 8,350 National employees were now working for Pan Am. Seawell had to raise National's pilots' wages to match those of Pan Am's pilots, and he had to increase their benefits packages to match those at Pan Am. The cost of acquisition was over half a billion dollars, and the year of acquisition was not even over.

The fleets of the two companies did not jibe. Although both carriers had 727s, the wide bodies were different: National had DC-10s and Pan Am had L-1011s. Each type of aircraft had a different power plant, whether Pratt & Whitney, Rolls Royce, or General Electric, and each had to be maintained and serviced by a mechanic specially trained and qualified on that engine. Each type of engine and each type of aircraft had to have parts and spares available and storage space to put them.

Prior to the acquisition of National, Pan Am appeared to be on the road back to profitability, and it was, in fact, sitting on significant cash. But that was the only good news; all the rest of the news was bad.

Matters were getting worse as the work forces of each company regarded each other warily. Pilot seniority has always been a fact of life in the airline industry. It is the measure by which a pilot knows what he is: a captain, a first officer, a journeyman, hired out, unemployed, furloughed, riding high, or down and out. It was, therefore, central to the pilots' interest in the merger to have their position in the seniority roster protected. A new seniority list was being prepared, one that would have to merge the two companies' seniority rosters into one new roster. The numbers, that's what the pilots called it, defined the pilots' past, present, and future.

Most of the Pan Am pilots were senior to the National pilots, so that if the respective rosters were to be merged on a chronological date basis, most of the National pilots would be at the bottom of the combined new roster. Captains would be first officers or even out of a job. A merger of the two rosters on the basis of relative position between the two, on the other hand, would mean that a National pilot with a seniority number of 100th from the top on the National roster might very well be many years junior to a pilot ranked 100th on the Pan Am roster, the effect being that a Pan Am pilot hired in 1965 might find himself serving under a National pilot hired in 1975. Each group of pilots was adamant about its view of the roster.

The issue was finally referred to binding arbitration. A complicated formula was decreed in March 1981 and the new Pan Am seniority list was posted. The result was not pleasing to either side, but it had to be accepted. On the National side, at least, the National 727 pilots retained their captains' positions. The rest had to sort out their numbers, most with a sense of disbelief.

When the two companies were combined, Pan Am had its domestic routes so long denied. But in 1980 it was losing a million dollars a day. The assets of Pan American included its landmark building astride Park Avenue in midtown Manhattan, with the Pan Am name emblazoned in 12-foot high letters for all to admire. Other assets included its hotel system and its coveted routes to almost every corner of the world. The options were considered by management, by the Seawell team, and it was obvious that some assets had to be converted to cash to satisfy the insatiable demands of the creditors. The Pan Am building was sold to Metropolitan Life Insurance Company for $400 million, but insolvency still loomed. Next came the Intercontinental Hotel chain, sold for $500 million. Deliveries of new airplanes were deferred, and unfilled orders were cancelled. General Seawell, no longer regarded as the savior of Pan American by the stockholders, retired early, in 1981.

Ed Acker took over Pan Am in 1981. Acker had been president of Braniff International in the 1970s and was acknowledged to have done a good job, leaving the company in good shape and with a better future before it. At length he wound up at Air Florida, a startup intrastate airline with revenues of less than $10 million a year as of 1977. In just three years, by 1980, Air Florida under his direction netted over $160 million.

Acker perceived his main job, like most of the new CEOs after deregulation, to secure givebacks from the union rank and file. After all, that was about the only place to look for relief. Everyone knew that the unions had had it too good during the old CAB days, and now it was time to get real. Typical of the time, wage and working condition concessions were agreed to by the unions, which represented 24,000 of the company's 33,000 employees, in return for a stock position in the company and, for the first time in the industry, a seat on the board of directors.

Yet, after Acker's first year as CEO, Pan Am lost $485 million. And the losses continued. The expected labor "snap backs," the increased pay to make up for the concessions given earlier by the unions, could not be made as scheduled because of the ongoing monthly losses. Negotiations did not produce any movement, and on February 28, 1985, the unions went out on strike. This was a new and unpleasant development for the old Pan Am pilots, who had always considered themselves as professionals, in service to their passengers and in league and in parity with the company.

Pan Am fired all the strikers, as was the custom, but in short order the sides came together, each claiming victory, and the strike was over. Everybody went back to work. But a strike is a serious financial blow to an airline, even a healthy one, and can be devastating to a crippled one like Pan Am in 1985.

In an ironic turn of events, the international routes were breaking even, but the long sought domestic routes of the former National Airlines were losing $250 million a year. Acker looked around for something else to sell; he came up with the Pacific routes so laboriously and bravely secured almost a half-century earlier. These were the routes of the Clippers; Hawaii and on to the romantic Orient, Singapore, Hong Kong, and Bora Bora. United wanted the Pacific routes, and shortly a deal was announced that United would buy the routes for $750 million. In the "first of a kind" deal, United agreed to take the sixteen 747 SPs (See Figure 28-1.) (the out-dated short range model), the six L-1011s, and a DC-10 that serviced the routes, as well as the personnel at Pan American who were dedicated to those routes. All told, the personnel transfer to United was about 2,700 employees, including managers, 1,200 flight attendants, and 410 pilots. These cost savings, and the influx of three quar-ters of a billion dollars, allowed the airline to continue its existence, at least for the time being.

By 1988, the United money was gone and Pan Am was still losing money. Terrorism had taken its toll on Pan Am: a takeover of a 747 in Karachi had ended badly in a highly publicized shootout. In 1988, Acker was out as CEO, and Tom Plaskett, fired by Lorenzo from Continen-tal, was in. More wage and work rules conces-sions for the unions were negotiated. Later, in 1988, Plaskett announced that Pan Am would have an operating profit for the first time in years. It was a great day. And then came December 21, 1988, the day Pan American would be ever identified with the small village of Lockerbie, Scotland. On the evening of that day the Clipper "Maid of the Seas" disintegrated at altitude, spreading itself, its passengers and crew, and all of their baggage over the Scottish countryside.

For days afterward, the forward section of the 747, painted in the white with blue trim col-ors of Pan American, was displayed on the evening news to the entire world as it lay on its side in an open field, a metaphor for the formerly great Pan American World Airways. Investiga-tion revealed that the flight was brought down by a terrorist bomb, but it did not seem to matter.

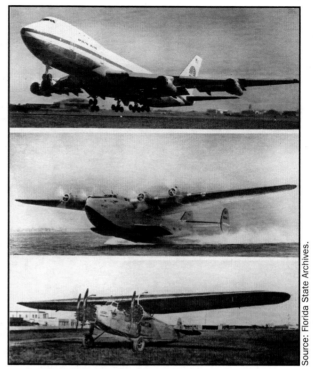

FIGURE 28-1 Boeing 747 (top), Boeing 314 (middle), Fokker F-7 (bottom).

Source: Florida State Archives.

Passengers did not fly Pan American in 1989, and Pan Am was losing $2 million a day.

In 1990, traffic picked up as the summer vacation crowd to Europe seemed to be coming back. Then, in August, Saddam Hussein invaded Kuwait. Passenger counts went down, and fuel prices went up. Plaskett could see the end com-ing. He had to sell something else. This was not like selling your blood, this was like selling your body parts. United wanted the crown jewels, the London routes. Pan American had been the first to fly to London from the States, in the Boeing 314 flying boat, over a half century earlier. Now fifty years of Pan American tradition in the Atlantic service was suddenly bestowed on United, and another Pan Am era was to be closed out for mere filthy lucre, some $400 million.

Many employees, as well as Wall Street observers, wondered at the point of it all. A morbid humorism was being circulated: "Pan Am is like a coyote caught in a trap. It's chewed off three of its legs and it's still in the trap."[1] The London deal included service from New York, Washington, Los Angeles, Seattle, and San Francisco, seven routes from London to Europe, as well as the Pan Am Washington to Paris route. What else was there left to sell? There was the Berlin service that Pan Am had faithfully husbanded over the years of the Cold War, the corridor through the Iron Curtain to the free world. Even though Germany was just being reunified after the collapse of the Soviet Union, Lufthansa wanted it, for $150 million. And so it went.

Pan Am was in its death throes, even if management would not admit it. It was now getting quite unseemly, with Airbus Industries taking back twenty Airbuses, and with Pan Am stock selling for 75 cents instead of $75. Pan American did not have enough money to pay its creditors. In January 1991, Pan Am went into Chapter 11. But even with the protection that Chapter 11 gave the airline from having to keep its creditors current, it was losing up to $3 million a day. The vultures gathered around, seeking to know whether the remains of the airline might be picked up cheap, or merged. The creditors' committee was interested, after all, since that was likely the only way unsecured creditors were going to get anything at all.

The biggest surprise was the interest of Delta Airlines, probably the most conservative airline of all, which in the summer of 1991 offered $310 million for Pan American World Airways. Finally, following hurried and intense negotiating sessions, a deal was closed between the creditors' committee and Delta. Delta would pay $416 million in cash and assume $389 million in pre-existing liabilities, making an immediate cash infusion of $80 million to prevent immediate shutdown. Pan American was to be salvaged as a corporation, 45 percent of its stock would be owned by Delta and creditors would hold the remaining 55 percent. Pan Am II, the new name of the restructured company that was to continue operation mainly down in the Caribbean, was set to emerge from Chapter 11 in December.

Pan Am ran through the $80 million deposited by Delta, and then another $35 million deposited by Delta. It seemed that Pan Am had no way to stop the bleeding, not even long

FIGURE 28-2 Pan American Field at Miami before the sale by Pan American to the city of Miami.

enough to be saved. Nobody apparently wanted to fly Pan American under bankruptcy circumstances. On December 3, 1991, Delta's lawyers advised the bankruptcy court that the deal was off. Delta would infuse no more money into Pan Am.

The Clipper "Goodwill," a Boeing 727, was the last Pan American airplane in the air after the company shut down. Pan Am operations directed the Clipper to Miami, to the airport that was first known as Pan American Field because Pan American had built it; to the airport that Pan Am had sold to the City of Miami in 1930 even when the city could not afford to finance the purchase—Pan Am had graciously bought the city's bonds. Pan American operations at Miami requested a last fly-by over the airport and the control tower approved. Down runway 12 to the southeast it flew, out over the first Pan Am hangars and the old marine terminal at Dinner Key in Biscayne Bay, where the clippers used to load up for South America. Reluctantly it seemed, the Clipper

FIGURE 28-3 Pan American Dinner Key Terminal.

Goodwill turned back to the airport; it came around, landed, and slowly taxied to the gate under saluting streams of water from airport fire trucks, sadly marking the end of an era.

Endnote

1. Gandt, Robert, *Skygods*, p. 289.

CHAPTER 29

Airline Labor Relations

© Alex Staroseltsev, 2008, Shutterstock.

It would be easy to excuse a person's confusion today when told that airline labor matters are governed by the Railway Labor Act.[1] But in 1936, when the RLA was made applicable to the neophyte airline industry, the differences between the two transportation systems was not at all clear. Both systems carried passenger and freight traffic in interstate commerce, across state lines, and from coast to coast. Both were considered quasi-public utilities obligated to conduct their operations in a manner consistent with the "public interest." And both were capable of causing severe disruption to the nation's commerce by labor-management disagreements and work stoppages.

We have already considered the temper of the times. The United States was deep into the Great Depression, distrust of the corporate world and capitalism was in vogue, unemployment was widespread, labor protective legislation was being cranked out of Congress, and membership in unions was high and on the rise. The airline industry seemed poised to take over from the railroads, which were on the wane, and it was assumed that the confrontational model of labor relations fashioned out of the experience of the railroads would serve the interests of labor and the nation in aviation as well.

But experience has shown that the airlines were not very much like the railroads after all; they were, in fact, very different. Aside from the fact that railroad labor relations arose out of the violent confrontations of the late nineteenth century, airlines were much more technologically oriented, the product of inventions and developments that had largely first come into being after the labor pattern of the railroads had already been established.

The job classifications (the "crafts" in the words of the RLA) were very different. The railroads had their train crews composed of engineers, firemen, brakemen, and conductors, which ranged from semi-skilled to laboring work, and owing to coal used for fuel, they were mostly soot-covered jobs. Job names like hostlers, boilermakers, car repair workers, maintenance of way laborers (gandy dancers), and blacksmiths filled the railroad roster. The airlines' occupational groups were pilots, powerplant mechanics, and clerical employees. Only baggage handlers, ground crew, and cleaners came close to matching the personnel types common on the railroads. The knowledge and skill requirements of the pilots and mechanics were federally mandated and tested. As time went on, many pilots came from the ranks of the college educated, and because of the federal limitations on hours flown, many of those would have second careers, some even professional careers based on advanced university degrees.

Railroad style unionism was promoted by the policies of the National Mediation Board (NMB), the federal body established under the RLA to mediate the relative positions of the two sides, which assumes a power-based equality of collective bargaining and promotes a "digging in" of the heels, rather than a cooperative effort based on a mutuality of interests approach. This has produced a history of labor strife marked by work stoppages and severe disruptions in the national transportation system over much of the life of the airline industry. Contributing to the encouragement of militant union activity has been a competition between the different unions' leadership to produce the best "package" in the industry, to set the standard for union gains. Resistance from management to such union activity was, during regulation, lessened due to the practice of the CAB of increasing rates and fares to cover the increase in employee wages and benefits. Management also appeared to be willing to trade off increased income from productivity gains due to technological advances, such as increased efficiencies associated with jet aircraft, to achieve peace with the labor unions.

Major Airline Unions

The major certified bargaining units (unions) in the airline industry are:

- The Air Line Pilots Association (ALPA), representing the majority of pilots
- The Allied Pilots Association (representing American Airlines pilots since 1960)
- The National Pilots Association (representing Air Tran pilots)
- The Southwest Airlines Pilots Association (Southwest pilots)
- Frontier Pilots Association (Frontier pilots)
- The International Association of Machinists and Aerospace Workers (IAM)
- The Association of Professional Flight Attendants (APFA)
- The Association of Flight Attendants (AFA)
- The Transport Workers Union (TWU), representing a range of employees from maintenance employees to flight attendants and dispatchers
- The Brotherhood of Railway, Airline and Steamship Clerks (BRAC), representing mostly clerical and passenger service employees
- The Aircraft Mechanics Fraternal Association
- The Communications Workers of America
- The International Brotherhood of Teamsters
- The Professional Airline Flight Control Association

Airline	Pilots	Flight attendants	Mechanics and related	Dispatchers	Fleet service/ramp
Alaska	ALPA	AFA	AMFA	TWU	IAM
America West	ALPA	AFA	IBT	TWU	TWU
American	APA	APFA	TWU	TWU	TWU
Continental	ALPA	IAM	IBT	TWU	(none)
Delta	ALPA	(none)	(none)	PAFCA	(none)
Northwest	ALPA	IBT	AMFA	TWU	IAM
Southwest	SWAPA	TWU	AMFA	SAEA	TWU
United	ALPA	AFA	IAM	PAFCA	IAM
US Airways	ALPA	AFA	IAM	TWU	IAM

TABLE 29-1 Unions representing selected crafts or classes at major passenger airlines as of February 1, 2003.

Most of the crafts of the largest nineteen airlines in the country, accounting for ninety-five percent of industry revenues, were unionized in 1977. Only Delta, which had a nonunion work force with the exception of its pilots (who are represented by ALPA), and Southern Airways deviated from the norm.

Strife and Presidential Interventions

From the time that the RLA was applied to the airline industry in 1936, there were no strikes until 1946, when the first Presidential Emergency Board (PEB) was established in a dispute between TWA and its pilots. Six more PEBs followed during the late 1940s, and then 19 occurred during the 1950s—11 during 1957 alone. These 1957 strikes involved Eastern, National, Capital, North-

east, Northwest, United, TWA, and American. Most of these involved the mechanics, although two were pilot initiated. Through 1978, the airlines had experienced a total of 191 strikes.

The number of strikes decreased significantly after deregulation. Only 16 strikes have been called since 1978, 12 of them before 1990. The duration of these strikes ranged from 2 years to 24 minutes. See Table 29-2 for a summary of strike incidences, presidential interventions, and nonstrike work actions between 1978 and 2002.

Presidential interventions may include the convening of a Presidential Emergency Board (PEB), or they may be limited to pressuring or "jawboning" with the parties. The President has also intervened in labor-management disputes to recommend binding arbitration. PEBs are normally not instituted except in circumstances

	Carrier	Union	Craft or class	Duration of negotiations	Dates of strike	Duration of strike
1	Alaska	IAM	Mechanics	2/17/84–6/3/85	3/4/85–5/4/85	2 months
2	American	APA	Pilots	6/30/94–5/5/97	2/15/97	24 minutes
3	American	APFA	Flight Attendants	11/18/92–10/10/95	11/18/93–11/22/93	5 days
4	American	TWU	Flight instructors	Not available	11/4/79	1 day
5	Continental	ALPA	Pilots	Not available	10/1/83–10/31/85	2 years
6	Continental	IAM	Mechanics	1981–1985	8/13/83–4/16/85	1 1/2 years
7	Continental	IBT	Flight engineers	Not Available	9/23/79–10/6/79	13 days
8	Continental	UFA	Flight attendants	Not available	12/5/80–12/21/80	16 days
9	Continental	UFA	Flght attendants	Not available	10/1/83–4/17/85	1 1/2 years
10	Continental	IAM	Flight attendants	1985–1989	3/15/89–12/15/89	9 months
11	Northwest	ALPA	Pilots	8/27/96–9/12/98	8/29/98–9/12/98	15 days
12	Northwest	IAM	Mechanics Flight kitchen	9/29/81–6/16/82	5/22/82–6/25/82	1 month
13	Southwest	IAM	Mechanics	Not available	1/13/80–2/1/80	19 days
14	United	ALPA	Pilots	1/30/84–6/17/85	5/17/85–6/14/85	29 days
15	United	IAM	Mechanics Ramp and stores Food services Dispatchers Security officers	10/1/78–5/24/79	3/31/79–5/27/79	2 months
16	USAir	IAM	Mechanics	2/14/90–10/13/92	10/5/92–10/8/92	3 days

Sources: NMB, airlines, and labor unions.

TABLE 29-2 Airline strikes that have occurred since deregulation through 2003.

	Carrier	Union	Craft	Amendable Date	Presidential Intervention Date	Actions Taken
1	American	APA	Pilots	8/31/94	2/15/97	Presidential Emergency Board
2	American	APFA	Flight attendants	11/1/98	2001	Presidential Emergency Board warning
3	American	APFA	Flight attendants	12/31/92	1993	Presidential recommends binding interest arbitration
4	Northwest	ALPA	Pilots	11/2/96	September 1998	Presidential Emergency Board warning
5	Northwest	AMFA	Mechanics	9/30/96	3/12/01	Presidential Emergency Board
6	United	IAM	Mechanics	7/12/00	1/19/02	Presidential Emergency Board

Sources: NMB and airlines.

TABLE 29-3 Number of presidential interventions since deregulation.

where significant interstate commerce disruption is expected to result. See Table 29-3.

Work actions, which is the term for union organized slow-downs, sick-outs, or other nonstrike activity, have increased since deregulation. Many of these disruptions go unheralded, but there have been 10 instances of such activity which have been recognized by various courts as being in violation of the RLA. Some of these nonstrike work actions are presented by labor in a context of safety concerns. One tactic used by Alaska flight attendants was a technique called "CHAOS" (Creating Havoc Around Our System) that involved intermittent but unpredictable walkouts. These tactics do not shut down the airline but attempt to make their point by harassment. See Table 29-4.

The Mutual Aid Pact

In 1958, the airlines entered into the Mutual Aid Agreement (MAA), also called the Mutual Aid Pact (MAP), which amounted to a self-insured strike fund. This airline cooperative agreement was to be in place for the next twenty years, until deregulation. Under this arrangement, the largest nine trunk carriers in the United States contributed to a fund from which amounts were paid to struck airlines to defray losses directly attrib-

utable to strike action. During the initial stage of MAP, the period 1958 to 1962, struck carriers received only "windfall benefits"—relatively small amounts equal to non-struck carriers' increased revenues realized due to the strikes. In the second stage of MAP, from 1962 to 1969, the plan assured that a struck carrier would recover at least an amount equal to 25 percent of the struck carrier's normal operating expenses. In the third stage, between 1969 and 1978, the fund paid a struck carrier between 35 and 50 percent of such expenses. At the beginning of the third stage, in 1970, local service carriers (feeder airlines) came into the program, along with the trunk carrier Western Airlines.

The major beneficiary of the strike insurance was Northwest, which received over $187 million, followed by National ($120.1 million) and TWA ($37.1 million). The three major contributors to the fund were United, American, and Eastern, none of which had actually benefited from the fund.

The unions fought the MAP from its inception in 1958, first before the CAB, which had to approve the plan, next by lobbying Congress, then by litigation brought in the courts, and finally in the collective bargaining arena. The unions lost on all fronts, and the MAP remained in force until the Airline Deregulation Act passed

	Carrier	Union	Craft	Work Action	Plaintiff Request	Date of Court Decision	Outcome
1	American	APA	Pilots	Sickout	TRO* sought	2/10/1999	Awarded
2	American	TWU	Mechanics	Slowdown	TRO sought	2001	Awarded
3	American	TWU	Mechanics	Slowdown	TRO sought	1998	Awarded
4	American	TWU	Mechanics	Slowdown	Injunction sought	1999	Granted
5	Delta	ALPA	Pilots	Refuse overtime	Injunction sought	2001	Granted
6	Northwest	AMFA	Mechanics	Refuse overtime	Injunction sought	5/11/2001	Granted
7	Northwest	IAM	Clerical Flight kitchen Stock	Slowdown	Injunction sought	2/25/1999	Granted
8	Northwest	IBT	Flight attendants	Sickout	Injunction sought	1/5/2000	Granted
9	TWA	IAM	Mechanics	Sickout and work stoppage	TRO sought	1998	Awarded
10	United	IAM	Mechanics	Slowdown	Injunction sought	7/1/2002	Granted

Sources: NMB, airlines, and courts.

*A "TRO" is a temporary restraining order, which requires the union to cease the offending activity.

TABLE 29-4 Court-recognized, nonstrike work actions since deregulation through 2003.

Congress in 1978. The ADA provided that the MAP as approved by the CAB would terminate, and that any subsequent plan entered into by the airlines would be constrained by very specific rules and requirements. Thus far, the provisions of the ADA have effectively terminated the strike insurance fund of the airlines.

It should be noted that the MAP was used to great advantage by Texas International beginning with Frank Lorenzo's takeover of that airline and during his battles with that airline's unions in the early 1970s. During the period 1970 to 1974, Texas International received over $11 million from the fund, while paying in only $732,000. Rumblings of discontent over Lorenzo's activities were heard even from the other airlines.

Airline Labor Relations after Deregulation

The Airline Deregulation Act initiated two primary changes in the *status quo ante* in the airline industry that were to have profound effects in labor rela-
tions. First, the practical effects of competition from new entrant, nonunion carriers were largely beyond the negotiating parameters practiced by the incumbent carriers and their unions; that is, concessions in wages and rules to match the startups would have been rejected out of hand by the unions as being too severe. This provided the start-ups with the advantage of being able to provide essentially the same service as the major airlines at greatly reduced rates and fares, and still make a profit. Second, the effects of economic pressures outside the airline industry, such as recession, fuel prices, and interest rates, could no longer be assuaged or compensated for by the CAB. The airlines and their unions, in other words, were going to have to learn to deal with each other in the real world where profit margins, or the lack thereof, were going to drive the relationship.

The overall economic climate that prevailed after the passage of ADA was first seen as a limited decline that turned into a recession by 1980, followed by a deeper sustained recession into the early years of the 1980s. Interest rates soared to 20 percent and inflation went into double digits.

The OPEC fuel embargo caused fuel prices to rise from \$.40 in 1978 to \$1.15 in 1980. The airlines' bottom line was hit hard. There was no safety net to prevent bankruptcy, as Braniff faltered and then fell. Management practices, at Braniff for instance, which completely misapprehended the effects of deregulation, compounded the problem. Between 1979 and 1984, the airlines as an industry lost \$4 billion. Other airlines followed Braniff into insolvency, including Air Florida, Air New England, and Laker.

Between 1979 and the end of 1984, 47 airlines filed under the bankruptcy act.

The takeover tactics of Lorenzo, and the creation of subsidiary airlines of incumbent carriers, like New York Air as a nonunion carrier owned by unionized Texas International, constituted wake-up calls to union leadership. Incursions by startups caused a general reassessment by both management of incumbent carriers and their unions. The apparent willingness, even eagerness, of pilots to work for these new carriers without the benefits of union representation was proven by the large number of applicants for the relatively few available positions.

ALPA and the Crew Size Issue

When technological advances in the railroad industry introduced the diesel locomotive to render obsolete the steam locomotive, and with it the firemen who had been necessary to stoke the steam locomotive's fireboxes, the unions successfully fought the railroads' attempts to eliminate the firemen's position. The firemen thenceforth sat in the engine with little or nothing to do and were paid their regular wage. The name given to this development was "feather-bedding," and it effectively reduced the productivity gains that diesel technology had produced.

When the DC-9 and the Boeing 737 were introduced into the airline fleet in the 1960s, the FAA certified these new types for operation with two-pilot crews. ALPA adopted a hard stance against the FAA certification on the 737, and refused to fly the aircraft with a two-pilot crew. United was originally the largest purchaser of the 737, and to avoid a pilot strike during the regulated 1960s, United agreed to binding arbitration to resolve the issue notwithstanding the FAA certification. In spite of the FAA certification and the proven experience of other airlines, like Lufthansa and Piedmont, that were flying the 737 with two-pilot crews with spotless safety records, the arbitration panel surprisingly ruled that safety concerns mandated that the United 737s be operated with three-pilot crews.

ALPA's stance was now further hardened and extended to the upcoming new Boeing types, the 757 and 767. At ALPA's National Convention in 1980, the delegates voted for a nationwide strike by March 1, 1981, if the crew-size issue on the new aircraft types was not resolved in favor of a three-pilot crew by that date. Such a strike would be a blatant violation of the provisions of the RLA, as ALPA well knew, and as the strike date approached, ALPA pressed for the appointment of a Presidential Task Force to review the FAA's prior certifications. In July 1981, the Task Force reported its findings that safety concerns did not justify the use of three-pilot crews on the new types of aircraft under consideration.

Prior to the publication of the Task Force report, United had concluded that its short haul routes serviced by the 737 would have to be discontinued or severely cut back, with significant pilot furloughs. Although United had reported a profit in 1978 of \$296 million, the subsequent years of 1979 and 1980 resulted in losses of \$235 million and \$65 million, respectively. In a first-of-its-kind turnabout, ALPA under these circumstances reversed its position on the crew size issue and announced that it would accede to the findings of the Task Force. Reminiscent of the days of old, however, ALPA did extract a concession from United, namely, that the airline would agree never to form a startup, nonunion subsidiary like New York Air.

The PATCO Strike

The Professional Air Traffic Controllers Organization (PATCO) walked off their jobs on August 3, 1981, in violation of the Civil Service Reform Act of 1978 (CSRA), which forbids strikes among civil service workers. That same day, President Reagan went on radio and television to announce that any striker who did not return to the job within 48 hours would be fired, and would also be permanently prohibited from being reemployed at any federal agency in the future. Of those controllers who went on strike (some 4,199 did not), 875 returned to work before the expiration of the deadline set by the President. The remainder of the strikers, over 11,000 controllers, were fired.

The FAA had made preparations to meet the strike. Controller positions were staffed by those who had refused to strike, supplemented by supervisors, military personnel, and retirees who were called back. Within ten days the ATC system was operating at about 70 percent effectiveness. The FAA recruited new trainees and ran them through its Air Traffic Service Academy to fill the remaining vacancies. When the air traffic system regained full operational capacity less than two years later, a head count showed that there were twenty percent fewer controllers required to run the system safely and efficiently, implicit proof that ATC was over-staffed when the strike began.

PATCO was decertified as the bargaining agent for FAA controllers. The FAA and the Airline Transport Association filed civil lawsuits seeking damages and injunctive relief, and the PATCO strike fund, which in August 1981 held over $3 million, was impounded to pay damages and fines. Criminal proceedings were commenced and federal court contempt orders were entered.

The controllers hired after the PATCO strike subsequently formed their own union, The National Air Traffic Controllers Union (NATCO), which represents controllers today.

Response from other union groups in support of the strike was muted. ALPA, in fact, publicly countered PATCO assertions that the ATC system was unsafe. Any tepid support voiced for the strike was seen as merely symbolic. Still, union leadership countrywide was apprehensive over the effect of such a devastating defeat suffered by any labor organization. They could not help but notice the overwhelming support that the administration's response to the strike had engendered.

The strike caused large airline losses at a time when the airlines were having a difficult time due to deregulation and the economic downturn then ongoing. It inconvenienced millions of air travelers, and reinforced the wisdom of the anti-strike provisions applicable to federal employees. Unions also took note of the public resentment generated by the strike and by the disruptions that it caused. It might even be concluded that the PATCO strike and its aftermath had a chilling effect on militant union activity— during the ensuing three-year period there were only two strikes in the airline industry, an IAM strike against Northwest in May 1982 and another IAM strike in August 1983, this time against Lorenzo's Continental. Each of the IAM strikes deserves further comment.

The strike against Northwest was called by the mechanics after negotiations had produced agreements with all of the other crafts. It was also generally conceded that the company's offer to IAM was substantial. Union solidarity, most visibly expressed by a refusal by one union's members to cross picket lines set up by different unions, has been a traditional and effective tool in job actions. When IAM struck Northwest, the pilots crossed the picket lines and continued to fly, as did the flight attendants represented by the Teamsters, thereby greatly reducing the effectiveness of the strike.

The Continental strike is technically still in progress given that Continental's entry into Chapter 11, and the subsequent firing of its employees under the *Bildisco* decision, caused the loss of all of those employees' jobs.

Concession Bargaining

Wage concessions first appeared as a result of the financial setbacks experienced by Eastern in the middle of the 1970s, before deregulation. Eastern's unions agreed to a one-year wage freeze in 1975, and in 1976 signed on to a new employee participation plan, known as the Variable Earnings Program (VEP), under which employees would return 3.5 percent of their wages to the company beginning in 1978 in return for profit sharing.

In 1981, the unions at Braniff agreed to a 10 percent wage reduction, but Braniff went into liquidation shortly thereafter anyway. Pan American unions agreed in October 1981 to a 10 percent wage cut, in return for an employee stock ownership plan and a seat on the board of directors. This was the first time that labor had negotiated a seat on any airline's board, and of the thirteen largest carriers in the United States, it was the only board seat. At United, the pilots gave work rule concessions, agreeing to more flying time and to the crew-size issue. They also gave up some bonus pay provisions.

Concession bargaining appeared to be limited to situations where the financial condition of the airline had been directly impacted by either claimed economic conditions or the effects of deregulation, or both. It also is clear that concession bargaining most often resulted in a *quid pro quo* back to the unions, as well as a "snap back" provision designed to reinstate the wage concession when the carrier was again financially stable.

Concession bargaining included wage reductions, work rule changes, delay or elimination of future wage increases, current wage freezes, and reductions in vacation allowances and fringe benefit reductions. Concession bargaining also appears to have been most effective with pilots and flight attendants, but less so with the mechanics. In fact, for many years IAM refused

further wage concessions after the Braniff agreement in 1981. The practice of concession bargaining continued over the ensuing years.

In April 2003, American employees agreed to $1.8 billion in wage, benefit, and work rules concessions to help the airline avoid bankruptcy. That same month, United employees represented by ALPA, Association of Flight Attendants (AFA), the International Association of Machinists and Aerospace Workers (IAM), the Transport Workers Union (TWU), and the Professional Airline Flight Control Association (PAFCA) agreed to $2.2 billion in average yearly savings to avoid liquidation. Through January 2003, US Airways employees agreed to over $1 billion in cuts to avoid liquidation. Of the three airlines, only American was able to remain out of bankruptcy.

Two-Tiered Wage Agreements

Two-tiered wage agreements, or b-scale wages, are a form of concession bargaining that first arose at American Airlines in 1983. The b-scale refers to a wage rate applied to workers solely on the basis of their having been hired after a specified date. The plan is, therefore, prospective in benefit rather than immediate. Once in place at American, the two-tier system rapidly proceeded through the ranks of most carriers, and was readily adopted. By 1986, with the exception of Braniff and Continental, all major carriers had the system in place for at least one craft of employees, and 70 percent of all union contracts carried b-scales.

The agreement typically involves a gradual "payoff," or a limited period during which the new employee will be paid under the reduced pay scale. The plan typically will be merged with the higher wage scale, usually within five years. The wage reduction historically has ranged from 20 percent to 45 percent.

Airline Union Characteristics

From a historical point of view, the machinists' union, IAM, can be considered to remain the most intransigent in labor negotiations. IAM is a centralized union with bargaining units outside of the airline industry. As a union with strong, central leadership that generally controls ultimate decision making in negotiations and concessions, there is a more consistent negotiating position throughout the union, and much less fragmentation due to local union authority. Mechanics are also less affected by either work stoppages or the fear of long-term unemployment due to bankruptcies of their employers since they are readily employable at other carriers or outside of the airline industry. One drawback to IAM is the fact that it represents significant numbers of much less skilled, or even unskilled, workers both within and outside of the industry. Aircraft cleaners and other ground employees, in some locations, are able to control the union. It is apparent that the interests of these disparate groups are not identical.

Pilots, 90 percent of whom are represented by ALPA, are all employed with the airline industry, and their mobility within the industry is seriously constrained by the seniority system employed on all airlines. They are also much more impacted by work stoppages or by carrier bankruptcies since they have no comparable opportunities outside of the industry, or even within the industry due to the seniority rosters. Finally, local ALPA chapters have had much more autonomy than IAM and have been more amenable to concession bargaining on an individual carrier basis.

Flight attendants traditionally have had less bargaining power than pilots and mechanics. They were organized much later than the other two crafts, and they were less unified. In the early 1980s, there were eleven bargaining units representing flight attendants. Their training is much less extensive than pilots or mechanics,

and there is no FAA certification requirement. Flight attendants, in other words, can be more easily replaced.

The Progression of Labor Impacts due to Deregulation

Mergers and acquisitions in the middle of the 1980s reduced the total number of major carriers and consolidated their workforces. Pilot retraining and certification became more problematic as pilots were required to qualify in aircraft types inherited in the mergers. New entrant airlines continued to hire personnel at comparatively reduced wages and with fewer benefits.

While airline labor costs remain the largest single area of expense, wages and benefits of incumbent carrier employees have trended lower throughout the period of deregulation. While there have been short periods of wage increases during periods of airline profitability, these gains have been given back as the legacy airlines have consistently come under increasing financial stress. After each period of recession, the airlines have requested and received concessions from employees and their unions. These concessions have generally tended to only delay the consistent decline in profitability of the incumbent airlines.

By September 2005, there had been 162 bankruptcy proceedings initiated by carriers since 1978. In most of these cases, airline management has gone back to labor representatives for additional concessions. By and large, labor has had the choice of (1) not cooperating with management and letting the airline go into liquidation (as in the case of Eastern), (2) not cooperating with management and letting the airline go into Chapter 11, where labor contracts are routinely abrogated or modified without labor's consent with resulting loss of wages, benefits, and jobs, or (3) agreeing to concessions in a cooperative attempt to sustain the viability of their employer.

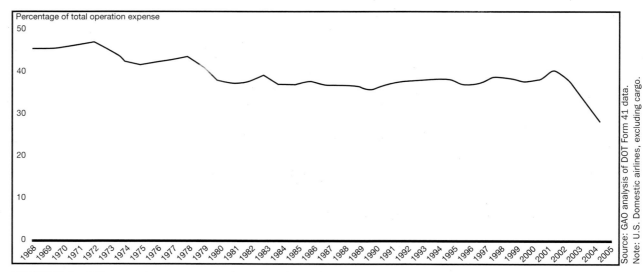

Source: GAO analysis of DOT Form 41 data.
Note: U.S. Domestic airlines, excluding cargo.

FIGURE 29-1 Airline employee compensation as a share of total operating expenses, 1968–2005.

	2004	2005	Change (%)
Pilots and Copilots	81,951	**84,302**	2.9
Other Flight Personnel	5,174	**4,316**	(16.6)
Flight Attendants	98,138	**91,469**	(6.8)
Mechanics	66,215	**59,406**	(10.3)
Aircraft and Traffic Service Personnel	239,901	**238,014**	(0.8)
Office Employees	36,949	**36,158**	(2.1)
All Other	41,169	**39,191**	(4.8)
Total Employment	569,498	**552,857**	(2.9)
Average Compensation[1]			
Salaries and Wages	$56,094	**$52,732**	(6.0)
Benefits and Pensions	17,647	**16,175**	(8.3)
Payroll Taxes	4,065	**4,148**	2.0
Total Compensation	$77,806	**$73,055**	(6.1)

[1]Major and national passenger airlines only.

Source: Air Transport Assn.

TABLE 29-5 Airline employment in 2005 U.S. airlines—average full-time equivalent (FTEs).

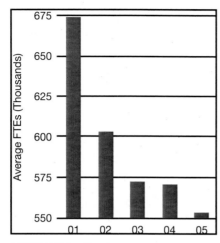

FIGURE 29-2 Employees.

In all cases, it has been the airline employee who has consistently given up the most under deregulation. The competitive forces of a deregulated air transportation industry have left no other alternative.

Summary

Studies[2] conducted on the impact of deregulation through 1992 on the primary crafts of pilots, mechanics, and flight attendants tend to show that:

1. Mechanics empirically suffered no loss in wages or benefits directly attributable to deregulation.

2. The average flight attendant experienced reductions in real earnings of 12 percent by 1985 and 36 percent by 1992 due to deregulation.

3. Pilots earnings were 12 percent lower in 1985 and 22 percent lower in 1992 than they would have been expected to be in the absence of deregulation.

Although there have been no empirical studies accomplished on these issues to bring these data up to date, it is likely that all labor groups are increasingly equally affected by the exigencies of deregulation.

Endnotes

1. To review the provisions of the RLA and its mandated procedures for the resolution of labor disputes, refer to Chapter 14.

2. Cremieux, Pierre-Yves, "The Effect of Deregulation on Employee Earnings: Pilots, Flight Attendants and Mechanics, 1949–1992," *Industrial and Labor Relations Review*, Vol. 49, No. 2, January 1996.

CHAPTER 30

The Progression of Deregulation

© Johnny Kuo, 2008, Shutterstock.

When Congress passed the Airline Deregulation Act in 1978, there existed no empirical data, nor any experience, to reliably predict what would happen to the U.S. air carrier industry under deregulation. During the three years that Congress held hearings on the matter before the Act was actually passed, scores of proponents and opponents testified. The arguments made for deregulation were largely just that, arguments, and they were premised on anecdotal data. Economic theory was given much credence, but it was still just theory. The effect that deregulation would have on the nation and the airline industry was unknown, and there was little basis or experience from which to project any reliable conclusion.

In Chapter 36 we will briefly review the history of the airlines under deregulation. But here, let us look at the results of the period since 1978, and how we got to where we are today.

Airline Fares

A study conducted by the Government Accounting Office (GAO) in the early 1970s concluded that airline fares under the CAB regulated system were anywhere from 22 percent to 50 percent higher than they would be under a deregulated system. The actual results of deregulation on median airline fares is depicted in Figure 30-1, and as of the end of the year 2005, airline fares were almost 40 percent less, in 2005 dollars, than in 1980. Fares have declined the most in long-distance and heavily trafficked markets, and the least in shorter-distance and less-traveled markets.

For many years after deregulation, most of the price benefit went to leisure travelers, who were not constrained to fly on short notice, like the business traveler. Due to computer reservation systems and the yield management programs available to the incumbent airlines, ticket prices were discounted most heavily for those who could purchase early. The airlines were able to charge much higher fares for those who could not plan very far ahead.

In the early years of deregulation, the system of yield management and other competitive pricing schemes resulted in an almost indecipherable pricing regimen, where the passenger in 20A, for example, may find that his fare is twice that of his seatmate in 20B, for no discernible reason. Business fares actually increased after deregulation, at one time by as much as 70 percent over similar fares charged during the CAB era.[1]

Recent evidence, however, discloses that businesses that were punished by the economic

237

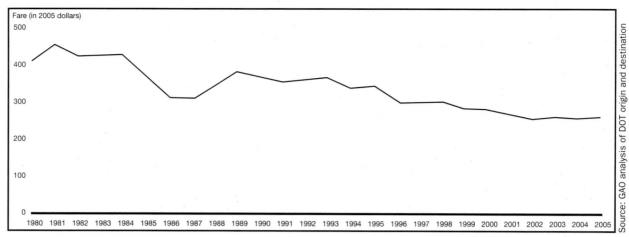

Fare (in 2005 dollars)

Source: GAO analysis of DOT origin and destination survey data.

FIGURE 30-1 Median fares have declined almost 40 percent since 1980 as measured in 2005 dollars.

downturn beginning in 2000 began to resist such disparate pricing. Corporate travel offices were set up for the express purpose of economizing on costs of air travel. By 2002, airlines began to reduce fares across the board, and an increased corporate use of the Internet caused some tempering of fare disparity. Fares still remain higher at "fortress hubs," where one or two airlines have disproportionate market share, and at some small airports where there is little or no competition.

Passenger Travel

Passenger enplanements since 1978 have increased dramatically.

➡ In 1978, 275 million people flew on domestic airlines. By 1995, that figure had doubled, to 548 million. In 2000, the number had increased to 693 million. Because of 9-11, passenger travel dropped significantly, to a low of 641 million in 2002, but by the end of 2005, passenger enplanements were almost 780 million.

➡ Airline departures increased from 5 million in 1978 to 11.5 million in 2005.

Number of Carriers

The number of carriers has increased. In 1938 when the CAB took over regulation of the airlines, there were 16 trunk carriers; by 1978, that number had shrunk to 10 airlines, although small and feeder lines had brought the total number of airlines to 43. In 2000, there were a total of 90 airlines operating in the United States, of which 10 were classified as "major" airlines, a rough equivalent to the trunk airlines of regulation days.

The number of carriers operating in any given year since deregulation has fluctuated greatly. This variation has been referred to as the "ebb and flow" of entrants by former CAB chairman John E. Robson. A variety of reasons has been given for new entrant failures: inexperienced management, unrealistic business plans, lack of solid financial backing, public doubts about airlines' reliability, and poorly conceived pricing structures.

At the end of 2005, there were 138 domestic airlines operating in the U.S., including 20 Majors, 33 Nationals, 31 Regionals, and 55 Commuters.

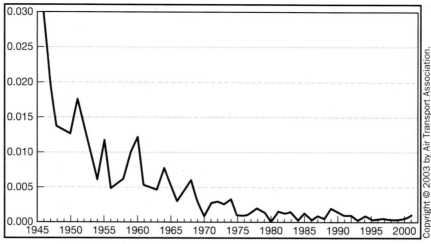

FIGURE 30-2 Safety record of U.S. airlines—fatal accidents per million aircraft miles.

Market Share

After deregulation, and for many years, at least through 2001, the incumbent airlines increased market share over that which existed during CAB regulation. In 1978, for instance, the five largest (incumbent) airlines took in 66 percent of domestic revenues. This control of market share was recited by proponents of deregulation during the Congressional hearings to demonstrate the anti-competitive impact of CAB regulation. In 2001, the five-carrier share had increased to 72 percent, revealing a central failure of deregulation theory. By the end of 2006, however, market share of all incumbent (legacy) airlines had fallen to 55 percent. This resulted, at least in part, due to the fact that after 9-11 four of the largest U.S. airlines went into Chapter 11 bankruptcy reorganization and all legacy airlines cut capacity.

Safety

The airline accident rate has been steadily declining since the 1940s. With the introduction of jet aircraft into the civilian airline fleet, the rate of decline increased even faster, so that by the late

1980s, the total annual number of airline accidents had become historically miniscule. Commuter carriers, flying more turboprop equipment than their larger brethren, have had a proportionately higher accident rate, but over the last two decades even that rate has declined by 90 percent. Since deregulation, the overall fatal accident rate per million miles flown has averaged 0.0009, compared to 0.0135 during the forty years of regulation. It can be logically surmised that the difference in the accident rate before and after deregulation probably has more to do with the technological advance of aircraft and equipment than with regulation. It should be remembered that deregulation did not extend to safety issues. The airline industry remains today one of the most heavily regulated endeavors in the world.

Employment

Through the year 2000, the number of airline employees had increased by 50 percent, to almost 675,000. This increase was reflected across all related industries, like airport security, and construction projects at airports and access to airports. Beginning in 2001, however, airline

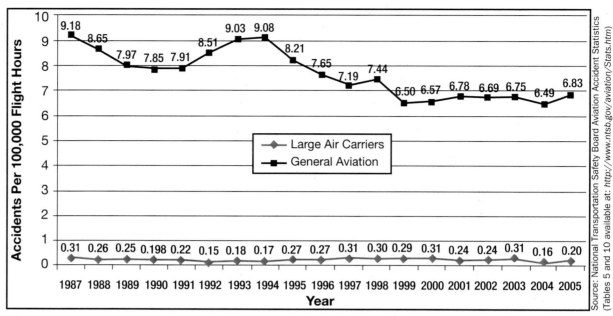

FIGURE 30-3 Accident rates.

jobs declined for the five consecutive years ending in 2005, to just over 550,000.

The Evolution of Operating Practices

The air carrier industry has passed through a series of changes or "waves" since deregulation in 1978.[2] The initial wave was the creation of the hub and spoke system. The second wave was the inauguration of low-fare, point-to-point service, pioneered by Southwest Airlines. The third wave was the entry into the airline fleet of the regional jet. The fourth wave, now in process, is the abandonment of the financial and operational model of the legacy carriers from the period of CAB regulation.

Hub and Spoke

Before deregulation, it was said that if you traveled in the Southeastern part of the United States and you wanted to get to heaven, you would have to go through Atlanta and change planes.

Delta Airlines is credited with creation of the hub and spoke concept that it centered in Atlanta, and, as discussed earlier, Delta began this service during the 1940s at the behest of the CAB in order to bring service to small outlying communities in the Southeast. The other trunk airlines that operated during regulation, however, were all point-to-point carriers.

After deregulation, the opportunities to serve when and where the airlines wanted, coupled with the economic necessity to fill their airplanes with as many passengers as possible, caused the adoption of the hub and spoke system nationwide. This system had two main advantages to the traveler:

➡ The passenger who lived in the hub city gained access to a greatly increased number of destinations directly from the hub airport.

➡ The passenger who lived in one of the smaller communities at the end of a spoke, who may not have had any service under regulation, was offered access to the same greatly increased number of destinations after one stop at the hub airport.

Year	Passenger Fatalities	Passenger Serious Injuries	Total Passenger Enplanements (millions)	Million Passenger Enplanements per Passenger Fatality
1987	213	39	458	2.2
1988	255	44	466	1.8
1989	259	55	468	1.8
1990	8	23	483	60.4
1991	40	19	468	11.7
1992	25	14	494	19.8
1993	0	7	505	No Fatalities
1994	228	15	545	2.4
1995	152	15	561	3.7
1996	319	19	592	1.9
1997	2	21	648	324.0
1998	0	12	650	No Fatalities
1999	10	46	676	67.6
2000	83	11	701	8.4
2001	483	7	629	1.3
2002	0	11	619	No Fatalities
2003	19	10	654	34.4
2004	11	3	711	64.6
2005	18	2	743	41.3
2006	47	4	750	16.0

Notes

· Injuries exclude flight crew and cabin crew.

· Since March 20, 1997, aircraft with 10 or more seats used in scheduled passenger service have been operated under 14 CFR 121.

TABLE 30-1 Passenger injuries and injury rates, 1987 through 2006, for U.S. air carriers operating under 14 CFR 121.

Hub and spoke brought to the airlines a much more efficient use of aircraft by allowing many more destinations to be served using far fewer airplanes. By way of example, if a carrier had 20 airplanes engaged in point-to-point service between city pairs, as was the case before deregulation, the number of origin and destination operations (O&D) would be limited to 20. In the hub and spoke system, the O&D number would suddenly jump to 400 (20 × 20).

The hub and spoke system has drawn complaints, too.

➡ First, passengers were said to be traveling "around their elbow," being required to stop at hub airports that were considerably distant from a direct line of travel, and losing the main advantage of jet aircraft, which is speed and the efficient use of time. According to this view, these passengers were traveling at the convenience of the airline, not themselves.

➡ Second, the system produced the natural result that the dominant airline gained tremendous market share at the hub city, a potential anticompetitive development. Dominated hubs include Atlanta (Delta), Denver (United), Detroit (Northwest), and Chicago (American and United).

➡ Third, the system required that all aircraft returning to the hub do so at or about the same time in order to make connections with aircraft departing from the hub to new destinations. This confluence of activity placed a huge strain on air traffic control and airport operations.

The introduction of these relatively short-haul operations altered the airlines' needs as to types of aircraft. Boeing, it is said, was in the process in the late 1970s of phasing out production of the 737. This decision was reversed after deregulation due to the adoption of the hub and spoke system, and production of 737 aircraft soared. The hub and spoke system also gave rise to an entirely new line of short-range aircraft, like the MD-80. Suddenly there was less need for the larger, fuel hungry 747s, and a general downsizing of aircraft began.

Low Fare, Point-to-Point Service

Southwest Airlines was a wholly intrastate carrier before deregulation, having been founded in 1971. It had developed a no-frills approach to air carrier service that it brought to the interstate market after deregulation, gradually expanding in a deliberate and cautious way. It used just one type of aircraft, the 737, thereby greatly reducing its parts inventory requirements and the training of its airframe and powerplant people, as well as its pilots. Southwest chose secondary airports, like Love Field in Dallas and Midway Airport in Chicago, where the turn-around time for its aircraft would be minimized. This practice avoided the congestion, the ATC delays, and the airport confusion that were becoming symptomatic of the hubs. Southwest's success moved it into the top ten airlines in the United States during the

1990s, and it continued to expand its service into the eastern United States market, opening up service to underserved or unserved airports. In 2006, Southwest had grown to be the second largest air carrier in the country as measured by passengers carried.

The success of Southwest caused startup airlines (increasingly known as "low cost carriers") to imitate its model of low cost and no frills, thereby creating even more service to even more destinations. The legacy airlines also began, in self-defense, to imitate the model of Southwest by creating subsidiaries that provided the same kind of no frills service and that used lower-paid crews operating a single type of airplane, just like Southwest.

The Regional Jet

The concept of the "regional aircraft" was born after World War II to describe the kind of airplanes used by "feeder airlines" authorized by the CAB to supplement the mainstay air carrier fleet. These airplanes were thus described to differentiate them from the long-haul aircraft flown by trunk carriers. At first these aircraft were older aircraft previously flown by the trunk lines, like the DC-3, Convair 240, 340, and 440, and the first commercial turboprop, the Vickers Viscount.

During the late 1950s and early 1960s, a new kind of turboprop was conceived to service the short-haul and feeder market. These were airplanes like the high-winged, 28-seat Fokker F27, delivered in 1958, and larger iterations of the same basic design. The F27 and its successor types would go on to become the most successful turboprop of all time. In 1963, the low-winged Avro 748 turboprop took to the skies, carrying over 20 passengers.

Turboprops worked well in this market, as their operating characteristics allowed them to service smaller airports, and their fuel economy was much better than turbojets. After deregulation, and during the 1980s, other manufacturers entered the 30 to 40 seat commuter market, like deHavilland with the Dash 8, also a high-wing turboprop. While these turboprops were well liked by passengers because of their relative roominess, they were slow compared to jets.

The regional jet (RJ) was introduced into the aviation community in 1992 by the Canadian aircraft manufacturer, Bombardier, with its 50-seat CRJ100 (Canadair Regional Jet), in part fashioned on its business jet, Challenger 604. In 1998, the company announced a stretched version holding 64 to 70 seats, designated the CRJ700, Series 701, and the 75-seat CRJ700, Series 705. A 90-seat version, CRJ900, joined the fleet in 2001. Canadair had some 55 percent of the regional jet market in 2002.

The Brazilian aircraft manufacturer, Embraer (Empresa Brasileira de Aeronautica, South America) entered the field in 1996 with the ERJ-145, with 50 seats. The 35-seat ERJ-135 was introduced into service in June 1999 to begin replacing the Brasilia, Embraer's turboprop workhorse. In 1999, Embraer launched a new family of twin-engined passenger aircraft consisting of the EMB-170, 175, 190, and 195 jets with seating in the 70 to 110 range. The first of this new family, the 170, flew on February 19, 2002. Embraer claimed about 40 percent market share of the regional jet market in 2002.

The Embraer 190 received FAA certification in September 2005. JetBlue Airways took the first delivery of this 98 seat RJ and has an order for 100 more. These new RJs are state-of-the-art airplanes, which rely on digital modeling and virtual reality concepts in its design. This airplane has an all digital cockpit and is equipped with fly-by-wire flight controls except for ailerons. Winglets at the wing tips are standard. The fuselage design features the "double bubble" idea, instead of the traditional circular cross section, which provides the look and feel of a larger cabin.

The Sukhoi Superjet 100, is a 75 to 95 seat RJ, developed by the Russian aerospace firm Sukhoi in collaboration with Ilyushin and Boeing, and is set to be launched in September 2007. The Chinese are in the developmental stage of an RJ called the ARJ 21, with 80 seats for the first phase production and 100 seats for its next phase. This airplane is expected to be certified by the Chinese Civil Aviation Administration in 2008.

There have been few other entrants into the RJ production market. (See Figure 30-4.) Fairchild Dornier, a subsidiary of the U.S.-German partnership, Fairchild Aerospace Corporation, marketed the 329Jet. Production stopped with Fairchild's financial reverses in the 1990s. The only other manufacturer of regional jets was Aero International, a consortium composed of Aerospatiale, Alenia, and British Aerospace. The Bae 146 series became the Avro RJ series (RJ 70/85/100) and 160 of these were produced before BAE Systems announced their discontinuation in the last quarter of 2001.

During the 1990s, RJs began to replace the turboprops used by commuter airlines. (Figure 30-5.) As airlines reconfigured and modified their hub and spoke concepts to utilize RJs, these small jets became commonplace and relatively popular in that service. (See Figure 30-6.) The regional jets are faster, the engines are more reliable, and engine maintenance costs are lower. But compared to turboprops, the original small RJs were much more expensive to operate on a per seat basis. They were also more cramped than the larger turboprops, had less carry-on storage space, had lavatory issues, and minimal flight attendant service. As seen above, the trend in RJ size has consistently been toward larger and larger aircraft.

As the new RJ designs have increased their seating capacity, the line between between a medium-sized jet and a so-called RJ is being blurred. The Airbus 319, for instance, is normally configured for 124 seats, not much larger than the latest RJs. The original RJ concept that emerged during the 1990s of producing jets to replace similar sized turboprops is apparently

Producer	Aircraft	Capacity (class)	Mfg. Year	Airline
McDonnell Douglas	DC-9-10	60/78 seats (1/2 cl)	1965–67	NW/TW/YX
	DC-9-30	84/100 seats (1/2 cl)	1967–82	NW/TW/YX/US/CO
	DC-9-40	112 seats (2 cl)	1967–79	NW/TW
	DC-9-50	122 seats (2 cl)	1975–81	NW/TW
British Aerospace/ Aero International (Regional)	BAe 146-100 (Avro RJ70)	86 seats (1 cl)	1982–	UA
	BAe 146-200 (Avro RJ85)	86/89 seats (1/2 cl)	1983–	UA/NW
	BAe 146-300 (Avro RJ100)	100 seats (1 cl)	1988–	UA
Boeing	717	106 seats (2 cl)	1999	n/a
Bombardier	CRJ-200	50 seats	1992–	DL
	CRJ-700	70 seats	1998–	n/a
Embraer	EMB-145	50 seats	1996–	CO/AA
	EMB-135	37 seats	1998–	n/a
Fairchild Aerospace	328 Jet	32–34 seats	1999	n/a
	728 Jet	70 seats	2001	n/a
	428 Jet	44 seats	2000	n/a
Fokker Aircraft	F28-4000	25/68 seats (1/2 cl)	1976–87	US/AS
	F-100	96/107 seats (1/2 cl)	1986–96	AA/JI
	70	78 seats (1 cl)	1994–96	Mesa

FIGURE 30-4 A wide array of "regional jets."

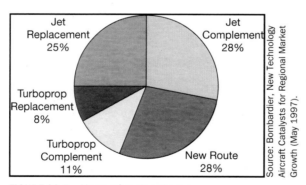

Source: Bombardier, New Technology Aircraft Catalysts for Regional Market Growth (May 1997).

FIGURE 30-5 Uses of regional jets.

being abandoned. Bombardier, for example, stopped production of its 50-seater in January 2006.

Because experience has shown that operating costs of RJs can make sense only on longer routes (400 miles seems to be the minimum), and as per seat operating costs have caused so-called "regional jets" to become larger, a market

is appearing for a new era of turboprop aircraft to fill that niche. Most short-haul routes are less than 350 miles. Rising fuel prices have only reinforced this idea. Turboprops use about 30 percent less fuel than RJs.

There are only two companies producing turboprops in the 40-seat-plus capacity range as of 2007: Bombardier and ATR. The economic factors discussed above have caused increased orders for these companies' turboprop aircraft.

The old deHavilland Dash 8 production unit, which delivered the first Dash 8 in 1984, was sold first to Boeing and then to Bombardier in 1992. Bombardier turboprops are the Q100, first delivered in 1984 (33–37 seats), the Q200, first delivered in 1989 (33–37 seats), the Q300, a stretched version of the 100 (48–50 seats) and the Q400, first delivered in 2000 (68–78 seats). These airplanes have been fitted with a computer controlled noise and vibration suppression system since 1996 (the "Q" denotes "Quiet"), and pro-

	1978	1996	Average Annual Growth Rate
Passengers Enplaned (millions)	11.3	61.9	9.9%
Revenue Passenger Miles (billions)	1.28	14.22	14.3%
Aircraft in Service	1,047	2,127	4.0%
Average Seating Capacity	11.9	25.1	4.2%
Average Trip Length (seat miles)	117	230	3.8%
Operating Airlines	228	109	−4.0%

Source: RAA Annual Report, AvStat Associates.

FIGURE 30-6   U.S. regional airline growth, 1978–1996.

duce a cabin decibel level equivalent to the CRJ regional jet. The Q400 has an impressive maximum cruise speed of 360 knots.

The European consortium ATR is a joint venture between EADS and Alenia Aeronautica. It produces the ATR 42-500 (48–50 seats) with a maximum cruise speed of 300 knots, and the ATR 72-500 (68–74 seats) with a maximum cruise speed of 276 knots.

As of January 2003, 90 percent of all regional jets were still used to service hub airports. As we have seen, this may be in the process of change, and JetBlue has announced that it intends to put its new fleet of EMB 190 aircraft (98 seats) to work overflying hubs on point to point service between city pairs.

Opening up smaller airports in point to point service by the use of RJs could also bring access to airline travel closer to home for the average traveler. Ninety percent of the country's population lives within 30 miles of an airport, yet only 64 airports (1 percent of all airports) serve 80 percent of passengers enplaned in the United States.[3]

The Fourth Wave—Demise of the Legacy Airlines Business Model

Pior to 9-11, the legacy carriers copied the Southwest model only by creating subsidiary operations patterned along the lines of Southwest, while maintaining their primary business models that evolved during CAB regulation.

After 9-11, four of the five largest legacy carriers entered Chapter 11 bankruptcy reorganization, where they secured approval to make substantive changes to their basic structure, including eliminating employee pension plans, securing reductions in wages, cutting capacity, and downsizing generally. These changes are discussed in more detail in Chapter 36. It is yet too early to see how these changes will affect the operations of legacy carriers, but it is not too heretical to suppose that the mainline operations of the legacy carriers may be gravitating to the Southwest model.

This conceivable development will be augmented by the NextGen policy (also discussed at length in Chapter 36) now in the planning stages in the Department of Transportation. Simply put, this complete transformation of the Air Traffic Control system from one of land-based navaids to a satellite-based navigation system, requiring on-board performance avionics and navigation capabilities, will likely drive new point-to-point operational models.

Endnotes

1. Kahn, Alfred E., The State of Competition in the Airline Industry, Statement before the U.S. House of Representatives Commission on the Judiciary, June 14, 2000.

2. The first three waves are suggested by Robert W. Poole, Jr. and Viggo Butler, "Airline Deregulation: The Unfinished Revolution," Reason Public Policy Institute.

3. Miles, Richard B., Testimony before the Aviation Subcommittee, Committee on Transportation and Infrastructure, U.S. House of Representatives, *Competition in the U.S. Aircraft Manufacturing Industry,* June 26, 2001.

CHAPTER 31

Deregulation and the Significance of Competition

© egd, 2008, Shutterstock, Inc.

If you were a traveler in the year 2000, 22 years after the airlines were deregulated, you would have been unable to fly nonstop between Springfield, Illinois, and Washington, D.C. No airline in the country offered this service. Instead, you would be required to go through either Chicago or St. Louis. Your airfare would be about the same, $470 in that year, whether you went through O'Hare using United Airlines or through St. Louis using American. But say that for personal reasons you wanted to drive to your first stop of Chicago or St. Louis, and then take the same flight from that airport on to Washington. Your airfare from either Chicago or St. Louis to Washington would now be about $1,200, between two to three times as much, even though the distance to Washington is shorter by 178 miles through Chicago and by 86 miles through St. Louis. The reason is summed up in three words: Lack of Competition.

United competed with American for the Springfield traffic to Washington. Springfield passengers had a choice of almost equal proportions, in distance, convenience, and service. And the price is about the same for our Springfield traveler whether he goes through Chicago or St. Louis. At Chicago, however, United has little competition for the Chicago to Washington traffic. United has what is known as a "fortress hub" in Chicago. The same situation exists in St. Louis with American. The fares are, therefore, much higher, even though the distance traveled is less.

A Look Back at the Arguments for Deregulation

It is clear that many of the arguments made in support of deregulation were theoretical only; there was no practical or empirical basis in the airline industry for them. Airline markets since deregulation have not performed as expected. What happened?

First, predictions made before deregulation did not foresee the evolution of the hub and spoke system, a system that was adopted by every incumbent carrier. Point-to-point service as a primary marketing or operations strategy has been maintained by only one major carrier, Southwest Airlines. The hub and spoke system has created major barriers to entry for the startup airlines.

Second, expectations that a simplified fare structure would be adopted, based on the assumption that startups with low operating costs would prevent the development or proliferation of complex fare structures, were not borne out.

The computer reservation systems of the incumbent airlines, coupled with the captured market produced by the hub and spoke system, allowed the proliferation of yield management principles first introduced by American Airlines in the 1970s. The application of these principles had a significant impact of rate structures. The widening of the gap between the price of unrestricted full fare tickets (purchased by the time-constrained or business passenger) to the price of the restricted low fares (purchased by the price-constrained, leisure class of passenger) has been due in large part to the workings of computerized yield management.

Third, it was predicted that there would be no "economies of scale" in a deregulated airline market. This expectation assumed that incumbent carriers would be unable to bring their size, their experience, their computer reservations systems, their borrowing power, their ownership of slots and gates, or the benefits of the unanticipated hub and spoke systems to create an advantage over smaller, startup airlines. The contrary, in fact, had been assumed, that the incumbent airlines would have difficulty in competing with the more efficient low-cost carriers that would emerge after deregulation. The lack of economies of scale argument had focused on the cost side of the equation, not on the revenue side. Experience has shown that there truly are few economies of scale on the cost side (e.g., costs of operation are not reduced because of economies of scale), but there are substantial economies of scale on the revenue side (e.g., the enhancement of revenues) due to the factors enumerated above. As a result, most of the startups that came into the market immediately after deregulation, not possessing these attributes, have vanished. Almost all of the major airlines in operation after deregulation are the very same large airlines that existed before deregulation.

The fact that the incumbent airlines were able to survive, and to expand, in spite of the lower costs of the smaller and more efficient startups, leads to the conclusion that there are economies of scale. Further, competitive responses of the incumbents to the entry of the startups in competing markets suggest the existence of anticompetitive practices by the incumbent lines, again possible because of the size and presence of the incumbent carriers. This leads to the next argument made for deregulation.

Fourth, it was said that airline markets were "contestable," that is, in a market where there are only relatively few participants to vie for and share the available market, low-cost carriers with low fares would necessarily cause the competing carriers to lower their fares. In actual practice, the market contestability theory has not proven out in the airline industry. Free entry into the market has been depressed by slot and gate unavailability. There has been an inequality of management acumen and operating experience. Costs associated with the beginning of operations are substantial, and they normally are not recovered in the short run. Predatory practices have been noticed, resulting in lowered fares by the incumbents to meet or exceed those charged by startups, by increases in capacity by the incumbents on the routes flown by the new entrant, and by the inauguration of new routes to compete with the new entrant. Marketing strategies, such as frequent flyer programs that grant advantages to the large, incumbent airlines, were not adequately considered initially.

Deregulation was supposed to foster competition. Competition is what gives to the consumer the best possible deal in price and quantity. Competition since deregulation has been primarily the result of new airlines entering the market, as well as established airlines entering new markets. Freedom to compete since the industry was deregulated, however, has not been uniform, and competition has been stifled in many ways. We will now take a further look at how the promise of deregulation has been compromised.

Barriers to Entry— Limiting Competition

One of the biggest reasons for the failure of deregulation to meet its promise of widespread competition has been the existence of barriers to entry of new airlines. Some of the barriers to entry were identified by opponents to deregulation, but some were not anticipated. The chief barriers to entry actually experienced will be discussed.

Slots

Since 1968, four of the most congested airports in the United States have been subject to "High Density Rules" (HDR), which limit the number of takeoffs and landings per hour. These airports—O'Hare, JKF, National (now Reagan National), and LaGuardia—began using a system of reservations under FAA authority known as "slots." A "slot" under this system is a reservation for an instrument flight takeoff or landing by an air carrier. A small number of slots are set aside for general aviation use.

During regulation, the slot system worked well since routes and access to these airports were controlled by the CAB. With deregulation, however, new airline companies appeared, and established airlines sought out new markets for themselves, greatly increasing the demand for access to these airports. In 1985, DOT revised its rules and procedures to allow slots to be bought and sold by airlines.[1] Slots became a limited commodity and subject to be traded like a commodity. Under the buy/sell rule, DOT retains ownership of the slots, so that they can theoretically be withdrawn at any time, but DOT grandfathered all slot allocations to airlines holding them as of December 16, 1985. DOT retained about 5 percent of outstanding slots and, in early 1986, distributed these in a random lottery to airlines having few or no slots.

Upon the expiration of the following ten year period, by the end of 1996, the General Accounting Office (GAO)[2] found that estab-lished (grandfathered) airlines had increased their total number of slots, while airlines that went into business after deregulation had lost slots. Slots held by startup airlines that went out of business were acquired by lenders (banks and other financial institutions) since these slots had been pledged as collateral to the lenders. The lenders were then free to transfer ownership rights to the slots to the highest bidder, which were often the established airlines. Established airlines also acquired slots by absorbing startup airlines by merger or buyout.

Slots have, therefore, become concentrated within the group of established carriers. In 1999, slot holdings at the four high density airports were:

➡ American Airlines, 32 percent
➡ U.S. Airways, 17 percent
➡ United Airlines, 28 percent
➡ Delta Airlines, 10 percent
➡ Northwest Airlines, 7 percent
➡ TWA, 4 percent

The four largest carriers controlled 87 percent of all slots, and the largest six airlines controlled 98 percent of all slots.[3] Because the number of slots is limited, slots have become very expensive, even if they can be bought at all. This situation is a disincentive to competition and is inequitable since the established airlines originally received the slots from the FAA at no cost.

As an alternative to sale, established airlines have leased slots to startup airlines. This procedure is anticompetitive, as well, since the established airlines often lease slots in order to avoid the "use or lose" rule imposed by the FAA. This rule requires the airline to use the slot at least 80 percent of the time or the slot will revert to the FAA. When the established airlines do lease slots, they typically do so only on a short-term basis, from 30 to 90 days. Entrant airlines find it difficult to justify start-up costs of new service at an airport with no guarantees of the right to continue to use slots, which are its only means of access to the airport and its market.

In 1994, by the FAA Authorization Act,[4] Congress authorized DOT to grant slot exemptions to new entrants where DOT found it to be in the public interest and based on "exceptional circumstances." Slot exemptions, unlike regular slots, could not be transferred. DOT interpreted this authorization narrowly and granted very few exemptions until GAO issued its 1996 report to Congress on the anticompetitive effect of the DOT interpretation. By 2000, DOT had amended its criteria such that, for example, slot exemptions at LaGuardia had been awarded to startup airlines Frontier, Spirit, Pro Air, AirTran, and American Trans Air. DOT also awarded 75 slot exemptions to recent startup JetBlue. Major airlines continued to oppose the relaxing of the slot allocations criteria of DOT.

In April 2000, Congress passed the Wendell H. Ford Aviation Investment and Reform Act for the 21st Century (AIR-21). (See Figure 31-1.) AIR-21 mandates the phasing out of the slot rules at LaGuardia, JFK, and O'Hare. The effective date for the elimination of all slot restrictions at O'Hare was July 1, 2002, and at the New York airports, January 1, 2007.

Upon expiration of slot controls at O'Hare in 2002, resulting congestion during peak hours caused serious delays at that airport. In consultation with affected airlines, the FAA issued an order limiting scheduled operations at ORD. This order is under review every six months, and the arrangement in place is not viewed as a long-range solution to congestion nor a substitute for slots.

Congressional elimination of the slot system raises a very pertinent question: What, if anything, should take its place? Slot control is a method of managing demand at airports. Slot control was initiated in the first place in order to respond to over-demand and to allocate access in an orderly manner. Slot control is also intended to minimize delays.

While the slot control issue affects only four airports, congestion and delays are increasing throughout the National Airspace System. Because of this combination of issues, DOT and FAA have coined a new approach to the problem: Congestion Management.

In October 2004, DOT and FAA contracted with NEXTOR, a cooperative group of university departments named the "National Center of Excellence for Aviation Operations Research," to carry out research on the question of congestion management alternatives, centered on operations at LGA. After the results of that endeavor were reported back to the federal government, in August 2006 the FAA issued a Notice of Proposed Rulemaking (NPRM) that addressed congestion management at LGA.

The proposed rule provided for slot allocations to be replaced with a concept known as Operating Authorizations (OAs). Each OA would have an expiration date so that the duration of the OAs would be from 3 to 13 years (after 3 years approximately 10 percent of the OAs would expire sequentially). No reallocation after expiration of the OAs was specified, although it is indicated that the use of market mechanisms (auction, for example) would likely be tried.

The NPRM also included an incentive structure designed to encourage the use of larger aircraft. The FAA has found that large carriers who control almost all slots at LGA are using LGA to serve their medium and large hubs, and that the average size aircraft operated into the airport has shrunk to 98 seats.

No final rule has been issued, but due to the expiration of slot controls as mandated by AIR-21, the FAA issued an interim rule effective January 1, 2007 which largely preserves the *status quo*.

"Congestion Management" is a concept that encompasses a number of different policies designed to reduce congestion and delay. Among these policies are (1) the imposition of landing fees during peak hours, (2) the expansion of the airside (runway) environment of the airport,

(3) reconfiguring runways and taxiways, especially to eliminate or minimize runway crossings, (4) incentives to airlines to use larger aircraft, and (5) the use of secondary and reliever airports.

Delays at O'Hare have caused the operator, the City of Chicago, to embark on two of the solutions mentioned, that of airside expansion and reconfiguration. O'Hare is undergoing a major renovation that will result in an eight-runway layout consisting of six parallel east-west runways and two crosswind runways. Overall delays will be reduced by 66 percent.

This kind of renovation and reconfiguration is not an option at LGA due to the physical land constraints there. It is located 8 miles from downtown Manhattan and bordered on three sides by water and by a multilane highway on the fourth side. It is, however, central to flight operations in the United States. One study showed that, on one particular day, "some 376 flights traveling to 73 airports experienced flight delays because their aircraft had passed through LaGuardia at least once that day."[5]

Gates

Exclusive, long-term gate leases restrict entry by new airlines at airports. A GAO survey in 1990[6] revealed that at the 66 largest airports in the United States, 85 percent of their gates were leased to established airlines under long-term and exclusive use arrangements. Most seriously affected have been Charlotte–USAir, Cincinnati–Delta, Detroit–Northwest, Minneapolis–Northwest, Newark–Continental, and Pittsburgh–USAir. This fact greatly contributes to the creation of fortress hubs, which is tantamount to the exclusion of competition from the market. In 1995, at all of these airports, with the exception of Newark, one carrier accounted for over 75 percent of all passenger enplanements.

Incumbent airlines will sometimes sublease gates to entrant airlines. These arrangements often carry with them inequities to the new air-line, such as being required to utilize the ground personnel of the lessor airline, usually at increased cost and diminished efficiency to the leasing airline. Occasionally, such subleases require that the entrant airline's aircraft be maintained by the lessor airline.

Perimeter Rules—LGA and DCA

In addition to the anticompetitive constraints of slot and gate access, at LaGuardia and at Ronald Reagan National, there is the additional constraint of perimeter rules. These restrictions require that all flights landing at these two airports be flights that do not originate in excess of a certain distance from the airport. The purpose of these rules was to promote the use of the relatively new JFK and Dulles airports as the long-haul airports for the area. In the case of LaGuardia, the New York Port Authority imposed a rule that nonstop flights in excess of 1,500 miles were prohibited from landing. At National Airport, federal law prohibits nonstop flights in excess of 1,250 miles.

The effect of these rules is to restrict entry, particularly in the case of startup airlines with hubs outside of the established perimeter. Under these rules, America West, the second largest airline started after deregulation, was precluded from serving these two airports from its Phoenix, Arizona, base of operations. At the same time, all seven of the largest, established airlines in the United States could easily serve these airports from one or more of their hubs.

In 2000 (Air-21) and 2003 (Vision 100), two federal statutes allowed DOT to award 44 new slots to airlines at DCA, 24 of which could be used for flights to cities more than 1,250 miles. These slots were awarded to airlines serving six cities (Denver, Las Vegas, Los Angeles, Phoenix, Salt Lake City, and Seattle). See Figure 31-1.

LaGuardia has one exemption to its perimeter rule—to Denver International.

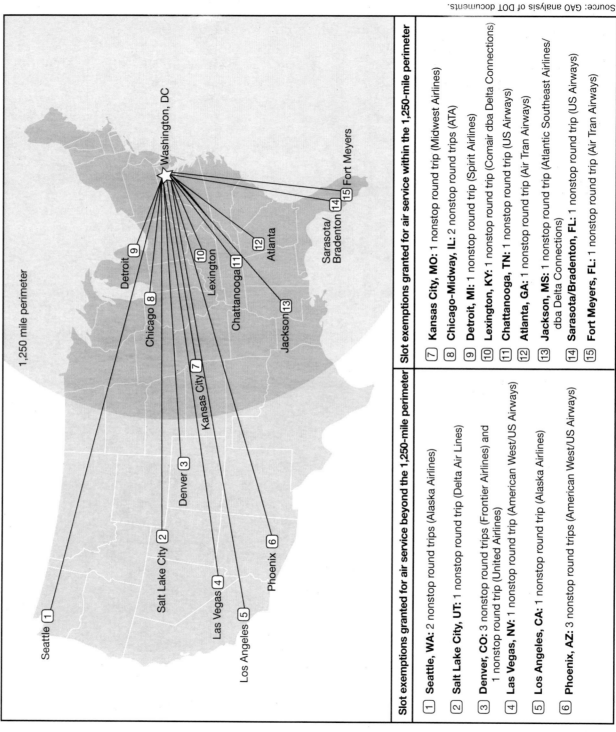

FIGURE 31-1 Summary of slot exemptions granted by DOT under AIR-21 and Vision 100 as of September 2006.

Slot exemptions granted for air service beyond the 1,250-mile perimeter

1. **Seattle, WA:** 2 nonstop round trips (Alaska Airlines)
2. **Salt Lake City, UT:** 1 nonstop round trip (Delta Air Lines)
3. **Denver, CO:** 3 nonstop round trips (Frontier Airlines) and 1 nonstop round trip (United Airlines)
4. **Las Vegas, NV:** 1 nonstop round trip (American West/US Airways)
5. **Los Angeles, CA:** 1 nonstop round trip (Alaska Airlines)
6. **Phoenix, AZ:** 3 nonstop round trips (American West/US Airways)

Slot exemptions granted for air service within the 1,250-mile perimeter

7. **Kansas City, MO:** 1 nonstop round trip (Midwest Airlines)
8. **Chicago-Midway, IL:** 2 nonstop round trips (ATA)
9. **Detroit, MI:** 1 nonstop round trip (Spirit Airlines)
10. **Lexington, KY:** 1 nonstop round trip (Comair dba Delta Connections)
11. **Chattanooga, TN:** 1 nonstop round trip (US Airways)
12. **Atlanta, GA:** 1 nonstop round trip (Air Tran Airways)
13. **Jackson, MS:** 1 nonstop round trip (Atlantic Southeast Airlines/ dba Delta Connections)
14. **Sarasota/Bradenton, FL:** 1 nonstop round trip (US Airways)
15. **Fort Meyers, FL:** 1 nonstop round trip (Air Tran Airways)

Marketing Strategies— Frequent Flyer Programs

Frequent flyer programs began in the early 1980s as a device to encourage customer loyalty incentive to a frequent traveler to use a chosen airline almost to the exclusion of all other competing airlines. The customers who fly the most, and usually at the highest fares, are business travelers whose costs of travel are usually paid by their employers, or accounted for as a business expense. Frequent flyer awards are based on miles flown with the airline that go directly to the passenger, not the employer. So far these awards have not been considered taxable. Thus, the frequent flyer has a potential personal and financial incentive to continue to fly with the sponsoring airline, often paying its highest fares. A new entry into one of these markets, whether by a startup or by an established airline, is very difficult.

Marketing Strategies— Code Sharing and CRS

Code sharing arrangements are devices used in advertising, sales, and reservations activities that allow originating airline designations to be carried through to connecting airlines' flight segments, including to the destination. These arrangements are often entered into between domestic and foreign airlines, or other end-to-end airlines, and between commuter carriers and major airlines. The first code sharing arrangement was approved by the United States government in 1983, when antitrust immunity was given to Pan American to advertise origin and destination points on international routes that actually lay on domestic inland routes operated by Empire Airlines, not Pan American. Empire Airlines became a feeder carrier to Pan Am, and was the first of many to come in the U.S. airline market. Code sharing is used to

eliminate potential competitors from picking up an airline's customers at interchange points by reserving the customer's seat, and issuing his ticket, utilizing only the code sharing partners' airlines. The code-sharing device is depicted in computer reservations systems in user-friendly ways that enhance the likelihood of selecting the code-sharing route from origin to destination. Often it is not readily apparent to the traveler that two or more separate airlines are involved in the itinerary.

> **❝British Airways believes that it is intrinsically deceptive for two carriers to share a designator code. ❞**
>
> —British Airways, comment on PDSR-85, Notice of Proposed Rulemaking, Docket 42199, 1984

Travel agents have been shown to prefer the airlines whose CRS they use. This has a dampening effect on the possibility that a new entrant airline will be selected in any given travel opportunity. Owners of computer reservations systems, which are limited to the established airlines, have more timely access to the booking data generated by the CRS, which in turn allows marketing decisions by the owning airline to be sooner and more accurately made.

As of the latter part of 1996, the major computer reservation systems utilized in the United States were owned as follows:

1. American Airlines owned 100 percent of the largest CRS (SABRE).

2. United and USAir owned 98 percent of the second largest (APOLLO).

3. Delta, Northwest, and TWA owned 95 percent of the third largest (WORLDSPAN).

4. Continental owned 33 percent of the fourth largest (SYSTEM ONE).

The Internet and Airport Competition Plans

Developments since the turn of the century have had a positive impact on competition in the airline industry. The aftermath of September 11 and the resulting economic downturn saw a significant increase in the use of the Internet by both business and leisure travellers for making travel arrangements directly with the airlines. This has the effect of countering some of the incumbents' economies of scale and CRS advantages. Another positive development has been the effect of AIR-21 provisions authorizing DOT to require Airport Competition Plans. This is discussed in Chapter 33.

Summary

The FAA has endeavored to minimize the anti-competitive impacts of CRS by ordering the elimination of all proprietary bias in these systems, which has had positive results. Frequent flyer programs are much more often cited as barriers to entry into markets than are computer reservation systems. Some argue that these programs are legitimate tools of the free enterprise system and a result of the competitive regimen of deregulation itself. Less justifiable in the competitive scheme anticipated by deregulation are the constraints to market entry and competition in general, demonstrated by the control of gates by established airlines and by the control of slots at the four airports affected.

GAO found that of the forty-three airports comprising the FAA's large hub classification, ten airports were significantly affected by barriers to entry. At these ten airports, fares were found to be generally much higher (on average higher by 31 percent) than at the remaining 33 large hub airports at which barriers to entry were not as significant. Some of these have adopted business practices that have made it difficult for entrant air carriers to serve their airports. GAO has specifically named Charlotte Douglas Airport, Greater Pittsburgh International Airport, Minneapolis–St. Paul International Airport, Detroit Metropolitan Airport, and Greater Cincinnati Airport.

The recent developments of the extensive use of the Internet for making reservations and the apparent beneficial effects of Airport Competition Plans have yet to be fully evaluated.

Endnotes

1. FAR Amendment 93-49, 50 Fed. Reg. 52-180 (1985), 14 CFR pt 93.

2. General Accounting Office Report, *Airline Deregulation: Barriers to Entry Continue to Limit Competition in Several Key Domestic Markets* (Letter Report, GAO/RCED-97-4, October, 1996).

3. Dempsey, *Airport Monopolization: Barriers to Entry and Impediments to Competition,* Testimony before the United States House of Representatives, Committee on the Judiciary—Hearings on the State of Competition in the Airline Industry, June 14, 2000.

4. 49 USC sec. 41714.

5. Market-Based Alternatives for Managing Congestion at New York's LaGuardia Airport, Michael O. Ball, University of Maryland.

6. General Accounting Office Report, *Airline Competition: Higher Fares and Reduced Competition at Concentrated Airports,* (GA)/RCED-90-102, July 1990.

CHAPTER 32

Antitrust Enforcement after Deregulation

© Dan Barnes, 2008, Shutterstock, Inc.

" I fly because it releases my mind from the tyranny of petty things . . .**"**

Antoine de Saint-Exupéry

One of the recognized purposes of government is to protect the "public interest" under its constitutional authority to promote the general welfare. A full and complete definition of the term "public interest," is elusive. The concept of the public interest has, for example, been used to justify both the regulation of the airline industry and its later deregulation. It was invoked to justify the original restrictive regulation of the railroads in 1887 (The Interstate Commerce Act), and later used to justify financial assistance to the same railroads.

The nature of the activity deemed by society, or the government specifically, to be either in the public interest or against the public interest is often a function of the "times" or of the philosophy of the administration that happens to be currently in charge of running the government.

In this chapter we will look at how the government attempts to protect the "public interest," specifically in the air transportation industry. To do this we will have to review the history of Congressional legislation which makes it unlawful for the private sector or any business enter-

prise to prevent or limit competition. This legislation is referred to generally as "antitrust" legislation, and it is in the public interest because competition in the business sector is seen as beneficial to the public, resulting in cheaper and more available products and services.

When this legislation was enacted by the Congress, the aviation industry did not exist. It was enacted primarily to curb abuses by the railroad industry during the late 19th and early 20th centuries. When the commercial airline industry came along, the courts had to decide whether or how the antitrust statutes would or should be applied to airline transportation.

Once Congress had enacted this type of legislation in the form of statutes, it fell to the executive branch of government to enforce the law. The executive branch does this through its departments and agencies. Jurisdiction over the airlines has bounced around in the executive branch of government, being first exercised by the Department of Commerce, then the agency known as the Civil Aeronautics Board. After deregulation of the airlines in 1978, jurisdiction swung between the newly formed Department of Transportation (DOT) and the Department of Justice (DOJ), and finally, today, is shared by these two departments and their agencies.

The chronological sequence of statutory law and the agencies that have enforced that law are as follows:

1. The Sherman Antitrust Act (Statutory Law)
2. The Clayton Antitrust Act (Statutory Law)
3. The Civil Aeronautics Board (Executive Agency)
4. The Department of Transportation (Executive Department)
5. The Department of Justice (Executive Department)
6. A combination of the DOT and the DOJ

The Sherman Antitrust Act—Price Fixing and Trusts

Shortly after the appearance of large corporations in the late nineteenth century, it was deemed to be in the public interest to prevent concentrations of power that interfered with trade or reduced levels of economic competition. The Sherman Antitrust Act (1890) essentially prohibits any activity that:

1. fixes prices,
2. limits industrial output,
3. allocates or shares markets,
4. or excludes competition.

This activity can be in the form of combinations or cartels, or agreements between corporations or individuals to accomplish that purpose, often referred to as trusts. The second essential prohibition of the Act is to make illegal any attempt to monopolize any part of trade or commerce by any individual or corporation.

There is no "bright line" test as to what activity constitutes a violation of the Act, and it generally requires a court test and a judicial decision to settle the question of whether or not specific activity is a violation of the Act. Perceived violations of the Act are enforceable by the Department of Justice through litigation in the federal courts.

The Clayton Antitrust Act—Mergers, Acquisitions, and Predation

In 1914, Congress supplemented the Sherman Act by passing the Clayton Antitrust Act, which prohibits:

1. Companies within the same field from having interlocking boards of directors (thus, essentially the same management)
2. Forms of price cutting (predatory pricing) or other pricing discrimination
3. Acquisition of stock or assets of one company by another if the acquisition tends to lessen competition or to create a monopoly. Enforcement is carried out jointly by the Department of Justice, Antitrust Division, and the Federal Trade Commission.

The Civil Aeronautics Act and the Department of Justice

When the airline companies first appeared during the 1920s and 1930s, it was rightly presumed that they were subject to the same antitrust laws as everybody else. The Department of Commerce had jurisdiction over the railroads and regulated that industry through its agency known as the Interstate Commerce Commission (ICC). When commercial aviation began, what little regulation there was of the airlines was also administered in the Department of Commerce, first by the Aeronautics Branch and then by the Bureau of Commerce and the ICC. In 1938, however, as commercial aviation expanded and became more important to the nation, the airlines came under the special legislation of the Civil Aeronautics Act, applicable only to the airlines, and administered by the Civil Aeronautics Board. Although the Sherman and Clayton Acts did not specifically address the antitrust aspects of airline operation, the Federal Aviation Act of 1958 gave the CAB authority to approve all airline mergers and consolidations[1] and granted certain exceptions from the Sherman Act and other antitrust laws.[2] The broader question of whether or to what extent the airlines were subject to the Sherman and Clayton Acts was an open one until finally settled in 1963.

The Justice Department had long maintained that it had antitrust enforcement authority over the airlines, and DOJ brought suit against Pan American and W. R. Grace & Co., as well as their jointly owned subsidiary, Pan American–Grace Airways (Panagra). In defense, the airlines contended that the Civil Aeronautics Board had exclusive authority over airlines, including antitrust matters, and that the Justice Department had no authority to bring the action. The lower federal court sided with the Justice Department, holding that Pan Am had violated the Sherman Act by combining with its subsidiary, Panagra, in agreeing to not parallel each other's South American routes, effectively agreeing not to compete. In **Pan American World Airways, Inc. v. United States,**[3] the Supreme Court reversed the lower court holding and established that the CAB had primary jurisdiction over the airlines in matters of "unfair practices" and "unfair methods of competition," as well as to consolidations, mergers, and acquisitions. This became established law and remained so until the CAB was legislated out of existence effective January 1, 1985, by the provisions of the Airline Deregulation Act of 1978.

Before deregulation, mergers of airlines were rare. The largest was United Airlines and Capital Airlines in 1961. The norm was represented by Delta's acquisition of Northeast in 1972 based on the "failing airlines" doctrine of the CAB. Simply stated, the "failing airlines" doctrine described the CAB practice that prevented any airline bankruptcies during regulation by allowing, encouraging, and arranging for stronger carriers to absorb weaker ones.

The Department of Justice and CAB— 1978 to 1985

The Department of Transportation— 1985 to 1988

During the first years after deregulation, and before 1985, antitrust jurisdiction was divided between the DOJ and the CAB. The DOJ prosecuted price fixing violations of the Sherman Act and the CAB retained jurisdiction over mergers and acquisitions. When the sunset provisions of the ADA extinguished the authority of the CAB, jurisdiction over merger authority went to the Department of Transportation (in 1985). During this period, the DOJ function with respect to proposed mergers was limited to the submission of comments to the DOT. DOJ agreed with some of the DOT positions on mergers and acquisitions. In 1986 alone, in fact, some 25 airlines were involved in 15 mergers.[4]

But the DOJ strongly opposed two mergers that the DOT approved, namely, the TWA acquisition of Ozark and the Northwest acquisition of Republic, both in 1986. The DOJ opposition was based on the fact that the merged carriers operated hubs at common airports, thus only they provided nonstop service to many city-pairs. With the mergers, all competition was lost.

The DOT approved the acquisitions rationalizing that the *threat* of entry into those markets by other carriers, who would be free to enter because of deregulation, would deter anticompetitive practices by the merged carriers. This thesis, known as the contestability theory, proved to be incorrect, and fare increases and service reductions followed the mergers.

The Department of Justice—1988

The DOT's jurisdiction over mergers terminated effective December 31, 1988, and the DOJ then assumed sole responsibility for airline merger review. DOJ now has primary authority in air carrier cases to enforce all antitrust laws. There were relatively few merger proposals after 1988 (see Figure 32-1), but it was apparent that the laissez-faire governmental attitude (minimal government interference or regulation) of the middle 1980s had come to an end when authority was assumed by DOJ. In 1998, when Northwest, then the fourth-largest carrier in the United States, proposed to acquire a controlling interest in Continental, then the fifth-largest air carrier, the DOJ opposed the action. The challenge of the DOJ was based on the fact that the two carriers are each other's most significant competitors (or only competitors) in nonstop service between cities where they maintain their hubs. In its complaint against the carriers, the DOJ asserted that the proposal would cause higher ticket prices and diminished service for millions of passengers. This proposed merger has not occurred.

How Proposed Mergers and Acquisitions Are Reviewed

Carriers proposing to merge are required to provide notice to the DOJ and to the Federal Trade Commission (FTC). The DOJ reviews the proposed merger plan, usually within a period of 30 days, and if no competitive issues are discerned by DOJ, the parties are free to proceed. In some cases, DOJ may issue its request for additional information, which prevents further action toward merger by the carriers for another 20 days. Often, concerns of the DOJ are addressed in this manner and any issues are resolved without formal action. Other times, litigation is required to resolve the issues.

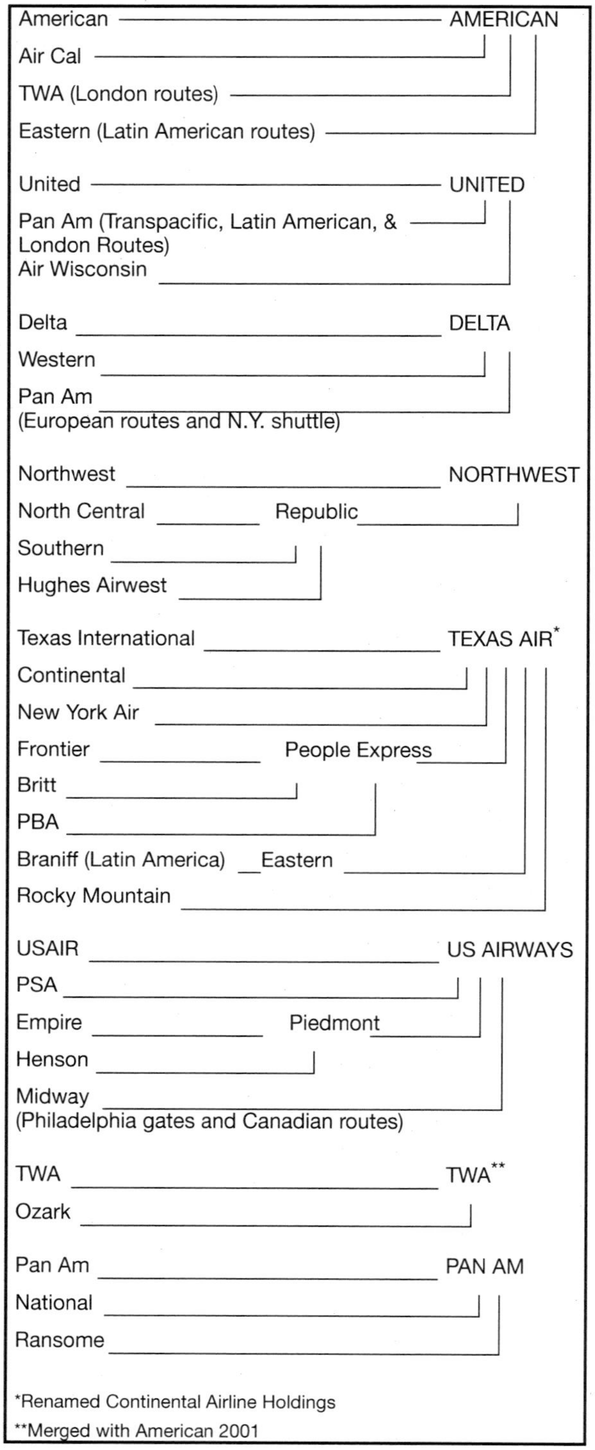

FIGURE 32-1 Major air carrier mergers, acquisitions, purchases, and consolidations through 2001.

The DOJ normally applies the provisions of Section 7 of the Clayton Antitrust Act, which prohibits the acquisition of stock or assets "where in any line of commerce or in any activity affecting commerce in any section of the country, the effect of such acquisition may be substantially to lessen competition, or to tend to create a monopoly." The statute provides the means for the proposed action to be prevented or delayed while the objections of the government are heard. The procedure reflects the fact that, once a merger process has begun or has been completed, it is very difficult to undo. Delay or prevention of the proposed merger activity is accomplished by the filing of a complaint in federal court and seeking a temporary restraining order or injunction to prohibit the airlines from proceeding with the proposed action.

The authority of the DOJ extends to instances involving the acquisition of relatively minor assets of one carrier by another, as in the case of gates or slots at airports. In 1989, for example, the DOJ moved to block the acquisition of Eastern's proposal to sell gates to USAir at Philadelphia International Airport, and again in 1991 when Eastern sought to sell slots and gates to United at Reagan Washington National Airport.

Finally, the DOJ has authority, jointly with the DOT, over airline acquisition of international route authority and mergers between domestic and foreign carriers. The DOT, in turn, works with the Department of State, which has final authority in dealing with foreign governments. The DOJ may challenge these proposals in the same manner as in domestic acquisitions.

The Department of Transportation after 1988

Even though the DOJ now has primary authority over domestic airline mergers and acquisitions, the DOT retains jurisdiction to regulate and investigate some aspects of domestic airline operations, including carrier fitness, ownership and advertising. DOT has express authority to prohibit unfair and deceptive practices and unfair methods of competition. Section 411 of the Federal Aviation Act, recodified as 49 U.S.C. 41712, provides:

> [The] Secretary may investigate and decide whether an air carrier . . . has been or is engaged in an unfair or deceptive practice or an unfair method of competition in air transportation . . . If the Secretary, after notice and an opportunity for hearing, finds that an air carrier . . . is engaged in an unfair or deceptive practice or unfair method of competition, the Secretary shall order the air carrier . . . to stop the practice or method.

DOT takes the position that it is authorized to prohibit conduct that does not amount to an actual violation of the antitrust laws, but is such that it could be considered anticompetitive under antitrust principles.[5]

Predation and Competitive Responses of Airlines

A government study begun in 1990[6] found that the hub and spoke system, adopted by all major airlines after deregulation, resulted in airlines charging premium prices to local passengers originating from dominated hubs. The study also found that low-cost point-to-point service, such as that developed by Southwest Airlines, provided an effective counter to local hub and spoke market power. Further, DOT found that the rapid growth of Southwest and the entry into the market of other low-cost carriers appeared to be correcting the lack of price competition at hubs. Thus, governmental action was not warranted.

By 1995, nearly 40 percent of domestic passengers flew from hubs with low-fare competition, causing some major carriers to emulate the low-cost point-to-point carriers by forming their own low-cost divisions. In 1998, DOT concluded that this competitive stimulus supplied by new-entrant carriers had subsided, and that the number of new-entry carriers had significantly declined. The reason, according to DOT, was because of anticompetitive activity on the part of some major airlines.[7]

Predatory activity by incumbent airlines generally occurs when other airlines, usually smaller discount airlines, seek to enter a market already served by the incumbent airline. The incumbent airlines may respond to this new competition by fare cuts, capacity increases by adding aircraft, or capacity increases by adding routes. The purpose of such activity is to maintain market power and to diminish or eliminate competition. Since the cornerstone of a successful air transport system under deregulation depends on fair competition among the participating air carriers, predatory activity is harmful to the success of the system and to the ultimate interest of the consumer. Maintaining competition requires the assurance that carriers can enter new markets fairly.

It has been cogently argued that the competitive responses of major hub carriers differ depending on which airline is supplying the competition. Major carriers' responses as to each other reflect a "live and let live" approach, that is, there is an implicit recognition that relatively equal financial strength and market power provide a control mechanism that allows a peaceful coexistence to be maintained in the competitive process. The competitive response against Southwest Airlines is more aggressive, but not destructively so, probably on the same basis, that Southwest is too large and too strong to kill. The competitive response to startups, however, is much more aggressive, including matching and even undercutting the startup low-cost fares and adding capacity to the routes of the interloper. Examples for evaluation include United versus Frontier, American versus Vanguard, Delta versus ValuJet, Northwest versus Sprint and Reno, and Continental versus Kiwi.

In 1998, DOT said:

DOT believes that the responses of some large, established major carriers at their hub cities to service by small, new-entrant airlines have inhibited competition, resulting in higher prices for many passengers and preventing a large sector of air travel demand from being efficiently served. These responses, which protect major carriers' ability to charge higher prices in local hub markets, involve temporarily selling such large numbers of seats at low fares, comparable to new-entrant fares, that by sacrificing profits in the short term, they force the new-entrant carriers to exit from the local market.[8]

DOT found that, once the low-cost carrier had been forced out of the market, the incumbent airline set its fares at least as high as they had been prior to the incursion by the new-entrant airline. It is believed that these anticompetitive practices against low-fare entrants caused new entries to virtually cease, beginning in the middle 1990s. No new companies made application to DOT for authority to begin operations during 1997 and 1998.

Having concluded that predatory activity by the incumbent airlines was, indeed, reducing competition, DOT in 1998[9] announced its new enforcement policy directed at curbing predatory activities by the major air carriers. Generally, DOT will regard an incumbent's competitive response to a new entry to be anticompetitive and predatory where it initiates fare cuts, capacity increases on the routes served by the new entry, and where the incumbent's tactics appear to be economically rational only if they force the new entrant to exit the market or reduce service.

DOT has announced its intention of working in cooperation with DOJ to prevent anticompetitive practices overall, and to prevent any unnecessary duplication of effort or hardships on the parties involved. DOT has also announced its intention to defer to DOJ primacy in the field in the event that DOJ concludes, in any particular case, that DOJ-invoked antitrust remedies (including initiating litigation against the air carrier) are the most efficient means of precluding anticompetitive practices

Anticompetitive Practices at Airports

In Chapter 31, we discussed barriers to entry and how slot and gate ownership can have the effect of limiting competition. In Chapter 33, Airports and Deregulation, we will talk about how the operation of airports can also have anticompetitive results. DOT has been concerned with all of these activities to the extent to which airlines participate in them. But DOT is also concerned with anticompetitive practices by the airport owners and operators themselves.

As we will see in Chapter 33, DOT oversight of anticompetitive practices by airport owners was severely curtailed until 2001. With the passage of the Wendell H. Ford Aviation Investment and Reform Act for the 21st Century (AIR-21), DOT was given an important tool to use in monitoring and preventing these practices. In order to participate in federal monies, airport owners and operators must now submit for DOT approval Competition Plans designed to insure that gate availability is equitably provided. Under this program, DOT can also monitor and, to some extent, control other anticompetitive and unfair practices associated with gate use, such as subleases, equipment leases, ground aircraft maintenance, and aircraft service agreements.

Endnotes

1. 49 USC sec. 1378.
2. 49 USC sec. 1384.
3. 371 U.S. 296 (1963).
4. Dempsey, Antitrust Law and Policy in Transportation: Monopoly Is the Name of the Game, 21 Ga. L. Rev. 505 (1987).
5. See *Pan American World Airways v. United States,* 371 U.S. 296, 306–308 (1963), and *United States v. CAB.* 766 F.2d 1107 (7th Cir. 1985).
6. GAO, Airline Competition: Higher Fares and Reduced Competition at Concentrated Airports, GAO/RECD-90-102; July 1990.
7. U.S. Department of Transportation, Statement of Enforcement Policy Regarding Unfair Exclusionary Conduct (Docket No. OST-98-3713, Notice 98-16) April 1998.
8. Ibid.
9. Ibid. This study was followed up by DOT in 2001, see: U.S. Department of Transportation, Enforcement Policy Regarding Unfair Exclusionary Conduct in the Air Transportation Industry (Docket ST-98-3713) January 17, 2001.

CHAPTER 33

Airports and Deregulation

© Terry Alexander, 2008, Shutterstock.

Throughout the period of Civil Aeronautics Board regulation of air carrier routes and rates, airports competed with each other for the limited amount of traffic that was available. Traffic was limited not only because CAB policy restricted the number of available routes, but because it also mandated high airfares. During the 1950s, 1960s, and most of the 1970s, airports maintained marketing departments whose functions included lobbying the airlines and the CAB for service.

After deregulation, by the year 2000, some 380 million more passengers a year were passing through America's airports than before deregulation. The problem was no longer one of how to secure more service; rather it was one of how to service the existing, and increasing, traffic.

Commercial-service airports were suddenly faced with the need for more gates and runways (airside expansion) and for more groundside support facilities (parking, restaurants, rental car counters, ticket counters, and shops). Methods of funding for renovation and expansion had to be addressed anew. The developing operational practice of the airlines known as hub and spoke, with its concentration of passenger arrivals and departures all at the same time, put severe pressure on airport operations. Control of existing gates had to be reevaluated in view of the increasing number of airlines requiring access to the limited number of gates. Environmental concerns, both from increased aircraft operations and from ground traffic to and from the airports, brought additional pressures on airport management practices.

The commercial air service industry consists of three essential components:

1. Air carriers
2. Air traffic control
3. Airports

While all three of these components must combine to function in an orderly and cohesive manner, the provisions of the Airline Deregulation Act directly controlled only the air carriers. In other words, only the air carrier portion of this combination had been deregulated. The federal government is solely responsible for the operation of the ATC system, and it is significantly involved in the operation of airports. Airports operate under a matrix of federal regulations, and commercial-service airports are all owned by local, regional, or state governments. While deregulation had unleashed the power and innovative potential of private enterprise in air carrier operations, the inherent limitations of government control in the ATC and airport sectors still overlay, and constrained, that potential. We will review how these factors have impacted modern airport operations.

Airport Ownership

There are around 18,300 airports in the United States, of which 5,300 are for public use. The majority of these airports (4,166) are publicly owned, and over 500 of these are commercial-service airports. Commercial-service airports are publicly owned airports that enplane more than 2,500 passengers annually in regularly scheduled passenger service. All of these airports are included in the FAA's National Plan of Integrated Airport Systems. While all such airports are currently publicly owned, a limited number have contracted out some of their operations to private, commercial management, primarily at medium hub airports.[1]

Airports are further classified by the FAA as

→ Large hub airports (at least 1.0 percent of total national enplanements)

→ Medium hub airports (less than 1.0 percent but more than .25 percent of total national enplanements)

→ Small hub airports (less than .25 percent but more than .05 percent of total national enplanements)

→ Non-hub airports

As of 1999, over 75 percent of all passenger enplanements occurred at large hub airports, 16 percent at medium hub airports, and 6 percent at small hubs. Less than 3 percent of all passenger traffic passed through non-hub airports (see Figure 33-1).[2]

Airport Funding for Operations and Capital Improvements

Each airport is operated under a master plan, the primary purpose of which is to provide safe and efficient air carrier service and to enhance airport capacity. Capital improvements include construction of new facilities or renovations of existing facilities. Sources of funding include:

→ Airport Revenue Bonds

→ The Airport Improvement Program (AIP)

→ Airport user charges

→ Passenger facility charges (PFCs)

→ State and local funding programs

Airport Revenue Bonds

Bonds are the primary means of financing airport capital development projects. Bonds are debt instruments (like I.O.U.s) issued by the airport owner to raise the money necessary for new construction or renovations. These bonds are tax-exempt and are known as General Airport Revenue Bonds (GARBs). GARBs accounted for 36 percent to 70 percent of airport capital development expenditures during the 1990s, a sum in excess of $3 billion per year. Projections for the time period 2007 to 2011 are for bond funds to account for 44 percent of planned capital projects.

A secondary source of revenue is derived from bonds known as Special Facility Bonds. These bonds are secured directly by the owner of the facility, such as a fixed base operation or aircraft maintenance facility, and the owner of the facility is usually responsible for paying off the principal amount of the bond and all interest charges.

Airport Improvement Program Funds (AIP)[3]

AIP funds are federal monies administered by the FAA. AIP grants are distributed both according to statutory formulas and FAA discretion. During the 1990s, AIP funds constituted 21 percent to 40 percent of the total airport capital development expenditures. The majority of AIP funding went to Landing Area Construction (52.9 percent) and Noise Control (11.1 percent). Airport owners or sponsors must provide a minimum of 10 percent share of any project funded by AIP grants.

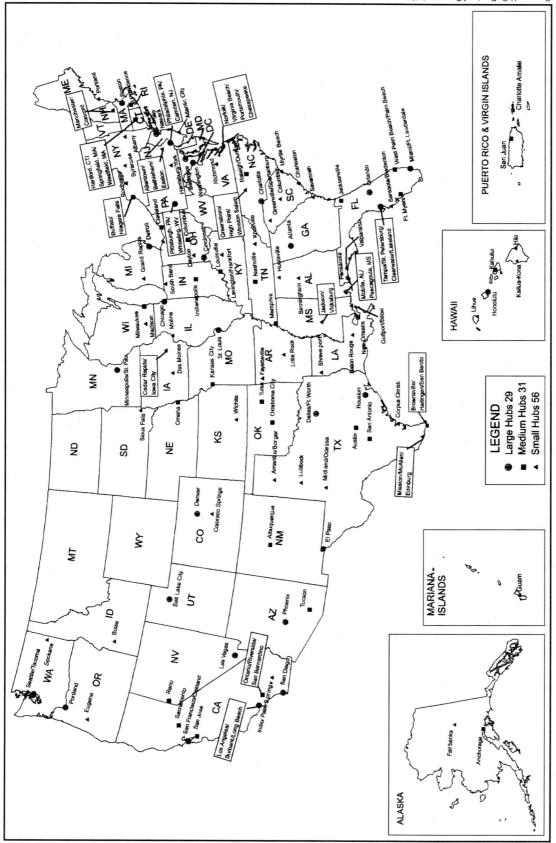

FIGURE 33-1 Airport activity statistics of certificated air carriers.

Airport User Charges

Airport user charges are either (1) aeronautical user charges or (2) non-aeronautical user charges.

1. Aeronautical user charges include landing fees, apron, gate-use or parking fees, fuel-flow fees and terminal charges for rent or use of ticket counters, baggage claims areas, administrative support quarters, hangars, and cargo buildings.

2. Non-aeronautical user charges include rentals to terminal concessionaires, automobile parking, rental car fees, and rents and utilities for hotel, gas station, and related facilities.

Passenger Facility Charges (PFCs)

In 1990, Congress authorized airports to charge a per-passenger enplanement fee to be used for the financing of airport capital improvements and the expansion and repair of airport infrastructure. A fee of up to $3 (fees over $3 require special justification pursuant to AIR 21, but as of April 1, 2007, only two applications out of 1,517 had been denied) per passenger may be imposed for the funding of three specific purposes: (1) to preserve or enhance safety, security or capacity, (2) to reduce noise or mitigate noise impacts, and (3) to enhance air carrier competition. Pending legislation (the 2007 FAA Reauthorization Act) would raise the PFC ceiling to $6.00. In 1996, PFCs accounted for 15 percent of total airport capital development expenditures. (See Figure 33-2.) Projections for the time period 2007 to 2011 are for PFCs to account for 20 percent of planned capital airport projects.

State and Local Government Programs

State and local funding is most often used as matching funds in order to receive federal support, although direct funding of maintenance

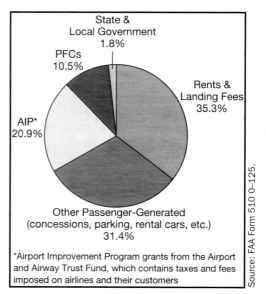

*Airport Improvement Program grants from the Airport and Airway Trust Fund, which contains taxes and fees imposed on airlines and their customers

Source: FAA Form 510 0-125.

FIGURE 33-2 98% of airport revenue comes from airport users: U.S. Airport Sources of Revenue, 2001.

projects is sometimes provided. During the 1990s, state and local funds accounted for 7 percent to 11 percent of airport capital development expenditures.

Airport Facilities Use Arrangements

Use of airport facilities, buildings, and land is normally arranged under use and lease agreements between the airport management and the user. Most of these agreements are between the airport owner and the airlines. These agreements generally fall into three separate categories: residual, compensatory, and hybrid agreements.

Residual Use and Lease Agreements

Under this type of agreement, airlines agree to assume the financial risk of running the airport. Airlines guarantee that the airport will not lose money by agreeing to make up the difference between total cost of operations and the total of non-airline revenue received by the airport.

These types of agreements originated during the period of regulation when traffic volumes were low and the airlines were much more powerful than after deregulation. The trade-off an airport makes when entering into this kind of agreement is two-fold:

1. The airport gives up the opportunity to make any profit in its operations since any surpluses are credited to the airlines.

2. The airport gives up the right to make autonomous decisions over capital expenditure programs because of provisions in the agreements, called "majority-in-interest" (MII) clauses.

These MII clauses allow the airline to approve or disapprove, or at least delay, specific capital projects, the costs of which would be included in the future charges to the airline.

Some of these capital projects (like construction of new gates) could benefit new entrant airlines into the airport, which would be adverse to the interests of the signatory airline. The right to disapprove the project, of course, is anticompetitive, so that the airline has been placed in a position of unfair advantage over its would-be competitor. These clauses are also against the public interest in having better, bigger, and more efficient airport facilities for use by passengers. MII clauses, however, do not give the airline approval authority over projects funded by AIP, PFCs, or special facility bonds, and airlines are legally barred from exercising veto rights over PFC-funded projects. Eighty-four percent of residual use and lease agreements have MII clauses, and the average length of the agreement at large hub airports is 28 years.

Compensatory Use and Lease Agreements

Under these types of agreements the airline pays only for the facilities and services actually used. The airport assumes the responsibility for meeting the costs of operation like any other owner. One survey reported that 20 percent of these types of agreements have MII clauses. Compensatory agreements, without MII clauses, allow the airport full latitude in the use of its funds and allow the incentive to add additional service in the interest of the public and the airport instead of the interests of the incumbent airlines at the airport.

Hybrid Use and Lease Agreements

These agreements typically exclude non-aeronautical uses (restaurants, rental car operations, etc.) from the residual pool, so that an airline's guarantee is limited to the cost of aeronautical operations only. The airport retains earned revenues from its non-aeronautical operations while being guaranteed a break-even on airfield activities. Seventy-four percent of these agreements contain MII clauses, the average length of which is 20 years. While these agreements are anticompetitive with respect to capital improvement and expansion projects, they do give to the airport the incentive to expand its non-aeronautical sources of income.

Gate Leasing Arrangements

Airport gates obviously are a finite commodity and an essential element of both airline service and competition in the airline industry. In combination with overriding use agreements, or as separate undertakings with airlines, airports have normally utilized three methods of allocating gate use to airlines serving that airport:

1. Exclusive-use contracts
2. Preferential-use contracts
3. Airport controlled gates

Exclusive-Use Arrangements

Exclusive-use arrangements typically assign to one airline the right to use and occupy gates and facilities for a specified duration, as well as the right to sublet or assign those gates and facilities conditioned on prior consent of the airport. These types of arrangements are recognized to constitute potential barriers to entry based on complaints by new entrant carriers that incumbent airlines hoard gates, require substantial sublease premiums, offer access at less preferable times, force the new entrant to use the incumbent's ground personnel, or refuse to sublease altogether. These arrangements also have the effect of hindering airport management from properly exercising its legislative mandate of providing equal, nondiscriminatory access to its federally-funded facilities. Moreover, since gate leases are considered assets in law, secured creditors of bankrupt carriers, like banks, can wind up possessing the proprietary rights to airport gates, and preventing recovery and use of those gates by airport management.

Exclusive-use gates remain the predominant arrangement at large hub airports, although their number fell between 1968 and 1992 from 63 percent to 55 percent. Projections are that by 2004 their use will be down to 40 percent. Exclusive-use gates at medium hub airports are less prevalent, constituting 35 percent of gate arrangements in 1992, down to 29 percent in 1998, with projections that by 2004 their uses will be down to 30 percent.

Preferential-Use Arrangements

Preferential-use arrangements normally give the tenant airline the primary right to use the facility only when it has operations scheduled. These arrangements constitute a shared control between the airport and the airline with an explicit contractual right remaining in the airport authority to allow use of the gate by other airlines. Importantly, this type of arrangement preserves the airports' ability to honor the legislative mandate of providing nondiscriminatory access to its facilities and to use the tenant's gates for new entrants.

Preferential-use agreements differ in their specifics, some containing "use-it-or-share-it" or "use-it-or-lose-it" requirements, as well as other types of recapture provisions. These types of gate arrangements have become more prevalent at large hub airports, increasing from 28 percent in 1992 to 32 percent in 1998, with projections that by 2004 their use will be up to over 46 percent. Reagan Washington National has reported a gate composition of all preferential-use gates, and Boston Logan expects to have all preferential-use gates beginning in 2002. Detroit Metropolitan Airport is in the process of transitioning to all preferential-use gates.

Airport-Controlled or Common-Use Arrangements

Airport-controlled or common-use arrangements are completely under the control of the airport authority. The airport may assign gate and facility usage on a temporary, per-turn basis or for a short-term duration. These types of arrangements have been popular in Europe and other foreign regions for some time. The concept has gained popularity to the point that it has acquired the acronym C.U.T.E., or Common Use Terminal Equipment, to describe what is being increasingly seen as the best way for an airport to organize its gates and check-in counter facilities.

The International Air Transport Association (IATA) has even issued a recommendation (No. 1797) favoring common use systems as a means of efficient and cooperative use of available terminal facilities worldwide.

Various proprietary contractors have developed expertise in assisting airports in setting up these common-use arrangements so that, rather than being blocked off, the available facilities can be distributed as needed to different airlines. These facilities include check-in counters, gates, holding rooms, and electronic equipment. The systems control and integrate all components necessary to the carrier, including computers, displays, and boarding pass printers and readers.

Two airports have all airport-controlled gates—Miami International with 121 gates and Phoenix Sky Harbor with 84.

DOT Interest in Airport Practices— Unfair Competition

Prior to 2001, the Department of Transportation's authority over the gate practices of commercial-service airports was severely limited.[4] While DOT had jurisdiction over the gate practices of airlines, constitutional principles prevented interference in policies and practices of state-owned airports.

With the passage of the Wendell H. Ford Aviation Investment and Reform Act for 21st Century (AIR-21), DOT was given authority to require certain large and medium hub airports to submit competition plans as a condition of receiving federal grant monies and as a condition for authority to impose PFCs at their airports. These airports (including those at which competition among the airlines was threatened by airline domination, gate control, and other anticompetitive practices) were required to provide DOT detailed information concerning their gate practices. DOT has used its authority to approve or disapprove these competition plans as a means to insure that gate practices at those airports are fair. This includes insuring broader access to gates by new entrant airlines.

Airline gate practices continue to be monitored by DOT to insure that airline control of gates does not unduly impede competition. Such authority could compel an airline to surrender control of airport gates, or prevent tying arrangements involving subleases by one airline to another, where, for example, the lease requires the use of the lessor airlines' ground forces by the lessee airline. So too may DOT apply its authority to situations where an airline, with market power, exercises it contractual rights

under a MII clause to block the construction of facilities for competitors merely to maintain its own monopoly power.

Airport Privatization

It would be fair to assert that the promise of airline deregulation has, to some extent, been compromised by continued government operation of the remaining two components of the air service industry: airports and air traffic control. Thirty years after deregulation of the airlines, airports are still run under principles similar to those applicable to the airlines prior to deregulation. It would also be legitimate to ask whether privatization of airports might not relieve some of the constraints now imposed on the air service industry, and whether many of the consumer complaints heard as a result of airline operations since deregulation might not be alleviated.

The international community is well out in front of the United States on this issue. Over one hundred foreign airports are now privatized, including Auckland, Buenos Aires, Dusseldorf, Johannesburg, London, Melbourne, and Rome. Others, such as the huge Frankfurt airport and Amsterdam's Schiphol, are partially privatized, and still others are in the process of privatization, including Hong Kong and Tokyo. Most of these airports are operated under a lease of the entire airport facility to a private operator on a long-term basis, usually 30 years or longer. The governmental owner of the airport normally retains ownership of the land and airport facilities.

Government-owned and managed airports are characterized as risk-averse, passive, and non-innovative. Privatized airports are more willing to take new risks, like expansion of facilities and gates. The lack of gates is cited as one of the constraints on new entrant airlines, which is a competitive disincentive. As we have seen, long-term leases with incumbent airlines allow a large degree of control to be lodged with those airlines, another competitive disincentive. Oxford

University has conducted recent research into airport management strategies and found that the management approach at privatized airports is significantly more "passenger-friendly" than at government-operated airports.[5]

At least one effort has been made toward privatization in the United States. In 1996, Congress passed the 1996 Airport Privatization Pilot Program. Under this statute, up to five airports, called "pilot program slots," were eligible for privatization, The owners of these airports were to be exempted from provisions of federal statutes that required repayment of prior federal grant monies to those airports and from restrictions on the use of proceeds of sale or lease of the airport to private persons or corporations.

As a result of airline lobbying, however, the statute provided that approval of the privatization would require consent of at least 65 percent, in landing weight, of the airlines serving that airport.

Only one airport has been privatized under this statute. Stewart Airport in Newberg, New York, received FAA approval in April 2000 of its 99-year lease to a British company. It was unable, however, to secure consent of the airlines serving the airport. As a result, the state of New York is required to use revenues derived from the lease of the airport for improvements to the airport or other state-owned airports.

In recent years there have been several additional applications for privatization, including New Orleans Lakefront Airport, a large general aviation field, and the State of Illinois for approval of its new Abraham Lincoln National Airport to be situated in Peotone, Ill. There is also activity by the City of Chicago toward potential privatization of Midway Airport in Chicago.

Under the 2007 FAA Reauthorization proposal, the number of "pilot program slots" would be increased to fifteen, and would eliminate the restrictions on the classification (sizes) of the applicant airports. It would also eliminate the airline approval requirement.

Wendell H. Ford Aviation Investment and Reform Act for the 21st Century (AIR-21)

On April 5, 2000, the far ranging Wendell H. Ford Aviation Investment and Reform Act for the 21st Century became law. This statute, designed to alleviate many of the intransient problems faced by the aviation infrastructure arising from deregulation, will increase funding for civil aviation in the United States by $10 billion over levels current at the time of its passage. Total authorized funding for federal aviation programs for the years 2001 to 2003 total $40 billion. The majority of the increased funding was earmarked for airport construction and improvement and for radar modernization. The major components of the law, broken out into the general categories that are affected, are outlined in the box on page 271.

It is recognized that deregulation was directed only at the economic regulation of the airlines, and that the aviation infrastructure, comprising the airports and the air traffic control system, were left in their pre-deregulation posture in 1978. Airports were unprepared—physically, financially, and legally—to deal with the developments in civil aviation wrought by deregulation. The ramifications of deregulation of the airlines were not fully appreciated at first, as they realistically could not have been, and only after some years' experience following deregulation has that experience now defined the major problems confronting the aviation infrastructure. An example of how the federal government is now addressing these concerns is discussed above as a result of the passage of AIR-21. It should be particularly noted that AIR-21 requires certain large and medium hub airports, as a condition of imposing PFCs at those airports, to submit a competition plan for DOT approval designed to assure a competitive environment. Central to this effort is gate use monitoring, gate sublease oversight, and procedures for gate assignment.

Box 33-1 The Major Components of the Wendell H. Ford Aviation Investment and Reform Act

1. Safety

   a. Increases FAA facilities and equipment budget by almost 50 percent for ATC system modernization

   b. Increases funds for runways and airport equipment

   c. Provides funding for FAA hiring and retention of controllers and inspectors

   d. Makes runway incursion prevention devices eligible for AIP funding

2. Competition

   a. Funding for new terminals, gates, and taxiways

   b. Abolishes slots at O'Hare in 2002; modified by FAA in 2004

   c. Abolishes slots at LaGuardia and Kennedy in 2007

   d. Creates 24 new slots at Reagan National, 12 of which are to be used for flights within the 1,250 perimeter and 12 to be used outside of the perimeter

   e. Requires certain and medium hub airports to submit a competition plan

3. Environment

   a. Increases funding for noise abatement

   b. Establishes guidelines for air tours over national parks

4. Small Communities

   a. Increases funding for non-hub airports

   b. Guarantees funding for general aviation airports

   c. Doubles the small airport fund

   d. Creates an incentive program to help airlines buy regional jets to be used to serve small airports

   e. Creates a new funding program to assist small airports to promote their air service

5. Large Airports

   a. Doubles the amount of annual passenger funding for primary airports (those with 10,000 or more passengers per year)

   b. Raises the cap on annual funding for large airports from $22 million to $26 million

   c. Doubles the funding for cargo airports

   d. Raises the cap on Passenger Facility Charges (PFC) by $1.50 (to $4.50) to facilitate airport improvements that cannot be funded through the Airport Improvement Plan (AIP). PFCs can only be used to fund airport projects that increase safety and competition or are used for noise abatement

6. FAA Reforms

   a. Creates an oversight board (similar to IRS reform legislation)

   b. Makes changes in FAA management structure to ensure spending integrity

   c. Creates a management board to oversee the ATC modernization program (the DOT is to consult with Congress in board appointments)

Airports had in place legally enforceable contracts with airlines and with others that could not, and in some cases, still cannot be abrogated or modified. The anticompetitive effects of these financial, legal, and physical constraints are only now being addressed, but at least they are now recognized to exist. Enlightened policies at DOT concerning competition and a proactive Congress concerning the funding needs of airports point to a remedying of the worst shortcomings present today in the aviation infrastructure.

Endnotes

1. U.S. Department of Transportation, FAA/OST Task Force, Airport Business Practices and Their Impact on Airline Competition, October 1999.

2. U.S. Department of Transportation, Bureau of Transportation Statistics, Airport Activity Statistics of Certificated Air Carriers, Summary Table ending December 31, 1999, BTSO 1-03, Washington, D.C.

3. See pp 185–186 for the history of the Airport Improvement Program.

4. This was because of long-standing constitutional principles which limited federal interference with the rights of the states and their subdivisions, as confirmed by the United States Supreme Court case of **Parker v. Brown,** 317 U.S. 341 (1943).

5. Cited in Poole, Robert W., Jr., "More Airline Competition—Yet Another Reason for Airport Privatization, Reason Public Policy Institute.

CHAPTER 34

Airports and the Environment

© Alex Staroseltsev, 2008, Shutterstock.

As a result of the industrialization of society and the growth of heavy industry during the late 19th and early 20th centuries, pollution of air and water became a significant by-product of progress. In the 1950s, prevailing wisdom held that such pollution was the inevitable price of such progress.

Visible air pollution was seen from stationary sources like plants and factories and in "smog" accumulations in places like the Los Angeles Air Basin due to automobile emissions. Industrial and municipality discharges into waterways caused wide-spread prohibitions against swimming and fishing due to health risks. Catastrophes like the Cayuga River fire (the river caught fire) and the Love Canal scandal (toxic waste seepage caused a declaration of a federal emergency) were high-profile examples of pollution. When jet transport aircraft were introduced into the air carrier fleet in 1958, the dense, black exhaust emissions created on takeoff at ground level and during climbout were vivid evidence of yet another encroachment on air quality levels.

Prior acceptance of pollution as an inevitable by-product of progress has now been roundly rejected. Current environmental policy is concerned with almost all aspects of the quality of life on earth. In this chapter we will briefly review the evolution of current policy generally, and we will look at how current policy has attempted to address the specific environmental impacts of aviation.

The Air Pollution Act and The Clean Air Act

The first attempt by Congress to address the problem came in the Air Pollution Act of 1955. Subsequent efforts to strengthen controls on pollution occurred in amendments beginning in 1963 in The Clean Air Act, which was amended almost yearly until 1970. That year proved to be a watershed year for environmentalists, with the passage of The Clean Air Act of 1970 (an amendment to the 1963 Act), which created the Environmental Protection Agency as an independent agency reporting directly to the President. Its broad authority is over control of pollution, noise, and radiation.

Although The Clean Air Act mandates a national policy, the statute gives state and local governments primary responsibility for regulation of pollution from power plants, factories, and other stationary sources. The EPA retains primary responsibility for "mobile source" pollution.

Aviation Impacts

Aviation activities impact the environment primarily in two ways: (1) engine-generated emissions into the air and (2) noise. Noise legislation has been addressed by the Congress in separate, specific legislation, and we will discuss those statutes later in this chapter. Engine emissions result from both aircraft operations and airport ground operations. Aircraft emissions and airport operations were not, at first, on the radar scope of the EPA. As it became more evident that airport operations were contributing to environmental concerns, however, the EPA initiated a study in 1999 to assess these impacts and has followed up with increased monitoring of aviation generated air pollution.

Aviation-Generated Air Pollution

Emissions associated with aviation are the result of burning fossil fuels that power aircraft, the

Pollutant	Representative Health Effects
Ozone	Lung function impairment, effects on exercise performance, increased airway responsiveness, increased susceptibility to respiratory infection, increased hospital admissions and emergency room visits, and pulmonary inflammation, lung structure damage
Carbon Monoxide	Cardiovascular effects, especially in those persons with heart conditions (e.g., decreased time to onset of exercise-induced angina)
Nitrogen Oxides	Lung irritation and lower resistance to respiratory infections
Particulate Matter	Premature mortality, aggravation of respiratory and cardiovascular disease, changes in lung function and increased respiratory symptoms, changes to lung tissues and structure, and altered respiratory defense mechanisms
Volatile Organic Compounds	Eye and respiratory tract irritation, headaches, dizziness, visual disorders, and memory impairment

TABLE 34-1 Representative Health Effects of Air Pollutants.

Pollutant	Representative Environmental Effects
Ozone	Crop damage, damage to trees and decreased resistance to disease for both crops and other plants
Carbon Monoxide	Similar health effects on animals as on humans
Nitrogen Oxides	Acid rain, visibility degradation, particle formation, contribution toward ozone formation
Particulate Matter	Visibility degradation and monument and building soiling, safety effects for aircraft from reduced visibility
Volatile Organic Compounds	Contribution toward ozone formation, odors and some direct effect on buildings and plants

TABLE 34-2 Representative Environmental Effects of Air Pollutants.

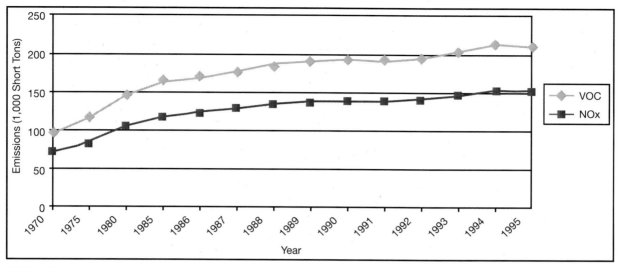

FIGURE 34-1 U.S. aircraft emission trends, 1970–1995.

equipment that services them, and the vehicles that transport passengers to and from airports. These pollutants include volatile organic compounds (VOCs), carbon monoxide, nitrogen oxides (NOx), particulate matter (PMs), and carbon dioxide (CO_2). As a group, these are considered deleterious to human health, to plant and animal life, and to the future of the planet. Comparatively, aviation-related activities are a minor contributor to total air pollution in the United States, comprising only 0.5 percent as of 2003. Projections of significant increases in commercial air traffic, however, have raised concerns about aviations's long-term effect on the environment.

Success in reducing particulate matter in the exhaust of jet engines was realized fairly early. This was due in part to the fact that this type of emission was the most noticeable and a solution was, therefore, quickly sought. In addition, jet engine-produced black smoke consists of fine carbon particles, partially burned fuel, and raw fuel. These PMs contain carcinogen content and descend to earth, creating health hazards. The reduction of exhaust smoke was accomplished by a more complete com-

bustion process whereby the hydrocarbons in jet fuel were converted to carbon dioxide and water.

Take off and landing operations produce the highest rate of PMs and NOx. Nitrogen oxides are a primary contributor to the formation of ozone, which is the most significant air pollutant in urban areas and which is a greenhouse gas in the upper atmosphere. Paradoxically, as innovative jet engine designs have produced more power while using less fuel and with lower carbon monoxide emissions, NOx emissions have increased due to their higher operating temperatures. Research is ongoing to find ways to reduce NOx.

Aircraft idle and taxi operations produce the highest rate of VOCs and carbon monoxide. Ground operated support equipment is mostly powered by gasoline or diesel engines, which produce VOCs, carbon monoxide, NOx, and PMs. Carbon dioxide, while not considered a pollutant in the lower atmosphere, can form ozone.

Airport operators have no direct control over aircraft emissions, although two foreign countries[1] have imposed landing fees based on the amount of aircraft emissions.[2] Primary regulation of aircraft

| Emission | Average Emission per Landing/Takeoff | | |
	Older Boeing 737 (pounds)	Newest Boeing 737 (pounds)	Changes
Nitrogen oxides	12.1	17.8	47% increase
Carbon monoxide	16.8	10.7	37% decrease
Hydrocarbons	1.2	1.1	10% decrease

Source: GAO.

Notes: Landing and takeoff data for U.S. aircraft in 2001 obtained from AvSoft. Emissions were calculated using FAA's Emissions and Dispersion Modeling System, version 4.01. The following variables were assumed to be the same for all
aircraft: (1) taxi-time: 15 minutes, (2) auxiliary power unit time: 26 minutes, and (3) ceiling height for emissions mixing with local air: 3,000 feet. The model's default was used for takeoff weight.

TABLE 34-3 Additional Information on Comparison of Older and Newest Model Boeing 737 Landing/Takeoff Emissions.

| Emission | Emission per Aircraft During Landing/Takeoff | | |
	Boeing 747-400 (pounds)	Boeing B777-200ER (pounds)	Changes
Nitrogen oxides	103.5	124.2	20 percent increase
Carbon monoxide	47.7	30.4	36 percent decrease
Hydrocarbon	4.1	2.4	41 percent decrease

Source: GAO.

Notes: Landing and takeoff data for U.S. aircraft in 2001 obtained from AvSoft. Emissions were calculated using FAA's Emissions and Dispersion Modeling System, version 4.01. The following variables were assumed to be the same for all aircraft: (1) taxi-time: 15 minutes, (2) auxiliary power unit time: 26 minutes, and (3) ceiling height for emissions mixing with local air: 3,000 feet. The model's default was used for takeoff weight.

The Boeing B77-200ER data is the weighted average (based on 2001 landings and takeoffs) for three different engines. The nitrogen oxides and other emission characteristics of these engines vary significantly.

The 58 Boeing 747-400s in the 2001 U.S. fleet have PW4056 engines and average 361 seats per aircraft. The 101 Boeing 777-200ERs in the 2001 U.S. fleet have the following engines: PW4090 (37 aircraft averaging 302 seats), GE90-90B (16 aircraft averaging 283 seats), and TRENT 892B-17 (48 aircraft averaging 249 seats). The three engine types for the Boeing 777-200ERs emit 138.6, 123.6, and 112.3 pounds of nitrogen oxides emissions per landing/takeoff, respectively.

TABLE 34-4 Additional Information on Comparison of Boeing 747 and 777 Emissions on a Per Aircraft Basis.

emissions is through EPA standards that apply to new engine designs. The EPA has elected to adopt international emission standards as set by ICAO. The FAA has been appointed by the EPA to function as the U.S. representative in formulation of these standards within ICAO. Engine manufacturers must now meet these standards in order to have new engines certified.

The imposition of emissions standards for new engines is a complex undertaking, since consideration must be given to the feasibility of mandating standards in view of the many other considerations inherent in engine manufacture, such as fuel efficiency, safety, and cost. Realizing this, the FAA and the EPA have established a consultation process known as "the stakeholders group," which includes representatives from government, airports, air carriers, and the aerospace industry. This group focuses on achieving lower aircraft emissions through a voluntary program because this strategy offers the potential for achieving desired goals with less effort and less time than a regulatory approach.

Airports are theoretically subject to nationally supervised state control of emissions through State Implementation Plans (SIPs). These plans must be submitted by the states to the EPA for reducing emissions in areas that fail to meet the National Ambient Air Quality Standards set by by the EPA under the Clean Air Act. The power of states in controlling pollution at airports is limited, however, since the EPA retains control of regulating mobile sources of emissions and because states are preempted from regulating aircraft operations generally. This is a federal responsibility (in order to maintain a consistent national policy) and the FAA is responsible for enforcing emission standards. For these reasons only three states have even attempted to target airports for emission reductions.[3] Operators of some of the busiest airports in the country have initiated voluntary programs to reduce emissions from sources over which they have control under the Voluntary Airport Low Emission Program (VALE). The goal of this program is to reduce emissions caused by ground service vehicles by investing in proven low-emission technologies, including alternative fuel vehicles.

Aircraft Noise

While air pollution considerations have become increasingly important in the years since jet transport aircraft were introduced into the civil aviation fleet in 1958, noise levels associated with the operation of jet transport aircraft at the nation's airports were an immediate concern to anyone within audible range. Jet noise had previously been limited to military operations, and most people were familiar with jet operations only as they were usually conducted at higher altitudes.

Citizens' groups became quite vocal about this intrusion into what had theretofore been a relatively peaceful coexistence with airport operations. Jet noise brought a new challenge to this attempt at coexistence. It took regulators until 1968 to accumulate enough anecdotal and empirical evidence to bring the matter successfully before the Congress. In that year, the first aircraft noise legislation was passed.

Aircraft Noise Abatement Act of 1968

That year the initial step was taken to confront what was coming to be recognized as not only an environmental issue, but also a health issue. The Aircraft Noise Abatement Act of 1968 required the FAA, in consultation with the new Environmental Protection Agency, to establish noise standards for aircraft and to apply them through issuance of civil aircraft certificates.

Noise Control Act of 1972 and Aviation Safety and Noise Abatement Act of 1979

In 1972, Congress passed the Noise Control Act, which amended the Federal Aviation Act of 1958 to specifically involve EPA in the regulation of airport noise. This was followed in 1979 by the Aviation Safety and Noise Abatement Act, which authorized the Secretary of Transportation to formulate a national aviation noise policy and authorized the FAA to promulgate regulations pursuant thereto, including "air noise compatibility planning." These regulations are contained in 14 Code of Federal Regulations, Part 150.

The FAA established a program under the 1979 statute to help airport operators develop comprehensive noise reduction programs. Known as the Part 150 program (derived from CFR Part 150), this voluntary program encourages airport operators to develop Noise Exposure Maps (NEM) and Noise Compatibility Programs (NCP). NEMs identify noise contours and land use incompatibilities. NEMS are used to evaluate existing noise impacts and to discourage future development not compatible with the airport plan. If FAA approves the NEM, the airport operator can submit an NCP, which describes measures that will improve noise and land use compatibility.

In 2005, 266 airports were participating in the Part 150 program and 226 airports had NCPs approved by the FAA. An FAA approved NCP allows an airport to obtain federal aid for noise mitigation projects. Since 1982, 247 airports have received a total of $4.3 billion for this purpose in addition to AIP noise grants (discussed below).

Airport Noise and Capacity Act of 1990

In 1990, *the first comprehensive airport* noise regulation statute, the Airport Noise and Capacity Act (ANCA), became law.

ANCA recognized that a national aviation noise policy was vital to the fitness of the country's air transportation system. Former Secretary of Transportation Skinner is on record as asserting that ANCA is "the most significant piece of aviation legislation since the deregulation act." ANCA effectively altered the landscape in matters of aviation noise.

Federal noise regulations in 1990 classified aircraft as Stage 1, Stage 2, or Stage 3 aircraft, with Stage 1 being the loudest. All Stage 1 aircraft have been phased out of service. ANCA mandated that no Stage 2 aircraft could be added to the fleet or imported into the United States after November 5, 1990, and that all unmodified Stage 2 aircraft be phased out of service by December 31, 1999. Stage 2 aircraft include the 727, DC-9, and early versions of the 737 and 747. These airplanes were developed in the 1960s and 1970s.

Stage 3 aircraft must meet separate standards for takeoff, landing, and sideline measurements, depending on the aircraft's weight and number of engines. Stage 3 aircraft are the newer and quieter 757, 767, and MD-80 series, later versions of the 737 and 747, and aircraft that have been retrofitted with quieter engines by the noise reducing "hush kits."

Under the provisions of ANCA, which apply to aircraft of at least 75,000 pounds certificated weight, airport operators were specifically regulated as to when and how they could restrict Stage 2 and Stage 3 aircraft operations at their local airports, reaffirming the supremacy of the federal government over aviation policy in the United States. Airport operators were prohibited from issuing unilateral restrictions on Stage 3 aircraft, since such aircraft comprise the state-of-the-art in aircraft noise. To paraphrase, the federal government in effect said, "This is the best we can do in engine noise, these are the airplanes that are necessary to be used in air transportation, and they will be allowed to fly no matter what the locals say." Any attempted local regulation of Stage 3 aircraft would thus amount to an unlawful usurpation of the federal prerogatives regarding aviation. Subject to due process safeguards, such as notice and opportunity to be heard, airport proprietors were allowed to apply certain reasonable restrictions on the operation of Stage 2 aircraft as long as such local authorities did not impair the national policy of "phase out" articulated in the statute.

In June 2001, the International Civil Aviation Organization (ICAO) adopted new, more stringent noise standards that went into effect on January 1, 2006. These standards mandate a noise reduction level of 10 dB below the standards previously required (Chapter 3). These standards are referred to as Chapter 4 standards by ICAO and Stage 4 standards by the FAA.[4]

Much of the work for the development of a Stage 4 noise standard has taken place in the ICAO Committee on Aviation Environmental Protection (CAEP), which was established by ICAO in 1983. The United States, as a member of ICAO, participates in the work of CAEP.

In 2005, the FAA, following the lead of ICAO, issued a rule that adopted a new noise standard for aircraft designs submitted after January 1, 2006. The new FAA rule requires new airplane type designs to comply with Stage 4 standards. This noise standard is intended to provide uniform noise certification standards for Stage 4 airplanes certificated in the United States and those airplanes that meet the new ICAO Annex 16 Chapter 4 noise standard. There is no weight limitation or exclusion for airplane type designs submitted after January 1, 2006; thus, all aircraft types will be subject to the Stage 4 noise standard.

Care should be taken to note the difference between the requirements of ANCA and the new FAA rule. ANCA, which requires compliance with Stage 3 standards, only applies to aircraft with certificated weight of 75,000 pounds and above. The new FAA rule, which requires new type designs to comply with Stage 4 standards, applies to all new airplane type design submissions, regardless of weight.

Although noise control of aircraft is exclusively a federal function, airport authorities and local governments do have the option to mitigate noise effects through land use controls, such as zoning and land acquisition, which the FAA agrees is the exclusive domain of state and local governments. Indeed, federal policy respecting Airport Improvement Program (AIP) funding favors the use of such funds for that purpose. Airport operators applying for funds for these purposes must design noise exposure maps and develop mitigation programs consistent with federal requirements to insure that noise levels are compatible with adjacent land uses. Noise compatibility projects include residential and public building sound insulation. They include land acquisition and relocating residents from noise sensitive areas. Airports have also installed noise monitoring equipment and noise barriers to reduce ground run-up noise.

ANCA also provides for additional funding sources by permitting the use of passenger facility charges (PFCs) for land use control. Airports have collected and used PFCs funds for noise studies and mitigation totaling $15 billion as of 2005.

Overall, ANCA provides a framework for the implementation of a national policy of aircraft noise control, and reaffirms that local governments have the continuing obligation to adhere to that policy and to cooperate with federal authorities to secure the achievement of such national interests. The policy is working. According to statistics supplied by FAA, exposure to airline noise has decreased significantly and consistently from 1975 to 2001. Airline noise levels are calculated using the number of persons exposed to 65 dbA, in millions. In 1975, some seven million people were subject to noise levels in excess of that number, while in 2001, the number of persons exposed to 65 dbA had declined to just 0.4 million. (See Figure 34-2.)

In 2005, FAA evaluation of the AIP set-aside program caused the FAA to set goals that will reduce residential and school populations exposed to aircraft noise at 65 dbA by 100,000 over the five year period from 2006 to 2010. (See Figure 34-3.)

Endnotes

1. Switzerland and Sweden.
2. The FAA has indicated that it does not believe that this program will be effective in reducing emissions.
3. California, Massachusetts, and Texas.
4. Aircraft must be built to meet noise certification standards established by ICAO, found in Annex 16, Environmental Protection, V. 1. The first generation of jet aircraft (707, DC-8) preceded the Annex 16 standards. These are Stage 1 aircraft. Chapter 2 of the Annex applied to aircraft built before 1977, and these are referred to as Stage 2 aircraft. Chapter 3 of the Annex covered the latest production aircraft, and are referred to by the FAA as Stage 3.

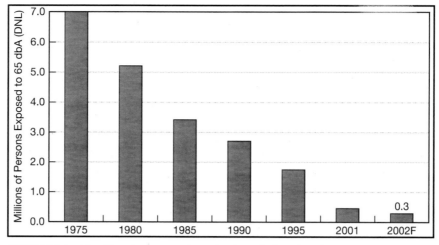

FIGURE 34-2 Significant progress in reduction of aircraft noise.

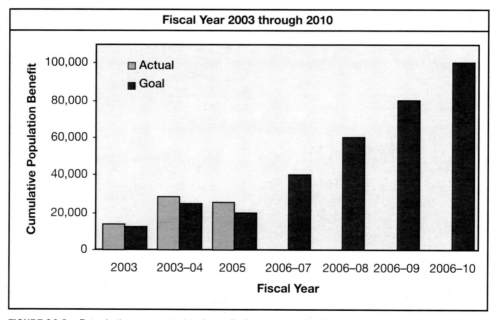

FIGURE 34-3 Population expected to benefit from noise funding.

CHAPTER 35

Deregulation in the Nineties

© Johnny Kuo, 2008, Shutterstock.

> " A recession is when you have to tighten your belt; depression is when you have no belt to tighten. When you've lost your trousers—you're in the airline business. "

Sir Adam Thomson

During the first three years of the last decade of the twentieth century (1990–1993), airlines in the United States had lost an amount of money equal to all the money that had ever been made in aviation in the United States since the first commercial flight. If this was what deregulation had wrought, then deregulation was obviously a tragic mistake. What is obvious is that deregulation has exposed the sensitive nature of the U.S. airline industry. This sensitivity results primarily from fluctuating economic conditions, often driven by geopolitical factors that affect fuel prices and travel demand. While deregulation gave air travel to the masses, it did so at the expense of the airlines' flexibility and any financial cushion in the airline industry. Competition has shaved profit margins so razor thin that almost any economic hiccup translates into problems for the industry. The industry has high fixed costs (the cost of labor and aircraft) that cannot be reduced quickly during these adverse economic conditions. Since fuel and labor costs account for over 50 percent of all airlines' expense, spikes in the cost of fuel are particularly debilitating to the airlines.

The following highlights provide a quick review of the airline experience in the 1990s.

The Economy

The early 1990s, like the early years of the two decades before, brought difficult economic times. In August 1990, Iraq invaded Kuwait, and another economic downturn began. Not only did fuel prices spiral upward (see Figure 35-1), but also travel was down. (See Figure 35-2.) Operating losses for the airlines in 1990 were $1.9 billion, in 1991 losses were $1.8 billion, and in 1992, they were $2.4 billion. A full year net profit was not recorded until 1995.

Leading up to the 1990s, the airlines as an industry had placed orders for over one thousand three hundred new jet aircraft, and the resulting crushing burden of debt pressed down on the airlines. Long-term airline debt, as reported by GAO in 1991, showed that during the 1980s, Eastern's debt increased from 79 percent to 473 percent; Pan Am went from 62 percent to 273 percent; TWA showed an increase from 62 percent to 96 percent.

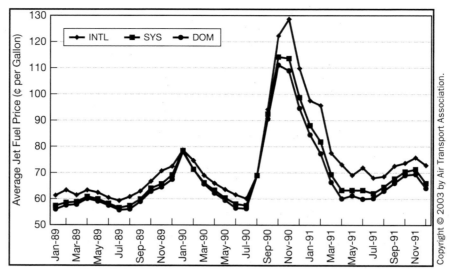

FIGURE 35-1 Jet fuel price 1989–1991. In July 1990, fuel price was at 57 cents. By October 1990, fuel price had soared to $1.14 a gallon.

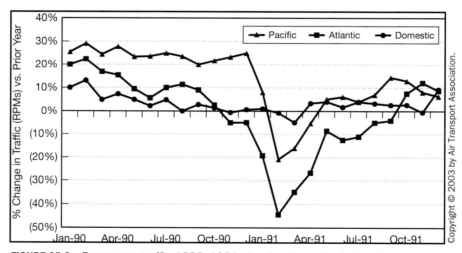

FIGURE 35-2 Passenger traffic 1990–1991 showing dramatic decline in international travel.

Liquidations and Chapter 11

By the early 1990s, Eastern had been liquidated, then Pan American followed. In 1992, Continental, America West, and TWA were all in Chapter 11, the second time for Continental.

Midway Airlines stopped flying and went into liquidation. Northwest was close to filing. In 1991, United had reported its biggest loss ever, and in 1992 its losses were three times greater than the year before. The year of 1993 did not look much better. The state of the airline industry was so fragile that a presidential commission was established to look into ways to ensure the survival of the industry.

Southwest Airlines

Only Southwest Airlines seemed to understand what was going on. While the major airlines were trying without much success to stop the bleeding, Southwest was raking in record profits. USAir had acquired PSA in California, and then began to cut back service on the north-south corridor. Southwest came in to fill the void, but at offbeat airports like Oakland and Burbank, and at seemingly ever decreasing fares. Then Southwest entered San Jose, where American Airlines operated out of the old AirCal quarters. When advised that Southwest was coming in, American did not even wait for the discount carrier to arrive; it cut back its services immediately, anticipating the losses to come in a one-on-one contest with Southwest.

❝ If the Wright brothers were alive today Wilbur would have to fire Orville to reduce costs. ❞

Herb Kelleher, Southwest Airlines, *USA Today*, 8 June 1994

Southwest was also headed east, for the first time in its history. Now Southwest would be in Baltimore (BWI), next to the seat of power in the District of Columbia. Southwest was now the eighth largest airline in the United States (United was first, followed by American, Delta, Northwest, Continental, USAir, and TWA), but it was different in at least one highly significant way: it had point-to-point routes (the 100 city-pairs most frequently traveled), and did not waste time getting in and out of large hub terminals.

American Airlines

American Airlines had doubled its debt in 1990 by aircraft purchases, and then in 1991 it had again increased it. By 1993, its long-term debt stood at $5.6 billion. Debt service of this kind could put American out of business any time its cash flow faltered. This put American in a bad negotiating posture with its unions, and American had been forced into agreeing to punishing wage rates in order to avoid strikes. Still, deregulation had taken a toll on employee wages. A 1992 study reported that average compensation of the airline employee went from $42,928 in 1978 to an inflation-adjusted $37,985 in 1988. Productivity during the same period increased by 43 percent.

Foreign Code Sharing

Code sharing is a practice that came into being in 1983, which allows an airline to advertise, as its own, a route from an origin to a destination, even though a part of that route is not actually flown by the advertising airline. Usually unknown to the passenger, a part of the route can be flown by a different airline using its own aircraft, its own pilots, and its own support infrastructure and staff, all of which entails utilizing its own procedures and rules. There is also a difference between airlines in their safety records.

The first foreign code share arrangement was approved by the Department of Transportation in 1993 in an arrangement that allowed KLM Royal Dutch Airlines to infuse capital into financially strapped Northwest Airlines. Although code sharing between airlines does not require a swap of assets or other financial investment between them, approval was initially given by the United States government to these arrangements in part due to the fact that additional financial stability was achieved in either one or both carriers. Following the KLM-Northwest code share arrangement, approval was given for a United Airlines-Lufthansa pairing, and shortly thereafter British Airways bought into USAir for $400 million and began code sharing.

United States airlines with these foreign code share arrangements could now pretend that they flew seamlessly beyond European gateways into the heart of Europe, and beyond, even though they did not. European carriers advertised in similar fashion, portraying an ability to fly to interior destinations in the United States beyond gateways. Although these arrangements constituted, in many cases, a deception to the flying public, they were actually a first step in the globalization of the world air transportation market.

United Airlines

By 1994, the need to cut costs further had caused United to enter into negotiations with its pilots to exchange stock equity for concessions in wages and working conditions. The pilots had, for some time, wanted some control over the future of the airline, particularly given their basic disagreement with management as to the proper way to run an airline. Wage concessions had been given before, but that had been a learning experience for the pilots. Now, wage concessions, if given, would have to be in exchange for stock. By the middle of 1994, a deal had been struck between the unions and management. The flight attendants opted out of the equity swap, but in return for hefty wage cuts and the agreement to implement b-scale wages for new hires, the other employees had an airline.

A New Wave of Startups

A new wave of startup airlines was entering the market during the middle 1990s, patterned largely on the Southwest model. This new breed was not like the first new entrants seen in the 1980s. Those original startups, although adhering generally to the principle of no-frills, had morphed into big organizations with large and varied types of airplanes, becoming not so very different from the "major" airlines of the day that they sought to distinguish themselves from. This "second generation" of entrants, in the middle 1990s, avoided the temptation to get big in a hurry, if at all, and contentedly found and filled a niche in the overall air service industry. New, small carriers like ValueJet, Kiwi, Reno Air, and UltraAir gradually made inroads on the domestic airline market, defying those who compared them with People Express and Texas Air.

Good Times Are Here Again

The recession of the early 1990s began to abate toward the middle of the decade. And just as deregulation had produced the greatest losses in the history of the airline business just a few years before, now profits began to rebound under deregulation:

➡ In 1994, American Airlines saw the highest quarterly profit in its history and in the history of any airline since the beginning of commercial aviation.

➡ TWA emerged from Chapter 11 and restructured—with a 45 percent employee ownership.

➡ Northwest avoided bankruptcy with an employee trade-off of stock for concessions.

Beginning in 1995, the financial picture for most airlines markedly improved, and continued to improve through the end of the decade. Net income for many airlines reached its peak that year as traffic figures spiraled upward in a continuation of a good economy and a climate of stable wages and fuel prices. Earnings for the industry continued to rebound:

➡ $2.3 billion in 1995

➡ $2.8 billion in 1996

➡ In 1997 almost doubling to $5.2 billion

➡ Down a bit in 1998 to $4.9 billion

➡ Back up in 1999 to $5.6 billion, although earnings derived solely from operations began to fall in 1999.

➡ Load factors also continued to increase, reaching a high of 72.4 percent in 2000, providing more income at the bottom line.

But there was trouble just over the horizon that nobody had foreseen.

CHAPTER 36

Airlines at the Beginning of the 21st Century

The airlines entered the new millennium riding the crest of the same wave that generally took the stock indices and corporate profits to their historical high point. The so-called dot.com computer and technological sector, now seen in context, propelled an economic "bubble" that burst in the year 2000. That year a downturn began in the economy that turned to concerns of a "bear" market, then to fears of a recession. Although passenger enplanements reached their all-time high in 2000 of 615 million, the airlines, like everyone else, were now on the backside of the wave.

The year 2000 saw the end of six years of relative prosperity in the air carrier industry. The downturn in air carrier profits actually began in 1998 but it was not until 2001 that adversity took hold. As the year progressed, it was forecast that the industry, as a whole, would experience a loss of perhaps $3 billion. This projected loss was of a magnitude somewhat comparable to the early years of the 1990s, but less than either 1990 or 1992. While this projected loss was substantial, it was still within the bounds of the cylical nature of the industry since deregulation.

September 11, 2001

The event that will forever be known as "September 11," a terrorist attack on the United States, occurred on September 11, 2001. It was focused on New York and Washington, D.C., respectively the nation's financial and governmental centers. The perpetrators were members of a fundamentalist Islamic group called al-Qaeda, all followers of a militant Islam sect headed by Osama bin Laden.

The selection of targets, the World Trade Center in New York, and the Pentagon in Washington, constituted a declaration of war on the institutions and ideals of the free world, and on the free enterprise system that had made possible the unprecedented strides in modern technology that it represented. It is ironic that the tools used by the terrorists to wreck such massive destruction upon that civilization were some of the very tools used to build the system, and which were themselves products of that system, the modern airliner.

American Airlines flight 11 was a Boeing 757 (see Figure 36-1) that departed Boston Logan for Los Angeles and was crashed into the north tower of the World Trade Center; United Airlines flight 175 was a Boeing 767 that departed Boston Logan for Los Angeles and was crashed into the south tower of the World Trade Center. (See Figure 36-2.)

American Airlines flight 77 was a Boeing 757 that departed Washington Dulles for

FIGURE 36-1 Boeing 757.

Image Courtesy of Corel.

Los Angeles and was crashed into the Pentagon in Washington, D.C.; United Airlines flight 93 was a Boeing 757 that departed Newark for San Francisco and crashed into a field in Pennsylvania after an apparent foiling of the terrorists' plans by passengers on board.

These aircraft were selected by the terrorists because of their size and because each one was a planned transcontinental flight heavily loaded with jet fuel which, when ignited upon impact, created an inferno larger than any that could have been accomplished by any transportable bomb available to the terrorists.

Immediately following the September 11 attack, all aircraft within the United States were grounded by federal order. The fact that the weapons used by the terrorists were airplanes caused the government to first ensure that no other aircraft could be used to the same effect. Implementation of the ground stop order was unprecedented in the history of aviation. The mechanism for the order was a relic of the Cold War and was originally conceived to prevent Soviet bombers from entering the United States while in the radar shadow of inbound commercial airliners. Within hours of its imposition, all flights within the borders of the United States were on the ground, and all inbound international flights had been turned back from America's borders. One of these, incidentally, was the Concorde, which was over the middle of the Atlantic Ocean at the time bound for New York. By the afternoon of September 11, FAA radars were eerily empty, reflecting only patrolling military fighter aircraft, particularly above the skies of the Northeastern United States.

Resumption of flight operations occurred incrementally, beginning with the repositioning of commercial aircraft, then resumption of domestic U.S. flag operations, and finally resumption of international flight operations. The federal order grounding all aircraft cost the airline industry over $330 million a day for the duration of the stoppage.

The attacks had a ripple effect on commercial losses, including insurance companies, travel services, the stock market, most commercial transactions, and, not least, on the confidence of the world citizen. But of all industry sectors affected, the airlines took the brunt of the blow. The airlines whose airliners were hijacked had to deal with not only the loss of the aircraft and crew, but with liability issues involving both death and property damage to those passengers on the airplanes and those in harm's way on the ground. The industry as a whole had to deal with the effect of the grounding, and the consequent disruption and loss of revenue while their expenses, including debt service on aircraft, continued unabated.

Congress and the President were quickly convinced that federal intervention was necessary to meet the financial needs of the United States air transportation industry. It was also clear that the nation had to address its overall security posture in the face of a new kind of enemy. A series

Image © PhotoDisc.

FIGURE 36-2 The Manhattan skyline prior to the terrorists' attacks of September 11, 2001.

of legislative initiatives was immediately begun in a Congress united in purpose. Several significant and complex new laws were passed in an almost unprecedented space of time.

The first of these, on September 22, 2001, was the Air Transportation Safety and System Stabilization Act, which, among other things, (1) provided compensation to the airlines for direct losses caused by the ground stop order and (2) created a fund to provide loans to qualifying air carriers. Second, the Aviation and Transportation Security Act addressed security upgrades that were needed to strengthen airports and the air transportation system generally. Third, a new Cabinet-level department, The Department of Homeland Security, was created to place within one executive department responsibility for all planning and procedures deemed necessary to enhance the security of the nation against similar types of threats.

The Air Transportation Safety and System Stabilization Act[1]

The main provisions of the statue provide:

1. Direct payments and loan guarantees

   a. All U.S. air carriers were eligible to share a $5 billion fund to compensate them for direct losses due to the federal ground stop order that resulted immediately after the terrorists' attack, and incremental losses incurred between September 11 and December 11, 2001

   b. Issuance of up to $10 billion in federal loan guarantees and credits to air carriers, subject to terms and conditions set by the President

2. Insurance and liability

   a. Limited the liability of air carriers, certified by DOT as victims of an act of terrorism, for losses suffered by third parties to $100 million in the aggregate (due to the terrorist act) with provisions for the government to assume all liability over that amount

   b. Prohibited the imposition of punitive damages against either the carrier or the government as a result of the terrorist act

   c. Granted DOT authority to reimburse air carriers for insurance premium increases due to September 11

3. Tax provisions extending certain tax due dates for air carriers

4. Creation of a victim compensation fund to compensate individuals (or their survivors) for injuries or death caused by terrorist-related aircraft crashes on September 11

The Act established the Air Transportation Stabilization Board, whose function was to administer the issuance of the $10 billion in federal loan guarantees to affected airlines. As a precondition to the issuance of any guarantees, the Board had to determine that:

1. Credit was not reasonably available to the airline at the time of the issuance

2. The intended obligation (the loan and the purpose for the loan) was prudently incurred

3. The transaction was a necessary part of maintaining a safe, efficient, and viable commercial aviation system in the United States

By the middle of 2002, some 400 air carriers had applied for compensation for direct losses as a result of September 11. The government had approved and paid $4.3 billion to 382 different carriers. The largest payments went to the largest airlines. United received almost $725 million, American received $656 million, and Delta got $595 million.

At the same time, the Stabilization Board continued to work through applications for loan guarantees. It quickly became clear that the Board was not going to rubber-stamp applications for the airlines. America West, the first to receive guarantees, was required to rework its application several times in order to satisfy the Board, and the guarantees were conditioned on the airline granting to the government warrants on one-third of the airline's stock. Warrants are options to purchase stock at a predetermined price.

The Board rejected other applications, including Vanguard Airlines's request for just $7.5 million in guarantees. Eleven other small airlines made applications, with varying results.

Major airlines were slow to apply, primarily because of the tough stance taken by the Board in the America West application. U.S. Airways did receive conditional approval for $900 million in guarantees dependent on the airline securing sizeable concessions from its employees. These concessions could not be secured as conditioned, and U.S. Air went into Chapter 11 in August 2002. United also applied for guarantees in an amount of $1.8 billion, but United was not able to convince its labor unions, particularly the machinists, to grant voluntary concessions that would satisfy the Board. In December 2002, UAL filed for bankruptcy protection under Chapter 11 of the Act. The other legacy carriers were just barely hanging on.

Aviation and Transportation Security Act[2]

The President of the United States signed the Aviation and Transportation Security Act on November 19, 2001. The Act created the Transportation Security Administration (TSA) (see Figure 36-3), placed in the Department of Transportation, which is charged with insuring the implementation of a sequenced series of enhanced security measures applicable to both aircraft and airports. These measures include installation of fortified cockpit doors on aircraft, implementation of new standards for airport baggage screeners, revitalization of the federal air marshal program, and the strengthening of airport perimeter areas. The statute transfers responsibility for aviation security from the Federal Aviation Administration to the TSA. The Security Act authorizes the TSA to impose user fees on both passengers and air carriers to help pay for these new security efforts. TSA was transferred from DOT to the Department of Homeland Security in 2003.

Homeland Security Act of 2002[3]

Congress passed the Homeland Security Act in November 2002, creating a new department in the executive branch at cabinet level known as the Department of Homeland Security. Former

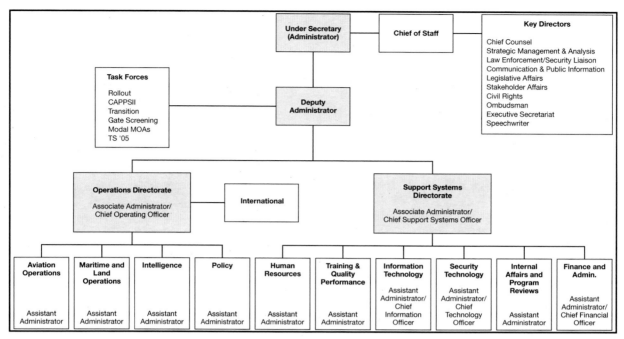

FIGURE 36-3 Organization of the Transportation Security Association (TSA).

Pennsylvania governor Tom Ridge was sworn in as the Department's first Secretary in January 2003. The primary missions of the Department are preventing terrorist attacks in the United States, reducing the country's vulnerability to terrorism, and minimizing damage in the event such attacks occur. The Department inaugurated its Federal Law Enforcement Training Center in Glynco, Georgia, where the Transportation Security Administration in April 2003 graduated the first 44 airline pilots certified as Federal Flight Deck Officers. These pilots were the first to be certified to carry firearms in the cockpit.

Aftermath of September 11

In the period beginning after 9-11, the nation's airlines faced many challenges. Superimposed on the preexisting economic decline was the impact of the terrorist attacks on the traveling public, which translated into an unprecedented decline in traffic. The drop in revenue passenger miles in 2001 was the largest in U.S. history.

The $3 billion industry loss for 2001 that was projected in early 2001 soon turned into more than twice that figure, $7.7 billion. In 2002, there was a slow recovery of traffic volumes, although they remained well below traffic levels from the previous year. The industry began to respond to these extraordinary market conditions immediately by reducing its labor force and by decreasing operations. But there were many factors in the days after 9-11 that were beyond the control of the airlines. We will review some of these factors.

Security Mandates

Prior to September 11, the airlines were responsible for conducting passenger screening under FAA guidelines. TSA took over this function upon its creation under the Aviation and Transportation Security Act. Fees on both passengers and the airlines were created to pay for this additional cost. These new security mandates, a direct result of the 9-11 attacks, constituted another

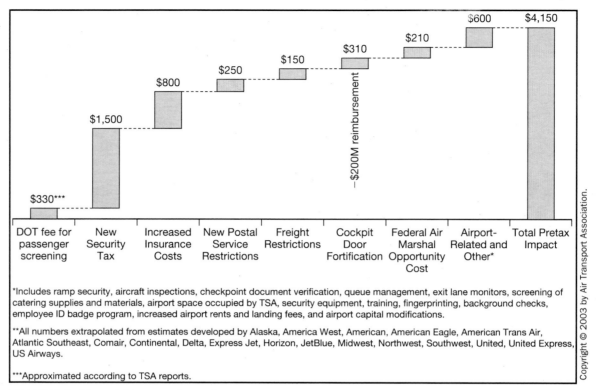

FIGURE 36-4 Financial impact of post 9-11 policies. Post 9-11 taxes, fees, and unfunded mandates have added more than $4 billion to the industry's annual burden.

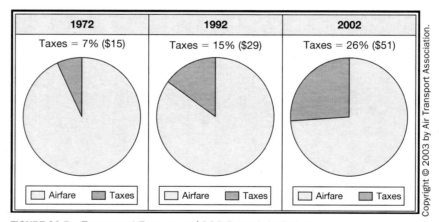

FIGURE 36-5 Taxes and Fees on a $200 Roundtrip Ticket.

financial impact on the already stressed airlines. These adverse effects result from direct, out-of-pocket costs borne by the airlines for unfunded security requirements, from payments made directly by the airlines and their passengers to the federal government, and from lost revenues due to these security policies. (See Figures 36-4 through 36-7.) The airline industry in 2003 was carrying a tax burden that was 76 percent higher than it was in 1992 and 240 percent higher than 1972.

Tax/Fee	1972	1992	2003	R/T***
Passenger Ticket Tax*	8.0%	10.0%	7.5%	nmf
Passenger Flight Segment Tax*	-	-	$3.00	$12.00
Passenger Security Surcharge	-	-	$2.50	$10.00**
Passenger Facility Charge	-	$3.00**	$4.50**	$18.00**
International Departure Tax	$3.00	$6.00	$13.40	nmf
International Arrival Tax	-	-	$13.40	nmf
INS User Fee	-	$5.00	$7.00	nmf
Customs User Fee	-	$5.00	$5.00	nmf
APHIS Passenger Fee	-	$2.00	$3.10	nmf
Cargo Waybill Tax*	5.00%	6.25%	6.25%	nmf
Frequent Flyer Tax	-	-	7.5%	nmf
APHIS Aircraft Fee	-	$76.75	$65.25	nmf
Jet Fuel Tax*	-	-	4.3¢/gal	nmf
LUST Fuel Tax*	-	0.1¢/gal	0.1¢/gal	nmf
Air Carrier Security Fee	-	-	TBD	nmf

*Tax applies only to domestic transportation; prorated on flights between mainland U.S. and Alaska/Hawaii

**Legislative maximum

***Single-connection roundtrip with $4.50 PFC

FIGURE 36-6 Federal aviation taxes and fees.

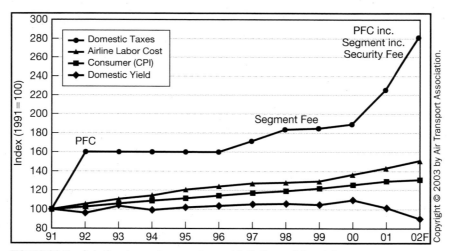

FIGURE 36-7 Aviation taxes have outpaced inflation, airline labor costs, and airfares.

Liability Insurance

Liability insurance costs after 9-11 were up more than threefold. War-risk insurance quoted by the commercial market is considered prohibitively expensive by the airline industry—as a result, partially subsidized war-risk insurance has so far been provided by the federal government through the Homeland Security Act. Even so, the cost to the airline industry is about $140 million a year. (See Figure 36-8.)

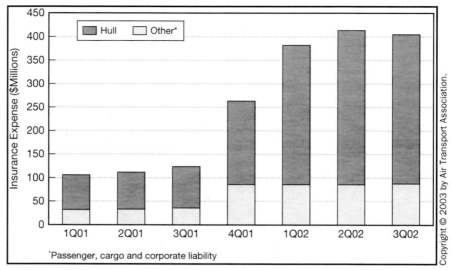

FIGURE 36-8 Airline Insurance Costs: 2001–02.

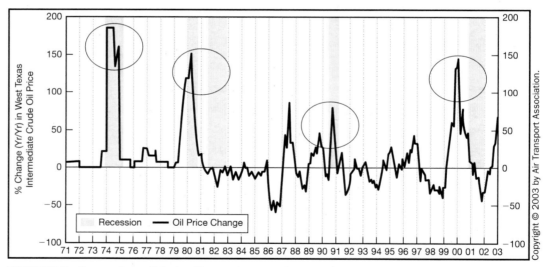

FIGURE 36-9 Comparison of fuel spikes and economic recessions.

Fuel Costs

The cost of fuel is the second largest operating expense faced by airlines. Fuel prices are inextricably interwoven with overall economic conditions. A close correlation can be observed between periods of recession and energy prices. (See Figure 36-9.) In spite of advances in fuel-efficient aircraft engines (the aircraft fleet in 2002 was almost three-times more fuel efficient than 30 years before), fuel prices continued to contribute heavily to the airlines' financial woes. During the first eleven months of 2002, jet fuel prices rose 27 percent, and from December 2002 to February 2003, those prices rose an additional 55 percent. Jet fuel prices more than doubled in the one-year period February 2002 to February 2003. The Air Transport Association says that each one-cent increase in the cost of jet fuel adds $180 million to the operating burden of the airline industry. (See Figure 36-10.)

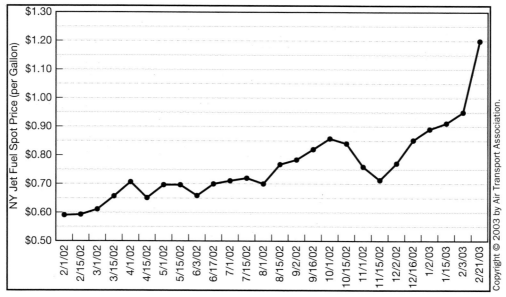

FIGURE 36-10 Market price of jet fuel.

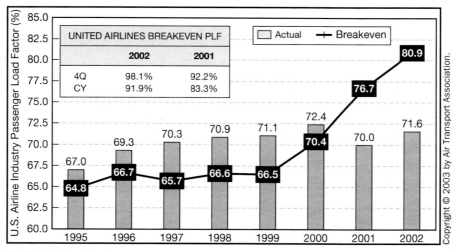

FIGURE 36-11 Breakeven passenger load factor at record highs.

Load Factors

After 9-11, the disparity between higher costs and declining load factors added to the losses the airlines experienced. Load factors overall had steadily increased since deregulation, reaching a 50-year record high of 72.4 percent. Because of September 11 and the rapid drop in passenger volumes, the load factor at the end of 2001 for all airlines was down to 71.3 percent. At the same time, due to falling fares and rising costs, the break-even load factor for 2001 rose to 77 percent, and for 2002 to 81 percent. (See Figure 36-11.)

Labor

In 2001, the airlines were coming out of a period of protracted wage negotiations with their labor groups, which resulted in agreements that significantly increased wages going forward for some years. Labor costs are the largest single expense factor faced by airlines, historically amounting to some 35 percent of total operating costs. The average airline employee in 2002 made $73,000 a year, including pension and insurance benefits. Because airlines require the service of highly skilled employees, their employees historically are highly paid. Airline wages were 53 percent higher than national averages. Following September 11, however, airlines were forced to reduce their workforce significantly, on average among the thirteen largest carriers by 14 percent, although at United the reduction was 20 percent and at USAirways it was an even greater 24 percent.

Fleet

Airlines reduced the number of aircraft in their fleets, by retirement, sale, or simply parking the airplanes. Especially targeted were less fuel-efficient and maintenance-intensive aircraft. The overall U.S. fleet was reduced to 4,717 aircraft. Orders on new aircraft were reduced, down by over 100 airplanes at the end of 2002 as compared with the end of the second quarter of 2001. (See Figures 36-12 through 36-14.)

At the end of 2002, only two major airlines ended up in the black. Southwest reported profits of $241 million, and JetBlue reported $55 million. The remainder of all major U.S. airlines reported substantial losses: American, $3.5 billion; United, $3.33 billion; Delta, $1.3 billion; Northwest, $766 million; Continental, $451 million; U.S. Airways, $1.66 billion. The combined losses of the industry exceeded $10 billion.

Bankruptcies

As we have seen, the Air Transportation Stabilization Board, which was set up to aid struggling airlines after 9-11, was not a rubber stamp operation to the airlines' petitions for money. Nevertheless, by 2004, the ATSB had paid out $7 billion in direct assistance and many billions more in indirect assistance in the form of loan guarantees, a tax holiday, and pension relief. But

all of this was not enough, or not soon enough, for some of the nation's airlines. We will review major filings below.

US Airways

On August 11, 2002, US Airways was the first carrier after 9-11 to seek bankruptcy protection. US Airways was the largest carrier at Washington–Reagan Airport, and as such was severely impacted by the airport's closure for an extended period of time. In Chapter 11, U.S. Airways made significant changes to its operating model. It became the first U.S. airline to eliminate the pensions of its pilots, affecting some 6000 employees. It became the first legacy carrier to eliminate complimentary meal service on domestic flights. As a part of its reorganization, it began a process of de-emphasizing its hub and spoke system, particularly in the Eastern U.S., in favor of point-to-point service similar to Southwest's successful model. While in bankruptcy, the airline received a government-guaranteed loan under the Air Transportation Stabilization Board.

United Airlines

After 9-11, then the sixth largest airline in the country, United applied for a government-guaranteed loan from the Air Transportation Stabilization Board. In December 2002, the Board voted to deny the application in spite of concessions previously given by its flight attendants and its pilots. The Board believed that United's labor burden was still too bloated to allow it to compete in the existing business environment. United filed for bankruptcy protection on December 9, 2002. In 2003, under bankruptcy court protection, United cut pilots' wages 30 percent. Pilots pay then ranged between $33,000 for new hires to a high of $195,000. It also terminated its employee pension plan, the second airline to do so. Both of these pension plans were transferred to the Pension Benefit Guaranty Corporation, a federal agency set up to protect employees' pensions.[4]

Fleet	6/30/01	12/31/01	6/30/02	12/31/02	Change
B727	480	333	259	224	(256)
MD80	631	573	561	554	(77)
DC10	133	111	96	72	(61)
DC9	311	274	272	268	(43)
DC8	118	80	78	77	(41)
F100	114	96	74	74	(40)
B717	28	43	13	13	(15)
L1011	20	15	13	13	(7)
B747	174	174	170	168	(6)
B737	1,296	1,277	1,303	1,294	(2)
A330	9	9	9	9	—
MD90	16	16	16	16	—
A310	41	43	46	45	4
A321	19	23	28	28	9
MD10	12	12	16	22	10
MD11	51	53	56	62	11
A300	89	94	101	104	15
B777	110	119	129	129	19
B767	333	344	359	363	30
B757	579	600	615	623	44
A319	158	177	196	210	52
A320	228	251	267	284	56
TOTAL	**4,950**	**4,717**	**4,677**	**4,652**	**(298)**

Copyright © 2003 by Air Transport Association.

FIGURE 36-12 Net change in mainline operating fleet—ATA U.S. members. ATA members are Airborne Express, Alaska Airlines, Aloha Airlines, America West Airlines, American Airlines, American Trans Air, Atlas Air, Continental Airlines, Delta Air Lines, DHL Airways, Emery Worldwide, Evergreen International, FedEx, Hawaiian Airlines, JetBlue Airways, Midwest Airlines, Northwest Airlines, Polar Air Cargo, Southwest Airlines, United Airlines, UPS Airlines, and US Airways.

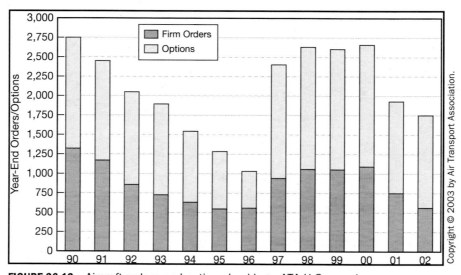

Copyright © 2003 by Air Transport Association.

FIGURE 36-13 Aircraft orders and options backlog—ATA U.S. members.

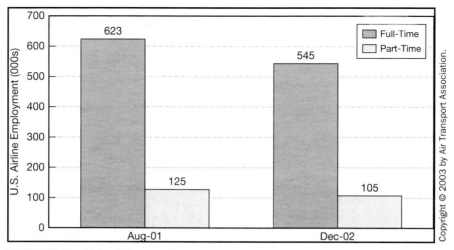

FIGURE 36-14 U.S. airline employment.

Delta Airlines

After 9-11, Delta Airlines continued its downward spiral, losing $10 billion between 2001 and 2005. The third largest carrier in the U.S., Delta entered Chapter 11 on September 14, 2005. Although Delta had been in financial straits for some time, its pilots pay ranged from $48,000 for beginning pilots to $275,000 for Boeing 777 captains. Delta froze its employee pension plan (which allowed Delta to forego any further contributions to the plan) by agreement with its unions. In September 2006, the Bankruptcy Court approved termination of Delta's pilot pension plan. Delta has preserved ground and flight attendants' pension plans based on the passage of the Pension Protection Act by Congress in 2006. This statute gives Delta (and Northwest) a period of 17 years to fund the employee plans.

Northwest Airlines

Northwest, the fourth largest U.S. carrier, entered Chapter 11 on the same day as Delta, September 14, 2005. Precipitating the filing, Northwest had been unable to win necessary wage concessions from its unions. In fact, Northwest had been operating for almost a month prior to filing with its unionized mechanics on strike. Like Delta, Northwest froze its employee pension plan in bankruptcy. Unlike other airlines in bankruptcy, Northwest preserved all of its pension plans.

As of September 14, 2005, four of the top seven carriers in the United States were in bankruptcy. They were all legacy airlines.

ATA Airlines

ATA was a new entrant airline, receiving its air carrier certificate in 1981, post deregulation. As the country's tenth largest air carrier, it filed for protection on October 22, 2004, citing fuel prices, competition, and lease payments on aircraft. This was necessary in spite of receiving an ATSB loan guarantee in the amount of $168 million in 2002. As part of its restructuring under bankruptcy protection, ATA agreed to sell its hub operation at Chicago Midway to AirTran, one of its major competitors. It also sold its slots at LaGuardia and Reagan National to AirTran.

Hawaiian Airlines

Founded in 1929 as Inter-Island Airways, Hawaiian Airlines has the distinction of being the oldest U.S. carrier never to have had a fatal accident in its history. Conditions after 9-11 forced HAL to begin a restructuring process, in which it negotiated significant concessions from its labor forces. The company was unable to satisfactorily restructure its aircraft leasing contracts, and entered bankruptcy in March 21, 2003.

Aloha Airlines

Aloha Airlines received its operating certificate in 1949. The company went private in 1986 with 100 percent ownership in two Hawaiian families. Aloha received a $45 million loan guarantee from the Air Transportation Stabilization Board in 2002, but by December 30, 2004, it was unable to continue operations outside of Chapter 11 bankruptcy. When it entered bankruptcy protection, it had repaid about half of the government-backed loan. The filing was attributed to competition factors, likely including its chief competitor, Hawaiian Airlines, which had already secured creditor relief from bankruptcy protection.

Mesaba Airlines (a Northwest link airline)

Mesaba began operations in 1944 as a feeder route in Minnesota. In 1984, it began flying exclusively for Northwest Airlines as a regional carrier. Mesaba depended on Northwest for all of its passengers and its entire schedule. When Northwest filed for bankruptcy protection on September 14, 2005, cash shortages, fleet changes, and other uncertainties were imposed on it by Northwest. It is not surprising, then, that Mesaba followed Northwest into Chapter 11, which it did on October 13, 2005. Mesaba was owed $30 million by Northwest when NW filed in September.

Beyond 9-11—Another New Beginning

A Glance over the Shoulder

Since it was economically deregulated in 1978, the airline transport industry has been in a struggle to define itself. Before government control and economic support were removed, the airlines were stable, reliable, and self-confident. With deregulation and its entry into the real world of private enterprise, the inherently fragile nature of the industry has been exposed.

In the thirty-year period since deregulation, the existence of the air carrier industry has been characterized by a cyclical "feast or famine" roller coaster ride. Short periods of prosperity have always been followed by periods of stress and financial loss. Each one of these cycles has been precipitated by overriding economic and political conditions, punctuated by high fuel costs, all of which have been largely beyond the control of airline management.

The business model that existed during the period of CAB control beginning in the 1930s, the model the legacy airlines operated under when deregulation began, has been tested and has now been found to be unworkable in the new competitive environment of deregulation. This was not true during the early years of deregulation, when the incumbent airlines' economies of scale (size, experience, computer reservation systems, gate and slot ownership, and control of the hub and spoke system) did, in fact, inhibit the success of new entrant airlines.

The predominance of the legacy airlines during the years immediately following deregulation turned out to be a transitional phase in the progression of the industry away from government control. But the challenges of a never-ending stream of new entrant airlines continued to apply pressure to the business model of these airlines, which were still constrained by high labor costs, high fixed costs, low fares, and ever-increasing debt incurred in an effort to continue to exist. Southwest Airlines, in particular, brought to the contest a new business model, one which during the more recent period of commercial aviation experience has provided an example to new entrant airlines. The "Southwest Effect," as its way of doing business and culture have been termed, has come to define how an airline can be run profitably in the deregulated world.[5]

New airlines continued to enter the field and, although most of them could not survive due to the economies of scale of the legacy carriers, the procession of new entrants seemed to be endless.

Gradually, the economies of scale of the legacy airlines began to give way to the more competitive styles used by the new breed of low-cost carriers.

Although the federal government abandoned direct economic regulation of the industry, it has brought to bear other aspects of regulation. Government oversight in the form of antitrust policy as administered by the Justice Department, in spite of significant lapses during the 1980s, halted anticompetitive mergers and acquisitions that characterized the immediate post-regulatory period.

The Department of Transportation assumed a new responsibility to insure that a more competitive environment existed. DOT did this by curbing predatory practices by legacy airlines and by removing barriers to competition at airports, notably with the requirement for airports to submit competition plans as authorized by AIR-21.

In each downturn in the cyclical evolution of the industry, judicious use has been made by airlines of the reorganization provisions of the bankruptcy act. With each filing in Chapter 11, the legacy airlines have taken another step in the direction of the new business model: renegotiation of labor contracts to reduce the number of employees, to reduce wages and benefits, and to permit outsourcing of work previously performed by unionized employees; eliminating employee pension plans; negotiation of debt reduction; and the consequent reduction of air fleets and physical plant.

Taking Stock

The survival of the air carrier industry in the days after 9-11 was no sure thing. Passenger volumes plummeted. Fares were lowered in an intensified competition for the available traffic. Enhanced airport security procedures, with its attendant delays, did not help. Added costs to the airlines included costs of intensified security (e.g., fortified cockpit doors), increased insurance premiums, and increased taxes. Fixed airline costs, like airplane lease payments and debt service ran on. There

was talk of nationalization of the industry or, at least, reregulation. Gloom prevailed.

The airlines began instituting drastic measures in an attempt to survive. In 2003, there was an 8 percent reduction in the number of aircraft as compared to 2000. New aircraft deliveries were postponed. Personnel layoffs resulted in 16 percent fewer jobs in 2003 than in 2000. By that year, some 140,000 jobs had been eliminated since 9-11.

Gradually, the industry began a sort of recovery. By the end of 2004, traffic volumes and capacity had surpassed 2000 levels. But limited pricing power (competition factors) yielded only moderate improvement. Cost-saving actions taken by the airlines after 9-11 improved the bottom line, but still the industry ran at a loss. Crude oil prices, which in 2004 had increased by 60 percent, added to the continuing financial stresses of the airlines. In 2005, fuel cost air carriers nearly $33 billion, twice what they spent in 2003.

The airlines continued to retire older, less-efficient airplanes, and by the end of 2005, over 600 aircraft had been parked as compared to 2001. Due to fuel efficiency progress in transport aircraft, the airlines in 2005 burned 400 million fewer gallons in their operations than in 2000, while carrying more passengers and cargo. But at the end of 2005, the industry was still operating in the red.

We have seen that between 2002 and 2005, eight major carriers had entered bankruptcy. By 2007, however, all major airlines that entered Chapter 11 post 9-11 had emerged from bankruptcy:

➡ June 2, 2005: Hawaiian Airlines

➡ September 27, 2005: US Airways. In Chapter 11, it merged with America West.

➡ February 1, 2006: United Airlines

➡ February 17, 2006: Aloha Airlines

➡ April 30, 2007: Delta Airlines

➡ May 31, 2007: Northwest Airlines

These transitions through reorganization have been largely at the cost of air industry labor groups and employees, and the stockholders of the companies. The one consistent winner through the years since deregulation has been the consumer. Domestic airfares have fallen 50.5 percent since 1978, adjusted for inflation. This phenomenon explains, in large part, the explosive growth that has been seen in air travel.

In 2005, the U.S. air carrier industry reported its first operating profit since 2000. Yet interest expense and other nonoperating costs left the airlines with a net loss of $5.7 billion.

By the end of 2006, for the first time since the turn of this century, U.S. air carriers had recorded a net profit. That year the airlines posted net income of $3 billion on $163.8 billion in revenues. Although fuel prices continued to increase. (See Figure 36-15) fuel efficiency also increased, by 22 percent over the year 2000. Passenger load factor increased to 79 percent. (See Figure 36-16). The airlines carried 12 percent more passengers in 2006 than in 2000, and they used 719 million fewer gallons of fuel in doing so. And they did it with fewer employees. Airline employment continued to decline, down to 544, 540. (See Figure 36-17 and Table 36-1.) The airline fleet continued toward modernization. (See Table 36-2 on page 303.) Yet, some airlines were more successful than others. Next we will take a closer look at that.

❝ Since 1978 the record pretty well shows that no start-up airline . . . has really been successful, so the odds of JetBlue having long-term success are remote. I'm not going to say it can't happen because stranger things have happened, but I personally believe P.T. Barnum was, in that respect, correct. ❞

(Ed. Note: P. T. Barnum, a 19th century showman and circus owner, is supposed to have famously said, "There is a sucker born every minute.")

Gordon Bethune, CEO Continental Airlines, commenting on the 70% rise in JetBlue's stock price in the days after its IPO. Continental's annual shareholder meeting, 17 April 2002

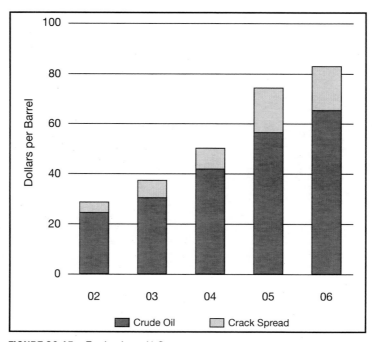

FIGURE 36-15 Fuel prices U.S.

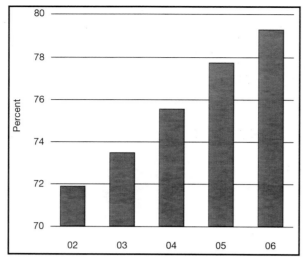

FIGURE 36-16 Passenger load factor.

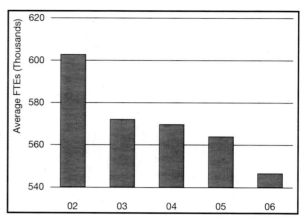

FIGURE 36-17 Employees.

U.S. Airlines—Average Full-Time Equivalents (FTEs)

	2005	2006	Change (%)
Pilots and Copilots	74,478	**69,181**	(7.1)
Other Flight Personnel	5,440	**4,824**	(11.3)
Flight Attendants	70,173	**76,919**	9.6
Mechanics	51,469	**47,335**	(8.0)
Aircraft and Traffic Service Personnel	288,542	**275,523**	(4.5)
Office Employees	36,537	**34,876**	(4.5)
All Other	35,827	**35,882**	0.2
Total Employment	562,467	**544,540**	(3.2)
Average Compensation[1]			
Salaries and Wages	$52,374	**$52,830**	0.9
Benefits and Pensions	15,931	**16,268**	2.1
Payroll Taxes	4,126	**4,100**	(0.6)
Total Compensation	$72,431	**$73,197**	1.1

[1]Passenger airlines only.

TABLE 36-1 Employment.

		ABX (GB)	Alaska (AS)	Aloha (AQ)	American (AA)	ASTAR (ER)	Atlas/Polar (5Y/PO)	Continental (CO)	Delta (DL)	Evergreen Int'l (EZ)	FedEx Express (FX)	Hawaiian (HA)	JetBlue (B6)	Midwest (YX)	Northwest (NW)	Southwest (WN)	United (UA)	UPS (5X)	US Airways (US)	Total
Airbus	A300				34	6					56							53		**149**
	A310										66									**66**
	A319														66		55		93	**214**
	A320												96		73		97		75	**341**
	A321																		28	**28**
	A330														24				9	**33**
Boeing	B-717											11		25						**36**
	B-727					29					104							31		**164**
	B-737		91	24	77			264	71							481	94		96	**1,198**
	B-747						38			13					33		30	11		**125**
	B-757				142			58	121						66		97	75	46	**605**
	B-767	33			73			26	104			18					35	32	10	**331**
	B-777				46			18	8								52			**124**
	DC-8	5				9												46		**60**
	DC-9	61													107					**168**
	DC-10										31				2					**33**
	MD-10										52									**52**
	MD-11										58							34		**92**
	MD-80		23		325				120					11						**479**
	MD-90								16											**16**
Embraer	E190												23						2	**25**
Total		**99**	**114**	**24**	**697**	**44**	**38**	**366**	**440**	**13**	**367**	**29**	**119**	**36**	**371**	**481**	**460**	**282**	**359**	**4,339**

Note: Values reflect mainline aircraft counts as of December 31, ( ) Airline code

Source: Air Transport Association

TABLE 36-2 ATA Member Airline Operating Fleet—2006.

Legacy Airlines vs. Low-Cost Carriers

So far, we have looked at the air transportation industry during this difficult period as a whole, or as a homogenous group. But the industry is actually now composed of two distinct types of airline: legacy and low cost. Differences in how each of these types of carriers have responded to recent pressures is revealing.

Legacy airlines are those that were in operation during the period of CAB economic regulation prior to 1978. They have long-standing union contracts with their work forces, they have fixed terminal facilities spread all over the United States, and they fly routes practically to any destination from any destination. Legacy airlines operate large hub-and-spoke facilities with thousands of employees and hundreds of aircraft. They fund contract operations with smaller regional airlines to provide service to smaller communities. They have traditionally relied on travel agents, computer reservation systems, in flight amenities, and larger aircraft.

Low-cost carriers, except for Southwest, entered the market after deregulation. Today's LCCs, for the most part, are to be distinguished from the new entrant airlines that came into the market during the late 1970s and the 1980s. These new LCCs are better capitalized and have better business plans and management than some of the earlier entrants. These LCCs have mostly depended on the Internet as the primary means of selling and distributing tickets, and as the medium for communicating with their customers. Websites and computer programs have increased the ability of these carriers to respond to their customers on an interactive basis and provide immediate information. They also provide a price transparency that empowers their customers. The routes flown by these low-cost carriers are mostly point-to-point using newer, smaller aircraft, and their work forces are generally younger and paid less than their legacy airline counterparts, while achieving greater productivity.

A government study[6] compared seven legacy carriers with seven low cost carriers[7] in the period after September 11. These carriers accounted for 90 percent of all domestic airline seat capacity in 2003.

This study showed that between October 1, 2001 and the end of 2003, legacy airlines reported a reduction in operating costs of 14.4 percent. These savings came from all areas of operation, but 43 percent came from labor. They reduced their seat capacity by 12.6 percent by reducing operations and increasing regional airline service. Low-cost carriers, to the contrary, increased their capacity by 26.1 percent as they took advantage of the pullback by the larger carriers. LCCs operating expenses *increased* during this period by 9.8 percent. While the cost-cutting measures aided the legacy airlines in the short term, their capacity constriction allowed the LCCs to increase market share from 23 percent to 33 percent by 2003. (See Table 36.3.)

Overall, legacy airlines have suffered devastating losses in recent years, while LCCs have held up well. (See Figure 36-18.) Between 2000 and 2003, legacy airlines unit costs (the cost to fly one seat one mile) have actually increased while fares have decreased. (See Figure 36-19.) The disparity between legacy airlines' costs and LCCs' costs is widening. It cost legacy airlines 2.1 cents more per seat mile to operate in 2000 than it did LCCs. By 2003, that differential had almost doubled, to 3.8 cents. (See Figure 36-20.)

Legacy airlines are also losing market share to the low-cost carriers. As of 2003, fares were below 2001 levels, even though passenger volumes had rebounded. Legacy carriers carried 10 percent fewer passengers in 2003 than they did in 2000, while LCCs carried nearly 40 percent more than they had in 2000. Legacy carriers are carrying fewer passengers and collecting less revenue. LCCs are flying more passengers at lower prices. (See Figures 36-21 and 36-22 on page 307.)

Looking Forward

The changes wrought in the airline industry, due both to the rigors of deregulation and the stress of 9-11, portends a more competitive and resilient air carrier industry. Significant technological improvements have been made in airframe design and in engines, producing a more efficient aircraft for the airlines going forward. Leaner and smarter operating procedures, and a growing similarity in workable business practices among the airlines, are resulting in cost savings that will be increasingly seen at the bottom line. And importantly, the industry is on the verge of a breakthrough in the way the U.S. air traffic system is operated.

The ATC system remains largely as it was designed and implemented in the 1950s. Attempts at modernization have not proven successful. The highways in the sky have become more and more crowded, and the equipment used by the federal government to keep air traffic moving and safe is mostly beyond "modernization." The FAA has warned that traffic delays in the seven years beginning in 2007 will increase a whopping 62 percent. If so, the system will be overwhelmed. In any event, the long view is that "modernization" is not what is needed. What is needed is an entirely new concept in air traffic control.

Rank	Airline	Enplanement
1	American Eagle[a]	14,869,258
2	ExpressJet[a]	13,664,642
3	SkyWest[a]	13,417,720
4	Airtran	13,178,118
5	Comair	12,637,210
6	JetBlue	11,731,733
7	Atlantic Southeast	10,427,885
8	American Trans Air	10,340,914
9	Mesa	9,122,237
10	Atlantic Coast	7,046,971
11	Air Wisconsin	6,954,187
12	Frontier	6,437,921
13	Pinnacle	6,362,805
14	Horizon	5,930,448
15	Chautauqua	5,608,947
16	Mesaba	5,427,694
17	Hawaiian	5,234,766
18	Spirit	4,592,640
19	Aloha	4,187,019
20	Trans States[a]	3,462,869
21	Executive	2,796,163
22	Midwest Express	2,376,304
23	PSA	2,030,870
24	Piedmont	1,948,292
25	Ryan International	1,626,437

Source: GAO analysis of U.S. Department of Transportation information.

[a]These airlines were transitioned into the ATOS program from 2003 through 2005.

TABLE 36-3 Number of Enplanements for the Top 25 Non-legacy Airlines, 2004.

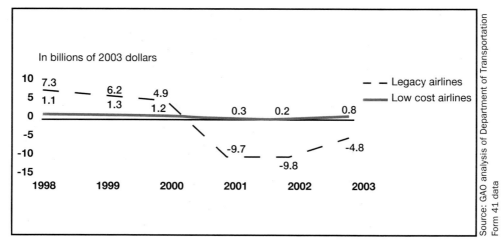

FIGURE 36-18 Legacy airlines have recorded nearly $25 billion in operating losses since 2001

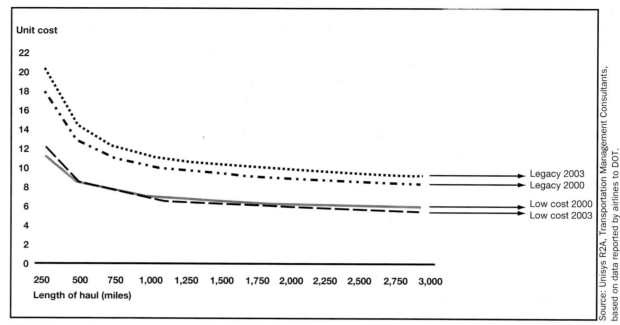

Source: Unisys R2A, Transportation Management Consultants, based on data reported by airlines to DOT.

FIGURE 36-19 Stage length cost curves, 2000 and 2003

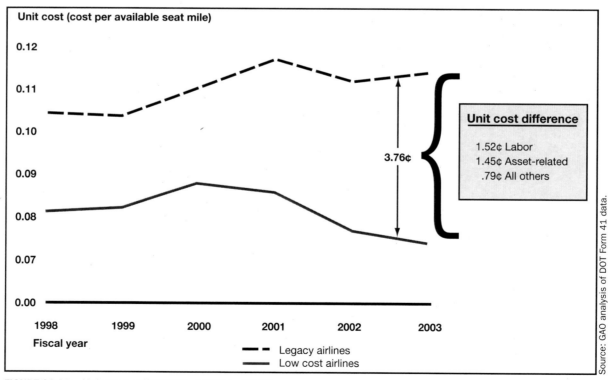

Source: GAO analysis of DOT Form 41 data.

FIGURE 36-20 Unit cost differential, 1998 to 2003

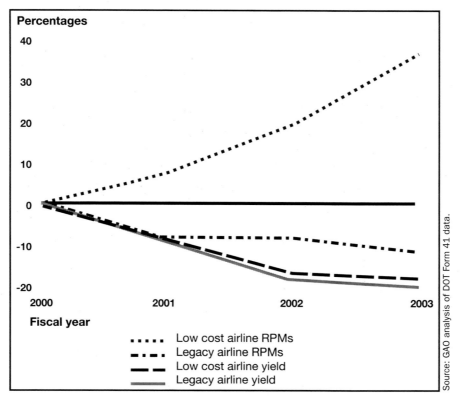

Source: GAO analysis of DOT Form 41 data.

FIGURE 36-21 Percentage change in airline fares and demand since 2000

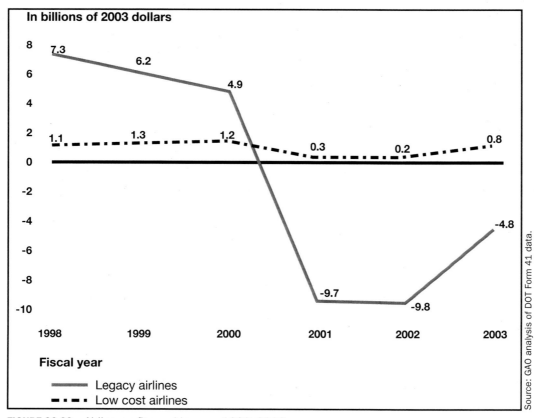

Source: GAO analysis of DOT Form 41 data.

FIGURE 36-22 Airline profits and losses, 1998–2003

Vision 100—Century of Aviation Reauthorization Act of 2003[8]

Next Generation Air Transportation System (NextGen)

This statute authorizes the development and launch of a Next Generation Air Transportation System. The concept involves moving from a system using ground-based radars to one using precision satellite-based navigation. This is a vast undertaking, and one that must be developed and implemented while the National Airspace System continues to be run full time by the FAA. To do this, the statute authorized the creation of the Joint Planning and Development Office (JPDO) to plan for and coordinate the transition to NextGen.

JPDO brings together a multitude of federal agencies[9] and organizations in the private enterprise sector.[10] The purpose of this enterprise is to insure that JPDO formulates a single vision that will effectively address the nation's needs for safety, capacity, and security in aviation.

It is important to emphasize that some of the technologies that will be required to make the NextGen system work are still being developed. The undertaking is so revolutionary and so massive that it will take the contributions and cooperation of all of the government agencies mentioned above as well as the various segments of the private enterprise community. These private enterprise entities include the airlines that will use the system, aircraft manufacturers, avionics companies, and research companies and consultants that are retained to provide technical expertise.

JPDO is developing several key documents that will form the foundation of NextGen planning: a Concept of Operations, an Enterprise Architecture, and an Integrated Work Plan.

➡ The Concept of Operations (ConOps) explains how the system will work and what it will look like.

➡ The Enterprise Architecture is like a set of blueprints. It defines the key capabilities of NextGen, how they fit together, the timing of their implementation, and how they affect the various members of the aviation community.

➡ The Integrated Work Plan will serve as a guide in developing the future needs for research and capital investment.

The NextGen system is based on the concept known as Performance-Based Navigation (PBN). PBN is basically a system of aircraft operations that maximizes on-board navigation capabilities and options while reducing ground-based control personnel and Navaids. PBN is based on two fundamental elements: Area Navigation (RNAV) and Required Navigation Performance (RNP).

RNAV as a general concept has been around for a long time. It was first implemented by using the Navaid system of VORs and other ground based facilities now in place. Avionics on board aircraft could "move" Navaids to any point in two-dimensional space, thus creating "waypoints" which could be used to fly direct routes. It was also subsequently used with LORAN airborne receivers in a similar manner for direct route navigation. The new RNAV system proposed in RNP uses satellite-based navigation and is much more sophisticated than previous concepts of RNAV.

Required Navigation Performance is a set of standards (parameters) by which departure, enroute, approach, and landing must be accomplished by aircraft in the National Airspace System, and requires the aircraft and its equipment to meet those associated performance standards. RNP contemplates a "trajectory" profile that will maximize the performance characteristics of jet aircraft and allow immediate climb to altitude and delayed, continuous descent to landing. This descent profile is known as Continuous Descent Approach (CDA). These procedures will reduce fuel burn, reduce noise in the ground environment, and reduce emissions, while expediting traffic flow.

RNP requires the use of a new technology called Automatic Dependent Surveillance–Broadcast (ADS-B), and associated subtechnologies known as Traffic Information Service-Broadcast (TIS-B) and Flight Information Service-Broadcast (FIS-B).

ADS-B is an aircraft-based surveillance technology that broadcasts once-per-second from the aircraft with its position, velocity, and identification. TIS-B is a ground-based broadcast service that provides secondary surveillance radar to enable a pilot to see other traffic in the air and on the ground. FIS-B provides weather and other noncontrol aeronautical information that allows pilots to operate more safely and efficiently.

Working closely with JPDO is the FAA, which will have the responsibility of implementing the system, integrating it with the current system, phasing out the old system, and making it all work. FAA has published its Roadmap for Performance-Based Navigation, which details the FAA's transition plans in three time periods: Near Term, Mid-Term, and Far-Term.

The Near Term Period extends from 2005 to 2010 and focuses on wide-scale RNAV implementation and the introduction of RNP for enroute, terminal, and approach procedures. It will assist in the alleviation of choke points at the 35 busiest airports in the FAA's Operational Evolution Plan (OEP). (See Table 36-4.)

The Mid-Term Period runs from 2011 to 2015 and contemplates a shift to predominately RNP operations for improving flight efficiency and airport access. The Mid-Term plan will employ RNAV extensively to improve flight operations.

The Far-Term Period includes 2016 to 2025 and expects operations to be conducted primarily under RNP. This period should realize optimization of airspace, automation enhancements, and modernization of communications and navigation.

RNP is expected to reduce air traffic controller inputs by 50 percent and to deliver considerable cost savings and curtailment of both

OEP 35 Airports

Atlanta Hartsfield–Jackson International	ATL
Baltimore–Washington International	BWI
Boston Logan International	BOS
Charlotte/Douglas International	CLT
Chicago Midway	MDW
Chicago O'Hare International	ORD
Cincinnati–Northern Kentucky	CVG
Cleveland–Hopkins International	CLE
Dallas–Fort Worth International	DFW
Denver International	DEN
Detroit Metro Wayne County	DTW
Fort Lauderdale–Hollywood International	FLL
George Bush Intercontinental	IAH
Greater Pittsburgh International	PIT
Honolulu International	HNL
Lambert St. Louis International	STL
Las Vegas McCarran International	LAS
Los Angeles International	LAX
Memphis International	MEM
Miami International	MIA
Minneapolis–St Paul International	MSP
New York John F. Kennedy International	JFK
New York LaGuardia	LGA
Newark International	EWR
Orlando International	MCO
Philadelphia International	PHL
Phoenix Sky Harbor International	PHX
Portland International	PDX
Ronald Reagan National	DCA
Salt Lake City International	SLC
San Diego International Lindbergh	SAN
San Francisco International	SFO
Seattle–Tacoma International	SEA
Tampa International	TPA
Washington Dulles International	IAD

Source: FAA Publication

TABLE 36-4 OEP 35 Airports.

airborne and ground delays. RNP is already being implemented in selected areas. These venues include Alaska airspace, Dallas–Ft. Worth (DFW), Hartsfield–Jackson Atlanta International (ATL), and Ronald Reagan Washington National (DCA).

RNP is not only being planned and implemented within the NAS system, but worldwide. It is being planned for oceanic airspace as well as under ICAO auspices and EUROCONTROL. The Roadmap is intended to provide airlines, manufacturers of avionics and aircraft, and other operators in the aviation industry with a guideline for future equipage and capability investments. ATC can thus more smoothly implement the transition process.

Why NextGen Is Necessary

In 2005, both major carriers and regional airlines saw significant increases in passenger enplanements, with regionals growing faster. International traffic increased almost twice as much as in domestic markets. By 2017, passenger demand is predicted to increase by a factor of 25 percent, to a total of 1 billion passengers.

General aviation is also expected to experience explosive growth. Piston aircraft are projected to increase at an annual rate of 1.4 percent, while business jets are expected to increase at the rate of 4 percent annually. Very light jets (VLJs) will add 400 to 500 aircraft to the NAS per year. Unmanned aircraft systems (UAS) will become routine.

Traffic demand on the ATC system, complicated by convective weather externalities, military operations, and security needs, will mandate greater flexibility in air operations. By 2017, the FAA says that traffic will peak at the nation's busiest airports at 30–40 percent above levels seen in 2005.

If the United States is to continue to provide a reliable, safe, and efficient air transportation system, the problem must be addressed now. NextGen may be the solution.

Endnotes

1. Pub.L. No. 107-42; 115 Stat. 230.
2. Pub.L. No. 107-71; 115 Stat. 597 (2001).
3. Pub.L. No. 107-296; 116 Stat. 2135 (2002).
4. The Pension Benefit Guaranty Corporation's (PBGC) single-employer insurance program is a federal program that insures certain benefits of the more than 34 million worker, retiree, and separated vested participants of over 29,000 private sector defined benefit pension plans. Defined benefit pension plans promise a benefit that is generally based on an employee's salary and years of service, with the employer being responsible to fund that benefit, invest and manage plan assets, and bear the investment risk. A single-employer plan is one that is established and maintained by only one employer. It may be established unilaterally by the sponsor or through a collective bargaining agreement
5. In January 2007, Southwest reported its 34th consecutive year of profitable operation.
6. Hecker, JayEtta Z., "COMMERCIAL AVIATION—Despite Industry Turmoil, Low Cost Airlines Are Growing and Profitable," Testimony before the Subcommittee on Aviation, Committee on Transportation and Infrastructure, House of Representatives, United States General Accounting Office, GAO-04-837T, June 3, 2004.
7. The legacy carriers were Alaska, American, Continental, Delta, Northwest, United, and US Airways. The low-cost carriers were AirTran, America West, ATA, Frontier, JetBlue, Southwest, and Spirit.
8. P.L. 108–176.
9. JPDO's partner agencies include the Departments of Transportation, Commerce, Defense, and Homeland Security; FAA; the National Aeronautics and Space Administration (NASA); and the White House Office of Science and Technology Policy.
10. Aviation groups, airport operators, manufacturers, and the aerospace industry.

PART VI

International Civil Aviation

Chapter 37   Treaties and International Civil Aviation Organizations

Chapter 38   Europe after World War II—The Rise of the European Economic Community

Chapter 39   American Deregulation and The European Union

Chapter 40   Global Deregulation Takes Off

Chapter 41   Global Aircraft Manufacturing

Chapter 42   Beyond Earth

Treaties and International Civil Aviation Organizations

© Dan Barnes, 2008, Shutterstock, Inc.

The concept of international air transportation emerged almost immediately with powered flight itself. Flight in lighter-than-air craft had been an international affair from the start. As the reality of powered flight neared, activity in both North America and Europe proceeded simultaneously. After the Wright brothers' success in 1903, Europeans immediately followed, developing their own brands and models of airplane.

International flight in heavier-than-air machines first occurred on August 22, 1906, when Louis Bleriot flew his monoplane across the English Channel from France to England. William Boeing was carrying airmail between Seattle and Vancouver in his Boeing B-1E seaplane in 1919 under agreement with both the United States and Canada. The International Air Traffic Association was organized in 1919 by six European air transport companies. It was obvious that mere boundaries could not contain the airplane and those who would use it in commerce. Still, under international law, borders could not be transcended with impunity, and it was clear early on that some kind of structure would have to be put in place to deal with the interaction between peoples of different cultures and different laws.

International Aviation Relations

Beginning in 1910 in Paris, international conferences between nations, attended by their appointed representatives, convened for the purpose of discussing and resolving issues related to international civil aviation. Representatives from nineteen European countries assembled that year in a meeting, now known as the Paris Conference, to consider the legal and practical requisites for international air commerce. Although little was immediately accomplished, a start had been made, and much of the work of that first conference resurfaced in the conferences of the future.

It is important to note the international legal distinction between the words *conference* and *convention*. A convention, as used in international civil aviation, means an agreement between nations, not yet rising to the status of a treaty, the latter of which only occurs upon ratification by the signatory nations. The word *conference* is used to describe the assembly or gathering where a convention might be agreed on.

In 1919, after World War I, representatives of the victorious nations, as well as Brazil and Cuba, adopted the Paris Convention, which established for the first time several important foundations for civil aviation. First, the Convention recognized that each nation has sovereignty over its own airspace, including its territories and colonies. Second, it followed the maritime law principle that each aircraft must have a national registration. Third, it established certain basic rules regarding the airworthiness of aircraft. Fourth, it adopted rules regarding the certification of pilots. Although the United States signed the Convention, it was not ratified. It would, however, become a model for the later enactment of statutes in the United States regarding the same subject matters.

In 1926, representatives from countries left out of the Paris meeting in 1919 adopted the Madrid Convention, which basically was the same agreement adopted in Paris in 1919. This agreement would have no substantial effect on later agreements in the field of civil aviation.

The Havana Convention of 1928 was an agreement between nations of the Western Hemisphere, and grew out of the Pan American Conference held in Santiago, Chile, in 1923. The provisions of this Convention were similar to those of the Paris Convention, but due to variations between the two, this Convention caused some commercial and operating uncertainties in the international community until the differences were finally resolved in 1944 at the Chicago Convention.

The Warsaw Convention—1929

At the same time that the hemispherical conferences were going on in the West, conferences were held in Europe, first in Paris in 1925 and then in Warsaw in 1929. Commercial air transportation between far-flung nations, including Europe and the United States, was being recognized as a probability since the significant aerial accomplishments of 1919. In that year the first transatlantic flight had been completed by the United States Navy in a Curtiss flying boat, NC-4, from North America to Lisbon via the Azores (requiring 57 hours of actual flying time). Englishmen Captain John Alcock and Lieutenant Arthur W. Brown made the first non-stop crossing from Newfoundland to Ireland (completed in just over 16 hours flying time). The English dirigible R-34 made a round trip from Scotland to Roosevelt Field, Long Island (between July 2 and July 8), and the first scheduled airplane passenger service was inaugurated between London and Paris. The primary concerns at the Paris and Warsaw conferences related to the lack of uniformity in commercial and legal transactions in international civil aviation. In 1929, the signatory nations established through the Warsaw Convention, effective on February 13, 1933, the first rules relating to carrier liability for passenger and cargo interests in international air transportation. The Warsaw Convention (Warsaw) provides the legal framework for the payment of claims for personal injury and death of passengers, claims for damaged goods, cargo and baggage, and claims for delay. Simply put, airlines must pay regardless of fault (strict liability) up to the limits of liability prescribed, subject to certain defenses set out therein. Warsaw also prescribed form and content for tickets, air waybills and other lading documents.

The Hague Protocol and the Montreal Agreement

Warsaw has been amended over its history, and its legal effect has been modified by separate agreements between nations. The original limitation of liability set forth in Warsaw was $8,300 per passenger for personal injury or death. This amount was doubled by operation of the Hague Protocol of 1955, effective in 1964. As inflation eroded the value of currencies the world over, the limitations of liability contained in Warsaw became effectively lower and lower. The United States, in 1965, let it be known that it would consider withdrawing from Warsaw if liability limits were not raised. This led to a voluntary accord, known as the Montreal Inter-Carrier Agreement, being signed in 1966 by all major foreign and U.S. carriers serving the United States. Under this agreement, limits of liability were raised to $75,000 per passenger for death or injury. This agreement was not an amendment of Warsaw, but a voluntary acceptance by the airlines of an increase in their potential liability. Any carrier desiring to fly into the United States was required to join the agreement. The Montreal Agreement was followed by a similar agreement between European civil aviation authorities, called the Malta Agreement, which increased those airlines' liability in such cases on international flights between their nations.

The Montreal Agreement was seen as an interim fix, and the United States continued efforts to have Warsaw formally amended or replaced. This led to two subsequent formal agreements, the Guadalajara Convention in 1961 and the Guatemala Protocol in 1971, but neither of these was ratified by the United States.

The Montreal Protocols in 1975 dealt with cargo issues arising under Warsaw, provided for increased liability limits and, importantly, eliminated the outmoded cargo documentation provisions of Warsaw. This step allowed the use of electronic commerce in international cargo transactions, eliminating the necessity of providing detailed air waybills and the like. This agreement was ratified by the United States in 1998.

IATA Inter-Carrier Agreement and IATA Measures of Implementation Agreement

In 1995, at the urging of the Department of Transportation, discussions were initiated between foreign and U.S. carriers under the auspices of IATA and ATA, to reach voluntary agreement to waive the limitations of liability set out in Warsaw. Later that year, these carriers signed the IATA Inter-Carrier Agreement (IIA) that committed the airlines to take action to waive the limitation of liability provisions of the Warsaw Convention. In 1996, the second step

was taken when many of them signed the IATA Measures of Implementation Agreement (MIA), which waived the Warsaw limitations up to 100,000 Special Drawing Rights (SDRs). SDRs are monetary units representing an artificial "basket" currency developed by the International Monetary Fund to replace gold as a world standard. Recently 100,000 SDRs represented approximately $130,000. By the middle of the year 2000, 122 international carriers, comprising more than 90 percent of the world's air transport industry, had signed IIA, with most of those also signing MIA. The effect of these developments is that any international passenger who qualifies would have an absolute right to receive a payment of approximately $130,000 regardless of airline fault.

The Montreal Convention—1999

As a result of the Band-Aid approach to fixing the deficiencies of Warsaw, the world international transportation community operated under a patchwork of rules governing liability and compensation in cases of loss. Under the auspices of ICAO, an international conference was convened in Montreal in 1999 and adopted what is now referred to as the Montreal Convention of 1999 (Montreal 99). The basic provisions of the Convention (Montreal 99) include: (1) imposition of strict liability for the first 100,000 SDRs of proven damages for passenger death or injury, (2) removal of all arbitrary limits of liability for amounts in excess of 100,000 SDRs for passenger death or injury (assuming there is carrier negligence), (3) increases the number of jurisdictions (countries) where suits may be brought than was allowed under Warsaw, and (4) clarifies carrier responsibilities under codesharing arrangements.

Montreal 99 was ratified by the United States on May 9, 2003, and entered into force as of November 4, 2003, as the Montreal Convention—1999.

The Chicago Conference

Toward the end of World War II, the United States invited representatives from the countries allied in the war effort against the Axis countries, as well as representatives from some of the neutral countries, to participate in an international conference on the subject of civil air transportation. World consensus was that there would be a mighty surge of international civil aviation and commerce after the expected end of hostilities. The United States at that time was in a preeminent position, *vis-a-vis* the rest of the world, to extend its influence all over the globe, and to capitalize on the great advantage that it held in international aviation as a result of the American air fleet produced during the war. American airplanes of the transport category had proliferated after wartime production began in 1941, and they had pioneered intercontinental routes in support of United States ground and naval personnel dispatched to all corners of the globe to meet the aggression of the Axis Powers. America, in fact, held a virtual monopoly on transport aircraft capable of intercontinental reach.

The Chicago Convention—1944

In November 1944, representatives from 54 countries attended the conference, since known as the Chicago Conference, at the end of which 32 countries signed a convention, the Chicago Convention, 1944, which established the International Civil Aviation Organization (ICAO) upon ratification of the convention by the required number of 26 countries. Ratification was accomplished on April 4, 1947, and at the invitation of the Canadian government, headquarters were established in Montreal. Legally, ICAO became a specialized agency linked to the Economics and Social Council of the United Nations.

The stated purposes of the Convention, to be administered and facilitated by ICAO, included (1) providing for the adoption of International Standards and Recommended Practices regulating international navigation, (2) providing recommendations for the installation of navigational facilities by the Contracting States, and (3) suggesting ways for the reduction of customs and immigration formalities. These purposes were to establish the fundamental basis for the safety, efficiency, and regularity of international civil aviation in the years to come.

The International Air Transport Agreement

During the Chicago Conference the United States pressed its view that international civil aviation would be served by adoption of "open skies," the concept of free flight over, to and from, and within the borders of the sovereign states represented at the Conference. It should be noted that "countries," in international treaty parlance, are known as "states," and exclusively referred to in that way. Of all the countries represented, only the United States was in a position to do any such flying. Known as the "Five Freedoms," this concept is outlined in the following box.

The Five Freedoms

1. Freedom One—The right of overflight without landing

2. Freedom Two—The right to land for reasons other than loading or unloading traffic, such as maintenance, fuel, or emergencies

3. Freedom Three—The right to carry traffic from a home country to a foreign country

4. Freedom Four—The right to carry traffic from a foreign country back to a home country

5. Freedom Five—The right to carry traffic between two foreign countries, as a part of an overall itinerary from or to a home country

---

The opposing view to "open skies" in 1944 was most forcefully stated by representatives of the United Kingdom. Britain believed that free and unlimited access by a foreign power to one's country and its markets was premature. England had no significant number of transport aircraft with which to take advantage of the open skies concept. Given the physical and financial state of its war-torn country, it was realized that it might take some years to be in a position to compete with the United States on any kind of a level playing field. The proposed agreement that would implement the Five Freedoms, officially known as the International Air Transport Agreement, informally referred to as the "Five Freedoms Agreement," was not generally acceptable to the main body of representatives present at Chicago, and only 19 countries were willing to sign it. It was not, therefore, effective, and is even less so today as many of the original signatories have withdrawn from it.

The Transit Agreement

The second agreement entered into at Chicago is known as the International Air Services Transit Agreement, or "Two Freedoms Agreement." This agreement embodies the first two freedoms, that is, overflight rights and landing rights for non-traffic reasons. Although signed by less than all conferees (100 nations had signed the "Transit Agreement" by 1992), this agreement became the basis upon which all future transit agreements would rest, and it established at least a minimum interactive relationship between the signatories. This agreement, therefore, may be considered to be one of the most significant results of the Chicago Conference.

The Bermuda Agreement

While the United Kingdom was not amenable to a multilateral treaty arrangement granting access to its markets, it was realized that the relationship between the United States and England was such that some sort of commercial aviation mutuality was in the interest of the United Kingdom. As the two most powerful leaders in the West to come out of World War II, the two governments agreed to have representatives meet in Bermuda in 1946 in an effort to reach an accord. The agreement that was reached was a compromise between the two positions previously articulated, and constituted the most important of the early bilateral (instead of multilateral) agreements to affect international civil aviation. The agreement essentially provided that

1. Fares and rates would have to be mutually acceptable to the two governments
2. Routes would have to be mutually agreed, and implicitly that there would be a *quid pro quo* for each route
3. Fifth Freedom rights (the carriage of traffic between two foreign countries without return to the home country) would be agreed on a case-by-case basis

The Bermuda Agreement became the model for future bilaterals between the United States and England and formed the model that would be used in other agreements between the United States and other foreign countries. Bilateral agreements have covered a variety of subject matters, including reciprocal recognition of pilot licenses, airworthiness standards for export aircraft, and radio communications.

Additional Conventions

International Recognition of Rights in Aircraft (Geneva Convention—1948)

Ninety-four countries had ratified this Convention as of 2002. The purpose of the treaty is to protect the rights of aircraft owners and others holding legal rights to the aircraft (such as security interests) when the aircraft crosses the borders of a signatory nation. One of the intended effects of the Convention was to encourage investors or financial institutions to more freely provide financing in the purchase of aircraft. Although a signatory to the Convention, Mexico filed a reservation to the effect that priority would be given by Mexican laws to "fiscal claims and claims made for work contracts" over claims asserted under the Convention. Sad stories are legend concerning the recovery of aircraft from Mexico.

Damage to Third Parties on the Surface Caused by Foreign Aircraft (Rome Convention—1952)

This Convention provides for the imposition of strict liability of the aircraft operator for damage caused to third parties on the ground, but places a limitation on the amount of compensatory damages. It also provides for the compulsory recognition of foreign judgments against the aircraft operator, so that a judgment secured in the injured parties' home jurisdiction may be enforced against the aircraft operator in the same manner as a domestic judgment.

Air Offenses Convention (Tokyo Convention of 1963)

This Convention is designed to insure that offenses committed on board an aircraft may be punished by authorities in the jurisdiction of the registration of the aircraft, no matter where the location of the aircraft may be when the offense is committed. The aircraft commander or his designees are empowered to prevent the commission of such acts and to take the offender into custody, and authorized to remove the offender from the aircraft. Signatories to the Convention are obligated to take all appropriate measures to prevent unlawful and forcible seizures of aircraft by persons on board and to restore control of the aircraft to the lawful commander of the aircraft.

Hijacking Convention (Hague Convention for the Suppression of Unlawful Seizure of Aircraft—1970)

As has been described above, the rash of hijackings that occurred in the 1960s caused international concern. Representatives met at The Hague to consider the problem and underscored international determination to do everything possible to prevent such actions and to ensure the severe punishment of perpetrators. Detailed provisions are set forth in the Convention concerning the establishment of jurisdiction by signatory nations in order to prosecute such offenses, including rights of nations to take offenders into custody and to prosecute or extradite them according to its provisions. As of 2002, 175 nations had ratified the Convention.

Convention for the Suppression of Unlawful Acts against the Safety of Civil Aviation (Montreal Convention—1971)

This Convention is concerned with unlawful acts other than those relating to the seizure of aircraft. The treaty defines a variety of acts deemed to constitute prohibited acts and makes those acts punishable by severe penalties. By a supplementary Protocol in Montreal in 1988, the enumeration of prohibited acts was expanded to include specific acts committed at airports serving international civil aviation.

Plastic Explosives Convention (Convention on the Marking of Plastic Explosives for the Purpose of Detection—1991)

The aim of this Convention is the prevention of unlawful acts involving the use of plastic explosives. Signatory nations are required to adopt measures to ensure the marking of plastic explosives that will assist in detecting such explosives. Specifically, the manufacture of plastic explosives is to be regulated to prevent the distribution of unmarked explosives, to provide for control of the transfer of marked explosives, and for their destruction under time limitations. The Convention contains specific descriptions of the concerned explosives, the detection agents to be used in marking them, and it creates an International Explosives Technical Commission to keep track of developments in the manufacture, marking, and detection of the explosives.

The International Civil Aviation Organization (ICAO)

ICAO officially came into being in 1947 as a result of the Chicago Convention, upon ratification by the requisite number of states. According to the mission statement of the organization, its aims and objectives are to develop the principles and techniques of international air navigation and to foster the planning and development of international air transport, so as to meet the needs of the international civil aviation community. The organization emphasizes its commitment, among other things, to facilitate:

1. The safe and orderly growth of civil air transportation

2. Aircraft design and operation for peaceful purposes

3. The development of airports, airways, and air navigation facilities for international civil aviation

Specifically, ICAO undertook to:

1. Establish international standards for aircraft airworthiness certification, flight crew certification, communications, and radio aids to navigation

2. Establish principles and procedures for the economic regulation of international routes, fares, frequency, and capacity

The use of English as the required language for communication between aircraft and air traffic control authorities in international civil aviation all over the world is an example of ICAO work.

ICAO adopts and publishes technical standards referred to as Standards and Recommended Practices (SARPs) that govern the interaction of civil air transportation the world over. These international standards provide uniformity and consistency that contribute to the safety and smooth operation of international civil aviation. ICAO proposes amendments and additions to SARPs as technology advances and conditions change. Satellite systems concepts, in the implementation stage as of 2002, will coordinate navigation, communications, and surveillance/air traffic management. The human element component of the equation is addressed through its TRAINAIR program, which is aimed at improving the quality and efficiency of aviation training, and the Human Factors program, which is directed toward reducing the impact of human performance limitations.

Other programs and efforts of the organization relate to education, the environment, including noise issues and emissions affecting the ozone layer, problems involving multiple taxation, airport and route facility management, statistics, economic analysis, legal matters including treaty drafting and interpretation of law, and security.

Security has been a subject of ICAO action since the early 1970s as a result of the hijacking of aircraft beginning in the 1960s. In 1974, ICAO adopted its Standards and Recommended Practices (SARPs) on Security, designated as Annex 17. The Annex is under constant review, and it has been amended ten times in order to respond to changing needs. The progression of emphasis in Annex 17 has been from hijacking, to sabotage, to baggage reconciliation with passengers, to screening of passengers and baggage and carry-on luggage. The latest revision on

December 7, 2001, dealt with challenges posed due to the events of 9-11.

Due to the disproportionately high aviation accident rate in Africa, beginning in 2007, ICAO is adopting a "new approach" toward carrying out its mandate to improve worldwide aviation safety as it relates to that region. Basically, ICAO intends to adopt a higher profile and assert its leadership role in the African region, raise awareness of the problem, and secure commitments from stakeholders and other interests. A study commission in 2006 found safety-related deficiencies that threaten the viability of civil aviation in Africa.

ICAO is at the center of the effort to coordinate the emerging globalization of the free market economy and provides assistance in bilateral and multilateral agreement models.

The International Air Transport Association (IATA)

The roots of IATA go back to 1919, the year that saw the world's first scheduled air transport service, when six "air transport" companies formed the organization known as the International Air Traffic Association. Membership was comprised solely of European carriers until Pan American joined in 1939. The present organization was founded in Havana, Cuba, in 1945, and was originally composed of 57 airlines mostly operating in Europe and North America. The purposes of the new organization were to promote safe and economical international air transport, to provide a means for collaboration of airline companies and to cooperate with the newly formed International Civil Aviation Organization (ICAO) as the representative of member airlines. As liaison to ICAO, through its members IATA supplied technical input for the Standards and Recommended Practices (SARPs) found in the Annexes to the Chicago Convention. IATA contributed to documentation and procedures standardization that

has allowed countries with differing languages and cultures to commercially interact with little difficulty. It also assisted in structuring a sound legal basis for international commercial transactions, meshing treaty law with existing air transport law of the United States. Ongoing work involves revision and modernization of the legal basis of carriage of persons and cargo in international aviation, as liability provisions of the Warsaw Convention have given way to subsequent amendments and superseding agreements.

After World War II, IATA began developing tariffs containing fares and rates (Traffic Coordination) for international carriage of passengers and cargo at meetings called Traffic Conferences, subject to the approval of the governments involved. A consistent schedule of rates and fares was also established, allowing airlines to accept each other's tickets on multisector itineraries, which in turn led to interlining between the world's airlines. It had been argued for years that IATA was, through its Traffic Coordination practices, engaged in price fixing that would normally be in violation of antitrust laws and in derogation of competition. Yet the United States, and other countries having similar laws, routinely granted antitrust exemptions for the activity. The truth was that international air transportation was among the least competitive industries in the world.

With the "father of deregulation," Alfred Kahn, at the helm of the CAB when deregulation was enacted in 1978, the deregulators turned their attention to international aviation. In 1979, hearings were conducted by the CAB in the United States to ascertain whether antitrust immunity should be removed from the Traffic Coordination activities of IATA. The world's airlines lined up in uniform opposition. The hearings concentrated on the North Atlantic routes, which was served by forty airlines. The Justice Department supported the CAB, but the Department of Transportation urged a "go slow" position. Nevertheless, on May 5, 1981, the

CAB issued a "show cause" order that raised the issue of whether antitrust immunity should be removed from IATA Tariff Coordinating Conferences. No decision was reached by the CAB prior to its demise at the end of 1984 pursuant to the "sunset" provisions of the Airline Deregulation Act. The Department of Transportation, having inherited the antitrust responsibilities of the CAB beginning in 1985, terminated the proceeding that year.

IATA, taking its cue, then reorganized itself into two parts, a Trade Association and a voluntary Traffic Conference, the latter dealing with the controversial issues of fare setting. In this way, IATA members sought to avoid further antitrust scrutiny of the United States antitrust regulators. No further proceedings have been initiated by the United States on this issue. IATA is still an influential trade association.

The organization has also served since the early days as the clearinghouse for interline accounting, and today services the accounts for 380 airlines. Multilateral Interline Traffic Agreements have been signed by most of the international carriers, which facilitates the seamless flow of passengers and cargo throughout the world.

CHAPTER 38

Europe after World War II—The Rise of the European Economic Community

© Terry Alexander, 2008, Shutterstock.

Since the 1950s, Europe has been on a journey to consolidate its economic power through a close association of its several states. Significant developments during that period are now having an important impact on the evolving global market. Specifically, the evolving equality between Europe and the United States, and the resulting competition between European and American commercial interests in international civil aviation, is a direct result of these developments. It is important, therefore, that we understand something of the history of the relationship between these two great areas of commerce.

The European-American Relationship

The primary advances in commercial aviation during the first part of the 20th Century were made in Europe. The French builder Deperdussin, for example, flew a 100-mile per hour airplane in 1912, a feat technologically far ahead of the Americans. European manufacturers supplied essentially all of the military aircraft used in World War I. French, German, and English manufacturers produced the world's most advanced aircraft designs and the most powerful aircraft engines. Further, the countries of Europe led the way in creating, organizing, and funding commercial passenger aviation immediately after World War I and began scheduled international aviation transportation as early as 1919. America had to play catch up during the 1920s, and American business interests had a hard time trying to figure out how the airplane could make any meaningful contribution to the progression of commerce in the United States.

The first airlines in the United States during the 1920s often looked to Europe to supply their aircraft needs. Juan Trippe, for example, began Pan American service in 1927 with Fokker trimotors, as that airplane set the standard with its cantilevered, mono-wing design. The Fokker departed from the biwing, wire-and-fabric airplanes of that and prior decades. This design was largely emulated in the Ford Trimotor in the 1920s. Beginning in the 1930s, however, the pendulum began to swing in favor of the Americans. This process began with the introduction in 1933 of the twin-engine Boeing 247, broadly acknowledged as the first modern airliner with its low mono-wing, retractable landing gear, and stressed all metal skin design. Concurrently with the emergence of the 247, the fortunes of the leading European manufacturer, Fokker, went into decline due to internal stress fractures occurring in its wooden wing. The first known failure of this wing caused the highly publicized crash of a Fokker Trimotor in 1931, resulting in the deaths of all passengers, including Notre Dame coaching legend, Knute Rockne.

In addition, the vast geographical area of America proved to be a fitting laboratory for the evolution of the commercial airliner. Navigational developments in the United States, beginning with its beacon system and followed by radio navigation, would lead the world in aviation technology as American airlines took to the skies.

Production of state-of-the-art transport aircraft intensified in the United States during the 1930s as Douglas inaugurated the highly successful Douglas Commercial (DC) series of airplanes. Lockheed joined the contest with the Constellation, Boeing countered with the first pressurized passenger airplane (the 309), and then came World War II.

The consolidation of military and political power by Germany during the 1930s, and the resulting devastation visited on the countries of Europe during the six years of World War II, left the United States in a position of preeminence in all things relating to commercial aviation by 1945. America had a ready-made fleet of commercial type aircraft, the most advanced of which included the Douglas DC-4 and the Lockheed Constellation. Immediately after the end of the war, advanced types of even larger aircraft began rolling off the American assembly lines, lines that had been set up during the war to produce the massive military airlift capacity of the Allies. The entire war production plant of the United States was now turned to peaceful and commercial ventures. At the same time, Europe lay in ruins.

In 1945, there was widespread hunger, unemployment, and housing shortages throughout the continent of Europe. Raw materials and foodstuffs were in short supply. Industries lay idle, or almost so, as much needed machinery and capital proved elusive. European cities were little more than acres of rubble, an estimated 500

million cubic tons of it in Germany alone. A breakdown of moral, social, and commercial life was threatened. The occupying forces of the Soviet Union were entrenched in much of Europe, and the expansionist Stalin government in power in the U.S.S.R. after World War II cast a covetous eye over the continent.

The Marshall Plan

Two years after the end of World War II, the situation in Europe was not much improved—in fact, whole segments of populations faced starvation. An economic depression loomed for the entire continent. Serious concerns were voiced in the United States over the deteriorating economic condition of Europe, and ideas were debated in foreign policy circles as to the best way to meet these concerns. By early 1947, preparations were complete for the initiation of a European economic recovery, a program that would come to be known as the Marshall Plan.

George C. Marshall was the Secretary of State in the Truman Administration in 1947. During the war he had been Army chief of staff and central in the military planning that had led to the defeat of the Axis Powers, particularly in Europe. He was considered indispensable in European affairs and he enjoyed considerable prestige with the United States Congress. In a speech to the graduating class at Harvard University on June 5, 1947, he proposed a solution for the European economic situation that was centered on the concept that the European countries would themselves set up a program for reconstruction, with the assurance of American assistance. The problem, he said, was:

The truth of the matter is that Europe's requirements for the next three or four years for foreign food and other essential products—principally from America—are so much greater than her present ability to pay that she must have substantial additional help or face economic, social, and political deterioration of a very grave character.

The remedy lies in breaking the vicious circle and restoring the confidence of the European people in the economic future of their own countries and of Europe as a whole.[1]

European response to this U.S. proposal of assistance was immediate and positive. A conference of sixteen European countries was arranged to meet in Paris in 1947. Twenty-two countries were invited to participate and all of those invited, except the Soviet Union and those countries under its control, attended. The Soviet Union, in fact, vigorously opposed the plan. The Paris conference led to the establishment of the Committee for European Economic Cooperation, and it was the forerunner of successive organizations that ultimately led to the existence of the European Union today.

In the United States, Congress passed the Economic Assistance Act of 1948, which became known as "The Marshall Plan." Congress appropriated in excess of $13.3 billion over the next four years and applied it to the European recovery plan. The plan has become known as the costliest, most successful, and arguably the most visionary international cooperative plan ever conceived in peacetime. It averted a postwar European depression and led to the economic recovery of the Western European countries, allowing an economic independence along with political stability that has endured. In addition to leading to the creation of the European Union, in due course it led to the creation of the Organization for Economic Development and Cooperation and to the North Atlantic Treaty Organization (NATO).

The Plan was amended in 1949 to include West Germany, the former foe of the United States and the other countries in Europe, which was a marked change from the victors' treatment of Germany after World War I. The inclusion of Germany was not only a benevolent and humanitarian act, it was a far-sighted move that quickly contrasted the free West German economy with that of the communist Soviet-controlled East Germany, and led to the establishment of a lasting progressive, free, and dynamic German economy. The Plan did not include Spain, which in 1948 was a dictatorship under Franco, and Spain was not invited to participate. At the same time, Spain had not been a combatant against Germany, and its economy and commercial infrastructure was relatively intact. (See Figure 38-1.)

To say that the Marshall Plan was a success would understate the facts. Europe gradually rebuilt, and its countries set about consolidating their common interests and strengths. The economic cooperation that spawned the European Community has gradually evolved into a legal, political, commercial, and social phenomenon—the end of which has not been seen.

In 1971, President Richard M. Nixon prophetically said of the American relationship with Europe:

The program which Secretary Marshall announced in 1947 served as a catalyst in helping the peoples of Western Europe release their boundless energies and express their abundant creativity. The Marshall Plan also created an environment in which the growth of strong ties within the Atlantic Community could be continually nourished.

The relationship between the United States and Europe is a dynamic one, susceptible, as we have seen, to constant, constructive change and thus touches on almost all aspects of our national well-being. This relationship is too critical to be taken for granted, too complex to be easily understood. We believe there is a great need for continuing study to enhance understanding of the relationship among all of our peoples.[2]

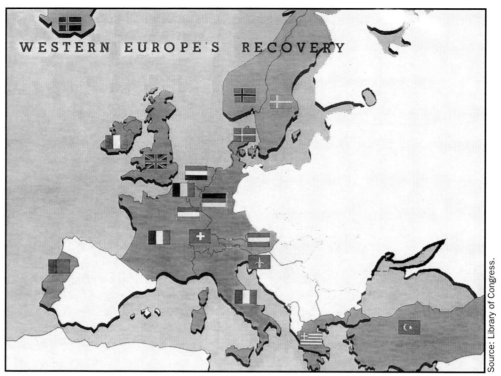

Source: Library of Congress.

FIGURE 38-1 Western Europe after World War II, showing countries that received aid under the Marshall Plan.

The Evolution of the European Community

In 1948, the major free nations of Europe created the Organization for European Economic Cooperation for the purpose of coordinating and administering the Marshall Plan for the economic recovery of Europe as a result of the devastating effects of World War II. Two years later, in 1950, the first significant step toward economic unification occurred with the agreement to pool coal and steel resources, which was entered into by those countries thereafter known as the "Six," and who were the original members of the European Community.[3] This was followed in 1951 with formalization in the Treaty of Paris, which established the European Coal and Steel Community. In 1953, the Six agreed to remove customs duties and quantitative restrictions on these raw materials, thus establishing for the first time a Common Market for coal and steel among those six countries.

In 1957, the Six signed the Treaty of Rome, establishing the European Economic Community (EEC). This agreement was to become the cornerstone of the present European Union, and is sometimes referred to as its "constitution." The Treaty of Rome is a comprehensive undertaking, articulating monetary policy, broad economic policy, and common commercial policy. It set goals for research and development, and for dealing with the environment, employment, discrimination, competition, and transportation. The Treaty also established the four governing bodies of the EEC: the Council, the Commission, Parliament, and the European Court of Justice.

Institutions of the EEC

The governmental entities created by the Treaty of Rome were entities in name only. They had been created and their responsibilities had been generally articulated. But boxes on an organizational chart must be given life by those who will take up the duty of beginning to perform the responsibilities assigned to them. The jurisdictional limits of each had to be established, and then tested one against the other. A pecking order had to be worked out. Bureaucratic motivations, goals, and energies had to be demonstrated. Results were measured. In the course of starting up a program as ambitious and unique as the European Economic Community, monumental uncertainties were expected and experienced, but they gradually gave way to a semblance of purpose and order. We will next review these governing entities and their duties, and we will then see how they came together to perform their joint function of pulling together the various disparate Member States into one cohesive, cooperative, and effective unit.

The **Council,** composed of representatives appointed from the Member States (one representative from each Member State), has both executive and legislative functions. It is charged with responsibility for ensuring that the objectives of the EC are realized, and put into practice. It may issue regulations and directives that are binding on Member States. Regulations are normally adopted based on recommendations of the Commission or Parliament. Work of the Council was compromised, particularly early on, by representatives' allegiances to their own government's interest, rather than to the collective interests of the EC. National governments still retain some powers not delegated to the EU.

Parliament is composed of elected representatives from the Member States (626 representatives elected by citizens of Member States).

From the first elections held in 1979, the Parliament has assumed a larger and more powerful role in the EU as a result of the 1992 Maastricht Treaty and the 1997 Amsterdam Treaty. The European Parliament, through these treaties, has progressed from a consultative body to a true legislative assembly. The Parliament is the only EU body that meets and debates in public, and it enacts the majority of European laws today. The legislative procedure for enacting legislation depends on a "codecision" process through which the Parliament and the Council are put on an equal footing, and together they enact laws proposed by the Commission. The members of Parliament are committed to act on behalf of the EC rather than at the behest of their constituency or their home governments, and sit in political groups instead of national delegations.

The **Commission** is headquartered in Brussels and is composed of 20 representatives appointed by the Member State governments (two commissioners from the larger Member States of Germany, France, Spain, Italy, and the United Kingdom, and one commissioner each from the smaller Member States of Belgium, Denmark, Greece, Ireland, Luxembourg, the Netherlands, Portugal, Finland, Sweden, and Austria). Due to the breadth of its administrative duties, it is the largest of the EU institutions, employing about half of all EU employees. The Commission is unique in that it is responsible for proposing all legislation to the European Parliament (for codecision with the Council). The Commissioners all swear an oath of independence, disclaiming any partisan influence from any source, and undertake to protect the interests of the European citizen, not the national citizen.

The Commission is in the nature of a Secretariat, having primarily executive duties, and its purpose is to see to it that the development of the EC conforms to the requirements of the Treaty of Rome. It has considerable autonomy in matters of competition, trade policy, and agriculture. It issues recommendations and opinions to the Council with the view to having the Council adopt binding regulations or directives to enforce compliance, specifically with regard to competition issues. The Commission has taken the lead in forcing compliance with the objectives of the Treaty of Rome, e.g., that the EC act as a cohesive force for the common good of the Member States rather than in their own national interests. The Commission has gradually accrued more power and responsibility since the 1980s, primarily as a result of decisions of the Court of Justice.

The **European Court of Justice** sits in Luxembourg and is the highest court in the EC. Its purpose is to interpret the Treaty of Rome and enforce its decisions on the Member States.

These bodies continue to serve in the present European Union.

By 1986, the EC had grown to 12 member states.[4] The European Union came into existence with the Treaty of Maastricht, signed in 1992. By 1995, the addition of Austria, Sweden, and Finland brought the number of countries in the EU to 15. In 2004, ten more countries were admitted.[5] By 2007, the total membership had risen to 27 with the addition of Bulgaria and Romania. Included in the purposes of the community are increased economic stability, expansion of economic activities, securing an improved standard of living, and the creation of a genuine, barrier-free internal market with the restoration and enhancement of the competitiveness of European industry. The key to realizing these goals was competition.

The Treaty of Rome and Air Transportation

The cornerstone of the dream of a unified Europe was that a reliable, common transportation system exist for the moving of people and goods. The Treaty of Rome incorporated this realization into Articles 85 and 86, which required the implementation of a common transport policy within the Community. Nevertheless, when the Council in 1962 adopted Regulation 17, which implemented those provisions of the Treaty, both air and sea transport were exempted.

The EC went further in 1968 and adopted a broad transportation policy applicable to commercial rail, road, and inland waterways, but not to sea and air transport. Air transportation policy within the EC was a difficult issue since each of the member states had, since of the Chicago Convention of 1944, regularly entered into bilateral agreements with other countries around the world. In addition, the airlines of Europe were heavily subsidized by their separate governments. They were generally understood to be and were treated as public utilities, and were considered part and parcel of the national image projected by the government. There was, therefore, very little progress made in the area of air transportation policy prior to 1986.

The Treaty of Rome also incorporated into Articles 85 and 86 specific provisions prohibiting anticompetitive activities and policies in the field of transportation by Member States. It was realized that any true integration of European economies would be impossible unless and until barriers to the smooth flow of commerce between them were removed.

By the middle of the 1980s, the competition rules of the Treaty of Rome had been applied to other forms of transportation and to virtually all other areas of commerce. Within the international aviation community, pressure had been building for some time to apply these rules to commercial aviation. The fact was that commercial aviation in the European Community had been left out of the integration that had proceeded with all other forms of commerce. At the same time, the Community found it hard to ignore the competitive effects of deregulation in the United States as U.S. airlines adopted policies and procedures in the running of their companies that produced more efficient operations, reduced overhead, and allowed reduced rates and fares. While some of the harsher realities of deregulation that had occurred in the United States were closely evaluated in Europe, it was realized by all concerned that Europe was going to have to compete with these American airlines on the international scene sooner or later.

Endnotes

1. http://www.loc.gov/exhibits/marshall/m9.html
2. http://www.loc.gov/exhibits/marshall/m12.html
3. France, Luxembourg, Italy, West Germany, Belgium, and the Netherlands.
4. In addition to the Six, there now was Ireland, Greece, Denmark, the United Kingdom, Spain, and Portugal.
5. Cyprus, Czech Republic, Estonia, Hungary, Latvia, Lithuania, Malta, Poland, Slovakia, and Slovenia.

CHAPTER 39

American Deregulation and the European Union

© Alex Staroseltsev, 2008, Shutterstock.

The sudden abrogation by the United States Congress of economic regulation of American airlines in 1978 caught the world by surprise. The air carrier industry worldwide, for practically its entire existence, had been operating under the benevolent supervision of national governments. But in the United States, although air carriers were subject to the economic control of the Civil Aeronautics Board, they operated within a greater free enterprise system that reflected the philosophy of the national government and American heritage. In Europe, governments after World War II largely embraced socialist economic philosophy and policies. Conceptually, the complete removal of all government economic control of the air carrier industry was a more difficult hurdle for Europeans than for Americans.

Airline management in the United States after deregulation was quick to embrace the competition of the free market. The competitive spirit had been there all along, as demonstrated by the rivalry between American Airlines and United Airlines during the 1970s, as they fought for market share even under CAB constraints. After deregulation, U.S. airlines simply joined the ranks of most other American businesses and operated under the same national laws that governed everybody else. Competition, after all, was what the American economy was all about.

In Europe, on the other hand, national governments were quite less ready to accept full free market principles in most economic endeavors. Philosophical concerns of government typically ran to issues of citizen welfare, access to medical treatment, worker benefits and other social entitlements, not to the state of competition in routine business affairs. With the prospect of privatization of air transport, all of these social concerns were present. Added to these concerns was anxiety over the loss of government control in directing the future of their airlines as organs of national influence.

Moreover, the demonstrated economic turmoil, bankruptcy, and labor strife that American deregulation had unleashed in the United States presented a foreboding view of the future under deregulation, and constituted another justification for European pause. The countries of Europe and the institutions of the EC debated the pros and cons of deregulation and its effect on the greater economy. Their approach was one of caution. The consensus generally formed was that air transport should be more the object of a policy of "liberalization" of regulation than an "abrogation" of regulation. And the discussion dragged on.

Then there was the matter of national diversity. The history of Europe through the first half of the twentieth century is a history of

331

conflict based largely on nationality or allegiances. European wars were the historical rule, not the exception. But after World War II, Europeans began to believe that things could be different. The countries that made up the EEC had agreed in the Treaty of Rome to embark on a more enlightened path for the future of Europe; cooperation and free competition, without national constraints, was the course set to be followed. But when it came to implementing the vision, old habits proved hard to break. National interests proved difficult to ignore, particularly given the history of the continent. Progress was slow.

In short, the United States was far more prepared to deal with the radical idea of economic deregulation of the airlines (read free competition) than were the states of Europe. Still, the Treaty of Rome had been signed and ratified; it was the law. It had been the law, in fact, for over 20 years when American deregulation came along in 1978. The institutions of the European Community had been set up, and they were staffed and operating. Many of those who had been charged with making the EC a reality were serious about their charge, and none more so than those within the European Commission.

Liberalization of Air Transport in the European Community

During the first twenty years of the EC, the European Council was unable to come to any consensus as to how to break down the State-sponsored anticompetitive barriers and practices that characterized European airlines, even though this was clearly its mandate. The European Commission, chafing at the lack of movement in this area, began the "liberalization" process with its Memorandum No. 1 in 1979, which dealt primarily with the existence of high tariffs between Member States. The Commission does not have authority to enact binding regulations, but only proposes to the Council, which has that authority. The Com-

mission, therefore, used the "Memorandum" vehicle as a gentle prod to the Council.

When the Council had failed to take action by 1984, the Commission published its Memorandum No. 2. This position paper was an expansion of the positions taken in Memorandum No. 1, and contained further, comprehensive proposals aimed at breaking down anticompetitive practices in air transportation among the Member States. The paper dealt with the intransigence of Member States in implementing Common Market unification strategies required by the Treaty of Rome, and emphasized the need for a unified European Community position in view of the effects of deregulation in the United States.

Further, between the Commission's Memorandum No. 1 and Memorandum No. 2, the Parliament brought an action against the Council in the European Court of Justice seeking a declaration that the Council had failed in its duty to act in promoting a common transportation policy. While the decision of the Court of Justice was wide-ranging, the decision did agree that the Council had effectively eschewed its responsibilities regarding air transport. With the rendering of this opinion of the Court of Justice, the Council had effectively been chastised by all three of the other EC institutions.

In April 1986, the European Court of Justice rendered its decision in the case of *Nouvelles Frontieres.*[1] This decision removed any remaining doubt that air transport was subject to the competition rules of the Treaty of Rome. The court held, in effect, that if the Council failed to act on competition issues, the Commission could issue a "reasoned decision" under Article 89 that would have the effect of putting competition issues into litigation for resolution. This decision constituted an "end run" around the Council, giving the Commission direct means to address the issue of competition in air transport matters.

Strengthened by *Nouvelles Frontieres,* later in 1986 the Commission sent letters to ten European airlines alleging that they had violated the anticompetitive provisions of the Treaty of

Rome by price fixing, capacity limitations, and various other practices. In due course, negotiations between the carriers and the Commission led to the implementation of restrictions of some of these anticompetitive practices for the first time.

After years of stagnation regarding the question of "liberalization" in the European air transport industry, things were now beginning to happen. The Single European Act,[2] an agreement ratified by the Member States in February 1986, and which went into force on July 1, 1987, effectively laid the necessary groundwork for the creation of the European Union. Its intendment was to finally create a true internal market in the Community, one in which restrictions on the movement of goods, services, people, and capital were eliminated. Additionally, by its amendment of the voting procedures used within the European Council (it eliminated single state veto and mandated majority vote), the Council was freed from its preexisting paralysis on a number of issues, including the issue of a common transport policy regarding aviation. No longer could one Member State veto action by the Council. No longer could minority bickering between nations within the twelve-member Council thwart the efforts of the majority toward full integration of Member States and the elimination of frontiers. At last, the Treaty of Rome had teeth.

Advent of the European Union

Although it had taken 30 years to accomplish, by 1987 the basis for broad European cooperation had finally been achieved. It had taken the separate efforts of all of the EC institutions to make it happen: the Commission, by its Memorandum No. 1 and Memorandum No. 2; the Parliament, by its civil action against the Council; the European Court of Justice, by its decision in the **Nouvelles Frontieres** case; and finally, the Single European Act. Henceforth, national autonomy would take a back seat to the unity of the European Union.

Competition Rules in Air Transport

Now it was the turn of the Council to take the leading role in implementing the goal of full economic integration by restructuring air transport policies. The Council, in 1987, adopted regulations (the Competition Rules) designed to apply the rules of competition, mandated by the Treaty of Rome, to scheduled air transport. These regulations applied only between Member States, not to internal domestic traffic nor to operations between a Member State and a non-Member State. Air transport operations to third-party states were, and had been, controlled by bilateral agreement beginning after the Chicago Convention in 1944.

The Council regulations came in three phases, or "packages" as they were called, between 1987 and 1993. The third set of regulations, effective on January 1, 1993, effectively satisfied the goal of air transport liberalization mandated by the Treaty of Rome. This group of regulations dealt with the important issues of fares, market factors (slot allocations, capacity, etc.), computer reservation systems, ground handling, cargo services, mergers, and subsidies.

In addition, by 1993 there had already begun a trend toward privatization of national airlines. British Airways was the first of the national airlines to privatize, in 1987, followed by Icelandair, and others were well on the way to privatization, like KLM (39 percent government owned), Sabena (53 percent), SAS (50 percent), Lufthansa (48 percent). Still others, like Air France, Iberia, and Olympic remained wholly government owned, but the trend toward privatization had been started. By the end of 2002, KLM and Iberia were fully privatized. Privatization among other international airlines is shown in Figure 39-1.

Predation and Merger

The Council's competition rules are mainly enforced by the Commission. Commission investigations of predation and mergers can be compared to those of the United States Department of Justice. With respect to mergers, the EU and the United States agreed in 1991 to coordinate their activities so as to reduce the likelihood of significant discrepancies existing in their anti-competition rules and policies regarding transatlantic mergers and acquisitions.[3]

Government Subsidies

Economic Issues Affecting Competition

National airlines of the European countries had been the object of national pride, support, and ownership for many decades, as discussed above. Under the new regulations of the Council effective in 1993, however, subsidization of national airlines was recognized to be a major problem and impedi-

ment to the goal of free competition within the EU. Still, such a long-standing and venerable practice was a difficult subject for the Commission to approach. In 1994, the Commission adopted a complex set of "guidelines" as a statement of policy, and a basis for potential enforcement, on the subject of government aid of airlines.

The guidelines apply not only to carriers but to the operations "accessory to air transport." These activities would include flight schools, duty-free shops, and airport facilities. **Notably, aircraft manufacturing subsidies were not included in the guidelines, an omission that effectively removed any consideration of the consortium Airbus Industrie from**

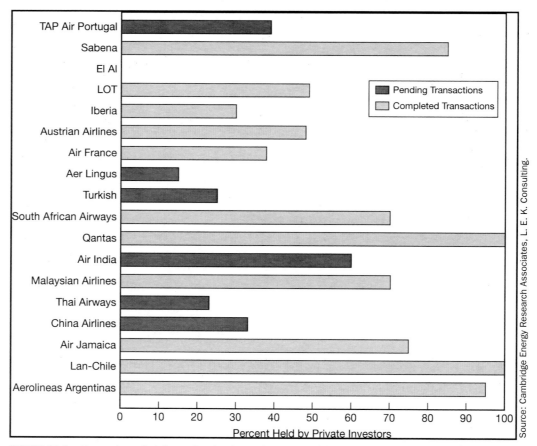

FIGURE 39-1 Examples of airline privatizations since the 1980s.

the policy of non-subsidy.[4] State aid to airports and funds for new airport construction were also not included in the scope of the guidelines.

The thrust of the rules governing subsidies is to prevent any operator from achieving a competitive advantage over any other operator based in the EU countries. The guidelines recognized at least five types of government aid that would be objectionable and contrary to the purpose of the EU. Direct operational subsidies are the most obvious and flagrant form of state aid. Aid in the form of state "investment" came under scrutiny by the Commission and became subject to evaluation using certain tests and criteria to determine if the aid is really "direct subsidy" in disguise. Other forms of state aid may include:

➡ capital injection
➡ loan financing
➡ loan guarantees
➡ the granting of exclusive rights

Noneconomic Issues

The EU institutions have also assumed responsibility for certain noneconomic issues that have direct bearing on air transport. Included in these issues are:

➡ Air traffic control
➡ Noise
➡ Carrier liability
➡ Accident investigation

Air Traffic Control

In 1961, the European Economic Community (EEC) was composed of just the original six members. Air traffic control after World War II had been the responsibility of each of their individual national governments. One of the first attempts at consolidation by the EEC was the coordination of air traffic within their severely restricted airspace. Beginning that year, the EEC created the agency known as EUROCONTROL, which took charge of air traffic control over the greater part of Europe.

In 1999, almost 40 years after establishment of the EEC, the European Commission recommended changes to EUROCONTROL that would bring about a more unified and efficient air traffic control system. By 1999, the organization had grown to 15 Member States, and the EEC had become the substantial sovereign entity known as the European Union. One of the recommended changes to the operation of EUROCONTROL was the creation of the concept known as "Single European Sky."

Later in this chapter we will review the historical evolution of EUROCONTROL, the transition of air traffic control under the Single European Sky concept and the proposed development of a satellite-based air traffic control system.

Noise Limitations

Reduction of noise levels on and around airports worldwide has received much attention. Excellent progress has been made in this area as decibel levels of operating aircraft have progressively been reduced and as land use management and other methods of noise reduction have been adopted. Europe's urban concentrations have made airport noise limitation a critical issue, and the EU has been aggressive in this area. Some EU practices, however, have caused consternation to foreign carriers and their governments. It is alleged, for instance, that the EU noise restrictions adopted by the Council have been applied in order to manage and restrict market access to foreign aircraft manufacturers, notably in the United States (Boeing). The argument is made that such restrictions are actually a form of "protectionism" for Airbus Industrie. These arguments note that EU noise limitations are significantly more limiting than ICAO standards.

Air-Carrier Liability

Until recently, air-carrier liability was governed by the terms of the Warsaw Convention of 1929, as modified by subsequent protocols and voluntary carrier agreements. A complete overhaul of the system was completed in 1999 (the Montreal Convention of 1999), and it entered into force as of November 4, 2003, among ratifying nations.[5] In 1997, the European Council adopted regulations that defined carrier liability of EU operators, increasing their potential liability (100,000 SDRs). These regulations are mandatory for EU-based operators but non-EU operators may exempt themselves from their operation through tariff clauses if notice to passengers is properly given.

Accident Investigation

In 1994, the Council adopted regulations designed to harmonize accident investigations within the EU, and outside the EU in some circumstances, by providing guidelines and requirements to be observed by Member States. National governments have had responsibility under the Chicago Convention for coordinating investigations of air crashes and incidents for fifty years. The action by the Council standardizes the procedures and requires reports to be filed with the Commission.

Aviation Agencies of the European Union

The European Civil Aviation Conference (ECAC)

The European Civil Aviation Conference is an independent body of 42 Member States that is closely integrated with ICAO, as anticipated by Article 55 (a) of the Chicago Convention. ECAC was founded in 1955 at the behest of the fledgling European Council to be to the pan-European states what ICAO is to the entire world. As ECAC has matured over the period of one-half century, its functions have been expanded, and it has become the only Europe-wide organization with the membership and expertise capable of responding to the complex needs of the European air transport industry.

ECAC's stated objectives include the promotion of continued development of a safe, efficient, and sustainable European air transport system that seeks to harmonize civil aviation policies and practices among its member states and the major industrialized countries of the world. It has become the essential forum for discussions of every major civil aviation topic and regularly conducts seminars and international symposia on various issues. It concerns itself with the environment, noise, accident investigation, security, immigration, certification, and airport policy and land-use management.

ECAC works closely with the European Commission in aviation affairs and is funded by the European Council. The aviation safety responsibilities of ECAC are currently carried out by the Joint Aviation Authorities and by its successor organization, the European Aviation Safety Agency (EASA).

The European Joint Aviation Authorities (JAA)

JAA was organized in 1970 as a group of civil aviation authorities from separate European states, formed to cooperate in producing "Joint Airworthiness Requirements" (JARs) for certification of aircraft and other products jointly produced in Europe and to facilitate the export and import of such products between European States. Since 1989, JAA as an organization has been cohesively associated as a body with ECAC and is charged with taking care of the regulatory activities in aviation safety under the oversight of ECAC. The ECAC itself concentrates on policy issues, security, and the environment as they relate to civil aviation.

JAA's primary function is to ensure that JAA Member States achieve a consistent level of aviation safety through the cooperation of its members. It expects to coordinate the transition of such activities from JAA to a permanent European Union agency responsible for all civil aviation safety to be known as the European Aviation Safety Agency (EASA) upon final approval by the European Council. EASA became operational in 2003 and will ultimately be responsible for rule-making, certification, and standardization of rules to be applied by the national aviation authorities.

JAA has developed and adopted Joint Aviation Requirements (JARs) in the areas of aircraft design and manufacture, aircraft operations and maintenance, and the licensing of aviation personnel. It also develops administrative and technical procedures for the implementation of JARs once they are adopted. Since 1996, for instance, JAA has had the responsibility of running the Safety Assessment for Foreign Aircraft (SAFA) program for ECAC. While ICAO has undertaken the overall role of developing and implementing safety standards worldwide, SAFA is an ECAC program that complements ICAO based on a "bottoms up" approach. Under this program, JAA conducts ramp inspections of aircraft throughout its Member States utilizing Standards of ICAO Annexes 1 (Personnel Licensing), 2 (Operations of Aircraft), and 3 (Airworthiness of Aircraft).

Since 2000, JAA has had a fully operational database, completely computerized, which is the repository for all reports completed as a result of the ramp inspections Europewide. In 2001, 25 states performed 2,706 inspections, up from 75 inspections in 1996. JAA action taken as a result of these inspections ranges from simple discussions with aircraft commanders concerning minor items to grounding of the aircraft until corrective action is taken for serious violations. Notification of the responsible Civil Aviation Authority of the aircraft's home country usually follows the notation of a violation. In repeated or egregious cases, entry permits of the aircraft operator may be revoked.

JAA seeks to maintain a high level of cooperation and coordination with the FAA in the United States, and more recently with the appropriate safety regulatory authorities of Russia and other former communist countries that now have joined the JAA, as well as with Canada, Japan, Australia, and others. With respect to the FAA, JAA says that it seeks to harmonize the relationship between FARs and JARs as they relate, particularly, to:

1. Design and manufacture, operation and maintenance of civil aircraft and related products and parts
2. Noise and emissions from aircraft and aircraft engines
3. Flight crew licensing

JAA has been regarded as the European equivalent of the FAA, and, in many respects, that is an accurate comparison. The JAA has been criticized by the United States, however, as having a protectionist agenda, that is, it has adopted regulations for the express purpose of promoting European aviation to the detriment of competitors from outside of the EU, particularly the United States. In June 1997, for instance, the JAA attempted to adopt rules that would have required flight training for European pilots to be conducted at flight schools that are 51 percent owned by Europeans. Although this requirement was dropped after objection by United States interests, the new regulation still severely restricts flight training at facilities outside of the EU countries, and makes it difficult to convert a license issued by the FAA into one acceptable under the JAA regulation. This regulation was justified by the JAA on the basis of safety, although even a cursory analysis of the rationale will disclose that basis to be a sham. It is a unilateral trade restriction designed to promote European flight schools to the detriment of similar schools located in the United States.

As to the function of JAA coordinating with foreign safety regulatory authorities, like the FAA, on the certification of products and services, JAA has made the process of securing its approval of U.S. manufactured products very difficult. Approval by JAA is a requirement before any such American product can be exported to Europe. The approval is designed to be a validation of FAA or other certification, not a new and complete recertification regimen imposed by the JAA. Allegations have been lodged that JAA is abusing this validation process to delay or prevent sales of U.S. aviation products in Europe. One example cited is the difficulty the Gulfstream V has had in securing JAA approval for sale in Europe, difficulty that has resulted in years of delay and the expenditure of millions of dollars. Another example is the Cessna X, which required in excess of four years and the expenditure of $3 million to secure JAA approval. In order for a new aircraft type manufactured in the U.S, and certified by the FAA, to be approved for export to Europe, JAA review requires as much as 52 percent of the time it took the FAA to certify the new type in the first place. This compares with 15 to 17 percent of the time the FAA takes to certify foreign aircraft for sale in the United States.[6]

These JAA practices will need to be monitored in the future. Other difficulties for U.S. manufacturers concern extreme noise limitations for aircraft operations in the EU. Whether JAA approval practices will change upon the transition to the permanent body, EASA, remains to be seen. These European practices may create trade issues that transcend anything previously experienced in world aviation commerce, and may have ramifications that affect the overall global aviation market. At a minimum, these practices violate the spirit of international trade agreements and impair the promise of the global market place. These practices by the EU, termed "Regulatory Nationalism," are receiving increasing scrutiny by United States government authorities.[7]

The European Commission works closely with JAA to facilitate the requirements of JARs becoming law through EU legislation, so that they become legally binding on EU member states. Funding of JAA activities comes from Member States' contributions (56 percent), income from the sale of publications and training (28 percent), and user charges or EU grants. Member States' contributions are based on a proportional system using the size of the member's aviation industry as the index. Under this system, some 52 percent of such member contributions come from France, Germany, and the United Kingdom.

As of January 1, 2007, the JAA entered an official "transition" phase designed to mark the absorption of JAA functions into EASA. The former JAA is now known as JAA-T, or JAA in Transition. Combining the offices of JAA with EASA in Cologne, Germany, began on March 1, 2007.

European Aviation Safety Agency (EASA)

EASA became operational in 2003 under European Parliament and Council authority. It is an independent EU body accountable to the Member States and the EU institutions. Its responsibility is aviation safety and aviation's impact on the environment. The agency promulgates safety and environmental rules applicable to the entire EU aviation community.

EASA's main tasks include:

➡ Rule-making, that is, drafting safety legislation for the European Commission

➡ Standardization programs and inspections to insure uniform implementation of EU aviation safety legislation in all Member States

➡ Type certification of aircraft, engines, and parts

➡ Data collection, analysis, and research to improve aviation safety

→ EASA is scheduled to expand its role in European aviation safety in 2008 by extending is rule-making authority to civil aviation operations, licensing of crews within the EU, certification of non member States airlines, as well as playing a key role in the safety regulation of airports.

→ The agency is also developing close working relationships with safety organizations in other countries (like the FAA) and with ICAO with the goal of harmonizing safety standards and procedures.

EASA will eventually take over all of the functions of JAA.

European Air Traffic Control

By 2007, EUROCONTROL had grown in size to include 37 countries, and now is comprised of most of the Member States of the EU, only Latvia and Estonia being non-members. Countries outside of the EU are also members, extending from Turkey in the east to Ukraine to Norway. Notably, Iceland is not a member.

EUROCONTROL was a marked improvement over the existing systems of the 1950s, but with increasing activity and congestion, by the 1990s EUROCONTROL was under scrutiny by the European Council. Traffic flow regimens were still mostly national, not European, and EUROCONTROL operation was divided among five regional flow management centers, all separately operated by their own national administrations.

The European Commission proposed inaugurating a new and unified control system that would operate independently of any national government control. This new system has been dubbed "Single European Sky" (SES).

SES is an ambitious initiative to reform the architecture of European air traffic control and to meet future capacity and safety needs. In 2004, the Council and the European Parliament endorsed the Single European Sky legislation that will integrate all European air traffic control in the European Community. A package of four regulations is included in this enabling legislation.

1. The framework regulation: This sets out the overall objectives for the Single European Sky initiative—"to enhance current safety standards and overall efficiency for general air traffic in Europe, to optimize capacity meeting the requirements of all airspace users and to minimize delays."

2. The airspace regulation: This concerns the use and organization of airspace, both for the civil and military requirements of Member States.

3. The service provision regulation: This mandates that common standards are to be applied for all navigation services provided.

4. The interoperability regulation: This looks to insure the integration of all systems from whatever source. The systems include eight areas: airspace management, air traffic flow management, air traffic services, communications, navigation, surveillance, aeronautical information services, and meteorological information.

This is a work in progress. The final product will include the standardization of air traffic systems across Europe, the common licensing of air traffic controllers, and the reconfiguration of European airspace into functional blocks irrespective of national borders. EUROCONTROL's function within the transition framework has not been fully decided, but its participation will be essential to a successful completion of this program.

SESAR (Single European Sky ATM Research Program)

Air Traffic Management (ATM) is a concept much the same as Air Traffic Control (ATC) in the United States. Like ATC, Europe has struggled to keep up with increasing demands imposed on the system by burgeoning passenger numbers.

SESAR might be compared to the NextGen program in the United States, and, like the Joint Planning and Development Office (JDPO), the planning segment of NextGen in the U.S., it is a forward-looking program that involves all of the entities that operate within the air transport system. These include civil and military agencies of government, legislators, industry, operators, and users. These entities will be central to the defining, committing to, and implementing of a pan-European ATM system.

The SESAR program is separated into three sequential phases into the future:

Definition Phase (2005–1008)

Development Phase (2008–2013)

Deployment Phase (2014–2020)

During the first phase, a European Master Plan will be presented. In the second, work will be based on the results of the definition phase, will build the future air traffic control system, and will synchronize plans for deployment and implementation. During the third phase, the plan and the development phases will come together for implementation.

SESAR will incorporate the European Global Navigation Satellite System (GNSS) known as Galileo, into the ATM system to be launched. Details of the manner and means by which the new system will operate have not been disclosed, but it might be presumed that it will evolve in a similar manner to the NextGen plan in the United States. Part of the U.S. plan, in fact, is to reach out to the global community so that the several systems now on the drawing boards might be developed with the requirements of the others in mind. It makes sense that these satellite-based air traffic control systems be compatible to the extent possible so that the globalization of the air transport system will extend, not only to marketing and governmental policy developments, like deregulation and open-skies, but to operational considerations, like air traffic control, to enhance the seamless transition of air transport operations over the globe.

The Case for Convergence[8]

Almost from page one in this book, we have seen that the North American continent and the European continent have been in a more or less symbiotic relationship since colonial times. They were at the forefront of the Industrial Revolution, and the advances and progress of that great movement were shared. In aviation, these two geographic areas moved forward together; sometimes in competition and sometimes in cooperation.

We now see that these two continents together represent 70 percent of the world Gross National Product. Trade between the United States and the EU comprises 40 percent of total world trade, and air traffic on transatlantc routes make up 60 percent of the global aviation market. A new Open Skies treaty has been signed as of April 2007 which deregulates commercial air transport between the United States and the European Union countries. Now they each are about to enter a new world of air transportation based on space technology.

There appears to be no insurmountable reason that both GPS, in the American system, and Galileo, in the Eurpean system, cannot talk to each other. Or, at least, their representatives can talk to each other. Since both systems will, no doubt, be based on the Required Navigation Performance System, which requires onboard capabilites for aircraft to function within it, it seems imperative that the two systems be, in that regard, compatible.

This intercontinental symbiosis should consist of three parts:

1. Air transport policy—This first layer contemplates a bridge between the EU and the United States. In this context there is a common understanding of the requirements in the greater global community of what drives the effort to achieve results that will be conducive to the greater good of the public.

2. Air Traffic Control—This essential element connects the air traffic control precedures and concepts of the United States FAA and European Eurocontrol or SES.

3. Private Enterprise—This layer involves industry-to-industry relations. Companies in the United States, like Boeing, Honeywell, and Rockwell Collins, are participating in the SESAR program with European companies. This brings antagonists like Boeing and Airbus face-to-face in a unified effort to bring a common benefit to the world population.

The point is this: The moving economic and political forces in the world are approaching a common understanding of the benefits available to all in the expansion of global commerce. As geopolitical forces give way to the economic power of a freed world population, and as the economic power of the corporate world is likewise freed from preexisting governmental restraints, we see that there exists a communality in these forces that will support a new day in the global air transport industry. Technological advances will enhance the efforts of private enterprise to provide a better system of air transportation, both within each of the two continents and between them. The transatlantic link between the continents will be the key to the growth of a viable global air transport industry, which will become less and less nationally oriented in the future. We can expect to see less identification with national interests and more of a realization of the communality between peoples of different nationalities and origins.

Summary

Entering the beginning of a new millenium, the EU was finally organized and configured to fulfill the broad goals originally set in the Treaty of Rome. The institutions of the EU had taken form and their relationships with each other were well-defined. The anticompetitive policies of the EU and its predecessor organizations had given way and the competition rules were in place. The national airlines of Europe were continuing to be privatized. Europe was finally positioned to deal with American deregulation of civil air transportation and the coming era of globalization of the world economy.

Endnotes

1. Minestere Public v. Lucas Asjes, 3 C.L.R. 173, Eur. Ct. R. 1425.

2. Common Mkt. Rep. (CCH) p. 202.7 (1978).

3. Agreement Between the Government of the United States of America and the Commission of the European Communities Regarding Application of Their Competition Laws, 1995 O. J. (L95) 47.

4. The Airbus Industrie v. Boeing struggle will be discussed in chapter 43.

5. See discussion in chapter 37.

6. Lipinski, William O., An Evaluation of the U.S.—EU Trade Relationship <http://www.house.gov./lipinski/aviation.htm>

7. *Competition in the U.S. Aircraft Manufacturing Industry*, Testimony before the Subcommittee on Aviation of the Committee on Transportation and Infrastructure, U.S. House of Representatives, July 26, 2001, U.S. Government Printing Office.

8. This section will incorporate the arguments and observations of Victor Aguado, director general of Eurocontrol.

Global Deregulation Takes Off

© Johnny Kuo, 2008, Shutterstock.

Worldwide, the air transport industry is a major factor in the economic health of nations.

There are some 900 airlines the world over, and they operate nearly 22,000 aircraft. Over 2 billion passengers travel on the world's airlines, with projections for 2.3 billion enplanements by the year 2010. Over 40 percent of the world's manufactured exports travel by air, and in 2006 the air transport industry provided, directly and indirectly, 29 million jobs for the global workforce.[1] North American airlines carry about 40 percent of the world's air passengers, with European carriers accounting for 26 percent and the Asia/Pacific region's airlines at 24 percent. Latin American, Middle Eastern, and African carriers account for the remainder.

The aviation transport industry generates wealth, employment, taxes, tourism, and related benefits for each nation with a viable air transport system. It is obvious, therefore, that it is in the national interest of such countries to be and remain competitive in the global air transport market. As we have seen, the airline industry has historically been regulated internally by their home governments and, except for the United States, state-owned airlines have been the general rule. Regulation of international air transport has been accomplished as a part of international relations, primarily by means of the bilateral agreement format between nations. Prior to the Airline Deregulation Act of 1978 in the United States, therefore, regulation by governments around the world, supplemented by the traffic coordination activities of the International Air Transport Association (IATA), had maintained a more or less stable international marketing environment.

For more than a quarter of a century in the United States, the cost benefits to air travelers and shippers directly attributable to the competitive influences of deregulation have become apparent. The numbers of enplanements and the number of flights have been greatly increased as many more people have taken to the air as the primary means of travel. These benefits have come at a price, however, in the form of bankruptcies of air carriers, losses to labor in the form of wages and benefits, and inconvenience and delays to air travelers. Nevertheless, the domestic air transport policy of the United States government of a free and competitive air carrier system has been clearly extended to the international arena. That policy was officially announced in 1992 by the Department of Transportation to be one of Open Skies.

Open Skies, as articulated by the United States, embraces full deregulation of international air transportation. This concept includes:

1. Unrestricted access to airlines to operate between international gateways by way of any point and beyond to any point (outside of the destination country) at the discretion of airline management

2. Unrestricted service opportunities, so that airlines are free to decide the frequency, capacity, and equipment necessary to service market demand

3. Freedom of airlines to set prices

Still not included as a part of Open Skies are cabotage rights (freedom to serve domestic traffic within the United States from another U.S. city) and foreign control of U.S. airlines (this maintains the current limitation of foreign ownership of U.S. carriers).[2]

The policy of the United States, as established by the Department of Transportation and the State Department, does support liberalization of long-standing cabotage rules and the 70-year-old policy restricting foreign ownership of U.S. airlines. The U.S. Congress, on the other hand, has failed to approve any change in these constraints to full deregulation. In 2006, in fact, the United States Congress was still opposed to increasing foreign ownership of U.S. airlines.[3] This disagreement over the future of airline deregulation is an example of the Constitutional separation of powers. In this case, the rift pits the policy-making perogatives of the Executive Branch against the law-making perogatives of the Legislative Branch.

The administration's policy also calls for the end of subsidies by foreign governments of national airlines, including state ownership, protectionism, or financial assistance of any kind, since these activities produce market-distorting results in a competitive system.

Within the European Unions, the separate governments of the Member States insisted on retaining their individual rights to negotiate and enter into bilateral traffic agreements as they chose, particularly with the United States. The European Commission, on the other hand, insisted that the right to negotiate and sign international traffic agreements lay with the EU, not the individual Member States.

Relying on its prior success at consolidating powers, the Commission in 1995 began to lobby hard for authority to regulate all Bilaterals affecting the EU nations. Neil Kinnock, the former British Laborite, as the Transport Commissioner threatened to bring the issue before the European Court of Justice. When that threat failed, the Commission sued six Member States.[4] That litigation was halted by agreement, but when Member States continued to pursue unilateral talks with the United States on the terms of Bilaterals, the Commission again sued, this time adding Germany and the United Kingdom.[5]

A standoff ensued on this issue in the EU. After Kinnock was replaced by Loyola de Palacio as Transport Commissioner, this issue appeared to have been relegated to secondary importance, and EU Member States continued to negotiate directly with the United States in Open Skies Bilaterals. France and the United States, for instance, signed an Open Skies agreement in January 2002, which contained the standard freedoms enumerated above.

In 2002, however, the European Court of Justice ruled that the practice of EU Member States negotiating Bilaterals directly with the United States was incompatible with EU law. The Court did not, however, strike down the existing Bilaterals, so international traffic continued under those preexisting agreements.

In addition to Open Skies bilateral agreements between countries, the United States advocates and approves strategic sharing alliances between U.S. carriers and foreign carriers under "antitrust immunity" agreements with those carriers. Under this arrangement, the alliance partners are free to set prices and to otherwise combine their resources in order to maximize marketing strategies that insure to the benefit of the international traveling public. These alliances have produced significant results.

According to the DOT,[6] implementation of alliances under Open Skies agreements has resulted in increases in passenger traffic numbers, decreases in prices, and the tapping of entirely new segments of populations that are now availing themselves of international air travel for the first time. Travelers from "behind European gateways" who had never been serviced in the transatlantic market were of particular note.

The First Multilateral Open Skies Agreement

On November 15, 2000, agreement was reached between the United States and four of its aviation partners for a comprehensive liberalization of aviation services: the first multilateral Open Skies agreement. Brunei, Chile, New Zealand, and Singapore, countries from diverse areas of the globe, agreed with the United States to unrestricted service by the airlines of each country to, from, and beyond the other's territory, as well as unrestricted destinations, routes, number of flights, and prices charged. This agreement promises to become a model for future arrangements with other countries under the United States concept of international competition.

Deregulation and the United Kingdom

In contrast to the apparent worldwide move toward liberalization, efforts to secure agreement with the U.K. failed, and the restrictions in the current bilateral agreement between the United States and Britain, known as Bermuda 2, are severe. Bermuda 2 was signed 30 years after the original agreement between these countries,[7] and while the new agreement relaxed some of the requirements and restrictions of the original pact, air transportation between the two countries remains heavily constrained. This "anachronistic agreement," as labeled by the Secretary of Transportation,[8] still limits the number of cities in the two countries that can be served, the number of airlines that can serve the market, the fares that can be charged, and the level of service that can be provided. Under Bermuda 2, for instance, only American Airlines and United Airlines are allowed to serve Heathrow airport.[9]

According to the DOT, the U.K. position is nothing other than protectionism of British Airways, which opposes entry into the world of free and fair competition. The effect of the British position has created a degree of British isolation in an increasingly progressive European aviation community.

Breakthrough—Open Skies Agreement between the United States and the European Union

The decision of the European Court of Justice in 2002, holding that Bilaterals between Member States and the United States were in violation of EU law, posed a significant problem for the EU States, as well as for the United States. It did, however, provide an opportunity to pressure the United Kingdom into finally seriously addressing the issue of globalization and relaxation of the constraints imposed by Bermuda 2.

In 2006, agreement was reached between negotiators for the U.S. and the E.U. for an Open Skies agreement for all EU Member States, including the U.K. Open Skies agreements are, technically, treaties between nations and, as such, in the United States these agreements must obtain Congressional approval. The Congress that year refused to approve the Open Skies agreement that had been negotiated, primarily on the basis that the agreement relaxed the law applicable to foreign ownership of U.S. airlines.

The negotiating teams went back to work, and in 2007, a new Open Skies agreement was reached, but this time the ownership rules were preserved, as well as historical cabotage restraints.[10] This new Agreement was signed on April 30, 2007, by the representatives of the EU and by the Department of State of the U.S. The Agreement was originally slated to go into effect in October, 2007, but due to objections posed by the U.K., the effective date has been moved back to March 30, 2008. This was, in part, to allow Heathrow airport to complete new terminal construction to enlarge its facilities in anticipation of the significant increases in traffic that the Agreement will cause.

The Agreement also contains exit provisions that will allow the EU to renounce the agreement in 2010 if the issues of cabotage and airline ownership are not liberalized. The Agreement will have to be approved by the Congress, but it is anticipated that, this time, the skies will be opened between the U.S. and the EU.

The EU has voiced one additional complaint. They say that the U.S. has the better part of the deal since U.S. airlines are permitted to fly into any EU country and then fly from that country into any other EU country. Although U.S. airlines may not fly from one point in any one country to another point in that same country, U.S. airlines do have a sort of cabotage right if the EU is considered a single sovereign entity. For instance, a U.S. airline will be permitted to land at Heathrow, pick up passengers and fly on to Paris, while an EU airline, landing at JFK, will not be permitted to proceed with passengers to Dallas, or any other U.S. city.

Summary

By 2007, the United States had concluded Open Skies agreements with 67 countries. The U.S.-EU agreement will increase that number even more. The leadership of the United States in promoting competition in international air transportation has yielded significant benefits to the international traveling public, and it has set the pattern for the expansion of a deregulated air transportation system across the globe.

Endnotes

1. *The Economic Benefits of Air Transport,* 2000 edition, The Air Transport Action Group, 33 Route de l'Aeroport, P.O. Box 49, 1215 Geneva 15, Switzerland.

2. In 2007, foreign ownership of U.S. airline companies is permitted to be in excess of 50 percent of voting and nonvoting stock, but only 25 percent of voting shares.

3. The first proposal for an Open Skies agreement with the European Union, which contained liberalization of foreign ownership rules, was voted down in the Congress even though is was supported by the Administration.

4. The countries sued were Austria, Belgium, Denmark, Finland, Luxembourg, and Sweden. Bruce Barnard, Kinnock Perseveres in Fight for EU-Wide Air Talks With U.S., J. Com., June 20, 1995, at 2B.

5. Dempsey, Paul, Competition in the Air: European Union Regulation of Commercial Aviation, *Journal of Air Law and Commerce,* Summer 2001.

6. U.S. Department of Transportation, International Aviation Developments—Global Deregulation Takes Off (First Report) December 1999; U.S. Department of Transportation, International Aviation Developments, Second Report—Transatlantic Deregulation—The Alliance Network Effect, October 2000.

7. The original Bermuda Agreement was signed in 1946.

8. Slater, Rodney, Testimony before the Aviation Subcommittee, U.S. House of Representatives, February 15, 2000.

9. United's transatlantic routes to Heathrow dated back to the days when Pan American was the only international U.S. carrier. These routes were sold by Pan American to United in 1989, just before Pan Am's liquidation.

10. Ownership of U.S. airlines is limited to 25 percent of voting stock in the airline. Cabotage, the prohibition for foreign airlines to carry revenue traffic between two U.S. cities, was also preserved.

CHAPTER 41

Global Aircraft Manufacturing

© egd, 2008, Shutterstock, Inc.

The preeminence that the United States enjoyed in commercial aviation at the end of World War II declined in almost direct proportion to the emergence of Europe as an economic world power. The consolidation of the energies and talents of the industrial leaders of Europe under the umbrella of cooperation first initiated by the Marshall Plan would have a direct and profound impact on the future of international aviation. The most remarkable part of this evolution was in the field of commercial airplane manufacture.

The great aircraft production companies of the United States, primarily Boeing, Douglas, McDonnell, and Lockheed, produced the world's most marketable commercial aircraft between 1933 and 1980. Others around the world made forays into this elite club of aircraft producers from time to time, but none remained competitive. The competition was between these American companies, and it was vigorous and constant. But it was mostly an American intramural contest.

European Aircraft Manufacturing

The most notable efforts at international competition for the American giants came from deHavilland (British) and Sud Aviation (French). American aircraft producers, for the most part,

produced aircraft in response to demand. This was true, for instance, with the 247, produced by Boeing for United Airlines, and then the DC series of airplanes produced by Douglas, first for TWA and then for American Airlines. It was the customers themselves, the airlines, that really drove the process of design. It was the airlines that were instrumental in setting the parameters and establishing the specifications for new aircraft. Usually, it was only when the broad outlines of needed aircraft types were supplied by the airlines did the imaginations and talents of engineers come into play. This was in keeping with the American free-enterprise system. Except for military aircraft, the extreme research and development costs of new aircraft were financed by the aircraft production companies, subject to the rules of supply and demand, and to the eternal truism that business could continue only so long as the company made a profit.

After World War II, therefore, American aircraft manufacturers were slow to convert commercial aircraft production to jets because the U.S. airlines did not believe that they would be profitable. Instead, American aircraft manufacturers produced airliners with bigger and bigger reciprocating engines, like the DC-6, DC-7, and the Constellation. Thus, the Americans almost gave away the game. As we have seen, the British manufacturer,

347

deHavilland, spearheaded the development of the commercial jet transport with the Comet in the early 1950s. deHavilland jumped out to a big technological lead in the new vibration-free commercial transport of the future, and it would have been a gigantic marketing success except for the pressure failures of the fuselage, which brought the company to grief and dashed the hopes of the English. That same failure gave the Americans time to catch up, and they did with the Boeing 707 and the Douglas DC-8.

In France, Sud Aviation of Toulouse emerged after World War II as the foremost exponent of civil air transport manufacture on the continent. Sud, with government money, developed the first rear-mounted jet engine in the Caravelle in 1957. The Caravelle would become the prototype for American designs later on, like the Boeing 727 and the DC-9. But the European aircraft companies did not prevail. Many factors made it difficult for any single European company, whether sponsored by its national government or not, to compete with the United States aircraft companies even two decades after World War II. America was possessed of vast resources, and its companies took advantage of them, whether natural, economic, or technological. America did not have to rebuild its infrastructure after the war; to the contrary, the industrial requirements placed on the United States by World War II had only made American industry stronger.

The leaders of Europe realized that the small nations of the continent would be better served by an overall different approach in the postwar period than had ever been taken before. The benefits obtained by the United States from the synergy of its varied geographical, technological, and industrial parts was obvious to Europeans. Europe's postwar cooperative effort is, most likely, the result of emulation of America's vast natural cooperative enterprise, but on an international, intra-European basis.

We have seen how the EEC came into existence with the Treaty of Rome in 1957, and we have followed its evolution thereafter. Aircraft manufacturing was part of the European vision even then.

The Concorde

Sud Aviation and deHavilland were the only two passenger jet manufacturers in the world in the middle of the 1950s when the British government set up the Supersonic Aircraft Committee, using both industry and government people to study the feasibility of commercial supersonic flight. By 1959, the Committee had concluded that supersonic flight was, indeed, a workable idea. Projections were made for technical goals, like aircraft speed, and for practical realities, like development costs and sales costs. The British government awarded contracts to begin research and development to Bristol Aircraft and to Hawker-Siddeley. Bristol Aircraft, along with English Electric and Vickers Aircraft, became the British Aircraft Corporation (BAC) in 1959. Hawker-Siddeley absorbed deHavilland, Blackburn Aircraft, and Folland Aircraft in 1960.

The French government was also very interested in the possibilities of supersonic commercial flight. With directives from the English and French governments to their national industry counterparts to cooperate, the companies undertook studies for a joint design. By 1962, the two governments were committed to the project, and the agreement for the collaborative effort was signed. The agreement provided that the two countries would share equally in the funding of the project, in the accomplishment of the work, and in the enjoyment of the benefits—a true joint venture in law. The project was entrusted to two English companies and two French companies. The airframe and fuselage components were the responsibility of the British Aircraft Corporation (BAC) and Sud Aviation. The jet engines were the responsibility of Rolls Royce and SNECMA, the latter a French mercantile combination.

Progress was slow and laborious. Language, culture, vision, standards of measurement (metric or English), and national pride were all impediments to progress. By 1964, a more or less workable form of cooperation had emerged, and the British version of a long-haul SST had been accepted. The French had prevailed on the name, "Concorde," rather than the English "Concord." The market for the Concorde, however, had not been established. Contrary to American practice, there were no known users for this technological marvel, although it was assumed that the national airlines of Britain (BEA and BOAC) and France (Air France) would certainly sign on. Juan Trippe, in 1963, ever the entrepreneur, the visionary, and adventurer, took out options for six Concordes in the name of Pan American Airways.

The other contenders in the supersonic transport (SST) research and development race were the United States and the U.S.S.R. The United States committed to funding 75 percent of the research and development costs, but further agreed to reimburse the working aircraft companies, Boeing and Lockheed, their 25 percent contribution if the project were cancelled. The United States, the U.S.S.R., and the Europeans (Britain and France) appeared in the late

1960s to be in a hotly contested race to produce the first SST. The American design was bigger and faster than Concorde. The American SST, while still existing only on paper, garnered 122 options, outpacing the Concorde, which had 74 options. In December 1967, the first Concorde test model (001) left its hanger at Sud Aviation in Toulouse. Shortly thereafter, the British contribution (002) was rolled out at the BAC plant at Filton, England.

The tangible existence of the Concorde, something that could be seen and touched (see Figure 41-1), caused options from airlines around the world to pick up significantly, including options taken out by some United States airlines. Japan Airlines and Lufthansa took options. But opposition to the new aircraft technology was picking up also. Environmental groups complained of probable ozone depletion, excessive noise levels, and sonic booms. Socialists believed Concorde was an elitist, capitalist project that was to be paid for by the worker. Controversy swirled, and enthusiasm waned.

The U.S.S.R. version, the TU-144, was proceeding in secret consistent with Soviet practices. The TU-144 was dubbed "Concordski"

FIGURE 41-1 Concorde.

Image Courtesy of Corel.

because of its remarkable resemblance to the design parameters of the Concorde, but it was actually slightly ahead of Concorde in the production schedule.

The burgeoning SST rivalry between America and Europe began to take on a cautionary, wary aspect. The debate on the SST was taking its toll, and the longer the debate went on, the more questions arose, until those in opposition to the project began to gain the upper hand, at least in the United States. In 1971, the United States Congress abruptly cancelled funding for the SST as too expensive, as well as too controversial. The United States had spent over $1 billion in the effort. Some felt that national pride had suffered; for this was the second time[1] that America had seemingly shirked its proper leadership role in a new technology. On the other hand, America had put men on the moon only two years before and brought them successfully home again. But conservative, rational thought prevailed, and for better or worse, commercial supersonic flight became a purely European affair.

The Concorde and Soviet SST both flew at the Paris Air Show in 1973. Competition, even enmity, between the two programs was exacerbated by the general Anglo-French belief that industrial espionage by the Soviets was the main reason that the TU-144 so closely matched their Concorde. As the TU-144 prepared for takeoff for its aerial display, it was reported that the French air controllers informed the Soviet pilots that their display time had been cut in half. The tower also failed to inform them that a French Mirage fighter would be closely shadowing the TU-144 while in flight. The TU-144 initiated a steep climb during its performance, rising several thousand feet within a few seconds, and it is speculated that when the Soviet pilot suddenly and unexpectedly saw the Mirage close by, he initiated an evasive maneuver that overstressed the SST. The TU-144 plummeted to earth, killing all on board and also eight people in a nearby French village. The cause of the crash was never the subject of complete agreement.

The Tu-144 went into service in December 1975 flying mail and freight, and in November 1977 in passenger service for Aeroflot. Aeroflot conducted only 55 passenger flights with the SST, the last of which was June 1, 1978.

Deliveries of the Concorde began in December 1975. Air France ultimately bought four and BOAC took five. But that was it. Pan American was the first to cancel its options in 1973. Things got worse for Concorde. Every single option taken out on the Concorde was, in turn, cancelled. The oil crisis of 1973 and the world recession delivered the *coup de grace* to the viability of the Concorde's commercial future. The price of the Concorde had soared from its first estimates (made in 1962) of $3 million to a prohibitive $47.5 million in 1974.

Tallying up the costs to the British and French governments was also a dismal undertaking. With only the national airlines of those two countries committed to the airplane, the losses were to be high. Not only that, but the much-vaunted prestige of the project, the European renaissance in aircraft manufacture, and the vanquishing of the American behemoths, was all going down in flames. In fact, the entire affair was beginning to look like a gigantic boondoggle.

Landing rights for the Concorde at the airports of the world were hard to come by. The problem of sonic booms limited its routes at supersonic speeds mainly to sparsely occupied lands or over the oceans. The engine noise on approach and takeoff was horrific. Another problem was its limited range. The Concorde could not make it to South Africa from Europe because no African nation would allow it to land for refueling. It could not land in the United States until 1976 in Washington, D.C., and until 1977 in New York. Soon after, service was terminated to Washington due to lack of traffic. The Concorde was proving to be a commercial failure.

Except for British Airways (BOAC and BEA merged to form BA in 1974) and Air France, the national airlines of the countries that paid to produce it, no Concorde was ever pur-

> 66 An aircraft which is used by wealthy people on their expense accounts, whose fares are subsidized by much poorer taxpayers. 77

Denis Healey, British Labour Party, regards the Concorde

chased by any other airline. The dream of reestablishing a European aircraft manufacturing presence in the world, fueled primarily by the French, was shattered. As commercial aviation stood at the brink of a revolution in mass transit, with aircraft becoming larger and with more seats, Concorde was flying the wrong way. Such a small, elite market could never sustain Concorde's costs.

To many, it looked like the American giants were secure. But Concorde was only the first round.

Airbus Industrie

The situation was this in 1967: The Europeans had committed to Concorde, but many had begun to have second thoughts about its viability. The good news was that the international European cooperative effort that was joined in 1959 actually did produce what it had intended, and had overcome considerable adversity in doing so. But the effort had been draining. Much capital, international goodwill, and energy had been expended on a project with no guarantee of success.

In the United States, the Americans in 1967 were still in the SST research and development trial period, but the idea of the wide-bodied jet was where their hearts were. In the American way, the airlines could see the possibilities. Boeing had committed to building the 747, which would fly in February 1969. Lockheed had completed the design of the L-1011 Tristar, and the DC-10 was in the works and would fly by 1971. Although the major effort of the Europeans had

been devoted to the Concorde, there had also been, since 1964, some rather disorganized discussion among Europeans of a cooperative effort on a wide-bodied jet. In 1967, a book entitled *Le Defi Americain* was published.[2] The title translates to "The American Challenge," but its central premise embraced the frustrations and loss of pride felt by many in European government and business circles: the United States industrial machine had taken over the world economy by means of a synergy between corporations and the American national government, and the other nations of the world, including those in Europe, had been reduced to little more than consumers of American commercial success. The case was laid out that European pride and tradition dictated a leadership role for it in world affairs, including business, and that the governments of Europe must cooperate with industry, to include subsidization where necessary, to create a national identity worthy of providing competition to the American behemoth. To do otherwise was to relegate Europe to the role of a vassal state of America.

The European interest in a subsonic wide-bodied commercial airliner lay largely with England and France and their national airline counterparts, mainly British European Airways (BEA) and Air France. The German Arbeitsgemeinschaft Airbus (working group Airbus) was formed in 1965, and its members were brought into the discussions with the English and the French. By 1967, specifications for a new airplane had been agreed upon (a 300 passenger, twin-engine, with the name "Airbus"). The governments of all three countries that year signed the first of a series of agreements to put the plan into operation, and Airbus was on its way.

In 1967 there were no large twin-engine jets. The consensus in the aeronautical community was that large aircraft, and those engaged in transoceanic routes, were required to have a minimum of three engines. Thirty-five years earlier, the same discussion had surrounded the emergence of the first modern airliners, as the prototype of the commercial airliner proceeded from the Trimotors to the twin-engined Boeing 247, and DC-1. As then, the decision to go with a twin-engine prototype was to set the standard for the industry. The people at Airbus were just starting to demonstrate the innovative thinking that would become, in time, one of the trademarks of the consortium. The failure of the American manufacturers to realize the importance of the twin-engine commitment, or to even consider the Airbus venture a legitimate competition, gave Airbus a head start.

Major funding for the venture was originally broken out as 37.5 percent British (Hawker-Siddeley and Rolls-Royce), 37.5 percent French (Sud Aviation), and 25 percent West German (Arbeitsgemeinschaft Airbus). The original prototype was to be a 300 passenger airplane with two new Rolls-Royce engines (the RB.207) then in the design stage, and much of the British commitment in money to the consortium was based on their use. The lead designer of the new aircraft was a Sud Aviation engineer by the name of Roger Beteille. He noticed that most of the Rolls-Royce effort was going into a smaller engine (the RB.211) that was to be used on the Lockheed Tristar. He suspected that the British financial backing to Rolls for the Airbus project was actually being applied to the RB.211, and he had misgivings that the new Rolls engine (the RB.207) would actually be produced.

Beteille began a redesign of the proposed aircraft. The new design reduced the airplanes' capacity to 250 seats so that existing engines could be used. Ironically, the new design was a specification first written in 1966 by Frank Kolk, chief engineer at American Airlines. With this development, the British withdrew their support. Due to the Concorde debacle, there was not much confidence in some quarters for the new project in the first place, and the U.K. left the consortium.

This development had the potential for sinking the entire Airbus effort. The two major partners had been the U.K. and France, allies against Germany during World War II, and they regarded the Germans primarily as "metal benders."[3] The

British departure left an unexpected, significant financial shortfall. The Germans, anxious to rehabilitate their image and enter the international commercial aviation arena for the first time since World War II, agreed to provide the majority of the funding necessary to fill the void left by the departure of the British. During the year of British participation, Hawker-Siddeley had been assigned wing development for the Airbus. When British funding was withdrawn, the question arose as to what to do about the work already performed by the English. Demonstrating a continuing commitment to innovation, the Germans agreed to fund the British company to the amount of 60 percent of development costs of the wing. Hawker-Siddeley was left to fund the remainder. This truly was international cooperation, and largely as a result, the German Defense Minister, Franz-Josef Strauss, was made the first president of Airbus.[4]

Thus was constructed the loose arrangement between West Germany and France for the funding of the prototype for Airbus. Although the financial commitment was one between the national governments, the actual participants were the national companies Messerschmitt-Bolkow-Blohm (MBB) and VFW-Fokker (German) and Aerospatiale (the name taken by the merged Sud Aviation, Nord Aviation, and Societe d'Etudes et de R'ealisation d'Engine Balistiques, or SEREB), and funding for the airplane was channeled through these companies. In 1970, Airbus GIE (Groupement d'Interet Economique), a form of consortium under French law, was formed.

A GIE is a French legal invention similar to a joint venture that was originally intended to be used by distressed French vineyards. It does, however, provide some very generous and unusual benefits to its participants, such as conferring a tax-free status and allowing nonreporting (no publication) of expenses and income. This is very convenient for a geopolitical manufacturing entity in competition with foreign private corporations like Boeing, and would become the subject of some international ill will as competition between the Europeans and the Americans intensified in later years. By 1971, the consortium was comprised of Aerospatiale (French, 47.9 percent), Deutsche Airbus GmbH (successor to MBB) (German, 47.9 percent), and Construcciones Aeronauticas S.A. (CASA) (Spain, 4.2 percent). Hawker-Siddeley was a subcontractor.

The launch date set for the A300, the type name given to the first production Airbus, was 1974. Procedures employed for the coordination of the construction of the airplane were simplified and streamlined as a result of the experience with Concorde, although each of the national partners insisted on their share of the construction pie. Different parts of the aircraft were put together in different countries (wings in Britain, fuselage and empennage in West Germany, fuselage, forward sections and flight deck in France) and flown to Toulouse for final assembly. In spite of the clumsiness of separate fabrication for the various elements of the airplane, it was delivered ahead of schedule. Two aircraft were built to the specifications designed for the A300B, and these first flew on October 28, 1972, and February 5, 1973, with General Electric CF6-50A turbofans. The new transport was configured to carry 225 passengers, and it would do so with only two engines and with a flight deck crew of just two pilots. The airplane was certified by 1974 and was on budget. This was a good beginning.

The American wide-bodies were already on the market by the time the A300 came on line. The names of Boeing, Douglas, and Lockheed were known quantities in the world aviation market, and their products had stood the test of time. Airbus Industrie was another matter. When it came to sales, the airlines of the world did not seem quite ready to trust the new contender. The national airlines of the major participants, of course, signed on for the airplane. Air France took six and Lufthansa three. Iberia initially placed an order, but then withdrew it. Korean Airlines agreed to buy the A300 in September 1974. The rest of the world took a wait-and-see attitude.

Airbus Industrie (AI) was geared up to produce four airplanes each month, but by the end of 1974 only ten airplanes had been sold. Projections were that it would require the sale of 360 A300s in order for the consortium to break even. In 1975, 33 orders were placed, and options were taken out on 22 more. Then the year 1976 passed without a single new sale. In fact, from the end of 1975 to May 1977, not a single order was received. The A300s were beginning to line up outside the assembly buildings in Toulouse. It was looking like a repeat of the Concorde.

Management at AI believed the key to success lay in two areas: (1) breaking into the American market would "beard the lion in his own den," and (2) creating a "family" of aircraft, planes that were basically similar but that provided a range of options, to appeal to the different requirements of airlines all over the world. With the dearth of sales through 1976, however, the basic strategy would have to be confined to AI's first goal, breaking into the American market. With all the A300s sitting on the tarmac in Toulouse, there would not yet be any addition to the "family."

The Competition Begins

AI decided to set up an American marketing presence. A former president of American Airlines, George Warde, was made a vice-president of AI in charge of North American sales and set up offices in New York City. The presence of a member of the inner circle of United States airline executives, talking up the attributes of the A300 began to put a somewhat different light on the matter. Eastern Air Lines was the first American airline to succumb. Eastern in 1976 was cash strapped, and AI came to the table ready to deal. The resulting agreement allowed Eastern to "try out" the A300 with no commitment to buy. This was aggressive marketing never before heard of in all of the years of commercial airplane sales. AI even took financial responsibility for the maintenance of the airplanes during the trial and for any costs associated with getting the A300 fully certified in the United States. The only cost that Eastern agreed to bear was the training of its pilots in the A300.

Eastern discovered that the A300's performance surpassed its specifications, burning less fuel than advertised, for instance, and that the airplane performed flawlessly and with great reliability. Moreover, it was cheaper than the American wide-bodies. Negotiations between Eastern and AI for a significant deal were started. AI was not through being innovative. In response to the claim of the airline that it really only needed 170 of the 260 seats in the A300, AI agreed to charge Eastern for only 170 seats, and if more seats were filled in actual usage, Eastern would pay more accordingly. As novel as the prior concessions made by AI were, this was truly precedent setting, unheard of marketing. The operating ratio for Eastern's flying of the A300 was suddenly cut by one-third.

In 1977, Frank Borman, head of Eastern Air Lines, signed up for 23 A300s for immediate delivery, took out options on nine more, and placed orders for 25 additional to-be-modified A300s. AI had achieved a major breakthrough. Not only was the sale worth $778 million, but also at least as significant, the great American airline market had been penetrated. And the American giants were beginning to take notice.

The first requirement for success that had been established by AI management was the breaking into the influential and pervasive U.S. airlines market. This hurdle in 1978 appeared to be doable. The second requirement for success, the creation of a line or "family" of associated aircraft types, was now ready for serious further consideration in Toulouse. The second member of the family was to be the A310, with a truncated fuselage and seats for something over 200 passengers, depending on configuration. The A310 was announced in July 1978 with orders already received from Lufthansa and Swissair.

Marketing in the United States was immediately initiated with the Big Four: American, Delta, TWA, and United. Although no sales were recorded with the United States airlines at that time, AI was received in airlines' offices as a legitimate competitor to the American aircraft manufacturers for the first time. Perhaps better yet for AI, the competition had caused Boeing, whose 767 ultimately beat out the A310 with the U.S. airlines, to reduce its prices to the airlines by some $1 million per plane. Airbus was beginning to emerge as a force to be reckoned with. Not only were their airplanes worthy contenders in the airline market, but Airbus was now seen by the airlines as a bargaining tool in dealing with the American aircraft production companies.

By 1979, only Eastern Air Lines of the U.S. carriers had bought Airbus. But the rest of the world was beginning fill their fleets with the A300 and A310. At the end of that year, AI had booked sales for 256 airplanes to 32 different airlines. The A300 had established a track record, as had Airbus Industrie itself. The consortium appeared to be here to stay. The airplane was proven reliable, safe, and economical to operate.

The Airbus strategy to break into the American airline market had centered on its North American presence through George Warde. Now Airbus wanted to expand its global marketing efforts to the East. The "silk route strategy" involved a campaign from Europe to the Middle East and on to the Orient. AI was now beginning to win contracts in direct competition with Boeing and the other American producers. And the national influence of both the United States and France was being called into play. State visits were scheduled to countries whose national airlines were in the market for new airliners, and marketing was mixed with diplomacy. Geopolitics proceeded hand-in-hand with airliner sales talk. Countries seeking admission into the EU told of pressures being brought by EU representatives to buy Airbus products. These results were mixed, but it was Airbus that was having more success. These tactics have continued on into the 21st century.[5] In 1979 and 1980, AI concluded orders in Indonesia, the Philippines, Malaysia, Pakistan, Iran, Egypt, Kuwait, Lebanon, and Saudi Arabia. The "silk route" strategy was clearly working. In 1981, Airbus was the world leader in sales of wide-bodied jets, with Boeing second and McDonnell Douglas third. But Airbus' success thus far was about market penetration, not profits. Airbus Industrie was still a government, taxpayer-funded operation, and its long-range existence was still an open question.

The American Giants

As Airbus Industrie was being birthed in the late 1960s, and as it fought for world legitimacy as a producer of commercial aircraft during the decade of the 1970s, the venerable aircraft companies of the United States were also undergoing stressful change. By the 1970s, the American commercial aircraft manufacturing community was fairly well defined as Boeing, McDonnell-Douglas, and Lockheed. The competition between these three companies (Douglas Aircraft Company was merged with McDonnell in 1967) extended all the way back to the 1930s and had been a nip and tuck affair for most of that time. Boeing had successfully broken into commercial jet transport production with the 707, largely as a result of its design of that aircraft as a tanker (the KC-135) for the U.S. Air Force. The head-to-head competition between the 707 and the DC-8 has already been reviewed. We also know that during the 1950s and 1960s Lockheed made the decision to produce only turboprop commercial aircraft (the Electra) instead of pure jets. When they appeared, the Boeing 737 and the Douglas DC-9 were both successful.

With the coming of the era of the wide-bodies, the three-way American competition was renewed. Boeing had taken an enormous gamble

in the late 1960s with the decision to produce the 747. Shortly thereafter, McDonnell-Douglas had entered the field with the DC-10. Lockheed followed with the L-1011 Tristar.

The L-1011 would prove to be the last offering Lockheed would make to the commercial aircraft industry. Ultimately, Lockheed was able to sell only about half (244) of the number of L-1011s necessary to break even on the research and development costs incurred, and the company would end up losing some $2.5 billion on that airplane. Production was stopped at the end of 1981, and Lockheed retired from the production of commercial aircraft for good.

The DC-10, which was a direct competitor to the L-1011, was even more star-crossed than the 1011. Three high visibility incidents involving the DC-10[6] hurt its position in the market, and by 1988 production of the DC-10 had ceased, also leaving McDonnell-Douglas short of a break-even position.

Of the three American giants, only Boeing succeeded in getting into the black with its original wide-body entrant, the 747. The decision to build the 747 required a commitment on the part of Boeing to risk essentially the entire net worth of the company in the process. The research and development costs, and the extraordinarily expensive production costs[7] meant that the 747 had to be a big winner in the world wide-body sales contest for Boeing to be able to survive. The 747 was in service by 1969, but during the early years of the next decade, the Gulf oil crises and the world recession caused sales to droop significantly. The economic downturn was so significant that by 1971, Boeing had to lay off over 60 percent of the staff that it had in place in 1968. The great Boeing organization was close to extinction. But Boeing held on during the middle years of that decade, and by 1978, things were beginning to look up, ironically at just about the same time that Airbus was making its initial inroads into the American airplane market.

Boeing's sales of the 747 were picking up internationally (83 orders) as nations used the beautiful big airplane as a symbol of national pride, painted in its national airline's colors. In 1978, both the 757 and the 767, utilizing the twin-engine concept for larger airliners pioneered by Airbus, were launched with pre-sales assured. Orders were received for a total of 461 airplanes, a yearly record. By the end of the decade, Boeing was ascendant, and its domestic competitors were just hanging on. Although McDonnell-Douglas had on its drawing boards the new MD-11, the world commercial aircraft production competition was beginning to look like a competition between Airbus and Boeing.

The U.K. Rejoins Airbus

The British, left out of the world commercial aircraft production business since it departed Airbus Industrie in 1968, had a change of heart during the middle of the 1970s and began exploring ways to get back in. The British government had discussed possible ventures with the Americans, both Boeing and McDonnell-Douglas, but no agreement was reached. They then turned back to the continent and, in 1979, the United Kingdom once again joined AI as a partner, only this time in a junior status. The participating British partner was the nationalized British Aerospace (Bae), the name of the recently merged British Aircraft Corporation and Hawker-Siddeley. The new consortium was arranged thusly: Germany, 37.9 percent; France, 37.9 percent; the U.K., 20 percent; and Spain, 4.2 percent. The new consortium was now more in the spirit of the emerging European Community.

Funding the "Family"

Since the original departure of the British in 1968, the A300 had become a reality and a relative success, and the German and the French governments had bankrolled it. When discussions within AI turned to expanding the "family"

of aircraft to the A310, the four governments that now constituted Airbus Industrie found themselves in less than full agreement about how the new project should be paid for. At the beginning of the 1980s, the nominal participants in AI were British Aerospace, Deutsche Airbus, Aerospatiale, and CASA. These companies were national organs of their governments, and were the operational devices through which the respective governments had cooperated in creating a world presence in commercial aircraft manufacture. The national governments had used a variety of financial models to fund the costs of development of the A300, such as having the nationalized participant company borrow the funds from a national bank and then guaranteeing up to 100 percent of the loan. Usually, the arrangement did not contemplate repayment of the funds except on successful sales of the airplane.

By the time the subject of funding the new A310 came under discussion around 1978, the national governments were becoming circumspect at the thought of just how much more money was going to be required to keep the Airbus Industrie experiment propped up. While there was hopeful talk about timetables when profits might be expected, the national governments nevertheless agreed to continue to fund Airbus, with or without profits. The Airbus experiment would continue at the expense of European taxpayers. The West German government, the most accommodating of the group, agreed to fund 90 percent of the Deutsche Airbus outlay (up to DM 1.5 billion or $750 million), with a repayment formula based on sales of the A320. The British government had contributed £50 million to British Aerospace (Bae) at the time of reentry into the consortium, and now authorized a loan in the amount of £250 million through 1988. Bae would be required to repay £50 million during the 1990s with the remainder to be repaid from the proceeds of aircraft sales. The French government signed on for 75 percent of Aerospatiale's development costs and arranged a bank loan for it, of FF 380 million, through a collection of French banks. The banks did not charge interest until production aircraft were flying, and repayment was conditioned on sales of the A320.

Market share for Airbus in 1975 was 10 percent. By 1977, it was 26 percent. By 1979, Airbus had 81 aircraft in service with the airlines of the world. Although the 767 had been launched by 1978, the first one had not been rolled out. Meanwhile, the "whitetails" (completed but unsold airplanes without airline livery) were lined up on the tarmac in Toulouse. Some airlines liked the idea of going to the manufacturing plant and being able to fly their purchase away. Airbus orders had reached 256 by the end of 1979, orders given by 32 different airlines, and AI that year sold more wide-bodies than any other producer in the world.

Success continued into the 1980s. In 1981 Airbus was again number one in sales for wide-bodies. It was time to enlarge the "family." (See Figure 41-2 and Figure 41-3.) This time the decision went for scaling down aircraft size. The single aisle option was chosen and the airplane was designated A320. In 1984, the A320 was launched. But Airbus was still suffering growing pains and international friction between the partners. Although the four governments had approved the go-ahead for the new aircraft, second-guessing within the separate governments was rampant. There were threats of pulling out of the project followed by counter threats relative to the numbers of jobs that would be lost if the project were abandoned, and on and on. The construction and assembly procedure used by AI was not designed for economy, and that raised a related concern: how to make the production of the A320 more efficient. The assembly procedure was designed specifically to accommodate the work forces and economies of the four partners, all located in their separate homelands. The A300 and A310 series airplanes were built in stages and then assembled in Toulouse, at the insistence of the French. Wings were constructed in England; forward, upper

FIGURE 41-2 The Airbus family.

center, and aft portions of the fuselage, as well as portions of the empennage were put together in Germany; the French built the forward section of the airplane, including the flight deck, part of the fuselage, and the engine pylons. All of these parts had to be delivered to Toulouse, by Boeing aircraft ironically, and assembled.

Much the same procedure was utilized for the production of the A320. With production of two different types already underway and certified, with world acceptance of the Airbus product now a fact, and with market share on the rise, attention was turned to considerations of efficiency. Little improvement was realized with the A320, but at least efficiency was now a management topic of discussion with some priority. This effort was enough to pull the partners together sufficiently to see the project through to completion. The A320 first flew in 1987.

Although the A320 experienced a rough beginning (preproduction orders in 1984 and 1985 lagged behind Boeing and even the DC-9, with less than 15 percent and 8 percent market share respectively for those years), the decision to launch the A320 turned out to be correct. Its market was for users of the older 737-200 Boeing series, and in spite of an economic recession in the middle 1980s, the A320 appealed to cost-conscious airlines because of its efficiency. Orders were almost immediately received from many world airlines, including Air France, British Caledonian, Adria Airways, Air Inter, and Cyprus Airways. In 1986, orders were received for over 100 A320s.

In 1985, market share for Airbus jumped to almost 45 percent of the world commercial aircraft market. Boeing was first, but McDonnell-Douglas was third. And the penetration of the American market was continuing. American Airlines ordered 15 A320s that same year under yet another financial innovative arrangement: American could return the airplanes at any time on 30 days notice. In law, this comes pretty close to a 30-day lease. In 1986, Northwest ordered ten A320s and agreed to buy 90 more in successive batches, a transaction ultimately in the range of $3.2 billion to the coffers of Airbus. Airbus was on a roll. In 1987, the consortium launched the A330/340, two-engine or four-engine models of essentially the same airplane. The 330 used the same basic fuselage and the same wing as the 340 but with only two engines. The long-range 340 was configured with four engines. Production costs savings were palpable, but the funding was still coming from the governments instead of from profits. The percentage of government contribution, however, was falling. With the A330/340, Airbus required 65 percent government help. Aerospatiale was funded FF 6 billion, the British ponied up £450 million to British Aerospace, and Germany gave up DM 3 billion. No details of the German arrangement were publicized, as is often the case under GIE consortium format, but it appears that the British and French loans were made without repayment being required except on sales of the new production aircraft. While the financing arrangements were largely well appreciated in Europe, the whole subsidization process was beginning to raise the

ire of the United States as Boeing continued to lose market share. These developments will be discussed in the next section.

Then in 1989 came the first of the variations of the A320 series with the slightly longer 321, to be followed into the 1990s with the A319, and then the shortest of all, the 318. (See Figure 41-3.) In 1991, it appeared that Airbus would not be a repeat of Concorde after all. AI management thought it was time for a little expounding. Some perspective on the Airbus Industrie journey is gained from a lecture given that year at the Cranfield management school in England by Jean Pierson, the managing director of Airbus:

> Aviation has changed the way we live, the way we do business. Aviation has allowed us to consider mankind for the first time in the context of truly global village. And the European contribution to this has been significant. . . . In the span of twenty years, a short time in our industry, Airbus Industrie has managed to restore European civil aircraft manufacturing to its proper place in the market. Let us go back to 1970 for one minute. Imagine if I had gone to a bank and said, "I have just started a management team from various European countries. I intend to make large aircraft to compete with Boeing. Will you lend me $1 billion? You may lose all of it. Or you may start to make some money twenty years from now." I leave to your imagination the welcome I would have had. No financial institution would have taken on such a risk, or if it had the interest rates would have been simply prohibitive. It was therefore up to the governments of each of the countries participating in Airbus Industrie to substitute themselves for the bankers and assume such risks.[8]

Pierson had put the issue in plain view. European governments were using taxpayer money to compete with American business in the manufacture of large commercial aircraft, and doing so without apology. It was the European

Years	Months	Highlights
1969	May	A300 go-ahead
1970	December	Creation of Airbus Industrie
1972	October	A300 first flight
1974	May	A300B2 entry into service
1975	June	A300B4 entry into service
1978	July August	A310 launch A300B4 convertible passenger/cargo
1980	December	A300-600 series go-ahead
1982	April	A310 first flight
1983	March July	A310-300 go-ahead A300-600 first flight
1984	March	A320 launch
1985	December	A310-300 entry into service
1987	February June December	A320 first flight A330/A340 launch A300-600R first flight
1988	February March	A320 certification A320 first delivery
1989	November	A321 launch
1991	October	A340 first flight
1992	November December	A330 first flight A340 certification
1993	January March June October December	A340 first delivery A321 first flight A319 launch A330 certification A330 first delivery A321 certification
1994	January September	A321 first delivery A300-600ST first flight
1995	January September November	A319 first flight A300-600ST certification A330-200 launch
1996	January April	A300-600ST entry into service A319 certification A319 first delivery
1997	June	A340-500/-600 launch A319 Corporate Jet launch
1999	April	A318 launch
2001	January April	Airbus Integrated Company A340-600 first flight
2002	January February May August December	A318 first flight A340-500 first flight A340-600 certification A340-600 entry into service A340-500 certification

FIGURE 41-3 Evolution of Airbus.

national governments who were actually competing against American business. Boeing is an American corporation, whose coffers are not filled by government payments of money as a national policy. Its stock is publicly held by individual investors, subject to the economic rules of business relating to profit and loss, and it was taking a relative drubbing from Airbus Industrie. Part of that drubbing was directly due to "dumping," or the sale of aircraft to Boeing's competitors (the airlines of the world) for less than cost because European taxpayers were footing the bill. Airbus could afford to be innovative due to the European governments' financial guarantees, a course of action that would be considered foolhardy in the real business world. What consumer would not be delighted with such deals?

What was now pointed up was the basic conflict in the social philosophies of European and American governments as to the **role of government,** at least as concerns the aerospace industry. In the preceding chapters we have detailed how the EU had been in the process of gradually receding from nationally imposed barriers to free trade. It was beginning to look like this was not to be the case with aerospace.

How this impasse plays out and what may be expected from this implacable difference between the EU and the United States will be discussed later in this chapter. But first, let's review the overall status of commercial aircraft manufacturing worldwide.

International Aircraft Production into the 21st Century

In this book we have traced aircraft manufacturing throughout the 20th Century. We have seen how American aircraft producers began to dominate the field during the 1930s, and how they reached preeminence after World War II. We have documented the rise of European competition to American dominance in aircraft production by

Aircraft	Description	Seats	Max	Launch Date	1st Flight	1st Delivery	Production to Cease
A300	2 engine, twin aisle	228–254	361	May 1969	28 October 1972	May 1974	July 2007
A310	2 engine, twin aisle, modified A300	187	279	July 1978	3 April 1982	Dec 1985	July 2007
A318	2 engine, single aisle, shortened 6.17 m from A320	107	117	Apr 1999	15 January 2002	Oct 2003	
A319	2 engine, single aisle, shortened 3.77 m from A320	124	156	June 1993	25 August 1995	Apr 1996	
A320	2 engine, single aisle	150	180	Mar 1984	22 February 1987	Mar 1988	
A321	2 engine, single aisle, lengthened 6.94 m from A320	185	220	Nov 1989	11 March 1993	Jan 1994	
A330	2 engine, twin aisle	253–295	406–440	June 1987	2 November 1992	Dec 1993	
A340	4 engine, twin aisle	239–380	420–440	June 1987	25 October 1991	Jan 1993	
A350	2 engine, twin aisle	270–350		Dec 2006	2011 expected	mid-2013	
A380	4 engine, double deck, quad aisle	555	853	2002	27 April 2005	Oct 2007	

FIGURE 41-4 Airbus family.

the emergence of Airbus Industrie beginning in 1970, and we have followed the unparalleled success of Airbus Industrie under the European subsidy system into the late 1990s. As the 21st century began, there were only two international manufacturers of large commercial jet aircraft, Boeing and Airbus, and each was in parity with regard to market share. In 1999, in fact, Boeing was forced, for the first time since 1945, to accept second place in the number of total aircraft ordered. (See Figure 41-5.)

As the new century begins, we observe that the international aircraft production arena is not static, but dynamic. The aerospace industry is still arguably the most important industry in the world, as advanced countries strive to position themselves in the world market possessed with a capacity to build commercial aircraft. Development of this industrial sector is viewed as of particular importance in the economic and industrial policy of these nations. Implicit in such a viable commercial jet aircraft capacity are links to national security, the generation of technology, positive contributions to the balance of payments from exports, the creation of jobs, and national prestige.

Large commercial aircraft (LCA) production going into the 21st century is a complex and diversified endeavor composed of the two

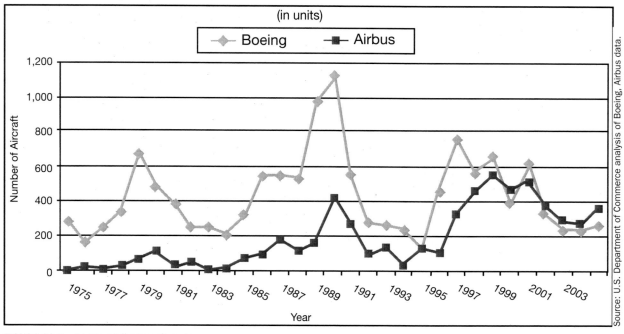

Source: U.S. Department of Commerce analysis of Boeing, Airbus data.

FIGURE 41-5 Large civil aircraft orders.

primary aircraft producers (Boeing and Airbus), producers of LCA jet engines, and major suppliers of the aerospace industry (the global supply chain). We will defer the discussion of the titanic contest between Boeing and Airbus until later in this chapter. But first, we will examine the suppliers of the subsystems necessary to make it all work.

Large Commercial Jet Engines

Three companies dominate the field of large engine suppliers: General Electric Aircraft Engines (GEAE), of the United States, Pratt & Whitney (P&W) of the United States, and Rolls-Royce PLC of the United Kingdom. In addition to these three, there are both domestic and international joint ventures composed of other companies in combination with these three, or combinations between these three. These include:

➡ CFM International—a joint venture composed of SNECMA Moteurs (France) and GEAE

➡ International Aero Engines, Inc.—a joint venture composed of P&W, Rolls-Royce,

MTU of Germany, and the Japanese Aero Engines Company

➡ The Engine Alliance LLC—a joint venture composed of GEAE and P&W to produce engines for the A380

GEAE, P&W, and Rolls-Royce produce the engines for practically all Boeing and Airbus models, as well as for Bombardier and Embraer regional jets. These companies also provide overhaul, repair, and fleet management services.

P&W was the largest producer of aircraft engines 30 years ago (see Figure 41-6), producing four of every five engines used in the commercial fleet. Although P&W is expected to double its annual deliveries for long-haul wide-body jets over the next 20 years, it is also expected to continue to lose market share to the other participants. Deliveries of LCA jet engines is depicted in Figure 41-7.

General Electric Aircraft Engines

As seen in Figure 41-7, GEAE is predominant in the delivery of jet engines. There are at least three areas in which the company has a proven

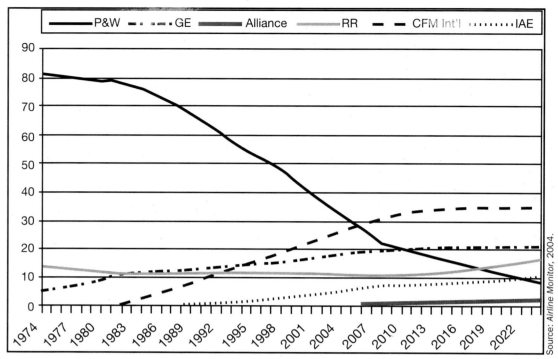

FIGURE 41-6 Large civil aircraft engines in service.

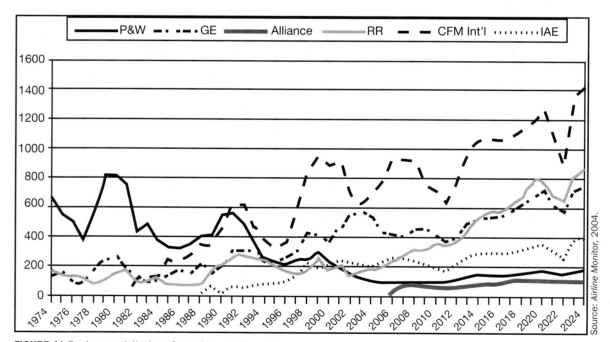

FIGURE 41-7 Large civil aircraft engines delivered.

advantage. (1) It is the exclusive provider of all jet engines for Bombardier's line of regional jets, as well as the two larger Embraer regional jets—the ERJ-170 and the ERJ 190. (2) It is also the supplier of the CFM-56 engines used exclusively by the Boeing 737 line of aircraft. The CFM-56 is produced by the GEAE joint venture with with SNECMA Moteurs of France. (3) It recently entered into a joint venture with the Japanese manufacturer Honda for the production of an engine to be used on small jets.

Pratt & Whitney

P&W is the venerable company we first encountered in Chapter 11 (Horsepower), which was formed through the vision and efforts of Fred Rentschler. Rentschler (while at Wright Aeronautical) produced the Wright "Whirlwind" engine used by Charles Lindbergh to cross the Atlantic in 1927. When he founded P&W, the company began producing the "Wasp" and "Hornet" engines used exclusively by the U.S. Navy on it first carrier airplanes. Today, P&W in combination with its multinational partners produces the V2500 engine used on narrow-body Airbus aircraft, and has ventures in Russia, China, Germany, Japan, and South Korea. It also produces engines for most of the Boeing and Airbus lines.

Rolls-Royce PLC

Rolls-Royce, like the other two LCA engine producers, provides engines for most Boeing and Airbus models. In 1995, Rolls-Royce acquired the American firm, Allison Engine Company, and it has a manufacturing presence in 26 states in the U.S. Through this connection, it supplies the engines for the smaller Embraer ERJ 135 and ERJ 145 regional jets.

The Global Supply Chain— Major Suppliers

Suppliers provide the materials and products that are incorporated into aircraft and engines produced by the major aircraft and engine manufacturers. They are located all over the world and number in the tens of thousands. We will review the major suppliers located in the United States, Europe, Japan, South Korea, China, Russia, Taiwan, and Indonesia.

United States

There are eight major civil aerospace suppliers in the United States. (See Figure 41-8.) At one time, U.S. suppliers were completely dependent on U.S. prime manufacturers. Due to the global

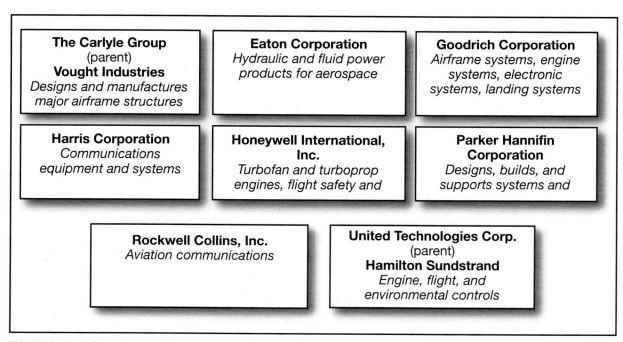

FIGURE 41-8 U.S. major suppliers.

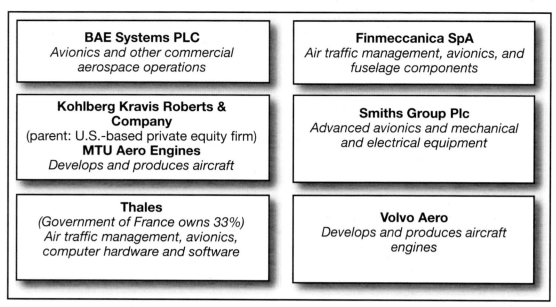

FIGURE 41-9 European major suppliers.

aspects of the supply chain, these producers today participate in the wider manufacturing process around the world. Some of these even participate as risk-sharing partners with LCA manufacturers in aircraft such as the A380 and the Embraer 170 and 190.

Europe

Figure 41-9 shows the major Eurpean suppliers of LCA products. These companies supply to both European and U.S. prime manufacturers. Although there is a small degree of government ownership interest in these companies, privatization efforts in Europe have succeeded in converting most of the aerospace supply industry into private equity holdings.

Russia

Since the disintegragtion of the Soviet Union, Russian aerospace companies have pulled back from a position of being prime manufacturing souces of large commercial aircraft. In 2007, their market share stood at 1 percent of the world market. Russian companies have, however, part-

nered with Boeing, beginning in 1990, to supply engineering and technical expertise in the 777 and 787 programs.

In July 2001, the parent company of Airbus, EADS, signed a cooperation agreement with the Russian Aerospace Agency agreeing to invest over $2 billion over the next decade on projects including the A320 and A380. As in similar Airbus transactions, this arrangement may be tied to the purchase of Airbus products since Aeroflot immediately thereafter agreed to purchase 18 new Airbus planes. In 2007, Airbus announced that it had signed a risk-sharing partnership (for a 5 percent stake) with Russia's new United Aircraft Corporation (see below) for A350 construction. Simultaneously, Aeroflot announced an order for 22 A350s.

Sukhoi, the Russian fighter jet maker, is currently engaged in development of a new regional jet, the Superjet-100, which is designed to compete with Bombardier and Embraer. The Superjet-100 is to be available in 75- and 95-seat models and is slated to go into production in 2008. Up until the Paris Air Show in 2007, all orders for the RJ came from Russian carriers (Aeroflot was the largest at 30 airplanes), but at that time Sukhoi announced orders for ten of the aircraft from the Italian airline, ItAli.

The Kremlin's new industrial policy seeks to combine state ownership with foreign technology and investment in an attempt to revive heavy industry in the country. The Russian government is consolidating the country's aerospace industries into a large holding company known as United Aircraft Corporation (UAC), which is owned 90.1 percent by the government. This move recognizes that the separate Russian industries have been largely marginalized since the fall of the Soviet Union. UAC will bring under one roof the well-known aircraft makers MiG, Tupolev, Ilyushin, Yakolev, and Sukhoi. The Russian government has pledged to supply at least $12 billion in subsidies to UAC over the next decade.

The Superjet-100 is being produced through cooperative agreements with foreign companies to supply engines (SNECMA—France), avionics (Thales—France), Goodrich (wheels and brakes—U.S.), and Boeing in a consulting capacity.

Japan

The Japanese government, from the end of the United States military occupation of that country in the 1950s, has been committed to the support of a commercial aircraft capacity. Two months after the occupation ended, in July 1952, the legal basis for government support of the industry was set down in the Aircraft Industry Manufacturing Law, which was followed in 1954 with the First Aircraft Industry Promotion Law. These laws subsequently caused heavy subsidization of the aircraft industry. The aircraft industry in Japan is composed of companies that are highly diversified, and allocation of resources and talent to their aircraft production divisions has been a cautious affair due to opportunities elsewhere in the aviation market. Government support to these industries, however, has been liberal, although not so much as in Europe. Japanese state aid has taken the form of direct subsidy, loan guarantees, the forgiving of loans, launch aid, and guarantees against production phase losses.

Japanese aerospace industrial policy is administered by the Ministry of Economy, Trade and Industry (METI), which plans and directs the development of the country's largest aircraft companies. METI arranges favorable financing that reduces the companies' risk, and coordinates the work undertaken in Japan under license, or as subcontractors, to foreign companies. Thus, the four largest aircraft industry manufacturers (Mitsubishi Heavy Industries, Kawasaki Heavy Industries, Ishikawajima-Harima Heavy Industries, and Fuji Heavy Industries) have participated in and controlled all such major contracts and programs.

In the 1980s, METI (then known as the Ministry of International Trade and Industry, or MITI) encouraged a strategy for Japanese aerospace companies that emphasized two essential components: (1) undertaking a partnership or subcontract role in international aerospace programs (primarily American) and (2) specializing in advanced component and subsystem technologies. Because the Japanese government has been willing to fund large portions of the development costs of new projects, Japanese companies have been appealing to Western companies as partners in such projects. As a result, the Japanese have become a major supplier of critical subcomponents and assemblies, and have become indispensable to the prime contractors. Japanese firms have been heavily involved in the Boeing 777. Boeing now says that it can no longer build an airplane without the Japanese.[9] The contributions of the Japanese extend to components, subsystems, electronics, and instrumentation, all essential to modern aircraft in some of their most technical aspects. Japanese companies are also significant risk-sharing partners with Boeing in the new 787 program.

This relationship is not one-sided. Japan is Boeing's largest customer for twin-aisle aircraft. Through the year 2002, Japan had ordered 644 Boeing aircraft worth some $61 billion. In the last decade, 78 percent of the airplanes oerdered by Japanese customers have been Boeing products.

By utilizing the "partnering" strategies managed by METI, the Japanese firms have avoided substantial risk and overhead costs that accompany design, manufacture, and marketing of new commercial aircraft types. Gradually, the Japanese have been introduced to advanced technology that was perfected through funding by the United States, as in the FS-X program, all with relatively minimum investment. Although Japan has yet to field its own large commercial jet aircraft, METI has placed this goal as a top priority. Currently, Japanese companies produce small jet and turboprop aircraft and helicoters, military aircraft and trainers, and space launch vehicles.

All of this has not gone unnoticed by Airbus. Seven Japanese suppliers are currently lined up to supply parts for the A380 over a period of twenty years, for a total of $850 million.

China

Aerospace manufacturers in the People's Republic of China are owned by the national government. The primary government enterprises controlling aircraft products are known as China Aviation Industry Corporation I (AVIC I), which focuses on large- and medium-sized aircraft, leasing and general aviation aircraft, and China Aviation Industry Corporation II (AVIC II), which produces small aircraft, feeder aircraft, and helicopters. Since 1993, all interfaces between China's aerospace industry and foreign producers have been coordinated through these China Aviation Industry Corporations (prior to 1999, this interface was known as Aviation Industries of China (AVIC).

Chinese strategy involves entering into equal partnerships with foreign manufacturers through joint production contracts, and thereby securing the technological and industrial background necessary to develop the aerospace presence it envisions for the 21st Century.

The primary aircraft production companies of China are Xian Aircraft Company, Shanghai Aviation, Chengdu Aircraft Corporation, and Shenyang Aircraft Manufacturing Company. Among the joint production contracts the Chinese have undertaken are assemblies of the MD-82 and MD-90, and vertical fin and horizontal stabilizers for the Boeing 737. Boeing has plans to build a maintenance, repair, and overhaul center to service B-777 aircraft in Shanghai. Pratt & Whitney, starting in the late 1980s, established joint ventures to manufacture turboprop engines for Chinese Y-series aircraft. More recently, Embraer has entered into a joint venture in China for production of their regional jets, including the ERJ 135/140/145 in Harbin, China.

These joint contract arrangements extract significant concessions from the partnering companies, and involve investment and technology transfers to the Chinese. With its large labor force and extremely cheap wage scales, China is in a position to offer significant cost savings in aircraft production, but the ultimate cost to the West may be high. Exports from China to the United States consist mainly of consumer goods, toys, and clothing. The United States finds it difficult to compete with China in the production of these goods. The Chinese are now importing about the only thing the West has left to export, its technology.

Both Boeing and Airbus are actively pursuing expansion of these partnering arrangements in China. China is seen as the single most important market for new LCA sales over the next 20 years. Air traffic in China tripled between 1980 and 2004, and passenger traffic is expected to grow at a rate of 8.5 percent per year over the next 20 years.

Available LCAs in China are few. There are only 1,100 registered aircraft in the entirety of the country, compared to 219,000 in the United States. Predictions are that some 2000 large- and medium-sized aircraft will be added to the Chinese airlines over the next two decades. At the end of 2004, Chinese airlines had ordered 103 new Boeing aircraft, and in January 2005, Boeing announced that six Chinese airlines had ordered 60 of the new 787 models. Airbus has also claimed significant Chinese orders.

The government of China appears set to supplement its aircraft needs of the future with Chinese produced airplanes. This will, no doubt, be made easier by the technology transfers that are implicit in the partnering arrangements that have long existed with Western aircraft producers. China's first business size jet (Little Eagle 500) took to the air in 2003. AVIC I is in the development phase of the first Chinese regional jet, the ARJ 21. AVIC I is currently seeking FAA certification for the ARJ 21.

While China for some time will be a source of supply, a risk-sharing partner, and a customer for Western produced aircraft, it is clear that China intends to become a competitor in the world aircraft market at some point in the future.

South Korea

As is the case with all Asian countries involved in aerospace participation, the South Korean government has been an integral part of that country's aerospace industry. The Korea Aerospace Research Institute (KARI) does research and development in aerospace issues and cooperates with other government and with private sector interests in that effort. The government has provided the country's main aerospace company, Korea Aerospace Industries, Ltd. (KAI) with all of its required funding for military R&D projects, and 50 percent of its funding for civil R&D projects. Through 1999, the industry in South Korea had received about $2.75 billion in government funding.

The South Korean aerospace industry is comprised of two companies, the aforementioned KAI, which is the larger of the two and which was created by the government in 1999 by the consolidation of Samsung Aerospace, Daewoo Heavy Industries, and Hyundai Space and Aircraft Company. KAI has had a long relationship with U.S. civil and military firms, and by far the largest part of KAI's activities relate to military and defense products. The other aerospace entity is Korean Air Lines, which is also the major airline operator. KAL has an extensive history of supplier contracts with Boeing, Airbus, and McDonnell Douglas.

Partnering relationships with European and other countries has been minimal, although in 1999 KAI entered into a joint venture with the EU company Eurocopter for development of the South Korean Light Helicopter Program.

The government of South Korea seeks to raise its profile in the aerospace industry on the global stage, and has advocated the creation of an Asian consortium similar to Airbus Industrie that would include China, Singapore, and India for the production of a 100–200 seat commercial jet.

Taiwan and Indonesia

Taiwan's main efforts in the field are through Taiwan Aerospace Corporation. As seen in almost all cases of foreign cooperation in assemblies of American aircraft, and in return for access to that foreign country's markets, offsets and technology transfers are demanded, and most often apparently given.

The Indonesian government owns and controls its sole aerospace production company, Industries Pesawat Terbang Nusantara (IPTN). This company produces military and commercial aircraft under license, makes aircraft parts for Boeing and Airbus, manufactures a homegrown turboprop series of medium weight aircraft, and has embarked on a design phase of a commercial twinjet, designated the N-2130, which is an 80 to 130 passenger airplane depending on configuration. Labor in Indonesia is exceedingly cheap, with skilled workers earning a fraction of their American or European counterparts. Japan has even begun to outsource to Indonesia part of the work it previously contracted for with Boeing, becoming, in essence, a broker.

Airbus vs. Boeing: International Trade Background

For much of its history, Airbus Industrie has been a collection of governments that used nationalized corporations as a cover to produce commercial airliners. The cost of the development and production of these airplanes was borne by the taxpayers of the countries that constituted Airbus Industrie. Airbus Industrie was formed and exists as a manufacturing presence for the essential purpose of competing with private American corporations in the business of aircraft manufacturing.

Trade (exporting and importing of goods) between nations and their citizens has had a long history, governed by rules imposed by national governments. Sometimes these rules are unilateral, that is, one nation may impose duties or tariffs on imports from other countries, often in order to protect that nation's own producers. Sometimes these rules are the result of agreements between two or more nations, designed to accommodate the interests of all parties. These agreements usually involve compromises on the part of each country, but with a view toward a fair and balanced approach to international trade that does not give either party an undue advantage over the other.

Historically, it is generally agreed that unilateral trade action is counter-productive. The imposition of tariffs on imports from a foreign country usually results in retaliatory action by that country by the imposition of tariffs against the first country. The imposition of tariffs is also an artificial control on the trade of goods that raises the price of those goods, and reduces the availability of those goods in the marketplace.

The reciprocal of this practice is free trade, based on market principles that establish the demand, the supply, and the price of goods. The basis of free trade is competition. Competition provides the most variety, the most availability, and the cheapest price based on supply and demand. It is the basic concept behind the deregulation of the domestic U.S. commercial aviation industry and the resulting globalization of deregulation seen since then.

Subsidy is also a unilateral national policy that skews free market trade. While there are various types of subsidy recognized in economic analyses, in the context used here they have the same general effect as tariffs. Tariffs impose a penalty on foreign producers for the advantage of domestic producers by making foreign goods more expensive or less available. Subsidies likewise favor domestic producers to the disadvantage of foreign producers by making domestic goods cheaper or more available.

After World War II, the advanced nations of the world came together in an effort to create an open multinational trading regimen to promote free and unfettered access by all nations to the benefits of world free enterprise. Barriers to trade were seen to have contributed to, if not caused, some of the world's most ruinous events. The Great Depression of the 1930s, for instance, had been a world-wide economic calamity, and it had a direct influence on the rise of National Socialism in Germany, which led to World War II. It benefited communist expansion in the U.S.S.R., which was seen as an alternative form of legitimate government and a remedy for the evils of capitalism.

Today, international trade is governed by the World Trade Organization (WTO), which will be discussed below. Before the establishment of the WTO, there were four main international trade agreements relevant to our discussion:

1. The GATT agreement
2. The 1979 GATT Aircraft Code
3. The GATT Subsidies Code
4. The 1992 Agreement between the United States and the European Community on Trade in Civil Aircraft

The first multinational agreement, The General Agreement on Tariffs and Trade (GATT), dates to 1947. The purpose of GATT was simply to minimize the barriers to free trade between nations, like tariffs imposed by governments, so as to spread the benefits of the world economy to all nations, large or small. Elimination or restriction of national or regional barriers was the key, so that access to markets was allowed to all nations.

GATT governed the global trading system. Aircraft manufacturing was not, *per se,* one of the issues directly contemplated by the agreement. Moreover, during the evolution of the EC, aircraft manufacturing was excluded from the competition rules adopted by the European Council beginning in 1988. Much of international civil aviation was an orphan in the world of international rules of trade. This was not so much a problem immediately after World War II because there was no world competition in aircraft manufacturing. The great American aircraft companies carried on a competition wholly within the national boundaries of the United States. That competition was fierce, but it was not international. With the advent of Airbus Industrie, the world competitive situation changed, and without any particular significant event, aircraft manufacturing gradually became subject to the rules of world trade.

The *status quo* in the United States after World War II included a duty (tariff) on imported aircraft of 6 percent, which predated the war. This was of no real consequence since there were no significant aircraft producers outside of the United States. But when Airbus Industrie began seriously producing commercial aircraft for sale to customers in the United States, that import duty was certainly a disincentive to buying Airbus products. This was a concern to the Europeans.

From the American point of view, the emergence of the Airbus consortium financially backed by the governments of Europe, was also of concern. The United States held the position that aircraft, which had been excluded from the ambit of GATT, ought to be included.

The result was a compact that was formalized during the Tokyo Round of GATT in 1979, known as The Agreement on Trade in Civil Aircraft, signed by the United States and the European Community, as well as 20 other nations. Its purpose was to bring commercial aircraft within the ambit of GATT, including restrictions on subsidy. By its terms, tariffs were also agreed to

be eliminated on aircraft, aircraft engines, and parts. Although the Aircraft Code was successful in eliminating most tariffs, the same could not be said concerning subsidy. Part of the problem was due to the language used in the Aircraft Code, which called for the "best efforts" of the signatories in curtailing such practices. Exactly what a "subsidy" was, in law, was not clearly defined. But it was also clear that there was a lack of commitment on the part of some countries. Subsidy had been a way of life for many years, particularly in Europe, and many of the airlines operating in those countries were government-owned. There was little to no distinction made in European government when it came to the Airbus subsidy issue. The result was a general disregard for the Aircraft Code's intent.

In the absence of some workable disputes-resolution forum, talk was heard of trade wars and protectionist legislation (Congressionally imposed tariffs on imports). The degree of agitation seemed to be directly proportional to the success of Airbus, and temperatures in the halls of government in the United States and in Europe rose and fell accordingly. Boeing was far and away the biggest exporter of American manufacturing and technology, and its welfare was a national concern, particularly if its woes could be attributed to concerted, unfair trade practices by foreign powers. But determining the cause of any company's successes or failures has never been an exact science, and blaming Boeing's loss of market share to Airbus shenanigans was, at best, an educated guess. Due to the secretive nature of the GIE form of existence under French law, no one could be certain how much subsidy there was.

There was, after all, little doubt that Airbus did produce safe, reliable, operationally economical, state-of-the-art aircraft (fly-by-wire, composite constructed, super-critical wing) that pleased airlines, the crews that flew them, and passengers. Further, America would be hard pressed to justify any complaint against fair competition, since that was the idea supporting the entire free market system. Another confounding problem was that, during the 1980s, Boeing's fortunes were rocketing skyward. Sales in 1987 were an all-time high of $15 billion, three times the level just a few years before. Orders to be filled were over $33 billion. Boeing had more liquidity (cash) than it had had in 20 years. And the future looked even better, so it was hard for the government to get too exercised over the matter of subsidies to Airbus.

The problem of potential unfair trade practices by Airbus was approached, therefore, in a circumspect way, and the pace of dealing with the problem was slow and deliberate. American manufacturers had far more aircraft in Europe or the United States than Airbus. A trade war, which would have imposed tariffs on Airbus products imported into the United States, would have been met with reciprocal duties imposed on Boeing and McDonnell-Douglas products imported into Europe. Thus, American aircraft sales would have suffered more than Airbus sales, which would have been counter-productive. Second, an action under section 301 of the 1974 Trade Act, which authorized an expansion of the retaliatory action by the United States to any and all imported goods from countries deemed guilty of unfair trade practices, was too much like a nuclear weapon. Like the mutually assured destruction (MAD) standoff between the United States and the U.S.S.R. that existed during the cold war, nobody did anything. Third, taking the matter to GATT for decision was a calculated risk. Although most knowledgeable people believed that the United States would prevail in such a contest, no one could be sure. The course of action thought to be the safest and most feasible was direct negotiation with the Europeans, which had begun in 1985.

Over the next seven years, the two sides thrust and parried, postured and threatened, although no formal action was taken. But some aspects of the dispute were clear. First of all, Airbus had no operating capital of its own. It was basically a legal fiction, a name under which a group of individuals appointed by the European governments managed and directed the construction of aircraft by the four participating corporate partners. Airbus Industrie performed no manufacturing itself. Except for British Aerospace, which completed privatization in 1985, the remaining three corporations were wholly owned by the governments of France, Germany, and Spain. The separate corporations of the consortium occupied the dual roles of owners (partners) and also of contractors. The work was parceled out to the four corporations, and the European governments covered all financial shortfalls experienced by the corporations by direct payments to them, or in the form of loans and other financial devices. From its beginnings in 1970, on into 1990, the Airbus consortium was the recipient of state subsidies of some $26 billion, with minimal repayments to the funding governments.[10] Applying accepted economic and accounting analyses, the entire Airbus enterprise was found to have not been commercially tenable.[11] In effect, without direct government subsidy and other state aid to its contractors, Airbus Industrie would never have existed in the first place.

The four countries that participated as backers for the consortium have apparently justified their contributions, at taxpayer expense, on the basis of four criteria:

1. Job creation for their citizens
2. The hope of technological advances in aerospace
3. National pride
4. Creation of European competition to U.S. dominance in aircraft production

Because these justifications are not intended to actually provide a financial return on investment in the American sense, Airbus Industrie could sell its aircraft at artificially low prices, and it was and is not yet financially constrained in its sales innovations to purchasing airlines. Airbus Industrie took advantage of this position to a very great extent beginning with the sales to

Eastern Air Lines in 1977, and it has become the Airbus *modus operandi* since.

The Europeans maintained that the great American aircraft producers also received government aid, particularly from military contracts. While it is true that American manufacturers have benefited from Department of Defense initiatives from time to time (the 707 prototype was the result of the KC-135 tanker research and development program), this result was incidental, and not the object or purpose of government policy. Any trade benefit to the American aircraft producers was the result of spillover from legitimate (not unfair trade) practices conducted in the national interest.

After six years of unavailing discussions with the EC, and with no relief in sight, the United States initiated the legal dispute process under GATT in 1991. With the stakes having been raised, the parties then intensified their efforts at resolution. In 1992, agreement was reached between the United States and the European Commission[12] that, for the moment, quieted the dispute. This agreement, which applies to aircraft with 100 or more seats:

1. Prohibited subsidies for *production* of aircraft (not R&D)
2. Limited subsidies for *development* of new aircraft to 33 percent with a repayment schedule at real interest rates
3. Prohibited revisions to existing subsidy agreements that would make them more favorable to Airbus
4. Provided restraints against unreasonable government intervention in aircraft marketing and procurement activities
5. Increased transparency of both direct and indirect government support activities

The Agreement had no effect on aircraft already launched, so that all Airbus aircraft except for the Super Jumbo 3XX (now known as the A380), were exempted from its operation. In addition, many of the provisions of the compromise agreement were couched in language so vague and ambiguous that enforcement of its terms was rendered very problematical, indeed. This result was regarded by most as an Airbus victory.

The World Trade Organization

In 1994, The World Trade Organization (WTO) was created as a result of the final accords of the Uruguay Round of GATT. The WTO began operation on January 1, 1995. This replacement for GATT was designed to establish a new legal framework to insure that trade laws of the various member nations conformed to the evolution of the new world economy and its multilateral trade system. The goal of the WTO is to facilitate the international movement of products, goods, and services for the betterment of the signatory countries and their citizens. The rules of trade between these nations are based on the WTO agreements that have been negotiated and signed by member countries, which as of 2007 numbered 150. Disputes between members are referred to the disputes resolution procedures set up by the WTO agreements. These agreements are the basis of the WTO multilateral trading system, and they bind member countries contractually to adhere to established rules and trading rights.

While certain new areas of commerce have been the subject of negotiation under the WTO format, like telecommunications in 1997 and agriculture in 2002, no further work has been done in the field of aerospace. This is likely due to the fact that, historically, there are few commercial aircraft-producing nations.

Airbus vs. Boeing: The Road to War

By 2004, it had become clear that the 1992 agreement between the U.S. and the European Commission was still not sufficient to resolve the outstanding issues between the U.S. and the EU. As had been predicted, the ambiguities in the terms of the agreement were interpreted by each of the parties in ways that were most favorable to their own positions. The United States had expected the agreement to lead to a progressive reduction of subsidies. According to the U.S., it became instead an excuse for continued subsidization of Airbus.

By October, 2004, the United States had concluded that the EU was not willing to consider an end to subsidies for large commercial aircraft. Deciding that it had no choice, the United States invoked the dispute resolution procedures available under the auspices of the WTO.

On October 6, 2004, the U.S. withdrew from the 1992 agreement and filed its request with the WTO for consultations on the subsidy issue. This is the first step in the process of a two-party dispute resolution of trade issues. The EU responded by requesting consultations on alleged U.S. subsidies to Boeing (primarily payments under Department of Defense contracts and in the form of research and development on military projects, as well as civilian contracts issued by NASA and the FAA). These consultations resulted in a second agreement, this one dated January 11, 2005, which contained bilateral objectives broadly directed to the ending of subsidies. But within months of signing the new agreement, the EU had changed its position. In fact, in March 2005 Airbus confirmed that it had applied to all four of the EU governments having ownership interests in Airbus for A350 launch aid. The U.K., German, and French governments promptly stated their support and announced that they would provide over $1 billion in subsidies for the A350.

The U.S. Trade Representative stated before Congress in May, 2005, that once again the EU was disregarding the terms of agreements, voluntarily entered into, designed to resolve the subsidy issue. (A comparison of the U.S. and EU positions on the January 11, 2005, Agreement are set forth below.) It was concluded by the United States that it had no alternative than to invoke the next step under WTO procedures for resolution of this dispute. Accordingly, on May 31, 2005, the U.S. requested a dispute settlement panel to be convened. On the same day, the EU filed its counter-request. This procedure is similar to the filing of a complaint and a counter-claim in a civil court, with the expectation of securing a resolution binding on both of the parties. This was the declaration of war.

It should be noted that, when the 1992 agreement was entered into between the U.S. and the EU, Airbus controlled 30 percent of the global large commercial aircraft market. By 2005, Airbus controlled over 50 percent.

Airbus vs. Boeing: A Review of the Grievances

Both the United States and the EU have good cause to protect their commercial aircraft producing companies. The contribution made by these companies to each of their international balance of trade ledgers is very significant. A discussion of this aspect of global commercial aircraft production is treated later in this chapter. But more than that, the U.S. and the EU have very different views of the companies themselves. In America, Boeing is generally regarded by the population at large as just another corporation. In Europe, on the other hand, Airbus is considered a symbol of national pride, and a collective achievement representing parity with the United States in international stature.

The arrival of the A380, for instance, caused these reactions in Europe: The Prime Minister of Great Britain, Tony Blair, was quoted as saying, "Airbus demonstrates we can achieve more together in Europe than we ever can alone. Working together in Europe means we can compete with anybody in the world."[13] French President Jacques Chirac announced: "It is a technological feat and a great European success. . . . When it takes to the skies it will carry the colors of our continent, and our technological ambitions to even greater heights."[14]

Beyond the matter of the A380, when Boeing announced the launch of the 787 Dreamliner, Airbus countered with the A350. It was the declaration of subsidy for the A350 that has brought the matter before the World Trade Organization.

May 31, 2005   **A Comparison of Current U.S. and EU positions and the Jan. 11, 2005 Agreement**

U.S.-EU Agreement on Terms for Negotiation to End Subsidies for Large Civil Aircraft.	Current U.S. Position	Current EU Position
1. The objective is to secure a comprehensive agreement to end subsidies to large civil aircraft producers in a way that establishes fair market competition for all development and production of LCA in the European Union and the United States.	- Yes	- No (wants initial agreement to reduce, not eliminate subsidies, with elimination at some distant date)
2. At present, the companies concerned in the EU are Airbus and its principal shareholders, and in the US, Boeing.	- Yes	- Yes
3. The agreement will be negotiated within three months.	- Flexible on new time frame	- Flexible on new time frame
4. (a) The agreement will be negotiated between and apply to the United States and the European Union.	- Yes	- ? (EU is now insisting that Japan must be included)
(b) These parties will subsequently work together to broaden the agreement to include as parties other countries with civil aircraft industries, or countries with risk sharing roles relevant to the objective of the agreement.	- Yes	- No (wants to broaden at outset)
5. (a) During the negotiations the parties will not request establishment of WTO panels relating to the pending disputes.	- Yes	- Yes
(b) During the negotiations, within the time frame foreseen in paragraph 3 above, the parties will make no new government support commitments for LCA development or production.	- Yes	- No (EU unwilling to continue standstill on new government launch aid during negotiations)
6. The Parties will use the definition of subsidies in the ASCM. The parties will agree on an illustrative list of subsidies to be covered by the agreement which elaborates the ASCM definition. They will use this list to reach agreement on which form of subsidy should be prohibited, actionable or permitted.	- Yes	- ? (EU has consistently sought to expand the definition beyond the WTO)
7. The agreement will be enforced through transparency and strong dispute settlement procedures.	- Yes	- Yes
8. In negotiating the agreement the parties will establish agreed terms and conditions under which either may withdraw at a future date. On the one year anniversary of the agreement, the parties will review its operation, including whether progress on international participation in it is sufficient to prevent circumvention of its objectives and to justify its continuation.	- Yes	- Yes

FIGURE 41-10   Trade facts.
Office of the United States Trade Representative

The U.S. Position

The basic complaint brought by the United States is that Airbus is the recipient of European tax-generated funds that are used in the research and development of new airplane types that are conceived and produced in direct competition with Boeing products. These funds do not have to be repaid under certain conditions, including instances in which the loans are forgiven outright (Germany forgave almost DM 7 billion in 1994), or in situations where the funded research is unproductive, or if new aircraft is not commercially successful. Airbus does not operate under basic economic constraints, and can market its products in direct competition with Boeing without the necessity to concern itself with the probability of profitable returns on investment. This type of "launch aid" constituted some $4 billion for the A380, and was provided by France, Germany, the U.K., Spain, Holland, Finland, Belgium, Italy, and Sweden.[15] There is no comparable source of funds available to any American corporation, including Boeing.

Funding for Airbus is also believed to be at below-market rates. This, too, upsets the international equilibrium of competition. In addition, each of the participating Airbus countries has its own finance agency (like the U.S. Export-Import Bank). Each of these government agencies underwrites sales of Airbus airplanes by offering subsidized financing to potential buyers.

Military contracts between the parent companies of Airbus and the EU or their separate governments are significant. In 2003, military sales of EADS and Bae to the EU surpassed Boeing military sales to the U.S. government, $29.7 billion to $27.4 billion.

Civilian research and development in the EU is controlled by an agency known as the Sixth Framework Program for Research, Technology Development and Demonstration Activities (FP6). EC documents imply that activities of FP6 are primarily aimed at promoting Airbus over Boeing, instead of simply aiding scientific progress in general. An official EU publication stated that its aerospace industry support is designed "to strengthen, by integrating its research effort, the scientific and technological bases of the European aeronautics and space industry and encouraging it to become more competitive at the international level."[16]

The individual governments of the EU also provide aid to Airbus in various ways. The Toulouse factory of Airbus is government provided. Airbus shops in Germany are built with government funds. Other construction is provided by the governments of Spain, France, and the U.K. The U.S. Department of Commerce states that more than $1 billion in infrastructure aid has been doled out to Airbus.[17]

The EU Position

The EU complains primarily about the money received by Boeing through military and civilian research and development contracts. Boeing is actually second to Lockheed Martin in Pentagon-awarded contracts. Although Boeing received $82 billion in government contracts between 1998 and 2003, less than one-fourth of that money was for R&D.

The EU maintains that R&D funding provides indirect benefits to Boeing and can be applied to commercial endeavors. This is exacerbated by higher defense spending in the U.S. than in Europe. The U.S., since World War II, has assumed the role of defender of Western freedoms, while the nations of Europe have placed relatively little emphasis on defense concerns. In addition to military contracts, Boeing receives money from NASA and the FAA under civilian research contracts.

The Export-Import Bank of the United States is the American equivalent of the European finance agencies mentioned above. The mission of the Export-Import Bank is to support transactions that commercial markets are unable to finance for the benefit of American industry. Its basic programs include direct loans to foreign buyers of U.S. goods and services and guarantees of commercial loans to foreign buyers. It attempts to level the playing field by neutralizing the effects of export credit subsidies from foreign governments. These loans are low-interest, and are, simply stated, partially funded by American taxpayers. Between 1998 and 2004, Ex-Im issued loans and long-term guarantees for $53 billion of U.S. exports. Almost $28 billion was for Boeing aircraft. For this reason, some refer to Ex-Im as "Boeing's Bank," although only about 20 percent of Boeing's exports receive Ex-Im financing.

Less direct federal funding comes in the form of the U.S. Department of Commerce promotion of American goods overseas, including the products of Boeing.

Boeing also receives various financial support from state sources, including the State of Washington (the unemployment insurance rate was lowered in order to induce Boeing to build the 787 at its Everette plant; the legislature reduced the state's "business and occupation" tax only for the aerospace industry, and then provided a credit against that tax for R&D expenditures; the state created a sales tax exemption on computers used in the design of aircraft, and provided property tax breaks for specific locations that Boeing was planning to build shops.) The City of Chicago and the State of Illinois combined to induce Boeing to relocate its headquarters by offering a $63 million deal, including a $1 million buyout of office space required by Boeing. It is estimated that Boeing will benefit by some $3 billion over 20 years. It should be recognized, however, that state and municipal incentives to all kinds of industrial companies (from all nations) is a long-standing practice designed to improve their tax base and to provide employment opportunities to local citizens.

Large parts of the 787 are to be manufactured in Japan. The government of Japan has provided launch aid to risk-sharing contractors in that country that will be to the ultimate benefit of Boeing, and to the ultimate detriment of Airbus. The EU has requested that Japan be included in the WTO proceedings. The United States has rejected this.

Overview of the Dispute

Both sides have claimed, even after the filings for WTO intervention, that they would prefer a negotiated settlement to the issues raised. Some government people say that this would be the best solution, if it can be achieved. There are many good reasons for this approach:

➡ In an era when closer political and commercial ties are being sought between most nations of the world, through globalization and other means, the WTO proceedings will likely have a significantly divisive impact on other areas of intended cooperation.

➡ It is possible that unintended consequences, undesired by either side, could be the result of a world body like the WTO taking on such a matter of such individual importance to the two greatest commercial centers in the world. Any WTO decision that enhances aerospace competition from other world governments, such as certain economic powers in Asia, could adversely affect both the U.S. and the EU.

➡ Many question whether the relatively new and inexperienced WTO is capable of undertaking such a complex and politically charged question in the first place.

➡ Precedent in the history of civil aviation matters submitted to the WTO, such as the dispute between Canada and Brazil over subsidies to the makers of regional jets in those countries, where the WTO upheld the positions of both parties, indicate that little change can be expected from WTO rulings in these matters.

➡ The international division of labor, suppliers, and technical expertise currently engaged by both Airbus and Boeing in producing aircraft has to some degree negated the national aspects of the Airbus and Boeing products. In a real sense, both of these companies are international in scope.

➡ Both Airbus and Boeing serve important customers on both sides of the Atlantic, and all over the world. How a WTO ruling would affect them is unknown.

The proper goal for the future of the global commercial aircraft production industry should be the elimination of government subsidies. Whether the WTO proceeding is the best way to accomplish this goal remains to be seen.

Airbus Restructured

Except for the subsidy issue for Airbus, privatization continues moving forward under the auspices of the EU and the Treaty of Rome. In 2001, Airbus Industrie was converted from its structure as a GIE consortium into a corporate legal form of existence, with shares of stock being issued to the corporate successors of the former government corporations that had made up Airbus Industrie, GIE. At the time of its restructuring, AI was constituted as a single integrated company with 80 percent of its stock owned by The European Aeronautic Defence and Space Company (EADS)[18] and 20 percent by BAF Systems (United Kingdom).

EADS is a large aerospace corporation (second only to Boeing) and shortly after its formation was comprised of The Lagardere Group and the French state under the name "SOGEADE" (French, 30 percent, successor to Aerospatiale-Matra), SEPI, a Spanish government holding company (Spanish, 5.5 percent, successor to CASA), DaimlerChrysler Aerospace AG (German, 30 percent successor to Deutsche Airbus), and public holdings (34.5 percent). The composition of Airbus under its corporate form, therefore, adheres to the national divisions of ownership and control that hearkened back to the days of the Concorde consortium. The stockholders in EADS after its formation, with the exception of the French government (15 percent) and SEPI (5 percent), were all fully privatized.

The privatization of EADS and Airbus began something of a reversal beginning in 2006 when DaimlerChrysler and Lagarere reduced their holdings from 30 percent to 22.5 percent. The French government increased its share by 2.25 percent and a Russian state-controlled bank took a 5 percent share. The Russian government is seeking an additional stake in EADS as of 2007.

In 2006, BAE sold its 20 percent interest in Airbus back to EADS. BAE is reportedly seeking closer business connections with U.S. aerospace companies.

The control of EADS has been traditionally based on a split management format, with dual Chief Executive Officers. The two CEOs have been selected based on their national origin, one German and one French. Most everything about EADS, and about Airbus, reflects this duality between German and French interests. All Airbus aircraft are assembled either in Hamburg, Germany, or in Toulouse, France. Factories and labor forces are also about evenly divided in order to preserve jobs in both countries (although wing structures have been fabricated in England and sub-assemblies in Spain).

The Airbus philosophy of maintaining a power balance between its major partners has saddled the business with many inefficiencies and frictions. Problems with schedules and costs in the production of the A380 (discussed below) have created turmoil within EADS and Airbus, resulting in the reshuffling of management of both companies. These problems have also pointed up the cost to the bottom line of inefficiencies that were previously tolerated. As of 2007, a power struggle appears to be underway between German and French interests (and governments) for greater control of EADS and Airbus, with the French position being for greater national government control. At the same time, due to a falling stock price of EADS on European Stock Exchanges, there was agreement that the company had to be streamlined and made more profitable. This process was begun in 2007, and may result in a more Westernized (and a less socialistic-paternalistic) approach to running the company.

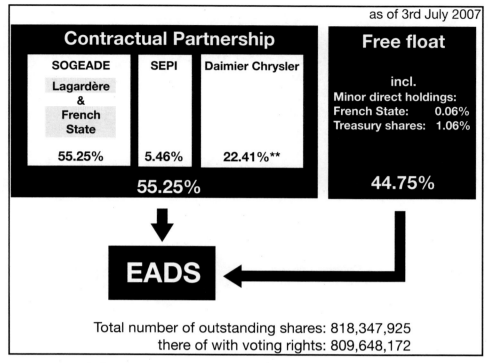

FIGURE 41-11 Stock ownership of Airbus Industrie.

In 2007, the dual CEO management format of EADS was modified to a more traditional corporate setup. The group is now arranged with a German national as the Chairman of the Board of Directors, a French national as the CEO, a German national as the President of Airbus (headquartered in Toulouse) and a French national as the Chief Operating Officer of Airbus.

As Airbus approaches its first delivery of the A380 in 2007, it is in the throes of serious changes to its structure and operations model. There are national divisions within the companies not previously seen. There seems to be a conflict within the group as to whether there should be more or less government control. However this conflict may be resolved, it does appear certain that the French and German governments will be granted a "golden share" in EADS, which is the right of either government to veto certain decisions of EADS' management in the name of national security.

Regulatory Nationalism

The EU has exhibited a tendency to adopt rules, regulations, and legislation that has the effect of punishing foreign imports, especially and specifically those from the United States, while favoring products and services produced within the EU countries. This tendency has been termed "Regulatory Nationalism." Examples of EU activity cited to support this view include:

1. Discriminatory rules applied to extended range twin engine aircraft manufactured in the United States that conveniently have no application to tri-jet aircraft produced in France

2. Flight training proposals that require European pilot training to be conducted at flight schools owned at least 51 percent by Europeans

3. Certification and validation processes conducted by EU agencies that require almost half as long to validate American-made aircraft and parts as it took the FAA to certify initially

4. European noise regulations that impact American-made aircraft and technological fixes, like "hush kits," leaving Airbus in a preferred position[19]

By various means and methods, the EU appears to be intent on challenging the American dominance in aerospace. Some of those means and methods are provocative from the standpoint of free trade agreements and statements of intent on the subject by the EU.

Challenge to America

Thirty-five years after the European call to arms manifested in *Le Defi Americain* (The American Challenge),[20] the Europeans have come a long way in answering that call. And the Europeans are intensifying their efforts and focus. The European Commission in 2000 published a report entitled "European Aeronautics: Vision for 2020." The thrust of this report is a statement of commitment to become the foremost producer of aerospace products in the world by the year 2020. Over the period 2000 to 2005, the EU projected that it would invest some $800 million in research and development. The report states, in one paragraph:

> A generation ago, higher, further, faster were the imperatives for any vision of the future of air transport. Now they are more affordable, safer, cleaner, quieter, reflecting the need to combine cost-effectiveness with the uncompromising attachment to safety and environmental objectives. The key to securing these objectives is investment in research and technology, with a strategy that can meet the demand of the market and the needs of the European community.

The challenge now is to America: Does the United States have the will to confront the energetic, focused, and nationally-financed onslaught that the EU presents? The further challenge to America is how to deal with the aftermath of September 11. Both of these conditions, and many others, impact the position of the U.S. aerospace industry.

In 2001, a federal Commission on the Future of the U.S. Aerospace Industry was constituted, composed of six appointees by Congress and six appointees by the Executive branch. The Commission's charter includes the comprehensive review of the current competitive situation with recommendations for national action to insure the longevity and competitive viability of America's aerospace industry. The final report of the Commission was issued in November 2002.[21]

The Commission's Final Report sounded an urgent alarm: "We stand dangerously close to squandering the advantage bequeathed to us by prior generations of aerospace leaders. We must reverse this trend and march steadily towards rebuilding the industry."[22] The Commission made a number of recommendations:

➡ Government must commit to sustained investment in the national aerospace sector and facilitate private investment in it.

➡ The U.S. air transportation system must be transformed as a national priority, including rapid deployment of a new, highly automated air traffic management system.

➡ The U.S. should create a space imperative which will partner the Department of Defense, NASA, and industry in innovative space technologies, especially in the areas of propulsion and power.

➡ The nation should adopt a policy that brings together government, industry, labor, and academia to allow an integrated view of national aerospace goals and efforts.

➡ The government should establish a national aerospace policy and create a government-wide management structure, including a

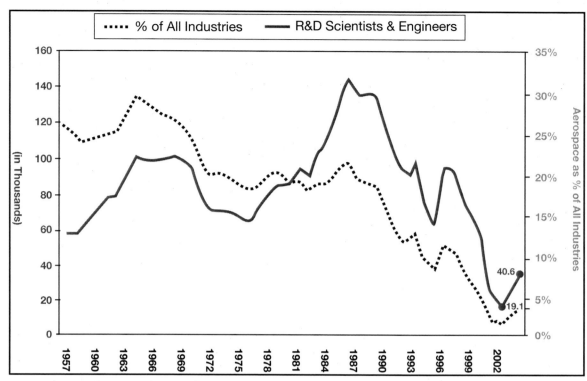

FIGURE 41-12 R&D scientists & engineers employment in aerospace and as % of all industries.

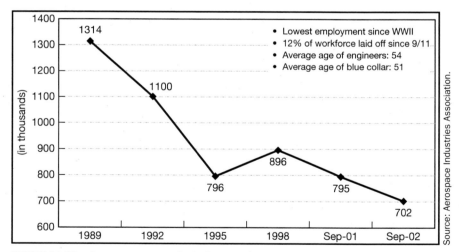

FIGURE 41-13 Aerospace manufacturing employment.

White House policy coordinating council, an aerospace office in the ORB, and a joint committee in Congress.

➡ Export-import regulations must be reformed to allow free movement of products and capital across international borders, and for-

eign government market intervention, such a subsidies to their aerospace industries, should be neutralized either voluntarily through agreement with such countries or by providing similar support for U.S. industry as necessary.

➡ Creation of a new business model to promote the aerospace industry driven by increased government investment and innovative government and industry policies that stimulate the flow of capital into the sector.

➡ Reverse the decline in a scientifically and technologically trained aerospace workforce, addressing the failure of American education in math, science and technology.

➡ The federal government should significantly increase its investment in basic aerospace research.

A glance at the charts on page 379 graphically displays the concerns of the committee.

A response by government can already be seen in the passage in 2003 by Congress of Vision 100, the basis of moving the NextGen transportation system forward. Boeing (and the private sector) are meeting the European challenge in the large commercial aircraft production arena. Below we will discuss the specifics of the Airbus and Boeing programs and the aircraft that are being offered to the world's airlines today.

There is other important news. Aerospace exports have picked up from the lows seen in the early years of this decade, and positive trade balances in the aerospace industry overall have increased over the last few years. In fact, the aerospace sector in the United States was highly successful in 2006, with deliveries expected to exceed $184 billion. This is an increase of more than 8 percent over 2005, which was, itself, a record year. (See Figure 41-17.)

Most of the sales of large commercial aircraft over the last few years have been to foreign customers, due to the depressed state of U.S. airlines and the bankruptcies seen in the legacy airlines during the early years of this decade. It is expected that U.S. customers will soon begin to add to their fleets from the offerings of Boeing and Airbus, so that the financial health of the industry is expected to continue to be good.

Why It Matters

To paraphrase government findings,[23] the aviation sector in the United States is critical to national security, to the free movement of people and articles of commerce, and to our quality of life. The first Gulf War, and the recent deployment of American forces in the conflict in Iraq beginning in 2003, demonstrates the need for a viable aviation infrastructure in the interest of National security. In 2000, U.S. carriers enplaned almost 700 million passengers and flew almost a billion passenger miles, accounting for 25 percent of all individual trips of over 500 miles, 50 percent of all trips over 1,000 miles, and 75 percent

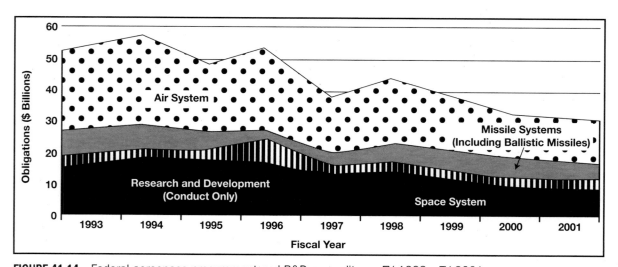

FIGURE 41-14 Federal aerospace procurement and R&D expenditures FY 1993—FY 2001.

over 2,000 miles. Airfreight carries 27 percent of the value of the nation's exports and imports and has grown at over 10 percent annually.

> ❝ More than any other sphere of activity, aerospace is a test of strength between states, in which each participant deploys his technical and political forces. ❞
>
> **French Government report, 1977**

There are 650,000 Americans employed in high quality aviation jobs. Labor productivity in the aviation sector, due to technology gains, has averaged 4.6 percent over the last 40 years, compared to 2 percent for industry as a whole in the United States. Technological advances over the last 40 years have resulted in ten-fold improvements in aviation safety, a doubling of fuel efficiency, reductions in environmentally harmful emissions, and significant reductions in noise.

The aviation sector uses a broad base of technologies—from computing and simulation to advanced materials—supporting the high technology industrial base of the United States. Aviation manufacturing is and has been for many years the largest surplus producer to the balance of trade, adding tens of billions of dollars annually. (See Figure 41-15.)

While it is unlikely that the United States will emulate the government-centered approach adopted by the EU, there do appear to be a number of legitimate areas that policy of the United States government, consistent with its commitment to private enterprise, can be instrumental. Some of these areas are discussed next.

Research and Development

After World War II, federal funding for R&D was driven primarily by Cold War considerations and by national space endeavors. Space spending declined over the years since 1969, the year America landed the first man on the moon. With the demise of the Soviet Union in 1991, defense

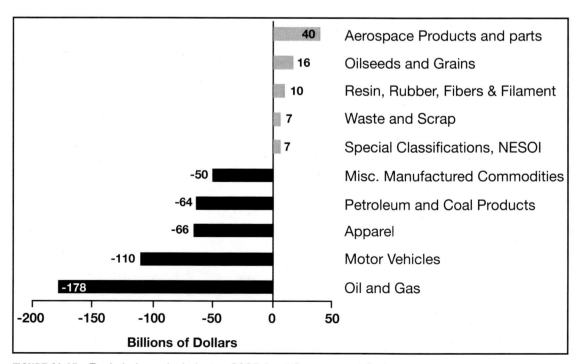

FIGURE 41-15 Trade balance by industry, 2005 (best five vs. worst five).

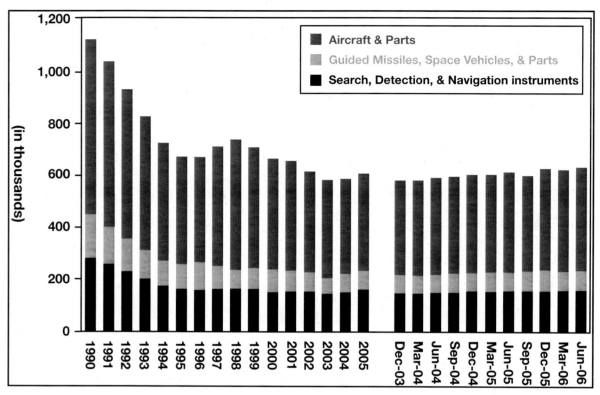

FIGURE 41-16   Aerospace employment.

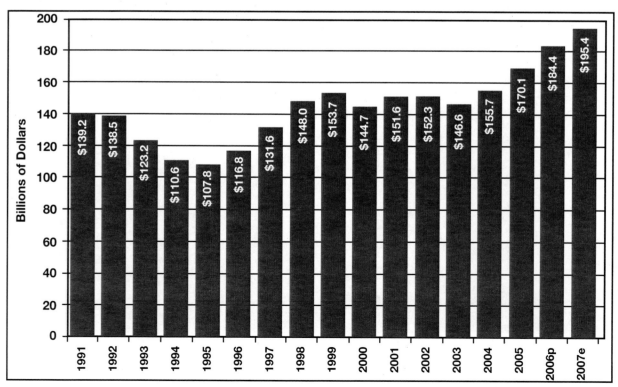

FIGURE 41-17   Aerospace industry sales.

spending was drastically reduced. R&D funding, for instance, dropped from $26 billion to $500 million. Downward trends in R&D funding were (and still are) seen in deteriorating wind tunnels, laboratories, and test ranges. This lack of investment is reflected not only in loss of R&D production, but also in the human element, the scientists and engineers needed to maintain United States leadership in aerospace. As R&D spending has been reduced, so has the number of scientists and engineers employed in the U.S. aerospace industry. From a high of 144,800 scientists and engineers employed in 1986, that number has fallen in 1998 to 77,000. (See Figure 41-12 and Figure 41-14.)

Since 2003, this downward trend has begun to reverse, at least to some degree, as seen in federal R&D expenditures, foreign trade balance increases, and aerospace industry sales. Projections indicate that, at least for the near future, these increases are likely to continue. (See Figures 41-16 Through 41-21.)

Tort (Liability) Law in the United States

Overall, the United States has the most liberal liability law in the world. The success and prominence of the plaintiff lawyers' bar has a heavy lobbying impact on the Congress and on the Legislatures of the fifty states. Current liability law in the United States favors the recovery of large sums of money by injured plaintiffs or by the legal representatives of persons killed in transportation or industrial mishaps. Product liability laws in force in all of the fifty states make it unnecessary in most cases to even prove negligence if it can be alleged by the plaintiff's attorney that a "defective" condition in the manufactured product (the airplane, for instance) was a cause of the injury or death. Efforts by business and industry to reign in the tide of multimillion dollar jury awards, including placing a "cap" on the amount of recoverable damages in certain types of cases, have met with failure in the U.S. Senate. Plaintiff lawyers are some of the largest contributors to Senators and Representatives in

the Congress, as well as on the state level. Large jury awards against commercial manufacturers translate into higher costs of doing business, with a concomitant higher price for the finished product. These factors severely curtailed, and almost ended, the light (general aviation) aircraft market during the 1970s and 1980s, until Congress finally enacted remedial legislation imposing curbs on the liability of manufacturers of small aircraft.[25]

Production of Regional Jets

No American aircraft company produces a regional jet. When regional jet sales are included in total aircraft sales for the world market, United States market share stands at 35 percent. As we have seen, regional jet sales are expected to increase dramatically as airport and enroute congestion become more and more of a problem for the traveling public. At present there are no government incentives for American aircraft companies to invest in the research, development, and plant capital outlay that would permit a competitive regional jet to join this important future market.

National Air and Space Administration (NASA)

NASA has traditionally provided significant R&D support to the aerospace industry as a consequence of federal projects, like the space program, undertaken by the government. The results of this R&D are made available, as a rule, not only to American industry, but also to European companies. Fly-by-wire technology, for instance, was developed by NASA for United States military aircraft and for the Space Shuttle. But it was Airbus that first incorporated this technology into commercial aircraft. European funding of R&D, by contrast, has been supplied directly to aircraft manufacturers (Airbus) and has ranged all the way from basic research to development and production. The fruits of European R&D, moreover, are closely held by European governments. This disparity in sharing technology is not likely to improve.

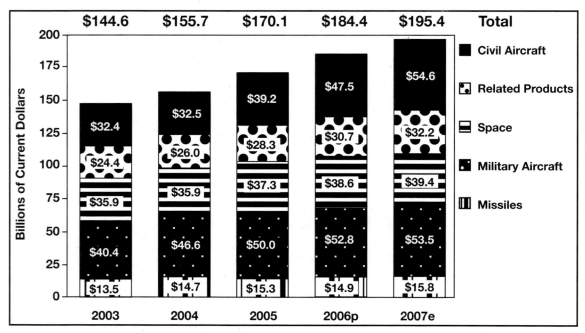

FIGURE 41-18 Aerospace industry sales.

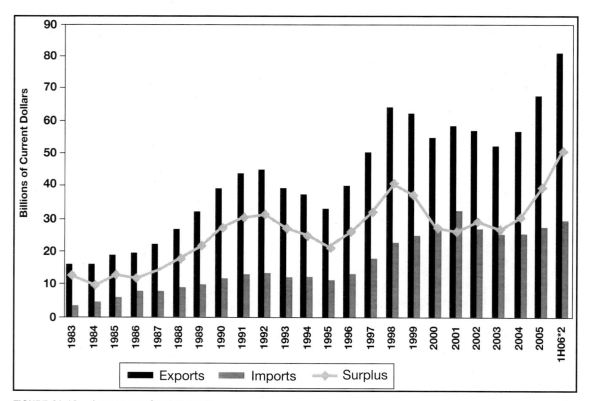

FIGURE 41-19 Aerospace foreign trade.

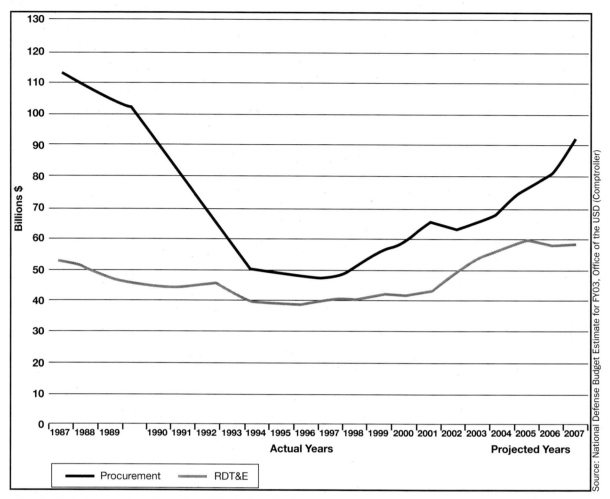

FIGURE 41-20 FY 1987—FY 2007 DoD budget authority.

Entering the 21st century, NASA acknowledges that dramatic change in funding, and military and space spending, are going to impact the way business is done. In 1971, for example, the military accounted for 55 percent of the overall aircraft market, while in 1998 it was down to 31 percent. Military spending on turbojet engines was even more reduced. Over that same time frame, General Electric declined from 70 percent military to 20 percent. During the 1950s, there were 45 aircraft development programs. During the 1980s there were only six. R&D expenditures are reduced in the same manner.

NASA points out that existing air traffic and airport systems in both the United States and around the world are reaching full capacity. Delays are increasing with no relief in sight. Computer models relied upon by NASA, based on operations at the country's top 64 airports (80 percent of enplanements), indicate that annual delay costs will increase to $13.8 billion by 2007 and to $47.9 billion by 2017, absent significant changes in the system. In addition to this, the nearer the system gets to its capacity limits, the less flexibility it has to cope with any type of disruption. Any isolated problem within the system, like a thunderstorm, creates missed connections, severe delays, and canceled flights that spread throughout the system. A dependable transportation system cannot operate with so little flexibility.

The "spill-over" effect of these occurrences, or externalities, are costs to the airlines, added stress to ATC and airport operations, and inconvenience to the traveling public. The private sector has little capacity to deal with these effects. NASA, however, is working through a number of programs, like Aviation Systems Capacity, to address these issues. These potential solutions could impact aircraft design. The NextGen Air Transportation System is under study and development, as earlier discussed.

The NASA Vision and Strategy for the Future

NASA believes that aviation has reached the point where evolutionary technology will not solve the transportation problem. The question is not whether it will be Boeing or Airbus that prevails in the intensifying competition in world aircraft production, but rather, which company or companies will be able to reinvent themselves to utilize new, revolutionary technologies to break through constraining market barriers and create a new playing field. Markets that are constrained by factors like "externalities," that defy solutions through evolutionary technology, breed new technologies. The railroads did it to the horse and buggy, semiconductors did it to vacuum tubes, and the airlines did it to the railroads.

NASA has made it clear that it is not interested in protecting any outmoded industrial base. It has no intention of perpetuating the past and helping industry better compete in a constrained market that does not serve the American public. Its purpose is to assist in providing the nation with a workable, flexible, competitive, and secure transportation system. That means that NASA intends to pioneer revolutionary technologies that will break through today's market barriers.

This is exciting stuff. It is also complex, and in a sense, almost science fiction. In NASA's own words,[26] here is the plan:

> First, we are focusing on the public good—not the maintenance of yesterday's industrial base. When we do this we create new opportunities. For example, NASA is focusing on the mobility of the U.S. people in our Small Aircraft Transportation System (SATS) program. Let me describe SATS. Over 90 percent of the U.S. population live within 30 miles of an airport. However, most of the airports are small, non-towered and without radar surveillance. We also do not have a very small, smart, safe and efficient fleet of aircraft to use this network of airports. In other words, most of the U.S. airport infrastructure falls outside the modern air transportation system. But this does not have to

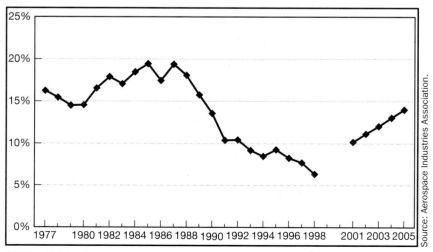

FIGURE 41-21 Aerospace share of national R&D funding.

Source: Aerospace Industries Association.

be the case. Utilizing GPS, a relatively inexpensive suite of electronics and sophisticated software we could turn these "dumb" airports into "smart" airports that would allow them to actually leapfrog onto a new era of intelligent, flexible airport facilities. It is also possible to enable a new generation of aircraft that can support this network of intelligent small airports. The first steps down this path are being made by new companies like Eclipse Aviation, using NASA technologies to produce inexpensive, safe small jets that will provide air taxi service point-to-point to small airports. The SATS program is focused on enabling this future. So, in focusing and innovating on mobility NASA is creating new opportunities for U.S. industry and we are already seeing new companies being formed. The future is unfolding before us if we choose to look.

Second, we are focusing on revolutionary "leap-frog" technologies—this means integrating radical new technologies such as information technology, nano-technology and biologically-inspired technologies into the traditional aerospace sciences to open up new pathways for innovation. For example, we can now envision a wing that "morphs" its shape, a structure that heals itself, and a control system that senses and controls its own operation down to the molecular level.

Third, we will develop a new era of engineering tools and processes. Assured safety, high mission confidence, fast development times, and efficiency in developing revolutionary aerospace systems must become the benchmarks of our future engineering culture. To meet these needs, NASA will develop the tools and system architecture to provide an intuitive, high-confidence, highly networked engineering design environment. This interactive network will unleash the creative power of teams. Engineers and technologists, in collaboration with all mission or product team members, will redefine the way new vehicles or systems are developed. Designing an aerospace vehicle from the atomic-level, engineering teams will have the ability to accurately understand all key aspects of its systems, its operating environment, and its mission

before committing to a single piece of hardware or software. We will drive the design cycle time back down from the nine-plus years it takes today to three to four years while increasing the quality of design.

Fourth, we must train the next generation of scientists and engineers. If we are to truly develop an entirely new approach to aerospace engineering and our aerospace transportation systems, we must motivate our students by focusing on the incredible range of innovation and opportunity that is possible and educate them so they can make it reality.

An Uncertain Future

If the NASA vision becomes national policy, the federal government will provide whatever assistance, control, and direction may be necessary to ensure a reliable, safe, and efficient transportation system. That system will bear little resemblance to the present one. Air traffic control will become a partnership between NASA technology and FAA operational oversight. Navigation and precision approaches to landing will be completely based on Department of Defense Global Positioning System technology, supplemented by Wide Area Augmentation System (WAAS) to ensure reliable signal availability over the entire United States. Airborne self-separation will revolutionize enroute traffic practices and eliminate the constraints of "corridor" routes. Expensive ILS and other in-place precision approach systems will be eliminated in favor of onboard satellite navigation. Small airports (over 5,400 in the United States) served by small commercial jets on point-to-point service will maximize use of the airport infrastructure and reduce the gridlock of the hub airport system, better serving the traveling public. Much of this vision is already on the drawing boards of government under the Next Generation Air Transportation System (NextGen) authorized by Congress in 2003 as discussed in Chapter 36.

The NASA vision goes beyond revolutionizing the airspace system. It envisions a revolution in "aviation vehicles" based on efficiency, functionality, and environmental compatibility. These aircraft will no longer be an assembly of multiple mechanically-connected parts. They will be constructed of "smart" materials containing embedded sensors, functioning like the nerves of a bird, that gauge wing pressures and send signals to the embedded actuators, that act like the muscles of a bird, to cause wing reformation and shape to optimize efficiency of the wing. NASA claims to be at the leading edge of the technology—nanotechnology—to make all this happen. The material to be used in the construction of these aircraft, carbon nanotubes, have the promise to be 100 times stronger than steel while weighing only $\frac{1}{6}$ as much.

The look of the aircraft of the twenty-first century will depart from the familiar airplane designs of the twentieth century. Commercial jet transport aircraft of today, the aircraft being built by Boeing and Airbus, use the same basic configuration that ushered in the Boeing 707, and the turbojet engines that were developed beginning in the 1950s. NASA believes that the evolutionary technology that produced the wonderful flying machines of the 20th Century is near its end, and that the era of radically new technology is at hand.

It is not possible at this point to predict how the events of September 11, 2001, will affect the NASA vision. The long-range impact of global terrorism on the airlines of the world, especially those of the United States, is also not presently knowable. What we do know is that U.S. airlines in 2003 entered another period of economic stress. The unsettled international situation resulted in a sharp decline in airline travel and took a heavy financial toll on the airline industry worldwide, including new aircraft orders. Since then, some recovery has been seen, as discussed in Chapter 36, but the air carrier system is still fragile.

A discussion of the effects of the War on Terrorism is presented elsewhere.[27] Concerns are being debated in the United States Congress relating to the vulnerability of the commercial aircraft to shoulder-launched missiles, and whether commercial airliners should be equipped with missile counter-measure defenses. The projected costs for equipping the entire U.S. fleet are enormous. How these costs would be borne, and what this additional burden to the final production cost of a large commercial aircraft would be (the A380 cost approaches $300 million today), remains an open question.

Airbus Beginning the 21st Century

The European governments that support and fund Airbus are clearly committed to continuing their joint efforts to make Airbus the primary LCA producer in the world. Since its beginnings in 1970, Airbus has fielded a type of aircraft to compete with all types of aircraft produced in the United States, with one exception: the 747.

The Boeing 747 has enjoyed unparalled success since its inauguration in 1969, and it has remained unchallenged for almost 40 years. It has been one of the primary purposes of Airbus, and the national governments of Europe, to break the dominance of the American large commercial aircraft manufacturers, and it has been largely successful except in the case of the 747. During the 1990s, airplane manufacturers began exploring the market for a successor to the 747, with even larger seating capacity. Airbus began its design process in 1994 with the design goal for a prototype that would operate at 15 to 30 percent of the operating costs of the 747. This process evolved into the 3XX program, which incorporated a two-deck concept.

The A380

The A380 was launched in December 2000. It is designed to take over the role that the Boeing 747 has occupied for nearly the last 40 years. This airplane will, at 555 seats in three classes, carry 35 percent more passengers than the 747-400 (853 passengers in single class), and will produce half the noise at takeoff. Engines are either Rolls-Royce Trent 900 or Engine Alliance GP7200. Composite materials make up 25 percent of the airframe by weight. It will have a maximum takeoff weight of 1,235,000 pounds.

The program started with a development budget of €8.8 billion. The development costs have grown to over €12 billion as of 2007, of which European governments have contributed at least one-third.

Manufacturing of components began in 2002, and the first completed aircraft was rolled out of its hangar in Toulouse on January 18, 2005. The airplane is built in separate structural sections in France, Germany, Spain, and the U.K., and these sections are transported to Toulouse by surface transportation due to their size. Due to the sale of the British interest (BAE) in Airbus in 2006, the Germans may take over wing construction in the future, particularly if the wing is redesigned. After assembly, new aircraft are flown to Hamburg for interiors and painting.

Airbus had announced 55 launch customers back in 2000. By roll-out, orders had grown to 149. The first production model took to the air three months later on April 27, 2005. By March 2007, nine A380 aircraft had flown, and five of these have been committed to the aircraft's testing phase. Evacuation certification trials occurred on March 26, 2006 when 853 passengers and 20 crew were evacuated in 78 seconds (90 seconds was the certification time limit). EASA and FAA certification for carriage of up to 853 passengers was given three days later. The aircraft received its type certification from both agencies on December 12, 2006.

Production of the 380 has been beset with problems that have resulted in a two-year delay in delivery. The first delay was announced in June 2005, pushing projected first delivery to Singapore Airlines to the last quarter of 2006. A year later, in June 2006, a second delay of six to seven months was announced. By this time, the

share price of EADS stock had fallen almost 30 percent. These problems also led to the resignations of the Airbus CEO, Gustav Humbert, and EADS CEO, Noel Forgeard. Still another delay was announced in October 2006.

These delays have resulted in cancelled orders (FedEx and UPS cancelled orders for the freighter version in 2007), an earnings shortfall at Airbus of at least €4.8 billion, and a push-back of the first delivery to Singapore Airlines to at least October 2007. Purchasers are also owed substantial penalties by Airbus due to the delays in delivery.

Airports and terminals must be reconfigured in certain ways to accommodate the A380. Although the airplane can land or take off on any runway that can take a 747, taxiways and aprons will require modifications in some cases. Aircraft bridges may have to be beefed-up. Terminal gates will require enlarged parking areas and multiple jetway bridges to access the aircrafts' two levels. Service vehicles capable of reaching the upper deck of the A380 will have to be acquired. Since all of these requirements carry with them substantial cost to the airports, it is not surprising that not all large airports have chosen to make these investments. Notable among these is Hartsfield Airport in Atlanta. There will, however, be some advantages to airports accepting the 380, including reduced pressure on slots, and increased revenue based on PFC charges and landing weight charges. It is estimated that there will be 20 airports worldwide by 2007 and 40 airports worldwide by 2010 that will be capable of accepting the A380.

The first delivery of the 380 (Singapore Airlines) was purchased in a 485-seat configuration and is planned to be used on the London-Singpore-Sydney route. Qantas is the customer for the second aircraft delivery in 2008, and it plans to put the aircraft in service on the Melbourne-Sydney-Los Angeles route in a 501-seat configuration. Air France's 380 will be used on the Paris to Montreal and New York routes.

Airline	EIS	Type			Engine	
		A380-800	A380-800F	Options	EA	RR
Air France	2009	12		2		
China Southern	2008	5				
Emirates[57]	2008	55				
Etihad Airways	2013	4				
ILFC	2013	10		4	4	
Kingfisher Airlines	2010	5		5		
Korean Air	2008	5		3		
Lufthansa[58]	2008	15		10		
Malaysia Airlines	2008	6				
Qantas[59]	2008	20		4		
Qatar Airways	2010	5		2		
Singapore Airlines[60]	2007	19		6		
Thai Airways	2010	6				
Virgin Atlantic	2013[61]	6		6		
Unidentified VIP customer		1				
Sub-totals		**174**	**0**	**42**	**82**	**81**
Total		**174 (firm: 165)**			**163**	

FIGURE 41-22 A380 orders.

The superjumbo market represented by the 747/380 types is estimated to be 5 percent to 10 percent of the entire LCA market as measured by value of annual deliveries. The smaller wide-body jets, by contrast, constitute 50 percent of the market. Airbus first projected a break-even production run of 270 aircraft, but that was raised to 420 due to costs of delays, and is expected to be raised yet again. There are only 165 firm orders for the A380 as of the middle of 2007 (See Figure 41-22), so Airbus has a long way to go to reach its break-even point. Many stumbling blocks could lie along the way, including the degree of acceptance that the airplane receives from airlines and passengers after it is put in service, the number of airports that incur the modification costs to accept it, and the world economy (including terrorist threats) in the near term.

It might be worthwhile at this point to reflect that Boeing, in the mid 1960s, literally gambled its entire future on the success of the 747. Had the 747 been a market failure, there would be no Boeing Aircraft Company today. But the 747 was not a market failure, it was a resounding success and the envy of every aircraft producer in its day, and is still today. With the A380, Airbus may be setting out on a similar gamble.

The A350

After Boeing announced the 7E7 concept in 2003, Airbus responded with a modification of its A330, which it called the A330-200Lite. The announcement of this proposal was roundly panned by the airlines, so that Airbus was required to literally go back to the drawing board. In 2004, Airbus announced the A350 project, which was a new aircraft using the A330 fuselage but with new wings, engines, and horizontal stabilizer. It also incorporated composite materials instead of metals used in the 330.

Customers again reacted with negative comments, saying that the Airbus response was a "band-aid" reaction to the new Boeing 787. Realizing that the 250–300 passenger airplane market was at risk, Airbus undertook a major redesign of the airplane, which resulted in a wider fuselage. This new iteration was called the A350 XWB (extra-wide body).

Launch of the A350XWD was delayed due to the problems in production of the A380 (discussed above), and because of uncertainty as to how the development costs of the new airplane would be borne. On December 1, 2006, the EADS Board of Directors gave approval for the official launch of the A350XWB, with costs to be paid from cash-flows. (Launch aid was subsequently offered by European governments, which precipitated the WTO action discussed above.) Development costs approximate $10 billion. Whether government launch aid will, in fact, be received is still an open question.

The airplane will be 52 percent composite construction, 20 percent aluminum, 14 percent titanium, 7 percent steel, and 7 percent the balance, similar to the 787. Rolls-Royce has committed to supplying engines for the airplane, and Airbus is in talks with General Electric in order to be able to offer a choice of engines to customers.

The first airplanes to be delivered, in 2013, are known as the A350-900 and will seat 314 passengers in three classes. The A350-800, although numbered lower, will actually enter service later, in 2014, and will seat 270 passengers in a three class arrangement. In 2015, a third iteration, the A350-1000, with 350 seats will be fielded. (See Figure 41-23 for complete specifications.)

Boeing Beginning the 21st Century

In March 2001, Boeing unveiled a new concept in large aircraft called the "Sonic Cruiser." This airplane would be designed to fly just below the speed of sound, at around 0.95–0.98 Mach, or 15 to 20 percent faster than wide-body production aircraft now in use. This increase in speed figures out to time-savings of about one hour for every 3000 miles traveled. This design significantly departs from the standard, incorporating a delta wing configuration, twin rudders, rear-mounted engines, and canards located forward on the fuselage, just aft of the cockpit. The Sonic Cruiser would accommodate 200 to 250 passengers in three classes with a range of 6000 to 9000 miles.

By the middle of 2002, however, Boeing's consultations with user airlines had created some doubt that current economic conditions would support the successful marketing of the Sonic Cruiser. By the end of 2002, Boeing announced its decision to forego putting the Sonic Cruiser into production.

Instead, in January 2003 Boeing announced that it had refocused its developmental efforts on the 7E7, a more conventional wide-body jetliner carrying 200–250 passengers on routes between 7000 and 8000 nautical miles. While the 7E7 is not a futuristic design like the Sonic Cruiser, it does plan to heavily incorporate advanced technology. Boeing has lagged behind Airbus in the incorporation of new technology into its aircraft designs. Although such technology was available, Boeing held back that technology in the 737 NG, for instance, in order to keep that new airplane as similar as possible to the existing 737 design in use by Southwest Airlines, the launch customer for the 737 NG. Not until the development of the 777 did Boeing incorporate similar modern technology as that used on Airbus aircraft.

The "E" in its 7E7 designation denotes improvements in efficiency, economics, environmental performance, and enabling technologies

Model	A350-800	A350-900	A350-1000
Cockpit Crew		Two	
Passengers	270 3-class	314 3-class	350 3-class
	312 2-class	366 2-class	412 2-class
Length	198 ft 6 in (60.5 m)	219 ft 3 in (66.8 m)	242 ft 3 in (73.8 m)
Wingspan		209 ft 10 in (64 m)	
Wing Area		4,740 ft^2 (440 m^2)	
Wing Sweepback		35°	
Height		55 ft 5 in (16.9 m)	
Fuselage Width		19 ft 4 in (5.90 m)	
Cabin Width		18 ft 4 in (5.60 m)	
Cargo Capacity	26 LD3	36 LD3	44 LD3
Maximum Takeoff Weight	540,000 lb (245,000 kg)	580,000 lb (265,000 kg)	650,000 lb (295,000 kg)
Cruise Speed		.85 March (561 mph at 40,000 ft)	
Maximum Cruise Speed		.89 March (587 mph at 40,000 ft)	
Range, Loaded	8,300 nm (15,400 km)	8,100 nm (15,000 km)	8,000 nm (14,800 km)
Max. Fuel		39,682 US gal (150,000 L)	
Service Ceiling		43,000 ft (13,100 m)	
Engines (2×)		RR Trent XWB	
Max. Thrust	75,000 lbf	87,000 lbf	95,000 lbf

FIGURE 41-23 Specifications.

developed during the examination of the Sonic Cruiser concept. In April 2004, All Nippon Airways became the launch customer for the 787, but still while the aircraft was known as the 7E7. On January 28, 2005, Boeing designated the aircraft as the 787.

The 787

The 787 features lighter weight construction using 50 percent composite, 20 percent aluminum, 15 percent titanium, 10 percent steel, and 5 percent the balance. The fuselage is all-composite (carbon fiber reinforced plastic). The composite fuselage allows higher cabin humidity for greater passenger comfort since composite materials do not corrode. The cabin air conditioning system features ozone removal from outside air, removal of bacteria and viruses through HEPA filters, and a filtration system that removes odors, irritants, and gaseous contaminants. Larger windows will allow passengers to view the horizon. Cabin width is 15 inches greater than the A330/340 (but 5 inches less than the proposed A350).

Boeing says that the airplane will be 20 percent more fuel-efficient than competing aircraft. The efficiency gain is provided by aerodynamic improvements (one-third), lighter weight materials (one-third), and from engines (one-third). The 787 has a new electric architecture that eliminates bleed air from the engines for systems operation and also replaces hydraulic power with electrically powered compressors and pumps. Notably, the A350 as now designed will still use bleed air for its systems.

Engines will be provided by either General Electric (GEnx) or Rolls-Royce (Trent 1000). For the first time in commercial aviation, either engine

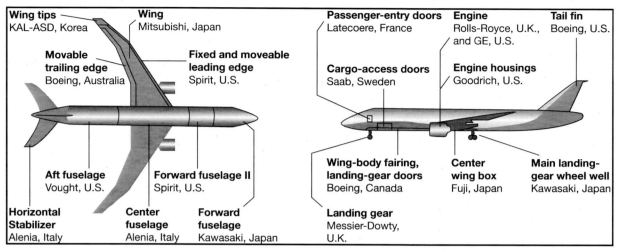

FIGURE 41-24   Joint effort: Parts for the Boeing 787 are manufactured around the globe.

can be fitted to the aircraft without modification due to engine and aircraft interface design.

Production is a worldwide affair, with wings being manufactured in Japan (Mitsubishi Heavy Industries), horizontal stabilizers made by Alenia Aeronautica of Italy, fuselage sections by Alenia, Kawasaki Heavy Industries (Japan), Vought (Charleston, SC), and Spirit AeroSystems (Wichita, KS). Latecoere (France) produces passenger doors and cargo doors are made by Saab (Sweden). The landing gear is provided by Messier-Dowty (France) and the integrated standby flight display and electrical power conversion system is supplied by Thales (France). Overall, 35 percent of the airplane is being built by risk-share partners in Japan. Avionics and flight control are the domain of U.S.-based Honeywell and Rockwell Collins. Flight Dynamics is studying forward-looking infrared as part of the heads-up display system, which will allow pilots to "see" at night or through any type of obscuration.

Final assembly will occur at Boeings' Renton, Washington, plant. The various subassemblies that have been outsourced to the various contractors mentioned above will be shipped, when complete by those contractors, to the Boeing plant aboard modified 747s dubbed "Dreamlifters."

In 2007, Boeing announced production problems related to "supply chain" issues and to its decision to outsource much of the airplane's design and construction. For some years, Boeing has used foreign contractors, particularly in Japan, to build significant parts of its aircraft. This procedure has been highly successful. With the 787, Boeing increased outsourced participation in the overall design and fabrication significantly. This decision was calculated, in part, to reduce the overall production schedule from six years to four years. Because the 787 is a completely new type of airplane, however, and because of the advanced materials and technologies that are incorporated into it, specifications, tolerances, and other technical issues have to be worked out on an on-going basis. Language differences have contributed to the delay in securing required changes, as has the fact that some of the contractors are working half a world away from Boeings' headquarters.

The first 787 was rolled from its hangar on July 8, 2007. In October 2007, Boeing conceded that its production schedule would be delayed by at least six months. While this will affect first flight and flight test dates, Boeing still expects to be able to deliver the first production 787 to its first customer, All Nippon Airways, by the end of 2008. Boeing plans to offer the airplane in three models, sequenced for delivery from 2008 to 2010. See Figure 41-25 for the list of customers for the three types of 787 being offered.

Customer	EIS†	787-3	787-8	787-9	787-10††	TBA†††	Options	Rights	GE	RR
Aeroflot	2014					22				
Aeromexico	2011		2						*	
Air Berlin	2013		25				10	15		
Air Canada	2010		37				23		*	
Air China	2008		15							*
Air India	2008		27						*	
Air New Zealand	2011			8			12			*
Air Pacific	2011			5				3	*	
ALAFCO (Leasing Company)	2012		22[1]						*	
All Nippon Airways	2008	30	20				50			*
Arik Air	2014			3						
Arkia Israel Airlines	2012			4						*
Avianca	2010		10					10		*
Aviation Capital Group			5							
Azerbaijan Airlines	2010		3						*	
Boeing Business Jet			3[4]	4					1	1
CASGC	2008		3[2]							
China Eastern Airlines	2008		15						*	
China Southern Airlines	2008		10						*	
CIT Aerospace (Leasing Company)	2012		10						3	
Continental Airlines	2009		8	17					*	
Ethiopian Airlines	2008		8	2					*	
First Choice Airways	2009		12						*	
Garuda Indonesia	2011		10							
Hainan Airlines	2008		8						*	
Hong Kong Airlines	2008					10				
Icelandair	2010		4					3		*
ILFC (Leasing Company)	2010		73	1					20	40
Japan Airlines	2008	13	22				15		*	
Jet Airways	2011		10							
Kenya Airways	2010		9				4			
Korean Air	2010		10				10		*	
LAN Airlines	2011					26	10			
LCAL (Leasing Company)	2009		6	9						9
LOT Polish Airlines	2008		8				1	5		*

Customer	Year									
Monarch Airlines	2010		6					4		*
Northwest Airlines	2008		18				50			*
Pegasus Aviation Finance (Leasing Company)	2009		6							*
PrivatAir (BBJ)			1[4]							
Qantas	2008		15	50[3]			20	30	*	
Qatar Airways	2010		30[5]				30		*	
Royal Air Maroc	2008		4				1		*	
Royal Jordanian Airlines	2010		2				2			
S7 Airlines	2014		15					10		
Shanghai Airlines	2008		9						*	
Singapore Airlines	2011			20			20			
Travel Service			1					1		
TUF Group	2010		11							
Uzbekistan Airways			2							
Vietnam Airlines	2010		4				11			
Virgin Atlantic Airways	2011			15			8	20		
Unidentified Customers			12			6			2	
Sub totals		**43**	**531**	**138**		**64**	**257**	**121**	**325**	**175**
TOTALS		\<— **776 (683 firm, 93 pending††††)** —>					**378**			

† Entry into service.

†† Boeing has not officially launched the 787-10.

††† Type to be announced.

††††Entries shaded in light gray have been announced, but a firm contract has not yet been signed.

1. ALAFCO will sell 12 of their 22 787s to Kuwait Airways. [1]

2. Xiamen Airlines cancelled its order for 3 787-8s in favor of the 737NG. Boeing has indicated that CASGC will reallocate these aircraft to another Chinese carrier.

3. Qantas has announced its intention to convert 20 options to 787-9s plus 20 purchase rights to options, but a firm contract has not yet been signed.

4. PrivatAir's order has been accounted for by Boeing as a Boeing Business Jet (BBJ) order.

5. Boeing has confirmed that Qatar is the customer of 30 787s ordered on April 5th though not in a press release. [2]. Further according to Flight International, Qatar has 30 options and has selected GEnx engines for their 787s. [3]

FIGURE 41-25 Boeing 787 Orders and Options.

The 787 is a success already. Pre-delivery, it has an unprecedented order backlog of 776 orders from 52 different customers. State another way, the 787 is sold out through 2014.

In view of worldwide economic conditions prevailing at the beginning of the 21st Century, airlines are not willing to commit to technology that will not reflect increases at the bottom line. "E" technology is much more likely to create efficien-cies that increase the financial returns of the world's airlines than is marginally increased speed capabilities of jetliners. The public appears content for the moment with the subsonic speeds that were attained a half-century ago. As if to underscore the point, Air France and British Airways announced that the removal of the Concorde from scheduled airline service effective, respectively, in April 2003 and in October 2003. (See Figure 41-25.)

Photos courtesy of Zaheer Karanjia

FIGURE 41-26 Last Scheduled Flight of the British Concorde, October 24, 2003, on Its Approach to Landing at Heathrow.

The 747-8

On November 14, 2005, Boeing launched the 747-8 program, which is designed to bring the new technologies seen in new Boeing and Airbus types to the venerated 747 line. The 747-8 will seat 467 passengers in three classes of service, which is 51 more passengers than in the 747-400. This will be the only airplane in the world market in the 400-seat category, and will fill the gap between the 555-seat A380 and the 365-seat Boeing 777. The airplane is scheduled to become available in 2010.

The freighter version of the 747 is a proven airplane with freight haulers, and the 747-8 will carry 23 more tons than the 747-400. Due to the two-year delay in delivery of the A380, both FedEx and UPS cancelled their orders for that aircraft and have elected to go with the 747-8, which will be available in the freighter version in 2009. The freighter version has 18 firm launch orders, 10 from Cargolux of Luxembourg and 8 from Nippon Cargo Airlines.

Both the passenger and freighter versions of the 747-8 will have an increased maximum take-off weight of 960,000 pounds. Boeing says that it will represent a new benchmark in fuel efficiency and noise reduction, allowing operation into more airports and during more hours of the day. Aerodynamic improvements are said to be "major," including drag-reducing winglets, and will have new avionics, new flight deck design, and the latest in in-flight entertainment systems. Overall, the 747-8 will incorporate the innovative technologies of the 787, including 787-technology engines.

In comparison with the A380, Boeing says that the 747-8 will consume 10 percent less fuel per passenger. The 747-8 is the only superjumbo that fits today's airport infrastructure, which will increase the destinations available to the airplane's operators.

Beginning the 21st Century— The Global Duopoly

The competition between Airbus and Boeing looks to be close to equilibrium, with the near term promising efficient and conventional designs. The current gambles of Airbus (A380) and Boeing (787), which is where the development costs were spent in the latest competitive round, appear to be bets, in turn, on the future direction of air traffic control, the commitment of airports to reconfigure their infrastructure for the A380, and the preferences of the airline passenger of the future.

ORDERS

	2006	2005	2004	2003	2002	2001	2000	1999	1998	1997	1996	1995	1994	1993	1992	1991	1990	1989
Airbus	791	1055	366	284	300	375	520	476	556	460	326	106	125	38	136	101	404	421
Boeing	1044	1002	272	239	251	314	588	355	606	543	708	441	125	236	266	273	533	716

DELIVERIES

	2006	2005	2004	2003	2002	2001	2000	1999	1998	1997	1996	1995	1994	1993	1992	1991	1990	1989
Airbus	434	378	320	305	303	325	311	294	229	182	126	124	123	138	157	163	95	105
Boeing	398	290	285	281	381	527	491	620	563	375	271	256	312	409	572	606	527	402

FIGURE 41-27 Orders and deliveries.

The A380, for example, is poised to take advantage of the dreaded hub and spoke system, while the smaller 787 appears better situated for city-pair utilization, and possible free-flight, when that possibility materializes. Moreover, in fielding the "semi-competitor" 747-8 to the A380 without duplicating the developmental costs already incurred in the 787, Boeing is making strides in the large aircraft market without incurring the costs and delays that Airbus has seen in the A380 program. The A350 is still a paper project, and depending on events, may remain so for the foreseeable future.

These events include the outcome of the World Trade Organization proceedings over the Airbus subsidy issue now pending before that body. These events also include the degree to which the terrorist threat impacts global commercial aviation.

Globalization of airliner production through the contracting out of sub-assembly fabrications, development of new technologies, and engine manufacture, moreover, will likely tend to keep this competition close, and of an international nature. Such interdependence is increasingly looking more like integration. Airbus, for instance, says that 40 percent of its total procurement budget is spent in the United States, providing over $5.5 billion to American companies and their employees per year. Much of the American aerospace industry, like Rockwell Collins, Honeywell, and General Electric, for years have been subcontractors and suppliers to Airbus, and for each of their employees working on Airbus products, there are some two or three employees in other American companies supplying them. The same thing, to a more or lesser degree, can be said of the effect of Boeing's global outsourcing practices.

With the spread of these international contributions to both Boeing and Airbus aircraft production, it will become more difficult for either the United States or the European Union to assert sovereign dominion over the aircraft manufacturing process in the world to come.

Endnotes

1. America had lagged in putting jet technology to use in the 1950s.

2. Servan-Schrieber, Jean-Jacques, Penguin Books, Harmondsworth, 1967.

3. Sweetman, Bill, Air & Space Magazine, October/November 2003.

4. Lynn, Matthew, Birds of Prey, Four Walls Eight Windows, 1997; a revised edition first published by Reed International Books, Ltd., London, 1995, p. 108.

5. These include (1) EU pressure on The Czech Republic to apply tariffs to Boeing products, *Regular Report on Czech Republic's Accession,* Commission of European Communities, October 9, 2002; (2) German advice to a Turkish Parliamentarian, on the question of EU membership, to "let 80 percent of the airplanes you buy be Airbus," *The U.S. Jet Transport Industry,* p. 84; (3) on December 31, 2004, the EU imposed a tariff on Thailand perfume, but stated that these tariffs could be avoided if the Thai government bought six A380s, "Tsunami-hit Thais told: Buy six planes or face EU tariffs," *The Scotsman,* January 18, 2005.

6. Two baggage door pressure failures and one engine departure from the aircraft. The first pressure failure occurred in June 1972 out of Detroit, but the American Airlines crew was able to land safely. The second pressure failure occurred in March 1973, and the Turkish Airlines aircraft crashed outside of Paris with 346 fatalities. The second crash occurred on May 25, 1979, at Chicago O'Hare when the left engine separated from the wing on takeoff, with 273 fatalities.

7. An entirely new plant and facility had to be built at a new site in Everett, Washington, due to the size of the 747.

8. Quoted in Lynn, Matthew, Birds of Prey, Four Walls Eight Windows, 1997; a revised edition first published by Reed International Books, Ltd., London, 1995, p. 153, 154.

9. Foreign Governments Target Aerospace Technologies and Jobs, <http://lights.com/epi/virlib/Studies/1995/jobso/foreignng.PDF>

10. "An Economic and Financial Review of Airbus Industrie," Gellman Research Associates (1990). Prepared for the U.S. Department of Commerce, International Trade Administration.

11. Ibid.

12. Agreement concerning the Application of the GATT on Trade in Civil Aircraft to Large Civil Aircraft.

13. "Airbus Superjumbo Unveiled," *Press Association,* January 18, 2005.

14. "Airbus Unveils A380, a Giant Fit for 555," *The New York Times,* January 19, 2005.

15. "The U.S. Jet Transport Industry," p. 69.

16. "Decision of the European Parliament and the Council relating to the Sixth Framework Programme," *Official Journal of the European Communities,* August 2002.

17. "The U.S. Jet Transport Industry," p. 80.

18. EADS is the result of the merger of Aerospatiale Matra SA (France), Daimler Chrysler Aerospace AG (Germany, successor to Deutsche Airbus), and CASA (Spain).

19. *Competition in the U.S. Aircraft Manufacturing Industry,* Testimony before the Subcommittee on Aviation of the Committee on Transportation and Infrastructure, U.S. House of Representatives, July 26, 2001, U.S. Government Printing Office.

20. The central premise embraced the frustrations and loss of pride felt by many in European government and business circles: the United States industrial machine had taken over the world economy by means of a synergy between corporations and the American national government. See footnote 2.

21. The Report may be accessed at: http://www.aerospacecommission.gov/AeroCommissionFinalReport.pdf.

22. Ibid., p. vi.

23. Venneri, Samuel L., Associate Administrator, Office of Aerospace Technology, NASA, Statement before the Subcommittee on Aviation, Committee on Transportation and Infrastructure, U.S. House of Representatives, July 26, 2001.

24. Douglas, John W., Aerospace Industries Association of America, Testimony before the House Transportation and Infrastructure Subcommittee on Aviation, July 26, 2001.

25. General Aviation Revitalization Act, Pub. L. No. 103–298, 108 Stat. 1552 (codified as amended at 49 U.S.C. sec. 40101).

26. Venneri, Samuel L., supra.

27. See chapter 36.

CHAPTER 42

Beyond Earth

© Dan Barnes, 2008, Shutterstock, Inc.

❝ The Earth is the cradle of humanity, but mankind cannot stay in the cradle forever. **❞**

Konstantin Tsiolkovsky

Thirty-eight years before the Wright brothers' first flight, and two years before even the transcontinental railroad was completed, wild fantasies of space exploits, a genre later to be known as "science fiction," hit the presses. In Jules Verne's *From Earth to the Moon,* published in 1865, three members of an American gun club travel to the moon aboard a spaceship launched from a columbiad[1] located in Florida. The story bears an uncanny parallel to the U.S. Apollo program that operated from Cape Canaveral, Florida, to the moon 100 years later.

Between Jules Verne and Apollo, however, there was much work to be done.

The Founding Fathers of Rocketry

The progression of rocketry from literary fancy to scientific reality is generally credited to three men, all of whom worked separately from each other at about the same time. All were inspired by Jules Verne.

Konstantin Tsiolkovsky (1857–1935) was a provincial math teacher who spent most of his life in the small Russian town of Kaluga. Tsi-

olkovsky was a theoretician in aerodynamic flight, working through some of the same problems the Wright brothers did at about the same time. His theories extended into jet propulsion and rocketry, as well as to the mechanics of living in space. In 1895 he published *Dreams of the Earth and Sky,* in which he described the mining of asteroids.

Tsiolkovsky's primary work, *Exploration of the Universe with Reaction Machines,* was

© Bettmann/CORBIS.

FIGURE 42-1 Konstantin Tsiolkovsky.

published in 1903 and is generally recognized as containing the first scientifically provable theories on the use of rockets in space. His writings are very detailed, including his specification for a mix of liquid oxygen and liquid hydrogen to fuel the engine of his theoretical spacecraft. Hydrogen was first liquefied in 1898, and it is nothing short of amazing that this mixture propels the Space Shuttle today. Tsiolkovsky was a true theoretician, never attempting to prove his theories by practical applications, like building models or attempting motor or flight tests. In spite of the volume of his publications, his work was not widely known outside of Russia.

Robert Goddard (1882–1945) was inspired not only by Jules Verne's writings but also by another science fiction tome, H. G. Well's *The War of the Worlds.* He dedicated himself to aeronautics and space issues from an early age, and his first article, *The Use of the Gyroscope in the Balancing and Steering of Airplanes,* was published by *Scientific American* in 1907.[2] After earning a Ph.D. in physics in 1911, he registered two patents describing multistage launchers and liquid and solid propellant rockets, which became central to the progression of rocket science. By 1916, his work was being partially subsidized by the Smithsonian Institution.[3]

Goddard's 1919 manuscript entitled *A Method of Reaching Extreme Altitudes,* published by the Smithsonian in 1920, is regarded as a seminal work in the pioneering of rocketry. He continued his experimentation with rockets, launching the first liquid-fueled rocket on March 16, 1926, in a cabbage patch near Auburn, Massachusetts. Although it rose only 184 feet in 2.5 seconds, it proved the workability of liquid-fuel propellants in rockets.

Like many who had gone before, much of Goddard's work was met by mocking and scorn, particularly by the press, and most particularly by The New York Times.[4] Although he withdrew from public view and conducted his experiments in as much privacy as possible, Goddard still attracted notoriety with each rocket launch. Launch failures and ensuing ground fires caused the Massachusetts State Fire Marshal to prohibit Goddard from conducting any further tests in the state.

Charles Lindbergh found Goddard's work fascinating and full of promise, and contacted him in November 1929. Lindbergh was famous by this time, and the lending of his name and credibility to Goddard's experimentation was invaluable. Through the influence of Lindbergh, Daniel Guggenheim agreed to fund Goddard's research in the amount of $50,000 beginning in 1930. Goddard continued to receive support from the Guggenheim Foundation in the ensuing years.[5]

Seeking open space and relative solitude, in July, 1930, Goddard relocated to, of all places, Roswell, New Mexico,[6] where he continued his research and experimentation until the beginning of World War II. He experimented with rocket control through movable vanes and rudders, as well as the use of gyroscopes. His rockets carried aloft the first payload, a barometer and a camera. Details of

Nasa's GRIN gallery from Nasa Headquarters Images (Center: HQ)

FIGURE 42-2 Robert Goddard on March 16, 1926 with the first liquid-fueled rocket.

all of his work were published in 1936 in the treatise, *Liquid Propellant Rocket Development.*

Efforts to interest the United States government in his work were unsuccessful. But not everyone was unable to grasp the potential of his work. The new government of Germany, which took power in January 1933, was highly interested in Goddard's work. The National Socialist German Workers Party, also known by its acronym, the "Nazi Party" led by Adolf Hitler, was very interested indeed.

Hermann Oberth (1894–1989) was born in Romania but lived his life in Germany. He was one of the first to discover the works of Konstantin Tsiolkovsky, during the 1920s. He published the book, *The Rocket into Interplanetary Space,* in 1923. This book presented theories very similar to Goddard's, but Oberth denied that he had had the benefit of Goddard's work beforehand.[7] Oberth conducted his own experiments during the 1920s, and in 1929 published an updated version of his previous book under the title of *The Road to Space Travel.*

Largely due to Oberth's efforts, rocketry became popular in Europe during the 1920s. In 1928, Wernher von Braun, while attending a boarding school in northern Germany, happened on Hermann Oberth's book *(The Rocket into Interplanetary Space).* Fascinated, he launched himself into a program of physics and mathematics that would prepare him for the fledgling science of rocketry. By 1930, von Braun was a student at the Technical University of Berlin, where Oberth was an instructor. An amateur rocketry group inspired by Oberth's book, known as the "Spaceflight Society," held meetings on the Berlin campus, and von Braun became a member. It was here that he met Oberth, and as a result von Braun was selected to assist Oberth in his liquid-fueled rocket motor tests. At this time von Braun was introduced to Goddard's work, and he followed up with his own research into Goddard's publications through scientific journals and publications.

The German Army began its rocket program in 1931. When it came to power in 1933, the Nazi government placed the advancement of rocketry high on its military "want list." At the time, the terms of the Versailles Treaty (the 1918 agreement that ended World War I) prohibited Germany from developing military aircraft, but it said nothing about rocketry, mainly because practical rocketry was unknown to anyone except to a handful of engineers. The German Army began recruiting bright University students with credentials and interest in rocket science.

By 1933, von Braun was working on his doctoral dissertation in physics. Because of a research grant from the German Army, von Braun began collaborating on a secret solid-fuel program at the ballistic weapons center at Kummersdorf. The Kummersdorf site was moved to Peenemunde on the Baltic coast in 1936. Peenemunde was the secret laboratory and test site for the development of the V-2 rocket, which is recognized as the immediate precursor of the launch

FIGURE 42-3 Hermann Oberth (foreground) Wernher von Braun (near right).

vehicles later used in the U.S. space program. The V-2 was the first practical rocket, 46 feet in length and weighing 27,000 pounds. It flew at speeds in excess of 3,500 miles an hour and delivered a 2,200-pound warhead 500 miles away. It was put to use against Allied targets, including London, in September 1944.

With the approach of Allied forces toward the end of World War II, von Braun arranged the defection of about 125 of his top rocket scientists and engineers, who brought with them their plans, drawings, and test results. Von Braun and his "rocket team" became the backbone of the United States' ballistic missile program after World War II, and ultimately were largely responsible for the development of the Saturn V super launch vehicle that propelled the Apollo modules to the moon. Although von Braun was central to the perfection of rocket science in its practical aspects, he is considered in the "second generation" of rocket pioneers.

Space: The New Frontier

From a technical perspective, atmospheres have no "end"; they just get progressively thinner. During the 1950s, it was generally known in the scientific community that, beyond some altitude, the physics of flight changed drastically. The principles for flight in the atmosphere, or the science of aeronautics, were fairly well understood. The principles for flight without an atmosphere, or the science of astronautics, were less understood. Some believed that these two disciplines needed some definition as to their separation.

There is no "bright line" that determines where outer space begins. NASA accords astronaut status to any individual who travels above 80 kilometers (50 miles). Yet atmospheric drag becomes evident on reentry at 75 miles above the earth's surface.

The venerable Federation Aeronautique Internationale,[8] which was founded in 1905, has ever since that time been accepted worldwide as the arbiter of aeronautical records. Through this private organization, the physicist Theodore von Karman in 1957 proposed a formula for the calculation of a boundary that would establish the beginning of space. One of the characteristics of aeronautical flight is the concept of lift, which is a function of speed through the atmosphere, among other things. The thinner the atmosphere, the faster the airplane must fly in order to gain the lift necessary to remain aloft. Karman proposed an altitude of approximately (the exact altitude depends on certain variables) 100 kilometers (62.1 miles) as the separation point based on his calculations that a space vehicle would have to travel faster than the speed necessary to obtain orbital velocity in order to maintain aeronautical lift. In other words, aerodynamic lift becomes less than centrifugal force.

This became the internationally accepted boundary to space, and it is known as the "Karman Line." The Federation Aeronautique Internationale is now the recognized keeper of all records that are established in astronautics.

Sputnik

Before October 4, 1957, humankind had always conducted its affairs below this boundary. On that date, the Space Age began with the orbiting of the artificial earth satellite known as "Sputnik," which was launched by the Soviet Union (Union of Soviet Socialist Republics, or U.S.S.R.) on a military rocket. This accomplishment, while heralded by the scientific community, caused considerable distress in the nations of the West.

After World War II, the Soviet Union had asserted dominion over the countries of Eastern Europe, and it was the titular head of the Communist World. The People's Republic of China, the name of the communist government that controlled that country beginning in 1949, and the People's Republic of North Korea, also fell into this camp. Communist controlled governments, considered by the West to be bent on world domination, extended from Northern Europe to the Pacific Ocean. The hostile relationship that emerged after World War II between the nations of the West and the Communist Bloc countries had been termed the "Cold War" by Winston Churchill in 1948, but there had been a shooting war on the Korean Peninsula between these factions from 1950 to 1953, and millions of people, both civilians and combatants, had died.

The Soviet Union had perfected nuclear weapon capability well before 1957, and with the launch of Sputnik, it was clear that the U.S.S.R. now had the capability to deliver these weapons on intercontinental ballistic missiles. Now also, for the first time since Roman law had established that national sovereignty extended from the ground upward to infinity, the sovereign skies of the Western countries were being violated every 90 minutes by the unauthorized passage overhead of the Russian satellite. Its "beeping" radio signal every few seconds only punctuated their helplessness.

The geopolitical contest between the Western powers and the Communist Bloc countries was one of brutal competition, and it was considered a philosophical, social, and, if necessary, a military fight to the death. But in the midst of this perilous world scene, there was some precedent for cooperation and good will among nations, based on scientific inquiry. Worldwide cooperative endeavors known as the International Polar Year in 1884, the Second International Polar Year in 1934, and the International Geophysical Year beginning in 1957 stood as hopeful examples of the advancement of humankind through peaceful cooperation.

People worried which way the Space Age would take them.

Scientific Cooperation— Precedent for Space

The Space Age arrived during the International Geophysical Year (IGY), which was actually an 18-month period that extended from July 1, 1957, to December 31, 1958. The IGY was an international effort to coordinate worldwide measurements and data collection of geophysical (earth, oceans, atmosphere) properties, as well as to investigate an expected peak of sunspot activity and a number of solar eclipses. It was apolitical and non-nationalistic, coordinated by the International Council of Scientific Unions, and 67 nations participated.

The American participation was done under the auspices of the National Academy of Sciences, with the stated goal: ". . . to observe geophysical phenomena and to secure data from all parts of the world. . . ." The IGY sought to capitalize on the many innovative technologies that were appearing after the Second World War, including computers, rocketry, and radar.

The International Geophysical Year was patterned on two previous international scientific undertakings. The first was the International Polar Year (IPY), which took place from 1881 to 1884, now known as the 1882 IPY. It was the first series of coordinated international expeditions ever undertaken to the Polar Regions. The project was inspired by the Austrian explorer, Carl Weyprecht, who believed that nations should put aside their competition for geographical dominion and, instead, fund a series of coordinated expeditions dedicated to scientific research. Eleven nations participated in the effort, and 12 stations were established and maintained in the Arctic for the three-year period.

A second expedition was conducted on the 50th anniversary of the first, and it became known as the 1932 Polar Year, or the Second International Polar Year. The Second IPY was promoted by the International Meteorological Organization to take advantage of several new technologies, such as precision cameras and high frequency radio, and to investigate the newly discovered "Jet Stream." Forty countries participated and 40 permanent observation stations were established in the Arctic. The contribution of the United States was the establishment in Antarctica of the meteorological station on the Ross Ice Shelf during the second

Byrd expedition. The Second IPY was primarily concerned with the investigation of meteorology, magnetism, atmospheric science, and the mapping of ionospheric phenomena that advanced radio science and radio technology.

Many scientific accomplishments have been recorded through these three international cooperative endeavors. Because of the IGY, for example, scientists defined the mid-ocean ridges (furthering the understanding of the effects of plate tectonics and verifying the formation of continental shapes), discovered the Van Allen radiation belts, charted ocean depths and currents, studied Earth's magnetic field, measured upper atmospheric winds, and studied Antarctica in great detail.

The Antarctic Treaty

The work of the IGY led directly to the Antarctic Treaty of 1959, which regulates international relations concerning Antarctica. Antarctica is the only continent on Earth without a native human population, and none of the continent has been appropriated under claim of right of discovery. The treaty's main aim is to establish Antarctica as a continent to be used by all nations for peaceful purposes and for cooperative scientific research. Military activity, weapons testing, nuclear testing, and radioactive waste disposal are prohibited. The Treaty went into effect on June 23, 1961, and over 40 nations are signatory to it.

The Antarctic Treaty is a singular achievement by the governments on Earth, and it stands in stark contrast to the history of nationalistic exploration and colonization that began with the Spanish expeditions led by Columbus in 1492. One of the reasons that Antarctica was never colonized, of course, is the fact that its climate has been inhospitable to long-term human presence. It is obvious that outer space possesses the same characteristics, even more so. The existence of

the Antarctic Treaty, then, held out some hope in many quarters of the world that the Space Age might bring a more hopeful future to humankind.

The Space Race Begins

Compounding the frustration of the United States over Sputnik, the Soviets launched a second, and larger, satellite (Sputnik 2) on November 3, 1957. This one carried a live animal, a dog named Laika, into orbit. Laika is believed to have survived only for a few hours due to an inability to properly regulate temperature in the capsule. But the Soviets were obviously making strides in space. The propaganda value to the U.S.S.R. was significant.

On January 31, 1958, the United States finally launched its first earth satellite, Explorer 1. Although smaller than either Sputnik 1 or Sputnik 2 (Explorer 1 weighed 30.8 pounds compared to 184 pounds for Sputnik 1 and 1,120 pounds for Sputnik 2), it accomplished more than the Sputniks; its mission payload Geiger counter was responsible for the discovery of the Van Allen radiation belts.[9]

While the launch of Explorer leveled the playing field, it also launched the contest that would preoccupy the world for the next 30 years, the Space Race. The shock of Sputnik also caused the United States to swiftly create a permanent federal agency dedicated to the exploration of space. All U.S. nonmilitary space activities were placed in the venerable, prestigious National Advisory Committee on Aeronautics (NACA).[10] In 1958, Congress passed the National Aeronautics and Space Act, which converted NACA into NASA, and charged the agency with the broad mission to plan, direct, and conduct aeronautical and space activities, to involve the nation's scientific community in its mission, and to disseminate information about its activities.

The stage was now set; the actors (the United States and the Soviet Union) took their places on the stage; the world audience looked on; the only trouble was nobody had a script.

Who Owns Outer Space?

Like the crossing of the Rubicon, traversing the Karman Line marked a point of no return for humanity.

In the context of the Cold War, the potential for disaster was palatable. ICBMs were now a reality, and there was no defense. Mutually Assured Destruction (MAD) was the acronym of the day, and it was a chillingly accurate description of what any miscalculation by either (later any) nuclear power would bring. This was the Wild West on an international level, without a sheriff.

In the context of international civil law, however, many people held out hope. It had been remarked by both astronauts (American) and cosmonauts (Soviets) that national boundaries on Earth were not discernable from space. Boundaries on earth, of course, imply the sovereignty of nation-states, and they have been the cause of wars since time immemorial. But there was something about being in space that seemed to strike a humanistic, rather than a nationalistic, chord in those first space travelers.

In 1945, the United Nations was founded among the world's sovereign states in the hope that it could provide a forum for the peaceful consideration of issues between states as an alternative to war. The United Nations is large, and through its organizations (its committee structure), programs (such as trade and food programs), and specialized agencies (such as WHO, the World Health Organization), it has assumed many and varied roles in the international community.[11]

In 1958, the United Nations set up an ad hoc committee called the Committee on the Peaceful Uses of Outer Space (COPUOS) consisting of 11 Member States. COPUOS became a permanent committee in the U.N. in 1959, with 24 members. Among the purposes of this body were the promotion of international cooperation in space, the encouragement of continued research and dissemination of information concerning space, and the study of legal problems arising relating to the exploration of outer space.

The main question confronting CUPUOS was whether a coherent form of international law could be brought to govern human interaction in outer space. If so, what form should it take? In view of international tensions at the time, this was a daunting task.

Terrestrial Precedents

It had been proposed, prior to Sputnik, that international relations with respect to the high seas should be precedent for space. To understand why, we will take a quick look at the concept of national sovereignty and how it relates to the high seas.

National sovereignty implies complete legal authority over an area or a population, which is defined by established national boundaries. Nations that bound the oceans have historically extended their sovereignty from their coastlines into the oceans for a defined distance. These areas are known as "territorial waters" and for many years the standard limit was three miles.[12] The high seas begin at the point territorial waters end.

Since Roman times, national sovereignty also extended "ad coelum," the Latin phrase meaning "to the sky." With the advent of airplanes, this doctrine was applied by international law above the territory of all nations, for as high as airplanes could fly. In all cases, that was in Earth's atmosphere. It continued to be applied to the sky, at least within earth's atmosphere, even after the launch of the first artificial earth satellites,[13] but by custom and acceptance, it has not been applied to flights above the Karman Line.

The legal relationships between sovereign nations are governed by international law. As we saw in chapter 37, international law has developed primarily through the agreement of two or more nations in the form of treaties, which become binding upon ratification and entry into force. In addition, sources of international law derive from "customary international law," which is based on universally accepted principles and general practice. These principles are often based on concepts of right and wrong, ethics, and responsibility.

All land masses on Earth are "owned" by sovereign nations with the exception of Antarctica. As we have seen, international law concerning that continent is now the subject of treaty. The other 70 percent of the Earth, known alternatively as "international waters" or the "high seas," since the early 18th Century has universally been accepted by custom as "free seas." Hugo Grotius[14] in 1609 set out in a dissertation called Mare Liberum (free seas) the logical premise and argument for a natural right residing in all nations and in all peoples to have free access and use of the seas. The concept of free seas implies the right of passage, the right of navigation, the right to fish, and the right to trade. The seas, being unbounded by man and incapable of possession, constitute an equitable, common benefit to the human race.[15]

Although it was a shock to the average citizen, the orbiting of Sputnik came as no surprise to either the scientific or legal community. In the scientific world, in fact, it had been an advertised feature of the International Geophysical Year that an artificial earth satellite would be launched before December 31, 1958, but it had always been assumed that it would be launched by the United States. In the international legal community, debate and discussion had been occurring for some years on many of the questions that were expected to arise once orbiting satellites were a reality.

There had been significant discussion, for instance, of whether the "ad coelum" doctrine would or should apply in outer space, but there was no agreement. Persuasive arguments were made for each position. But when Sputnik was launched, all of the sterling legal arguments were suddenly rendered irrelevant. Sputnik was a scientific and technological fact, and there was nothing anyone could do about it. It became clear that law was going to have to follow science.[16]

There was not one objection by any nation that its national sovereignty was being violated by Sputnik's transits overhead. There was now an acceptance of a limit to national sovereignty somewhere around the Karman Line. But more importantly, the conclusion was compelling that outer space was, indeed, like the high seas. As Grotius had said, "What cannot be possessed is necessarily free for all to use."

The precedent of international maritime law influencing space law was a good thing. Since nations had been sharing the seas for millennia, there was now some basis to believe that the Earth-based international community might, after all, be able to agree on how to use outer space in a peaceful way.

Another terrestrial precedent is Aviation Law. When airplanes became capable of overflying borders into another country's airspace, leaders of those countries sat down together and worked out the details that extended maritime law principles to aviation and devised new rules required by the new aviation technology. Examples of these include the Paris Conference of 1910 and the Paris Convention of 1919. (Refer to chapter 37.) As aircraft became capable of longer range and higher flight, international civil aviation was born to replace, in large part, the maritime passenger industry and to supplement the maritime shipping trade.

The future for international civil aviation was set by the Chicago Convention of 1944. Recognizing the increasing importance to the world of aviation after World War II, contracting nations agreed to set up a structure for the adoption of international regulations, standards, and procedures that would govern and control essentially all aspects of international flight.[17]

But in the years just after the first launches of artificial earth satellites, there were still only two participants in outer space, the U.S. and the

U.S.S.R., and they were still engaged in the "Cold War." It was obvious that some bilateral accommodation between these two powers would have to accompany, if not precede, any effective peaceful solution to the problems of outer space.

Treaties Affecting Outer Space

The Limited Test Ban Treaty of 1963

Escalating tensions and the growth of nuclear armaments during the 1950s had caused talks between the United States and the U.S.S.R to commence in 1955 over the issue of the testing of such weapons. Radiation fallout from atmospheric tests by both sides had accidentally contaminated people and areas far removed from the test sites. Apprehension over the cumulative effect of contamination of the environment and possible genetic damage to the population was shared by most civilized countries.

The United States and the Soviet Union both had actually detonated nuclear devices above the Karman Line, the highest at 540 kilometers (335 miles). The effects of these explosions were varied, and their visual effects were quite spectacular, but the destruction of the electronic components of satellites in low earth orbit by electromagnetic pulses was a common result. During the Cuban missile crisis in October 1962, both the United States and the Soviet Union detonated several high altitude devices as a show of force. The most significant, destructive effects of nuclear detonations in space occurred during this time, on October 22, 1962, when the Soviets exploded a device at an altitude of 290 kilometers. Electromagnetic impulses at ground level in Kazakhstan fused 570 km of overhead telephone line, started a fire that burned down a power plant, and shut down 1,000 km of buried power cables.

The next year, in 1963, the United States and the Soviet Union agreed to prohibit nuclear weapons tests "or any other explosion" in the atmosphere, under water, or in outer space. The inclusion of outer space in this essentially terrestrial agreement created a benchmark for future agreement on outer space.

The Committee on the Peaceful Uses of Outer Space, COPUOS, got off to a good start after is creation in 1959, although it was not involved in the Limited Test Ban Treaty of 1963. During its early years, the number of committee members was small. The committee operates on the basis of consensus (agreement), not majority vote. This means that all members of the committee must agree as to all points on any issue. With fewer members on the committee, consensus was easier to achieve. As the years passed, more members joined the committee, so that now it has expanded to 67 in number. COPUOS has created drafts for five treaties since its formation; all were agreed to between 1967 and 1979. We will now look at each of these.

The Outer Space Treaty of 1967

The cumbersome title, "The Treaty on the Principles Governing the Activities of States in the Exploration and Use of Outer Space, Including the Moon and Other Celestial Bodies," is commonly called The Outer Space Treaty. This treaty is to Space Law what the Magna Carta is to English Common Law, and what the Treaty of Rome is to the European Union. It is the most inclusive and authoritative document for human governance in space, and it is the basis for all treaties that have come after it. It is modeled on the Antarctica Treaty, which was drafted for much the same reason in 1959, as was the Outer Space Treaty in 1967.

Like the Antarctica Treaty, it is a "no armament" treaty. It seeks to prevent a new form of colonial competition in outer space. The treaty covers the entire outer space environment, including the moon and other celestial bodies. It entered into force on October 10, 1967.

The main provisions of the Outer Space Treaty provide:

➡ The use and exploration of outer space is to be carried out for the benefit of all.

➡ Outer space is not subject to national appropriation by claim of sovereignty.[18]

➡ Activities in outer space are to be in accordance with international law.

➡ Outer space is to be free of nuclear weapons or other weapons of mass destruction.

➡ Military bases and testing of weapons are forbidden, although military personnel may be used for scientific research and other peaceful purposes.

➡ Astronauts are envoys of mankind and shall be rendered all possible assistance in the event of accident, distress, or emergency landing on any State's territory or on the high seas.

➡ States launching objects into outer space are liable for any damage caused.

➡ Launched objects shall remain the property of the State or party that launched it.

➡ Use and exploration of outer space is to be carried out without interference to other States, and a procedure for consultation between States is provided for this subject.

➡ States will inform all concerned, including the public, of intended space activities.

The treaty is broadly worded and, therefore, does not purport to provide definition on many issues. Implicit in the drafting is the expectation that other, more specific agreements would be crafted in the future to address specific concerns as needed.

The United States is a signatory to this treaty.

The Rescue Treaty of 1968

The full title is "The Agreement on the Rescue of Astronauts, the Return of Astronauts and the Return of Objects Launched into Outer Space."

Its purpose is to give specificity to the provisions of the Outer Space Treaty that call for the rendering of aid to astronauts and the return of space crews and property launched into space.

The Rescue Treaty creates obligations on contracting parties, both as to crew and as to objects launched into space, who learn of any accident, unintended landing, or crew distress, to immediately:

➡ Notify the launching authority or make a public announcement, and notify the Secretary-General of the UN.

➡ Rescue crew and render assistance, even if on the high seas.

➡ Return the crew to the launching authority.

➡ Return the space object to the launching authority.

The words of the treaty express the sentiment that astronauts are the "envoys of mankind," and that all nations shall have the attitude toward them that reflects the spirit of international cooperation and assistance.

The United States is a signatory to this treaty.

The Liability Treaty of 1972

This treaty is fully titled as "The Convention on International Liability for Damage Caused by Space Objects." It recognizes one of the truisms of human existence, that there can and will be unintended consequences attached to human endeavors, and when those consequences result in damage to others, there should be a defined process to address those consequences by the payment of money damages.

The Liability Treaty sets out a complex regimen designed to cover essentially every possible scenario in which damage results from the launch of any space object. It incorporates principles of tort law, contract law, strict liability, indemnity and other legal concepts that are beyond the scope of our discussion. The basic operation of the treaty, however, follows.

The treaty makes the launching state (or any state that procures a launch by another state) absolutely liable for any damage caused by the launched object that occurs either on the surface of the Earth or to aircraft in flight. The liability is on the contracting party (the country that signs the treaty) even though the launch may be made by a private company. The liability attaches to the state even though there is no fault, or negligence, connected with the launch in any way. This is known as "strict liability."

By way of example, assume that the country of Malaysia contracts with Boeing Launch Services to launch a satellite from Cape Kennedy. The launch results in a collision with an Airbus 300 operated by Air France, killing all foreign passengers and crew and destroying the aircraft. The debris falls in the ocean on the high seas and damages a Russian warship and members of its crew. Who is liable?

The short answer is that the United States, as the signatory country to the treaty, would bear the liability in the first instance. The liability would be to Air France for the value of the Airbus, for damages to the families of the passengers and crew for loss of life, for damages for the value of onboard baggage and cargo, for damages to the warship to the state of Russia, and for damages to sailors aboard the Russian ship.

If neither the United States, nor Malaysia (which procured the launch) is guilty of any fault or negligence, then the United States would have an action under the treaty to recover half of its payout from the state of Malaysia, assuming it was also a signatory to the treaty. The United States (and Malaysia) would have a possible right of indemnity against Boeing Launch Services, under the laws of the United States, for which the U.S. would be made whole for all payments made.

The treaty separately addresses the situation where a space object belonging to launching state (State A) is damaged by a space object belonging to a second launching state (State B). If the space object that is damaged is on the surface of the earth, the rules are the same as stated above, that is, strict liability. But if the damaged space object is anywhere else (in the atmosphere or in outer space), then the state that launched the damaging space object (State B) is liable to State A only if State B is somehow at fault, or negligent, which causes the damage. This distinction recognizes, for example, that a collision of satellites or launch vehicles in motion may be the fault of either one or the other launching states, or both, and that proof of that fault should be a precondition to liability.

Liability may be avoided by the launching state, even under strict liability, if the launching state can prove that the damage was caused by the claimant's gross negligence or intentional act.

The treaty also does not apply to claims made by citizens of the launching state against the launching state (for example, an American against the U.S.), since that would be a matter of national, not international, law.

Claims for compensation are presented through diplomatic channels, or through the United Nations.

There have been only a few claims made under the Liability Treaty since it entered into force. The first, and perhaps the most notable, was Cosmos 954. Cosmos 954 was a 46 foot-long, 5 ton Soviet reconnaissance satellite powered by a nuclear reactor. The "spy satellite" was on a sensitive and secret mission designed to locate and track U.S. nuclear submarines. The reactor core failed to attain nuclear-safe orbit (800 miles high) and remained in a lower orbit that decayed within a year to re-entry in 1978.

The United States had begun tracking the satellite from the time of its launch, September 18, 1977, and was aware of its sagging orbit by December 1977. The U.S. began diplomatic conversations with the Soviets to try to determine the extent of the risk, such as a critical mass explosion on reentry or on impact with the ground. The Soviets cooperated, but were circumspect due to the satellite's mission. The U.S. wanted answers about the enrichment of the uranium on board.[19]

The trajectory for reentry placed the satellite over North America, possibly near New York City. U.S. and Canadian technical forces stood by awaiting the event. The satellite actually crashed into the Northwest Territory of Canada, spreading radioactive fuel over a large area.

A joint American-Canadian effort was undertaken to recover radioactive material, the search covering over 48,000 miles in area. The U.S. sent a U-2 and a KC-135 to check for high-altitude radiation, along with a 44-man team of military technicians. The Canadians sent in a nuclear-accident team of 22 people in radiation suits to find and collect debris. The Soviets naturally offered to help, but Canada declined the offer.

The cleanup continued into October 1978 and consisted of locating, recovering, removing, and testing the debris and normalizing the affected area. Most of the recovered debris was radioactive, some to a lethal degree. The government of Canada presented to the U.S.S.R. its claim in the amount of $6,041,174.70 relying on the Liability Treaty, the Outer Space Treaty, and general principles of international law dealing with the violation of national sovereignty.

The claim resulted in extended negotiations over the course of the next three years between Canada and the U.S.S.R., resulting in a settlement of the claim for a total of just $3 million. The nature of the defense presented by the U.S.S.R that would cause the Canadian government to accept less than half its claim is not known, but it is likely related to the fact that Canada refused the offer of assistance made by the U.S.S.R. before the cleanup began. In law, this is known as a failure to mitigate (or lessen) one's own damages.

The United States is a signatory to this treaty.

The Registration Convention of 1976

Officially termed "The Convention on the Registration of Objects Launched into Outer Space," the Registration Treaty requires launching states to maintain a register of launched objects, and to furnish to the United Nations certain basic information, including:

➡ The name of the launching state
➡ The designator of the space object or its registration number
➡ Date and territory or location of the launch
➡ Basic orbital parameters, including nodal period, inclination, apogee, and perigee
➡ General function of the space object
➡ A registration list of space objects that are no longer in orbit

In addition to providing a launch registry for general housekeeping purposes, it is expected that the registry will assist in identifying space objects that are involved in claims of liability and also serve as a basis for helping to clean up space debris.

The United States is a signatory to this treaty.

The Moon Treaty of 1979

"The Agreement Governing the Activities of States on the Moon and Other Celestial Bodies," or the Moon Treaty, is yet another follow-on treaty that proceeds from the first space treaty, the Outer Space Treaty. Each of the treaties that have been adopted since the Outer Space Treaty has added more detail and definition to the general principles enunciated in the first treaty. The Moon Treaty, however, is considered by most as a "failed" treaty because the specific, additional language used has met with opposition from the major space-faring countries.

The basic stumbling block in the treaty is the use of the words "common heritage of mankind" to describe the nature of the moon and its resources, as well as the other celestial bodies. The treaty provides for the establishment of an international regime to govern the exploitation of these resources when such exploitation becomes feasible.

The general interpretation of this language is that all nations of the world have equal rights to the resources of the heavens, irrespective of whether or not they put forth any effort or incur any risk, financial or otherwise, in development of ways and means to recover those resources. Any plan to develop these resources would ostensibly require approval of all nations on earth, which would be impracticable.

The rejection of the Moon Treaty follows a similar rejection of the terrestrial Law of the Sea Treaty (Referred to gleefully by its detractors as LOST). In 1982, the United Nations conceived the Law of the Sea Treaty as a means of control and governance of the world's oceans. The breadth of the treaty was such that it sought to regulate deep-sea mining, as well as such controversial areas as the ocean environment. Like the Moon Treaty, LOST failed to gain support from the major developed nations since it was viewed as an attempt to create a new world order based on a system for the redistribution of the world's wealth. This new system rejects the free-market system of risk and reward for a global collectivist regimen like socialist central planning. Under this scheme, ocean resources would necessarily have to be shared among all mankind. This approach is seen mainly as a benefit to third-world countries.

Most knowledgeable people feel that the provisions of the Moon Treaty materially narrow the intent and provisions of the Outer Space Treaty, although the latter uses similar words of description, "the common Province of all mankind." The meaning of the latter phrasing, found in the Outer Space Treaty, was that no single country could claim outer space or other celestial bodies as its own in the colonial sense, but it did permit the extraction of resources. The "common heritage of mankind" language and related provisions of the Moon Treaty means that the celestial resources may not be extracted unilaterally by any single nation.

The United States is not a signatory to this treaty.

The International Space Station Agreement

The competitive aspects of the space race resulted in much duplication of effort and fiscal waste. During the 1980s, the Soviets had the Salyut and Mir space stations, the U.S. had planned Space Station Freedom, the European Union had planned Columbus, and the Japanese, Kibo. With the demise of the U.S.S.R., the United States initiated discussions with the E.U., Russia, Japan, and Canada in the early 1990s concerning a joint effort to build a significant, lasting international space station. The project, named the International Space Station (ISS) was jointly announced in 1993, and it attempted to combine the best features of all of the existing or planned national space stations.

The primary agreement authorizing the ISS is a treaty signed on January 28, 1998, by the 15 participating countries[20] known as the Space Station Intergovernmental Agreement (IGA). The IGA provides for a long-term cooperative framework for the design, development, operation, and utilization of the ISS.

In addition to the IGA, there are two additional levels of agreements contemplated, called "Memoranda of Understandings." The IGA designates NASA as the Manager of the ISS, and these additional agreements are between NASA and the space agencies for the other participating partners[21] or with agencies of countries other than the original 15 participants.[22] These supplementary agreements deal with the specifics of the management and operation of the ISS, including criminal jurisdiction and codes of behavior.

The IGA provides for the participating countries to extend their jurisdiction into outer space with the ISS. Each country, therefore, will retain jurisdiction and responsibility for the parts of the ISS it registers and for its nationals who are on board. This aspect of the IGA establishes that, for instance, the law of the EU will apply to activities within the European Columbus Laboratory module. Thus, national law applies to criminal and liability issues, and is the basis for the protection of intellectual property rights arising on the ISS.

The first section of the ISS was placed in orbit in November 1998, followed by two additional sections soon after. The ISS is in Low Earth Orbit which ranges between 199 miles to

215 miles above the earth. On November 2, 2000, the first crew, consisting of two Russians and one American, took up residence. The ISS is powered by electricity generated by the sun, it generates it own oxygen on board, and recycles waste and water. The ISS is still being assembled, and when complete, it will have 1,200 cubic meters of pressurized space, or about the size of the interior of a Boeing 747.

Activity aboard the ISS centers on research in "experiment modules," which by 2010 will all be in place. Research fields include biology (including biomedical research and biotechnology), physics (including fluid physics, materials science, and quantum physics), astronomy, and meteorology. The goals of this research include developing an understanding of, and the technology to deal with, long-term human presence in space, developing methods for the more efficient production of materials, developing new ways to treat disease, achieving more accurate measurements than is possible on Earth, and a better understanding of the universe.

Commercial Space Transportation— End of a Government Monopoly

For many years after the launch of Explorer I in 1958, conventional wisdom and generally held perception was that space activities were, and should be, the exclusive domain of national governments. Only NASA, the military services, and the National Reconnaissance Agency[23] were permitted or able to engage in launch activity. Although some commercial payloads were placed in orbit as early as the 1960s, the launching of them was strictly a government business. This view prevailed in spite of the fact that the United States has long based its successful economic system on private enterprise, with the role of government being limited and supportive of the private engines of commerce. This government-private sector symbiosis was the dynamic partnership that we described at the beginning of this book, and it

has been the norm in every industrial, technical, and a scientific advance seen in the United States.

The Commercial Space Launch Act of 1984

The "government only" perception began to change during the 1980s. Europe's Arianespace began offering launch services in 1983. This was followed by President Reagan's **Executive Order 12465** signed in 1984, which authorized U.S commercial space launch activity with the words "in order to encourage, facilitate, and coordinate the development of commercial expendable launch vehicle (ELV) operations by private United States enterprises." Up to that time, all U.S. commercial satellites had been launched on rockets owned and operated by the United States government. The Executive Order was followed by passage in Congress of the Commercial Space Launch Act that same year, which directed the Department of Transportation to "encourage, facilitate, and promote commercial space launches." DOT set up the Office of Commercial Space Transportation to address the transition from government to commercial operations. In 1989, the U.S. government decided to stop launching commercial payloads on the Space Shuttle, in part because of the Challenger disaster that occurred in 1986. This spurred commercial launch interest even more.

The Commercial Space Launch Act established a comprehensive licensing structure that enabled launch operators to comply quickly and efficiently with existing federal regulations. The statute also authorized the licensing of nonfederal launch sites, from which commercial space launches would occur, in addition to commercial launches from federal sites. In 1995, the licensing responsibility was transferred from the DOT to the FAA's Office of Commercial Space Transportation (FAA/AST), which now licenses and regulates U.S. commercial space launch and reentry activity, including launch vehicles. It also licenses nonfederal launch sites.

Commercial Space Launch Activity

The first licensed commercial space launch occurred in March 1989. By October 2006, federally licensed commercial space launches had numbered 179. From 1989, the number of annual launches increased each year through 1997 with a high that year of 24 launches. Beginning in 1998, launch activity leveled off, and even began to decline on an annual basis. In 2005 and 2006, there were 15 commercial space launches each year. For historical and forecast launch and satellite data, see Table 42-1 and Figures 42-4, 42-5, and 42-6.

2007	2007	2008	2009	2010	2011	2012	2013	2014	2015	2016	Total	Average
GSO Forecast (COMSTAC)	23	22	21	23	19	22	21	21	19	19	210	21.0
NGSO Forecast (FAA)	34	18	34	30	22	14	13	10	8	8	191	19.1
Total Satellite	**57**	**40**	**55**	**53**	**41**	**36**	**34**	**31**	**27**	**27**	**401**	**40.1**
GSO Medium-to-Heavy	17	18	16	17	13	16	15	15	13	13	153	15.3
NGSO Medium-to-Heavy	11	8	8	5	4	3	2	4	2	2	49	4.9
NGSO Small	6	5	5	4	2	2	2	2	2	2	32	3.2
Total Launches	**34**	**31**	**29**	**26**	**19**	**21**	**19**	**21**	**17**	**17**	**234**	**23.4**

TABLE 42-1   Commercial Space Transportation Satellite and Launch Forecasts.

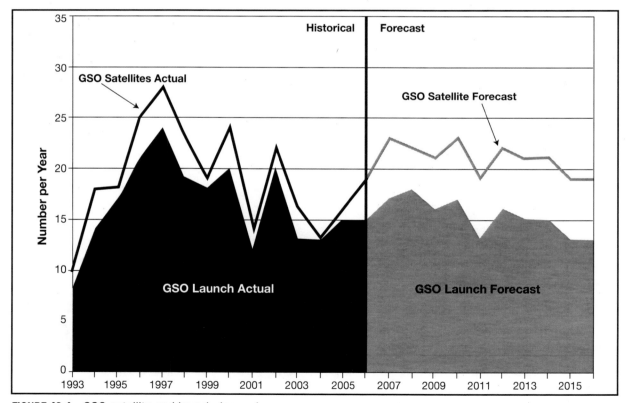

FIGURE 42-4   GSO satellite and launch demand.

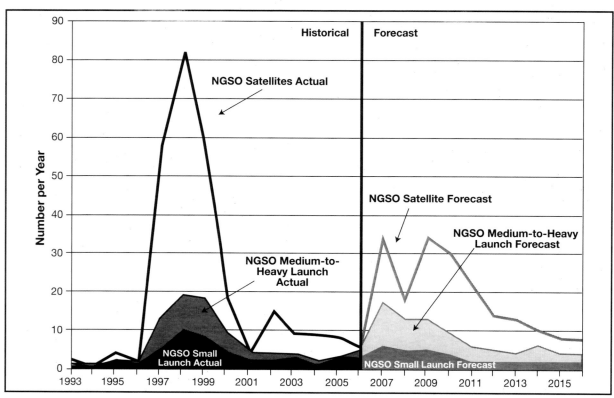

FIGURE 42-5 NGSO satellite and launch demand.

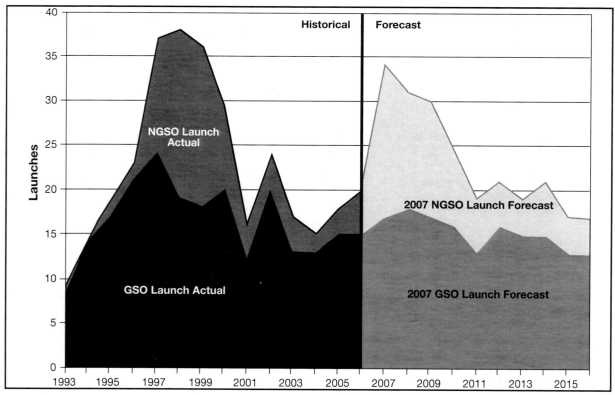

FIGURE 42-6 Combined GSO and NGSO launch forecasts.

Until the 1990s, most commercial satellites were telecommunications orbiters that were placed in geostationary orbit (GSO). The geostationary orbit is a unique, circular orbit plane directly above the earth's equator. By "unique" is meant that there is only one GSO, which is the orbital plane at zero degrees inclination. A satellite placed in this orbit will appear to hover directly over the same point on earth above the equator at all times.[24] A GSO satellite orbits at an altitude of about 22,236 miles above Earth. Since GSO is unique, the number of satellites that can be placed in it is limited. A system of slots is being monitored by the United Nations to insure fairness in allocation of GSO participation among nations.

Since 1997, satellites have also been placed in Low Earth Orbit (LEO) or nongeosynchronous orbit (NGEO)[25] in order to serve new markets in commercial mobile telephones, data messaging, and remote sensing.

Commercial Launch Sites

In addition to the federal launch facilities used as sites for commercial space launches, the federal regimen contemplates the creation of numerous nonfederal (private or state-owned) spaceports around the country. (See Figure 42-7. U.S. Space Transportation Industry, Sites and Locations by U.S. FAA Regional Boundaries.)

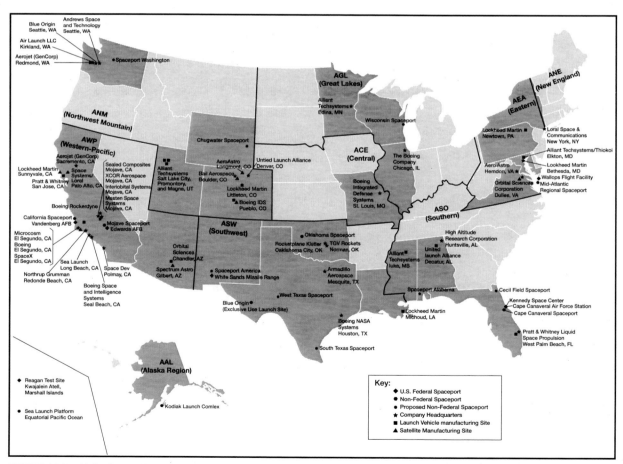

FIGURE 42-7 U.S. Space Transportation Industry.
Sites and Locations by U.S. FAA Regional Boundaries.

By 2006, the FAA/AST had licensed seven launch sites in the U.S. The first four licensed are coastal sites: California Spaceport (at Vandenberg Air Force Base), Cape Canaveral Spaceport (at Cape Canaveral Air Force Station), Mid-Atlantic Regional Spaceport in Virginia (at Wallops Flight Facility), and in Alaska (at Kodiak Launch Complex). The fifth was the first inland site licensed, Mojave Spaceport (Edwards Air Force Base). In June 2006, the FAA/AST licensed the Oklahoma Spaceport on the site of a former military air base (Clinton-Sherman) at Burns Flat, OK. In September 2006, Corn Ranch (Blue Origin) Spaceport in Van Horn, Texas received FAA approval.

As state governments are increasingly interested in developing spaceports within their borders, the FAA/AST foresees a network of nonfederal launch sites throughout the United States. (See Figure 42-8. U.S. Spaceports.) A New Mexico site near White Sands Missile Proving Grounds, 25 miles from Las Cruces, known as Spaceport America, is expected to receive FAA/AST approval in 2008. Richard Branson of Virgin Atlantic plans to operate a tourist space company, to be called Virgin Galactic, from the site.

U.S. commercial launches to GSO are made from either Cape Canaveral Air Force Base or from the platform operated by Sea Launch in the Pacific. Launches to NGSO can occur from any U.S. launch site.

SpaceShipOne (SS1)

On April Fool's day, April 1, 2004, FAA/AST granted the first license ever issued for a private, suborbital flight. The award went to a company founded by aeronautical pioneer Burt Rutan, Scaled Composites. Rutan, an aerospace engineer, gained a reputation for developing new, unconventional airplane designs built of strong, light, composite materials. In 1986, his Voyager aircraft was the first to fly around the world without refueling.

Just one year before being awarded the federal license, Scaled Composites revealed that it was working on a spacecraft design to compete for the Ansari X Prize.[26] At the time, there were 27 announced competitors for the prize. The Ansari X Prize, in the amount of $10 million, was offered by the X Prize Foundation for the first private, nongovernmental launch of a reusable manned spacecraft, capable of carrying three people into space with safe return, twice within a two-week period. The Ansari X Prize is patterned after the early 20th century practice of awarding monetary prizes to aviators in order to spur greater achievements in the then-nascent aviation field. In particular, it is reminiscent of the Orteig Prize of $25,000 that was posted by Ray Orteig in 1919 for anyone who successfully completed a nonstop flight between New York and Paris. The Orteig Prize was claimed by Charles Lindbergh in 1927. (See chapter 13. See also The NASA Centennial Challenges below.)

The Ansari X Prize stipulated that the spacecraft exceed 100 kilometers as the required threshold of space (the Karman Line) at 62.1 miles above the earth. The SS1 flights originated from the Mojave Airport Civilian Flight Test Center (now Mojave Spaceport) in California. SpaceShipOne was aerially launched from a specially Rutan-designed carrier jet called "White Knight." The spacecraft was powered by a hybrid rocket engine that used nitrous oxide (laughing gas) as the oxidizer and synthetic rubber as the fuel. (See Figures 42-9, 42-10 on page 421, and 42-11 on page 422.)

The first competitive flight in the Ansari X Prize competition occurred on September 29, 2004, achieving an altitude of 102.9 kilometers and a maximum speed of 2.92 mach. On October 4, 2004, SpaceShipOne duplicated its earlier successful suborbital flight, this time to 111.996 kilometers and a maximum speed of 3.09 mach. That date was the 47th anniversary of the first Sputnik flight.

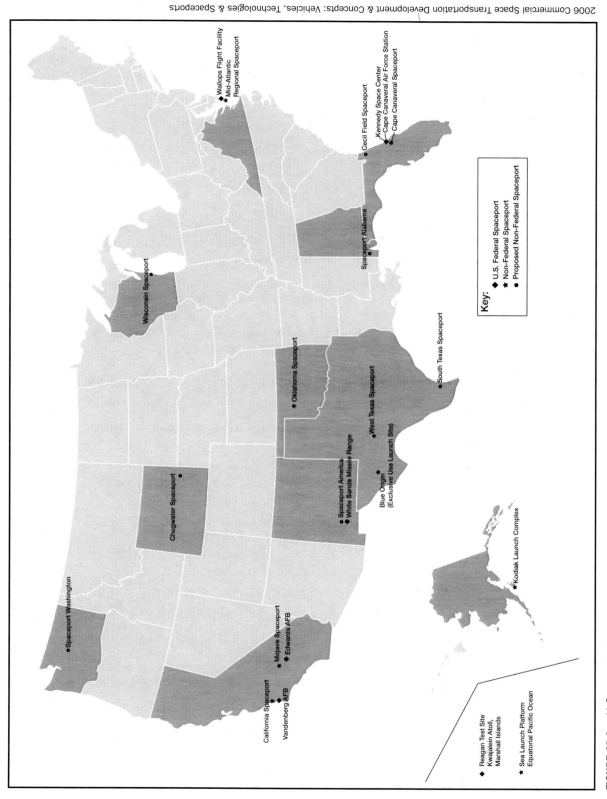

FIGURE 42-8 U.S. spaceports.

Launch service providers today include:

International Launch Services, a partnership between Lockheed Martin and several Russian firms, with experience dating back to 1995. As of 2006, ILS had made 100 launches, 97 of which were successful. In 2006, Lockheed's interest was acquired by Space Transport, Inc. ILS uses the Russian Proton rocket for its launches.

United Launch Services, a joint venture between Boeing and Lockheed Martin, began operations at the end of 2006. ULS uses the Atlas V, Delta II, and Delta IV rockets.

Orbital Sciences Corporation, was founded in 1982 and has completed over 500 launches. It uses the Minotaur, Pegasus, Taurus, and OSP-2 Minotaur IV rockets.

Sea Launch is a consortium of private companies from the United States, Russia, Ukraine, and Norway that was established in 1995. It launches satellites from a mobile sea platform located in the Pacific Ocean at the equator, using Russian-Ukrainian Zenit-3SL rockets. As of January 2007, it had launched 24 rockets, with two failures.

Arianespace is a French company founded in 1980 and comprised of the French space agency CNES, and the French aerospace companies, EADS and SAFRAN. It holds a large percentage of the market for the launch of satellites to the geostationary transfer orbit, from which the satellites are boosted into GSO. Arianespace has completed more than 130 commercial launches since 1984.

Antrix Corporation is the marketing element of the Indian Space agency, known as Indian Space Research Organization. It operates the Indian rocket, the Polar Satellite Launch Vehicle.

Eurockot Launch Services, a joint venture between EADS Astrium and a Russian company; launches satellites into Low Earth Orbit.

ISC Kosmotras, a Russian, Ukrainian, and Kazakhstanian consortium established in 1996, uses the Dnepr rocket.

SpaceX, the popular name for the Space Exploration Technologies Corporation, has never launched a payload into space. It is in the process of testing the new ELV known as "Falcon," and has experienced one failure and a second, partial failure that achieved orbital velocity while losing telemetry. The third launch, from Vandenberg Air Force Base, is scheduled to carry a Naval Research Laboratory satellite.

Starsem, is a European-Russian company created in 1996 to commercialize the former U.S.S.R. Soyuz rocket. It calls itself "the Soyuz company," saying that it "brings together the all key players in the production, operation and international marketing of the world's most versatile launch vehicle." The 1,724th launch of a Soyuz rocket was accomplished on September 14, 2007.

China Great Wall Industry Corporation (CGWIC) is a subsidiary of China Aerospace Science and Technology Corporation and is the only commercial organization authorized by the Chinese government to provide international commercial launch services. CGWIC has conducted at least 24 international launches using the Long March rocket, successfully orbiting 30 foreign satellites.

TABLE 42-2 Launch Service Providers.

FIGURE 42-9 White Knight lifting SpaceShipOne.

FIGURE 42-10 SpaceShipOne.

Scaled Composites plans to begin flight testing its next phase, SpaceShipTwo in late 2007. This space plane will be more powerful than SS1 and is expected to attain 120 kilometers altitude. This will be the vehicle that will be used in the Virgin Galactic flights beginning in 2009 that will carry tourists into space.

Scaled Composites plans orbital flights using its planned SpaceShipThree, assuming success in its Virgin Galactic venture. Orbital flight is much more difficult to achieve than is suborbital flight since the speed necessary to gain escape velocity is on the order of 7 to 8 times that required to reach suborbital altitudes. While SpaceShipOne reached the Karman Line while accelerating to less than 3 mach, orbital vehicles will require 25 mach to achieve

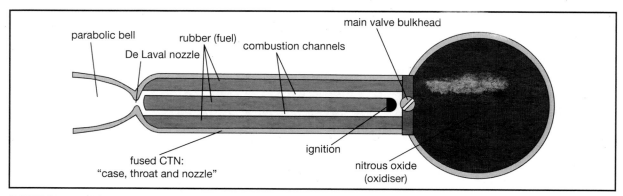

FIGURE 42-11 Hybrid rocket engine used by SS1.

escape velocity. Reentry is also much more complex, since all of the excess speed must be dissipated on reentering Earth's atmosphere.

On July 25, 2007, an explosion during testing of the SpaceShipTwo rocket engine killed three Scaled Composite employees and seriously injured three others. Engine testing was put on hold by the company and it is not known what effect this accident will have on its future.

Reusable Launch Vehicles

SpaceShipOne was the first reusable launch vehicle (RLV) to be deployed since the X-15 rocket plane (1959–1968). The Space Shuttle is a partially reusable launch and space vehicle, with only the orbiter and the solid rocket boosters being reusable. The external fuel drop tank breaks up on reentry after being jettisoned. A significant characteristic of an RLV is the considerably lower cost required to access the space environment. In this regard, the Space Shuttle cannot be considered an RLV of this type since it requires over two months and a substantial ground support crew to refurbish the vehicles for relaunch. The total refurbishment cost is also higher than some ELVs. Moreover, the planned retirement of the Space Shuttle in 2010 has created a need for the development of new technologies to support future missions.

Both commercial and government efforts at developing reusable launch vehicles for orbital flight, beginning in the 1990s, have been largely unsuccessful.[27] There is, however, significant interest in suborbital RLV possibilities, especially in the tourism area. The success of SpaceShipOne portends the likelihood that space tourism will be a reality in the near future.

Manifesting the widespread interest in reusable launchers, here is an impressive list of private companies now continuing development of their own programs:

- Blue Origin (New Shepherd Launch System)
- Armadillo Aerospace (Quad)
- Sea Star Microsatellite Launch Vehicle (MSLV)
- Interorbital Systems (Neptune)
- Rocketplane Kistler (K-1 and Rocketplane XP)
- SpaceDev (Dream Chaser)
- SpaceX (Falcon 9)
- Sprague Astronautics (Altairis)
- TGV Rockets, Inc (Michelle-B)
- SCOR Aerospace (Xerus)

The proliferation of private investment in this segment of space activity is largely due to the **Commercial Space Launch Amendments Act of 2004.** This statute amounts to a declaration that the United States government supports the commercialization of human space flight, and by this law it intends to encourage private investment and participation in expanding this frontier. Among the findings of Congress that require this legislation are: (1) the goal of opening space to the American people and to their private commercial enterprises should guide federal space investments, policies, and regulation; (2) private industry has begun to develop commercial launch vehicles capable of carrying human beings into space; (3) greater private investment in these efforts will stimulate the commercial space transportation industry; and (4) space transportation is inherently risky.

This statute creates the structure for the regulation of private space activities and frees the fledgling industry from the patchwork of regulations that had been applied to it, and which inhibited investment and freedom to innovate. The regulatory scheme previously in place at the FAA/AST was designed for unmanned expendable launch vehicles, not suborbital human space flight. The cost of complying with ELV regulations was a disincentive to RLV launches. Moreover, existing FAA/AST regulations did not cover passengers and crew, which are at the heart of the emerging RLV industry.

The NASA Centennial Challenges

In 2003, NASA started a new program known as "The Centennial Challenges" based on a recommendation of the National Academy of Engineering in 1999. This recommendation was that Congress should encourage federal agencies to experiment more extensively with inducement prize contests in science and technology. The NASA Centennial Challenges were named in recognition of the Wright brothers' first flight 100 years before.

The "Challenges" set up a monetary prize format similar to that discussed above, and which actually relates back to the British prize of twenty thousand pounds sterling offered in 1714 for a reliable method of determining longitude on a ship at sea. (Refer to pages 4 and 5 above.)

The NASA Challenges typically coordinate the competitions with private foundations, like the X-Prize Foundation, the Spaceward Foundation, or others, which actually run the events. The Challenges are announced annually and range over a wide spectrum of scientific and technical issues. Examples from the 2007 competition include the Astronaut Glove Challenge (to devise the best performing glove for space use), the Moon Regolith Oxygen Challenge (the extraction of oxygen from lunar soil), and the Suborbital Payload Challenge (to achieve suborbital altitudes that provide enough linger time for the kind of microgravity research NASA needs).

But the most fascinating Challenges for our purposes relate to the proposed technology that will put humans and objects into space without the use of rocket propulsion. These Challenges are subparts of the larger "space elevator" concept that was first mentioned by Konstantin Tsiolkovsky in the late 19th century, and then more specifically proposed by a Russian engineer (Yuri Artsutanov) in the 1960s. The basic idea is to anchor a tether (a ribbon with a diameter half that of a pencil) at a point on earth that will extend into outer space, to a point beyond the geosynchronous orbit. A counterweight positioned at the space end of the tether would provide enough inertia through the rotation of the earth (centripetal force) to keep the length of the tether taut. Payloads would be attached to the tether for delivery into space.

When first proposed, and even in 1960, the idea was assigned to science fiction because there existed no material strong enough to construct a workable tether. In 1991, science discovered a new class of molecule known as the carbon nanotube, which possesses over twice the strength necessary to make the tether work.

"Elevator 2010" is an organization of the Spaceforward Foundation, which, working with NASA, is sponsoring a 5-year $4 million technology prize competition designed to find the core technologies necessary to design and build the Space Elevator. The NASA-funded Centennial Challenge that relates to these endeavors is the Tether and Beam Challenge, which is broken down into two separate Challenges: The Tether Challenge and The Beam Power Challenge. These were the first two Challenges announced by NASA in March 2005.

The Tether Challenge is a competition to construct a tether of sufficient strength to accommodate the requirements of the ribbon. The prize the first year was $50,000. Because no competing tether surpassed the base-line strength tether by 50 percent, no money award was made. The requirements for the 2006 competition, likewise, went unmet. The award money has increased to $500,000 for 2007.

The Beam Power Challenge is a competition to build a wireless lifting mechanism, called a climber system, powered by electricity from a ground electrical outlet that is "beamed" (wirelessly) to the climber apparatus. The beam is a high-power low-intensity laser. The lifting mechanism must lift a payload a prescribed height within a prescribed time. Like the Tether Challenge, no contestant was able to claim the Beam Power Prize during the first two years of competition. One team's robot ascended a distance of 55 meters in 57 seconds, which was only two seconds too slow to claim the prize. The prize for 2007 is $500,000.

The goal of the competition is to prove, by 2010, that the Space Elevator is a compelling, workable technology, and to have identified the scientific and engineering group that will build it.

The Bigelow Aerospace Competition— America's Space Prize

A second competition has been announced by Bigelow Aerospace, a private aerospace contractor located in Nevada. This company has offered a prize in the amount of $50 million, valid through January 10, 2010, for producing a privately funded, reusable vehicle capable of performing the following feats:

➡ The spacecraft must reach a minimum altitude of 400 km (250 miles).

➡ The spacecraft must reach a minimum velocity sufficient to complete two full orbits at altitude before returning safely to Earth.

➡ The spacecraft must carry no less than a crew of five.

➡ The spacecraft must dock or demonstrate its ability to dock with a Bigelow Aerospace expandable space habitat and be capable of remaining on station for at least six months.

➡ The spacecraft must perform two consecutive, safe, and successful orbital missions within a period of 60 calendar days.

Time will tell whether these prize competitions will advance the cause of space development in any fashion similar to that of the ancestor competitions of long ago. It should be a compelling exercise for students in this course to monitor the success of these extraordinary competitions.

Vision for Space Exploration— A Statement of National Purpose

For many years after the launch of Sputnik, the competitive aspects of the Space Race between the United States and the U.S.S.R. spurred space advances and development. These were the days of setting new records over the whole spectrum of space activity. These "firsts" included the first human in space, the first woman, the longest time in space, the first "spacewalk," and so on.

A Brief History

During these early years, the space race included the race to the moon. Both the U.S. and the U.S.S.R. successfully sent unmanned probes to the moon, but it was the United States, as a result of the Apollo program, that was to win the race. Beginning with Apollo 8, Americans left Earth's orbit and ventured out into deep space. At first orbiting the moon without landing, it was not until Apollo 11, on July 20, 1969, that man first set foot on the moon.[28]

The Apollo program successfully landed six missions on the surface of the moon. Apollo 11 through Apollo 17 were landing missions to the moon, but due to a severe, life-threatening explosion aboard Apollo 13 enroute to the moon, that landing mission had to be scrapped. Only through superior scientific and engineering skill, determination, and a bit of luck was the Apollo 13 crew successfully retrieved from space to a safe landing by NASA personnel and the onboard crew.

The Soviet human moon orbiting and landing program faltered during the Apollo launches, and the Soviets settled for low earth orbit experimentation through its orbiting space station program. To date (circa 2007), only three countries have placed humans into space utilizing their own launching systems. In addition to the United States and the U.S.S.R., in October 2003, the People's Republic of China successfully launched its first astronaut into orbit on the Shenzhou 5 launch vehicle. All other programs, including the European Hermes and the Japanese Hope-X programs, have been cancelled.

Human spaceflight since the Apollo missions has been limited to Earth orbit. The Space Shuttle program in the United States has met with both success and failure, with two catastrophic flights in Challenger (explosion of the external tank caused by booster rocket failure on launch in 1986 with complete loss of crew) and Columbia (disintegration of the orbiter on reentry in 2003 with complete loss of crew). Additionally, the public and Congressional enthusiasm for human spaceflight seemed to wane as the space program became more mundane and as costs for the program came under greater Congressional scrutiny.

The Vision

In 2004, President Bush announced a new space policy for the country termed "Vision for Space Exploration." Its purpose was to give new direction to the American space program and regain public enthusiasm for space exploration. The new program sets out an ambitious agenda:

➡ The International Space Station is to be completed by 2010.

➡ The Space Shuttle is to be retired by 2010.

➡ Replacement of the Space Shuttle, a program called Orion (successor to the Crew Exploration Vehicle), should be operational by 2014.

➡ A new generation of reusable and partially reusable launch vehicles should be developed using Space Shuttle technology, called Shuttle-Derived Launch Vehicles. These launchers include the Ares I, Ares IV, and the Ares V. The new concept will be to use the Ares I for crew lift and the bigger, more expensive Ares V for cargo lift. These are to be the launchers for further moon exploration. (See Figure 42-12.)

➡ Renew moon exploration by launching robotic missions to the moon by 2008 and crewed missions to the moon by 2020.

➡ Continue the exploration of Mars with robotic missions to be followed by crewed missions.

There is no clear national consensus for Vision for Space Exploration program that could be compared to that of the early years of space activity. Yet there is substantial hope that the new frontier of space can once again capture the imagination of humankind. It is also hoped that the cooperative efforts that have evolved between nations since the end of the Cold War, particularly as to the International Space Station, will be applied to deep-space exploration. Such an effort would not only spread the cost and economic feasibility of space exploration, but would also further the aspirations of those thinkers and

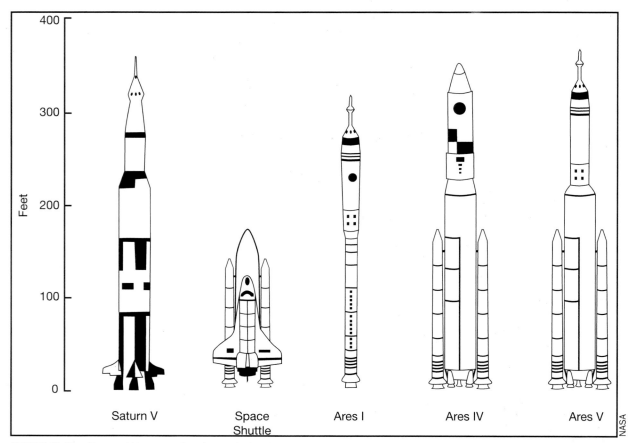

FIGURE 42-12 Saturn V, space shuttle, and shuttle-derived launch vehicles (Ares 1, Ares IV, & Ares V) shown by relative size.

The Role of Government

The federal government today plays a critical, supportive role in the United States commercial space transportation industry. At the beginning of the space age, while it assumed complete control of space activities, the government partnered with private industry to provide for the nation the best and safest space program in the world. As space technology and experience evolved, the government once again stepped aside as the commercial opportunities manifested themselves, and during the Reagan years it invited in the great American enterprise

planners of 50 years ago that space can, indeed, be the hope of humanity.

system to take over. American business and technology has responded in a resounding fashion, as the launch industry has promoted the evolution of new markets. At first these markets were communications, requiring communication satellites, then came direct television, bringing satellite television into American homes, then came data services, and then satellite radio. The commercial remote sensing industry was born, and with all of these came the need for more satellites and support ground equipment.

The federal government has now shifted from providing the only launch capability in the country to becoming a customer for the private commercial launch providers. In 2004, 10 of the 16 launches of U.S. built expendable launch vehicles carried government payloads, valued at $975 million. Government, in fact, was instrumental in the development of the current generation of commercial launch vehicles, including the Delta 4 and Atlas 5 rockets. The government also supports the launch industry by building and maintaining launch facilities from Cape Canaveral Air Force Base in Florida to Vandenberg Air Force Base in California.

These activities have all relied upon expendable launch vehicles.

The Commercial Space Launch Amendments Act of 2004 (CSLAA) was passed by Congress in December 2004. This law specifically addresses the emerging suborbital, crewed flights that will take passengers into space in reusable space vehicles. This statute was, itself, boosted into being by the success of the Space-ShipOne flights. Its overriding premise is that the federal government should not "over regulate" this new industry for fear that, in so doing, it will stifle the innovation necessary to make the concept succeed. Those now in the forefront of experimentation are compared to the early pioneers in aeronautical flight at the beginning of the last century. These current pioneers need a regulatory environment that will allow them room to experiment and take chances as they develop the space concepts of the future.

The government has decided that regulation will not be the enemy of innovation. Remembering the early days of aviation presented earlier in this book, we saw that the first regulation of aviation by the federal government occurred in 1926, some 23 years after the Wright brothers' first flight. As with the development of law after the first Sputnik orbited earth, it was clear that law must follow, not lead, technology. Just as government oversight of aviation safety gradually developed as aviation itself developed, so too will government oversight of the commercial space industry evolve.

According to statements made by FAA representatives to Congress, the government is placing its oversight emphasis on the protection of the public, not the participants. Given the experience of the industry regarding the failure rate of expendable launch vehicles, which is about 10 percent of all attempts, it is recognized that space launches are a relatively dangerous activity. FAA efforts are directed, therefore, not to the over-protection of those who voluntarily place themselves in harm's way as a part of the industry itself, but to the bystanders of the process, the public. In this regard the oversight process employed by the FAA has been successful. There have been no deaths or serious injuries, nor any significant property losses, as a result of FAA-monitored commercial launch activity.

It may be expected, however, that once commercial launch activity is removed from federal launch sites, with their isolated locations and ranges, and with their strict safety regulations and controls, there may be greater likelihood of harm to the general public. The regulatory regime of CSLAA provides for launch operators to maintain an under-layer of liability insurance, but provides for the federal government to indemnify or reimburse operators for losses to third parties in excess of that insurance up to the sum $1.5 billion. The removal of this financial risk is important to private investment.

The federal government, through CSLAA and other support activities, has recognized that the promise of space has been largely unmet for the first 50 years of space activity. If the government's encouragement of commercial space exploration and human space occupation is answered by the private sector, the future for the "fourth environment" of space[29] will be a giant leap for mankind, indeed.

Endnotes

1. A large caliber muzzle loading gun able to fire heavy projectiles

2. Refer to chapter 8 for a review of the impact of *Scientific American* on the early aviation community.

3. Refer to chapters 6 and 7 for a review of the Smithsonian's impact on the early work in aeronautics by Samuel Langley and the Wright brothers, and to Appendices 1 and 2 for comments by Dr. Alexander Graham Bell at the Smithsonian in 1913 about their experiments.

4. On July 17, 1969, the day after the launch of Apollo 11 for the moon landing, the Times issued a "correction" to its 1920 mocking editorial of Goddard's 1919 treatise. It concluded: "The Times regrets the error."

5. Refer to chapter 13 for a discussion of the Guggenheim family and their contributions to early aviation and research in the U.S.

6. Roswell would become famous as the site of the alleged alien space ship crash in 1947.

7. It is known that several score of the 1750 copies of Goddard's 1920 Smithsonian Report did reach Europe.

8. The F.A.I. awarded Amelia Earhart a "flying certificate" before the U.S. began licensing pilots. See chapter 13.

9. The Van Allen radiation belts are bands of trapped plasma (charged particles) radiation that surrounds the Earth along the magnetic field. The belts are closely related to the aurora borealis and are capable of damaging earth satellites.

10. Formed in 1915, we first encountered NACA back in chapter 9.

11. For instance, the International Civil Aviation Organization (ICAO) is a specialized agency of the U.N. Refer to chapter 37 for the discussion on the creation of ICAO as a result of The Chicago Convention of 1944.

12. The three mile limit was established by custom and acceptance because that was the distance that a nation could defend its territory from shore by the use of cannon in the 18th Century. By the middle of the 20th Century, most maritime nations claimed a 12 mile limit in order to extract mineral resources, to protect fish stocks, and as a means to enforce pollution controls.

13. The Soviets shot down the U.S. U-2 reconnaissance aircraft flown by Francis Gary Powers over Soviet territory on May 1, 1960.

14. Grotius was a Dutch philosopher and legal theorist who became known as the "father of international law."

15. At various times, a few nations have attempted to lay claim to the high seas. The Romans claimed the waters of the Mediterranean Sea, the English claimed the North Sea and the English Channel, and Denmark claimed the Baltic Sea. None of these claims could be sustained.

16. COPUOS has never adopted a legal or a scientific definition for "outer space." The scientific evidence is that the maximum altitude of stable aerodynamic flight is considerably lower than the minimum altitude for stable orbital flight. This band of "no man's land" is so wide that a specific altitude denoting the boundary between the atmosphere and outer space would necessarily have to be arbitrary.

17. Refer to chapter 37 for a review of the Chicago Conference.

18. The South American country of Colombia, on behalf of equatorial states, in 1975 claimed sovereignty over a 5.5 degree segment of the geostationary orbit (GSO). The GSO is the circular orbit in which a spacecraft has an orbital period exactly equal to the period of rotation of the Earth. This period, 23 hours, 56 minutes, allows the spacecraft to remain in the same place relative to the earth at all times. The claims of the equatorial countries have been rejected by COPUOS.

19. Uranium 235 and Plutonium 239 are the most practical fuels for space reactors. U-235 is much less harmful than Plutonium 239.

20. The U.S., Canada, Japan, the Russian Federation, and 11 Member States of the European Union, (Belgium, Denmark, France, Germany, Italy, The Netherlands, Norway, Spain, Sweden, Switzerland, and the United Kingdom).

21. ESA, the European Space Agency; CSA, the Canadian Space Agency; RKA, the Russian Federal Space Agency; and JAXA, the Japanese Aerospace Exploration Agency

22. NASA contracted with the Brazilian space agency, AEB, for the use of Brazilian equipment on board ISS.

23. The NRO is an agency of the Department of Defense and builds and operates the nation's reconnaissance satellites.

24. A geostationary orbit must first be geosynchronous, that is, equal to the earth's rotational period. The difference is that a geosynchronous orbit may or may not be in the equatorial plane. If it is not, it will appear to move above and below the equator (changing latitude location) as viewed from earth, although it will remain at the same line of longitude at all times. A geostationary satellite, however, will remain in the equatorial plane at all times and over the same point on earth at all times. Geostationary satellites have a zero inclination. These two types of orbits are often referred to interchangeably, but incorrectly.

25. NGSO or NGEO satellites are all satellites not in GSO or GEO. LEO satellites orbit from lowest achievable orbit to about 2,400 km, Medium Earth Orbit (MEO) satellites orbit from 2,400 km to GSO.

26. The X Prize is titled after Anousheh Ansari, a female Iranian who immigrated to the United States as a teenager, unable to speak English. She gained financial success through her own superior efforts in the computer and technology fields, founding Telecom Technologies in 2001. She became a member of the X Prize Foundation Vision Circle, and in 2006 became the first female private space explorer when she traveled to the International Space Station as part of the Expedition 14 crew.

27. For example, the Kistler Aerospace K-1 project was terminated in 2000 due to lack of funding. The K-1 technology is under review by NASA, however, in order to further examine its feasibility. Government programs for RLVs that have been terminated include the X-33 and X-34 programs.

28. Neil Armstrong was the first human to stand on the moon. Jim Lovell, also on the Apollo 11 crew, was the second.

29. The first three "environments" are land, sea, and air.

Excerpts from the Address of Dr. Alexander Graham Bell in Presenting the Langley Medal to Mr. Gustave Eiffel and to Mr. Glenn Curtiss in 1913

On the sixth of May 1896 a steam engine provided with wings made a successful flight in the air over the Potomac River at Quantico, Virginia about sixty miles from Washington, D.C. There was no man in the machine, yet it pursued its way steadily through the air, continually rising until its power gave out, when its propeller stopped and it descended so gently to the water that it was immediately ready for another flight.

The second flight was equally successful, and though the total distance was not great, barely exceeding one half mile, it succeeded in demonstrating to the world the practicability of mechanical flight by machines heavier than the air and driven by their own motive power.

The production of this machine was really the culminating point of the researches of the late Secretary of the Smithsonian Institution, Dr. Samuel Pierpoint Langley, and the Smithsonian Institution very properly celebrates the sixth of May as "Langley Day."

For many years before 1896 Professor Langley, being assured in his own mind of the practicability of mechanical flight had devoted himself to scientific experiments with aeroplanes, that is, with flat surfaces or planes driven edgeways through the air, at varying angles of incidence to the horizon. In his usage the aeroplanes, while applicable to the wings of a flying machine, was not applicable to the machine itself. The machine as a whole he called an aerodrome, from the Greek work aerodromos, "traversing the air." In the terminology employed by him aerodromics is the art of traversing the air—the art of aerial locomotion; and an aerodrome was a machine for traversing the air.

The knowledge that so eminent a man as the Secretary of the Smithsonian Institution, believed in the possibility of mechanical flight and was carrying on scientific experiments to attain that end, proved a great stimulus and encouragement to many less eminent men who were working along the same lines under the discouragement and ridicule from the incredulous world . . . I was the only witness of this remarkable flight outside of the workmen employed. I may perhaps be pardoned for saying a few words about it. Professor Langley had met with so many failures that, though hopeful, he was somewhat doubtful of the result, and he invited me to witness the experiment on the condition that I was the only man he knew whom he could bear to be a witness of a failure.

I found a houseboat containing all his apparatus anchored in the little Bay of Quantico and, on the roof, his machine was arranged ready to be shot off by a huge catapult. It was a huge model, thirteen feet from tip to tip, . . . and sixteen feet from head to tail, the whole propelled by a wonderfully light steam engine of Professor Langley's own design.

I had a boy row me out on the bay where I thought I could get a good snapshot of the machine when it leaped into the air, while Professor Langley, too nervous to be close to the scene of operations, retreated to the shore, and I saw him standing lonely on the end of a little pier with the wooded shore behind him.

Then the whirr of the propellers was heard and the catapult was released causing the machine to shoot out into the air almost horizontally. Then came the critical moment. Would it fall into the water? Would it strike against the trees that surrounded the bay? Or would it ascend and clear them? The queries were soon answered. For the huge bird-like machine gracefully soared from twenty to thirty feet above the tops of the trees, turning slightly as it rose, and made a beautiful flight of over half-a-mile, when the steam was exhausted the propellers stopped and it began to come down.

The descent was as fascinating as the ascent, and it glided gracefully to the surface of the water. The workmen employed hailed the success of the experiment with loud cheers, in which I joined. It was picked up and found to be practically uninjured except for a wetting. The experiment was then repeated with even greater success than before.

The prophecy received its fulfillment but not until the beginning of the twentieth century. In 1898 the Board of Ordinance & Fortification, after carefully studying the flight of 1896, appropriated $50,000 to enable Langley to experiment with a full sized aerodrome carrying a man. This was not completed until 1903, and on August 8 of that year a quarter-sized model of it propelled by a gasoline engine made a beautiful public flight.

On September 7, 1903, the full-sized aerodrome, carrying Mr. F. W. Manley, as aviator, was tried on the Potomac, but when the catapult was released, the aerodrome sped along the track on the top of the houseboat attaining sufficient headway for normal flight; but at the end of the rails it was jerked violently down at the front, and plunged headlong into the river. It was subsequently discovered that the guy post that strengthened the front pair of wings had caught in the launching ways, and bent so much that those wings lost all support.

A second launching was attempted on the Potomac River near Washington, on December 8, 1903. This time the rear guy post was injured, crippling the rear wings, so that the aerodrome pitched up in front and plunged over backwards into the water. Fortunately the aviator, Mr. Manly, received no injury in either case.

It will thus be seen that Langley's aerodrome was never successfully launched, so that it had no opportunity of showing what it could do in the air. The defect lay in the launching mechanism employed and not in the machine itself, which is recognized by all experts as a perfectly good flying machine, excellently constructed and made long before the appearance of other machines.

Langley's efforts at aviation were received with public ridicule, and he found it impossible to obtain the necessary funds to try the experiment again. Professor Langley was of a very sensitive nature and the public ridicule with which his efforts were received had a good deal to do with the illness which caused his death. Not very long after the accident he received a paralytic stroke, and after partially recovering from this, another stroke ended his life in 1906. . . .

The second and last trial of Langley's aerodrome occurred December 8, 1903, and on December 17 of that same year, the Wright brothers made their first flight in their gliding machine provided with a 16 HP engine and two screw propellers. Little or nothing was known of this flight by the general public. The Wright brothers removed their machine to Dayton, Ohio. During 1904 and 1905 numerous flights were made in Dayton, Ohio, culminating in a flight of eleven miles on September 26, 1905. These were all in secret. After this, field practice with them ceased for more than two years to enable them to preserve the secrecy which they had hitherto maintained.

A few statements concerning their success leaked out into the public press, but were generally received with incredulity and unbelief.

A competent scientific investigator was sent from France to Dayton, Ohio to investigate the truth of the rumors that had appeared in the newspapers of success that had found their way into the press. He was unable to obtain any definite information concerning the trials that had been made, but by interviewing the neighboring farmers he was able to satisfy himself that flights had actually been made, and so reported to his principals in France, and it was from France that America received the first authentic news that the Wright brothers had actually flown.

Then M. Archdeacon stirred up the patriotic spirit of the French, not to be beaten by America, and offered his prize . . . of FF3000 to be awarded to the first person who should sail or fly twenty-five meters, under certain conditions.

The whole art of aerial locomotion originated in France. In 1783, the Montgolfiers produced the balloon, their hot air balloon, and in the same year M. Charles and the Brothers Roberts gave us the hydrogen balloon. After the lapse of 100 years, Nadar issued his celebrated manifesto in which he advocated the heavier than air flying machine, rather than the balloon, and started the controversy between the lighter-than-air and the heavier-than-air camps, which has lasted to our day, and is not settled yet. . . .

On August 22, 1906, M. Santos-Dumont made a tentative flight in his new "aeromobile," and on October 23, 1906 he ran this strange machine swiftly over the ground and glided boldly into the air, flying above the excited spectators at a speed of twenty-five miles an hour, and covering a distance of two hundred feet, thus gaining the Archdeacon Cup.

This was the first public flight in the world, made without any certain knowledge of the previous secret flights made by the Wright brothers in America.

From this time the French have been feverishly active in the field of aviation. In October 1907 the Aerial Experiment Association was organized with the object of constructing a practical aerodrome, driven through the air by its own motive power, and carrying a man. This was a mere experimental association, financed by my wife, and consisting of the late Lt. Selfridge, Mr. F. W. Baldwin, Mr. Glenn H. Curtiss, Mr. J. A. D. McCurdy and myself. On March 12, 1908, the Association succeeded in raising its first aerodrome, the Red Wing, into the air from the ice on Lake Keuka, near Hammondsport, N.Y. Mr. F. W. Baldwin was the aviator on this occasion, which constituted the first public flight of an aerodrome in America. The Wright brothers, of course, had previously flown, but nothing was known with certainty at that time concerning their achievements. Then in that same year, 1908, the Wright brothers for the first time appeared publicly in flight. Wilbur Wright in Europe, and Orville Wright in America, startled the world with their achievements, and proved themselves to be the master of their art. . . .

Excerpts from Remarks of Dr. Alexander Graham Bell before the Board of Regents of the Smithsonian Institution on February 13, 1913 on the Award of the Langley Medal

Since the award of the Langley Medal to the Wright brothers three years ago, there has been great activity in the field of aviation. The war departments of the different nations have been constantly at work, but little is known concerning the character of the advances made. So far as the public are aware the chief progress has related to details of construction and improvement in motive power. The advance has been much greater in the *art* than in the *science.*

There has, however, been considerable advance in the science of aerodromics along the lines laid down by our late Secretary, Dr. S. P. Langley, and by M. Gustave Eiffel, Director of the Eiffel Aero-Dynamical Laboratory in Paris.

In 1907 M/Eiffel published the results of experiments made at the Eiffel Tower; in 1911, he published the results of his experiment at the aerodynamic laboratory in Paris on the resistance of the air in connection with aviation, and these results have been of great value to aerial engineers in designing and construction flying machines. Indeed his works upon the subject have already become classical. . . .

In spite of the great advances that have been made in the art of aerodromics we are confronted with a long list of fatalities to aviators, for whose protection there remains a great deal yet to be done. There has been one very notable development in this direction, made by an American, Mr. Glenn R. Curtiss of Hammondsport, N.Y.

In 1908, the Aerial Experiment Association, of which Mr. Curtiss was a member, discussed the advisability of have flying machines so constructed as to enable them to float, and to rise from the water into the air, as an element of safety. In pursuance of these ideas, the Association's aerodrome No. 3, the "Curtiss June Bug" was attached to pontoons and an experiment was made on Lake Keuka on November 6, 1908. Although the speed on the water appeared to be satisfactory, the machine failed to rise in the air, but the occasion formed the starting point for Mr. Curtiss' independent researches.

After the dissolution of the Association, March 31, 1909, Mr. Curtiss continued his experiments to find a practical solution of the problem, and in May 1910, he made that remarkable flight from Albany to New York City over the Hudson River, a distance of 152 miles in 2 hours 52 minutes, with two light pontoons attached to his machine, to enable it to float should it come down into the water.

In 1911 Mr. Curtiss continued his efforts to construct a machine that would not only float, but would rise from the water into the air, and in January 1912, he succeeded in doing this in San Diego Bay, California. "On January 26, 1912" he says "the first success came": and on January 27, 1912, the Aero Club of America awarded him the Collier Trophy for his accomplishment.

In February 1912, he demonstrated the use to the Navy of such machines by flying to the U.S. Armored Cruiser "Pennsylvania" . . . alighting in the water beside the vessel. The machine was hoisted up on the vessel's deck, and then again lowered into the water without damage, showing the possibility of handling such machines without special equipment. He then rose from the water and flew back to the starting point.

By July 1912, he had developed the remarkable machine he calls "the flying boat," which represents the greatest advance yet made along these lines. It develops great speed upon the water and also in the air, and is equally at home in either element. The world is now following Mr. Curtiss' lead in the development of flying machines of this type.

Great experience in the handling of aerial machines is necessary before aviators can safely make extended flight over land, where a fall might be fatal. The successful development of the hydro-aerodrome now enables this experience to be gained over water without serious danger to life or limb; and marks a notable advance in the direction of safety that might well be recognized by the Smithsonian Institution by the award of a Langley Medal to Mr. Glenn M. Curtiss.

Blazing the Trail to Chicago

The first person account of the original survey flight from New York to Chicago on September 5, 1918, made to determine the feasibility of carrying airmail between those two cities, by Max Miller, Aerial Mail Pilot No. 1. Miller died on September 1, 1920 when his mail plane caught fire in the air and crashed.

Blazing the air trail to Chicago would have been a "cinch" if I had started at 6 A.M. on September 5th, as had been planned. This would have enabled me to start one hour ahead of the storm, and I could have reached Chicago by evening without trouble.

I left Belmont Field, Long Island, at 7:08 A.M., with a good wind in back of me, flew over the City of New York, the Hudson River and Hoboken, and headed west 284 degrees.

There was a bank of low clouds near the ground and another layer of clouds at a high altitude. I kept right between them and flew on my compass course. I could not see the ground, but ran for about two hours and at ten o'clock I came down through the lower strata of clouds and landed one mile from Danville, N.Y., about 155 miles from New York City. There I inquired to find out my bearings and found that I was not more than two miles out of my course. I did not kill the motor, but left it running, and after five minutes started up again and headed for Lock Haven.

I entered the fog which hung low over the ground and over the tops of the mountains, and I figured that it would take me about three-quarters of an hour to make Lock Haven. I came down and saw the field through a notch in the mountains and made a good landing. My motor was missing, so I changed spark plugs which took me about an hour, filled up with oil and gas, got a couple of sandwiches, and left about 11:45 A.M.

I climbed up through the fog again and went on over the mountains. I sailed on my compass course for an hour, 283 degrees, and I figured I was about 100 miles further on. Then I came down to see where I was and get my bearings, and the first thing I knew I hit the top of a tree. That sure gave me a good scare. I hustled back up again into the fog, determined to get plenty of altitude and keep on going as long as my gas held out.

I went fifty miles, and then I found my radiator was leaking and I came down and I saw a town with a fair going on. There was such a mob of people that I did not land there, but went on about twenty miles to a town named Cambridge. I inquired where I was and was told "Jefferson." On looking on my map I found a town called Jefferson lying to the north of my route, so on leaving I headed toward the south in order to cross the route again; but I found that it was Jefferson

Country, PA, instead of the town of Jefferson, Ohio, and I went about 150 miles out of my way before reaching Cleveland, where I had to remain all night on account of darkness.

The next morning I got my radiator fixed and rested up after being buffeted about by the storm and rain, and got away at 1:35 P.M. for Bryan on the compass course of 275 degrees, a little south of due west about 140 miles. I had to stop several times to fill up my radiator with water. The weather was very much better, and I was able to make Bryan, where I was received by Postmaster Jordan and got away at 4:35 P.M. I skirted the southern shore of Lake Michigan and arrived over Grant Park at an altitude of 5,000 feet at 6:55 P.M.

I circled around and made a good landing and was received by Postmaster Wm. B. Carlile, Mr. Chas. Dickenson, President of the Aero Club of Illinois, Capt. B. B. Lipsner, Superintendent of Aerial Mail Service, Mr. Thos. Downey, Assistant Superintendent of Mails, Mr. James O'Conner, Director of the U.S. War Exposition, Mr. James Stevens, Secretary of the Aero Club of Illinois, and Mr. Augustus Post, Secretary of the Aero Club of America, who had come on from New York to witness the inauguration of the first aero mail service between New York and Chicago.

The weather on the return trip was much better. I started from Chicago on September 10, at 6:26 A.M. I carried about three thousand pieces of mail. The weather looked so good that I expected to make a record trip. There was some haze on the ground, but not nearly enough to prevent landmarks being distinct. Just as I was over Cleveland, I found a broken connection in the radiator and I landed there to get it repaired.

This took some time, but I got away from there by 4:30 P.M., in time to make a pleasant flight to Lock Haven, one of the scheduled stops, before dark, a distance of 210 miles. I stayed at Lock Haven all night, leaving there at 7:20 A.M. As a path finding trip it was an immense success. We gathered a lot of information which will be very valuable in the future trips.

The radiator trouble was the only thing that prevented me from making the trip within the ten hours set. If I had had a spare aeroplane even, I could have done it. We will, of course, have spare machines for the permanent route, so it will not happen again.

Excerpts from Lindbergh's Log of His Solo Flight from New York to Paris

New York to Paris

Charles Lindbergh was already being treated like something of a celebrity even before he departed New York for Paris. He and the Spirit of St. Louis had been ready to fly since Monday, May 16, 1927, but the weather was dreadful in New York and points north. Since his arrival in New York he had been feted and greeted by dignitaries ranging from William McCracken, the Assistant Secretary of Commerce for Aeronautics to Harry Guggenheim, Tony Fokker, Rene Fonck, C. M. Keyes of the Curtiss Company, Charlie Lawrance, the air-cooled radial engine pioneer, and Theodore Roosevelt, Jr.

The press had been pushy and ever-present, and the week had been very tiring. On Thursday, the 19th, Lindbergh visited the Wright factory in Paterson, New Jersey, and attended the theater that night, including a trip backstage. He did not arrive at his hotel until after midnight, and he was scheduled to arise at 3:00 A.M. to go out to Roosevelt Field to make the final decision for takeoff as weather had been reported improved. He was too keyed up to sleep.

In the pre-dawn gloom of Roosevelt Field on Friday, May 20, 1927, the clouds hung low and a light rain was falling. The weather was reported as still improving, and a high-pressure area is moving in over the North Atlantic. After the Spirit of St. Louis is towed into takeoff position and fueled, the wind shifts to a tailwind. The engine on run-up is thirty revolutions low due to the weather, the mechanic said.

As Lindbergh himself explains the situation:

Plane ready; engine ready; earth-inductor compass set on course. The long, narrow runway stretches out ahead. Over the telephone wires at its end lies the Atlantic Ocean; and beyond that, mythical as the rainbow's pot of gold, Europe and Paris. This is the moment I've planned for, day and night, all these months past. The decision is mine. No other man can take that responsibility. The mechanics, the engineers, the blue-uniformed police officers standing there behind the wing, everyone has done his part. Now, it's up to me.

Their eyes are intently on mine. They've seen planes crash before. They know what a wrong decision means. If I shake my head, there'll be no complaint, no criticism; I'll be welcomed back into their midst, back to earth and life; for we are separated by something more than the few yards that lie between us. It seems almost the difference between the future and the past, to be decided by a movement of my head. A shake, and we'll be laughing and joking together, laying new plans, plodding over the wet grass toward hot coffee and a warm breakfast—all men of the earth. A nod, and we'll be separated—perhaps forever.[1]

The Flight

7:52 A.M. Takeoff from Roosevelt Field, Long Island, New York. Mud, rain, and fog complicate the departure. Lindbergh clears telephone wires at the end of the runway by only 20 feet.

8:52 A.M. Over Rhode Island, 100 miles from Roosevelt Field, 3500 miles to go. Altitude 600 feet; Airspeed 102 miles per hour; Ceiling 2000 feet; Visibility 5 miles; True course 51 degrees; Compass course 63 degrees.

9:52 A.M. Between Boston and Cape Cod. Altitude 150 feet; Ceiling 4000 feet; Visibility unlimited; Airspeed 107 miles per hour; True course 56 degrees; Compass course 70 degrees.

10:52 A.M. Over water. Burning 16 gallons of gasoline per hour. Altitude 50 feet; Ceiling unlimited; Airspeed 104 miles per hour; True course 57 degrees; Compass course 73 degrees.

11:52 A.M. Approaching Nova Scotia. Altitude 200 feet; Airspeed 103 miles per hour; True course 58 degrees; Compass course 78 degrees. He is six miles southeast of course.

12:52 P.M. Over Nova Scotia. Wind is 30 miles per hour from the West forcing a crab correction of 15 degrees. Altitude 700 feet; Airspeed 102 miles per hour; True course 60 degrees; Compass course 82 degrees. Storm clouds are forming.

1:52 P.M. Beginning the seventh hour, over Nova Scotia. 3000 miles to go. Altitude 900 feet; Ceiling 1500 broken; Airspeed 101 miles per hour; True course 61 degrees; Compass course 84 degrees.

2:52 P.M. Still over Nova Scotia. Altitude 600 feet; Airspeed 96 miles per hour; True course 64 degrees; Compass course 89 degrees. Storm recedes to the North. Lindbergh sees fog, his most dreaded condition, directly ahead.

3:52 P.M. Leaving Cape Breton Island for a 200 miles stretch of water to Newfoundland. Altitude 500 feet; Airspeed 94 miles per hour; True course 64 degrees; Compass Course 91 degrees. Lindbergh is fighting the urge to sleep. Sleep is winning.

4:52 P.M. Over ice fields in the Atlantic. Altitude 150 feet; Airspeed 95 miles per hour; True course 73 degrees; Compass course 102 degrees. Lindbergh has trouble holding course, causing repeated corrections.

5:52 P.M. Placentia Bay, along the southeastern coast of Newfoundland. Altitude 300 feet; Airspeed 92 miles per hour; True course 70 degrees; Compass course 100 degrees.

6:52 P.M. Sunset over Newfoundland. Altitude 700 feet; Airspeed 98 miles per hour; True course 68 degrees; Compass course 99 degrees. Lindbergh has covered 1100 miles in 11 hours, exactly. Never before has an airplane overflown Newfoundland without landing. Lindbergh leaves the continent of North America.

7:52 P.M. Over an iceberg laden Atlantic. Altitude 800 feet; Airspeed 90 miles per hour; True course 65 degrees; Compass course 97 degrees. Fog below and 5 miles visibility above. Lindbergh begins a climb to 7500 feet to stay out of clouds. He figures he has a strong tailwind.

8:52 P.M. Nighttime over the Atlantic. Altitude 9300 feet; Airspeed 90 miles per hour; True course 66 degrees; Compass course 99 degrees. During the next hour Lindbergh will be forced into towering clouds where he will begin to pick up ice at 10500 feet. He sets a limit of 15000 feet as his maximum altitude to escape clouds. He considers descending into warmer air.

9:52 P.M. Clear of clouds in haze, cloud formations farther away. Altitude 10500 feet; Airspeed 87 miles per hour; True course 66 degrees; Compass course 99 degrees. The moon begins to rise.

10:52 P.M. Altitude 10200 feet; Airspeed 86 miles per hour; True course 69 degrees; Compass course 99 degrees. Now 1500 miles from New York, 2100 miles to go. Lindbergh is losing the battle to stay awake. He is still angling on a northward course on the great circle route. Soon the course will turn southward. Lindbergh starts confusing stars overhead with the lights of non-existent ships at sea.

11:52 P.M. Altitude 10000 feet; Airspeed 90 miles per hour; True course 70 degrees; Compass course 103 degrees. Clear above clouds.

12:52 A.M. Closer now to Europe than America. Altitude 9600 feet; Airspeed 88 miles per hour; True course 72 degrees; Compass course 106 degrees. High thin overcast. Lindbergh only wants sleep, nothing else. Yet he realizes that sleep means death and failure. He must be intermittently sleeping: He makes repeated course corrections in excess of 10 degrees in both directions.

1:52 A.M. 1800 miles to Paris. Altitude 9000; Airspeed 87 miles per hour; Lindbergh fails to record his true course or his compass course. Lindbergh begins to wonder what difference a few degrees can make. Figuring out his new heading is beyond his resolve and his ability. Suddenly, he realizes that it is daylight again.

2:52 A.M. Beginning the 20th hour. Altitude 8800 feet; Airspeed 89 miles per hour; Ceiling: flying between cloud layers. True course and compass course not recorded. The altimeter has not been reset since Newfoundland, by flying close to the water. That was 8 hours ago. He descends to near sea level and determines that he has a quartering tailwind there. But he encounters fog and begins a climb to 1500 feet. He frequently loses control of the airplane as he fights sleep, but recovers each time.

During the 21st hour. Lindbergh misses the 3:52 A.M. log entry. He reasons that it's not worth the effort anyway. He is so tired that he cannot both control the airplane and make entries in the log. He has energy enough only to fly the airplane and keep track of fuel management. The Spirit of St. Louis has 5 fuel tanks: a nose tank, a fuselage tank, a left wing tank, a center wing tank, and a right wing tank. He switches tanks hourly.

4:52 A.M.   Still on instruments. He wonders what happened to the forecast high-pressure area that was supposed to be over the North Atlantic. His log entries are confined to fuel management. Over and over again he falls asleep with his eyes open, knowing all the time this is what's happening, but unable to prevent it. (p. 387) He finds himself just above the mountainous ocean waves, flying in salt spray form the wave tops. He climbs.

6:05 A.M.   The 23rd hour. No entries again. What difference does it make, he wonders. No entries in the log for over 3 hours. Lindbergh flies above, below and between layers of clouds.

The 24th hour.   Lindbergh decides to abandon any further effort to keep his log. He figures that he is 2300 miles from New York, 1300 miles from Paris, and maybe 700 miles from Ireland. But he is beginning to realize that he can no longer accurately deal with figures.

_____

Endnote

1. The Spirit of St. Louis, p. 182.

Women in Early Aviation

Women had been involved in aviation, in one way or another, since Elisabeth Thible of Lyons, France, went aloft in a hot air balloon in 1784. By 1834, some twenty-two women had piloted their own balloons on the continent of Europe. In 1886, Mary H. Myers set an altitude record of over 20,000 feet (without oxygen) in a balloon above the fields of rural Pennsylvania, and in 1903, Cuban born Aida de Acosta became the first woman to pilot a powered machine in flight in a dirigible over Paris, France.

The first woman to earn a pilot's certificate anywhere in the world was Raymonde de Laroche, a French adventuress who also raced early motorcars. Granted a license by the Federation Aeronautique Internacionale (F.A.I.) on March 8, 1910, she was seriously injured four months later when she crashed during an air race competing against the likes of Louis Bleriot. Both legs were broken, as was one arm, and she sustained head and internal injuries. Two years later she was again back to racing the primitive airplanes of the day. She was killed in an airplane crash in 1919 in which she was riding as a passenger.

Helene Dutrieu was licensed shortly after. She flew nonstop over the 28 mile stretch from Ostend to Brugges, in Belgium, only five months after her first flight. She entered an air race in Florence, Italy, in May 1911 and, as the only woman in the field, triumphed over her 15 male competitors to win the Italian King's Cup. She was also known for her avant-garde ways: she flew airplanes without wearing a corset.

The first American woman to make a solo flight was Blanche Stuart Scott on September 6, 1910, although without official observers to confirm, she would not receive official acknowledgment. She had previously gained some measure of notoriety by driving an Overland motorcar from San Francisco to New York in 1910 as a publicity stunt for the Willys-Overland Company, the automobile manufacturer. Driving through the country was so simple and uncomplicated, she showed, even a woman could do it. At the time, Glenn Curtiss had founded an exhibition-flying troupe that performed around the country. Miss Scott was taught to fly at Hammondsport, N.Y. by Glenn Curtiss himself, and she became a daring and successful member of the troupe, making up to $5,000 a week at a time when the average weekly salary for men was $300 and for women was $144.[1]

Official recognition for the first woman to solo an airplane in the United States was given to Bessica Raiche, who had earned a doctor of medicine degree at Tufts Medical School in 1903. Along with her husband, a New York City attorney, they built their own biplane in the living room of their Mineola, N.Y. summer home. When it was ready, they removed the front wall of the house and rolled it out into the street. Mineola Field was a center for early aviation activity and it was there in 1907 that they first tested their machine. Their airplanes went through several iterations, but by 1910 they had completed a Curtiss-type pusher biplane that was propelled by a 40 horsepower engine. Lateral control was achieved by a sort of wing flap connected to a harness worn by the pilot, which operated the wing flaps when the pilot leaned one way or the other. First trials on September 15, 1910, resulted in a crash with Bessica at the controls, but by September 26, repairs had been made and she completed the first official solo of the aircraft by an American woman. The Aeronautical Society of New York presented her with a medal in commemoration of the event with the words "the

nation's first intentional solo by a woman." Although the husband and wife airplane construction team built additional aircraft, and sold them, they each in time returned to their professions of medicine and law, apparently content with their adventure.

Harriett Quimby is easily the most acknowledged of the early women aviators. (See Figure App 5-1.) She was a newspaper and periodical reporter in the early 1900s, living first in San Francisco and then in New York City. She was the first American woman to earn her license (number 37) from the F.A.I. on August 2, 1911. She gained international recognition as the first woman to fly the English Channel when she crossed from Dover to Hardelot, France, 25 miles south of Calais, in a borrowed Bleriot monoplane on April 16, 1912. Her brief but illustrious flying career came to an end on July 1, 1912, when she fell from her new Bleriot monoplane over Boston Harbor before 5,000 spectators. Seatbelts were not worn in those days.

Source: Library of Congress.

FIGURE APP 5-1 Harriet Quimby was the first American woman to earn her license from F.A.I. on August 2, 1911.

It is not generally appreciated that early women aviators taught men to fly. A German, Melli Beese, started a flying school in 1912 in Berlin, and the Englishwoman Hilda Hewlett taught World War I British pilots in fighter aircraft. In the United States, Marjorie Stinson instructed Canadian airmen slated for service in Britain, having taught over 100 before she had reached the age of 22. Marjorie Stinson was the youngest licensed female pilot in the United States at age 20, and her sister, Katherine, was the fourth woman in this country to be licensed by F.A.I. Katherine also became the first woman to fly the U.S. Mail (in Montana), and became known as one of the most daring aerobatic, or stunt pilots as they were then known, in the country. She made a flying tour of Japan and China in 1916, performing aerobatic maneuvers previously unseen in those countries, for crowds that numbered in excess of 25,000 people. In the process she became an icon for the women of those countries, whose prevailing customs were even more restrictive for women than those in the West.

Victor Carlstrom set the American nonstop distance record on November 2, 1916 by flying 452 miles on a course between Chicago and New York. Less than three weeks later, Ruth Law, who had earned her license in 1912, broke that record over the same course by flying 590 miles from Chicago to Hornell, New York. It should be remembered that this was the route over the Allegheny Mountains that would claim the lives of many airmail pilots in the years to come. Upon reaching New York City the next day, she was acclaimed in newspapers the country over, and was feted in a series of banquets attended by President Woodrow Wilson, Admiral Robert E. Peary, the first man to set foot at the North Pole (April 6, 1909), and Captain Roald Amundsen, first to the South Pole (December 14, 1911).

During the 1920s, women continued to enter the field of aviation, and to continue to expand the limits of their participation. Adrienne Bolland, a Frenchwoman who was licensed in 1920, set an aerobatic record by performing 212 consecutive loops that year. She then had her airplane shipped to Argentina and flew it from Mendoza to Chile, becoming the first woman to cross the Andes by airplane on April 1, 1921.

Facing both gender and race barriers to her aspirations, Bessie Coleman became the first black female pilot licensed by F.A.I. on June 15, 1921. She was taught to fly at Ecole d'Aviation des Freres in Le Crotoy, France, and was the only woman in her 62-person class. Bessie Coleman had arrived in France by way of Atlanta, Texas, her birthplace, and from Chicago, where she had lived after leaving Texas. Her two older brothers had been in the U.S. Army in France during World War I, and had returned with stories of life there, and especially about women aviators. Bessie was befriended by the publisher of *The Chicago Defender,* Robert Abbott, who assisted her in her aspirations to travel to France for flying lessons. On her return to the United States, he sponsored flying exhibitions, which featured her as "the world's greatest woman flyer." She attained countrywide recognition on her own merit, and became an advocate for equal rights for all people. She was killed when she fell from the open cockpit of her biplane on April 30, 1926 while preparing for an exhibition in Jacksonville, Florida.

Sophie Mary Pierce (later Lady Mary Heath), was an Irishwoman who emigrated to England and became known for her athletic prowess as a member of the Great Britain Athletics Olympic Team in the early 1920s. She wrote *Athletics for Women and Girls: How to Be an Athlete and Why* in 1925, which followed her presentations to the International Olympic Committee that same year. She shared the world record for the women's high jump and became British javelin champion. In 1926 she was granted a commercial airplane license by the International Commission for Air Navigation after successfully contesting the Commission's ban on awarding commercial licenses to women. She held several altitude records for light planes. In 1927–28, less than a year after Lindbergh's solo flight over the Atlantic, she made the first solo flight from Capetown, South Africa to Cairo in an Avro Avian monoplane, and then extended that with a flight on to London. She then began a tour of England and the United States, being received by President and Mrs. Coolidge in 1928. The Jacksonville Journal recorded her visit to that Florida city on January 4, 1929:

She made the wings fast in flying position, climbing around the plane like a great cat . . . She was clad in a colorful cretonne smock and wore high, soft leather boots . . . She spun the propeller and started the engine herself while a score of men and boys stood open-mouthed in a semi-circle.

These were some of the women who preceded Amelia Earhart.

Endnote

1. <Camps, Enriqueta, Universitat Pompeu Fabra, April 2001, http://www.clarku.edu/faculty/brown/papers/camp1.pdf>.

Calbraith Perry Rodgers

A Wright brothers' airplane (a model B, modified for the flight) would be the first airplane to fly coast-to-coast in the United States in 1911, piloted by a nearly deaf, cigar smoking 32 year old motorcycle racer and yachtsman of independent means. This was Cal Rodgers, great-grandnephew of Captain Oliver Hazard Perry (who defeated a British squadron at the Battle of Lake Erie in the War of 1812), and the great-grandson of Commodore Matthew Calbraith Perry (who was in command of the U.S. Navy contingent that sailed into Tokyo Bay in 1853), the latter being credited with the opening of feudalistic and xenophobic Japan to U.S. and international trade for the first time. Cal Rodgers wanted to follow in his esteemed forefathers' footsteps, but he was denied admission to the United States Naval Academy due to the hearing deficiency that had resulted from an onset of scarlet fever when he was six years old.

It could be said that Cal Rodgers had been at loose ends for most of his adult life. At six feet four inches tall, he had excelled at football in college, but thereafter he seemed to be unable to find his niche. He was never required to work for a salary due to his financial station, and he spent his days after college in "gentlemen's" pursuits and in amateur sports adventures. Cal's cousin, Lt. John Rodgers, was in 1911 a recent graduate of the Naval Academy, and he had been assigned to take flying lessons at the Wright brothers' flying school in Dayton, Ohio (Huffman Prairie) as a part of the fledgling Naval Aviation program. It was there during the first half of 1911, while visiting with his cousin, that Cal Rodgers encountered his first airplane up close.

Cal received ninety minutes of flight instruction from Orville Wright and considered that he was ready for solo flight. Orville disagreed, so Cal just bought one of the Wright's Model Bs and took off on his own. He entered his first aerial competition in July 1911, and in August, he won $11,000 at the International Aviation Meet in Chicago for endurance aloft.

Not quite one year earlier, in October 1910, publisher William Randolph Hearst had offered a prize of $50,000 for any person who could fly coast-to-coast within a period of thirty days from start to finish. In spite of no serious threat to the prize money from anyone else, Rodgers decided that he could win that endurance prize as well. Orville Wright, again, disagreed with the brash Rodgers, believing that the state of the aviation art had not progressed to the point where any flying machine could endure such a trial. Undaunted, Rodgers lined up financial support from the

Chicago meat packer J. Ogden Armour, who had just inaugurated a new five cent soft drink called the "Vin Fiz." Armour seized on the idea of a cross-country publicity campaign as being just the right promotion for his new drink and agreed to finance the venture. (See Figure App 6-1.)

The modified Model B was dubbed the "Vin Fiz" and carried the designation "EX," which denoted that it was for exhibition flying. The primary distinguishing characteristic of the Model B was the absence of the forward elevator, or canard, which had been the primary vertical control device on all prior Wright models, including the "A." The Model B was larger than the EX, with a wingspan of 38.5 feet to only 32 feet for the exhibition model. Both craft used twin pusher-type propellers chain driven by the 35 horsepower water-cooled motor, but the EX was built specifically for the stresses of exhibition flying. It carried no instruments, and Rodgers sat in an open chair located on the lower wing structure, completely exposed to the elements.

Armour also agreed to commission a three-car train to accompany the cross-country effort and to carry a contingent of mechanics and support personnel, including the famed Charley Taylor, who had built the Wright internal combustion engine used in the first successful flight of the Flyer at Kitty Hawk. The train, known as the "Vin Fiz Special," was pulled by a steam engine, and consisted of a day coach, a Pullman sleeping car, and a "hangar" car containing tools, spare parts, and a Palmer-Singer automobile with which to fetch Rodgers and return him to the Pullman at the end of each day. Both Cal's mother and his wife, Mabel, went along for moral support, as did a revolving assortment of friends, dignitaries, and newspaper reporters.

The adventure began on September 17, 1911 at the Sheepheads Bay Race Track on Long Island, where he lifted off to begin the first leg of the 4,000-mile odyssey (See Figure App 6-2.). His route would necessarily follow railroad tracks in order to make use of the "Vin Fiz Special" maintenance crew, but also because there were no

FIGURE APP 6-1 Cal Rodgers just before beginning his cross-country odyssey on Sept. 17, 1911.

navigation aids to guide his progress, nor were there any aerial charts, airports, or support facilities of any kind. The "iron compass," the railroad tracks that would still be used to guide the first airmail pilots later in the decade, ran westerly toward the great city of Chicago, on the far side of the daunting Allegheny Mountains. These same mountains would provide the greatest obstacle to the establishment of successful cross-country airmail in the years to come, but now they lay directly ahead of Rodgers.

Although exact historical sources are scarce, it appears that Rodgers elected to proceed northwest from Sheepheads Bay, to Middletown, New York, for his first leg of 84 miles, which he accomplished easily and, as he said, he "didn't even knock the ashes off my cigar." But this pleasant beginning was not to be a harbinger of good things to come. Although the northwest route would avoid the harshest portions of the vaunted Alleghenies, flat land it was not. The troubles began as he left Middleton when he crashed on takeoff. Difficulties continued as he made his way west toward Elmira, New York, then down into Pennsylvania, and finally on into the flat country of Ohio.

By October 9, 1911, Rodgers had made it only to Chicago. He was just one third of the way across the country and it was becoming obvious that the Hearst time limitation for the prize money could not be met. He reached an accommodation with the Armour organization, nevertheless, to press on, prize or no prize. At Chicago the route turned south, partly because of the established rail lines and cities lying in that direction and partly to prepare for the southern circumvention of the highest portions of the Rocky Mountains. At stops along the way, crowds increased in size and enthusiasm. In Kansas City, the authorities closed the schools to celebrate the remarkable effort.

Enroute, the mechanics were kept busy refurbishing the Vin Fiz after the constant mishaps encountered on takeoff and landings. An accurate tabulation of the number of crashes over the course of the journey is not available to us, but estimates range from sixteen to thirty-nine, depending on the prevailing distinction between a "hard landing" and a "crash." Cal fared little better than the airplane, and he flew

FIGURE APP 6-2   Flight of the "Vin Fiz," 1911.

in bandages over most of the route and in leg casts over some of it.

By the time he and the Vin Fiz hobbled into Pasadena, California on November 5, 1911, it had been 49 days since he lifted off from the East Coast. A crowd estimated in number from 10,000 to 20,000 was there to greet him. He had made some 69 stops and had logged a total of 82 hours and 4 minutes airborne. But he was not quite through proving his point: he wanted the wheels of the Vin Fiz to kiss the Pacific waters. On November 12 he took off for the 20-mile hop to Long Beach and the Pacific Ocean only to experience after just 8 miles one of his worst crashes of all, at Compton. Rodgers was hospitalized with internal injuries and a fractured ankle, and his recuperation forced a further delay until December 10, when he finally was able to complete his meandering and perilous coast-to-coast expedition. Crowds cheered as Rodgers taxied the weary Vin Fiz into the lapping surf of the Pacific, his ever-present cigar clenched in his teeth. It had been 84 days since he left Sheepheads Bay.

Cal Rodgers had become a celebrity, as his progress had been faithfully heralded by the countries' newspapers during the course of the journey. As King of the Tournament of Roses Parade on New Year's Day 1912, he flew over the gathered marching bands and floats, dropping carnations to those assembled there. He was awarded a medal by the Aero Club of New York later that month, with President of the United States Taft in attendance.

Back in California on April 3, 1912, he was observed to take off from Long Beach, not far from where he had brought his continental odyssey to its tortured end. He proceeded out over the Long Beach pier and was seen flying along with a flock of seagulls when his new Wright Model B suddenly dived into the Pacific Ocean. Calbraith Perry Rodgers did not survive. An investigation concluded that a seagull had been impacted by the airplane and had lodged between the articulating surfaces of the rudder, rendering control hopeless.

Cal Rodgers' accomplishment has been relegated to the status of a footnote in the annals of aviation history, yet it stands as one of the many similar stories of the sacrifices of the gallant pioneers of flight. He was one of those who placed his love of flying and his capacity to endure ahead of his own safety and comfort.

❝ If you are looking for perfect safety, you will do well to sit on a fence and watch the birds; but if you really wish to learn, you must mount a machine and become acquainted with its tricks by actual trial. ❞

—Wilbur Wright, from an address to the Western Society of Engineers in Chicago, 18 September 1901.

Accidents Involving Passenger Fatalities

U.S. Airlines (Part 121) 1982–Present

The NTSB wishes to make clear to all users of the following list of accidents that the information it contains cannot, by itself, be used to compare the safety either of operators or of aircraft types. Airlines that have operated the greatest numbers of flights and flight hours could be expected to have suffered the greatest number of fatal-to-passenger accidents (assuming that such accidents are random events, and not the result of some systematic deficiency). Similarly, the most used aircraft types would tend to be involved in such accidents more than lesser used types. The NTSB also cautions the user to bear in mind when attempting to compare today's airline system to prior years that airline activity (and hence exposure to risk) has risen by almost 100% from the first year depicted to the last.

Date	Location	Operator	Aircraft Type	Passengers Fatal	Passengers Surv
1/13/82	WASHINGTON, DC	AIR FLORIDA	BOEING 737-222	70	4
1/23/82	BOSTON, MA	WORLD AIRWAYS	MCDONNELL DOUGLAS DC-10-30	2	198
7/09/82	NEW ORLEANS, LA	PAN AMERICAN WORLD AIRWAYS	BOEING 727-235	137	0
11/08/82	HONOLULU, HI	PAN AMERICAN WORLD AIRWAYS	BOEING 747-100	1	274
01/09/83	BRAINERD, MN	REPUBLIC AIRLINES	CONVAIR 580-11-A	1	29
10/11/83	PINCKNEYVILLE, IL	AIR ILLINOIS	HAWKER SIDDELEY HS-748-2A	7	0
01/01/85	LA PAZ, BOLIVIA	EASTERN AIR LINES	BOEING 727-225	21	0
01/21/85	RENO, NV	GALAXY AIRLINES	LOCKHEED 188C	64	1
08/02/85	DALLAS/FT WORTH, TX	DELTA AIRLINES	LOCKHEED L-1011-385-1	126	26

Continued

Date	Location	Operator	Aircraft Type	Passengers	
				Fatal	Surv
09/06/85	MILWAUKEE, WI	MIDWEST EXPRESS AIRLINES	DOUGLAS DC-9-14	27	0
12/12/85	GANDER, NEWFOUNDLAND	ARROW AIRWAYS	DOUGLAS DC-8-63	248	0
02/04/86	NEAR ATHENS, GREECE	TRANS WORLD AIRLINES	BOEING 727-231	4	110
02/14/87	DURANGO, MX	PORTS OF CALL	BOEING 707-323B	1	125
08/16/87	ROMULUS, MI	NORTHWEST AIRLINES	MCDONNELL DOUGLAS DC-9-82	148	1
11/15/87	DENVER, CO	CONTINENTAL AIRLINES	MCDONNELL DOUGLAS DC-9-14	25	52
12/07/87	SAN LUIS OBISPO, CA	PACIFIC SOUTHWEST AIRLINES	BRITISH AEROSPACE BAE-146-200	38	0
08/31/88	DALLAS/FT WORTH, TX	DELTA AIRLINES	BOEING 727-232	12	89
12/21/88	LOCKERBIE, SCOTLAND	PAN AMERICAN WORLD AIRWAYS	BOEING 747-121	243	0
02/08/89	SANTAMARIA, AZORES	INDEPENDENT AIR	BOEING 707	137	0
02/24/89	HONOLULU, HI	UNITED AIRLINES	BOEING 747-122	9	328
07/19/89	SIOUX CITY, IA	UNITED AIRLINES	MCDONNELL DOUGLAS DC-10-10	110	175
09/20/89	FLUSHING, NY	USAIR	BOEING 737-400	2	55
12/27/89	MIAMI, FL	EASTERN AIR LINES	BOEING 727-225B	1	46
10/03/90	CAPE CANAVERAL, FL	EASTERN AIR LINES	MCDONNELL DOUGLAS DC-9-31	1	90
12/03/90	ROMULUS, MI	NORTHWEST AIRLINES	MCDONNELL DOUGLAS DC-9-14	7	33
02/01/91	LOS ANGELES, CA	USAIR	BOEING 737-300	20	63
03/03/91	COLORADO SPGS, CO	UNITED AIRLINES	BOEING 737-291	20	0
03/22/92	FLUSHING, NY	USAIR	FOKKER 28-4000	25	22
07/02/94	CHARLOTTE, NC	USAIR	DOUGLAS DC-9-30	37	20
09/08/94	ALIQUIPPA, PA	USAIR	BOEING B-737-300	127	0
10/31/94	ROSELAWN, IN	AMERICAN EAGLE	ATR-72-212	64	0
12/20/95	CALI, COLOMBIA	AMERICAN AIRLINES	BOEING B-757	152	4
05/11/96	MIAMI, FL	VALUJET AIRLINES	MCDONNELL DOUGLAS DC-9	105	0
07/06/96	PENSACOLA, FL	DELTA AIRLINES	MCDONNELL DOUGLAS MD-88	2	140
07/17/96	MORICHES, NY	TRANS WORLD AIRLINES	BOEING 747	212	0
08/02/97	LIMA, PERU	CONTINENTAL AIRLINES	BOEING 757-200	1	141
12/28/97	PACIFIC OCEAN	UNITED AIRLINES	BOEING 747	1	373

Date	Location	Operator	Aircraft Type	Passengers	
				Fatal	Surv
06/01/99	LITTLE ROCK, AR	AMERICAN AIRLINES	MCDONNELL DOUGLAS MD-80	10	129
01/31/00	POINT MUGU, CA	ALASKA AIRLINES	MCDONNELL DOUGLAS MD-83	83	0
09/11/01	NEW YORK CITY, NY	AMERICAN AIRLINES	BOEING 767-200	81	0
09/11/01	NEW YORK CITY, NY	UNITED AIRLINES	BOEING 767-200	56	0
09/11/01	ARLINGTON, VA	AMERICAN AIRLINES	BOEING 757-200	58	0
09/11/01	SHANKSVILLE, PA	UNITED AIRLINES	BOEING 757	37	0
11/12/01	BELLE HARBOR, NY	AMERICAN AIRLINES	AIRBUS INDUSTRIE A300-600	251	0
01/08/03	CHARLOTTE, NC	US AIRWAYS EXPRESS	Beech 1900	19	0
10/19/04	KIRKSVILLE, MO	CORPORATE AIRLINES	British Aerospace Jetstream 32	11	2
12/19/05	MIAMI, FL	CHALKS OCEAN AIRWAYS	Grumman G-73T	18	0
08/27/06	LEXINGTON, KY	COMAIR	Bombardier CRJ-100	47	0

The NTSB wishes to make clear to all users of the preceding list of accidents that the information it contains cannot, by itself, be used to compare the safety either of operators or of aircraft types. Airlines that have operated the greatest numbers of flights and flight hours could be expected to have suffered the greatest number

U.S. Commuters (Part 135) 1982–Present

The NTSB wishes to make clear to all users of the following list of accidents that the information it contains cannot, by itself, be used to compare the safety either of operators or of aircraft types. Airlines that have operated the greatest numbers of flights and flight hours could be expected to have suffered the greatest number of fatal-to-passenger accidents (assuming that such accidents are random events, and not the result of some systematic deficiency). Similarly, the most used aircraft types would tend to be involved in such accidents more than lesser used types. The NTSB also cautions the user to bear in mind when attempting to compare today's airline system to prior years that airline activity (and hence exposure to risk) has risen by more than 35% from the first year depicted to the last.

Date	Location	Operator	Aircraft Type	Passengers Fatal	Surv
02/21/1982	PROVIDENCE, RI	PILGRIM AIRLINES	DEHAVILLAND DHC-6	1	9
12/09/1982	NEAR KLAWOCK, AK	TYEE AIRLINES, INC.	DEHAVILLAND DHC-2	7	0
08/17/1983	PEACH SPRINGS, AZ	LAS VEGAS AIRLINES	PIPER PA-31-350	9	0
03/05/1984	CUMBERLAND, MD	CUMBERLAND AIRLINES	PIPER PA-31	2	0
07/21/1984	TAU, MANUA	ISL SOUTH PACIFIC ISLAND	DEHAVILLAND DCH-6-300	1	10
08/02/1984	VIEQUES, PR	VIEQUES AIR LINK, INC. BRITTEN	NORMAN BN-2A ISLANDER	8	0
08/24/1984	SAN LUIS OBISPO, CA	WINGS WEST AIRLINES, INC.	BEECH C-99	13	0
09/07/1984	NAPLES, FL	PROVINCETOWNBOSTON AIRLINES	CESSNA 402C	1	4
12/06/1984	JACKSONVILLE, FL	PROVINCETOWNBOSTON AIRLINES	EMBRAER BANDEIRANTE EMB-110P1	11	0
12/17/1984	BAINBRIDGE, NY	SUSQUEHANNA AIRLINES, INC.	PIPER PA-23-250	2	0
02/04/1985	SOLDOTNA, AK	NORTH PACIFIC AIRLINES	BEECH 65-A80	7	0
02/06/1985	ALTUS, OK	ALTUS AIRLINE, INC.	CESSNA 402B	1	0
04/26/1985	NEW YORK, NY	NEW YORK HELICOPTERS	AEROSPATIALE SA360C DAUPHIN	1	5
08/25/1985	AUBURN, ME	BAR HARBOR AIRLINES	BEECH 99	6	0
09/23/1985	GROTTOES, VA	HENSON AIRLINES	BEECH B99	12	0
11/01/1985	BETHEL, AK	HERMENS AIR, INC.	CESSNA 208	1	2
03/13/1986	ALPENA, MI	SIMMONS AIRLINES	EMBRAER EMB-110P1	2	5
10/28/1986	ST. CROIX, VI	VIRGIN ISLAND SEAPLANE SHUTTLE	GRUMMAN G-73	1	12

Date	Location	Operator	Aircraft Type	Passengers	
				Fatal	Surv
01/15/1987	KEARNS, UT	SKY WEST AIRLINES INC. (SKY WEST AIRLINES/ WESTERN EXPR)	SWEARINGEN SA-226TC	6	0
03/04/1987	ROMULUS, MI	FISHER BROTHERS AVIATION INC. (NORTHWEST AIRLINK)	CASA C-212-CC	7	9
04/01/1987	ANCHORAGE, AK	WILBUR'S FLIGHT OPERATIONS (WILBUR'S INC.)	CESSNA 402	1	0
11/23/1987	HOMER, AK	RYAN AIR SERVICE, INC.	BEECH 1900C	16	3
12/23/1987	KENAI, AK	SOUTH CENTRAL AIR, INC.	PIPER PA-31-350	5	2
12/23/1987	MAUNALOA, HI	PANORAMA AIR TOURS (PANORAMA AIR TOURS)	PIPER PA-31-350	7	0
01/19/1988	BAYFIELD, CO	TRANS COLORADO AIRLINES (TRANS COLORADO)	FAIRCHILD SA-227-AC	7	8
02/19/1988	CARY, NC	AVAIR, INC. (AMERICAN EAGLE)	FAIRCHILD SA-227-AC	10	0
04/19/1989	PELICAN, AK	CHANNEL FLYING SERVICE	DEHAVILLAND DHC-2	1	0
07/30/1989	HAINES, AK	SKAGWAY AIR SERVICE	PIPER PA-32-301	2	2
10/28/1989	HALAWA, MOLOKAI, HI	ALOHA ISLANDAIR	DE HAVILLAND DHC-6-300	18	0
12/26/1989	PASCO, WA	NPA/UNITED EXPRESS (UNITED EXPRESS)	BRITISH AEROSPACE BAE-3101	4	0
09/03/1990	KALTAG, AK	FRONTIER FLYING SERVICE	PIPER PA-31-325	3	6
02/01/1991	LOS ANGELES, CA	SKYWEST AIRLINES, INC.	FAIRCHILD SA-227-AC	10	0
04/05/1991	BRUNSWICK, GA	ATLANTIC SOUTHEAST AIRLINES	EMBRAER EMB-120RT	20	0
07/10/1991	BIRMINGHAM, AL	L'EXPRESS AIRLINES, INC.	BEECH C99	12	1
08/20/1991	KETCHIKAN, AK	TEMSCO HELICOPTERS, INC. (TEMSCO AIRLINES)	PILATUS BRITTEN-NORMAN BN-2A-26 ISLANDER	3	0
09/11/1991	EAGLE LAKE, TX	CONTINENTAL EXPRESS	EMBRAER 120	11	0
12/10/1991	TEMPLE BAR, AZ	LAS VEGAS AIRLINES, INC.	PIPER PA-31-350	4	0
01/03/1992	GABRIELS, NY	COMMUTAIR (USAIR EXPRESS)	BEECH 1900C	1	1
01/23/1992	CLEWISTON, FL	AIR SUNSHINE INC.	CESSNA 402C	1	0
06/07/1992	MAYAGUEZ, PR	EXECUTIVE AIR CHARTER, INC. (AMERICAN EAGLE)	CASA 212	3	0
06/08/1992	ANNISTON, AL	GP EXPRESS AIRLINES, INC.	BEECH C99	2	2
10/27/1992	SAIPAN, MP	PACIFIC ISLAND AVIATION, INC.	CESSNA 310R	2	0
10/31/1992	GRAND JUNCTION, CO	ALPINE AVIATION (ALPINE AIR)	PIPER PA-42	2	0

Continued

Date	Location	Operator	Aircraft Type	Passengers	
				Fatal	Surv
11/08/1992	KIANA, AK	BAKER AVIATION INC.	CESSNA 402C	2	0
04/03/1993	NOME, AK	RYAN AIR SERVICE, INC	CESSNA 207	1	0
07/12/1993	LAS VEGAS, NV	AIR NEVADA AIRLINES	CESSNA 402C	2	0
12/01/1993	HIBBING, MN	EXPRESS AIRLINES II, INC. (NORTHWEST AIRLINK)	JETSTREAM BA-3100	16	0
01/07/1994	COLUMBUS, OH	ATLANTIC COAST AIRLINES (UNITED EXPRESS)	JETSTREAM 4101	2	3
12/13/1994	MORRISVILLE, NC	FLAGSHIP AIRLINES (AMERICAN EAGLE)	BAE JETSTREAM 3201	15	5
08/21/1995	CARROLLTON, GA	ATLANTIC SOUTHEAST AIRLINES (DELTA CONNECTOR)	EMBRAER EMB-120RT	7	19
11/19/1996	QUINCY, IL	GREAT LAKES AVIATION (UNITED EXPRESS)	BEECH 1900	10	0
01/09/1997	IDA, MI	COMAIR	EMBRAER 120	26	0
02/08/1997	ST. THOMAS, VI	AIR SUNSHIHE	CESSNA 402C	2	2
04/10/1997	WAINWRIGHT, AK	HAGELAND AVIATION	CESSNA 208B	4	0
06/27/1997	NOME, AK	OLSON AIR SERVICE	CESSNA 207	1	0
11/08/1997	BARROW, AK	HAGELAND AVIATION SERVICES	CESSNA 208B	7	0
09/05/1999	WESTERLY, RI	NEW ENGLAND AIRLINES	PIPER PA-32-260	2	2
12/07/1999	BETHEL, AK	GRANT AVIATION	CESSNA 207	5	0
09/18/2000	NUIQSUT, AK	CAPE SMYTHE AIR SERVICE	PIPER PA-31T3	4	5
10/03/2001	DECATUR ISLAND, WA	WEST ISLE AIR	CESSNA 172N	2	0
10/10/2001	DILLINGHAM, AK	PENINSULA AIRWAYS	CESSNA 208	9	0
07/13/2003	TREASURE CAY, BAHAMAS	AIR SUNSHINE	CESSNA 402C	2	7
12/14/2006	PORT HEIDEN, AK	PENINSULA AIRWAYS	PIPER PA-32-301	1	0

The NTSB wishes to make clear to all users of the preceding list of accidents that the information it contains cannot, by itself, be used to compare the safety either of operators or of aircraft types. Airlines that have operated the greatest numbers of flights and flight hours could be expected to have suffered the greatest number of fatal-to-passenger accidents (assuming that such accidents are random events, and not the result of some systematic deficiency). Similarly, the most used aircraft types would tend to be involved in such accidents more than lesser used types. The NTSB also cautions the user to bear in mind when attempting to compare today's airline system to prior years that airline activity (and hence exposure to risk) has risen by more than 35% from the first year depicted to the last.

updated September 2005

Administrative Law Judge (ALJ)—A person appointed pursuant to civil service regulations to hold hearings and make determinations of fact and law. Most commonly in aviation, ALJs conduct trials de novo as first level appeals in FAA certificate actions against airmen.

Aerial Experiment Association—A scientific association formed in 1907 by Alexander Graham Bell and consisting of Bell, Glenn Curtis, J. A. D. McCurdy, F. W. Baldwin, and Lt. Thomas Selfridge. The purpose of the organization was to study aeronautics and to design and build a practical airplane.

Aerodrome—The name given by Samuel P. Langley to the flying machine he designed in 1893. His aerodrome no. 5, a 14 pound model powered by small steam engine, flew for a distance of over one-half mile in 1896. The aerodrome employed "planes" (wings), or flat horizontal surfaces mounted to the fuselage, to achieve lift.

Air Transport Association—Trade association composed of U.S. certificated air carriers.

Airport Improvement Program Funds (AIP)—Funds derived primarily from taxes on passenger tickets and aviation fuels used in non-commercial operations and used to pay for improvements to the nation's airports and air traffic control system.

Airship—A lighter than air, elongated balloon-like vehicle with engines for propulsion and external devices (rudders and elevators) for control.

Airway—A route through navigable airspace defined by aids to navigation designated by the FAA, 10 miles in width, and that extends upward from the beginning of navigable airspace to 27,000 feet altitude.

Airworthiness—Term used to describe the legal or mechanical status of an aircraft with regard to its readiness for flight.

Antarctica—The Earth's southernmost and fifth-largest continent. It has an area of 5,400,000 square miles, of which 108,000 (2 percent) is ice-free. It has the highest average elevation of all the continents, and is the driest, coldest, and most windy. It has very little precipitation and is, therefore, the largest desert in the world. Animals that have adapted to its environment include penguins, various kinds of seals, and several species of birds.

Apogee—In an elliptical orbit path, the point at which a satellite is farthest from the Earth.

Arianespace—The French company (Arianespace SA), founded in 1980, which undertakes the production, operation and marketing of the Ariane 5 rocket launcher. It was the world's first commercial space transportation company.

Assembly Line—An innovation employed in the assembly of early Ford automobiles that required workers to perform essentially the same task or tasks on each automobile in the assembly process as the automobile being assembled slowly proceeded down the assembly line by means of a mechanized conveyor.

Astronautics—A branch of engineering (astronautical engineering) that deals with machines designed to work outside of the Earth's atmosphere. The science of the design, construction, and operation of spacecraft.

Atmosphere, Earth's—The layer of gases surrounding the planet, which are retained by Earth's gravity. It is composed of nitrogen (78 percent), oxygen (20.95 percent), argon (.93 percent), carbon dioxide (.038 percent), and trace amounts of other gases. The atmosphere absorbs ultraviolet radiation and reduces temperature extremes of day and night periods.

Available Seat Mile (ASM)—Statistical measure used to describe one seat flown one mile. An aircraft with 100 seats flown a distance of 100 miles represents 10,000 ASMs.

Axis Powers—An alliance of Germany, Italy, and Japan before and during World War II.

Cabotage—Originally, the term for coastwise shipping within the borders of a single country so as to effect commerce between two or more points within that country. In international civil aviation, it describes the practice reserved to domestic airlines only to serve a second point (airport) within a single country from an initial point (airport). Cabotage has not been granted so far in international civil aviation.

CAM Routes—Contract airmail routes awarded by the U.S. post office department beginning in 1925 to companies and individuals in the private sector, granting to them the exclusive right to carry U.S. mail by air between designated points in the country.

Certificate of Public Convenience and Necessity—A certificate granted by the Department of Transportation upon a finding that an air carrier utilizing aircraft with a seating capacity in excess of 60 seats has met the fitness requirements set out in the federal aviation regulations.

Chapter 11—The section of the United States bankruptcy code (11 U.S.C. 1113, et. seq.) designed to allow a corporation to reorganize its operations under the protection of the bankruptcy court and to secure temporary relief from claims of creditors during the period of reorganization. Invoking the provisions of chapter 11 allows the corporation to continue operations even though it is technically bankrupt (liabilities exceed assets).

Civil Aeronautics Administration—Agency of the United States created by the 1940 amendments to the Civil Aeronautics Act of 1938 and charged with the administration of non-military safety programs, air traffic control, and airway development. It was one of the forerunners of the Federal Aviation Administration.

Civil Aeronautics Board—Independent board formed by the 1940 amendment to the Civil Aeronautics Act of 1938 for the purpose of administering the economic regulation of the airlines. The CAB ceased to exist on December 31, 1984, pursuant to the provisions of the Airline Deregulation Act of 1978.

Civil Reserve Air Fleet (CRAF)—Designation of aircraft of U.S. certificated carriers that may be activated, with crew, for exclusive military use in the national interest in cases of emergency.

Code of Federal Regulations (CFRs)—Codification of federal agency regulations that are promulgated by such agencies pursuant to authority given in statutes passed by the congress of the United States. The CFR is arranged into 50 titles, each dealing with a different subject matter, and it is revised and updated annually.

Code Sharing—Marketing devices used by airlines in advertising, sales and reservations that allow originating airlines designations (two letter code) to be carried through to connecting airlines flight segments, even though such subsequent segments are conducted by an entirely different airline.

Cold War—A period of conflict, tension, and competition between the United States and the Soviet Union between the late 1940s until the early 1990s. The Cold War period was characterized by costly defense spending, a massive arms race in conventional and nuclear weapons, and proxy wars.

Common Law—Law that is a result of contested cases between parties in litigation and which results in opinions handed down by courts. Common law was the "judge-made" law of England that was in use in the colonies prior to the American Revolution, and which was adopted by the newly created states of the new American republic. Common law is to be distinguished from statutory law, or legislation, which is created on the federal level in the Congress of the United States, and on the state level in the various legislatures of the states.

Computer Reservation Systems (CRS)—A development made possible by the advent of real-time computer technology beginning in the 1960s, applied to the complexities of airlines' passenger reservations operations. CRS became a major marketing tool for the airlines during the 1980s, and provided immediate analytical perspectives in airline operations not previously possible, including information that allowed last minute seat pricing changes to optimize passenger load factors. Several airlines own these systems and they are used by travel agents.

Convention—An international agreement among nations governing international civil aviation operations.

Department of Transportation—Cabinet level department of the United States government created by congress in 1966, and which began operations in 1967. The legislation, for the first time, gathered into the DOT all federal agencies and functions having to do with any aspect of transportation. The administration of aviation was placed within a new agency called the Federal Aviation Administration. Upon its creation, the Department of Transportation was the fourth largest department in the federal government.

Depression—A period of economic stress that persists over an extended period, accompanied by poor business conditions and high unemployment.

Deregulation—Term used in referring to the Airline Deregulation Act of 1978, which ended the economic regulation of the airlines by the federal government.

Dirigible—See airship.

Due Process—Constitutional guarantee given to all persons in the United States by the fifth and fourteenth amendments to the U.S. constitution that life or liberty may not be taken or abridged by the federal government or any state government without certain procedural and substantive safeguards being observed. Among these are the right to confront witnesses and to cross examine them, the right to a fair trial before an impartial jury, the right to competent counsel, and the right to just compensation for property taken by the government in the public interest.

Enplanements—Term used to describe the number of passengers boarding a flight.

Essential Air Service—Government subsidized airline service to rural areas of the U.S. made necessary by effects of airline deregulation in 1978.

Export-Import Bank—Governmental agency designed to support transactions between domestic suppliers and foreign consumers by providing financing that is not available in the commercial markets.

FAA/AST—The Office of Commercial Space Transportation in the Federal Aviation Administration that approves all commercial rocket launch operations. This Office regulates launch sites, publishes quarterly launch forecasts, and holds annual conferences with the space launch industry. FAA/AST was created by the Commercial Space Launch Act of 1985.

Federal Register—Published under the authority of Congress five days a week, providing official notice of agency proposed rule making, adoption of rules and regulations, and congressional activities.

Federation Aeronautique Internationale (FAI)—A nongovernmental, nonprofit international organization founded in 1905 whose basic aim is the furthering of aeronautical and astronautical activities worldwide. It has some 100-member countries. FAI establishes rules for the control and certification of world aeronautical and astronautical records.

Four Course Radio Range—The first non-visual navigation system ever developed. It utilized low frequency radio waves to transmit steady morse code signals as a homing device to airplanes along the first airways.

General Agreement on Tariffs and Trade (GATT)—Created in 1947, GATT was a multinational agreement designed to promote and allow unfettered access by all nations to the benefits of world free enterprise by reducing protectionist barriers to free trade. It was replaced in 1995 by the World Trade Organization.

General Maritime Law—The common law of admiralty, or the law of the sea, originating in England and adopted by the United States after the American Revolution.

Geostationary orbit—A geosynchronous orbit in the Earth's equatorial plane, directly above the equator. A GSO has zero degrees of inclination and remains in the equatorial plane at all times. To an observer on Earth, it will appear to remain motionless in the sky. Also called a "Clarke Orbit" due to the first use of the phrase by science fiction writer, Arthur C. Clarke in 1945. Satellites in GSO orbit in the direction of the Earth's rotation at an altitude of approximately 22, 240 miles above mean sea level. A GSO orbital period is equal to the Earth's rotational period, known as the sidereal day.

Geosynchronous orbit—An orbit around the Earth with an orbital period identical to the sidereal rotation period, or the period of Earth rotation. A geosynchronous orbit differs from a geostationary orbit in that the former may have an inclination from the equatorial plane, so that it passes above and below the plane of the equator during the Earth day.

Guggenheim Fund—A charitable fund established in 1926 by Daniel Guggenheim for the promotion of aeronautics. The fund paid for the establishment of engineering programs at universities, including aeronautical engineering degree programs at Stanford, MIT, Harvard, and others. Competition sponsored by the fund resulted in the first STOL (short takeoff and landing) ever built. The fund was responsible for many other innovations that greatly contributed to the safety of aviation.

Hub and Spoke—The system of airline operations that concentrates the arrival and departure of multiple scheduled aircraft at one central airport (the hub) at or near the same time to allow passengers (arriving from one of the outlying feeder airports at the end of the spoke) to connect with other arriving flights at the hub (each arriving from a different outlying airport) in order to continue their flight to a different outlying destination airport. The system allows maximum utilization of smaller aircraft by airlines but places a huge strain on air traffic control and airport facilities.

ICBM—Intercontinental ballistic missile, or long-range missile designed for the delivery of nuclear weapons. All five of the nations with permanent seats on the United Nations Security Council have operational ICBM systems. France and the United Kingdom have submarine launch capacity and China, the Russian Federation, and the United States have both submarine and land-based launch capability.

Inclination—The angle between an orbital path and a plane of reference. The most common plane of reference used in artificial earth satellite orbit is the equatorial plane. The angle of inclination is stated in degrees.

Institute of Medicine, The—Chartered in 1970 as a component of the National Academy of Sciences, the IOM is a nonprofit organization specifically created to give advice to the federal government on matters of biomedical science, medicine, and health.

International Air Transport Association (IATA)—Association of international air carriers operating as a trade association with liaison responsibilities to the international civil aviation organization (ICAO). IATA also serves as the clearinghouse for interline accounting, servicing the accounts of 380 airlines.

International Civil Aviation Organization (ICAO)—An organ of the United Nations created in 1947 by the Chicago Convention. It has facilitated the integration of international airline operations since World War II, including the adoption of standards for navigation, communication, and aircraft certification.

Joint Aviation Authorities—Association of European countries formed in 1970 for the purpose of coordinating standards for certification of aircraft, and since 1989 it has been charged with coordinating safety efforts similar to the FAA in the United States. Responsibility for aviation safety within the European union is expected to be taken over on a permanent basis by the European Aviation Safety Agency (EASA).

Labor Union—An organized association of workers, often in a trade, formed to protect and further their rights and interests.

Laissez-Faire Policy—Governmental abstention from interfering in economic or commercial affairs.

Load Factor—The percentage of available seats that are filled with paying passengers. Revenue passenger miles divided by available seat miles.

Low Earth orbit—An orbit around the Earth ranging from an altitude of 124 miles to 1240 miles above the Earth's surface. Most human activity in space has been conducted in LEO orbits.

Major Carrier—An airline with annual revenues of more than $1 billion.

Marshall Plan—A program inaugurated by the United States, and participated in by most of the Western European nations, designed to provide economic assistance to the nations of Western Europe in the aftermath of World War II. It was the single most effective and successful international cooperative plan ever conceived in peacetime, and was responsible for the economic recovery of those war-torn nations after 1945.

Medium Earth orbit—An orbit around the Earth above LEO (at a high of 1240 miles) and geosynchronous orbit (around 22,240 miles). The most common use for satellites in this region is for navigation (GPS satellites orbit at around 12,552 miles). Orbital periods for MEO satellites is from 2 hours to 12 hours.

Minimum Wage—Legislatively mandated hourly wage that, at a minimum, must be paid to all qualifying workers by affected employers.

Monopoly—Control or advantage obtained by one supplier or producer over the commercial market within a given region. The market condition existing when only one economic entity produces a particular product or provides a particular service. The term is now commonly applied also to situations that approach but do not strictly meet this definition.

Monroney Aeronautical Center—Location of FAA aircraft registry and recordation activities, airman records branch, the civil aeromedical institute (CAMI), and training center. It is located in Oklahoma City, OK.

Mutually assured destruction (MAD)—A doctrine of military strategy in which a full-scale use of nuclear weapons by one of two opposing sides would effectively result in the destruction of both. It is an evolutionary defense strategy based on the concept that neither the United States nor its enemies will ever start a nuclear war because the other side will retaliate massively. MAD is a product of the 1950s that has little relevance to the major defense threats of the 21st century.

National Academy of Engineering, The—Founded in 1964, the NAE operates under the same Congressional Act of Incorporation that established the National Academy of Sciences, and performs the same functions for the federal government in engineering matters as does the NAS in scientific matters.

National Academy of Sciences, The—Created by statute and signed into law by Abraham Lincoln on March 3, 1863, the NAS is an honorific society of distinguished scholars engaged in scientific research. It investigates, examines, experiments, and reports upon any subject of science or art whenever called upon to do so by any department of the government.

National Academies, The—Composed of four separate organizations (the National Academy of Sciences, the National Academy of Engineering, the Institute of Medicine, and the National Research Council), this collection of experts serves in a pro bono capacity as a public service to address critical national issues and to give advice to the federal government and the public.

National Advisory Committee for Aeronautics (NACA)—Established by the United States government in 1915 to direct and conduct research and experimentation in aeronautics. NACA was formed because of the perception that the United States had fallen behind the European countries in the emerging field of aeronautics during World War I. NACA was the forerunner of NASA.

National Carrier—An airline with annual revenues of between $100 million and $1 billion.

National Mediation Board—Agency created by the Railway Labor Act (RLA) to mediate major issues arising under the RLA with a view to avoiding strikes, work stoppages, and interruptions of national transportation services.

National Reconnaissance Office, The—The NRO was established in 1960 to develop the nation's satellite reconnaissance systems. It is part of the Department of Defense, and is one of the 16 intelligence agencies in the United States. It designs, builds, and operates the reconnaissance satellites of the U.S. government.

National Research Council, The—A component of the National Academies, the mission of the NRC is to improve government decision making and public policy, increase public education and understanding, and promote the acquisition and dissemination of knowledge in matters involving science, engineering, technology, and health.

National Transportation Safety Board—Created by the Department of Transportation Act of 1966, the NTSB is now an independent federal agency charged with the primary responsibility of investigating transportation accidents, making findings of the "probable cause" of such accidents, and making recommendations for system improvements to assist in preventing future accidents. It is responsible under Part 830 of the Federal Aviation Regulations for receiving notification of aircraft accidents and incidents and for administration of the aviation disaster family assistance act.

Nodal period—The time that elapses between successive passages of a satellite through successive ascending nodes (or descending nodes) of an artificial Earth satellite. An orbital node is one of the two points where the satellite's orbit crosses a plane of reference. The most common plane of reference is the Earth's equatorial plane. Orbits that are contained in the plane of reference are called non-inclined. Orbits that cross the plane of reference are in inclined orbits.

Notice of Propose Rulemaking—The Administrative Procedures Act requires that all agencies in the United States government provide notice to the public of any intent to adopt new rules or regulations, setting for the particulars of the proposed rule and the basis for its adoption.

Part 121 Regulations—FAA safety regulations applicable to commercial operations of aircraft with 10 or more seats.

Part 135 Regulations—FAA safety regulations applicable to commercial operations of aircraft with fewer than 10 seats.

Passenger Facility Charges (PFCs)—A per passenger enplanement fee charged by airports, collected by airlines in addition to the passenger airfare, to be used for financing airport capital improvements.

Patent—The governmental grant of a right, privilege, or authority. A patent granted to an invention recognized by industry or the scientific community as pioneering, unexpected, and unprecedented.

Peenemunde—Situated in the northeast of Germany on the Baltic coast, this area was occupied by the German Reich Air Ministry in 1936 as a research center. Its location permitted rocket test flights over water with monitoring capability for some 200 miles along the coast. Experimentation and development of rocket systems, radar systems, and night-navigation were conducted here.

Perigee—In an elliptical orbit path, the point at which a satellite is closest to the Earth.

Perimeter Rules—Restrictions applied to arriving aircraft at New York LaGuardia and Washington National (now Reagan) that requires arriving nonstop flights to have originated within a certain radius, in miles, from the airport (1,500 miles for LaGuardia and 1,250 miles for National). The purpose of perimeter rules was to encourage the use of JFK airport and Dulles airport, which were then relatively new.

Predatory Practices—Unfair exclusionary airline practices designed to prevent or minimize competition from other airlines, usually competition from new entrant or smaller airlines.

Presidential Emergency Board—A panel of experts appointed by the President of the United States pursuant to the provisions of the Railway Labor Act whose function is to make a last-ditch effort to effect a compromise between labor and management to prevent a work stoppage and consequent disruption of national transportation services.

Recession—Period characterized by a sharp slowdown in economic activity, declining employment, and a decrease in investment and consumer spending.

Reconnaissance satellite—An Earth observation satellite or communication satellite deployed for military or intelligence purposes, also known as a "spy satellite."

Regional Carrier—An airline with annual revenues of less than $100 million whose service generally is limited to a particular geographic region.

Rubicon—A river in northern Italy flowing eastward from the Apennines to the Adriatic Sea. "Crossing the Rubicon" is a popular idiom meaning to go past a point of no return. Julius Caesar crossed the river in 49 B.C. deliberately as an act of war.

Saturn V—A multistage liquid-fuel expendable rocket used in the NASA Apollo and Skylab programs.

Sidereal day—The period of time needed for the Earth to complete one complete rotation around its axis. The sidereal day is about four minutes shorter than the solar day.

Slots—A device initiated by the FAA in 1969 in an attempt to alleviate congestion at four airports in the U.S.—Chicago O'Hare, Washington National (now Reagan), New York JFK, and New York LaGuardia. The procedure grants to participating air carriers a specific time and date for either landing or taking off from one of these airports.

Smithsonian Institution—In 1826, James Smithson, a British scientist, drew up his last will and testament, naming his nephew as beneficiary. Smithson stipulated that, should the nephew die without heirs (as he would in 1835), the estate should go "to the United States of America, to found at Washington, under the name of the Smithsonian Institution, an establishment for the increase and diffusion of knowledge among men."

Solar day—The average period of time needed for the sun to return to its highest point (24 hours).

Statute—A written law enacted by a legislative body.

Tariff—Publication of an air carrier in which notice is provided of fares and rates, and any special rules or conditions upon which the transportation of persons or property is subject.

Trial de Novo—A proceeding that is conducted as an original proceeding to find facts based on the presentation of evidence in the proceeding and to make conclusions of law applicable to the case based on the facts presented.

Van Allen radiation belts—Two layers of radiation outside of the earth's atmosphere extending from 400 to 40,000 miles into space. The belts are named for James A. Van Allen, the American astrophysicist who first predicted the belts. The charged particles of which the belts are composed circulate along the Earth's magnetic lines of force extending from the area above the equator to the North pole, to the South Pole, and circle back to the equator. These particles are believed to originate in periodic solar flares and become trapped by the Earth's magnetic field. They are responsible for the aurora borealis.

Versailles Treaty—The peace treaty that officially ended World War I between the Allied and Associated Powers and Germany. The treaty is generally regarded as punitive against Germany, requiring Germany to accept full responsibility for causing the war, to disarm, to make substantial territorial concessions and to pay reparations. The terms of the treaty caused widespread resentment in Germany, and became the focal point for radical political activity during the 1920s in Germany. The National Socialist Party, led by Adolf Hitler, used its extremely punitive provisions as justification for many of its territorial expansions and its rearmament during the 1930s.

Widebody Aircraft—Aircraft with more than one aisle in the passenger cabin, such as the Boeing 747, 767 and 777, L-1011, DC-10, and Airbus A300 and A310.

William J. Hughes Technical Center—Center for research and development programs conducted by the FAA. It is located near Atlantic City, N.J.

Wing-warping—Innovation by the Wright brothers employed on their gliders, and later on the Flyer, that effected a bending of the outer trailing edges of the upper and lower wing surfaces by means of ropes and pulleys manipulated by the operator that allowed, for the first time, a means to control lateral stability of the machine in flight. The U.S. patent office granted patent no. 821,393 to the Wrights on May 22, 1903.

World Trade Organization (WTO)—Successor to GATT effective in 1995, the WTO governs international trade in all respects. The goal of the WTO is to facilitate the international movement of products, goods, and services for the betterment of signatory countries and their citizens.

Yield—Average revenue per revenue passenger mile expressed in cents per mile.

Yield Management—The process made possible by computers that allows airlines to set and revise prices for a particular flight based on real-time information.

Zeppelin—Large airship originally built by Ferdinand Adolf von Zeppelin in 1900. Zeppelins were used in passenger service and in war, the last of which was the Hindenburg, which burned upon attempting to dock at Lakehurst, N.J., in 1937 after a transatlantic voyage.

———, *Airlines 101-A Primer for Dummies,* The Airline Monitor, November 1998.

———, *Airlines Treat Patron 'Like Cattle' Feds Say,* Aviation Week and Space Technology, August 7, 2000.

———, *Chronology of Presidential Emergency Boards Under the Railway Labor Act,* Catherwood Library, School of Industrial and Labor Relations, Electronic Archive, Miscellaneous Documents <http://www.ilr.cornell.edu/library/e archive/miscellaneous/?pqge.airlines%2Fairlines>, 2002.

———, *A Chronology of Strikes in the Airline Industry,* Catherwood Library, School of Industrial and Labor Relations, Electronic Archive, Miscellaneous Documents <http://www.ilr.cornell.edu/library/e archive/miscellaneous/?page=airlines%2Fairlines>, 2002.

———, *Federal and State Coordination: Aviation Noise Policy and Regulation,* 46 Administrative Law Review 413–427, 1994.

———, *Hell's Bells,* Smithsonian Magazine, May 2002, pp. 28–29.

Air Transport Association, *Airlines in Crisis—The Perfect Storm,* 2003.

Air Transport Association, *2002 Annual Report,* 2002.

Air Transport Association, *The Airline Handbook,* 2001.

Air Transport Association, *State of the U.S. Airline Industry: A Report on Recent Trends for U.S. Air Carriers,* 2002.

Air Transport Association, *U.S. Air Carrier Industry Review and Outlook,* Talk by David Swierenga, Chief Economist, Air Transport Association, to National Business Economics Issue Council, Las Vegas, Nevada, February 12, 2002.

Air Transport Association, *U.S. Carrier Industry Review and Outlook,* 2002.

The Airline Builders, Time-Life Books, 1981.

Allied Pilots Association, *The Birth of APA,* http://www.alliedpilots.org/index.asp, 2002.

Ambrose, Stephen, *Nothing Like It in the World: The Men Who Built the Transcontinental Railroad 1863–1869,* Simon and Schuster, New York, 2000.

Bailey, Elizabeth E., *Airline Deregulation: Confronting the Paradoxes,* Regulation, Vol. 15, No. 3, Summer 1992.

Borenstein, Severin, *Hubs and Higher Fares: Dominance and Market Power in the United States Airline Industry,* Rand Journal of Economics, Vol. 20, 1989, pp. 47–92.

Bornstein, Aaron, *Grounded. Frank Lorenzo and the Destruction of Eastern Airlines,* Simon and Schuster, New York, 1990.

Costello, Frank J., *The Lessons of Airline Deregulation,* Zuckert, Scoutt, and Rosenberger, LLP, web site. www.zsrlaw.com.

Cremieux, Pierre-Yves 1996. *The Effect of Deregulation on Employee Earnings: Pilots, Flight Attendants, and Mechanics, 1959–1992,* Industrial and Labor Relations Review, Vol. 49, No. 2 (January) pp. 223–242.

Crouch, Tom D., *The Bishop's Boys: A Life of Wilbur and Orville Wright,* W. W. Norton and Co., New York, 1990.

David, Carl, *The Impact of Deregulation on the Employment and Wages of Airline Mechanics,* Industrial and Labor Relations Review, Vol. 39, No. 4, July 1986.

Dempsey, Paul Stephen, *Airport Monopolization: Barriers to Entry and Impediments to Competition,* Testimony before the United States House of Representatives, Committee on the Judiciary-Hearings on the State of Competition in the Airline Industry, June 14, 2000.

Dempsey, Paul Stephen, *Antitrust Law and Policy in Transportation: Monopoly is the Name of the Game,* 21 Ga. L. Rev. 505 (1987).

Dempsey, Paul Stephen, *Competition in the Air: European Union Regulation of Commercial Aviation,* Journal of Air Law and Commerce, Summer 2001.

Dooley, Frank J., *Déjà vu for Airline Industrial Relations,* Journal of Labor Research, Vol. XV, No. 2, Spring 1994.

Douglas, John W., Aerospace Industries Association of America, Testimony before the Subcommittee on Aviation, Committee on Transportation and Infrastructure, U.S. House of Representatives, July 26, 2001.

Emme, Eugene M., comp., *Aeronautics and Astronautics: An American Chronology of Science and Technology in the Exploration of Space, 1915–1960* (Washington, D.C.: National Aeronautics and Space Administration, 1961) pp. 26–32.

Gandt, Robert, *Skygods,* William Morrow and Company, Inc., New York, 1995.

General Accounting Office Report, *Airline Competition: DOT's Implementation of Airline Regulatory Deregulation* (GAO/RECD-89-93, June 28, 1989).

General Accounting Office Report, *Airline Deregulation: Barriers to Entry Continue to Limit Competition in Several Key Domestic Markets,* (Letter Report, GAO/ RCED-97-4, October 18, 1996).

General Accounting Office Report, *Changes in Airfares, Service, and Safety Since Airline Deregulation* (GAO/T-RECD-96-126, April 25, 1996).

Groenewege, Adrianus D., *Compendium of International Civil Aviation,* International Aviation Development Corporation, 1996.

Hendricks, Wallace and Feuille, Peter and Szersen, Carol, *Regulation, Deregulation, and Collective Bargaining in Airlines,* Industrial and Labor Relations Review, Vol. 34, No. 1, October 1980.

Heppenheimer, T. A., *Turbulent Skies,* John Wiley and Sons, 1995.

The jetAge, Time-Life Books, 1982.

International Air Transport Association, History of IATA, http://wwwl.iata.org/about/history.htm, 2002.

International Civil Aviation Organization, History of ICAO, http://www.icao.int/, 2002.

Kahn, Alfred E., *Change, Challenge, and Competition: A Review of the Airline Commission Report,* Regulation, Vol. 16, No. 3, 1993.

Kahn, Alfred E., Statement before The United States House of Representatives, Committee on the Judiciary, *The State of Competition in the Airline Industry,* June 14, 2000.

Kelly, Fred, *The Wright Brothers: A Biography Authorized by Orville Wright,* Ballentine Books, New York, 1956.

Komans, N. A., *Bonfires to Beacons,* Smithsonian Institution Press: Washington, D.C. 1989.

Leonhardt, David with Michelene Maynard, *Troubled Airlines Face Reality: The Cheap Fares Have a Price,* New York Times, August 18, 2002.

Lindbergh, Charles A., *The Spirit of St. Louis,* Charles Scribner's Sons, New York, 1953.

Lipinski, William O., *An Evaluation of the US.—E.U. Trade Relationship* <http://www.house.gov./lipinski/aviation.htm>, 2002.

Lynn, Matthew, *Birds of Prey,* Four Walls Eight Windows, New York 1977; a revised edition first published by Reed International Books, Ltd., London, 1995.

Miles, Richard B., *Competition in the U.S. Manufacturing Industry,* Testimony before the Aviation Subcommittee, Committee on Transportation and Infrastructure, U.S. House of Representatives, June 26, 2001.

Morrison, Steven A. and Winston, Clifford, *The Evolution of the Airline Industry,* Brookings Institution, Washington, D.C., 1995.

Nannes, John M., Deputy Assistant Attorney General, Antitrust Division, *The Importance of Entry Conditions in Analyzing Airlines Antitrust Issues,* Talk before the Industrial Aviation Club, Washington, D.C., July 20, 1999.

Nannes, John M., Deputy Assistant Attorney General, Antitrust Division, *Statement Before the Committee on Transportation and Infrastructure,* United States House of Representative Concerning Antitrust Analysis of Airline Mergers, June 13, 2000.

Nay, Leslie A., *The Determinants of Concession Bargaining in the Airline Industry,* Industrial and Labor Relations Review, Vol. 44, No. 2, June 1991.

Northrup, Herbert R., *The New Employee Relations Climate in Airlines,* Industrial and Labor Relations Review, Vol. 36, No. 2, June 1983.

Northrup, Herbert R., *The Rise and Demise of PATCO,* Industrial and Labor Relations Review, Vol. 37, No. 2, June 1984.

Peterson, Barbara and Glab, Jonas, *Rapid Descent,* Simon and Schuster, New Mexico, 1994.

Petzinger, Thomas, Jr., *Hard Landing,* Three Rivers Press, 1996.

Poole, Robert W., Jr., *More Airline Competition—Yet Another Reason for Airport Privitization,* Reason Public Policy Institute, December 1999.

Poole, Robert W., Jr. and Butler, Viggo, *Airline Deregulation: The Unfinished Revolution,* Reason Public Policy Institute, March 1999.

Robson, John E., *Airline Deregulation—Twenty Years of Success and Counting,* Regulation, Spring 1998, pp. 17–22.

Rowe, Jonathon and Cahn, Edgar, *Time Dollars,* Rodale 1992.

Sampson, Anthony, *Emperors of the Sky: The Politics, Contests, and Cartels of World Airlines,* Random House, 1984.

Servan-Schrieber, Jean-Jacques, *Le Defi Americain,* Penguin Books, Hammondsworth, 1967.

Slater, Rodney, Testimony before the Aviation Subcommittee, Committee on Transportation and Infrastructure, U.S. House of Representatives, February 5, 2000.

Solberg, Carl, *Conquest of the Skies,* Little Brown and Company, 1979.

Sterling, Robert, Eagle: *The Story of American Airlines,* St. Martins Press, 1995.

Sterling, Robert, *Howard Hughes' Airline: An Informal History of TWA,* St. Martin's/Markk, 1983.

Thierer, Adam D., *20th Anniversary of Airline Deregulation: Cause for Celebration, Not Re-regulation,* The Heritage Foundation, April 22, 1998.

Thomas, Steven L., and Officer, Dennis, and Johnson, Nancy Brown, *The Capital Market Response to Wage Negotiations in the Airlines,* Industrial Relations, Vol. 34, No. 2, April 1995.

Thronicroft, Kenneth W., *Airline Deregulation and the Airline Labor Market,* Journal of Labor Research, Vol. X, No. 2, Spring 1989.

Time Magazine, *Hunting the Predators,* Vol. 151, No. 15, April 20, 1998.

U.S. Department of Transportation, Bureau of Transportation Statistics, *Airport Activity Statistics of Certificated Air Carriers,* Summary Tables: Twelve Months Ending December 31, 1999, BTSO 1-03, Washington, D.C. 2001.

U.S. Department of Transportation, Bureau of Transportation Statistics, *Airport Activity Statistics of Certificated Air Carriers,* Summary Tables ending December 31, 1999, BTSO1-03, Washington, D.C. 2001.

U.S. Department of Transportation, FAA/OST Task Force, *Airport Business Practices and Their Impact on Airline Competition,* October 1999.

U.S. Department of Transportation, FAA Strategic Plan, 1998. http://api.hq.faa.gov/spo pubs.htm# ANCHOR98 3, 2002.

U.S. Department of Transportation, *Enforcement Policy Regarding Unfair Exclusionary Conduct in the Air Transportation Industry* (Docket No. ST-98-3713) January 17, 2001.

U.S. Department of Transportation, *International Aviation Developments—Global Deregulation Takes Off (First Report),* December 1999.

U.S. Department of Transportation, *International Aviation Developments, Second Report—Transportation Deregulation—The Alliance Network Effect,* October 2000.

U.S. Department of Transportation, *Statement of Enforcement Policy Regarding Unfair Exclusionary Conduct,* (Docket No. OST 98-3713, Notice 98-16) April 1998.

U.S. Department of Transportation, *Statement of U.S. International Air Transportation Policy,* Federal Register, Vol. 60, No. 85, May 3, 1995.

Venneri, Samuel L., Associate Administrator, Office of Aerospace Technology, NASA, Statement before the Subcommittee of Aviation, Committee on Transportation and Infrastructure, U.S. House of Representatives, July 26, 2001.

Wilson, John R. M., *Turbulence Aloft: The Civil Aeronautics Administration Amid Wars and Rumors of Wars, 1938–1953,* Washington: Government Printing Office, 1979.

Winston, Clifford, *Economic Deregulation: Days of Reckoning for Macroeconomists,* Journal of Economic Literature, Vol. 31, No. 3, September 1993, pp. 1263–1289.

Wright, Nancy Allison, *The Reluctant Pioneer and Air Mail's Origin,* Air Mail Pioneers News, 1998–2001.

Zagorin, Adam, *Hunting the Predators,* Daily Magazine, Vol. 151, No. 15, April 20, 1998.

Cases

Minestere Public v. Lucas Asjes, 36 L. R. 173, Eur. Ct. R. 1425.

National Labor Relations Board v. Bildisco, 465 U.S. 513 (1984).

Pacific Air Transport v. U.S; Boeing Air Transport v. U.S.; United Airline Transport Corporation v. U.S., 98 Ct. Cl. 649 (1942).

Pan American World Airways v. United States, 371 U.S. 296, 306–208 (1963).

Panama Refining Co. v. Ryan, 298 U.S. 388, 55 S. Ct 241, 79 L. Ed 446 (1935).

United States v. CAB, 766 F.2d 1107 (7th Cir. 1985).

Statutes

Interstate Commerce Act

Feb. 4, 1887, ch 104, 24 Stat. 379, 49 USCS §§ 1–22, 25–27, 153, 153 nt., 301–312, 314–327, 901–923, 1001–1022.

Elkins Act

Elkins Act (Interstate Commerce)
Feb. 19, 1903, ch 708, 32 Stat. 847, 49 USCS §§ 41–43.

Hepburn Act

Hepburn Act (Interstate Commerce)
June 29, 1906, ch 3591, 34 Stat. 595, 49 USCS § 20 (11, 12).

Mann-Elkins Act

June 18, 1910, ch 309, 36 Stat. 539, 49 USCS §§ 1, 4, 6, 10, 13, 15, 16, 20, 50.

Transportation Acts

Feb. 28, 1920, ch 91, 41 Stat. 456, 49 USCS §§ 1–6, 10–18, 19a, 20, 20a, 26, 27, 71–74, 76–80, 137, 141, 142, 316, 1361 nt.

May 8, 1920, ch 172, 41 Stat. 590, 49 USCS § 75.

Aug. 13, 1940, ch 666, 54 Stat. 788, 40 USCS § 316.

Jan. 7, 1941, ch 938, 54 Stat. 1226, 49 USCS § 73.

Oct. 25, 1972, P.L. 92–550, 86 Stat. 1163, 49 USCS § 66.

Nov. 6, 1978, P.L. 95–598, 40 USCS § 316.

Airmail Acts

Feb. 2, 1925, ch 128, 43 Stat. 805 (See 39 USCS § 5401 et seq.).

Feb. 21, 1925, ch 283, 43 Stat. 960.

June 3, 1926, ch 460, 44 Stat. 692.

March 8, 1928, ch 149, 45 Stat. 248.

May 17, 1928, ch 603, 45 Stat. 594.

March 2, 1929, ch 478, 45 Stat. 1450.

April 29, 1930, ch 223, 46 Stat. 259.

March 27, 1934, ch 100, 48 Stat. 508.

June 12, 1934, ch 466, 48 Stat. 933.

June 19, 1934, ch 652, 48 Stat. 1102.

June 26, 1934, ch 762, 48 Stat. 1243.

Aug. 14, 1935, ch 530, 49 Stat. 614.

Aug. 24, 1935, ch 638, 49 Stat. 744.

Aug. 20, 1937, ch 718, 50 Stat. 725.

Jan. 14, 1938, ch 9, 52 Stat. 6.

April 15, 1938, ch 157, 52 Stat. 218.

June 23, 1938, ch 601, 52 Stat. 997.

July 6, 1945, ch 274, 59 Stat. 451.

Aug. 14, 1946, ch 963, 60 Stat. 1062.

June 23, 1948, ch 607, 62 Stat. 576.

June 29, 1948, ch 717, 62 Stat. 1097.

July 3, 1948, ch 830, 62 Stat. 1261.

Aug. 30, 1949, ch 523, 63 Stat. 680.

May 27, 1958, P.L. 85–426, 72 Stat. 138.

Aug. 23, 1958, P.L. 85–726, 72 Stat. 808.

Air Commerce Act of 1926

May 20, 1926, ch 344, 44 Stat. 568 (See 49 USCS
§§ 1301, 1472, 1473, 1507–1509).

Aug. 5, 1950, ch 591, 64 Stat. 414 (See 49 USCS
§§ 1472, 1473, 1509).

Oct. 11, 1951, ch 495, 65 Stat. 407 (See 49 USCS
§ 1509).

Aug. 8, 1953, ch 379, 67 Stat. 489 (See 49 USCS
§ 1508).

Railway Labor Act

May 20, 1926, ch 347, 44 Star. 577 (See 15 USCS
§§ 21, 45) 18 USCS § 373; 28 USCS §§
1291–1294; 45 USCS §§ 151–163, 181188.

June 21, 1934, ch 691, 48 Stat. 1185, 45 USCS
§§ 151–158, 160162.

April 10, 1936, ch 166, 49 Stat. 1189, 45 USCS
§§ 181–188.

Jan. 10, 1951, ch 1220, 64 Stat. 1238, 45 USCS § 152.

Aug. 31, 1964, P.L. 88–542, 78 Stat. 748, 45 USCS
§ 154.

June 20, 1966, P.L. 89–456, 80 Stat. 208, 45 USCS
§ 153.

April 23, 1970, P.L. 91–234, 84 Stat. 199, 45 USCS
§ 153.

Oct. 15, 1970, P.L. 91–452, 84 Stat. 930, 45 USCS
§ 157.

Aug. 4, 1988, P.L. 100–380, 102 Stat. 896.

Oct. 19, 1994, P.L. 103–380, 108 Stat. 3512.

Dec. 29, 1995, P.L. 104–88, 45 USCS § 151.

Oct. 9, 1996, P.L. 104–264, 45 USCS § 151.

Norris-La Guardia Act (Labor Disputes)

March 23, 1932, ch 90, 47 Stat. 70, 29 USCS
§§ 101–115.

Nov. 8, 1984, P.L. 98–620, 29 USCS § 110.

National Labor Relations Act

July 5, 1935, ch 372, 49 Stat. 449, 29 USCS
§§ 151–166.

Motor Carrier Act

Aug. 9, 1935, ch 498, 49 Stat. 543, 15 USCS § 77c; 49
USCS §§ 1–5, 6–13, 15–17, 19–20a, 22, 26, 27,
301–327.

Civil Aeronautics Act of 1938

June 23, 1938, ch 601, 52 Stat. 973 (See 49 USCS
§§ 1301–1542).

Federal Airport Act

May 13, 1946, ch 251, 60 Stat. 170, 49 USCS
§§ 1101–1119.

Federal Aviation Act of 1958

Aug. 23, 1958, P.L. 85-726, 72 Stat. 731, 14 USCS
§§ 81, 82, 90; 15 USCS § 45; 16 USCS § 7a;
31 USCS § 686; 48 USCS §§ 485–485d; 49 USCS
§§ 212, 486 nt., 1101, 1102, 1103, 1105, 1108,
1111, 1116, 1151, 1152 and others; 50 USCS
§ 123; 50 USCS Appx §§ 1622–1622c.

Airport and Airway Development Act of 1970

May 21, 1970, P.L. 91–258, 84 Stat. 219, 49 USCS §§ 1701 et seq., 1701 nt., 1711–1727.

Nov. 27, 1971, P.L. 92–174, 85 Stat. 491, 49 USCS §§ 1711–1715, 1717.

June 18, 1973, P.L. 93–44, 87 Stat. 88, 49 USCS §§ 1711, 1712, 1714, 1716, 1717.

Feb. 18, 1980, P.L. 96–193, 49 USCS §§ 1711 et seq.

April 7, 1986, P.L. 99–272, 49 USCS Appx § 1741.

Oct. 22, 1986, P.L. 99–514, 49 USCS Appx § 1741.

Noise Control Act of 1972

Oct. 27, 1972, P.L. 92–574, 86 Stat. 1234, 42 USCS §§ 49014918; 49 USCS § 1431.

Airport Development Acceleration Act

June 18, 1973, P.L. 93–44, 87 Stat. 88, 49 USCS §§ 1513, 1711, 1712, 1714, 1716, 1717.

Airline Deregulation Act of 1978

Oct. 24, 1978, P.L. 95–504, 49 USCS §§ 1301, 1301 nt., 1302 et seq.

Feb. 15, 1980, P.L. 96–192, 49 USCS § 1341 nt.

Oct. 31, 1994, P.L. 103–429, 49 USCS Appx § 1301 nt.

Motor Carrier Act of 1980

July 1, 1980, P.L. 96–296, 49 USCS § 10101 nt.

Sept. 20, 1982, P.L. 97–261, 49 USCS § 10706 nt.

Jan. 6, 1983, P.L. 97–424, 49 USCS § 10927 nt.

Oct. 30, 1984, P.L. 98–554, 49 USCS § 10927 nt.

Nov. 18, 1988, P.L. 100–690, 49 USCS § 10927 nt.

Nov. 16, 1990, P.L. 101–615, 49 USCS § 10927 nt.

Staggers Rail Act of 1980

Oct. 14, 1980, P.L. 96–448, 49 USCS § 10101.

Dec. 21, 1982, P.L. 97–375, 49 USCS S 1654a.

Airport Improvement Program Temporary Extension Act of 1994

May 26, 1994, P.L. 103–260, 26 USCS § 9502; 49 USCS Appx §§ 1348 nt., 2201 nt., 2204, 2206, 2207, 2212.

Oct. 31, 1994, P.L. 103–429, 49 USCS Appx § 2204.

Airport and Airway Improvement Act of 1982

Sept. 3, 1982, P.L. 97–248, 49 USCS §§ 2201 et seq.

Oct. 2, 1982, P.L. 97–276, 49 USCS § 2207.

Jan. 6, 1983, P.L. 97–424, 49 USCS §§ 2204, 2205, 2206.

Dec. 30, 1987, P.L. 100–223, 49 USCS Appx §§ 2226, 2227.

Aug. 14, 1988, P.L. 100–393, 102 Star. 971.

Nov. 3, 1988, P.L. 100–591, 49 USCS Appx § 2205.

Aug. 4, 1989, P.L. 101–71, 49 USCS Appx § 2212.

May 4, 1990, P.L. 101–281, 49 USCS Appx § 2210.

Nov. 5, 1990, P.L. 101–508, 49 USCS Appx §§ 2201–2207, 2227.

Oct. 31, 1992, P.L. 102–581, 49 USCS Appx §§ 2201–2212, 2226c, 2227.

May 26, 1994, P.L. 103–260, 49 USCS Appx §§ 2204, 2206, 2207, 2212.

Airport Noise and Capacity Act of 1990

Nov. 5, 1990, P.L. 101–508, 49 USCS Appx §§ 2151 nt., 21512158.

Federal Aviation Administration Research, Engineering, and Development Authorization Act of 1994

Aug. 23, 1994, P.L. 103–305, 49 USCS §§ 40101 nt.

Wendell H. Ford Aviation Investment and Reform Act for the 21st Century

April 5, 2000, P.L. 106–181, 114 Star. 61, 49 USCS § 40101 nt.

Sherman Anti-Trust Act (Trusts)

July 2, 1890, ch 647, 26 Stat. 209, 15 USCS §§ 1–7.

July 7, 1955, ch 281, 69 Stat. 282, 15 USCS §§ 1–3.

Oct. 8, 1982, P.L. 97–290, 15 USCS § 6a.

Clayton Act (Anti-Trust Act)

Oct. 15, 1914, ch 323, 38 Stat. 730, 15 USCS §§ 12–27, 44; 29 USCS § 52.

Dec. 29, 1950, ch 1184, 64 Stat. 1125, 15 USCS §§ 18, 21.

July 7, 1955, ch 283, 69 Stat. 282, 15 USCS §§ 15a, 15b, 16.

July 23, 1959, P.L. 86–107, 73 Stat. 243, 15 USCS § 21.

Sept. 12, 1980, P.L. 96–349, 15 USCS §§ 15 et seq.

Dec. 29, 1982, P.L. 97–393, 15 USCS § 15.

Oct. 4, 1984, P.L. 98–443, 98 Stat. 1708, 15 USCS §§ 18, 21.

Aug. 9, 1989, P.L. 101–73, 15 USCS § 18a.

Nov. 16, 1990, P.L. 101–588, 15 USCS §§ 15a, 19, 20.

Dec. 17, 1993, P.L. 103–203, 15 USCS § 19.

Dec. 29, 1995, P.L. 104–88, 15 USCS § 18, § 21, § 26.

Feb. 8, 1996, P.L. 104–104, 15 USCS § 18.

Oct. 27, 1998, P.L. 105–297, 15 USCS § 27a.

Nov. 12, 1999, P.L. 106–102, 15 USCS § 18a.

INDEX

A

Abbott, Robert, 443
Accident investigations, 88, 336
  National Transportation Safety
    Board (NTSB), 178
Accidents, safety and accident rates,
    239, 240, 241
"Accidents Involving Passenger
    Fatalities," 449–454
  U.S. airlines (1982 to present),
    449–451
  U.S. commuters (1982 to present),
    452–454
Accounting, 3
Acker, Ed, 220–221
Acosta, Aida de, 441
ADA. See Airline Deregulation Act
    of 1978
Ad coelum doctrine, 407, 408
Ader, Clement, 32
Administration of Aviation, 135
ADS-B. See Automatic Dependent
    Surveillance-Broadcast
Aerial Experiment Association, 39, 51,
    56, 57, 58, 60, 62, 431, 433
Aerial Steam Transit Company
    (1843), 31
Aero Club de France, 50
Aero Club de Saitte, 50
Aero Club of America, 57
Aerodromes, 55
  Model No. 4, 37–39
Aerodynamics, 31
Aeromarine West Indies Airways, 82
Aeronatutics Branch, Department of
    Commerce, 88, 92, 114
Aeronautical charts, 88
Aeronautical Division, U.S. Army
    Signal Corps, 55, 56
Aeronautical engineering programs, 91
Aeronauts, 28
Aerospace employment and industry
    sales, 382, 384
Aerospace foreign trade, 384
Aerospace share of national R&D
    funding, 386
Agrarian societies, 8
AIPs. See Airport improvement funds

AIR-21. See Wendell H. Ford Aviation
    Investment and Reform Act for
    the 21st century
Airacomet (XP-59), 152
Air agency certification, 173
Airbus Industrie, 168, 222, 334,
    351–353, 356–360, 388–391.
    See also Global aircraft
    manufacturing
  A300, 167, 168, 353, 354, 356
  A310, 354, 356
  A319, 243, 358
  A320, 357, 358
  A321, 358
  A330/340, 358
  A350, 372, 390–391
  A350-1000, 391, 392
  A380, 184, 371, 372, 388–390, 398
  Airbus GIE, 352–353
  orders and deliveries, 397
  stock ownership of, 377
Air carriers in World War II, 140
Air Commerce Act (1926), 88, 92, 113,
    178, 181
Aircraft airworthiness standards, 87, 88
Aircraft and trained pilots in 1914, 63
Aircraft carriers (ship), 77
Aircraft certification, 172–173
Aircraft emission trends, 275
Aircraft industry, before the Civil
    Aeronautics Act (1938),
    129–131
Aircraft noise, 277–280
Aircraft Noise Abatement Act (1968),
    172, 277
Aircraft Production Board, 64, 76
Aircraft Registry, 176
Air Force One, 156
Air France, 350
Airline Deregulation Act of 1978
    (ADA), 191, 197–199, 237, 257
Airline fares, 237–238, 247, 301
  percentage change in fares and
    demand since 2000, 307
Airline labor relations, 225–235
  after deregulation, 229–230, 233
  airline employment, 234, 235
  airline union characteristics, 233

"CHAOS" (Creating Havoc Around
    Our System), 228
concession bargaining, 232
crew size issue and ALPA, 230
employee compensation, 234
job classifications, 225
major airline unions, 226–227
Mutual Aid Pact (MAP), 228–229
National Mediation Board
    (NMB), 226
PATCO strike, 231
Presidential Emergency Board
    (PEB), 227
and Railway Labor Act (RLA),
    225, 227
strikes and presidential interventions,
    227–228
two-tiered wage agreements, 232
work actions (non-strike activity),
    228, 229
Airline management, 144
Air Line Pilots Association (ALPA),
    109, 164, 226, 233
Airline profits and losses
    (1998–2003), 307
Airlines, 87–103. See also Airlines
    before the Civil Aeronautics
    Act; Airline labor relations;
    Jet age
  Aerial Steam Transit Company
    (1843), 31
  Aeromarine West Indies
    Airways, 82
  after World War II, 143–147,
    149–150
  Air Commerce Act (1926), 88, 92
  Airmail Act of 1925 (Kelly Act) and
    1928 amendments, 101
  Airmail Act of 1930 (McNary Watres
    Act), 99–103
  airship passenger service, 29, 30
  airways for airmail, 101
  airways for navigation, 88, 92–93
  Aviation Corporation (AVCO),
    97–98, 107, 114
  Big Four, 103, 106, 108
  Big Four progenitors, 98–99
  coach or tourist class, 145

471

Daniel Guggenheim Fund for the Promotion of Aeronautics, 90, 91–92
employee protection, 197
first class travel, 143, 166
first passenger (DELAG), 29
and government, 8
and international shipping, 8
and labor, 8
and the labor movement, 8
from mail carriers to airlines, 97
marketing schemes of, 192
Morrow Board, 87–88
National Advisory Committee for Aeronautics (NACA), 87
North American Aviation (NAA), 97, 108
organized airline labor, 203
passenger service, 100
in post World War II, 143–147, 149–150
and railroads, 8
scheduled passenger service, 81, 194
service to small communities, 197
St. Petersburg-Tampa Airboat Line, 81
time to cross the continent, 147
transatlantic travel, 149, 150
Transcontinental Air Transport (TAT), 98, 99, 115
transcontinental travel, 147
types of domestic aircraft utilization, 146
United Air Transport, 97
uses for, 192
in World War II, 137–141
Airlines at the beginning of the 21st century, 287–310
aftermath of September 11, 291–299
AIR-21, 300
air fares, 301
airline profits and losses (1998–2003), 307
air traffic control (ATC) system, 305, 310
Air Transportation Safety and System Stabilization Act (2001), 289–290
Air Transportation Stabilization Board (ATSB), 296
antitrust policy, 300
Area Navigation (RNAV), 308
Automatic Dependent Surveillance-Broadcast (ADS-B), 309

Aviation and Transportation Security Act, 289, 290, 291
background, 299–300
bankruptcies, 296–299, 300, 301
Century of Aviation Reauthorization Act of 2003 (Vision 100), 308–310
Continuous Descent Approach (CDA), 308
Department of Homeland Security, 289
economies of scale, 300
employment, 298, 301, 302
Enterprise Architecture, 308
EUROCONTROL, 310
financial impact of post 9-11 policies, 292
fleet, 296, 297, 303
Flight Information Service-Broadcast (FIS-B), 309
fuel costs, 294–295, 300, 301
future, 305
Homeland Security Act (2001), 290–291, 293
Joint Planning and Development Office (JPDO), 308, 310
labor, 295–296
legacy airlines vs. low-cost carriers (LCCs), 304, 305, 310
liability insurance, 293–294
load factors, 295, 302
Next Generation Air Transportation System (NextGen), 308–310
operating profits, 301
Operational Evolution Plan (OEP) 35 airports, 309
Pension Benefit Guaranty Corporation (PBGC), 310
percentage change in fares and demand since 2000, 307
Performance-Based Navigation (PBN), 308
Required Navigation Performance (RNP), 308, 309, 310
security mandates, 291–292
September 11, 2001, 287–289
stage length cost curves, 306
taking stock, 299–303
taxes and fees on a $200 roundtrip ticket, 292
Traffic Information Service-Broadcast (TIS-B), 309
Transportation Security Administration (TSA), 290, 291
unit cost differential, 306

Airlines before the Civil Aeronautics Act, 113–131
Air Commerce Act (1926), 113
airmail service (1926–1936), 122
Big Four, 113, 114–120
American Airlines, 114
Eastern Air Lines, 114–115
TWA, 115–119
United Airlines, 119–120
Civil Aeronautics Act (1938), 113, 119
condition of airlines, 129–131
lesser lines, 120
National Advisory Committee on Aeronautics (NACA), 113–114
Pan American Airways, 120–129
revenue sources of airline companies, 123
Airmail, 67–74, 88
aircraft used, 68, 70, 71
Airmail Act of 1925 (Kelly Act), 84–86
Airmail Act of 1930 (McNary Watres Act), 99–103, 106, 107
airmail routes in 1934, 107
Army pilots, 67
"blind" flying, 70
civilian pilots, 70
contract airmail (CAM) routes, 84–85
federal funding for, 67
first cross-country route, 14
first experimental route, 68–69
Foreign Airmail Act (1928), 103, 121
international, 121
lighted airway, 73, 74
National Advisory Committee for Aeronautics (NACA), 65
navigation and instrumentation, 70, 73
night flying, 65, 71
privatization of, 81–86
scheduled service, 69–71, 73
service (1926–1936), 122
transcontinental route, 71, 72–73
Airmail Act of 1925 (Kelly Act), 84–86
and 1928 amendments, 101
Airmail Act of 1930 (McNary Watres Act), 99–103
Airmail Act of 1934 (Black-McKellar Act), 106–108, 113, 119
Airman Records Branch, 176
Air marshals, 185
Airmen certification, 172
Air navigation facility certification, 173

Air Offenses Convention (Tokyo
Convention of 1963), 318
Air Pollution Act (1955) and Clean Air
Act (1970), 273–277
Airport and Airway Development Act,
176, 185, 186
Airport and Airway Trust Fund, 186
Airport Competition Plans, 254
Airport improvement funds (AIPs), 264
Airport Improvement Program, 176,
186, 272
Airport Noise and Capacity Act
(1990), 278
Airport Privatization Pilot Program
(1996), 270
Airports, 143, 181–187
Air Commerce Act (1926), 181
Airport and Airway Development
Act, 176, 185, 186
Airport and Airway Trust Fund, 186
Airport Improvement Program,
176, 186
aviation excise tax structure, 187
background, 181–183
certification of, 173, 186
Civil Aeronautics Act (1938), 182
civil airport construction, 182, 184
Development of Landing Areas for
National Defense, 182
electronic screening of passengers, 185
environmental issues, 184, 185
Federal-Aid Airport Program
(FAAP), 185
Federal Airport Act (1946),
183–184, 185
landing "fields," 181
metal detectors at gates, 185
new national policy, 185–186
prohibited carry-on items, 185
security, 184–185
Surplus Property Act (1944), 182
Airports and deregulation, 263–272.
See also Airports; Deregulation
activity statistics, 265
AIR-21, 266, 269, 270–271
airport improvement funds (AIPs), 264
Airport Improvement Program, 272
Airport Privatization Pilot Program
(1996), 270
background, 263
classification of, 264
compensatory use and lease
agreements, 267
DOT interest in airport practices—
unfair competition, 269

FAA Reauthorization Act (2007),
266, 270
facilities use arrangements, 266–267
funding for operations and capital
improvements, 264–266
gate leasing arrangements, 267–269
General Airport Revenue Bonds
(GARBs), 264
hybrid use and lease
arrangements, 267
National Plan of Integrated Airport
Systems, 264
ownership of airports, 264
passenger facility charges (PFCs), 266
privatization of airports, 269–270
residual use and lease agreements,
266–267
revenue sources, 264, 266
state and local government
programs, 266
statistics on airports, 264
user charges, 266
Airports and the environment, 273–280.
See also Airports
aircraft emission trends, 275
aircraft noise, 277–280
Aircraft Noise Abatement Act
(1968), 277
Air Pollution Act (1955) and Clean
Air Act (1970), 273–277
Airport Noise and Capacity Act
(1990), 278
aviation-generated air pollution,
274–277
aviation impacts, 274
Aviation Safety and Noise
Abatement Act (1979), 277
environmental effects of air
pollutants, 274
Environmental Protection Agency, 273
health effects of air pollutants, 274
International Civil Aviation
Organization (ICAO), 276, 278
National Ambient Air Quality
Standards, 277
Noise Control Act (1972), 277
pollution of air and water, 273
Air Safety Board, 135
Airships (dirigibles), 29–31
passenger service, 29, 30
and World War I, 29
Air Traffic Control (ATC), 159, 160,
305, 310, 387
Air Traffic Service Academy, 231
Contract Tower Programs, 175

estimated controller losses and
planned hires, 174
and the FAA, 175
future of, 387
NATCO, 231
PATCO strike, 231
satellite-based navigation system, 245
training center for controllers, 176
Air Traffic Control, Inc., 134
Air traffic management (ATM), 339
Air Transport Association, 135
Air Transportation Safety and System
Stabilization Act (2001),
289–290
Air Transportation Stabilization Board
(ATSB), 296
Airways
for airmail, 101
for navigation, 88, 92–93
Western Air Express ("Model
Airway"), 91
Airworthiness Directives (ADs), 172
Alcock, John, 314
Allegheny Airlines, 165
Allied forces
World War I, 63
World War II, 137
Aloha Airlines, 299
Altimeter, 92
American Airways (American Airlines),
98, 106, 107, 114, 194, 195
debt and recovery in the nineties,
283, 284
route structure in 1937, 114
American Export Airlines, 217
American Railway Union (ARU), 21
American Society of Civil Engineers, 33
America West, 282
Amphibious aircraft, 61, 62
Amsterdam Treaty (1997), 327
Amundsen, Roald, 443
Ancient Phoenicians, 3
Antarctica Treaty, 406, 409
Anticompetitive practices, 192
at airports, 261
Antitrust enforcement after deregulation,
255–261. *See also* Deregulation
Airline Deregulation Act (1978), 257
anticompetitive practices at
airports, 261
background, 255–256
chronological sequence of statutory
law, 256
Civil Aeronautics Act and the DOJ,
256–257

Civil Aeronautics Board (CAB), 257
Clayton Antitrust Act of 1914
     (mergers, acquisitions, and
     predation), 256, 259
  competition, 255
  Department of Justice (1988),
     258–259
  Department of Justice and CAB
     (1978–1985), 257
  Department of Transportation
     (1985–1988), 257
  Department of Transportation after
     1988, 259–261
  failing airlines doctrine, 257
  major air carrier mergers, acquisitions,
     purchases, and consolidations
     through 2001, 259
  mergers, 257
  *Pan American World Airways, Inc. v.
     United States*, 257
  predation and competitive responses
     of airlines, 259–261
  public interest, 255
  reviewing proposed mergers and
     acquisitions, 258–259
  Sherman Antitrust Act of 1890 (price
     fixing and trusts), 256
Antitrust laws, 197
Antitrust policy, 300
APOLLO, 153, 206, 207
Apollo program, 401, 425, 428
Archdeacon, M., 431
Area Navigation (RNAV), 308
Ares launchers, 425, 426
Armour, J. Ogden, 446
Army Air Corps
  carrying airmail, 106, 113
  World War II, 138, 139
Arnold, Hap, 138, 152
Around the world flights
  Earhart, 96
  Hughes, 103, 118, 119
  Post, 103, 119
Artsutanov, Yuri, 423
Asia (Asu), 3
Assembly line, 22
Astrolabe, 4
Asu (east), 3
ATA Airlines, 298
Atlantic routes, Pan American Airways,
     128, 129
ATM. *See* Air traffic management
ATSB. *See* Air Transportation
     Stabilization Board
Authorization Act (1994), 250

Automatic Dependent Surveillance-
     Broadcast (ADS-B), 309
Automobiles, 22, 65
  electric self-starter, 75
AVCO. *See* Aviation Corporation
Aviation and aircraft manufacturing
     war effort, World War II, 137,
     139–141
Aviation and Transportation Security
     Act, 289, 290, 291
Aviation Corporation (AVCO), 97–98,
     107, 114
Aviation Disaster Family Assistance
     Act, 180
Aviation excise tax structure, 187
Aviation-generated air pollution,
     274–277
Aviation Medical Examiners, 176
Aviation regulation, 77
Aviation Safety and Noise Abatement
     Act (1979), 277
Aviation vehicles, 388
Avro 748 turboprop, 242
Axis forces
  World War I, 63
  World War II, 137
Azimuth location (bearing), 160

B
Bakes, Phil, 203, 204, 205, 210
Baldwin, Casey, 57
Baldwin, Frederick W., 55, 57, 431
Baldwin, Thomas Scott, 55
Ball, Clifford, 85
Balloons, 27, 28–29
Baltimore and Ohio Railroad, 11
Bankruptcy, 192, 233, 296–299,
     300, 301
  after 9-11, 239
  Aloha Airlines, 299
  America West, 282
  ATA Airlines, 298
  between 1979 and 1984, 230
  Braniff Airways, 230
  Chapter 7, 199
  Chapter 11, 199
  Continental Airlines, 204, 212,
     231, 282
  Delta Airlines, 298
  Eastern Airlines, 211
  Frontier Airlines, 210
  Hawaiian Airlines, 298–299
  insolvency, 198
  labor contracts, 204
  Mesaba Airlines, 299

Midway Airlines, 282
*National Labor Relations Board v.
     Bildisco*, 204, 210, 231
  in the nineties, 282–283
  Northwest Airlines, 298
  Pan American, 222, 282
  reorganization process, 199
  TWA, 215–216, 282, 284
  United Airlines, 296
  United States Bankruptcy Act,
     198–199
  United States Constitution, 198–199
  US Airways, 296
  voluntary and involuntary, 198
Barnstormers, 67, 88
Barriers to entry of new airlines,
     249–252, 254
Battle of England, World War II, 138
Beam Power Challenge, 424
Beese, Melli, 443
Bell Aircraft, 152
Bell, Alexander Graham, 38, 39, 52,
     62, 427
  and Curtiss, 55, 57, 59, 60
  Langley Medal presentation address,
     429–431
  remarks to the Board of Regents of
     the Smithsonian Institution,
     433–434
Benoist XIV flying boat, 81, 82
Berg, Mrs. Hart O., 50
Bermuda Agreement, 317, 346
Bermuda Two Agreement, 345
Beteille, Roger, 352
Bethune, Gordon, 301
Bigelow Aerospace Competition, 424
Big Four, 103, 106, 108, 113, 114–120
  progenitors of, 98–99
"Birdflight as the Basis of Aviation"
     (Lilienthal), 32–33
Black, Hugo, 105–106, 113, 119, 192
Blair, Tony, 372
Blanchard, Jean Pierre, 28
"Blazing the Trail to Chicago" (Miller),
     435–436
Bleriot, Louis, 58, 313, 441
Blimps (non-rigid airships), 29, 30, 31
"Blind" flying, 70
Boeing Company, 62, 64, 86, 107, 355,
     391–396. *See also* Global
     aircraft manufacturing
  B-1E seaplane, 313
  B-17, 117, 137, 139, 151
  B-24, 139
  B-45 Tornado, 152

B-47 Stratojet, 152, 155
B-52, 153
B-247, 115, 116, 161, 168, 323, 347, 352
B-307, 117, 118, 119, 137, 141
B-309, 324
B-314, 128, 130, 221
B-314A, 129
B-377 Stratocruiser, 149, 151, 156, 166
B-707, 155, 156, 157, 163, 166, 348
B-727, 164, 348
B-737, 164, 165, 203
B-747, 165, 166, 184, 221, 351, 356
B-747-8, 396
B-757, 287, 288, 356
B-767, 168, 356
B-787, 372, 392–393, 394–395, 398
wind tunnel, 155
Boeing, William, 77, 85–86, 97, 313
Bolland, Adrienne, 443
Bolschevik Revolution in Russia, 22
Borman, Frank, 168, 354
Boyd, Alan S., 169
Boyle, George, 68, 69, 73
Braniff Airways, 106, 120, 198, 230
Branson, Richard, 418
Breyer, Stephen, 194, 203
British Aircraft Corporation (BAC), 348, 356
British Airways, 350
British Comet, 153–154
British Overseas Airways Corporation (BOAC), 153
Brotherhood of Locomotive Firemen, 21
Brown, Arthur W., 314
Brown, Walter Folger, Postmaster General, 99–103, 105–106, 108, 113, 115, 213
Bryan, Charlie, 209, 210
Buckley, William F., 211
"Bumped," 140
Bureau of Air Commerce, Department of Commerce, 88, 107
Bureau of Lighthouses, Department of Commerce, 134
Burr, Donald, 201, 202, 203, 209, 210
Bush, George W., 425
Business, government involvement in, 8
"Buzz bomb" (Germany), 76
Byrd, Richard E., 83, 89, 94, 406
Skyward, 94

C

C-47, 140
C-54, 138, 140
CAA. *See* Civil Aeronautics Administration
CAB. *See* Civil Aeronautics Board
Cabotage rights, 344, 346
Califano, Joseph A., 169
Capital Airlines, 145
Capitalism, 14–15, 17, 20
Caravelle, 163, 348
Caribbean, 120, 124
Carlile, William B., 436
Carlstrom, Victor, 443
Carlzon, Jan, 212
Carrier liability, 335–336
CARs. *See* Civil Aeronautic Regulations
Carter, Jimmy, 191, 194, 218
Cavendish, Henry, 28
Cayley, Sir George, 31
Central Pacific, 13
Century of Aviation Reauthorization Act of 2003 (Vision 100), 308–310
Certificate of Convenience and Necessity, 136
Certification
of airports, 173, 186
Federal Aviation Administration (FAA), 172–173
Chanute, Octave, 41, 42, 47, 59
Progress in Flying Machines, 33–35
"Recent Experiments in Gliding Flight," 34
"CHAOS" (Creating Havoc Around Our System), 228
Chapter 7 and 11, 199. *See also* Bankruptcy
Charles, Jacques Alexandre Cesar, 28, 431
Charters or "nonskeds," 144, 145, 193, 194, 195
Chicago Conference, 316, 317, 428
Chicago Convention (1944), 314, 316, 333, 336, 408
Child labor laws, 22
Chile, 125
China National Aviation Corporation, 126, 127
Chirac, Jacques, 372
"Chosen Instrument," Pan American Airways, 139, 217, 218
Christianity, 7
Chronometer, 5
Churchill, Winston, 405
Cities in U.S. in 1880, 17

Civil Aeromedical Institute (CAMI), 176
Civil Aeronautic Regulations (CARS), 159
Civil Aeronautic Rules (CARs), 171
Civil Aeronautics Act of 1938 (McCarran-Lea Act), 109, 113, 119, 133–136, 161, 182
Amendment to (1940), 135
Certificate of Convenience and Necessity, 136
Civil Aeronautics Administration (CAA), 135–136, 161, 169
Civil Aeronautics Authority, 159
Civil Aeronautics Board (CAB), 135, 136, 144, 161, 169, 192, 193, 257
and the DOJ, 256–257
Civil Aeronautics Administration (CAA), 135–136, 160, 161, 169
Civil Aeronautics Authority, 135, 159
Civil Aeronautics Board (CAB), 135, 136, 161, 169, 192, 193, 257
post World War II, 144
Civil Air Regulations, 135
Civil War, 14, 19
balloons in, 28
Class warfare, 20, 22
Clayton Antitrust Act of 1914 (mergers, acquisitions, and predation), 22, 108, 256, 259
Clean Air Act (1970), 273–277
Clipper Goodwill, 223
Clipper Ships, 62, 126, 129, 141, 221, 223
Coach or tourist class, 145
Code of Federal Regulations, 159, 172
Cold War, 222, 409, 425
Mutually Assured Destruction (MAD), 407
Coleman, Bessie, 443
Collective bargaining, 226
under the Railway Labor Act, 111
Colombia, 121
Comet (British), 153–154
Commercial Space Launch Act of 1985, 176–177
Commercial Space Launch Act of 1984, 414
Commercial Space Launch Amendments of 2004, 422–423
Commercial space transportation, 176–177, 414–418, 414–423
Commission on the Future of the U.S. Aeorspace Industry, 378–380

Committee on the Peaceful Uses of Outer Space (COPUOS), 407, 409, 428

Commodities, 191

Common law, 16

Common Use Terminal Equipment (C.U.T.E.), 268

Commuter market, 243

Compensatory use and lease agreements, 267

Competition
  and deregulation, 192, 195, 197, 247–254, 248
  free, 332
  rules in air transport, 333

Computer reservations systems, 205–209
  APOLLO, 153, 206, 207
  and code sharing, 246, 253
  IBM, 206
  PARS, 206, 215
  SABRE, 206, 207, 253
  SAGE, 206
  SYSTEM ONE, 253
  and travel agents, 207, 208
  WORLDSPAN, 253

Concession bargaining, 232

Concorde, 348–351, 396

Congestion management, 250–251

Consolidated Commodore, 124–125, 129

Constellation, 137, 138, 143, 144, 145, 149, 151, 347

Constitutional concepts, 3

Consumerism, 8

Contact flying, 70

Continental Airlines, 120, 231, 282
  takeover by Lorenzo, 204–205, 210, 211, 212

Continuous Descent Approach (CDA), 308

Control in heavier than air powered flight, 27

Convair 240, 340, 440, 242

Convention for the Suppression of Unlawful Acts against the Safety of Civil Aviation (Montreal Convention—1971), 318

Conventions and conferences, 313

Convergence (intercontinental symbiosis), 340–341

Coolidge, Calvin, 90, 95, 181, 444

Cooper, D.B., 185

Cord, E.L., 98, 114

Corporate raiders, 204. *See also* Lorenzo, Francisco A.

Corporations, 8, 14–15, 19, 198

Coupe de Michelin Trophy, 50

Cox, Archibald, 203

Cradle of Civilization, 7

Crandall, Robert, 193, 207, 208

Crew size issue and ALPA, 230

CRJ100, 243

CRJ700, 243

CRJ900, 243

Cross-staff, 4

CRS. *See* Computer reservations systems

Curtiss Aeroplane and Motor Company, 63–64

Curtiss, Glenn, 39, 49, 55–62, 63, 441
  Aerial Experiment Association, 56, 57, 58, 60, 62
  Curtiss Aeroplane and Motor Company, 61, 63
  Curtiss-Baldwin dirigible balloon, 55, 56
  flying boat and amphibious aircraft, 61, 62
  Gold Bug, 58, 59
  Herring-Curtiss Company, 59
  Jenny, 61, 63–64, 65
  June Bug, 58, 59, 61
  Langley Medal, 429, 431, 433, 434
  motors by Curtiss, 55, 56
  NC-4 (first plane to cross the Atlantic), 62
  Oriole, 61–62
  Red Wing, 56
  San Diego International Air Meet, 59
  Silver Dart, 58
  and U.S. Navy, 60–61
  White Wing, 56–57
  and Wright brothers, 59–60

C.U.T.E. *See* Common Use Terminal Equipment

Cutting, Bronson, 133

Cyclone, 77

D

Damage to Third Parties on the Surface Caused by Foreign Aircraft (Rome Convention—1952), 318

Daniel Guggenheim Fund for the Promotion of Aeronautics, 90, 91–92

Da Vinci, Leonardo, on manned flight, 4, 31

Dayton-Wright Company, 64, 76

DC-1, 116, 117, 161, 168, 352

DC-2, 114, 117, 119

DC-3, 114, 117, 119, 140, 143, 242

DC-4, 137, 138, 140, 141, 143–144, 144, 149, 151, 324

DC-6, 149, 150, 153, 155, 347

DC-7, 149, 150, 153, 157, 347

DC-8, 155, 156, 157, 163, 348

DC-9, 164, 165, 348

DC-10, 167, 168, 219, 351

Debs, Eugene V., 21

Ded or dead reckoning, 70, 73

Deeds, Edward, 75, 76, 77

De facto deregulation, 194, 195

Defi Americain, Le (*The American Challenge*), 351, 378

DeHavilland, 347

De Havilland Comet, 153, 155, 348

DeHavilland DH-4, 64

DELCO, 75

Delta Airlines, 106, 120, 298
  hub and spoke system, 240
  and Pan Am, 222

Department of Commerce, 169
  Aeronatutics Branch, 88, 92, 114
  Bureau of Air Commerce, 88, 107
  Bureau of Lighthouses, 134

Department of Homeland Security, 289

Department of Justice, 258–259
  and CAB (1978–1985), 257

Department of Transportation, 169–180, 257
  after 1988, 259–261
  Federal Aviation Administration (FAA), 170–177
  interest in airport practices—unfair competition, 269
  National Transportation Safety Board (NTSB), 177–180
  and slot exemptions, 250
  sub-agencies to be included in, 170

Department of Transportation Act (1966), 177

Dependent worker class, 8

Deregulation, 237–245. *See also* Airports and deregulation; Antitrust enforcement after deregulation; European Union and American deregulation; Global deregulation
  Airline Deregulation Act of 1978 (ADA), 191, 197–199, 237
  airline fares, 237–238, 247
  Airport Competition Plans, 254
  arguments for, 247–248
  background and prelude to, 191–195

barriers to entry of new airlines, 249–252, 254

Braniff International Airways case history, 198

code sharing and computer reservation systems (CRS), 246, 253

and competition, 192, 195, 197, 247–254, 248

congestion management, 250–251

de facto deregulation, 194, 195

demise of the legacy airlines business model, 245

economic nature of transportation, 191–192

economies of scale, 248

employment, 239–240

factors contributing to, 193–195

frequent flyer programs, 253

gates, 251

hub and spoke, 240–242, 247

the Internet and Airport Competition Plans, 254

low fare, point-to-point service, 242, 247

market contestability theory, 248

marketing strategies, 253

market share, 239

nature of regulated transportation, 192–195

in the nineties, 281–285

Notice of Proposed Rulemaking (NPRM), 250

number of carriers, 238

Operating Authorizations (OPs), 250

operating practices, 240

and Pan American Airways, 217–223

passenger travel, 238

perimeter rules, 251

regional jets, 242–245

safety and accident rates, 239, 240, 241

slot system, 249–251, 252

United States Bankruptcy Act, 198–199

Wendell H. Ford Aviation Investment and Reform Act for the 21st century (AIR-21), 250, 251, 252, 254, 261

yield management principles, 248

De Rozier, Jean Francois, 28

De Saint-Exupéry, Antoine, 255

Development of Landing Areas for National Defense, 182

Dickenson, Charles, 85, 436

Dinner Key Terminal, Pan American Airways, 223

Dirigibles (airships), 29–31

Distance Measuring Equipment (DMF), 160

Dixie Clipper, 129

Dole, Elizabeth, 215

Domestic aircraft utilization, 146

Domestic routes, and Pan American Airways, 218

Domestic travel space priority system, World War II, 140

Donovan, William J., 125

Doolittle, Jimmy, 92

Douglas Commercial, 324

Downey, Thomas, 436

Downsizing, 199

Dreams of the Earth and Sky (Tsiolkovsky), 401

Dual mandate, Federal Aviation Administration (FAA), 176

Dutrieu, Helene, 441

E

EADS. *See* European Aeronautic Defense and Space Company

Earhart, Amelia, 93–97, 428, 444

EASA. *See* European Aviation Safety Agency

Eastern Air Transport (Eastern Air Lines), 97, 98, 106, 108, 114–115

route structure in 1937, 114–115

takeover by Lorenzo, 209, 210–211

ECAC. *See* European Civil Aviation Conference

ECC. *See* European Economic Community

Eccles, R.A., 134

Economic nature of transportation, 191–192

Economic necessity basis of government regulation, 15

Economics of Regulation, The (Kahn), 193, 194

Economies of scale, 248, 300

Education, Federal Aviation Administration (FAA), 176

Eiffel, Gustave, 429, 433

Eisenhower, Dwight D., 217

Elder, Ruth, 95

Electric self-starter, 75

Electronic screening of passengers, 185

Elkins Act (1903), 16

ELVs. *See* Expendable launch vehicles

Ely, Eugene, 60

Embraer, 243

Employee stock ownership plan (ESOP), 204

Employment, 234, 235, 298, 301, 302

compensation for, 234

and deregulation, 239–240

pay givebacks and salary cuts, 199, 204, 209

protection for, 197

Enforcement, Federal Aviation Administration (FAA), 174–175

English common law, 16

English inventiveness, and the Industrial Revolution, 7–8

Enterprise Architecture, 308

Environmental effects of air pollutants, 274

Environmental issues, airports, 184, 185. *See also* Airports and the environment

Environmental Protection Agency, 273

Ereb (west), 3

ESOP. *See* Employee stock ownership plan

Etienne, Jacques, 28

EUROCONTROL, 310, 335, 339

Europe (Ereb), 3

Europe after World War II, 323–329

Amsterdam Treaty (1997), 327

European-American relationship, 323–324

European Economic Community (EEC), 326–329, 348

European Union (EU), 328

Maastricht Treaty (1992), 327, 328

the Marshall Plan, 324–326, 347

North Atlantic Treaty Organization (NATO), 325

Organization for European Economic Cooperation (1948), 326

the "Six," 326, 329

Treaty of Rome (1957), 326, 328

Treaty of Rome and air transportation, 328–329

European Aeronautic Defense and Space Company (EADS), 376–377

"European Aeronautics: Vision for 2020," 378

European aircraft manufacturing, 167, 168, 347–353

European-American relationship, 323–324

European Aviation Safety Agency (EASA), 336, 337, 338–339

European Civil Aviation Conference (ECAC), 336
European Economic Community (EEC), 326–329, 348
European exploration and discovery, 4
European Joint Aviation Authorities (JAA), 336–338
European Union (EU) and American deregulation, 328, 331–341, 344, 345–346
  accident investigation, 336
  airline privatizations, 334
  air traffic control (EUROCONTROL), 335, 339
  air traffic management (ATM), 339
  background, 331–332
  carrier liability, 335–336
  competition rules in air transport, 333
  convergence (intercontinental symbiosis), 340–341
  European Aviation Safety Agency (EASA), 336, 337, 338–339
  European Civil Aviation Conference (ECAC), 336
  European Joint Aviation Authorities (JAA), 336–338
  free competition, 332
  global commerce, 341
  Global Navigation Satellite System (Galileo), 340
  government subsidies, 334–335
  liberalization of air transport, 332–333
  noise limitations, 335
  noneconomic issues, 335
  Nouvelles Frontieres, 332, 333
  predation and merger, 333–334
  SESAR (Single European Sky ATM Research Program), 339–340
  Single European Sky (SES), 339
  Treaty of Rome, 332–333, 341, 348
Expendable launch vehicles (ELVs), 414
Exploration of the Universe with Reaction Machines (Tsiolkovsky), 401–402
Explorer 1, 406, 414

F
F-86, 153
FAA/AST, 176–177
FAAP. *See* Federal-Aid Airport Program
Facilities use arrangements, 266–267
Factory system, 8, 22
Failing airlines doctrine, 257

Farley, James, Postmaster General, 106, 115, 117, 127, 198
FARs. *See* Federal Aviation Regulations
Fatalities by transportation mode, 180. *See* "Accidents Involving Passenger Fatalities"
"Feather-bedding," 230
Federal agencies, 16
Federal-Aid Airport Program (FAAP), 185
Federal Airport Act (1946), 183–184, 185
Federal Aviation Act (1958), 150–161, 169, 170, 197
Federal Aviation Administration (FAA), 16, 170–177
  Authorization Act (1994), 250
  certification, 172–173
  commercial space transportation, 176–177
  dual mandate, 176
  education, 176
  enforcement, 174–175
  functions of, 171
  funding, 176
  glider classification, 27
  investigation, 174
  operations, 175–176
  Reauthorization Act (2007), 266, 270
  registration and recordation, 176
  regulation, 171–172
Federal Aviation Agency, 161, 169, 170
Federal Aviation Reauthorization Act (1996), 177
Federal Aviation Regulations (FARs), 16, 171, 174, 175, 180
Federal Register, 135
Federal Trade Commission (FTC), 258
Federation Aeronautique Internacionale, 94, 404
Feeder airlines, 146, 165, 192, 242
Feldman, Al, 204
Female pilots, 93–97
Ferris, Richard, 193, 208
Feudal system, 7
First class travel, 143, 166
First coast-to-coast airplane flight, 445–448
First passenger (DELAG), 29
FIS-B. *See* Flight Information Service-Broadcast
Fisher Body, 64
Fleet, 296, 297, 303
Fleet, Reuben, 68

Flight attendants, 233, 235
Flight beginnings, 27–39
  Aerodrome Model No. 4, 37–39
  balloons, 27, 28–29
  dirigibles, 29–31
  gliders, 31–35
  heavier than air powered flight, 27, 31, 37–39
  "lighter than air" craft, 27
  planaphore, 32
Flight crew members, 164–165
Flight Information Service-Broadcast (FIS-B), 309
Flight schools, 62, 159
Flyer I, II, and III, Wright brothers, 45, 57, 58
Flying boat and amphibious aircraft, 61, 62
Flying boats and multiengine planes, Pan American Airways, 121
Flying Machine Trust, 59–60
Flying shuttle, 7
Fokker designs, 63, 85, 89, 113
  F-10 Super Trimotor, 91
  Fokker F27, 242
  Fokker F-7, 83, 123, 221
  Fokker Trimotor, 115, 120, 121, 323, 324
Fokker, Tony, 437
Fonck, Rene, 89, 437
Ford Air Transport, 82, 84
Ford, Gerald, 194
Ford, Henry, 22, 82
Ford Motor Company, 82
Ford Trimotor, 83, 85, 113, 323
Foreign code sharing, 283–284
Foreign control of U.S. airlines, 344
Foreign object damage (FOD), 183
"Four course radio range," 92–93
Free enterprise, 8
Free market, 192
Free market exchange, 7
Free market techniques, 199
Free trade, 368
Frequent flyer programs, 253
Friendship Airlines, 212
From Earth to the Moon (Verne), 401
Frontier Airlines, 204, 209, 210
Frye, Jack, 108, 115, 117, 118, 119, 138, 211, 213
FTC. *See* Federal Trade Commission
Fuel (kerosene), 157
Fuel costs, 294–295, 300, 301
Fuel prices, 230, 282

Funding, Federal Aviation
      Administration (FAA), 176
Future
   of the airlines, 305
   Global aircraft manufacturing,
      387–388

G

Galileo (Global Navigation Satellite
      System), 340
Gambetta, Leon, 28
Gann, Ernest K., 135
GARBs. *See* General Airport Revenue
      Bonds
Gardner, Edward, 70
Gas turbines, 151
Gate leasing arrangements, 267–269
   airport-controlled or common-use
      arrangements, 268–269
   exclusive-use arrangements, 267–268
   preferential-use arrangements, 268
Gates, airport, 251
GATT. *See* General Agreement on
      Tariffs and Trade
General Agreement on Tariffs and
      Trade (GATT), 368–369, 371
General Airport Revenue Bonds
      (GARBs), 264
General Electric Company, 152
General Motors, 97, 115
Geostationary orbit (GSO), 415, 416,
      417, 428
German Arbeitsgemeinschaft Airbus,
      351, 352
German Luftwaffe, World War II,
      63, 138
Glider classification, 27
Gliders, 31–35
Global aircraft manufacturing,
      347–399
   aerospace employment and industry
      sales, 382, 384
   aerospace foreign trade, 384
   aerospace share of national R&D
      funding, 386
   Airbus GIE, 352–353
   Airbus Industrie, 351–353, 356–360,
      388–391
      A300, 353, 354, 356
      A310, 354, 356
      A319, 358
      A320, 357, 358
      A321, 358
      A330/340, 358

A350, 372, 390–391
A350-1000, 391, 392
A380, 371, 372, 388–390, 398
   orders and deliveries, 397
   stock ownership of, 377
Airbus vs. Boeing
   Airbus restructured, 376–377
   EU position, 374–375
   global duopoly, 396–398
   international trade background,
      367–371
   overview of the dispute, 375–376
   review of the grievances, 372
   road to war, 371–372
   U.S. position, 374
the American giants, 355–356
Boeing, 391–396
   B747-8, 396
   B787, 292–393, 394–395, 398
   orders and deliveries, 397
British Aircraft Corporation (BAC),
      348, 356
challenge to America, 378–380
Commission on the Future of the
      U.S. Aeorspace Industry,
      378–380
the competition begins, 353–359
the Concorde, 348–351, 396
Defi Americain, Le (*The American
      Challenge*), 351, 378
European Aeronautic Defense and
      Space Company (EADS),
      376–377
"European Aeronautics: Vision for
      2020," 378
European aircraft manufacturing,
      347–353
future, 387–388
   airports, 389
   air traffic control, 387
   aviation vehicles, 388
   nanotechnology, 388
   navigation, 387
   NextGen, 387
General Agreement on Tariffs and
      Trade (GATT), 368–369, 371
German Arbeitsgemeinschaft Airbus,
      351, 352
global supply chain, 363–367
   China, 366–367
   Europe, 364
   Japan, 365–366
   Russia, 364–365
   South Korea, 367

Taiwan and Indonesia, 367
United States, 363–364
governmental role, 359
Hawker-Siddeley, 348, 352, 356
importance of, 380–387
   background, 380–381
   NASA vision and strategy for the
      future, 386–387
   National Air and Space
      Administration (NASA), 383,
      385–386
   national security, 380
   production of regional jets, 383
   research and development, 381, 383
   tort (liability) law in the U.S., 383
large civil aircraft orders, 361
large commercial jet engines,
      361–363
   General Electric, 361–363
   Pratt & Whitney, 363
   Rolls-Royce PLC, 363
regulatory nationalism, 377–378
Small Aircraft Transportation System
      (SATS), 386
Soviet TU-144, 349, 350
Sud Aviation, 348
supersonic transport (SST), 349
   trade balance by industry
      (2005), 381
   the twenty-first century, 359–363
   World Trade Organization (WTO),
      368, 371, 375–376, 398
Global commerce, 341
Global deregulation, 343–346. *See also*
      Deregulation
   cabotage rights, 344, 346
   European Union, 344, 345–346
   first multilateral Open Skies
      agreement, 345
   foreign control of U.S. airlines, 344
   International Air Transport
      Association (IATA), 343
   North American airlines, 343
   number of airlines in the world, 343
   Open Skies, 343–346
   subsidies by foreign government, 344
   United Kingdom, 345
Global Navigation Satellite System
      (Galileo), 340
Global Positioning System (GPS),
      175, 340
Global supply chain, 363–367
Gloster Aircraft Company, 152
Gnomon, 4

Goddard, Robert, 402–403, 428
  *Method of Reaching Extreme
    Altitudes, A,* 402
  *Use of the Gyroscope in the
    Balancing and Steering of
    Airplanes, The,* 402
Goering, Hermann, 63
Gold Bug, 58, 59
Goodyear Company, 30
Gordon Bennett Cup, 58
Gordon, Bill, 94
Government
  See also Deregulation; Labor
    movement
  and airlines, 8
  basis of regulation, 15–16
  Clayton Antitrust Act (1914), 22
  common law, 16
  interstate commerce, 12, 15
  involvement in business, 8
  and labor movement, 22, 23
  laissez-faire economics, 8, 15
  Morrow Board, 87–88
  Pacific Railroad Act (1862), 13
  positive and negative intervention
    by, 12
  public interest or quasi-public, 15,
    17, 103, 191, 193, 208, 225,
    255, 386
  railroads and the public, 8, 11, 12
  role in global aircraft
    manufacturing, 359
  role in space, 426–427
  Sherman Antitrust Act (1890), 21–22
  statutory law, 16
Government subsidies, 334–335
GPS. *See* Global Positioning System
Grayson, Frances, 95
Great Depression, 22, 105, 108–109,
    129, 225, 368
  Works Progress Administration
    (WPA), 182
Great Northern Railroad, 21
Great Society programs, 193
Grotius, Hugo, 408, 428
GSO. *See* Geostationary orbit
Guadalajara Convention (1961), 315
Guatemala Protocol (1971), 315
Guest, Frederick E., 94
Guggenheim, Daniel, 91, 402, 428
  Daniel Guggenheim Fund for the
    Promotion of Aeronautics,
    90, 91–92
Guggenheim, Florence, 91

Guggenheim, Harry, 91, 437
Gulf Wars, 380
  Iraq invading Kuwait (1990),
    212, 281
  Saddam Hussein invading
    Kuwait, 221
Gunpowder, 3
Gyrocompass and artificial horizon, 92
Gyroscopic instrument, 71

H
H-1 racer, 137
Hague Protocol, 314–315
Halaby, Najeeb, 169, 217, 218
Haldeman, George, 95
Halliburton, Erie, 102
Hamilton, Leslie, 95
Hang gliders, 32
Hargreaves, James, 7
Harriman, Averell, 97, 98, 114
Harrison, John, 4–5
Havana Convention (1928), 314
Hawaiian Airlines, 298–299
Hawker-Siddeley, 348, 352, 356
Hawker-Siddeley Trident, 163
Healey, Denis, 351
Health effects of air pollutants, 274
Hearst, William Randolph, 445
Heavier than air powered flight, 27, 31,
    37–39, 313
Heinkel 280, 152
Heinkel, Ernst, 152
Henderson, Paul, 73
Henson, William S., 31
Hepburn Act (1906), 16
Herring, Augustus, 35
Herring-Curtiss Company, 59
Hertz, John, 98, 115, 117, 118
High density rules (HDR), 249
High seas or international waters, 407,
    408, 428
Hijacking Convention (Hague
    Convention for the Suppression
    of Unlawful Seizure of
    Aircraft—1970), 318
Hijacking of aircraft, 184–185
Hindenburg disaster, 30
Hinson, Walter, 84
Hitler, Adolf, 63, 137, 403
Homeland Security Act (2001),
    290–291, 293
Hoover, Herbert, 87, 99, 105, 181
Hoover, Mrs. Herbert, 125
Hopson, Wild Bill, 71

Hornets, 77
Horsepower, 75–77
  Cyclone, 77
  Dayton-Wright Company, 76
  DELCO, 75
  Hornets, 77
  Rentschler, Fred, 75–77, 86
  Wasps, 77, 86
Hostile takeovers, 199, 202, 204, 212
Hub and spoke, 240–242, 247
Hughes, Howard, 103, 117–119
  and the Constellation, 138
  Hell's Angels, 118, 119
  at TWA, 137, 202, 213
Hybrid use and lease arrangements, 267

I
IATA. *See* International Air Transport
    Association
IATA InterCarriers Agreement and IATA
    Measures of Implementation
    Agreement, 315
IATA Tariff Coordinating
    Conference, 321
Ibarra, José Maria Velasco, 211
IBM, 206
Icahn, Carl, 208, 209
  and TWA, 213–216
ICAO. *See* International Civil Aviation
    Organization
IFR. *See* Instrument Flight Rules
IGY. *See* International Geophysical Year
ILS. *See* Instrument landing systems
Imperial Airways (British), 128
Independent Safety Board Act (1974),
    178, 180
Industrialization, and labor movement,
    19, 20
Industrial Revolution, 5, 7–9, 22
  factory system, 8
  from feudalism to mercantilism, 7
  government involvement in
    business, 8
  labor movement, 8
  railroads, 8
  roots in English inventiveness, 7–8
  steam engine, 8
  time line of events in industrial and
    technological development, 9
  working for a wage, 8
Instrumentation, 70, 73
Instrument flying, 92
Instrument landing systems (ILS), 175
Instrument Flight Rules (IFR), 159

Insurance, 3
Intercontinental symbiosis
        (convergence), 340–341
Internal combustion engines, 151
International shipping, and airlines, 8
International airline, Pan American
        Airways, 120
International airmail, 121
International Air Traffic Association, 313
International Air Transport Agreement
        ("Five Freedoms"), 316–317
International Air Transport Association
        (IATA), 145, 268, 320–321, 343
International Association of Machinists
        and Aerospace Workers (IAM),
        204, 210, 211, 231, 232, 233
International aviation relations,
        313–314
International Civil Aviation Organization
        (ICAO), 276, 278, 310, 316,
        319–320, 428
International Geophysical Year (IGY),
        405, 408
International law, 407–408
International Polar Year (IPY), 405
International Recognition of Rights in
        Aircraft (Geneva Convention—
        1948), 317–318
International route expansion, TWA, 213
International routes, 217, 218, 219
International shipping, 8
International Space Station Agreement,
        413–414, 425
International travel decline, 282
Internet and Airport Competition
        Plans, 254
Interstate commerce, 12, 15
Interstate Commerce Act (1887), 16,
        131, 191
Interstate Commerce Commission, 16,
        88, 107, 119, 169, 193
Intrastate carriers, 194, 242
Investigation of accidents, 88
    Federal Aviation Administration
        (FAA), 174
IPY. *See* International Polar Year
Islam, 7
Itasca (Coast Guard vessel), 96

J
J-57, 155
Jeffries, John, 28
Jenny, 61, 63–64, 65

Jet age, 149–157, 163–168. *See also*
        Airlines
    the British Comet, 153–154
    European aircraft builders, 167, 168
    fuel (kerosene), 157
    jet engine development, 150–153
    jumbo jets, 165–168
    regional jets, 163
    turbojet engine, 153
    turboprops, 154, 157, 163
    U.S. development, 155–157
JetBlue Airways, 243, 245, 250, 296, 301
Jet Capital Corporation, 201, 202
Jet engine development, 150–153,
        155–157
Job classifications, 225
Johnson, Kelly, 137
Johnson, Lyndon B., 169, 170, 193, 217
Johnson, Phil, 119
Joint Planning and Development Office
        (JPDO), 308, 310
JPDO. *See* Joint Planning and
        Development Office
Judaism, 7
Judge-made law, 16
Jumbo jets, 165–168
June Bug, 58, 59, 61

K
Kaempffert, Waldemar, *New Art of
        Flying, The*, 52
Kahn, Alfred, 204, 215, 320
    Economics of Regulation, The,
        193, 194
Kamal, 4
Karman Line, 404, 407, 408, 418, 421
Karman, Theodore von, 404
Kay, John, 7
KC-97, 156
Kelleher, Herb, 283
Kelly Act. *See* Airmail Act of 1925
        (Kelly Act)
Kennedy, John F., 217
Kennedy, Ted, 203
Kerosene, 157
Kettering, Charles, 75, 76
Keyes, C.M., 437
Keys, Clement, 97, 98, 100
Kinnock, Neil, 344
Kittinger, Joe, 28–29
Kitty Hawk flight on December 17,
        1903, Wright brothers, 17, 27, 45
Knight, Jack, 72

Kolk, Frank, 352
Kollsman, Paul, 92
Ku Klux Klan, 105

L
Labor contracts, 204. *See also*
        Bankruptcy
Labor movement, 19–23. *See also*
        Airline labor relations
    Air Line Pilots Association
        (ALPA), 109
    and airlines, 8
    American Railway Union (ARU), 21
    background and definitions, 19–20
    Brotherhood of Locomotive
        Firemen, 21
    Clayton Antitrust Act (1914), 22
    and government, 22, 23
    and industrialization, 19, 20
    minimum wage, 22
    National Mediation Board
        (NMB), 110
    Norris-LaGuardia Anti-Injunction
        Act (1932), 108
    organized airline labor, 203
    Panic of 1873 (recession), 20
    Panic of 1893 (recession), 21
    Presidential Emergency Board
        (PEB), 110
    Pullman Strike (1894), 20–21
    and railroads, 8, 19, 20
    Railway Labor Act (1926), 108–110
    rights of workers to organize and
        strike, 22
    Sherman Antitrust Act (1890), 21–22
    Strike of(1877), 20
    strikes, 20–21, 108, 109, 110
    ties to Mafia, 22–23
    trade guilds, 19
    union membership, 22
    working conditions, 22
    Workingmen's Party, 20
Labor relations, 295–296
LaGuardia, 182
La Guardia, Fiorello, 182
Lahm, Frank, 51
Laissez-faire economics, 8, 15
Land grants to railroads, 181
Landis, James, 202
Land mass transportation system
        (railroads), 8
Langley Laboratory, 87
Langley Medal, 52, 429–431, 433–434

Langley Memorial Aeronautical Laboratory, 65
Langley, Samuel P., 37–39, 41, 42, 48, 427, 429, 433
Laroche, Raymonde de, 441
Latin America, 120, 121, 128
Latitudinal position, 4
Law of the Sea Treaty (LOST), 413
Lawrance, Charles, 76, 437
Law, Ruth, 443
Lease agreements, 267
Le Bris, Jean-Marie, 31–32
Legacy airlines business model, demise of, 245
Legacy airlines vs. low-cost carriers (LCCs), 304, 305, 310
Legal basis of government regulation, 16
Lehman Brothers, 115
Lehman, Robert, 97, 98, 114, 118
Lemay, Curtis E., 218
Lend Lease Act, 138–139
Leveraged buyouts, 199, 202, 211, 212
Levine, Michael, 193
Liability insurance, 293–294
Liability Treaty of 1972, 410–412
Liberalization of air transport, 332–333
Liberty engine, 64
Licensing of pilots, 87, 88
Lifland, Burton, 212
Lift in heavier than air powered flight, 27
Lighted airway, 73, 74, 81
Lighter than air craft, 27, 313
Lilienthal, Otto, "Birdflight as the Basis of Aviation," 32–33, 41, 42, 43
Limited Test Ban Treaty of 1963, 409
Lindbergh, Anne Spencer, 90
Lindbergh, Charles A., 84, 87, 88–91, 138, 444
  airmail contractor, 88
  barnstormer and stunt man, 88
  and Goddard, 402
  log of solo flight from New York to Paris, 437–440
  non-stop flight between New York and Paris, 88–90, 94, 103
  and Pan American, 93, 103, 121, 124
  Spirit of St. Louis, 89, 437
  Transcontinental Air Transport (TAT), 90
  and Trippe, Juan, 90–91
  We (book), 94
Lipsner, Benjamin, 70, 436
Load factors, 295, 302

Local service lines, 146
Lockheed, 165, 324, 355
  C-5A, 165
  C-141 Starlifter, 165
  Electra, 118, 157
  Electra 10E, 96
  Hudson bombers, 139
  L-1011 Tristar, 166, 167, 168, 219, 351
  P-80, 153
  "Skunk Works," 137
Locomotive, 8, 11, 12
London Science Museum, 45
Longitudinal position, 4–5
Loran C, 175
Lorenzo, Francisco A., 199, 201–212
  business methods of, 212, 230
  computer reservations systems, 205–209
  Continental Airlines takeover, 204–205, 210, 211, 212
  departure of Lorenzo, 211–212
  Eastern Air Lines takeover, 209, 210–211
  Friendship Airlines, 212
  Jet Capital Corporation, 201, 202
  National Airlines, 202–203, 219
  New York Air, 203, 204, 208, 230
  "peanut fares," 202
  People Express, 203–204, 208
  People Express takeover, 209–210
  Texas International Airlines, 201–203, 204, 209, 210, 211, 212, 230
  TWA, 205, 206, 209, 214, 215
Louisiana Purchase, 12, 13
Low-cost carriers (LCCs), 242
  vs. legacy airlines, 304, 305, 310
Lowenstein-Wertheim, Anne, 95
Low fare, point-to-point service, 242, 247
Lufthansa Airlines, 164

M

Maastricht Treaty (1992), 327, 328
Madrid Convention (1926), 314
Mafia, Teamsters ties to, 22–23
Magna Carta, 3
Magnetic compass, 3
Magneto ignition, 64
Mail carriers to airlines, 97
Major air carrier mergers, acquisitions, purchases, and consolidations through 2001, 259

Manly, Charles, 38
Manned flight, 4
Mann-Elkins Act (1910), 16
Manufacturers Aircraft Association agreement, 65
Maritime trading centers, 3
Market contestability theory, 248
Marketing schemes of airlines, 192, 253
Market share, 239
Mars exploration, 425
Marshall, George C., 324
Marshall Plan, 324–326, 347
Martin, 62
  M-130, 126, 127, 129, 130
Martin, Glenn, 63, 64, 70, 76, 126
Marx, Karl, *Communist Manifesto*, 20, 22
Maxim, Hiram, 32, 42
McCracken, William, 125, 437
McCurdy, J.A.D., 55, 57, 431
McDonnell Douglas Corporation, 83, 166–167, 168, 355
  MD-11, 356
McDonnell, William, 83
McKinley, William, 37
Mechanics, 235
Mediterranean, 3, 7
Mercantile class, 7
Mergers, 202, 212, 257, 333–334
  Clayton Antitrust Act of 1914 (mergers, acquisitions, and predation), 256, 259
  major air carrier mergers, acquisitions, purchases, and consolidations through 2001, 259
  reviewing proposed mergers and acquisitions, 258–259
Mesaba Airlines, 299
Messerschmidt 262, 152
Metal detectors at gates, 185
Meteor (English fighter plane), 152
Method of Reaching Extreme Altitudes, A (Goddard), 402
Mickelson, George S., 180
Microwave landing systems (MLS), 175
Mid-air collisions, 160
Middle Ages, 7
Middle East, 7
Midway Airlines, 282
Military aircraft, 347
Miller, Max, 70, 73
  on "Blazing the Trail to Chicago," 435–436
Minchin, Fred, 95

Minimum wage, 22
MLS. *See* Microwave landing systems
Model A flyers, 49, 50, 51, 55
Model B, Model F, Model K, 52
Monroe Doctrine, 121, 131
Monroe, James, 131
Monroney Aeronautical Center, 175–176
Monroney, Mike, 161, 175
Montgolfier, Joseph Michele, 28
Montreal Agreement, 314–315, 315
Montreal Convention (1999), 315
Montreal Protocols (1975), 315
Moon exploration, 425
Moon Treaty of 1979, 412–413
Morgan, J.P., 50
Morrow Board, 87–88, 181
Morrow, Dwight, 87, 90
Morse code, 73, 92–93
Morse, Samuel, 17
Motive power. *See also* Propulsion in
        heavier than air powered flight
    for land transport, 5
Motor Carrier Act (1935), 131
Multilateral Interline Traffic
        Agreements, 321
Musick, Eddie, 123, 124, 127
Mutual Aid Pact (MAP), 228–229
Mutually Assured Destruction (MAD),
        Cold War, 407
Myers, Mary H., 441

N

NAA. *See* North American Aviation
NACA. *See* National Advisory
        Committee on Aeronautics
Nanotechnology, 388
NASA. *See* National Aeronautics and
        Space Administration
NASA. *See* National Air and Space
        Administration
NASA Centennial Challenges, 423–424
NASA vision and strategy for the
        future, 386–387
National, 120
National Advisory Committee for
        Aeronautics (NACA), 65, 87
    airmail service, 65
    Langley Memorial Aeronautical
        Laboratory, 65
    Manufacturers Aircraft Association
        agreement, 65
    night flights for mail, 65
National Advisory Committee on
        Aeronautics (NACA),
        113–114, 406

National Aeronautics and Space
        Administration (NASA),
        113, 176
National Air and Space Administration
        (NASA), 383, 385–386
National Airlines, 202–203, 219
National airports, 175
National Ambient Air Quality
        Standards, 277
National defense and aviation, 88, 113
National Labor Relations Act of 1935
        (Wagner Act), 109
National Labor Relations Board v.
        Bildisco, 204, 210, 231
National Mediation Board (NMB),
        110, 226
National Plan of Integrated Airport
        Systems, 264
National security, 380
National Socialism in Germany, 368
National Transportation Safety Board
        (NTSB), 177–180
    accident investigations, 178
    Air Commerce Act (1926), 178
    Aviation Disaster Family Assistance
        Act, 180
    fatalities by transportation mode, 180
    functions of, 177
    Independent Safety Board Act (1974),
        178, 180
    organization of, 178
    policies for investigations by
        mode, 179
National work programs, 22
NATO. *See* North Atlantic Treaty
        Organization
Navigation, 70, 73
    future of, 387
    open water, 4–5
    painting names of cities on
        rooftops, 92
    Pan American Airways, 121–122
    by radio, 71, 92, 175
    VHF Omnidirectional Radio (VOR),
        159, 160
Nazi Party, 403
NC-4 (first plane to cross the Atlantic),
        62, 314
"Near misses," 174
New Art of Flying, The (Kaempffert), 52
New Deal, 22, 105
Newton, Maurice, 70
New York Air, 203, 204, 208, 230
New York, Rio and Buenos Aires
        Airways (NYRBA), 124

Next Generation Air Transportation
        System (NextGen), 245,
        308–310, 340, 380, 387
NGEO. *See* Nongeosynchronous orbit
Night flying, 65, 71
Nixon, Richard M., 218, 325
NMB. *See* National Mediation Board
No-frills concept, 204
Noise Control Act (1972), 277
Noise limitations, 335
Noneconomic issues, 335
Nongeosynchronous orbit (NGEO),
        415, 416, 417, 428
Non-military aviation, 88
Non-rigid airships (blimps), 29, 30, 31
Noonan, Fred, 96
Norris-LaGuardia Anti-Injunction Act
        (1932), 108
North American airlines, 343
North American Aviation (NAA),
        97, 108
North Atlantic Treaty Organization
        (NATO), 325
North Central Airlines, 165
Northwest Airlines, 120, 284, 298
"No shows," 140
Notice of Proposed Rulemaking
        (NPRM), 250
Nouvelles Frontieres, 332, 333
NTSB. *See* National Transportation
        Safety Board

O

Oberth, Hermann, 403
    Road to Space Travel, The, 403
    Rocket into Planetary Space, The, 403
O'Conner, James, 436
Official Airline Guide (OAG), 207
Ohain, Hans von, 152
Oil crisis of 1973, 350
Open Skies, 316, 317, 343–346
Operating Authorizations (OPs), 250
Operating practices, 240
Operating profits, 301
Operational Evolution Plan (OEP) for
        35 airports, 309
Operations, Federal Aviation
        Administration (FAA), 175–176
Organization for European Economic
        Cooperation (1948), 326
Oriole, 61–62
Orion, 425
Orteig, Raymond, 88, 418
Outer Space Treaty of 1967, 409–410
Outsourcing, 199

Ownership of airports, 264
Ownership of outer space, 407–409
Ozark Airlines, 215

P

P-3 Convair, 157
P-51 Mustang, 140
Pacific Air Transport v. U.S.,et.al., 106
Pacific Railroad Act (1862), 13, 13–14
Pacific routes, Pan American Airways,
    125, 126, 127, 129, 221
Packard Motors, 64
Palacio, Loyola de, 344
Panama Refining Co. v. Ryan, 135
Pan American Airways, 98–99, 108,
    120–129, 222, 282
  airmail contract, 120
  and American Export Airlines, 217
  Atlantic routes, 128, 129
  before Civil Aeronautics Act (1938),
    120–129
  "Chosen Instrument," 217, 218
  Clipper Goodwill, 223
  Clipper Ships, 62, 126, 129, 141,
    221, 223
  and the Constellation design, 138
  and deregulation, 217–223
  Dinner Key Terminal, 223
  and domestic routes, 218
  extending route authority, 121, 124
  flying boats and multiengine
    planes, 121
  international airline, 120
  and Lindbergh, 90, 103, 121, 124
  merger talks, 218
  monopoly on international traffic, 217
  name change to "Pan American
    World Airways," 144
  and National Airlines, 219
  navigation, 121–122
  Pacific routes, 125, 126, 127, 129, 221
  Pan American Field (Miami),
    222, 223
  and Puerto Rican migration,
    144–145, 166
  route map of airways, 126
  and terrorism, 221
  and World War II, 139, 141
Pan American Conference, 314
Pan American Field (Miami), 222, 223
*Pan American World Airways, Inc. v.
    United States*, 257
Panic of 1873 (recession), 20
Panic of 1893 (recession), 21

Paris Convention (1919), 313–314, 408
PARS, 206, 215
Parsons, Charles, 150–151
Passenger airlines
  Aerial Steam Transit Company, 31
  airships (dirigibles), 29, 30
  DELAG as first, 29
Passenger facility charges
    (PFCs), 266
Passengers
  electronic screening of
    passengers, 185
  injuries and injury rates of, 241
  screening of, 291
Passenger service (airline), 100, 238
  scheduled, 81, 194
PATCO strike, 231
Patent law, 3
Patent "pool," 60
Patents granted in the United States, 3
  telegraph, 17
  to Wright brothers, 27, 47, 49, 59
Patterson, Pat, 119
PBGC. *See* Pension Benefit Guaranty
    Corporation
PBN. *See* Performance-Based
    Navigation
"Peanut fares," 194, 195, 202
Peary, Robert E., 443
PEB. *See* Presidential Emergency
    Board
Penaud, Alphonse, 32
Pension Benefit Guaranty Corporation
    (PBGC), 310
People Express, 203–204, 208
  takeover by Lorenzo, 209–210
Performance-Based Navigation
    (PBN), 308
Perimeter rules, 251
Perry, Matthew Calbraith, 445
Perry, Oliver Hazard, 445
Personal liberty, 3
Phipps, Amy, 94
Piedmont, 165
Pierce, Sophie Mary, 443
Pierson, Jean, 358
Pilcher, Percy, 33, 42
Pilotage, 70
Pilotless "flying bomb," 76
Pilots, 235
Pilot seniority, 219–220
Piston engine, 157, 310
Planaphore, 32
Plaskett, Tom, 221

Plastic Explosives Convention
    (Convention on the Making of
    Plastic Explosives for the
    Purpose of Detection—1991),
    318–319
Plutonium 239, 428
Point-to-point service, 242, 247
Pollution of air and water, 273
Position reporting, 160
Post, Augustus, 436
Post, Wiley, 119
"Powder Puff Derby," 95
Power Jets, Ltd., 151
Praeger, Otto, 67, 68, 71, 73
Predation
  Clayton Antitrust Act of 1914
    (mergers, acquisitions, and
    predation), 256, 259
  and competitive responses of
    airlines, 259–261
  and merger, 333–334
Presidential Emergency Board (PEB),
    110, 227
Pressurized airplanes, 117
Price fixing by the CAB, 194
Prime Meridian, 5
Privatization
  of airlines, 334
  of airmail, 81–86. *See also*
    Airmail
  of airports, 269–270
Profit motive, 3
Progress in Flying Machines
    (Chanute), 33–35
Prohibited carry-on items, 185
Prohibition, 82
Propulsion in heavier than air powered
    flight, 27, 32, 44
Public interest or quasi-public, 15,
    17, 103, 191, 193, 208, 225,
    255, 386
Puerto Rican migration, and Pan
    American Airways,
    144–145, 166
Pullman Palace Car Company, 21
Pullman Strike (1894), 20–21
Purdue University, 96
Putnam, George Palmer, 94, 95

Q

Quasi-public businesses, 15, 17, 103,
    191, 193, 208, 225, 255, 386
Quesada, Elwood R. "Pete," 161
Quimby, Harriett, 442

R

Radar, 150, 160, 161
Radio
    "four course radio range," 92–93
    for navigation, 71, 92, 175
    PIREPS (pilot weather reporting
        system), 91
    radiotelegraphy, 121–122
    VHF Omnidirectional Radio (VOR),
        159, 160
Raiche, Bessica, 441–442
Railroads, 8, 11–17. *See also*
        Government; Labor movement
    Air Brake law, 108
    and airlines, 8
    Baltimore and Ohio Railroad, 11
    Boiler Inspection Act, 108
    Central Pacific, 13
    construction funds, 13
    decline of, 17
    Elkins Act (1903), 16
    and government, 8, 11, 12, 15–16
    government control in World War I, 81
    Hepburn Act (1906), 16
    interstate commerce, 12
    Interstate Commerce Act (1887), 16
    and labor movement, 8, 19, 20
    land grants to, 181
    locomotive, 8, 11, 12
    Louisiana Purchase, 12, 13
    mail, 81
    Mann-Elkins Act (1910), 16
    maximum trackage, 17
    mergers of, 193
    Pacific Railroad Act (1862), 13–14
    and the public, 8, 11, 12
    rebates (kickbacks), 16
    regulation of, 193
    right of way for the roadbeds, 13
    safety and working conditions, 108
    Safety Appliances Act, 108
    steam engine, 8, 11, 12
    tariffs, 16
    telegraph, 13, 17
    transcontinental railroad, 12, 13–14
    Union Pacific, 13
    in World War II, 140
Railway Labor Act of 1926 (RLA),
        108–111
    and airline labor relations, 225, 227
Rand, James, 125
Reagan, Ronald, 175, 231, 414, 426
Rebates (kickbacks), 16
"Recent Experiments in Gliding Flight"
        (Chanute), 34

Reciprocating engines, 151
Reconstruction era, 14
Red Wing, 56
Regional jets, 163, 242–245, 383
Registration and licensing of aircraft, 88
Registration and recordation, Federal
        Aviation Administration
        (FAA), 176
Registration Convention of 1976, 412
Regulated transportation, 192–195
Regulation
    basis of, 15–16
    Federal Aviation Administration
        (FAA), 171–177
Religions, 7
Renaissance, 3
Rentschler, Adam, 75
Rentschler, Fred, 75–77, 86
Rentschler, William, 97
Required Navigation Performance
        (RNP), 308, 309, 310
Rescue Treaty of 1968, 410
Research
    research laboratory (NACA),
        113–114
    William J. Hughes Technical
        Center, 176
Research and development, 381, 383
Residual use and lease agreements,
        266–267
Reusable launch vehicles (RLVs),
        422–423
Revenue sources
    of airline companies, 123
    airports, 264, 266
Rickenbacker, Eddie, 108, 114, 115,
        117, 209, 211
Ridge, Tom, 291
Right of way for the railroads, 13
Rights of workers to organize and
        strike, 22
Rigid airships, 29
RLA. *See* Railway Labor Act, 225, 227
RLVs. *See* Reusable launch vehicles
RNAV. *See* Area Navigation
RNP. *See* Required Navigation
        Performance
Road to Space Travel, The (Oberth), 403
Robber barons, 15
Robson, John, 194, 204, 238
Rocket into Planetary Space, The
        (Oberth), 403
Rocketry, 401–404
Rockne, Knute, 115, 133, 324
Rodgers, Calbraith Perry, 445–448

Rodgers, John, 445
Rogers, Will, 95
Rolls, Charles, 50
Roosevelt, Franklin D., 103, 105–111
    Airmail Act of 1934 (Black-
        McKellar Act), 106–108,
        113, 119
    Army Air Corps carrying airmail,
        106, 113
    collective bargaining process under
        the Railway Labor Act, 111
    Great Depression and bread lines,
        105, 108–109
    Lend Lease Act, 139
    National Labor Relations Act of
        1935 (Wagner Act), 109
    New Deal, 22, 105
    Railway Labor Act (1926), 108–111
    Social Security Act (1935), 109
    Spoils Conferences on government
        mail contracts, 105–106
    wartime conferences, 141
Roosevelt, Theodore, Jr., 437
Roswell, New Mexico, 402
Rule of Law, 3
Rutan, Burt, 418
Ryan Airplane Company, 89

S

SABRE, 206, 207, 253
"Safe Aircraft Contest," 91
Safety of flying, 88, 91, 133–134, 159
    Federal Aviation Administration,
        170–171, 177
    and jumbo jets, 166
    research, 161
    safety and accident rates, 239,
        240, 241
Safety of workers, 22
Safety regulations, 88
SAGE, 206
San Diego International Air Meet, 59
Santos-Dumont, M., 49, 56, 431
Saturn V, 426
Scandinavian Airlines System
        (SAS), 212
Schultze, Charles, 169
Science fiction, 401, 423. *See also*
        Space
Science of astronautics, 404
Scientific American, 402, 427
    trophy, 57, 58, 59
Scientific cooperation, 405–406
Scott, Blanche Stuart, 441
Seawell, William T., 218, 219, 220

Second International Polar Year (IPY), 406
Security, airports, 184–185
Security mandates, 291–292
Selfridge, Thomas E., 50–51, 55–56, 57, 59, 431
September 11, 2001, 31, 287–289
    aftermath of, 254, 291–299
    and airport security, 185
    financial impact of post 9-11 policies, 292
Service to small communities by airlines, 197
SESAR (Single European Sky ATM Research Program), 339–340
Sextant, 4
Shank, Robert, 70
Sheppard, Morris, 67
Sherman Antitrust Act of 1890 (price fixing and trusts), 21–22, 108, 206, 256
Shintag, Bernard, 109
Short takeoff and landing (STOL) characteristics, 91
Shugrue, Martin, 211
Shute, Nevil, 149
Sikorsky, 62
    S-38, 123, 124
    S-40, 125, 126, 127
    S-42, 126, 128
    S-43, 129
Sikorsky, Igor, 124
Silver Dart, 58
Single European Sky (SES), 339
Six, Robert, 204
"Skunk Works," Lockheed, 137
Slot system, 249–251, 252
Smith, C.R., 107, 114, 155, 205
Smithsonian Institution, 35, 37, 41, 45, 62, 427, 428, 429, 433–434
Smith, Wesley, 70
Snook, Neta, 93
Social Security Act (1935), 109
Sociedad Colombo-Aleman de Transposes Aereos (SCADTA), 121
Solo transatlantic flights, 88–90, 94, 95, 103
Sonic booms, 350
South America, 120–121, 125
Southwest Airlines, 194, 195, 202, 240, 242, 245, 247, 283, 296, 299, 310
Soviet Union, collapse of, 222

Space, 401–428
    Antarctica Treaty, 406, 409
    Apollo program, 401, 425, 428
    Ares launchers, 425, 426
    Beam Power Challenge, 424
    Bigelow Aerospace Competition, 424
    commercial space transportation, 414–418, 414–423
        Commercial Space Launch Act of 1984, 414
        Commercial Space Launch Amendments of 2004, 422–423
        geostationary orbit (GSO), 415, 416, 417, 428
        launch activity, 415–417
        launch service providers, 420
        launch sites, 417–418
        list of private companies, 422
        nongeosynchronous orbit (NGEO), 415, 416, 417, 428
        spaceports, 418, 419
        Virgin Galactic flights, 421
    Committee on the Peaceful Uses of Outer Space (COPUOS), 407, 409, 428
    expendable launch vehicles (ELVs), 414
    Explorer 1, 406, 414
    Federation Aeronautique Internationale, 404
    government's role, 426–427
    history, 424–425
    Karman Line, 404, 407, 408, 418, 421
    Mars exploration, 425
    moon exploration, 425
    NASA Centennial Challenges, 423–424
    National Advisory Committee on Aeronautics (NACA), 406
    Orion, 425
    ownership of outer space, 407–409
    reusable launch vehicles (RLVs), 422–423
    rocketry, 401–404
        Goddard, Robert, 402–403
        Oberth, Hermann, 403
        Tsiolkovsky, Konstantin, 401–402
        V-2 rocket, 404
        Von Braun, Wernher, 403–404
    Saturn V, 426
    science of astronautics, 404
    scientific cooperation, 405–406
        International Geophysical Year (IGY), 405, 408

        International Polar Year (IPY), 405
        Second International Polar Year (IPY), 406
    space race, 406–407, 424
    SpaceShipOne (SS1), 418, 421, 422, 427
    SpaceShipThree, 421
    SpaceShipTwo, 421, 422
    space shuttle program, 414, 422, 425, 426
        Challenger, 414, 425
        Columbia, 425
    Sputnik, 404–405, 406, 408, 424, 427
    Sputnik 2, 406
    terrestrial precedents, 407–409
    Tether Challenge, 423–424
    treaties affecting outer space, 409–414
        International Space Station Agreement, 413–414, 425
        Law of the Sea Treaty (LOST), 413
        Liability Treaty of 1972, 410–412
        Limited Test Ban Treaty of 1963, 409
        Moon Treaty of 1979, 412–413
        Outer Space Treaty of 1967, 409–410
        Registration Convention of 1976, 412
        Rescue Treaty of 1968, 410
    "Vision for Space Exploration," 424–426
    "White Knight" lifting SpaceShipOne, 418, 421
Space launches, 176–177
Spaceports, 418, 419
Space race, 406–407, 424
Space reactors, 428
SpaceShipOne (SS1), 418, 421, 422, 427
SpaceShipThree, 421
SpaceShipTwo, 421, 422
Space shuttle program, 414, 422, 425, 426
    Challenger, 414, 425
    Columbia, 425
Sperry, Elmer, 92
Spinning jenny, 7
Spirit of St. Louis, 89
Spoils Conferences on government mail contracts, 105–106, 192, 213
Sputnik, 404–405, 406, 408, 424, 427
Sputnik 2, 406
SR-71, 137
Stage length cost curves, 306

Standardization of aircraft procedures, 135
"Standbys," 140
Start-up airlines, 242, 247, 248, 249, 250, 284
State and local government programs, airports, 266
Statutory law, 16
Steam engine, 8, 11, 12
Steamship, 8
Steel industry, 3
Stevens, James, 436
Stinson, Katherine, 443
Stinson, Marjorie, 443
Stock exchanges, 19, 105
Stout, William E., 82, 83
St. Petersburg-Tampa Airboat Line, 81
Stratoliners, 117, 137, 138, 139
Strauss, Franz-Josef, 352
Strikes, 20–21
    PATCO strike, 231
    and presidential interventions, 227–228
    Strike of 1877, 20
Stringfellow, John, 31
Stultz, Lou, 94
Subsidies by foreign government, 344
Sud Aviation, 347, 348
Sukhoi Superjet 100, 243
Super Constellation, 149, 150
Super jumbo jets, 371
"Supersaver" fare, 195
Supersonic aircraft transport program, 169
Supply and demand, 191–192
Surplus Property Act (1944), 182
SYSTEM ONE, 253

T
Taft, William H., 51
Tanager, Curtiss, 91
Tariffs, railroad, 16
TAT. *See* Transcontinental Air Transport
Taxes and fees on a $200 roundtrip ticket, 292
Taxpayer Relief Act (1997), 187
Taylor, Charles, 44, 446
Teamsters, ties to Mafia, 22–23
Technological accomplishment, 3–5
    ancient Phoenicians, 3
    Industrial Revolution, 5
    invention of the wheel, 3
    Magna Carta, 3
    manned flight, 4
    Mediterranean, 3, 7

motive power for land transport, 5
open water navigation, 4–5
rate of advance, 3, 4
Renaissance, 3
time line of events in industrial and technological development, 9
in wars, 63, 141, 150
Western Civilization, 3
Telegraph, 13, 17
Terrestrial precedents for space, 407–409
Territorial waters, 407
Terrorism
    and blimps, 31
    hijacking aircraft, 185
    and Pan American Airways, 221
    War on, 388
Tether Challenge, 423–424
Texas International Airlines, 194, 195, 201–203, 204, 209, 210, 211, 212, 229, 230
Thible, Elisabeth, 441
Thomson, Sir Adam, 281
Three mile limit, 428
Tillinghast, Charles, 213
Time Between Overhaul (TBO), 155, 157
Time line of events in industrial and technological development, 9
"Tin Goose," 84
TIS-B. *See* Traffic Information Service-Broadcast
Titanium, 155
Tort (liability) law in the U.S., 383
Trade, 368
Trade guilds, 19
Trade routes, 4
Trade unions. *See* Labor movement
Traffic Information Service-Broadcast (TIS-B), 309
Transatlantic flights, solo, 88–90, 94, 95
Transatlantic service, TWA, 143
Transatlantic travel, 149, 150
Transcontinental Air Transport (TAT), 90, 95, 98, 99, 115
Transcontinental railroad, 12, 13–14. *See also* Railroads
Transcontinental route, for airmail, 71, 72–73
Transcontinental travel, 147
    first coast-to-coast airplane flight, 445–448
    time to cross the continent, 147
Transit Agreement, 317

Transportation
    economic nature of transportation, 191–192
    regulated, 192–195
Transportation Security Administration (TSA), 180, 185, 290, 291
Travel agents, 153
    and computer reservations systems, 207, 208
Treaties affecting outer space, 409–414
Treaties and international civil aviation organizations, 313–321
    Air Offenses Convention (Tokyo Convention of 1963), 318
    Bermuda 2, 345
    Bermuda Agreement, 317, 346
    Chicago Conference, 316, 317, 428
    Chicago Convention (1944), 314, 316, 333, 336, 408
    Convention for the Suppression of Unlawful Acts against the Safety of Civil Aviation (Montreal Convention—1971), 318
    conventions and conferences, 313
    Damage to Third Parties on the Surface Caused by Foreign Aircraft (Rome Convention—1952), 318
    Guadalajara Convention (1961), 315
    Guatemala Protocol (1971), 315
    Hague Protocol, 314–315
    Havana Convention (1928), 314
    Hijacking Convention (Hague Convention for the Suppression of Unlawful Seizure of Aircraft—1970), 318
    IATA InterCarriers Agreement and IATA Measures of Implementation Agreement, 315
    IATA Tariff Coordinating Conference, 321
    International Air Traffic Association, 313
    International Air Transport Agreement, 317
    International Air Transport Agreement ("Five Freedoms"), 316–317
    International Air Transport Association (IATA), 320–321
    international aviation relations, 313–314
    International Civil Aviation Organization (ICAO), 316, 319–320

International Recognition of Rights in Aircraft (Geneva Convention—1948), 317–318
Madrid Convention (1926), 314
Montreal Agreement, 314–315, 315
Montreal Convention (1999), 315
Montreal Protocols (1975), 315
Multilateral Interline Traffic Agreements, 321
"open skies," 316, 317
Pan American Conference, 314
Paris Convention (1919), 313–314, 408
Plastic Explosives Convention (Convention on the Making of Plastic Explosives for the Purpose of Detection—1991), 318–319
Transit Agreement, 317
Warsaw Convention (1929), 314, 335
Treaty of Rome (1957), 326, 328, 332–333, 341, 348
and air transportation, 328–329
Trippe, Juan, 84, 85, 90–91, 99, 120, 125, 126, 144, 155, 156, 165, 166, 211, 217, 323, 349
Truman, Harry, 217
Trump, Donald, 211
Trunk airlines, 192, 193
TSA. *See* Transportation Security Administration
Tsiolkovsky, Konstantin, 401–402, 423
Dreams of the Earth and Sky, 401
Exploration of the Universe with Reaction Machines, 401–402
Turbine engines, 150–153
Turbinia, 151
Turbochargers, 151
Turbojet engine, 153
Turboprops, 154, 157, 163, 242–243
TWA, 98, 108, 115–119, 205, 206, 209, 214, 215, 215–216, 282, 284
bankruptcy, 215–216
before the Civil Aeronautics Act (1938), 115–119
demise of, 216
Hughes at, 137
and Icahn, Carl, 213–216
international route expansion, 213
name change, 213
transatlantic service, 143
in World War II, 141, 213
Two-tiered wage agreements, 232

U
U-2, 137
UAS. *See* Unmanned aircraft systems
Unilateral trade, 368
Union (airline) characteristics, 233
Union membership, 22. *See also* Labor movement
Union Pacific, 13
Unions, major airline unions, 226–227. *See also* Labor movement
Unit cost differential, 306
United Aircraft and Transport Corporation, 77
United Air Transport, 97
United Airways (United Airlines), 98, 107, 115, 119–120, 282, 284, 296
and Roosevelt administration, 119
routes in 1937, 119–120
suing the government, 119
United Kingdom, 345
United States Bankruptcy Act, 198–199
United States Code, 16
United States Constitution, 16, 23, 198–199
United States Patent Office, patents granted, 3, 17, 27
United States Post Office Department, 67, 107. *See also* Airmail
Universal or Zulu time, 5
Unmanned aircraft systems (UAS), 310
Uppercu, Inglis M., 82
Uranium 235, 428
US Airways, 296
U.S. Army Signal Corps, Aeronautical Division, 55, 56
Use of the Gyroscope in the Balancing and Steering of Airplanes, The (Goddard), 402
User charges, airports, 266
U.S. Navy, and Curtiss, Glenn, 60–61
U.S.S. Los Angeles (dirigible), 90
U.S.S.R.
after World War II, 324, 325
space race, 406–407
Sputnik, 404–405

V
V-2 rocket, 404
Valuejet crash in Florida, 177
Van Allen radiation belts, 406, 428
Verne, Jules, *From Earth to the Moon*, 401

Versaille Treaty (1918), 403
Vertical holding companies, 97–98, 106, 107
Very light jets (VLJs), 310
VFR. *See* Visual Flight Rules
VHF Omnidirectional Radio (VOR), 159, 160, 175
Vickers Viscount, 242
Victor (VOR) airways, 159, 160
Vin Fiz, first coast-to-coast airplane flight, 445–448
Virgin Galactic flights, 421
Vision 100, 251, 252, 380
"Vision for Space Exploration," 424–426
Visual Flight Rules (VFR), 159, 160, 161
VLJs. *See* Very light jets
Von Braun, Wernher, 403–404
VOR. *See* VHF Omnidirectional Radio
VORTACs, 175
Vought, Chance, 77, 97

W
WAAS. *See* Wide Area Augmentation System
Wages, working for, 8
Wall Street crash (1929), 98
Ward, Earl, 134
Warde, George, 353, 354
War of the Worlds, The (Wells), 402
War on Terrorism, 388
War Production Board, World War II, 138
Warsaw Convention (1929), 314, 335
Wasps, 77, 86
Watt, James, 8
We (book), (Lindbergh), 94
Weather conditions, 91, 92
reporting, 92
Wells, H.G., *War of the Worlds, The*, 402
Wendell H. Ford Aviation Investment and Reform Act for the 21st century (AIR-21), 250, 251, 252, 254, 261, 266, 269, 270–271, 300, 387
Wenham, Francis, 32
Western Air Express ("Model Airway"), 91, 115, 120
Western Civilization, 3
Wheel, invention of, 3
"White Knight" lifting SpaceShipOne, 418, 421

White Wing, 56–57

Whittle, Frank, 151, 152

Wide Area Augmentation System (WAAS), 175

William J. Hughes Technical Center, 176

Wilson, John R.M., 182

Wilson, Woodrow, 65, 68, 113, 443

Wind tunnels, 114, 155

Wolf, Stephen, 204

"Women in Early Aviation," 441–444

Women's Air Derby, 95

Woolen goods production, 7–8

Woolman, C.E., 106

Work actions (non-strike activity), 228, 229

Workers, rights of workers to organize and strike, 22

Worker safety, 22

Working conditions, 22

Working for a wage, 8

Workingmen's Party, 20

Works Progress Administration (WPA), Great Depression, 22, 182

WORLDSPAN, 253

World War I, 22, 63–65

    aircraft and trained pilots in 1914, 63

    Aircraft Production Board, 64

    and airships (dirigibles), 29

    Allied side aircraft, 63

    Axis side aircraft, 63

    Curtiss Aeroplane and Motor Company, 63–64

    Dayton-Wright Company, 64

    DeHavilland DH-4, 64

    Liberty engine, 64

    magneto ignition, 64

    National Advisory Committee for Aeronautics (NACA), 65

    patent "pool," 60

    technological advances, 63

    Versaille Treaty (1918), 403

    Wright-Martin Aircraft Company, 64

World War II, 137–141, 368

    airlines after, 143–147, 149–150

    airlines in, 137–141

    Allied forces, 137

    Army Air Corps, 138, 139

    aviation and aircraft manufacturing war effort, 137, 139–141

    Axis forces, 137

    Battle of England, 138

    "buzz bomb" (Germany), 76

    the chosen instrument, 139

    domestic travel space priority system, 140

    German Luftwaffe, 63, 138

    Lend Lease Act, 138–139

    non-rigid airships (blimps), 30–31

    and Pan American Airways, 139, 141

    War Production Board, 138

Wright Aeronautical Corporation, 64, 76

Wright brothers, 41–52, 427, 430, 431

    and the Aerial Experiment Association (AEA), 39, 51

    and Curtiss, Glenn, 59, 59–60, 60

    first interest in manned flight, 35

    Flyer I, II, and III, 45, 57, 58

    influences of Pilcher, Lilienthal, and Chanute, 33, 35, 41, 42, 43, 47

    kite building, 41, 42

    Kitty Hawk flight on December 17, 1903, 17, 27, 45

    and Langley, 35, 41

    Langley Medal, 433

    Military Flyer, 51

    Model A flyers, 49, 50, 51, 55

    Model B, 52, 445

    Model F and Model K, 52

    Orville, 43, 45, 49, 52, 58, 60, 62, 76, 90, 445

    patent, 27, 47, 49, 57, 59

    record setting accomplishments, 50

    Wilber, 41, 43, 49, 50, 51, 52, 59, 448

    "Wright Aeroplane and Its Fabled Performance, The" (*Scientific American*), 47–49

    Wright Company, 52, 59–60, 62

Wright, Katherine, 51

Wright-Martin Aircraft Company, 64, 76

Wright, Milton, 43

Y

Yankee Clipper, 129

Z

Zeppelin airship (dirigible), 29–30

Zeppelin, Ferdinand Adolf von, 29

Zulu or Universal time, 5